DEVIANT BEHAVIOR
AND
HUMAN RIGHTS

DEVIANT BEHAVIOR AND HUMAN RIGHTS

John F. Galliher
University of Missouri—Columbia

PRENTICE HALL
Englewood Cliffs, New Jersey 07632

taloging-in-Publication Data

Deviant behavior and human rights

ts / [edited by] John F. Galliher.

ferences.

ISBN 0-13-204066-2
    1. Deviant behavior. 2. Social justsice. 3. Abuse of rights-
-United States. 4. Corporations--United States--Corrupt practices.
I. Galliher, John F.
HM291.D4844 1991
302.5'42--dc20

90-7270
CIP

Editorial/production supervision and
   interior design: *Nancy Savio-Marcello*
Cover design: *Ben Santora*
Manufacturing buyer: *Ed O'Dougherty*

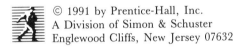 © 1991 by Prentice-Hall, Inc.
A Division of Simon & Schuster
Englewood Cliffs, New Jersey 07632

Printed in the United States of America

10 9 8 7 6 5 4 3 2 1

ISBN 0-13-204066-2

Prentice-Hall International (UK) Limited, *London*
Prentice-Hall of Australia Pty. Limited, *Sydney*
Prentice-Hall Canada Inc., *Toronto*
Prentice-Hall Hispanoamericana, S.A., *Mexico*
Prentice-Hall of India Private Limited, *New Delhi*
Prentice-Hall of Japan, Inc., *Tokyo*
Prentice-Hall of Southeast Asia Pte. Ltd., *Singapore*
Editora Prentice-Hall do Brasil, Ltda., *Rio de Janeiro*

to
Rea Bates Galliher

CONTENTS

PREFACE

Some argue that social scientists, unlike politicians and religious leaders, should merely attempt to describe and explain the events of the world but should never make value judgments based on those observations. Yet a value-free and nonjudgmental social science has no place in a world that has experienced the Holocaust, in a world having had slavery, in a world with the ever-present threat of rape and other sexual assault, in a world with frequent, unpunished crimes in high places, including the production of products known by their manufacturers to cause death and injury as has been true of asbestos products and continues to be true of the cigarette industry, and in a world dying from environmental pollution by these same large multinational corporations. This book will demonstrate that such corporations feel they owe no loyalty to the citizens of any culture or nation and thus in turn deserve no respect from social scientists and other citizens.

In the first section sociology's early efforts to arrive at some conclusions about the relationship between deviant behavior, human liberty, and social justice is explored. Section 2 describes powerful social institutions and customs that support oppression, including rape, racism, capital punishment, and genocide. Large-scale corporate crime is discussed in Section 3, as is the considerable legal freedom such organizations enjoy. Section 4 shows how legal institutions established to control abuses actually end up perpetuating such behavior. Section 5 analyzes the appropriate moral stance of the social scientist who is concerned with human liberty and survival.

Thanks go out to the following reviewers: Steven F. Messner, SUNY—Albany; Andre Modigliani, University of Michigan; and Richard Quinney, Northern Illinois University.

DEVIANT BEHAVIOR
AND
HUMAN RIGHTS

INTRODUCTION

Concerns with human rights only make sense if we depart from the common stance of contemporary sociology that adheres to a *value neutrality* (Sjoberg et al., 1984). The idea of value neutrality assumes that it is improper, and in fact impossible, for social scientists, as social scientists, to make moral or ethical judgments or take positions on political issues. According to this reasoning, social scientists who take these positions do so only as private citizens, not as social scientists. Whether they are registered Democrats, Republicans, or disenchanted radicals, they must not allow biases to influence their professional work in any fashion. In the real world it seems highly dubious that this is ever possible, as everything human beings do is influenced by their values, their work, their play, and their politics.

Sociologist Alvin Gouldner agrees. Value-free ''arguments appeal to reason but ignore experience'' (1962:199). He explains (1962:212):

I believe that, in the end, this segregation [of values and science] *warps reason by tinging it with sadism and leaves feeling smugly sure only of itself and bereft of a sense of common humanity* [emphasis in original].

If we would teach students how science is made, really made rather than as publicly reported, we cannot fail to expose them to the whole scientist by whom it is made, with all his gifts and blindness, with all his methods and his *values* as well. To do otherwise is to usher in an era of spiritless technicians who will be no less lacking in understanding than they are in passion, and who will be useful only because they can be used.

Gouldner then concludes (1962:212):

If sociologists ought not express their personal values in the academic setting, how then are students to be safeguarded against the unwitting influence of these values which shape the sociologist's selection of problems, his preferences for certain hypotheses or conceptual schemes, and his neglect of others. For these are unavoidable and, in this sense, there is and can be no value-free sociology.

These problems aside, nicely suited to this value neutrality is *cultural relativism,* which contends that various cultures' practices can only be described as different from one another, not judged as better or worse. Thus the beliefs and practices of the Swedes are merely different from those of the Russians, not better or worse. The Holocaust during World War II made such concerns of value neutrality and cultural relativism absurd. The Nazis really were worse than the Swedes, for example. More recently, apartheid in South Africa is recognized worldwide as not merely a *different* cultural prac-tice than found in other nations, but as morally repugnant. Indeed, to avoid making such judgments about Nazism or apartheid is in itself widely recognized as a moral outrage.

The demand for elementary human rights, some feel, runs the risk of ethnocen-trism whereby observers judge any cultural practice on the basis of how closely it matches their own. Given this risk, the skeptic may ask, Nazi illustrations aside, how can we arrive at these human rights that are presumably universal and thus be used to judge any given cultural practice? An answer to this question has been attempted by Rawls (1971). He has discussed the notion of the *original position* where people do not yet have information on the society into which they will be born, nor do they know what specific position they will occupy in any society. In this original position people are behind what Rawls has referred to as the *veil of ignorance.* If people are in the original position, Rawls argues, on the basis of self-interest alone, they will always choose a society where equality is at a maximum. To minimize their risk of future misery they will pick socialist Sweden, for example, over South Africa.

While both freedom and equality are important, Dworkin (1977) argues that equality is the more important of the two. If people have an equal input into their gover-nance, they have the means to guarantee their own freedom. Additionally, Hart (1961) found that people everywhere require protection from personal physical attacks, since, unlike tigers in the jungle or the sharks of the ocean, the human is inherently a very vulnerable creature. Thus, the requirements for equality and personal protection are the two universal qualities of human beings that can be used to determine whether their essential human rights are being protected.

The particular bases we will use for making moral judgments are found in such places as the United Nations Charter, which begins with its statement of purpose as follows (United Nations Conference, 1945:1):

WE THE PEOPLE OF THE UNITED NATIONS DETERMINED
to save succeeding generations from the scourage of war, which twice in our lifetime has brought untold sorrow to mankind, and to reaffirm faith in fundamental human rights, in the dignity and worth of the human person, in equal rights of men and women.

Moreover, the U.S. Declaration of Independence reads: "We hold these truths to be self-evident, that all Men are created equal, that they are endowed by their creator with certain unalienable Rights." This demand for social equality and dignity is precisely what the late Reverend Martin Luther King, Jr., emphasized during his lifetime. He argued that any laws that singled out blacks for inferior treatment to whites were morally repugnant (1963).

The United Nations Universal Declaration of Human Rights (1948/49:535–536) includes the following articles:

All human beings are born free and equal in dignity and rights.

Everyone has the right to life, liberty and the security of person.

No one shall be held in slavery or servitude.

No one shall be subjected to torture or to cruel, inhuman or degrading treatment or punishment.

All are equal before the law and are entitled without any discrimination to equal protection of the law.

No one shall be subjected to arbitrary interference with his privacy.

Everyone has the right to freedom of movement.

Everyone has the right to own property.

Everyone has the right to work, to free choice of employment.

Amnesty International has long made judgments about nations with great violations of human rights (Amnesty International Report, 1983). Amnesty International is particularly concerned when societies kill and torture their own citizens or imprison them because of their political beliefs. And the International Olympic Committee, on the basis of similar demands, has refused since 1968 to allow South Africans to participate in the Olympic Games (Epsy, 1980). Nazi genocide was condemned by four major world powers: France, England, the Soviet Union, and the United States. Although Nazi atrocities violated no German laws of the time, Nazi officials were still held accountable at the Nuremberg trials and they were punished for their acts of violence.

Clearly, cultural relativism will not suffice. According to cultural relativists all deviant behavior is the same if contrary to societal rules. For example, shoplifting and murder are thus lumped together in the United States; both are deviant behavior. And if not contrary to a given culture's rules, nothing is deviant. For example, genocide in Nazi Germany was not deviant. The problem of distinguishing offenses on the basis of seriousness has been a goal of students of deviant behavior for some time. Unfortunately, the distinction between victim and victimless crimes is not satisfactory (Schur, 1965). Victimless crimes include such offenses as prostitution, drug use, and illegal gambling. The problem with this distinction is that a relatively petty offense such as shoplifting is a crime with victims just as is genocide. Personal versus property crime is not satisfactory either, because the boundary is permeable. The massive theft of land from Native American tribes made their survival nearly impossible. The Federal Bureau of Investigation (FBI) distinction between serious Part I and less serious Part II crimes fares no better. Auto theft, and in fact, any theft, is classified as a Part I crime, whereas child abuse is a Part II offense. In the bizarre world of the FBI, stealing a Ford or a bicycle is more serious than beating a child.

HUMAN RIGHTS AND THEORETICAL FOCUS

Perhaps a better method of distinguishing offenses is between those that do and those that do not have institutional support. The Schwendingers have concluded that the ultimate crimes include imperialistic war, racism, sexism, and poverty (1970). As implied, these are listed because the power of the actors involved is such that they can create great harm and massive human suffering. Whether or not they are technically criminal violations is immaterial, since even Nazi genocide was legal under the German law of the period. The human rights orientation has the advantage of considering the human rights of both the victim and the aggressor, including prison inmates such as serial killers, as well as others who have been brutally executed and those on death row. What makes the crimes of serial killers so spectacular is that even without great political power they can cause many deaths, something usually reserved for behavior with institutional support such as water and air pollution, lynching, slavery, and genocide. As discussed in Section 3, the Johns-Manville Corporation was responsible for killing many thousands of people through asbestos poisoning.

The question is, When does deviant behavior encroach on these alleged human rights? The first cluster of essays analyzes the theoretical efforts to understand deviant behavior and together ultimately lead us toward an answer to the question of the relationship between deviant behavior and human rights. The earliest perspectives emphasized that deviance was considered to be anything that upset the established order, as the Mills (1943) paper demonstrates. These value judgments were sometimes cloaked in scientific language where communities were said to be disorganized to the extent they failed to uphold rural, Protestant values. Such guises were required, for social scientists soon began to claim to be objective and value-free. No consideration was given to whether this established order was just or fair. Mills implies the very modest right to deviate from middle-class rural norms. There is thus a right to refuse to assimilate and, for example, the right to hold to European values and practices. This includes the right to freedom of religion and lifestyle.

A later generation of social scientists stressed that deviance was merely what a given society determined to call it—nothing more nor nothing less. Labeling theory (which this perspective was called) was seen as a means of avoiding puritanical moral judgments, such as mentioned by Mills. Labeling theory has led to cultural relativism and the avoidance of imposing ethical judgments on those called deviant. Several authors whose essays are included here (see Liazos, Thio, Gouldner, and Schervish in Section 1) note that labeling theory studies only the poor and powerless. According to Schervish (1973), labeling theory assumes actors who are labeled are *passive* and also assumes an individualistic line of analysis, which implies that individuals face labelers totally *alone*, thus ignoring opposing interest groups. This bias leads to a fatalism and pessimism about the possibility of collective action from below. Yet, in fact, radicals have challenged the legitimacy of existing norms and have made demands for human rights.

If such a description of isolated powerlessness applies to anyone, it is to the poor and not to the wealthy. Thus it follows, according to Thio (1973), that the powerless alone are studied by social scientists because *the powerful can hide*. Thio implies the right of others to have the abuses of the powerful disclosed and even perhaps ultimately controlled. Hughes (1984) in Section 1 notes that in any research there is an underlying reason for conducting the research, a driving force that he calls the *major premise*. Typically, the major premise is not made explicit and not recognized. For example, investigations of the pathologies of the poor usually imply that there is something inherently inferior about these people that justifies their subordinate position.

According to Gouldner (1968), labeling theory and its ethos would have us concentrate on problems of the down-and-out, or underdog deviance such as prostitution and drug addiction. This perspective emphasizes their quaintness but involves no real commitment to them. It claims to be on the side of the underdog, but really is only *against* lower-level functionaries. It is, however, according to Gouldner, *necessary to under-*

stand the underdog to truly understand human suffering that is avoidable as a means of avoiding complacency. In this context we can learn something from the victims of slavery, rape, and lynching. Unlike radicals, Gouldner claims that labeling theorists have no interest in the power elite, for they argue that all superordinates in turn have superordinates over them. Thus the view of society they provide is where no one is really in charge and thus no one can be held responsible for institutionalized atrocities. This is precisely what the Nazi officials argued at the end of World War II, as reflected in the article by Hughes (1962) in Section 2. As in this case when the government is directly responsible, it often happens that no individuals are held accountable for savagery. This is true of American slavery, as well as American lynchings and its modern-day replacement, the death penalty.

Gouldner's implication is that sociologists should study the underdog with an intellectual passion, and that if and when they do, they will learn not only about the avoidable suffering of the poor but will also at the same time learn about the oppressive practices of the rich and powerful. The fact that only the powerless are labeled and thus only the powerless are studied, leaves *those at the top untouched,* according to Liazos (1972). Massive thefts of corporations, creation of slums, and waging of wars for profit are left unstudied in favor of "marihuana smokers" and "motorcycle gangs" (Liazos, 1972:107). The human right clearly implied here is the right not to die from poverty in a world of plenty. The organized crimes of the modern state are often neglected because social scientists and others confuse large-scale organized crime with the Mafia, as Chambliss (1971) and Smith and Alba (1979) demonstrate (see their articles in Section 3).

Contrary to the value-neutral claims of labeling theorists, their emphasis on the poor often makes the poor seem to be the most immoral. In avoiding ethical judgments of those called deviants, this perspective also avoids ethical judgments of the societies of which these deviants are a part (Gouldner, 1968). Neither the labeling theorists nor the earlier social scientists emphasizing a rural, Protestant order can address these issues of deviant behavior and human rights. The studies included in this book are intended to demonstrate the manner in which deviant behavior is a product of specific social and economic institutions, as are attempts to control deviance. These studies show massive violations of human rights for fair and equal treatment. Chambliss (1964) in Section 2 demonstrates that even the simple right of freedom of movement has been abridged by elites for purposes of economic gain. Indeed, some of these studies show how human life itself is held hostage by giant corporations and modern governments. If social science is to play a major role in disclosing the abuses of the rich and powerful, new professional ethics may be required, as the final two essays of this book conclude.

REFERENCES

Amnesty International Report
    1983   London: Amnesty International Publications.
Chambliss, William J.
    1964   "A sociological analysis of the law of vagrancy." Social Problems 12 (Summer): 67–77.
    1971   "Vice, corruption, bureaucracy, and power." Wisconsin Law Review 1971 (no. 4): 1150–1173.
Dworkin, Ronald
    1977   Taking Rights Seriously. Cambridge, Mass.: Harvard University Press.

Epsy, Richard
  1980   The Politics of the Olympic Games. Berkeley: University of California Press.
Gouldner, Alvin W.
  1962   ''Anti-Minotaur: The myth of a value-free sociology.'' Social Problems 9 (Winter):
         199–213.
  1968   ''The sociologist as partisan: Sociology and the welfare state.'' The American
         Sociologist 3 (May): 103–116.
Hart, H.L.A.
  1961   The Concept of Law. London: Oxford University Press.
Hughes, Everett C.
  1962   ''Good people and dirty work.'' Social Problems 10 (Summer): 3–11.
  1984   The Sociological Eye: Selected Papers. New Brunswick, N.J.: Transaction Books.
King, Martin Luther, Jr.
  1963   ''Letter from Birmingham jail.'' The Christian Century 80 (June 12): 767–773.
Liazos, Alexander
  1972   ''The poverty of the sociology of deviance: Nuts, sluts, and preverts.'' Social Prob-
         lems 20 (Summer): 103–120.
Mills, C. Wright
  1943   ''The professional ideology of social pathologists.'' American Journal of Sociology
         49: 165–180.
Rawls, John
  1971   A Theory of Justice. Cambridge, Mass.: Belknap Press.
Schervish, Paul G.
  1973   ''The labeling perspective: Its bias and potential in the study of political deviance.''
         The American Sociologist 8 (May): 47–57.
Schur, Edwin M.
  1965   Crimes Without Victims. Englewood Cliffs, N.J.: Prentice Hall.
Schwendinger, Herman, and Julia Schwendinger
  1970   ''Defenders of order or guardians of human rights?'' Issues in Criminology 5
         (Summer): 123–157.
Sjoberg, Gideon, Ted R. Vaughan, and Andree F. Sjoberg
  1984   ''Morals and applied behavioral research: A prefatory essay.'' Journal of Applied
         Behavioral Science 20: 311–321.
Smith, Dwight C., Jr., and Richard D. Alba
  1979   ''Organized crime and American life.'' Society 16 (March/April): 32–38.
Thio, Alex
  1973   ''Class bias in the sociology of deviance.'' The American Sociologist 8 (February):
         1–12.
United Nations Conference on International Organization
  1945   ''Charter of the United Nations together with the Statute of the International Court
         of Justice.'' U.S. Department of State Publication No. 2353. Conference Series
         74. Washington, D.C.: U.S. Government Printing Office.
United Nations Yearbook
  1948/49 ''United Nations Universal Declaration of Human Rights.'' New York: Columbia
         University Press.

1

INSTITUTIONS AND DEVIANCE
Theoretical Prospects

In the first selection, Mills observes that those who study deviance have a rural, middle-class bias with an emphasis on stability and order by focusing on deviation from social norms as a problem. Remember that, according to the argument developed by Gouldner, deviance theorists who rely on labeling theory condemn lower-level functionaries, not the institutions that really create the most misery. In the selection by Liazos, we see how students of deviance usually study the powerless and poor. Only the powerless are focused on by labeling theory, which is discussed by Thio. Schervish demonstrates that labeling theory emphasizes controlled and passive actors and has as well an individualistic bias. According to Hughes, there is an important hidden agenda in any research that researchers will nonetheless usually deny. The Schwendingers argue that one needs explicit moral criteria to develop a clear picture of a human rights–based definition of crime and deviant behavior, rather than leaving such judgments to the state.

THE PROFESSIONAL IDEOLOGY
OF SOCIAL PATHOLOGISTS

C. Wright Mills

An analysis of textbooks in the field of social disorganization reveals a common style of thought which is open to social imputation. By grasping the social orientation of this general perspective we can understand why thinkers in this field should select and handle problems in the manner in which they have.

By virtue of the mechanism of sales and distribution, textbooks tend to embody a content agreed upon by the academic group using them. In some cases texts have been written only after an informal poll was taken of professional opinion as to what should be included, and other texts are consulted in the writing of a new one. Since one test of their success is wide adoption, the very spread of the public for which they are written tends to insure a textbook tolerance of the commonplace. Although the conceptual framework of a pathologist's textbook is not usually significantly different from that of such monographs as he may write, this essay is not concerned with the "complete thought" or with the "intentions" of individual authors; it is a study of a professional ideology variously exhibited in a set of textbooks.[1] Yet, because of its persistent importance in the development of American sociology and its supposed proximity to the social scene, "social pathology" seems an

no one of the texts to be quoted exemplifies *all* the concepts analyzed; certain elements are not so visible in given texts as in others, and some elements are not evidenced in certain texts at all. In general, the documentary quotations which follow in footnotes are from the later editions of the following books: W. G. Beach and E. E. Walker, *American Social Problems* (1934); J. H. S. Bossard, (*a*) *Social Change and Social Problems* (1934) and (*b*) *Problems of Social Well-Being* (1927); C. H. Cooley, (*a*) *The Social Process* (1918), (*b*) *Human Nature and the Social Order* (1902, 1922), (*c*) *Social Organization* (1909); Edward T. Devine, (*a*) *The Normal Life* (1915, 1924), (*b*) *Progressive Social Action* (1933); R. C. Dexter, *Social Adjustment* (1927); G. S. Dow, *Society and Its Problems* (1920, 1929); M. A. Elliott and F. E. Merrill, *Social Disorganization* (1934, 1941); C. A. Ellwood, (*a*) *The Social Problem, a Constructive Analysis* (1915, 1919); (*b*) *Sociology and Modern Social Problems* (1910–35); H. P. Fairchild, *Outline of Applied Sociology* (1916, 1921); M. P. Follett, (*a*) *The New State* (1918), (*b*) *Creative Experience* (1924); James Ford, *Social Deviation* (1939); J. M. Gillette and J. M. Reinhardt, *Current Social Problems* (1933, 1937); J. L. Gillin, (*a*) *Poverty and Dependence* (1921, 1926, 1937), (*b*) *Social Pathology* (1933, 1939); J. L. Gillin, C. G. Dittmer, and R. J. Colbert, *Social Problems* (1928, 1932); E. C. Hayes, editor's introductions to texts in the "Lippincott Series"; W. J. Hayes and I. V. Shannon, *Visual Outline of Introductory Sociology* (1935); G. B. Mangold, *Social Pathology* (1932, 1934); H. A. Miller, *Races, Nations, and Classes* (1924); H. W. Odum, *Man's Quest for Social Guidance: The Study of Social Problems* (1927); Maurice Parmelee, *Poverty and Social Progress* (1916); H. A. Phelps, *Contemporary Social Problems* (1932, 1933, 1938); S. A. Queen and J. R. Gruener, *Social Pathology* (1940); S. A. Queen, W. B. Bodenhafer, and E. B. Harper, *Social Organization and Disorganization* (1935); C. M. Rosenquist, *Social Problems* (1940); U. G. Weatherly, *Social Progress* (1926).

C. Wright Mills (1943) "The Professional Ideology of Social Pathologists." *American Journal of Sociology* Vol. 49 (September): 165–180. Reprinted by permission of The University of Chicago, publisher.

[1]No attempt has been made to trace specific concepts to their intellectual origins. Only elements admitted into the more stable textbook formulations have come within my view: the aim is to grasp typical perspectives and key concepts. Hence,

appropriate point of entry for the examination of the style of reflection and the social-historical basis of American sociology.

The level of abstraction which characterizes these texts is so low that often they seem to be empirically confused for lack of abstraction to knit them together.[2] They display bodies of meagerly connected facts, ranging from rape in rural districts to public housing, and intellectually sanction this low level of abstraction.[3] The "informational" character of social pathology is linked with a failure to consider total social structures. Collecting and dealing in a fragmentary way with scattered problems and facts of milieux, these books are not focused on larger stratifications or upon structured wholes. Such an omission may not be accounted for merely in terms of a general "theoretical weakness." Such structural analyses have been available; yet they have not been attended to or received into the tradition of this literature. American sociologists have often asserted an interest in the "correlation of the social sciences"; nevertheless, academic departmentalization may well have been instrumental in atomizing the problems which they have addressed.[4] Sociologists have always felt that "not many representatives of the older forms of social science are ready to admit that there is a function for sociology."[5] However, neither lack of theoretical

ability nor restrictive channeling through departmentalization constitutes a full explanation of the low level of abstraction and the accompanying failure to consider larger problems of social structure.

If the members of an academic profession are recruited from similar social contexts and if their backgrounds and careers are relatively similar, there is a tendency for them to be uniformly set for some common perspective. The common conditions of their profession often seem more important in this connection than similarity of extraction. Within such a generally homogeneous group there tend to be fewer divergent points of view which would clash over the meaning of facts and thus give rise to interpretations on a more theoretical level.[6]

The relatively homogeneous extraction and similar careers of American pathologists is a possible factor in the low level of abstraction characterizing their work. All the authors considered[7] (except one, who was foreign born) were born in small towns, or on farms near small towns, three-fourths of which were in states not industrialized during the youth of the authors. The social circles and strata in which they have severally moved are quite homogeneous; all but five have participated in similar "reform" groups and "societies" of the professional and business classes. By virtue of their being college professors (all but three are known to have the Ph.D.), of the similar type of temporary posi-

---

[2] See Read Bain, "The Concept of Complexity," *Social Forces,* VIII, 222 and 369. K. Mannheim has called this type "isolating empiricism" ("German Sociology," *Politica,* February, 1934, p. 30).

[3] H. P. Fairchild, p. vii: "Dealing with applied sociology [this book] devotes itself to facts rather than to theories." James H. S. Bossard (a), p. xi: "In [*Problems of Social Well-Being*] an effort was made to consider chiefly in a factual vein, certain elements which seemed of basic importance. . . ." G. B. Mangold, p. viii: "The author has tried to select that which [of factual material] best illustrates problems and practical situations."

The quotations in the footnotes are merely indications of what is usual. The imputations presented must be held against the reader's total experience with the literature under purview.

[4] In Germany the academic division of specialties prior to the rise of sociology channeled sociological work into a formal emphasis. In America a somewhat comparable situation led to a fragmentalization of empirical attention and especially to a channeling of work into "practical problems."

[5] A. W. Small, *American Journal of Sociology,* May, 1916, p. 785, citing an editorial in the *American Journal of Sociology,* 1907.

[6] Such "homogeneity" is not, however, the only condition under which some common style of thought is taken on by a group of thinkers. Compare the formal conception of "points of coincidence" advanced by H. H. Gerth in *Die sozialgeschichtliche Lage der burgerlichen Intelligenz um die Wendes des 18 Jahrhunderts* (diss., Frankfurt A.M.) (V.D.I-Verlag, G.m.b.H. Berlin, N.W. 7). The entire question of the grounding of imputations in terms of social extraction and career-lines is an unfinished set of methodological issues. In this paper the major imputations advanced do *not* proceed upon career data as much as upon the social orientation implied by general perspectives and specific concepts, and by the selection of "problems."

[7] Information concerning twenty-four of the thirty-two authors was full enough to be considered. Five of the eight not considered were junior authors collaborating with persons who are included.

tions (other than academic) which they have held, of the sameness of the "societies" to which they have belonged and of the social positions of the persons whom they have married, the assertion as regards general similarity of social extraction, career, and circles of contact seems justified.[8]

A further determinant of the level of abstraction and lack of explicit systematization (beyond which the mentality we are examining does not easily or typically go) is the immediate purpose and the type of public for which they have presumably written. They have been teachers and their specific public has been college students: this has influenced the content and direction of their intellectual endeavors.[9] Teaching is a task which requires a type of systematization to which the textbook answers. Most of the "systematic" or "theoretical" work in "social pathology" has been performed by teachers in textbooks for academic purposes.[10] The fact that sociology often won its academic right to existence in opposition to other departments may have increased the necessity for *textbook* systematization. Such systematization occurs in a context of presentation and of justification rather than within a context of discovery.[11] The textbook-writing and the academic profession of the writers thus figure in the character and function of systematic theory

within the field.[12] Systematization of facts for the purpose of making them accessible to collegiate minds is one thing; systematization which is oriented toward crucial growing-points in a research process is quite another. An attempt to systematize on the level of the textbook makes for a taxonomic gathering of facts and a systematization of them under concepts that have already been logically defined.[13] The research possibilities of concepts are not as important as is the putting of the accumulated factual details into some sort of order.

But, even though the perspectives of these texts are usually not explicit, the facts selected for treatment are not "random." One way to grasp the perspective within which they do lie is to analyze the scope and character of their problems. What, then, are the selecting and organizing principles to be extracted from the range and content of these texts? What types of fact come within their field of attention?

The direction is definitely toward particular "practical problems"—problems of "everyday life."[14] The ideal of practicality, of not being

---

[8]The order of their respective experience has not been systematically considered. All career data on contemporary persons should be held tentatively: open to revision by knowledge not now publicly available.

[9]See above. A. W. Small, p. 754: ". . .the mental experience of the teacher-explorer in the course of arriving at the present outlook of sociologists . . . has also been due to the fact that many of the advances in perception or expression have been in the course of attempts to meet students' minds at their precise point of outlook." See C. Wright Mills, "Language, Logic, and Culture," *American Sociological Review*, October, 1939, for mechanisms involved in such determinations of the thinker by his public.

[10]This statement, as is widely recognized, holds in a measure for all American sociology. Cf., e.g., Pitirim Sorokin, "Some Contrasts in Contemporary European and American Sociology," *Social Forces*, September, 1929, pp. 57–58. "In America sociology has grown as a child nursed by the universities and colleges. . . American literature in sociology has been composed largely out of textbooks."

[11]Cf. Hans Reichenbach, *Experience and Prediction*, chap. i. See P. Sorokin's comment, op. cit., p. 59.

[12]J. L. Gillin (*a*), p. v: "My years of experience as a social worker and teacher have gone into the content and method of presentation." J. H. S. Bossard (*a*), p. 759: "In the preceding chapters, problems have been grouped on the basis of one underlying fact or condition. Obviously, this is an arbitrary procedure which can be justified only on the basis of pedagogical expedience"; p. xi: "The. . . is the method followed. . . .By way of defense, this seems simpler and pedagogically preferable"; p. xii: "The decision to omit them was made. . .second, because in an increasing number of colleges and universities, these particular fields are dealt with in separate courses."

[13]Cf. Fritz Mauthner, *Aristotle,* for the pedagogic character of the taxonomic logic of Aristotle. H. P. Fairchild, pp. 6–7: ". . .the essential features of the scientific method. . .are three in number. First, the accumulation of facts. . . . Second, the arrangement or classification of these facts according to some predetermined logical basis of classification. . . ." J. H. S. Bossard (*a*), p. 34: "It is the present contention that the scientific study of social problems which confines itself to mere description and classification serves a useful purpose."

[14]M. A. Elliott, *American Sociological Review,* June, 1941, p. 317: "The only problems which need concern the sociologists' theories and research are the real, practical problems of everyday living." Queen and Gruener, p. 42: "[In contradistinction to scientific problems] social problems. . .pertain directly to everyday life. . . .Their concern is usually 'practical,' and often personal." J. H. S. Bossard (*a*), p. 32:

"utopian," operated, in conjunction with other factors, as a polemic against the "philosophy of history" brought into American sociology by men trained in Germany; this polemic implemented the drive to lower levels of abstraction. A view of isolated and immediate problems as the "real" problems may well be characteristic of a society rapidly growing and expanding, as America was in the nineteenth century and, ideologically, in the early twentieth century. The depictive mode of speech and the heavy journalistic "survey" are intellectual concomitants of an expanding society in which new routines are rising and cities are being built.[15] Such an approach is then sanctioned with canons of what constitutes real knowledge; the practice of the detailed and complete empiricism of the survey is justified by an epistemology of gross description. These norms of adequate knowledge linger in an academic tradition to mold the work of its bearers. The emphasis upon fragmentary,[16]

practical problems tends to atomize social objectives. The studies so informed are not integrated into designs comprehensive enough to serve collective action, granted the power and intent to realize such action.

One of the pervasive ways of defining "problems" or of detecting "disorganization" is in terms of *deviation from norms*. The "norms" so used are usually held to be the standards of "society." Later we shall see to what type of society they are oriented. In the absence of studies of specific norms themselves this mode of problematization shifts the responsibility of "taking a stand" away from the thinker and gives a "democratic" rationale to his work.[17] Rationally, it would seem that those who accept this approach to "disorganization" would immediately examine these norms themselves. It is significant that, given their interest in reforming society, which is usually avowed, these writers typically assume the norms which they use and often tacitly sanction them.[18] There are few attempts to explain deviations from norms in terms of the norms themselves, and no

"Frankly, applied sociology is utilitarian. It is concerned with practical problems and purposes." Gillette and Reinhardt, p. 22: "The study of social problems constitutes the heart of sociology as a science. . . .Even so-called 'pure' sociology, or theoretical sociology, more and more devotes itself to these practical problems of society."

On the other hand, such writers as Ellwood, rising to a *very* high level of abstraction, conceive *formally* of "the social problem." C. A. Ellwood (*a*), pp. 13–14: "Some of us, at least, are beginning to perceive that the social problem is now, what it has been in all ages, namely, *the problem of the relations of men to one another*. It is the problem of human living together, and cannot be confined to any statement in economic, eugenic or other one-sided terms. . .it is as broad as humanity and human nature. . . .Such a statement [in terms of one set of factors] obscures the real nature of the problem, and may lead to dangerous, one-sided attempts at its solution." In terms of social and intellectual orientation, both ways of conceiving of "social problems" are similar in that neither is of a sort usable in collective action which proceeds against, rather than well within, more or less tolerated channels.

[15]See H. D. Lasswell, *Politics* (1936), p. 148; K. Mannheim, op. cit., pp. 30–31; and *Ideology and Utopia*, pp. 228–29.

[16]Gillin, Dittmer, and Colbert, p. 44: "There are hundreds of social problems, big and little." Queen and Gruener, p. 171: "We present here some of the problems of day by day living encountered by diabetics and cardiacs." J. H. S. Bossard (*a*), p. 33: "Certain particular social problems are coming to be reserved for applied sociology. Their selection has been determined less by logic or principle than by accident and historical development"; p. 44: "The more one deals with life's problems at first hand, the more one is impressed with their concreteness, their specificity, and their

infinite variety." Gillette and Reinhardt, p. 14: "From almost any point of view there must be a large number of social problems today"; p. 15: "This book is a treatise on a large number of social problems. It does not claim to consider them all. It repeatedly recognizes the plurality of problems in its treatment of the great problems."

[17]C. M. Rosenquist, p. 19: ". . .popular recognition of any social condition or process as bad, followed by any attempt to eliminate or cure it, serves as a criterion for its inclusion in a study of social problems. The writer merely accepts the judgment of public opinion. This is the method to be followed in this book." E. T. Devine (*a*), in Note to the Second Edition: "The object of Social Economy is that each shall be able to live as nearly as possible a normal life according to the standard of the period and the community."

[18]C. M. Rosenquist, p. 19: "Perhaps we may be on solid ground through a recognition of the capitalist system and its accompaniments as normal. We may then deal with its several parts, treating as problems those which do not function smoothly. This, it seems, is what the more reputable sociologist actually does." H. P. Fairchild, p. 59: ". . .some of the social conditions which are the natural and consistent outcome of an individualistic-capitalistic organization of industry, and hence are to be considered as normal in modern societies." Examination of discussions of such items as poverty in most of the texts confirms this assertion. J. L. Gillin (*a*), p. 495: "For serious depressions carefully planned unemployment relief schemes should be formulated before the depression is felt."

rigorous facing of the implications of the fact that social transformations would involve shifts *in them.*

The easy way to meet the question of why norms are violated is in terms of biological impulses which break through "societal restrictions." A paste-pot eclectic psychology provides a rationale for this facile analysis.[19] Thus, more comprehensive problematization is blocked by a biological theory of social deviation. And the "explanation" of deviations can be put in terms of a requirement for more "socialization." "Socialization" is either undefined, used as a moral epithet, or implies norms which are themselves without definition. The focus on "the facts" takes no cognizance of the normative structures within which they lie.

The texts tend either to be "apolitical"[20] or to aspire to a "democratic" opportunism.[21]

When the political sphere is discussed, its pathological phases are usually stated in terms of "the anti-social," or of "corruption," etc.[22] In another form the political is tacitly identified with the proper functioning of the current and unexamined political order; it is especially likely to be identified with a legal process or the administration of laws.[23] If the "norms" were examined, the investigator would perhaps be carried to see total structures of norms and to relate these to distributions of power. Such a structural point of sight is not usually achieved. The level of abstraction does not rise to permit examination of these normative structures themselves, or of why they come to be transgressed, or of their political implications. Instead, this literature discusses many kinds of apparently unrelated "situations."

About the time W. I. Thomas stated the vocabulary of the situational approach, a social worker was finding it congenial and useful. In M. E. Richmond's influential *Social Diagnosis* (1917) we gain a clue as to why pathologists tend to slip past structure to focus on isolated situations, why there is a tendency for problems to be considered as problems of individuals,[24] and why sequences of situations were not seen as linked into structures:

Social diagnosis. . .may be described as the attempt to make as exact a definition as possible of the situa-

[19]That is, an eclecticism that does not analyze in any adequate way the elements and theories which it seeks to combine. Cf. Reuter's critique, *American Journal of Sociology,* November, 1940, pp. 293–304.

[20]E. C. Hayes in the Introduction to H. A. Miller, p. x: "Not political action, the inadequacy of which Professor Eldridge (*Political Action*) has shown, nor revolution, the pathological character of which Professor Sorokin has demonstrated, but social interaction, the causal efficiency of human relationships, is the predominant factor in securing both order and progress."

[21]J. H. S. Bossard (*a*), pp. 14–15: "The constructive approach. . .may be summarized in one sentence: It is always possible to do something. . . Such an approach represents in welfare work that hopelessly incurable optimism which in political life we call democracy." Gillette and Reinhardt, pp. 16–17: "There are no certain rules to be followed step by step in the discovery of the solution. Our best resource is to employ scientific methods rigidly at every step. . .because of uncertain factors always present, we never can be sure that our conclusions are more than approximations of the truth. . . .Since we cannot completely control their activities. . . our cures must be partial and approximate." One type of link between democratic ideology and social pathology is shown in the following quotation, wherein a condition that deviates from the former is called pathological; the quotation also indicates a typical shying-away from all orders of domination other than that type legitimized traditionally, which is left open: H. A. Miller, p. 32: "When certain . . . psycho-pathological conditions are found, we may postulate an abnormal relationship as a cause . . . the particular form of pathology which is involved in our problem may be called the *oppression psychosis.* Oppression is the domination of one group by another." G. V. Price, reviewing Queen and Gruener, *Social Forces,* May, 1941, p. 566: "Without using

the word democracy in the doctrinal sense the authors have shown what its utilities are in reducing pathologies."

[22]M. A. Elliott and F. Merrill, p. 28: "The pathological phases of the political process include such anti-social behavior as delinquency, crime, disorder, revolt, and revolution. Corrupt political activity is an important example of such malfunctioning."

[23]Note the identification of "political action" with legislation: Gillin, Dittmer, and Colbert, p. 94: "It is an American practice to attempt to solve any and every sort of social problem through political action. As a result, our statute-books are loaded with 'dead-letter' laws that are not enforced simply because public opinion does not respect them, nor does it feel responsible for them."

[24]J. L. Gillin (*a*), p. 13: "Experience shows that rehabilitation is possible only when each case of poverty or dependency is taken separately and its difficulties handled with strict regard for all the attendant circumstances. . . .It must be done in terms of the individual, for. . .it cannot be done *en masse.*"

tion and personality of a human being in some social need—of his situation and personality, that is, in relation to the other human beings upon whom he in any way depends or who depend upon him, and in relation also to the social institutions of his community.[25]

This kind of formulation has been widely applied to isolated "problems" addressed by sociologists.[26] And the "situational approach" has an affinity with other elements which characterize their general perspective.[27]

Present institutions train several types of persons—such as judges and social workers—to think in terms of "situations."[28] Their activities and mental outlook are set within the existent norms of society; in their professional work they tend to have an occupationally trained incapacity to rise above series of "cases." It is in part through such concepts as "situation" and through such methods as "the case approach"[29] that social pathologists have been intellectually tied to social work with its occupational position and political limitations. And, again, the similarity of origin and the probable lack of any continuous "class experience" of the group of thinkers decrease their chances to see social structures rather than a scatter of situations. The mediums of experience and orientation through which they respectively view society are too similar, too homogeneous, to permit the clash

of diverse angles which, through controversy, might lead to the construction of a whole.

The paramount fact of immigration in American culture, with each wave of immigrants displacing the lower-class position of former waves and raising the position of the earlier immigrants, also tends to obscure structural and class positions.[30] Thus, instead of positional issues, pathologists typically see problems in terms of an individual, such as an immigrant, "adjusting" to a milieu[31] or being "assimilated" or Americanized. Instead of problems of class structure involving immigration, the tendency has been to institute problems in terms of immigration involving the nationalist assimilation of individuals. The fact that some individuals have had opportunities to rise in the American hierarchy decreases the chance fully to see the ceilings of class. Under these conditions such structures are seen as fluctuating and unsubstantial and are likely to be explained not in terms of *class position* but in terms of *status attitudes.*[32]

Another element that tends to obviate an analytic view of structure is the emphasis upon the "processual" and "organic" character of society. In Cooley, whose influence on these books is decisive, one gets a highly formal, many-sided fluidity where "nothing is fixed or independent, everything is plastic and takes influence as well as gives it."[33] From the standpoint of political action, such a view may mean a reformism dealing with masses of detail and furthers a tendency to be apolitical. There can be no bases or points of entry for larger social action in a structureless flux. The view is buttressed epistemologically with an emotionalized animus against "particularism" and with the intense ap-

---

[25]Richmond, p. 357; see also pp. 51 and 62.

[26]J. H. S. Bossard (*a*), p. 3: "Social problems consist of (*a*) a social situation, (*b*) which are. . . ." Gillette and Reinhardt, p. 15: "A social problem is a situation, confronting a group. . . ."

[27]J. H. S. Bossard (*a*), p. 57: ". . .the emphasis in our social thinking upon the situation as a unit of experience, as 'an aggregate of interactive and interdependent factors of personality and circumstance,' is in essence a recognition of the idea of the emergent. . . .Queen recognizes the implications of the situational approach very clearly in these words: 'For purposes of sociological analysis, a situation consists in relationships between persons viewed as a cross section of human experience, constantly changing. . .Thus we make of the concept "situation" an intellectual tool' " (S. Queen, "Some Problems of the Situational Approach," *Social Forces,* June, 1931, p. 481).

[28]See K. Mannheim, *Man and Society,* p. 305.

[29]Queen, Bodenhafer, and Harper, p. viii: Editor's Note by S. Eldridge: "The present volume. . .features the case approach to social problems."

[30]Note the lack of structure in the conception of "class": Gillette and Reinhardt, p. 177: "Viewing the matter historically, then, it appears that the chief cause of rigid *class systems* of society with their attendant evils is the prolonged concentration of wealth in the hands of a relatively few persons."

[31]See below, the concept of "adjustment."

[32]Gillin, Dittmer, and Colbert, p. 59: "The most fundamental cause of class and group conflict is the attitude of superiority on the part of one class, or group, toward another."

[33]*The Social Process,* pp. 44–45.

proval of the safe, if colorless, "multiple-factor" view of causation.[34] The liberal "multiple-factor" view does not lead to a conception of causation which would permit points of entry for broader types of action, especially political action.[35] No set of underlying structural shifts is given which might be open to manipulation, at key points, and which, like the fact of private property in a corporate economy, might be seen as efficacious in producing many "problems." If one fragmentalizes society into "factors," into elemental bits, naturally one will then need quite a few of them to account for something,[36] and one can never be sure they are all in. A formal emphasis upon "the whole" plus lack of total structural consideration plus a focus upon scattered situations does not make it easy to reform the status quo.

The "organic" orientation of liberalism has stressed all those social factors which tend to a harmonious balance of elements.[37] There is a minimization of chances for action in a social milieu where "there is always continuity with the past, and not only with any one element only of the past, but with the whole interacting organism of man."[38] In seeing everything social as continuous process, changes in pace and revolutionary dislocations are missed[39] or are taken as signs of the "pathological." The formality and the assumed unity implied by "the mores" also lower the chances to see social chasms and structural dislocations.

Typically, pathologists have not attempted to construct a structural whole. When, however, they do consider totalities, it is in terms of such concepts as "society," "the social order," or "the social organization," "the mores and institutions," and "American culture." Four things should be noted about their use of such terms: (a) The terms represent undifferentiated entities. Whatever they may indicate, it is systematically homogeneous. Uncritical use of such a term as "the" permits a writer the hidden assumption in politically crucial contexts of a homogeneous and harmonious whole.[40] The large texture of "the society" will take care of itself, it is somehow and in the long run harmonious,[41] it has "strain toward consistency" running through it;[42] or, if not this, then only the co-operation of all is needed,[43] or perhaps even a right moral feeling is taken as a solution.[44]

---

[34]Elliott and Merrill, p. 38: "One of the most significant concepts in the understanding of social problems is the idea of multiple causation."

[35]See above comments on political relevance. C. A. Ellwood (b) p. 324: "We may, perhaps, sum up this chapter by saying that it is evident that the cure of poverty is not to be sought merely in certain economic rearrangements, but in scientific control of the whole life process of human society. This means that in order to get rid of poverty, the defects in education, in government, in religion and morality, in philanthropy, and even in physical heredity, must be got rid of. Of course, this can only be done when there is a scientific understanding of the conditions necessary for normal human social life."

[36]J. L. Gillin (a), pp. 51–128: ". . .the modern theory of the causes of poverty has passed beyond any one-sided explanation to a many-sided theory." The following conditions of poverty and dependence are discussed: poor natural resources, adverse climate, adverse weather, insect pests, disasters, illness and diseases, physical inheritance, mental inheritance, adverse surroundings of children, death or disability of the earner, unemployment, lack of proper wages, traditions, customs, habits, advertising and instalment buying, fluctuations between costs of living and income, inequitable distribution of wealth and income, family marital relations, political conditions, unwise philanthropy, etc. After these discussions, *family cases* are presented as ". . .studies in causation."

[37]Whereas many socialist theories have tended to overlook the elastic elements that do exist in a society. Cf. K. Mannheim, *Politica*, pp. 25–26.

[38]C. H. Cooley (a), p. 46.

[39]See Max Lerner, *It Is Later than You Think*, pp. 14–15; and *Encyclopaedia of the Social Sciences*, article "Social Process." See documentation and consequences below.

[40]Gillin, Dittmer, and Colbert, p. 11: "All this group life is nicely woven into a system that we call society. . . ."

[41]Ibid., p. 15: "But the aim of society is ever directed to the task of bringing uniform advantages to all." C. A. Ellwood (b), p. 395: "Social organization may refer to any condition or relation of the elements of a social group; but by social order we mean a settled and harmonious relation between the individuals or the parts of a society. The problem of social order is then the problem of harmonious adaptation among the individuals of the group. . . ."

[42]It is significant that it was Sumner, with his tacit belief in "natural" order, who set forth the phrase and what it implies.

[43]Gillin, Dittmer, and Colbert, p. 13: "Since a community is made up of a number of neighborhoods, it is necessary that all cooperate in order to secure better schools, improved. . . ."

[44]J. L. Gillin (a), p. 133: "Only as a passion for social righteousness takes the place of an imperative desire for selfish advantage. . .will society do away with the conditions that

(*b*) In their formal emptiness these terms are commensurate with the low level of abstraction. Their *formality* facilitates the empirical concern with "everyday" problems of (community) milieu. (*c*) In addition to their "descriptive" use, such terms are used normatively. The "social" becomes a good term when it is used in ethical polemics against "individualism" or against such abstract moral qualities as "selfishness," lack of "altruism," or of "antisocial" sentiments.[45] "Social" is conceived as a "co-operative" "sharing" of something or as "conducive to the general welfare."[46] The late

eighteenth-century use of "society" as against "state" by the rising bourgeoisie had already endowed "society" with a "democratic" tinge which this literature transmits. (*d*) There is a strong tendency for the term "society" to be practically assimilated to, or conceived largely in terms of, primary groups and small homogeneous communities. Such a conception typically characterizes the literature within our purview.[47] In explaining it, we come upon an element that is highly important in understanding the total perspective.

The basis of "stability," "order," or "solidarity" is not typically analyzed in these books, but a conception of such a basis is implicitly used and sanctioned,[48] for some normative conception of a socially "healthy" and stable organization is involved in the determination of "pathological" conditions. "Pathological" behavior is not discerned in a *structural* sense (i.e., as incommensurate with an existent structural

now depress some classes of the population and exhalt others.''

[45]C. A. Ellwood (*b*), p. 84: ". . .increasing altruism is necessary for the success of those more and more complex forms of cooperation which characterize higher civilization and upon which it depends.'' G. B. Mangold, p. 17: "Without the spirit of altruism society would be but a sorry exhibition of the collective humanity that we believe has been made in the image of God.'' Conversely, the "anti-social'' is held to include certain abstract, moral traits of individuals. Elliott and Merrill, p. 43: "An analysis of the disorganization process suggests two types of anti-social forces: (1) the consciously directed anti-social forces and (2) the impersonal organic forces which are an outgrowth of the formalism discussed above. . .to advance their own selfish ends. These men are thoroughly aware of their anti-social attitudes. Social values have no meaning for them. . . .There has often been no socializing influence in the lives of those men. . . .Co-operation, or 'mutual aid,' the implicit counterpart of effective social organization. . . .Vice areas. . .function because of human appetites, because individual desires are more deeply rooted than any sense of the social implications. . . .The prostitute exists only because she is a means to man's sensual pleasure and satiety''; p. 44: "Sin, vice, crime, corruption, all consciously directed anti-social forces, offer a primrose. . . .'' G. B. Mangold, p. 59: "Unsocial habits lead to poverty; particularly do they degrade poverty into dependency. Chief among these vices is intemperance. Before the advent of prohibition it was. . . .'' Queen, Bodenhafer, and Harper, p. 4: "When there is. . .characterized by harmony, teamwork, understanding, approval, and the like, we may speak of organization. When the opposite is true and there is a. . .marked by tension, conflict, or drifting apart, we may speak of disorganization.''

[46]Gillin, Dittmer, and Colbert, p. 5: " 'The word [social] means conducive to the collective welfare, and thus becomes nearly equivalent to moral' [Cooley, *Human Nature and the Social Order*, p. 4]. . .it is this . . . meaning that comes closest to our interpretation . . .—'conducive to the collective welfare'—relationships, and products of relationships that are believed to foster and promote *group life,* and to insure *group survival.*''

[47]J. L. Gillin (*b*), p. 313: ". . .personal relationships. . .are the most important ties in the social organization. . . .'' C. A. Ellwood (*b*), pp. 3–4: "The tendency in the best sociological thinking is to emphasize the importance, for the understanding of our social life, of 'primary' or face-to-face groups''; p. 77: "Primary groups. . .are of most interest sociologically, because they exhibit social life at its maximum intensity, and because they are the bearers of the most vital elements in social life, especially the traditions of civilization''; pp. 79–80: "The chief importance of primary groups in our social life, however, is that they. . .furnish the 'patterns' which we attempt to realize in our social life in general''; pp. 84–85: "All human history has, from one point of view, been a struggle to transfer altruism and solidarity of the family to successively larger and larger groups of men''; pp. 90–91: "Primary, or face-to-face groups are the key to the understanding of our social life. . . .'' Gillin, Dittmer, Colbert, p. 282: ". . .the home is probably our most fundamental social institution. . . .''; p. 285: "Anything that endangers the stability of the family endangers society.'' J. H. S. Bossard (*a*), p. 555: "Family life is the focal point of virtually all of our social problems.''

[48]C. A. Ellwood (*b*), pp. 79–80: "The very ideal of social solidarity itself comes from the unity experienced in such [primary] groups.'' Elliott and Merrill, p. 581: "An ever-increasing number of persons living in the giant cities has become completely deracinated, cut off from all stable primary ties. They have lost not only their physical home, but often their spiritual home as well. Social disorganization breeds in these unattached masses of the urban proletariat. They furnish willing nuclei for robbery, brigandage, and revolution.''

type) or in a *statistical* sense (i.e., as deviations from central tendencies). This is evidenced by the regular assertion that pathological conditions *abound* in the city.[49] If they *"abound"* therein, they cannot be "abnormal" in the statistical sense and are not likely to prevail in the structural sense. It may be proposed that the norms in terms of which "pathological" conditions are detected are "humanitarian ideals." But we must then ask for the social orientation of such ideals.[50] In this literature the operating criteria of the pathological are typically *rural* in orientation and extraction.[51]

Most of the "problems" considered arise because of the urban deterioration of certain values which can live genuinely only in a relatively homogeneous and primary rural milieu. The "problems" discussed typically concern urban behavior. When "rural problems" are discussed, they are conceived as due to encroaching urbanization.[52] The notion of disorganization is quite often merely the absence of that *type* of organization associated with the stuff of primary-group communities having Christian and Jeffersonian legitimations.[53]

Cooley, the local colorist of American sociology, was the chief publicist of this conception of normal organization. He held "the great historical task of mankind" to be the more effective and wider organization of that moral

---

[49]J. L. Gillin (b), p. 411: "In the city we have a greater degree of disorganization in the sense in which we use that term' '; p. 410: ". . .in the simple and well-organized ties of country life. . .''; p. 409: "Recreation in the country is largely homemade. . . .In the city it is professional. . . .The patterns of behavior. . .are here again disorganized and new patterns have to be found." Gillette and Reinhardt, p. 116: "Cities exhibit all the social problems, save those peculiar to agricultural extractive pursuits." H. P. Fairchild, p. 304: "Since there are no *natural* facilities available to the majority of the *denizens* of cities for the gratification of the desire for dancing, it inevitably follows that provision is made on a commercial basis" (my italics). C. M. Rosenquist, p. 47: "The controls which were effective in the small, settled farm community no longer suffice in. . .the city. To this fact may be traced many of the conditions we speak of as social problems. . . ." W. G. Beach and E. E. Walker, pp. 102–3: ". . .men find their life interests and values in group membership and participation. The most influential groups are those which provide intimate, face-to-face relationships, as the family, the playground, the club, the neighborhood, and the small community. . . .Any wholesome and satisfying life must provide for a continuation of such small groups and institutional forms. . . .One of the most elusive and challenging problems arising from the growth of cities is that of preventing the complete disorganization of essential social groups. In the rural community. . . ." J. H. S. Bossard (a), p. 113: "The marked trend of population to the city and the rapid rise of large urban centers, together with their reflex upon the rural regions, constitute the basis of virtually every problem to be discussed in this volume."

[50]This is what Waller does *not* do in his provocative discussion of "humanitarian" and "organizing mores" ("Social Problems and the Mores," *American Sociological Review,* December, 1936, pp. 922–33).

[51]J. L. Gillin (b), p. 407: The home "developing as. . .rural" is considered "disorganized" in the city; p. 409: "[In the city] it is only the rebel, unable and unwilling to adjust himself to machine and organization, who retains personal independence. . . .The farmer, conscious that he lives by his own thinking. . .responds to his environment with a feeling of independence—a normal response. The city worker has no keen perception of his dependence upon nature." Elliott and

Merrill, p. 32: "However different this approach, the basic dilemma of civilization is the fundamental disparity of values and standards of universally accepted definitions of the situation."

[52]C. A. Ellwood (b), p. 281: "The reflex of the city problem is the rural problem." J. L. Gillen (b), p. 429: "[Urbanization] which has modified the solidarity of the rural family. . . ." W. J. Hayes and I. V. Shannon, p. 22: "Contacts. . .emanicate individuals from control of primary groups. . .this leads to setting up personal norms of behavior instead of conforming to group standards." (Implies no conception of *urban* types of norms.)

[53]The intellectual consequences of the rural to urban drift are much wider than the perspectives noted in the literature of pathology. In more general American sociology the writings of a man like E. A. Ross are to be understood in terms of a reaction of those oriented to a farmer's democracy against the growth of big business, in its control of railroads, etc. Another division of American sociology in which America's rural past is *intellectually* evident is "rural sociology" itself. This field shows the positive side of the matter, for here the yearning for the values associated with rural simplicity and neighborliness is even more noticeable. In this literature a primary, rural heritage is taken as the source of "stability" and is conceived as the reservoir of "values." Such straddling concepts as "urban" function to limit recognition of the urban character of dominant contemporary social structures. In a historical sense we need not argue with these emphases: the underlying form of American democracy and religion, e.g., has drawn much from the dominance of a rural society. And a rapid urbanization may well be only a veneer upon masses of rurally oriented personalities. But the kind of structural stability in America which grew from rural patterns is historical. In the world today the kind of stability that can—indeed, in part has—emerged from the hunger for those primary contacts historically associated with ties of blood and closeness to soil is a streamlined variety.

order and pattern of virtues developed in primary groups and communities.[54] Cooley took the idealists' absolute[55] and gave it the characteristics of an organic village; all the world should be an enlarged, Christian-democratic version of a rural village. He practically assimilated "society" to this primary-group community, and he blessed it emotionally and conceptually.[56] "There is reflected here," says T. V. Smith of Cooley—and what he says will hold for the typical social pathologist—"what is highly common in our culture, an ideal of intimacy short of which we do not rest satisfied where other people are concerned. Social distance is a dire fate, achieved with difficulty and lamented as highly unideal, not to say as immoral, in our Christian traditions. It is not enough to have saints; we must have "communion" of the saints. In order to have social relations, we must nuzzle one another."[57]

The aim to preserve rurally oriented values and stabilities is indicated by the implicit model which operates to detect urban disorganization; it is also shown by the stress upon *community* welfare. The community is taken as a major unit, and often it sets the scope of concern and problematization.[58] It is also within the framework of ideally democratic communities that proposed solutions are to be worked out.[59] It should be noted that sometimes, although not typically or exclusively, solutions are conceived as dependent upon abstract moral traits or democratic surrogates of them, such as a "unanimous public will."[60]

"Cultural lag" is considered by many pathologists to be the concept with which many scattered problems may be detected and systematized. Whereas the approach by deviation from norms is oriented "ideologically" toward a rural type of order and stability, the

---

[54]*Social Organization,* chap. v.

[55]G. H. Mead, "Cooley's Contribution to American Social Thought," *American Journal of Sociology,* XXXV, 701: "Cooley was Emersonian in finding the individual self in an oversoul." Cf. G. W. F. Hegel, *Lectures on the Philosophy of History* (London: Geo. Bell & Sons, 1884), especially pp. 39–44.

[56]Note the common association of urban "impersonality" and "formalism" with "disorganization." Elliott and Merrill, p. 16: ". . .lack of harmony between the various units of the social order is in a sense. . .exemplified by the impersonal nature of the social organization and the consequent process of social disorganization. . . .[cf. C. H. Cooley, *Social Process,* pp. 3–29]"; p. 574: "There is a very close relationship between formalism and disorganization, although at first glance the two states appear to be opposite poles in the social process. They are in reality sequential steps in the same great movement of disorganization, which grows out of formalism. . . ."

[57]*Beyond Conscience,* p. 111.

[58]C. A. Ellwood (*b*), p. 12: "All forms of association are of interest to the sociologist, though not all are of equal importance. The natural, genetic social groups, which we may call 'communities,' serve best to exhibit sociological problems. Through the study of such simple and primary groups as the family and the neighborhood group, for example, the prob-

lems of sociology can be much better attacked than through the study of society at large or association in general"; pp. 76–77: ". . .natural groupings, such as the family, the neighborhood, the city, the state or province, and the nation. They may be, and usually are, called *communities,* since they are composed of individuals who carry on all phases of a common life. Voluntary, purposive associations always exist within some community, whether large or small. Groups which we call 'communities' are, therefore, more embracing, more stable, less artificial and specialized than purely voluntary groups. For this reason communities are of more interest to the sociologist than specialized voluntary groups, and sociology is in a peculiar sense a study of the problems of community life." J. H. S. Bossard (*a*), pp. 49–50: "Acceptance of the community as a definite unit in social work and in social theory has become general during the past fifteen years. American participation in the World War was an important factor in bringing this about, first because the community constituted the basic expression of that democratic spirit which the war engendered, and second, the community was seized upon by the various war-time activities and drives as the most effective unit for the mobilization of the spirit and resources of the nation."

[59]Gillin, Dittmer, and Colbert, p. 15: ". . .*social work,* which means, scientifically developing and adjusting human relations in a way that will secure normal life to individuals and communities and encourage individual and community progress"; p. 47: ". . .it is important to keep in mind that the central problem is that of adjusting our social life and our social institutions, so that, as individuals and as communities, we may use and enjoy the largest measure of civilization possible, and promote further progress." M. P. Follett (*a*), Part III, has suggested that neighborhood groups be organized into political units. This would permit the expression of daily life and bring to the surface live needs that they may become the substance of politics. The neighborhood as a political unit would make possible friendly acquaintance; it would socialize people and would make for "the realization of oneness."

[60]J. L. Gillin (*b*), p. 97: "The 'liquor problem' is as acute in the United States today as it ever was in the past, perhaps even more so"; p. 101: "The solution must spring from an aroused and unanimous public will."

cultural-lag model is tacitly oriented in a "utopian"[61] and progressive manner toward changing some areas of the culture or certain institutions so as to "integrate" them with the state of progressive technology.[62] We must analyze the use made by pathologists of "lag" rather than abstract formulations of it.[63]

Even though all the situations called "lags" *exist* in the present, their functional realities are referred back, away from the present. Evaluations are thus translated into a time sequence; cultural lag is an assertion of unequal "progress." It tells us what changes are "called for," what changes "ought" to have come about and didn't. In terms of various spheres of society it says what progress is, tells us how much we have had, ought to have had, didn't have, and when and where we didn't have it. The imputation of "lag" is complicated by the historical judgment in whose guise it is advanced and by the programmatic content being shoved into pseudo-objective phrases, as, for example, "called for."

It is not enough to recognize that the stating of problems in terms of cultural lag involves evaluations, however disguised. One must find the general loci of this kind of evaluation and then explain why just this form of evaluation has been so readily accepted and widely used by pathologists. The model in which institutions lag behind technology and science involves a positive evaluation of natural science and of orderly progressive change. Loosely, it derives from a liberal continuation of the enlightenment with its full rationalism, its messianic and now politically naïve admiration of physical science as a kind of thinking and activity, and with its concept of time as progress. This notion of progress was carried into American colleges by the once prevalent Scottish moral philosophy. From after the Civil War through the first two or three decades of the twentieth century the expanding business and middle classes were taking over instruments of production, political power, and social prestige; and many of the academic men of the generation were recruited from these rising strata and/or actively mingled with them. Notions of progress are congenial to those who are rising in the scale of position and income.

Those sociologists who think in terms of this model have not typically focused upon the conditions and interest groups underlying variant "rates of change" in different spheres. One might say that in terms of the rates of change at which sectors of culture *could* move, it is technology that is "lagging," for the specific reason of the control of patents, etc., by intrenched interests.[64] In contrast to the pathologists' use, Veblen's use of "lag, leak, and friction" is a structural analysis of industry versus business enterprise.[65] He focused on where "the lag" seemed to pinch; he attempted to show how the trained incapacity of legitimate businessmen acting within entrepreneurial canons would result in a commercial sabotage of production and efficiency in order to augment profits within a system of price and ownership. He did not like this "unworkman-like result," and he detailed its mechanism. In the pathologists' usage the conception has lost this specific and structural anchorage: it has been generalized and applied to everything fragmentarily. This generalization occurs with the aid of such blanket terms as "adaptive culture" and "material culture."[66] There is no specific focus for a program of action embodied in the application of such terms.

Another model in terms of which disorganizations are instituted is that of "social change" itself.[67] This model is not handled in any one

---

[61]Cf. K. Mannheim, *Idealogy and Utopia,* for definitions of these terms.

[62]However, "lag" and "norms" are not unrelated: Queen, Bodenhafer, and Harper, p. 437: "Much of the discussion of cultural lags in the family assumes some kind of normal pattern which is commonly believed to have permanent validity because of the functions performed."

[63]See examples given in J. W. Woodard's "Critical Notes on the Cultural Lag Concept," *Social Forces,* March, 1934, p. 388.

[64]See, e.g., B. J. Stern's article in *Annals of the American Academy of Political and Social Science,* November, 1938.

[65]*The Engineers and the Price System; The Theory of Business Enterprise.*

[66]J. H. S. Bossard (*a*), p. 5: ". . .as Ogburn put it [W. F. Ogburn, *Social Change* (1922)] to the extent that the adaptive culture has not kept pace with the material culture, the amount of social ill-being has increased relatively."

[67]J. L. Gillin (*b*), p. 416: "Social disorganization is a function of rapidly changing conditions in people's lives." W. J. Hayes and I. V. Shannon, p. 20: "Social disorganization is an abrupt break in the existing social arrangements

typical way, but usually it carries the implicit assumption that human beings are "adjusted" satisfactorily to any social condition that has existed for a long time and that, when some aspect of social life changes, it may lead to a social problem.[68] The notion is oriented ideologically and yet participates in assumptions similar to those of cultural lag, which, indeed, might be considered a variant of it. Such a scheme for problematization buttresses and is buttressed by the idea of continuous process, commented on above; but here the slow, "evolutionary" pace of change is taken explicitly as normal and organized,[69] whereas "discontinuity" is taken as problematic.[70] The orientation to "rural" types of organization should be recalled. In line with the stress on continuous process, the point where sanctioned order meets advisable change is not typically or structurally drawn.[71] A conception

of "balance" is usual and sometimes is explicitly sanctioned.[72] The question, "Changes in what spheres induce disorganization?" is left open; the position taken is usually somewhere between extremes, both of which are held to be bad.[73] This comes out in the obvious fact that what a conservative calls *dis*organization, a radical might call *re*organization. Without a construction of total social structures that are actually emerging, one remains caught between simple evaluations.

Besides deviation from norms, orientation to rural principles of stability, cultural lag, and social change, another conception in terms of which "problems" are typically discussed is that of adaptation or "adjustment" and their opposites.[74] The pathological or disorganized is the maladjusted. This concept, as well as that of the "normal," is usually left empty of concrete, social content;[75] or its content is, in effect, a

---

or a serious alteration in the routine of group life causing maladjustment." H. W. Odum, p. 100: ". . .if one reviews the general categories of social problems already listed in previous chapters, it must be clear that most of them or their present manifestations are due to or accentuated by the process of social change."

[68]The point is made and acutely discussed by Rosenquist, pp. 8–10.

[69]Gillin, Dittmer, and Colbert, p. 48: "Social life and its products require long periods of time to develop and ripen. . . ." Gillette and Reinhardt, p. 13: "The larger proportion of social changes are small and simple, and resemble osmosis in the field of physics and organic life." This gradualism is related to the orientation to primary group relations and experiences and hence to the "sharing" conception of the social. E.g., Elliott and Merrill, p. 11: "Assimilation, on the other hand, is gradual and depends upon some degree of contact and communication, if there is to be any vital sharing of common experience (Cf. M. P. Follett, *Creative Experience*). . . ."

[70]Gillette and Reinhardt, p. 30: ". . .the need for thought about discontinuity in industry or education and about our dependence on proper training to keep society stabilized and progressive should be emphasized"; p. 21: "The habitual, daily, routine, conventional activities of life fortunately make up the greater part of life, most of the time. Often, however, they are broken across by social breakdowns, disturbances, and dislocations and the appearance of troublesome classes of persons." C. A. Ellwood (*a*), p. 230: ". . .revolution is not a *normal* method of social change; . . .it marks the breakdown of the normal means of social development; . . .it is not inevitable, but may easily be avoided by plasticity in social institutions and in the mental attitudes of classes and individuals. . . ."

[71]The notion of temporal contingency, at times extended to the point of historical irrationality, plays into the processual,

nonstructural characteristics of the perspective; notice also its commensurability with the apolitical and one-thing-at-a-time reformism. Elliott and Merrill, p. 3: "Life is dynamic. Life is ceaseless, bewildering change, and man, armed though he is with the experience of the past, can never be certain of the future. He must recognize that the immediate present is a constantly changing frame of reference and that future problems are a matter of chance for which the past offers no sure panacea."

[72]E. C. Hayes' Editor's Introduction to U. G. Weatherly, p. xii: "Realization that progressive change is not likely to be less in the generation next to come. . .and determination. . .to promote progress, is the normal attitude for every person who is animated by generous loyalty and. . . ." Weatherly, p. 138: "Both innovation and conservatism have their value, and the balance between them, which is an ideal attitude. . ."; p. 380: "Discipline and liberation are not two antagonistic processes; they are complimentary parts of the same process, which is social equilibration. They illustrate the law of physics. . .stability is reached only by a balance of forces."

[73]A. Ellwood (*a*), p. vii: "The aim of the book is to indicate the direction which our social thinking must take if we are to avoid revolution, on the one hand, and reactions, on the other."

[74]H. P. Fairchild, p. 35: ". . .it can be safely said that maladjustments are among the most numerous and important of all forms of abnormality, frequently being so extensive as to include entire social groups or classes."

[75]Gillin, Dittmer, and Colbert, p. 536: "All social problems grow out of *the* social problems—the problem of the adjustment of man to his universe, and of the social universe to man. The maladjustments in these relationships give us all our social problems. . . ." H. P. Fairchild, p. 16: "While the word 'normal' carries a fairly definite and, for the most

propaganda for conformity to those norms and traits ideally associated with small-town, middle-class milieux.[76] When it is an individual who is thought to be maladjusted, the "social type" within which he is maladjusted is not stated. Social and moral elements are masked by a quasi-biological meaning of the term "adaptation"[77] with an entourage of apparently socially bare terms like "existence" and "survival," which seem still to draw prestige from the vogue of evolutionism.[78] Both the quasi-biological and the structureless character of the concept "adjustment" tend, by formalization, to universalize the term, thus again obscuring specific social content. Use of "adjustment" accepts the goals and the means of smaller community milieux.[79]

At the most, writers using these terms suggest techniques or means believed to be less disruptive than others to attain the goals that are given. They do not typically consider whether or not certain groups or individuals caught in economically underprivileged situations can possibly obtain the current goals without drastic shifts in the basic institutions which channel and promote them. The idea of adjustment seems to be most directly applicable to a social scene in which, on the one hand, there is a society and, on the other, an individual immigrant.[80] The immigrant then "adjusts" to the new environment. The "immigrant problem" was early in the pathologist's center of focus, and the concepts used in stating it may have been carried over as the bases for a model of experience and formulations of other "problems." *The Polish Peasant* (1918), which has had a very strong influence on the books under consideration, was empirically focused upon an immigrant group.

In approaching the notion of adjustment, one may analyze the specific illustrations of maladjustment that are given and from these instances infer a type of social person who in this literature is evaluated as "adjusted." The ideally adjusted man of the social pathologists is

---

part, accurate implication to the mind of any intelligent person, it is nevertheless extremely difficult to define in concrete terms. . . .As commonly used to convey a definite idea, the word 'normal' means that which is in harmony with the general make-up and organization of the object under discussion—that which is consistent with other normal factors.''

[76]Elliott and Merrill, p. 17, correctly assert that in "Edward T. Divine's discussion of 'the normal life' the norm is the healthy and uneventful life cycle of the average middle-class man or woman. These persons are never subjected to the temptations of great wealth. Neither do they come in contact with poverty, crime, vice, and other unpleasantly sordid aspects of life [*The Normal Life,* pp. 5–8]. His discussion is thus a consideration of the 'normal standards' for the several ages of the bourgeoisie. . . .''

[77]When it is so hidden; but note the heavily sentimental endowment the term may receive: R. C. Dexter, p. 408: ''. . .few of the present generation of little ones, and fewer still of the next, will never see the sun or the green grass because of the sins of their parents or the carelessness of their physician; and thanks to our increasing provision for free public education, more and more adapted to the needs of the individual child, thousands of boys and girls will become intelligent, responsible citizens, worthy of a free nation, instead of pawns for unscrupulous politicians. All this and much more is due to social adjustments, made by the unceasing effort and sacrifice of men and women who. . . .''

[78]J. L. Gillin (*b*), p. 4: "Social pathology . . . is the study of the social patterns and processes involved in man's failure to adjust himself and his institutions to the necessities of existence to the end that he may survive and satisfy the felt needs of his nature.''

[79]J. L. Gillin (*b*), p. 8: "An individual who does not approximate these [socially approved] standards is said to be *unadjusted.* If he does not concern himself with living up to them, he is said to be demoralized or disorganized.'' R. C. Dexter, p. 407: "In this book the term Social Adjustment has been. . .used as applying to. . .the necessary task of

smoothing-off the rough edges and softening the sledgehammer blows of an indifferent social system. The term. . .is practically synonymous with social adaptation—the fitting of man to his complete environment, physical and social alike. Until the present it has been the especially maladjusted individual or group who has received the service of 'straighteners.' '' (Note *ideological* orientation of concept.)

[80]H. P. Fairchild, p. 34: "The other form of incompetence, which may be called 'maladjustment,' does not imply any lack on the part of the individual himself. . . .The man is all right, but he is not in the right place. Our immigrants furnish abundant examples of this form of incompetence. . . . But the foreigner is not by any means the sole example of maladjustment. Our modern life, particularly our modern city life, teems with cases of this sort.'' J. H. S. Bossard (*a*), p. 110 (under "The Immigrant's Problem of Adjustment"): "To most persons, life consists in large measure of habitual responses to the demands of a fairly fixed environment. When man changes his environment, new and perhaps untried responses are called for. New adjustments must be made, as we say.'' J. L. Gillin (*b*), p. 10: "Social pathology. . .arises out of the maladjustment between the individual and the social structure.'' Elliott and Merrill, p. 22: "Just as an effective social organization implies a harmony between individual and social interests, so a disorganized social order must involve a conflict between individual and social points of view.''

"socialized." This term seems to operate ethically as the opposite of "selfish;"[81] it implies that the adjusted man conforms to middle-class morality and motives and "participates" in the gradual progress of respectable institutions. If he is not a "joiner," he certainly gets around and into many community organizations.[82] If he is socialized, the individual thinks of others and is kindly toward them. He does not brood or mope

about but is somewhat extravert, eagerly participating in his community's institutions. His mother and father were not divorced, nor was his home ever broken. He is "successful"—at least in a modest way—since he is ambitious; but he does not speculate about matters too far above his means, lest he become "a fantasy thinker," and the little men don't scramble after the big money. The less abstract the traits and fulfilled "needs" of "the adjusted man" are, the more they gravitate toward the norms of independent middle-class persons verbally living out Protestant ideals in the small towns of America.[83]

---

[81]Gillin, Dittmer, and Colbert, pp. 16–17: "By *socialization* we mean the directing of human motives toward giving to 'even the least' of the members of the social whole the benefits of cultural development. Socialization is thus practically the opposite to *aloofness, selfishness, greed, exploitation,* and *profiteering.* It causes the individual and the group to *feel* their *oneness* with the social whole. . . .In brief, what society regards as *moral, i.e.,* good for the whole, becomes the aim of socialized individuals and groups. This being true, the improvement of society rests to a very large extent upon *moral progress.*"

[82]See Queen and Gruener, *Social Pathology: Obstacles to Social Participation.* These authors would deny this mode of statement, but such verbal denials must be tested against what they have done and the framework they have actually employed in defining pathologies. Their criterion of the pathological is correctly indicated in the subtitle of their book. Elliott and Merrill, p. 580: "There are various criteria by which the degree of individual participation may be measured roughly. . .whether or not he votes at elections. . .the individual's ownership of real or personal property. . .the degree of specific interest in community activities may be roughly measured by the number and character of the institutions to which the individual belongs, as well as voluntary community activities in which he participates. Communities in which there is a high percentage of individuals with a positive rating on the items listed above are logically those which are the most highly organized and efficient." (Note the character of the institutions, participation in which is defined as organized.)

[83]See above documentation; notice the Protestant ethical accent on *utility* and what it will do for one, apparently irrespective of social fact: Gillin, Dittmer, and Colbert, p. 106: "People who are useful, no matter what happens to their race or color, come to be liked and respected. Consequently, the central aim of a sound educational program should be to teach people to be useful. (Hart, Hornell, *The Science of Social Relations,* 1927, pp. 521–524)." In the following, note the norm of competitiveness: Elliott and Merrill, pp. 29–30: "Often, however, the individual cannot or will not compete. We then have the following pathological manifestations: '. . .the *dependent.* . .who is unable to compete; the *defective.* . .who is, if not unable, at least handicapped in his efforts to compete. The *criminal,* on the other hand, . . .who is perhaps unable, but at any rate refuses, to compete according to the rules which society lays down' (Park and Burgess, *Introduction to the Science of Sociology,* p. 560)." Among the traits thought to characterize "the good life from the standpoint of the individual," Odum, pp. 50–51, cites: "patience," "specialized knowledge of some particular thing," "skill," "optimism," "love of work," "dynamic personality," "moderation," "trained will power," etc. Cf., in this connection, K. Davis, "Mental Hygiene and the Class Structure," *Psychiatry: Journal of the Biology and Pathology of Interpersonal Relations,* February, 1938, pp. 55–65.

THE SOCIOLOGIST AS PARTISAN
Sociology and the Welfare State

Alvin W. Gouldner
Washington University

Sociology begins by disenchanting the world, and it proceeds by disenchanting itself. Having insisted upon the non-rationality of those whom it studies, sociology comes, at length, to confess its own captivity. But voluntary confessions should always be suspect. We should try to notice, when men complain about the bonds that enchain them, whether their tone is one of disappointed resentment or of comfortable accommodation.

In 1961, in an address to a learned society, I attacked what I took to be dominant professional ideology of sociologists: that favoring the value-free doctrine of social science. Today, only six years later, I find myself in the uncomfortable position of drawing back from some who found my argument against the value-free myth so persuasive. I now find myself caught between two contradictory impulses: I do not wish to seem ungrateful toward those who sympathized with my position, yet the issue is a serious one and I also do not want to encumber discussions of it with considerations of personal tact or professional courtesy.

In a nutshell: I fear that the myth of a value-free social science is about to be supplanted by still another myth, and that the once glib ac-

ceptance of the value-free doctrine is about to be superseded by a new but no less glib rejection of it. My uneasiness concerning this came to a head upon reading Howard S. Becker's paper which boldly raises the problem, "Whose Side Are We on?" Rather than presenting the storybook picture of the sociologist as a value-free scientist, Becker begins by stating that it is impossible for a social scientist to do research "uncontaminated by personal and political sympathies." We are told that, no matter what perspective a sociologist takes, his work must be written either from the standpoint of subordinates or superiors. Apparently one cannot do equal justice to both.

The most telling indication of just how large a change sociology has recently undergone may be seen not so much from the position that Becker takes but from the way his position is presented. There is nothing defensive in the manner that Becker rejects the older, nonpartisan conception of the sociologist's role. Instead, Becker presents his rejection of this position as if it needed no explanation; as if it were completely obvious to everyone; and as if there were nothing to argue about. His posture is not that of the cocky challenger but of a blasé referee announcing the outcome of a finished fight, and whose verdict must be obvious. More than anything else, this suggests that there has been a substantial change in the occupational culture of sociologists in the last decade or so.

Alvin W. Gouldner (1968) "The Sociologist as Partisan: Sociology and the Welfare State." *The American Sociologist* Vol. 3 (May): 103–116. Reprinted by permission of the American Sociological Association.

Becker's conception of the partisan sociologist would be unimportant were it simply an expression of his own idiosyncratic individuality. The fact is, however, that there is every reason to believe that he is voicing the sentiments of a substantial and probably growing number of sociologists, and, in particular, those whose interests focus upon the study of social problems, or the sociology of "deviant behavior." It is notable that the article in which Becker asks, "Whose Side Are We on?" was delivered originally as his Presidential Address to the Society for the Study of Social Problems. This implies that Becker's constituency was at least large enough to have elected him to this modestly notable position in the structure of American social science. In short, Becker does not speak for himself alone.

That Becker's is a representative voice is further indicated by his own writings on deviant behavior, especially his books *The Outsiders* and *Social Problems,* which are presently one of the two dominant standpoints in American sociology concerning the analysis of social problems. Becker, then, is a leading spokesman of a viable coterie of sociologists specializing in the study of social deviance, whose members include such able men as Howard Brotz, Donald Cressey, John Kitsuse, Raymond Mack, David Matza, Sheldon Messinger, Ned Polsky, and Albert J. Reiss; and this coterie in turn overlaps with a larger network that essentially comprises the "Chicago School" of sociology. Becker's plea for a partisan sociology may be regarded as a weather-vane signaling that new winds are beginning to blow. Yet the direction from which they come is not altogether clear.

Since Becker forcefully entitles his discussion, "Whose Side Are We on?", we might reasonably expect that he will, at some point, give a straightforward answer to his own straightforward question. Yet one reads it through and puts it down, only suddenly to notice that Becker gives no direct answer at all to his own question. Indeed, we pick it up once again to make sure that our first impression is correct and discover that this is indeed the case. If, in an effort to puzzle this through, we turn to Becker's earlier work, *The Outsiders,* we find that he does essentially the same thing there. In the culminating pages of that volume, he also asks: "Whose viewpoint shall we present?" And once again we find that no straightforward answer is given. If there is a difference between this volume and Becker's Presidential Address, it is that, in the earlier volume, he states explicitly that there is no basis in terms of which an answer to the question can be formulated. That is, he holds that neither strategic considerations, nor temperamental and moral considerations can tell us "to which viewpoint we should subscribe."

It seems equally clear, however, that, although Becker refuses explicitly to answer his explicit question, he does have an answer to it. If instead of looking at the explicit formulations advanced by Becker or other members of his group, we look, rather, at the specific researches that they have undertaken, we find that they unmistakably do adopt a specific standpoint, a kind of *underdog* identification. As I have said elsewhere, theirs is a school of thought that finds itself at home in the world of hip, drug addicts, jazz musicians, cab drivers, prostitutes, night people, drifters, grifters, and skidders: the "cool world." Their identifications are with deviant rather than respectable society. "For them, orientation to the underworld has become the equivalent of the proletarian identifications felt by some intellectuals during the 1930's. For not only do they study it, but in a way they speak on its behalf, affirming the authenticity of its style of life." Their specific researches plainly betray, for example, that they are concerned with and resent the legal straitjacket in which the drug addict is confined in the United States, or the degrading impact of the mental hospital on its inmates. In one part, this school of thought represents a metaphysics of the underdog and of the underworld: a metaphysics in which conventional society is viewed from the standpoint of a group outside of its own respectable social structures. At any rate, this is how it began; but it is not how it remains.

When Becker tells us that the world is divided into subordinates and superordinates, and that sociologists must look at the world from one side or the other, his implication seems to be that they should look at it from the standpoint of the deviant, of the subordinate, of the underdog. For these people, Becker says in his Presidential Address, are "more sinned against than sinning." The question arises as to why it is that, although Becker's leanings are clear enough, he chooses not to express them explicitly. Why is it that Becker does not declare openly for the standpoint of the underdog, since he clearly feels this way? If partisanship is inevitable, why doesn't Becker clearly state whose side *he* is on, rather than simply goading others to take a stand? There are probably both intellectual and practical reasons for Becker's failure to give a definitive answer to his own question—whose side are we on? First, I want to explore briefly some of the intellectual and practical factors that lead to Becker's reticence.

THE THEORY AND PRACTICE OF COOL

In *The Outsiders,* Becker makes it plain that his own theoretical contribution leads to a focus, not merely on the rule breakers or deviants, but also to a study of those who make and enforce the rules, and most especially the latter. Although much of Becker's concrete research has been on deviants, his own theory, which came later, has largely focused on rule-makers and rule-enforcers. A crucial stage, in what Becker calls "the deviant career," occurs when someone declares that someone else's behavior has violated the rules of their game. The deviant, in short, is made by society in two senses: first, that society makes the rules which he has broken and, secondly, that society "enforces" them and makes a public declaration announcing that the rules have been broken. The making of the deviant, then, entails a process of social interaction. That being the case, the deviant-making process cannot be understood unless rule-making and rule-enforcing procedures or persons are studied.

The question then arises as to *whose* standpoint shall be adopted when rule-*makers* or rule-*enforcers* are themselves studied. Shall we describe their behavior from their own "overdog" standpoint or from that of the "underdog" deviants? One answer is given by Becker's more general theoretical position, the tradition of George Herbert Mead, which requires that men—even if they are "overdogs"—be studied from the standpoint of their *own* conceptions of reality. The point here, of course, is that men's definition of their situation shapes their behavior; hence to understand and predict their behavior we must see it as they do. Becker's own specific theory of deviance, then, constrains him to look at the behavior of rule-*enforcers,* while his Meadian tradition requires him to look at it from *their* standpoint, rather than that of the deviant rule-breakers.

But this, by itself, would still create no difficulties. For, if Becker were entirely comfortable with this position, he would simply recommend that studies be conducted from the standpoint of *whoever* is being studied, be they rule-enforcers, rule-makers, or deviant rule-breakers. If he were to be consistent, then, Becker would answer the question, whose side are we on?, simply by stating that we are on the side of whomever we are studying at a given time. In other words, he would advocate the devotional promiscuity of sacred prostitution.

The reason that Becker cannot adopt this fairly obvious conclusion, and why he cannot give any answer to his question, is a simple one: his *sentiments* are at variance with his theories. Becker is sentimentally disposed to view the entire ambience of deviance from the standpoint of the deviant persons themselves. It is this that makes him sit on a fence of his own construction. Caught in the divergence between his theories and his sentiments, he is unable to answer his own question, whose side are we on? His sentimental disposition to see the world of deviance from the standpoint of the deviant conflicts with his theoretical disposition to take the standpoint of whichever group he happens to be studying. Becker "solves" this problem by raising the question, whose side are we on?, with such blunt force that makes the very question seem like an answer; and he evidences his own sentiments so plainly that he need not assert them and, therefore, need never take responsibility for them.

In suggesting that Becker has refused to answer his own question because of this conflict between his theories and his sentiments, I do not mean that this is the only reason for his reticence.

For there are other, more practical costs that would have to be paid were Becker (or anyone else) to announce such a position in a direct manner. A straightforward affirmation of sympathy with the underdog would, for one thing, create practical difficulties for Becker as a researcher. For he might one day wish access to information held by rule-enforcers and rule-makers who, in turn, might be dismayed to hear that Becker was disposed to view them from the standpoint of those whom they feel to be threats to society. Again, a straightforward affirmation of sympathy with the underdog or deviant might create a certain uneasiness among those who, either directly or indirectly, provide the resources which Becker, like any other research entrepreneur, requires. An outright expression of concern for or sympathy with the underdog thus conflicts with the sociologist's practical and professional interests. In other words: even genuine attachments to the underdog must be compromised with a tacit but no less genuine attachment to self-interest. We are, in short, also on our own side.

There is, I believe, still another reason why Becker fails to say whose side he is on. It has to do with the fact that he is not only on his own side and that, for all its underdog sympathies, his work is also on the side of one of the currently conflicting elites in the welfare establishment. But I must hold this for development at a later point. Becker's reticence about answering his own question, then, derives in part from a conflict between his sentiments and his interests, in part from a conflict between his theories and his sentiments, and, in part also, from a conflict within his sentiments.

There is still another way that Becker copes with the conflict between his sympathetic concern for the underdog and his equally human concern for more practical interests. We can see this if we notice the implicit irony in Becker's position, an irony that contributes importantly to the persuasiveness of his argument. Becker's central thesis is the impossibility of being value-free and the necessity of taking sides. In other words, he argues that real detachment is impossible. Yet one of the very things that makes Becker convincing is that he somehow manages to con-

vey a sense of dispassionate detachment. This is largely accomplished through his *style*. Written in a non-polemical and flaccid style, Becker's rhetoric conveys an image of himself as coolly detached, despite his own explicit argument that partisanship and involvement are inevitable. The limp sobriety of his style projects an image of him as someone who has no axe to grind. It is through his style, then, that Becker invites us to believe that it is possible for a work to be biased without paying intellectual costs.

In effect, Becker appears to hold that emotional blandness is somehow an effective antidote to partisanship. Indeed, at various points, one suspects that Becker believes that blandness is also an effective substitute for analytic probing and hard thought. As I shall later develop, Becker believes that the real enemy of good social science is not a one-sided value commitment, but, rather, something that he calls "sentimentality."

Thus, while Becker invites partisanship, he rejects passionate or erect partisanship. In the very process of opposing the conventional myth of the value-free social scientist, Becker thereby creates a new myth, the myth of the *sentiment-free* social scientist. He begins to formulate a new myth that tacitly claims there is such a thing as a purely cerebral partisanship, which is devoid of emotional commitment and "sentimentality." Underlying this is Becker's tacit assumption that these entail intellectual costs, and costs *alone*. It seems equally reasonable to believe, however, that passion and sentimentality serve not only to produce costs and intellectual blindness, but may just as likely serve to enlighten, and to sensitize us to certain aspects of the social world. Indeed, it may be suspected that it is precisely, in some part, because there are certain intellectual gains derived from emotionally tinged commitments that it is possible for social scientists to sustain such commitments. In short, sentimentality does not seem to be the heartless villain that Becker makes it out to be. It is Becker who is being "sentimental" when he fosters a myth that holds it possible to have a sentiment-free commitment.

To recommend that sociological researches be undertaken from the standpoint of subordinates or underdogs creates as many problems as it resolves. While such a standpoint expresses a sympathy that I share, I still feel obligated to ask: How do we know an underdog when we see one? Who and what are underdogs? What marks someone as an underdog? And we have to ask an even more difficult question: Why *should* we undertake our studies from the standpoint of the subordinate, underdog?

Becker may recognize the intellectual bind in which he has placed himself by inviting research from the standpoint of the underdog. But he has only begun to glimpse it. Although acknowledging that a superior may be a subordinate to someone else, he fails to recognize that this works both ways: everyone who is a subordinate, *vis-a-vis* his superior, is also a superior in relation to some third party. If we regard every man as both superior and subordinate, overdog and underdog, how then do we know and on what basis do we select the underdogs whose standpoint we shall take? Clearly, Becker presents no logical solution to this quandary; he can intend it to be resolved only by the impulses of the very sentimentality that he deplores. It is also likely that Becker never confronts this problem—with *which* underdog shall he sympathize?—because he tacitly assumes that good liberals will instinctively know, and always agree, who the true underdogs are.

Let me acknowledge, once for all, that I share Becker's underdog sympathies. Yet I also believe that sociological study from an underdog standpoint will be intellectually impaired without clarifying the *grounds* for the commitment. A commitment made on the basis of an unexamined ideology may allow us to feel a manly righteousness, but it leaves us blind.

SOCIOLOGY AND SUFFERING

The question then is: Are there any *good* reasons to conduct research from an underdog standpoint? One such reason may be that a feelingful commitment to the underdog's plight enables us to do a better job as *sociologists.* Specifically, when we study a social world from an underdog standpoint, we elevate into public view certain under-privileged aspects of reality. These are aspects of social reality that tend to be comparatively unknown or publicly neglected because they are dissonant with conceptions of reality held by the powerful and respectable. To take the standpoint of the underdog in our researches, then, does two things. First, it gives us new information concerning social worlds about which many members of our society, including ourselves, know little or nothing. Secondly, it may give us new perspectives on worlds that we had thought familiar and presumed that we already knew. To that extent, then, taking the underdog's standpoint does indeed contribute to the successful fulfillment of the intellectual obligations that we have as sociologists. It helps us do the distinctive job we have.

I have acknowledged a sympathy with the underdog and with impulses to conduct researches from his standpoint. Yet in searching for the justification of my sentiments I must also candidly confess that I see no special virtue in those who are lacking in power or authority, just as I see no special virtue that inheres in those who possess power and authority. It seems to me that neither weakness nor power as such are values that deserve to be prized.

The essential point about the underdog is that he suffers, and that his suffering is naked and visible. It is this that makes and should make a compelling demand upon us. What makes his standpoint deserving of special consideration, what makes him particularly worthy of sympathy, is that he suffers. Once we see this, however, the nature of our relationship to the underdog changes; correspondingly, the nature of the obligation that we experience as *sociologists* may also change.

First, we can recognize that there may be forms of human suffering that are unavoidable, that cannot be remedied in some particular society or at some particular time. Correspondingly, however, there are also forms of suffering that are needless at particular times and places. I think that it is the sociologist's job to give special attention to the latter, while recognizing that it is no easy task to distinguish between avoidable and unavoidable suffering, and while fearing that some will all too easily categorize certain kinds of suffering as unavoidable so that they may disregard them with comfort.

Moreover, I would also insist that even when men experience needless suffering, a suffering which is unavoidable, tragic, and truly a part of the eternal human condition, that they still deserve sympathy and loving consideration. It is vital for sociologists also to portray this unyielding part of the world. For this reason, I cannot imagine a humane sociology that would be callous to the suffering of "superiors." A sociology that ignored this would, so far as I am concerned, neither manifest a respect for truth nor a sense of common humanity.

But if all men suffer and to some extent unavoidably, is there any reason at all to feel a special sympathy for underdogs? Is there any reason to make a special effort to conduct research from their standpoint? I think that there is.

For one thing, the suffering of some is still simply and literally unknown to many in society. This is a special and important part of reality which, I think, is one of our important responsibilities to understand and communicate. The problem is not simply that there exists what Becker calls a "hierarchy of credibility"—in which men in power are presumably granted the right to declare what is real and true in the world around them. It is rather that these dominant conceptions of reality, sustained and fostered by the managers of society, have one common defect: they fail to grasp a very special type of reality, specifically the reality of the suffering of those beneath them. In failing to see this, what they must also fail to see is that those beneath them are indeed very much like themselves, in their suffering as in other ways.

This, in turn, implies that a sociology truly concerned with representing the standpoint of the underdog would most especially seek to communicate the character of his suffering, its peculiar sources and special intensity, the ways and degrees in which it is avoidable, the forces that contribute to it, and his struggle against it. The underdog's standpoint therefore deserves to be heard in sociology not because he has any special virtue and not because he alone lives in a world of suffering. A sociology of the under-

dog is justified because, and to the extent, that his suffering is less likely to be known and because—by the very reason of his being underdog—the extent and character of his suffering are likely to contain much that is avoidable.

Although Becker leans toward a sympathy and special consideration for the underdog's standpoint, and although the underdog's suffering is particularly visible, it is still one further paradox in Becker's discussion that we find him displaying no such concern for suffering. Rather, what we do find is a fear of such a concern, a fear that this concern will make us lose our cool. I would guess that it is in some part because of this fear that Becker makes such a point of rejecting "sentimentality."

Yet if it is not the suffering of the subordinate or the deviant that involves Becker—and others of his school—with the underdog, then what is it? It is my impression, from many years of reading their researches and of talking with them, that their pull to the underdog is sometimes part of a titillated attraction to the underdog's exotic difference and easily takes the form of "essays on quaintness." The danger is, then, that such an identification with the underdog becomes the urban sociologist's equivalent of the anthropologist's (onetime) romantic appreciation of the noble savage.

The Becker School's view embodies an implicit critique of lower middle class ethnocentrism, of small town respectability, of the paradoxical superiority that one ethnic can feel toward another. Indeed, one might say that theirs is most especially a critique of the uneducated middle classes. Now this is no mean thing, for the piety of these strata is certainly pervasive in the United States. Becker's rejection of their smug narrowness is wholesome and valuable.

At the same time, however, Becker's school of deviance is redolent of Romanticism. It expresses the satisfaction of the Great White Hunter who has bravely risked the perils of the urban jungle to bring back an exotic specimen. It expresses the Romanticism of the zoo curator who preeningly displays his rare specimens. And like the zookeeper, he wishes to protect his collection; he does not want spectators to throw rocks at the animals behind the bars. But neither is he eager to tear down the bars and let the animals go. The attitude of these zookeepers of deviance is to create a comfortable and humane Indian Reservation, a protected social space, within which these colorful specimens may be exhibited, unmolested and unchanged. The very empirical sensitivity to fine detail, characterizing this school, is both born of and limited by the connoisseur's fascination with the rare object: its empirical richness is inspired by a collector's aesthetic.

It is in part for this reason that, despite its challenging conception of a partisan sociology and its sympathy with the underdog, Becker's discussion is paradoxically suffused with a surprising air of complacency. Indeed, what it expresses is something quite different from the older, traditional sympathy with the plight of the underdog. Basically, it conceives of the underdog as a *victim.* In some part, this is inherent in the very conception of the processes by means of which deviance is conceived of as being generated. For the emphasis in Becker's theory is on the deviant as the product of society rather than as the rebel against it. If this is a liberal conception of deviance that wins sympathy and tolerance for the deviant, it has the paradoxical consequence of inviting us to view the deviant as a passive nonentity who is responsible neither for his suffering nor its alleviation—who is more "sinned against than sinning." Consistent with this view of the underdog as victim, is the more modern conception of him as someone who has to be managed, and should be managed better, by a bureaucratic apparatus of official caretakers. In short, it conceives of the underdog as someone maltreated by a bureaucratic establishment whose remedial efforts are ineffectual, whose custodial efforts are brutal, and whose rule enforcement techniques are self-interested. While it sees deviance as generated by a process of social interaction, as emerging out of the matrix of an unanalyzed society, it does not see deviance as deriving from specified master institutions of this larger society, or as expressing an active opposition to them.

The underdog is largely seen from the standpoint of the difficulties that are encountered when the society's caretakers attempt to cope with the deviance that has been produced in him by the society. Becker's school of deviance thus views the underdog as someone who is being mismanaged, not as someone who suffers or fights back. Here the deviant is sly but not defiant; he is tricky but not courageous; he sneers but does not accuse; he "makes out" without making a scene. Insofar as this school of theory has a critical edge to it, this is directed at the caretaking institutions who do the mopping-up job, rather than at the master institutions that produce the deviant's suffering.

It is in some part for this reason that the kinds of researches that are undertaken from this standpoint tend to exclude a concern with *political* deviance, in which men do actively fight back on behalf of their values and interests. We thus find relatively few studies of people involved in the civil rights struggle or in the peace movement. For however much these deviant groups are made to suffer, no one could easily conceive of them as mere victims well under the control of bureaucratic officialdom. It is not man-fighting-back that wins Becker's sympathy, but rather, man-on-his-back that piques his curiosity.

What we have here, then, is essentially a rejection of unenlightened middle class bigotry. And in its place is a sympathetic view of the underdog seen increasingly from the standpoint of the relatively benign, the well educated, and the *highly* placed bureaucratic officialdom: of the American administrative class. What seems to be a rejection of the standpoint of the superior is, I shall argue, actually only a rejection of the *middle-level* superior.

We may see this more clearly if we return to the problem that gives Becker his greatest uneasiness, the observation that every superior has his own superior, and, correspondingly, Becker's failure to observe that every subordinate has his own subordinate. (Lower than the prostitute is the pimp; lower than the pimp is the errand boy; and lower than the errand boy is the kid on the fringe of the gang who would like his job.) Now, since everyone may have someone or something above or below him, this does not make it more but less possible to know *which* subordinate's standpoint we should adopt. But this does not deter Becker for a moment. As he gayly says, "I do not propose to hold my breath until this problem is solved."

I, for my part, however, continue to be perplexed about the manner in which a specific stratum of underdogs comes to be chosen as the focus for an orienting standpoint. There is a hidden anomaly in any recommendation to look upon the world from the standpoint of underdogs. The anomaly is this: to a surprising degree, underdogs see *themselves* from the standpoint of respectable society; Negroes, in fact, often call one another "niggers." Thus, if we did study underdogs from "their own" standpoint we would, inevitably, be adopting the standpoint of the dominant culture. It is precisely insofar as the deviant and subordinate do accept a role as passive victims rather than as rebels against circumstances, that they do view themselves from the standpoint of the dominant culture.

In the very act of viewing deviants and subordinates from *their own* standpoint, we are bound to see them from the standpoint of respectable society and its dominant institutions. We will also see deviants in terms of conventional categories not only when we look upon them as passive victims, but, also, to the extent that they are looked upon from the standpoint of the bureaucratic caretakers who are publicly chartered either to put them into custody or to correct their behavior. Paradoxically, then, although Becker invites us to adopt the standpoint of the subordinate, and thereby presumably braves giving offense to respectable values, I believe that he himself is still using some version of the outlook of respectable society.

OMBUDSMAN SOCIOLOGY: CRITIQUE OF THE MIDDLE MAN

Becker seems to be adopting the position of the outcast. In point of fact, I believe that he is also embracing the position of "enlightened" but no less respectable liberalism toward the outcast. Becker appears to be taking up arms against society on behalf of the underdog. Actually, he is taking up arms against the ineffectuality,

callousness, or capriciousness of the caretakers that society has appointed to administer the mess it has created. Becker's argument is essentially a critique of the caretaking organizations, and in particular of the *low level* officialdom that manages them. It is not a critique of the social institutions that engender suffering or of the high level officialdom that shapes the character of caretaking establishments.

Much of deviant study today has become a component of the new style of social reform which is now engineered through caretaking public bureaucracies. The ideological standpoint implicit in Becker's School embodies a critique of the *conventional* welfare apparatus and of the *old* style welfare state, before it extricated itself from social movement reform. It is, as such, a critique of the ethnocentrism and the ineffectuality with which deviance is regarded and treated by certain of the local caretakers immediately responsible for it today. Becker's theoretical school is indeed taking sides; it is a party to the struggle between the old and the new elites in the caretaking establishments; between the welfare institutions inherited from the 1930's and those now promoted today; and between the "locals" working in the municipalities and the "cosmopolitans" operating from Washington, D.C. His ideology is, in each case, injurious to the former and supportive of the latter. If this is seen, it can be better understood how certain of the other difficulties in Becker's discussion are to be resolved. We therefore need a temporary detour to obtain a view of these difficulties.

Becker makes a distinction between the conduct of research in two settings: in political and non-political situations. He is moved to make this distinction because he wants to hold that accusations of bias against sociologists, and reactions to them, differ, depending upon whether the situation studied is political or not.

Becker holds that in *non*-political situations sociologists are more likely to accuse one another of bias when their studies adopt underdog perspectives, than when they look at things from the standpoint of superiors. The reason for this, he says, is that in these non-political situations there exists an accepted "hierarchy of credibility" which credits superiors with the right to define social reality in their spheres; since most sociologists, like others, tend to accept the established hierarchies of credibility, they therefore tend to view studies conducted from underdog perspectives as biased.

Now this is very curious. For what Becker is arguing is that most sociologists, who he says are liberal, will, despite this ideology, nonetheless identify with the overdog in their studies of non-political situations. In short, while most sociologists will presumably give free rein to their liberal ideologies when studying political situations, they will turn their backs on these same liberal ideologies, and act as if they were non-liberal, when studying non-political situations. If this is true, surely one must ask: How is this switch effected? What brings it about? Indeed, is it really a switch? We must consider the other side of the equation; that is, if we ask how some liberal sociologists come to identify with the underdog, we must also ask, how does it happen that others failed to do so?

Becker recognizes that *some* explanation is called for to account for sociologists' adoption of overdog viewpoints in their researches. He says that (in non-political situations) most sociologists tend to accept the dominant hierarchy of credibility. In other words, in these situations, most sociologists conduct their studies from the standpoint of responsible officials, says Becker, because they accept the standpoint of responsible officials. Becker's invocation of this tautology at least acknowledges that an explanation is in order. Yet when it comes to explaining why a minority of sociologists adopt an *underdog* standpoint in the same non-political situations, Becker does not even see that this, too, is a problem that needs explaining.

BLEAK HYPOTHESES

What, indeed, are the sources of these sociologists' identification with underdogs? Clearly we cannot simply hold that such an identification with the underdog stems predominantly from the sociologists' liberal ideology. For Becker is quite right in stating that most sociologists are politically liberal. It is clear therefore that many, if not most, who adopt the overdog standpoint

must share this liberal ideology. Thus, while the liberal ideology may be a necessary condition for adopting an underdog standpoint, it cannot be a sufficient condition for doing so. The question here, the most important question we ever confront in understanding how moralities and ideologies work in the world, is: By what specific mechanisms are men kept honest? In other words, how is it that they are made to conform to their ideologies or values?

It may be surprising, but there are actually many things that keep men—including sociologists—honest. First, remember, as Becker acknowledges, that an underdog standpoint is adopted by only a minority of sociologists. Being infrequent, a minority perspective is more likely to be visible in the larger professional community from whom sociologists seek recognition. Of course, such notice may take the form of hostile criticism. But while an underdog standpoint thus has its risks, it may also bring higher and quicker returns than the adoption of an overdog standpoint which, being common, tends to glut the market and to depress the price paid per individual contribution.

An underdog perspective may, then, be thought of as a career strategy more appealing to high variance betters who, in turn, are more likely to be found among the ambitious young. Bear in mind, however, that the larger professional audience to whom their work is addressed will for the most part conceive themselves as "liberals"—and on whose sympathy an underdog standpoint has some claim. Those adopting an underdog standpoint are, therefore, probably not engaged in as risky an undertaking as their minority position might imply. We are, in summary, suggesting a bleak hypothesis: sociologists with liberal ideologies will more likely adopt underdog perspectives when they experience these as compatible with the pursuit of their own career interests.

Implicit in this bleak hypothesis is the assumption that there is probably some positive relationship between the youth and low professional status, on the one hand, and the adoption of an underdog perspective, on the other. In brief, I would expect that younger intellectuals would, other things constant, be readier to adopt this high variance bet than older intellectuals. It may also be that older intellectuals who feel that they have been bypassed, or whose rewards have somehow not been appropriate, would also be more likely to adopt an underdog standpoint.

Correspondingly, I would also expect that as sociologists get older, as they become increasingly successful, more likely to live next door to or associate with those who are also successful, or themselves become involved in the practical management of public (including university) affairs, they too will come increasingly to adopt overdog standpoints despite their continued public professions of liberalism. Moreover, as sociologists become better established, recognized, and successful, they are—as they begin to move toward the zenith of their careers— risking more should they make a high variance wager on underdogs. The additional net advantage still possible to them is in this way diminished. In short, for the rising sociologist, identification with the underdog may mean greater risk than it does for the younger or less successful sociologists.

I would, however, suggest one important qualification concerning this disposition of older men toward increasing overdog standpoints. As they achieve (rather than merely approach) the zenith of their careers, the rewards that older sociologists are given for conformity to conventional overdog positions, are especially subject to a diminishing marginal utility; in the result some of them may be less subject to professional controls that dispose them to the conventional standpoints of their contemporaries. Thus some senior sociologists, beginning to think about the judgment of "posterity" rather than the views of their contemporaries, may return to the underdog standpoints of their youth. Moreover, as their own age group thins out through death, they may receive more encouragement from the young with whom they are not in competition, than from the middle aged; and they may begin to feel that the future of their reputations will be more enduringly affected by the judgment of the relatively young. These, at any rate, are some of the ways in which the career and personal interests of some older sociologists may dispose them to defy the es-

tablished hierarchy of credibility and to opt for the underdog. We might call it the "Bertrand Russell Syndrome."

But men are prompted to heed the voice of conscience and to abide by high principle by still other considerations. We can see some of these if we ask, how is it that the young, high variance betters are not brought under control by their elders in the course of their education, apprenticeship, and common research undertakings, and are in this way constrained to adopt the respectable overdog standpoints more congenial to the older? Here, again, things are not simple. In some part, the young men's underdog impulses will be protected by the academic ideology of collegiality, which nominally governs relationships. Thus even when working under the supervision of older men, the young men can lay claim for the protection of their underdog standpoints.

Once more, however, we must call attention to the role of bleak factors in keeping men honest. These essentially have to do with the ramifying and powerful role of the new funding structures in social science today which, in turn, are linked to the growth of the new welfare state and its new conceptions of social reform.

Nothing is more obvious than that these are plush times for American social scientists, and there is never any reason to underestimate the power of the obvious. So far as the older and better known men are concerned, they are often so fully funded that they may have little time to supervise their researches personally, to administer them with the continuing closeness that could effectively imprint their overdog identifications on the research. Sometimes the older men are so loosely connected with the researches they have funded that even basic research decisions are made by younger men from their different standpoints. Older men today are often constrained to surrender wide discretionary power to their juniors, if they are to keep them in today's seller's market in social research. The irony of the matter, then, is that the more successful the older man is in funding his research, the less successful he may be in having it conducted according to his lights: the research is less likely to be "his."

With the new funding situation and the greater ease of access to research money, it is now also much simpler for younger men to procure funds for themselves, for their own researches, and at an earlier age. Being their own masters, they can now more readily express their own underdog standpoint, insofar as they have one.

But it would seem that there should be a fly in this ointment. For the question that now arises is whether the new funding situation may simply mean that the younger men have only exchanged one master for another; for even if they are no longer subjected to the direct pressure of senior professors, they may now be subjected to the direct pressure of the funding agencies. In my opinion, this is exactly what has happened.

With growing ease of funding, younger men gain independent access to research resources at a time when their liberal underdog ideologies are still relatively strong and can shape their research. At the same time, however, the career gratifications of these funding opportunities, as well as the personal gratifications of being close to men of power, become vested interests that constrain to a dependency on the new sources of funding. Thus the younger man's more salient, underdog identifications now need to be accommodated to his new-found "appreciation" of overdogs. This is in part accomplished by submerging this "appreciation" in a subsidiary awareness that is maintained by a collegial reciprocity: each tactfully agrees not to look the other's "gift horse in the mouth." (There are, alas, "deviant" cases: e.g., those who make a career of denouncing Project Camelot and then themselves apply for a half-million dollar grant from the State Department.)

This accommodation of underdog identification to overdog dependencies is, quite apart from skillful rationalizing, not too difficult today. For the new funding agencies now desperately need information about underdogs; and these are not unreceptive even to researches conducted from the latter's standpoint, for much the same reason that colonial governments supported similar researches in anthropology. Overdogs in the welfare state—in Washington bureaucracies and New York foundations—are buyers of underdog research for much the same political reasons that the Johnson regime initiated the "war on poverty." To explore a few of the implications of this, I must revert to some of the larger institutional changes that come to a head in the welfare state.

Perhaps the crux here is the manner in which social reform in the United States has changed in character. What is new is not the "plight of the cities," however increasing their deterioration, but rather that this becomes an object of a measured "concern" rather than of "shame." What is new, in a somewhat larger historical perspective, is that the locus of reform initiatives and resources is increasingly found on the level of national politics and foundations, rather than in the political vitality, the economic resources, or the zealous initiatives of elites with local roots.

The reform of American cities was once a process that involved small businessmen, muckraking journalists, and local political machines, all of whom had some vital involvement and interest in their local communities. Today, however, with the changing structure, character, and ecology of the middle classes, many who might give leadership to urban reform live neither in the city itself nor in the still politically powerful rural areas, but live rather in suburbia and exurbia. The educated, bureaucratically employed, and highly mobile middle classes have a dwindling localistic attachment and a narrowing base of power on the *local* levels, which could provide them with the economic and political leverage to effectuate urban reform. They must, in consequence, seek a remedy not on the local but the national level.

As the locus of reform efforts moves upward from the local to the national level, the conception and meaning of social reform changes. The urban reforms being sought by this new middle class are now aimed at the reform of a community to which they are less tied by complex interests, urbane pleasures, or by a round of familiarizing daily activities. It is not "their" community that they now wish to reform—for their suburbs are decent enough as they view them. When they concern themselves with the plight of Negroes, it is not even "their" Negroes whom they seek to help, but Negroes viewed abstractly and impersonally.

Social reform now becomes an effort largely motivated by bland political appraisal, removed economic calculus, prudent forecasting, or a sense of pity and sympathy that becomes increasingly remote as it loses rooting in daily experience and encounter. The community to be reformed becomes an object, something apart from and outside the reformer. The nature of the reform becomes less a matter of moral zeal or even of immediate personal interest and more of a concern prompted by a long range appraisal and prudence. Social reform now becomes a kind of engineering job, a technological task to be subject to bland ''cost-benefit'' or ''system-analysis.'' The rise of the welfare state then means the rise of the uninvolved reformer: It means the rise of reform-at-a-distance. Reform today is no longer primarily the part-time avocation of dedicated amateurs but is increasingly the full-time career of paid bureaucrats.

Today civil rights reforms and the war against poverty are pursued by many in a Bismarckian mood. Reform is no longer prompted by the twinge of conscience or the bite of immediate personal interest but, rather, by ''reasons of state,'' and on behalf of the ''national interest.'' Personal liberalism becomes state liberalism. Liberalism changes in character from a matter of conscience, which had a penetrating claim upon private and daily decision, to electoral loyalty to the Democratic Party and to marginal differentiations in career strategies. The operational meaning of liberalism for the sociologist now tends to become calibrated in terms of the government agency for which he will work, or whose money he will take. From some current standpoints, for example, a truly ''liberal sociologist'' is one who will reject money from the Defense Department but will seek and accept it from the State Department!

The funding agencies of social science today, whether government agencies or massive private foundations, are essentially the welfare state's purchasing agents for market research: they are the instrumentalities of this new reform movement. They express the ''detached concern'' of educated but bureaucratically dependent middle classes who no longer have effective bases in localities; whose cosmopolitan sympathies are not personally and deeply engaged by a daily encounter with urban suffering; and whose fears are not deeply aroused by a close dependence upon the deteriorating urban community. Prodded partly by mild discomforts, vague forbodings, prudent extrapolations, partly by concern to maintain a decent image of themselves, and, not least, by the growing rise of the militant politics of public demonstrations, they approach the task of modern urban reform with a thin-lipped, businesslike rationality. This is the social context in which we can better understand some of the ramifying meanings of Becker's bland program for an underdog sociology. It is the larger context which makes it possible for some sociologists today to stay honest: that is, to implement their liberal ideologies with an effort at underdog indentification.

The superiors whose dominant ''hierarchies of credibility'' are resisted by this underdog sociology are essentially those whose powers remain rooted in, and hence limited by, the local level. The sociology of the underdog is a sociology that rejects the standpoint of only the *local* officials: the head of the medical school, the warden of the prison, the city director of the housing agency. In short, the respectables who are being resisted, and whose hierarchy of credibility is disputed, are those local officials who, for the most part, do not control access to large supplies of research funds.

TOWARD A NEW ESTABLISHMENT SOCIOLOGY

The new underdog sociology propounded by Becker is, then, a standpoint that possesses a remarkably convenient combination of properties: it enables the sociologist to befriend the very small underdogs in local settings, to reject the standpoint of the ''middle dog'' respectables and notables who manage local caretaking establishments, while, at the same time, to make and remain friends with the really top dogs in Washington agencies or New York foundations. While Becker adopts a posture as the intrepid preacher of a new underdog sociology, he has really given birth to something rather different:

to the first version of new Establishment sociology, to a sociology compatible with the new character of social reform in the United States today. It is a sociology of and for the new welfare state. It is the sociology of young men with friends in Washington. It is a sociology that succeeds in solving the oldest problem in personal politics: how to maintain one's integrity without sacrificing one's career, or how to remain a liberal although well-heeled.

The social utility of this new ideology is furthered by the fact that, for some while now, there has been a growing tension between the entrenched local welfare establishments and the newer and powerfully supported federally based agencies and programs of the "Great Society." These new federal agencies, headed by personnel with substantially greater education than the local elites, are presently attempting to implement their new programs against the resistance of the local notables. It is the ultimate function of the federally based programs to win or maintain the attachment of urban lower and working classes to the political symbols and machinery of the American state in general, and of the Democratic Party in particular. While the local caretaking elites usually share these political aims, they also feel that their own local prerogatives and position are threatened by the growth of programs over which they have less control, since they derive from national resources and initiatives. Becker's new underdog sociology functions to line up sectors of sociology against the "backward" resistance of the officialdom on the municipal level, and in favor of the most powerful "enlightened" sectors on the national level.

Essentially Becker's type of research does this because, in adopting the standpoint of the underdogs, it simultaneously shows how ignorant local caretakers are of this standpoint and how badly local caretaking officials manage their establishments. It must not be thought for a moment that Becker's work performs this ideological function through any intention to further the ambitions of the upper officialdom or by any intention to conduct his research in any narrowly conceived applied manner. It achieves its ideological consequences primarily by taking and revealing the standpoint of those for whom local caretaking officials are responsible and by "unmaking" the ignorance of these officials. This is not an incidental or trivial byproduct; rather, this is exactly what carries the political payload. For it is this discrediting of local officials that legitimates the claims of the higher administrative classes in Washington and gives them an entering wedge on the local level.

Becker's readiness to sacrifice the middle dogs to the top dogs can be gleaned when he states that there is no point in attempting to adopt the standpoint of middle level officialdom. Looking at the situation from the standpoint of middle level officials—in other words, from the standpoint of the prison warden, the school principal, the hospital administrator—simply leads to an infinite regression, says Becker.

This has a seeming persuasiveness, but it is too glib by far. First, it is by no means certain that an "infinite regress" problem is involved. Is it really true that every superior has a superior who, in turn, limits and prevents him from doing as he really would like? Isn't there some point at which the buck-passing ends? This would seem to be part of what C. Wright Mills had in mind when he spoke of the "power elite." We can, of course, maintain that even the highest officers of state in turn always require the consent of the governed. But this brings us back full circle; and we would then have to acknowledge that the very underdogs, who Becker says are more sinned against than sinning, are at least in part responsible for the sins against them; and why, then, should sociologists conduct their studies primarily from their standpoint?

It would seem that there is one way out of this impasse for Becker. He could say that it is not a matter of superiors and subordinates as such, but, rather, of the *institutions* governing their relationship. He might maintain that the need is not to study social situations from the standpoint of subordinates as an end in itself, but of conducting studies with a view to understanding how some are crushed by certain institutions, and how all alike are subjected to institutions that do not permit them to live as they wish. As I say, this position would be one way for Becker. But he neither sees it nor takes it. For this undercuts his "infinite regress" gambit and leads research inevitably to the doorstep of power; it would force the research focus upward, fastening it on the national levels.

Parenthetically, but not irrelevantly, I think that *radical* sociologists differ from liberals in that, while they take the standpoint of the underdog, they apply it to the study of overdogs. Radical sociologists want to study "power elites," the leaders, or masters, of men; liberal sociologists focus their efforts upon underdogs and victims and their immediate bureaucratic caretakers.

For all its difficulties, Becker's position does provide a vantage point for a criticism of local managers of the Caretaking Establishment, of the vested interests and archaic methods of these middle dogs. This is all to the good. But this vantage point has been bought at a very high price. The price is an uncritical accommodation to the national elite and to the society's master institutions; and this is all to the bad.

There is, I think, one other way in which Becker's position is too glib. It is premised upon a conviction (or sentiment) to the effect that, as he says in *The Outsiders,* while it may be possible to see a situation from "both sides," this "cannot be done simultaneously." This means, explains Becker, that "we cannot construct a description . . . that in some way fuses perceptions and interpretations made by both parties involved in a process of deviance . . . We cannot describe a 'higher reality' that makes sense of both sets of views." I assume this means that although the sociologist can, at some point, present the views of one group and then, at another point, present the views of a different group, that nonetheless, the sociologist's own standpoint—when he speaks in an omniscient voice—tends inevitably to favor one of these sides more than the other, to present one side more attractively than the other. This frank confession of human fallibility is so appealing that it seems almost churlish to question it. But I do.

One reason that Becker sees no way out of this impasse is because he is committed to a kind of interpersonal social psychology which, with all its humanistic merits, fails to see that men—superiors as well as subordinates—may be powerfully constrained by institutions, by history, and indeed by biology. Becker's position is largely that of the undefeated, pragmatic, historyless and still optimistic American to whom "everything is possible" in man-to-man, and manly encounter. If, however, we acknowledge that superiors no less than subordinates live within these limits—which may not be impossible to penetrate, but only costly to do so—we do not, I think, degrade their humanity but rather sensitize ourselves to it. We may then see that the issue not only entails a conflict between superiors and subordinates but a larger kind of human struggle. Such a perspective does not require us to restrain our sympathy for the underdog or ignore his special plight, but gives us a broader comprehension of it. To have a sense of man's common humanity does not demand a superhuman capacity to transcend partisanship. But a partisanship that is set within the framework of a larger humanistic understanding is quite different from one devoid of it. This is one difference between the merely political partisanship of daily involvements, and the more reflective and tempered partisanship which may well be such objectivity of which we are capable.

There are works of art that manifest this objective partisanship. The dramas of the great classical tragedians are magnificent case in point. What makes them great is their objectivity; and what makes them objective is their capacity to understand even the nobility of their Persian enemies, even the dignity of their "barbarian" slaves, even the bumbling of their own wise men. They do indeed express a viewpoint which in some sense does take the standpoint of both sides, and does so simultaneously. If great art can do this, why should this be forbidden to great social science? That it is not common is precisely what makes its accomplishment an expression of greatness.

Despite the inevitability of bias and the unavoidability of partisanship, the fact remains that two researchers may have the same bias but, nonetheless, may *not* be equally objective. How is this possible? Becker notes "that our unavoidable sympathies do not render our results invalid" and that, despite them, research must meet "the standards of good scientific work." This does not clarify the issue as much as we might wish, for there never was any suggestion that partisanship impaired the "validity" of research. There is also no doubt that partisanship does not necessarily impair the "reliability" of a research. The validity and reliability of researches are matters quite apart from their *objectivity.*

And it is primarily this last concern which is engaged when the problem of partisanship is raised. The question here is only whether partisanship necessarily vitiates objectivity, and, this in turn requires that at some point we clarify our conception of objectivity and of how it may be attained.

ONCE AGAIN: THE PROBLEM OF OBJECTIVITY

How, then, does Becker seek to enhance the objectivity of even partisan research? His views concerning this are sketchy in the extreme. Although he speaks of a need to maintain scientific standards, he quickly recognizes that there is no way in which we can be sure that sociologists will *apply* these standards "impartially across the board." He also expresses the qualified hope that, over the years, the accumulation of "one-sided" studies will gradually produce a more balanced picture of a social situation; but he also recognizes that this does not help the individual researcher in the here and now.

The remedies in which Becker apparently reposes greater confidence consist rather of two other things. First, he recommends that we honestly confess the partisan position we have adopted, openly acknowledging that we have studied the problem from the standpoint of only certain of the actors involved and not of all. Considering that Becker has himself refused openly to acknowledge his own underdog standpoint, this solution to the problem of objectivity is not entirely confidence inspiring. Secondly, Becker also recommends—and it is this that he seems to feel most strongly about—the avoidance of "sentimentality," whatever that may mean.

For my part, it seems to me that other things might be done.

For one, I would encourage a condemnation of complacency rather than of sentimentality. For it is complacency which allows us to think, *à la* Myrdal, that we have solved the problem of objectivity by good-naturedly confessing that, yes, we do indeed have a standpoint and by openly specifying what it is. Confession may be good for the soul, but it is no tonic to the mind. While the "heart may have reasons of its own," when it simply chooses to assert these without critical inspection, then reason must condemn this as complacency. Of course, it is a good thing for sociologists to know what they are doing; and it is a good thing for them to know and to say whose side they are on. But a bland confession of partisanship merely betrays smugness and naiveté. It is smug because it assumes that the values that we have are good enough; it is naive because it assumes that we know the values we have. Once we recognize that complacency is the mind's embalming fluid and once we move to overcome it, we are then forced to ask, what is it that is now making us so complacent?

The complacency of Becker and of his school of deviance derives in large measure from its own unexamined, comfortable commitment to political liberalism. It has wrapped itself in the protective covering of the liberal Establishment which dominates American sociology today, as well as American academic life in general. Becker blandly acknowledges, without making the least effort to explore its appreciable consequences, that "it is no secret that most sociologists are politically liberal. . . ." But it is complacency to allow ourselves to be appeased by a confession of the commonplace. To confess that most sociologists are politically liberal is like "confessing" that men are conceived in sexual intercourse. The question is whether Becker sees any *consequences* in the thing confessed. Without considering these, confession becomes a meaningless ritual of frankness.

The important problem is the exploration of the ways in which the political liberalism of many sociologists today affects the worth, the scope, the bite, and the objectivity of their sociology. The very blandness of his confession implies that Becker fails to grasp that liberalism today is not simply the conscientious and liberating faith of isolated individuals. Political liberalism today instead verges on being an official ideology of wide sectors of the American university community as well a broader strata of American life. For many American academicians, liberalism has now become a token of respectability, a symbol of genteel open-mindedness, the fee for membership in the faculty club; in point of fact, liberalism is also an operating code that links academic life to the political machinery of the Democratic Party.

Far from being the conscientious code of isolated individuals, much of liberalism today is the well-financed ideology of a loosely organized but coherent Establishment. It is the domaint ideology of a powerful group that sprawls across the academic community; that is integrated with American politics; that has its opinion leaders in various publications; that has its heroes whose myths are recited. Liberalism, then, is the mythos of one of the dominating American establishments; it is not simply the hard-won faith of a happy few. As the ideology of an establishment, such official liberalism has things to protect. It has reasons to lie. It has all the social mechanisms available to any establishment by which it can reward those who tell the right lies, and punish and suppress those who tell the wrong truths. In its meaner moments, it is an intellectual Mafia. It is not only, therefore, as Becker says, that "officials must lie because things are seldom as they ought to be." Like any other member of an establishment, the sociologist who is a political liberal is expected to lie along with his fellow members of the Establishment, to feel the rightness of their cause and a responsibility for its success.

The bias of the sociologist, then, does not derive simply from the fact that it is inherent in the human condition or in sociological research. The sociologist also lies because he is a political person. It would seem, however, that sociologists have no right to be complacent about anything that they, more than others, should have good reason to know makes liars of them. They thus have no right to be complacent about the intellectual consequences of their own liberalism.

The complacency that oozes from Becker's discussion, the vapid frankness of its confessional style, rests upon a simple sociological condition: upon the fact that it is allied with official liberalism, is embedded in the liberal Establishment, and is supported comfortably by the welfare state.

This still leaves the question as to whether there is any road toward objectivity, and what direction it might take. In my view, the objectivity of sociologists is enhanced to the extent that they critically examine all conventional "hierarchies of credibility," including their own liberal "hierarchy of credibility," which is today as respectable, conventional, and conformist as any. Becker acknowledges that it is sometimes possible to "take the point of view of some third party not directly implicated in the hierarchy we are investigating." This would, indeed, he agrees, make us neutral to the contending groups in the situation under study. But, he adds, this "would only mean we would enlarge the scope of the political conflict to include a party not ordinarily brought in whose view the sociologist has taken." But isn't this precisely one possible meaning of an avenue toward objectivity?

Isn't it good for a sociologist to take the standpoint of someone outside of those most immediately engaged in a specific conflict, or outside of the group being investigated? Isn't it precisely this outside standpoint, or our ability to adopt it, which is one source and one possible meaning of sociological objectivity? Granted, all standpoints are partisan; and, granted, no one escapes a partisan standpoint. But aren't some forms of partisanship more liberating than others? Isn't it the sociologists' job to look at human situations in ways enabling them to say things that are not ordinarily seen by the participants in them? This does not mean that the sociologist should ignore or be insensitive to the full force of the actors' standpoints. But it does mean that he himself must have a standpoint on their standpoint. Objectivity is indeed threatened when the actors' standpoints and the sociologists' fuse indistinguishably into one. The adoption of an "outside" standpoint, far from leading us to ignore the participants' standpoint, is probably the only way in which we can even recognize and identify the participants' standpoint. It is only when we have a standpoint somewhat different from the participants that it becomes possible to do justice to their standpoints.

There are, it seems to me, at least three other possible conceptions of sociological objectivity. One of these can be characterized as "personal authenticity" or "awareness," another can be termed "normative objectification," and the third may be called "transpersonal replicability."

To consider "normative objectification" first: when we talk about the bias or impartiality of a sociologist we are, in effect, talking about the sociologist as if he were a "judge."* Now, rendering a judgment premises the existence of conflicting or contending parties; but it does not imply an intention to *meditate* the difficulties between them. The function of a judge is not to bring parties together but is, quite simply, to do justice. Doing justice does not mean, as does mediation or arbitration, that both the parties must each be given or denied a bit of what they sought. Justice does not mean logrolling or "splitting the difference." For the doing of justice may, indeed, give all the benefits to one party and impose all the costs upon another.

What makes a judgment possessed of justice is not the fact that it distributes costs and benefits equally between the parties but, rather, that the allocation of benefits and costs is made in conformity with some stated normative standard. Justice, in short, is that which is justified in terms of some value. The "impartiality" or objectivity of the judge is an imputation made when it is believed that he had made his decision primarily or solely in terms of some moral value. In one part, then, the objectivity of the judge requires his explication of the moral value in terms of which his judgment has been rendered. One reason why Becker's analysis founders on the problem of objectivity is precisely because it regards the sociologists' value commitment merely as an inescapable fact of nature, rather than viewing it as a necessary condition of his objectivity.

Insofar as the problem is seen as one of choosing up sides, rather than a working one's way through to a value commitment, I cannot see how it is ever possible for men to recognize that the side to which they are attached can be wrong. But men do not and need not always say, "my country right or wrong." Insofar as they are capable of distinguishing the side to which they are attached, from the *grounds* on which they are attached to it, they are, to that extent, capable of a significant objectivity.

It should again be clear, then, that I do not regard partisanship as incompatible with objectivity. The physician, after all, is not necessarily less objective because he has made a partisan commitment to his patient and against the germ. The physician's objectivity is in some measure vouchsafed because he has committed himself to a specific value: health. It is this commitment that constrains him to see and to say things about the patient's condition that neither may want to know.

But in saying that the explication of the sociologist's value commitment is a necessary condition for this objectivity, we are saying little unless we recognize at the same time the grinding difficulties involved in this. For one, it is no easy thing to know what our own value commitments are. In an effort to seem frank and open, we all too easily pawn off a merely glib statement about our values without making any effort to be sure that these are the values to which we are actually committed. This is much of what happens when scientists conventionally assert that they believe only in "the truth." Secondly, a mere assertion of a value commitment is vainly ritualistic to the extent that the sociologist has no awareness of the way in which one of his commitments may conflict with or exclude another. For example, there is commonly some tension between a commitment to truth and a commitment to welfare. Third, we also have to recognize that the values in terms of which we may make our judgments may not necessarily be shared by the participants in the situations we have studied. Our objectivity, however, does not require us to share values with those we study, but only to apply the values that we claim are our own, however unpopular these may be.

---

*The next paragraph or so is indebted to the excellent discussion by Rostein Eckhoff, "The Mediator, the Judge and the Administrator in Conflict-Resolution," *Acta Sociologica,* Vol. 10, pp. 148–172.

In other words, this form of objectivity requires that we be on guard against our own hypocrisy and our need to be loved. This creates a problem because the values we may actually hold may differ from those we feel that we must display in order to gain or maintain access to research sites.

To come to another meaning of sociological objectivity, "personal authenticity." If the previous conception of objectivity, "normative objectification," emphasizes that the sociologist must not deceive *others* concerning the value basis of his judgment, then personal authenticity stresses that the sociologist must not deceive *himself* concerning the basis of his judgment. By personal authenticity or awareness, I mean to call attention to the relationship between the sociologist's beliefs about the actual state of the social world, on the one hand, and his own personal wishes, hopes, and values for this social world, on the other hand. Personal authenticity or awareness exists when the sociologist is capable of admitting the factuality even of things that violate his own hopes and values. People do differ in this regard, some having a greater capacity and need for self-deception and others possessing less talent to attain the comforts born of such self-deception. Not all conservatives are equally blind to the fragility of the *status quo;* not all radicals are equally blind to its stability.

In this sense, then, one form of sociological objectivity involves the capacity to acknowledge "hostile information"—information that is discrepant with our purposes, hopes, wishes, or values. It is not the state of the world, then, that makes information hostile, but only the state of the world in relation to a man's wants and values. Here, then, objectivity consists in the capacity to know and to use—to seek out, or at least to accept it when it is otherwise provided—information inimical to our own desires and values, and to overcome our own fear of such information.

Both forms of objectivity imply a paradoxical condition: namely, that one cannot be objective about the world outside without, to some extent, being knowledgeable about (and in control of) ourselves. In normative objectification, one of the central problems is to *know* our values, and

to see that such knowledge is problematic. In personal authenticity there is a need for a similar knowledge of the self, but for a knowledge that goes beyond values into the question of our brute impulses and of other desires or wants that we may not at all feel to be valuable. In both forms of objectivity, also, it would be foolhardy to expect that the requisite knowledge is acquirable through a simple process of frictionless "retrieval." Rather, we must expect that either form of objectivity entails some measure of *struggle* in and with the sociologist's self and, with this, a need for courage. It now should be clear why I have taken up the cudgels against complacency, for it is the very antithesis of the kind of moral struggle required for objectivity.

PROFESSIONALISM AND OBJECTIVITY

Insofar as the pursuit of objectivity rests upon what I must reluctantly call "moral character," we can also see another source from which sociological objectivity is deeply undermined today. It is undermined, from one direction, by a compulsive and exclusive cultivation of purely technical standards of research and of education, so that there is neither a regard nor a locus of responsibility for the cultivation of those very moral qualities on which objectivity rests. The truth is that to the extent that sociology and sociological education remain obsessed with a purely technical focus they have abdicated a concern with objectivity; it is merely hypocritical for those with such a standpoint to enter occasional accusations about other's lack of objectivity.

A second basic inner locus for our default with respect to the problem of objectivity is the growing transformation of sociology into a profession. This may seem paradoxical again, for surely professions profess value commitments, at least to client, if not public, welfare. Professions, however, do not tend to see value commitments as questions of personal commitment but tend, instead, simply to treat the values they transmit as non-problematic givens. Most civic professions tend to take the larger culture and institutions in their society as given. But it is precisely the peculiar nature of the sociologist's task to be able to take them as problematic. The development of professionalization among sociologists deserves to be opposed because it undermines the sociologist's capacity for *objectivity* in any serious sense. In effect, the growth of professionalization means the substitution of a routine and banal code of ethics for a concern with the serious kind of morality on which alone objectivity might rest.

A third specific conception of objectivity common to many American sociologists—and so common, in fact, that even C. Wright Mills agreed with it—is what has been termed "transpersonal replicability." In this notion, objectivity simply means that a sociologist has described his procedures with such explicitness that others employing them on the same problem will come to the same conclusion. In effect, then, this is a notion of objectivity as technical routinization and rests, at bottom, on the codification and explication of the research procedures that were employed. At most, however, this is an *operational* definition of objectivity which presumably tells us what we must *do* in order to justify an assertion that some particular finding is objective. It does not, however, tell us very much about what objectivity *means* conceptually and connotatively. It says only that those findings which are replicated are to be considered to be objective.

It is quite possible, however, that any limited empirical generalization can, by this standard, be held to be objective, however narrow, partial, or biased and prejudiced its net impact is, by reason of its selectivity. Thus, for example, one might conduct research into the occupational-political distribution of Jews and come to the conclusion that a certain proportion of them are bankers and Communists. Given the replicability conception of objectivity, one might then simply claim that this (subsequently verified) finding is "objective," and this claim could be made legitimately even though one never compared the proportions of bankers and Communists among Jews with those among Protestants and Catholics. It might be said that, without such a comparison among the three religions, one would never know whether the proportion of bankers and Communists among

Jews was higher or lower than that among Protestants and Catholics. But this objection would simply indicate the technical statistical condition that must be met in order to justify a statement concerning the Jewish *differential*. Insofar as one happens not to be interested in making or justifying a statement about this, the objectivity of the original statement remains defensible in terms of the technical conception of objectivity as replicability. Thus it would seem that the replicability criterion falls far short of what is commonly implied by objectivity.

This technical conception of objectivity is in part, but in part only, reminiscent of the manner in which Max Weber conceived of it. We might say that the current conception is a kind of mindless corruption of Weber's. Weber essentially thought of scientific objectivity as something left over. It was a residual sphere of the purely technical, a realm in which decisions should and could be made without thought of their ultimate value relevancies. Weber's approach to objectivity comes down to a strategy of segregation—the conscientious maintenance of a strict separation between the world of facts and the world of values. Weber's emphasis here, therefore, is not on the manner in which scientific objectivity depends upon value commitments; this tends tacitly to be assumed rather than deliberately insisted upon. Weber's stress is placed, rather, upon the separation and discontinuity of facts and values. As a result, one may come away believing that, to Weber, the objectivity of research need not be colored by the scientist's personal values or the manner in which these are arrived at and held. *En principe,* neither the sanity nor maturity of a scientist need affect his objectivity. The madman and the teenager can be as scientifically objective as anyone else in this view, so long as they adhere to purely technical standards of science, once having committed themselves to some problem. Weber's theory invites a fantasy that objectivity may, at some point, be surrendered entirely to the impersonal machinery of research.

The passionate artfulness with which Weber argues this case endows the world that he conjures in imagination to be mistaken for reality, and we may fail to notice just how *grotesque* this conjured world is. Actually, Weber's entire enterprise here is born of his attempt to overcome his conception of the world as grotesque by formulating a salvational myth of a value-free social science. Through this he strives to still his furious sense of uneasiness that the real world, in which science and morality do cohabit, is a world of mutually destructive incompatibles. Weber fantasies a solution in which facts and values will each be preserved in watertight compartments. The tensions and dangers of the conjunction of facts and values are to be overcome by a segregation of the sequential phases of research, so that: first, the scientist formulates his problem in terms of his value interests and, then, having done this, he puts his values behind him, presumably never again allowing them to intrude into the subsequent stage of technical analysis.

To overcome his experience of the world as grotesque, Weber formulates an incipient utopia in which the impure world is split into two pure worlds, science and morality. He then attempts to bridge the cleavage he has created by pasting these two purified worlds together, so that each is made sovereign in a different but adjacent period of time. The incongruity of the world has not so much been overcome as transcended in myth. The experienced unmanageability of the one world gives way to the promised manageability of the two worlds. The reality gives way to the myth, but the grotesqueness abides.

One central difference between Weber's and the current technical conception of objectivity is that Weber recognized that the technical sphere would have to be brought into some sort of alignment with the value sphere. The modern technical conception of objectivity, however, simply regards the value problem and its relation to the technical as either negligible or dull. It allows it to remain unclarified. The modern technical approach to objectivity also differs from the Weberian in a second way. The former takes it for granted that, somehow, social scientists will do the right thing. It assumes that, in some manner, there will be a mustering of motives sufficient to make social scientists conform with their technical standards and rules.

Commonly, the source of these motives is not explored. Sometimes, however, it is today held that the mutual inspection and the checks and balances of modern *professionalization* will suffice to keep social scientists honest. In short, it is assumed that the machinery of professionalism will make the machinery of science work.

This expectation underestimates the ease with which professionalism is corruptible as well as the power of the corrupting forces. Perhaps the most important example of this in the present generation was the work of the Warren Commission appointed by President Lyndon Johnson to investigate the assassination of President John Kennedy. Whatever one's conclusions concerning the substantive issues, namely, whether Lee Harvey Oswald was the assassin, and whether or not he alone or in conspiracy with others murdered President Kennedy, one miserable conclusion seems unavoidable: that there was scarcely a civic profession—the military, the medical, the police, the legal, the juridical—that was not involved in suppressing or distorting the truth, and which did not bow obsequiously to power. And I am far from sure that this was always motivated by a concern for the national welfare. The more that the respectable professions are transformed from independent vocations into bureaucratic and federally sponsored dependencies the more corruptible they will be in the future. Those who think that professional associations and universities will immunize the professions from the pressures and temptations of power have simply not understood the revelations about the CIA penetration into these very associations and universities. For these show that they were willing and eager parties to their own corruption in the name of a well-financed patriotic devotion.

For his part, however, Weber never assumed that the technical machinery of science would be self-winding and self-maintaining. For Weber, the maintenance of objectivity at least required a persisting moral effort to prevent one's personal values from intruding into purely technical decisions. The machinery was really never thought of as operating successfully apart from men's characters. Weber premises that, even in the purely technical stages of later research, work will be subject to an ongoing superintendence by the social scientist's moral commitment to "truth." Since the continued force of this personal value is conceived to be compatible with the maintenance of technical standards, its significance is left unexplicated. It is only implicitly, therefore, that Weber indicates that the objectivity of research depends continuingly, and not only in the early problem-formulating stages, upon something more than the technical machinery of research.

The question arises, however, as to the meaning of this extra-technical, "transcendental" commitment to the truth. Does it entail anything more than a commitment to the segregation of facts and values? Either it has some meaning beyond this or it does not. If it does not, then we are still left wondering how and why social scientists may be relied upon to adhere to this very segregation of facts and values: What endows it with binding force? If it does, and if the "truth" that it demands is something more than the mere application of technical standards alone, then it must entail something more than a belief in reliability or validity. If "truth" is not merely a summarizing redundancy for these terms it must be embedded with some conception that embodies or resonates value commitments that call for something more than pure truth alone.

The pursuit of "truth for its own sake" is always a tacit quest for something more than truth, for other values that may have been obscured, denied, and perhaps even forbidden, and some of which are expressed in the quest for "objectivity." Objectivity expresses a lingering attachment to something more than the purely technical goods of science alone and for more than the valid-reliable bits of information it may produce. In this sense, "truth for its own sake" is a crypto-ethic, a concealment of certain other substantive values through a strategy that, leaving them entirely in the open, diverts attention from them to another dramatically accentuated valuable: truth. The old Druidic sacred place is not destroyed; it is merely housed in an imposing new cathedral. In affirming that he only seeks the truth for its own sake, the scientist is therefore not so much lying as pledging allegiance to the flag of truth, while saying nothing about the country for which it stands.

What are the other values that lie obscured in the long shadows cast by the light of pure truth? In Western culture, these often enough have been freedom—the truth will set you free—and power—to know, in order to control. Underlying the conception of truth as objectivity there is, however, still another value, a faint but enduring image of the possibility of *wholeness.* One obvious implication of objectivity has commonly been to tell the "whole" story. The longing here is to fit the partial and broken fragments together; to provide a picture that transcends the nagging sense of incompleteness; to overcome the multiplicity of shifting perspectives. Underlying the quest for objectivity, then, is the hope of dissolving the differences that divide and the distances that separate men by uniting them in a single, peace-bringing vision of the world.

In such a conception of objectivity there is, I suspect, the undertow of an illicit yearning that links science to religion. Perhaps this conclusion is an illusion. Worse still, perhaps it is "sentimental." Yet it will not seem so fanciful if it is remembered that the modern conception of an objective social science was born with early nineteenth century Positivism. This set itself the task of creating both an objective social science and a new religion of humanity, each informing the other and aimed at reuniting society. The objectivity of the new sociology was, from its very beginnings, not an end in itself; it was clearly aimed at the enhancement of human unity and it then had the most intimate connection with an openly religious impulse.

The conception of objectivity has commonly projected an image of the scientist as linked to a higher realm, as possessed of a godlike penetration into things, as serenely above human frailties and distorting passions, or as possessed of a priest-like impartiality. The realm of objectivity is the higher realm of *episteme,* of *wahrheit,* of *raison,* of Truth, which have always been something more than sheer information. In other words, the realm of objectivity is the realm of the *sacred* in social science. But why has the quest for this realm been encrusted under the defensive conception of truth for its own sake?

Essentially the fate of objectivity in sociology

is linked with, and its fortunes vary with, the changing hopes for a peace-bringing human unity. Some power-tempted social scientists are simply no longer able to hear this music. Others may withdraw because their hope is so vital that they cannot risk endangering it by an open confrontation. For some, an open admission would be dissonant with their conception of themselves as tough-minded and hard-headed. Still others have a genuine humility and feel that the pursuit of this high value is beyond their powers. There are also some who doubt the very value of peace itself because, oddly enough, they want men to endure and to live, and they suspect that the successful quest for a peace-bringing unity spells death: they ask themselves, after unity and peace, what?

Perhaps what has been most discrediting to the quest for human unity is that, since its classical formulation, its most gifted spokesman have often had totalitarian proclivities: they came to be viewed as enemies of the "open society," who denied the value and reality of human difference. In short, the plea for human unity has often, and quite justifiably, been interpreted as a demand for a tension-free society that was overseen by a close superintendence of men from nursery to graveyard, and was blanketed with a remorseless demand for conformity and consensus. What has really been discredited, however, was this chilling version of the dream of human unity, although it remains extremely difficult to extricate the larger hope from the nightmare form that it was given.

Whether objectivity is thought possible comes down then to a question of whether some vision of human unity is believed workable and desirable. It comes down to the question, as C. Wright Mills once said, of whether there is still some vision of a larger "public" whose interests and needs transcend those of its component and contending factions. In this sense, one possible meaning of objectivity in social science is the contribution it might make to a human unity of mankind. But to make such a contribution the social sciences cannot and should not be impartial toward human suffering; they must not make their peace with any form of human unity that complacently accommodates itself to or imposes suffering.

At the same time, however, an empty-headed partisanship unable to transcend the immediacies of narrowly conceived political commitment is simply just one more form of market research. A blind or unexamined alliance between sociologists and the upper bureaucracy of the welfare state can only produce the market research of the liberalism. It rests upon the tacit, mistaken, but common, liberal assumption that the policies of this bureaucracy equitably embody the diverse interests of the larger public, rather than seeing that the bureaucracy is one other interested and powerful contending faction, and is more closely allied with some of the contenders rather than equally distant from all. It is to values, not to factions, that sociologists must give their most basic commitment.

THE POVERTY OF THE SOCIOLOGY
OF DEVIANCE
Nuts, Sluts, and Preverts*

Alexander Liazos
Regis College

C. Wright Mills left a rich legacy to sociology. One of his earliest, and best, contributions was "The Professional Ideology of Social Pathologists" (1943). In it, Mills argues that the small-town, middle-class background of writers of social problems textbooks blinded them to basic problems of social structure and power, and led them to emphasize melioristic, patchwork types of solutions to America's "problems," ranging from rape in rural districts to public housing, and emphasized the orderly structure of small-town America; anything else was pathology and disorganization. Moreover, these "problems," "ranging from rape in rural districts to public housing," were not explored systematically and theoretically; they were not placed in some larger political, historical, and social context. They were merely listed and decried.[1]

Since Mills wrote his paper, however, the field of social problems, social disorganization, and social pathology has undergone considerable changes. Beginning in the late 1940's and the 1950's, and culminating in the 1960's, the field of "deviance" has largely replaced the social problems orientation. This new field is characterized by a number of features which distinguish it from the older approach.[2]

First, there is some theoretical framework, even though it is often absent in edited collections (the Rubington and Weinberg (1968) edited book is an outstanding exception). Second, the small-town morality is largely gone. Writers claim they will examine the phenomena at hand—prostitution, juvenile delinquency, mental illness, crime, and others—objectively, not considering them as necessarily harmful and immoral. Third, the statements and theories of the field are based on much more extensive, detailed, and theoretically-oriented research than were those of the 1920's and 1930's. Fourth, writers attempt to fit their theories to some central theories, concerns, and problems found in the

©1972 by the Society for the Study of Social Problems. Reprinted from *Social Problems,* Vol. 20, No. 1, Summer 1972, pp. 103–120, by permission.

*The subtitle of this paper came from two sources. a) A Yale undergraduate once told me that the deviance course was known among Yale students as "nuts and sluts." b) A former colleague of mine at Quinnipiac College, John Bancroft, often told me that the deviance course was "all about those preverts." When I came to write this paper, I discovered that these descriptions were correct, and concise summaries of my argument. I thank both of them. I also want to thank Gordon Fellman for a very careful reading of the first draft of the manuscript, and for discussing with me the general and specific issues I raise here.

[1]Bend and Vogenfanger (1964) examined social problems textbooks of the early 1960's; they found there was little theory or emphasis on social structure in them.

[2]What I say below applies to the "labelling-interactionist" school of deviance of Becker, Lemert, Erikson, Matza, and others: to a large degree, however, most of my comments also apply to the other schools.

general field of sociology; they try to transcend mere moralizing.

The "deviant" has been humanized; the moralistic tone is no longer ever-present (although it still lurks underneath the explicit disavowals); and theoretical perspectives have been developed. Nevertheless, all is not well with the field of "deviance." Close examination reveals that writers of this field still do not try to relate the phenomena of "deviance" to larger social, historical, political, and economical contexts. The emphasis is still on the "deviant" and the "problems" *he* presents to himself and others, not on the society within which he emerges and operates.

I examined 16 textbooks in the field of "deviance," eight of them readers, to determine the state of the field. (They are preceded by an asterisk in the bibliography.) Theoretically, eight take the labelling-interactionist approach; three more tend to lean to that approach; four others argue for other orientations (anomie, structural-functional, etc.) or, among the readers, have an "eclectic" approach; and one (McCaghy, et al., 1968) is a collection of biographical and other statements by "deviants" themselves, and thus may not be said to have a theoretical approach (although, as we shall see, the selection of the types of statements and "deviants" still implies an orientation and viewpoint). A careful examination of these textbooks revealed a number of ideological biases. These biases became apparent as much from what these books leave unsaid and unexamined, as from what they do say. The field of the sociology of deviance, as exemplified in these books, contains three important theoretical and political biases.

1. All writers, especially those of the labelling school, either state explicitly or imply that one of their main concerns is to *humanize* and *normalize* the "deviant," to show that he is essentially no different from us. But by the very emphasis on the "deviant" and his identity problems and sub-culture, the opposite effect may have been achieved. The persisting use of the label "deviant" to refer to the people we are considering is an indication of the feeling that these people are indeed different.

2. By the overwhelming emphasis on the "dramatic" nature of the usual types of "deviance"—prostitution, homosexuality, juvenile delinquency, and others—we have neglected to examine other, more serious and harmful forms of "deviance." I refer to *covert institutional violence* (defined and discussed below) which leads to such things as poverty and exploitation, the war in Vietnam, unjust tax laws, racism and sexism, and so on, which cause psychic and material suffering for many Americans, black and white, men and women.

3. Despite explicit statements by these authors of the importance of *power* in the designation of what is "deviant," in their substantive analyses they show a profound unconcern with power and its implications. The really powerful, the upper classes and the power elite, those Gouldner (1968) calls the "top dogs," are left essentially unexamined by these sociologists of deviance.

I.

Always implicit, and frequently explicit, is the aim of the labelling school to humanize and normalize the "deviant." Two statements by Becker and Matza are representative of this sentiment.

In the course of our work and for who knows what private reasons, we fall into deep sympathy with the people we are studying, so that while the rest of society views them as unfit in one or another respect for the deference ordinarily accorded a fellow citizen, we believe that they are at least as good as anyone else, more sinned against than sinning (Becker, 1967:100–101).

The growth of the sociological view of deviant phenomena involved, as major phases, the replacement of a correctional stance by an *appreciation* of the deviant subject, the tacit purging of a conception of pathology by a new stress on human *diversity,* and the erosion of a simple distinction between deviant and conventional phenomena, resulting from intimate familiarity of the world as it is, which yielded a more sophisticated view stressing *complexity* (Matza, 1969:10).

For a number of reasons, however, the opposite effect may have been achieved; and "deviants" still seem different. I began to suspect this reverse effect from the many essays and papers I read while teaching the "deviance" course. The clearest example is the repeated use of the word "tolerate." Students would write that we must not persecute homosexuals, prostitutes, mental patients, and others, that we must be "tolerant" of them. But one tolerates only those one considers less than equal, morally inferior, and weak; those equal to oneself, one accepts and respects; one does not merely allow them to exist, one does not "tolerate" them.

The repeated assertion that "deviants" are "at least as good as anyone else" may raise doubts that this is in fact the case, or that we believe it. A young woman who grew up in the South in the 1940's and 1950's told Quinn (1954:146): " 'You know, I think from the fact that I was told so often that I must treat colored people with consideration, I got the feeling that I could mistreat them if I wanted to.' " Thus with "deviants;" if in fact they are as good as we are, we would not need to remind everyone of this fact; we would take it for granted and proceed from there. But our assertions that "deviants" are not different may raise the very doubts we want to dispel. Moreover, why would we create a separate field of sociology for "deviants" if there were not something different about them? May it be that even we do not believe our statements and protestations?

The continued use of the word "deviant" (and its variants), despite its invidious distinctions and connotations, also belies our explicit statements on the equality of the people under consideration. To be sure, some of the authors express uneasiness over the term. For example, we are told,

In our use of this term for the purpose of sociological investigation, we emphasize that we do not attach any value judgement, explicitly or implicitly, either to the word "deviance" or to those describing their behavior or beliefs in this book (McCaghy, et al., 1968:v).

Lofland (1969:2, 9–10) expresses even stronger reservations about the use of the term, and sees clearly the sociological, ethical, and political problems raised by its continued use. Yet, the title of his book is *Deviance and Identity*.

Szasz (1970:xxv–xxvi) has urged that we abandon use of the term:

Words have lives of their own. However much sociologists insist that the term "deviant" does not diminish the worth of the person or group so categorized, the implication of inferiority adheres to the word. Indeed, sociologists are not wholly exempt from blame: they describe addicts and homosexuals as deviants, but never Olympic champions or Nobel Prize winners. In fact, the term is rarely applied to people with admired characteristics, such as great wealth, superior skills, or fame—whereas it is often applied to those with despised characteristics, such as poverty, lack of marketable skills, or infamy.

The term "social deviants". . . does not make sufficiently explicit—as the terms "scapegoat" or "victim" do—that majorities usually categorize persons or groups as "deviant" in order to set them apart as inferior beings and to justify their social control, oppression, persecution, or even complete destruction.

Terms like victimization, persecution, and oppression are more accurate descriptions of what is really happening. But even Gouldner (1968), in a masterful critique of the labelling school, while describing social conflict, calls civil-rights and anti-war protesters "political deviants." He points out clearly that these protesters are resisting openly, not slyly, conditions they abhor. Gouldner is discussing political struggles; oppression and resistance to oppression; conflicts over values, morals, interests, and power; and victimization. Naming such protesters "deviants," even if *political* deviants, is an indication of the deep penetration within our minds of certain prejudices and orientations.

Given the use of the term, the definition and examples of "deviant" reveal underlying sentiments and views. Therefore, it is important that we redefine drastically the entire field, especially since it is a flourishing one: "Because younger sociologists have found deviance such a fertile and exciting field for their own work, and because students share these feelings, deviance promises to become an even more important area of sociological research and theory in the coming years" (Douglas, 1970a:3).

The lists and discussions of "deviant" acts and persons reveal the writers' biases and sentiments. These are acts which, "like robbery, burglary or rape [are] of a simple and dramatic predatory nature. . ." (The President's Commission on Law Enforcement and the Administration of Justice, in Dinitz, et al., 1969:105). All 16 texts, without exception, concentrate on actions and persons of a "dramatic predatory nature," on "preverts." This is true of both the labelling and other schools. The following are examples from the latter:

Ten different types of deviant behavior are considered: juvenile delinquency, adult crime, prison sub-cultures, homosexuality, prostitution, suicide, homicide, alcoholism, drug addiction and mental illness (Rushing, 1969:preface).

Traditionally, in American sociology the study of deviance has focused on criminals, juvenile delinquents, prostitutes, suicides, the mentally ill, drug users and drug addicts, homosexuals, and political and religious radicals (Lefton, et al., 1968:v).

Deviant behavior is essentially violation of certain types of group norms; a deviant act is behavior which is proscribed in a certain way. [It must be] in a disapproved direction, and of sufficient degree to exceed the tolerance limit of the community. . . . [such as] delinquency and crime, prostitution, homosexual behavior, drug addiction, alcoholism, mental disorders, suicide, marital and family maladjustment, discrimination against minority groups, and, to a lesser degree, role problems of old age (Clinard, 1968:28).

Finally, we are told that these are some examples of deviance every society must deal with: ". . .mental illness, violence, theft, and sexual misconduct, as well as. . .other similarly difficult behavior" (Dinitz, et al., 1969:3).

The list stays unchanged with the authors of the labelling school.

. . .in Part I, "The Deviant Act," I draw rather heavily on certain studies of homicide, embezzlement, "naive" check forgery, suicide and a few other acts. . .in discussing the assumption of deviant identity (Part II) and the assumption of normal identity (Part III), there is heavy reference to certain studies of paranoia, "mental illness" more generally, and

Alcoholics Anonymous and Synanon (Lofland, 1969:34).

Homicide, suicide, alcoholism, mental illness, prostitution, and homosexuality are among the forms of behavior typically called deviant, and they are among the kinds of behavior that will be analyzed (Lofland, 1969:1). Included among my respondents were political radicals of the far left and the far right, homosexuals, militant blacks, convicts and mental hospital patients, mystics, narcotic addicts, LSD and Marijuana users, illicit drug dealers, delinquent boys, racially mixed couples, hippies, health-food users, and bohemian artists and village eccentrics (Simmons, 1969:10).

Simmons (1969:27, 29, 31) also informs us that in his study of stereotypes of "deviants" held by the public, these are the types he gave to people: homosexuals, beatniks, adulterers, marijuana smokers, political radicals, alcoholics, prostitutes, lesbians, ex-mental patients, atheists, ex-convicts, intellectuals, and gamblers. In Lemert (1967) we find that except for the three introductory (theoretical) chapters, the substantive chapters cover the following topics: alcohol drinking, four; check forgers, three; stuttering, two; and mental illness, two. Matza (1969) offers the following list of "deviants" and their actions that "must be appreciated if one adheres to a naturalistic perspective:" paupers, robbers, motorcycle gangs, prostitutes, drug addicts, promiscuous homosexuals, thieving Gypsies, and "free love" Bohemians (1969:16). Finally, Douglas' collection (1970a) covers these forms of "deviance:" abortion, nudism, topless barmaids, prostitutes, homosexuals, violence (motorcycle and juvenile gangs), shoplifting, and drugs.

The omissions from these lists are staggering. The covert, institutional forms of "deviance" (part II, below) are nowhere to be found. Reading these authors, one would not know that the most destructive use of violence in the last decade has been the war in Vietnam, in which the U.S. has heaped unprecedented suffering on the people and their land; more bombs have been dropped in Vietnam than in the entire World War II. Moreover, the robbery of the corporate world—through tax breaks, fixed prices, low wages, pollution of the environment, shoddy goods, etc.—is passed over in our fascination with "dramatic and predatory" actions. Therefore, we are told that "while they certainly are of no greater social importance to us than such subjects as banking and accounting [or military violence], subjects such as marijuana use and motorcycle gangs are of far greater interest to most of us. While it is only a coincidence that our scientific interests correspond with the emotional interest in deviants, it is a happy coincidence and, I believe, one that should be encouraged" (Douglas, 1970a:5). And Matza (1969:17), in commenting on the "appreciative sentiments" of the "naturalistic spirit," elaborates on the same theme: "We do not for a moment wish that we could rid ourselves of deviant phenomena. We are intrigued by them. They are an intrinsic, ineradicable, and vital part of human society."

An effort is made to transcend this limited view and substantive concern with dramatic and predatory forms of "deviance." Becker (1964:3) claims that the new (labelling) deviance no longer studies only "delinquents and drug addicts, though these classical kinds of deviance are still kept under observation." It increases its knowledge "of the processes of deviance by studying physicians, people with physical handicaps, the mentally deficient, and others whose doings were formerly not included in the area." The powerful "deviants" are still left untouched, however. This is still true with another aspect of the new deviance. Becker (1964:4) claims that in the labelling perspective "we focus attention on the other people involved in the process. We pay attention to the role of the non-deviant as well as that of the deviant." But we see that it is the ordinary non-deviants and the low-level agents of social control who receive attention, not the powerful ones (Gouldner, 1968).

In fact, the emphasis is more on the *subculture* and *identity* of the "deviants" themselves rather than on their oppressors and persecutors. To be sure, in varying degrees all authors discuss the agents of social control, but the fascination and emphasis are on the "deviant" himself. Studies of prisons and prisoners, for example, focus on prison subcultures and prisoner rehabilitation; there is little or no consideration of the social,

political, economic, and power conditions which consign people to prisons. Only now are we beginning to realize that most prisoners are *political prisoners*—that their "criminal" actions (whether against individuals, such as robbery, or conscious political acts against the state) result largely from current social and political conditions, and are not the work of "disturbed" and "psychopathic" personalities. This realization came about largely because of the writings of political prisoners themselves: Malcolm X (1965), Eldridge Cleaver (1968), and George Jackson (1970), among others.[3]

In all these books, notably those of the labelling school, the concern is with the "deviant's" subculture and identity: his problems, motives, fellow victims, etc. The collection of memoirs and apologies of "deviants" in their own words (McCaghy, et al., 1968) covers the lives and identities of "prevert deviants:" prostitutes, nudists, abortionists, criminals, drug users, homosexuals, the mentally ill, alcoholics, and suicides. For good measure, some "militant deviants" are thrown in: Black Muslims, the SDS, and a conscientious objector. But one

---

[3]The first draft of this paper was completed in July, 1971. The killing of George Jackson at San Quentin on August 21, 1971, which many people see as a political murder, and the Attica prisoner rebellion of early September, 1971, only strengthen the argument about political prisoners. Two things became clear: a) Not only a few "radicals," but many prisoners (if not a majority) see their fate as the outcome of political forces and decisions, and themselves as political prisoners (see Fraser, 1971). Robert Chrisman's argument (in Fraser, 1971) points to such a conclusion clearly: "To maintain that all black offenders are, by their actions, politically correct, is dangerous romanticism. Black antisocial behavior must be seen in and of its own terms and corrected for enhancement of the black community." But there is a political aspect, for black prisoners' condition "derives from the political inequity of black people in America. A black prisoner's crime may or may not have been a political action against the state, but the state's action against him is always political." I would stress that the same is true of most white prisoners, for they come mostly from the exploited poorer classes and groups. b) The state authorities, the political rulers, by their deeds if not their words, see such prisoners as political men and threats. The death of George Jackson, and the brutal crushing of the Attica rebellion, attest to the authorities' realization, and fear, that here were no mere riots with prisoners letting off steam, but authentic political actions, involving groups and individuals conscious of their social position and exploitation.

wonders about other types of "deviants:" how do those who perpetrate the covert institutional violence in our society view themselves? Do they have identity problems? How do they justify their actions? How did the robber barons of the late 19th century steal, fix laws, and buy politicians six days of the week and go to church on Sunday? By what process can people speak of body counts and kill ratios with cool objectivity? On these and similar questions, this book (and all others)[4] provides no answers; indeed, the editors seem unaware that such questions should or could be raised.

Becker (1964), Rubington and Weinberg (1968), Matza (1969), and Bell (1971) also focus on the identity and subculture of "prevert deviants." Matza, in discussing the assumption of "deviant identity," uses as examples, and elaborates upon, thieves and marijuana users. In all these books, there are occasional references to and questions about the larger social and political structure, but these are not explored in any depth; and the emphasis remains on the behavior, identity, and rehabilitation of the "deviant" himself. This bias continues in the latest book which, following the fashions of the times, has chapters on hippies and militant protesters (Bell, 1971).

Even the best of these books, Simmons' *Deviants* (1969), is not free of the overwhelming concentration of the "deviant" and his identity. It is the most sympathetic and balanced presentation of the lives of "deviants:" their joys, sorrows, and problems with the straight world and fellow victims. Simmons demystifies the processes of becoming "deviant" and overcoming "deviance." He shows, as well as anyone does, that these victims *are* just like us; and the differences they possess and the suffering they endure are imposed upon them. Ultimately, however, Simmons too falls prey to the three biases shown in the work of others: a) the "deviants" he considers are only of the "prevert" type; b) he focuses mostly on the victim and his identity, not on the persecutors; and c) the persecutors he does discuss are of the middle-level variety, the agents of more powerful others and institutions.

Because of these biases, there is an implicit, but very clear, acceptance by these authors of the current definitions of "deviance." It comes about because they concentrate their attention on those who have been *successfully labelled as "deviant,"* and not on those who break laws, fix laws, violate ethical and moral standards, harm individuals and groups, etc., but who either are able to hide their actions, or, when known, can deflect criticism, labelling, and punishment. The following are typical statements which reveal this bias.

". . .no act committed by members of occupational groups [such as white-collar crimes], however unethical, should be considered as crime unless it is punishable by the state in some way" (Clinard, 1968:269). Thus, if some people can manipulate laws so that their unethical and destructive acts are not "crimes," we should cater to their power and agree that they are not criminals.

Furthermore, the essence of the labelling school encourages this bias, despite Becker's (1963:14) assertion that ". . .insofar as a scientist uses 'deviant' to refer to any rule-breaking behavior and takes as his subjects of study only those who have been *labelled* deviant, he will be hampered by the disparities between the two categories." But as the following statements from Becker and others show, this is in fact what the labelling school does do.

Deviance is "created by society. . .*social groups create deviance by making the rules whose infraction constitutes deviance,* and by applying those rules to particular people and labelling them as outsiders" (Becker, 1963:8–9). Clearly, according to this view, in cases where no group has labelled another, no matter what the other group or individuals have done, there is nothing for the sociologist to study and dissect.

Rules are not made automatically. Even though a practice may be harmful in an objective sense to the group in which it occurs, the harm needs to be discovered and pointed out. People must be made to feel that something ought to be done about it (Becker, 1963:162).

---

[4]With the exception of E. C. Hughes, in Becker (1964).

What is important for the social analyst is not what people are by his lights or by his standards, but what it is that people construe one another and themselves to be for what reasons and with what consequences (Lofland, 1969:35).

. . .deviance is in the eyes of the beholder. For deviance to become a social fact, somebody must perceive an act, person, situation, or event as a departure from social norms, must categorize that perception, must report the perception to others, must get them to accept this definition of the situation, and must obtain a response that conforms to this definition. Unless all these requirements are met, deviance as a social fact does not come into being (Rubington and Weinberg, 1968:v).

The implication of these statements is that the sociologist accepts current, successful definitions of what is "deviant" as the only ones worthy of his attention. To be sure, he may argue that those labelled "deviant" are not really different from the rest of us, or that there is no act intrinsically "deviant," etc. By concentrating on cases of successful labelling, however, he will not penetrate beneath the surface to look for other forms of "deviance"—undetected stealing, violence, and destruction. When people are not powerful enough to make the "deviant" label stick on others, we overlook these cases. But is it not as much a *social fact,* even though few of us pay much attention to it, that the corporate economy kills and maims more, is more violent, than any violence committed by the poor (the usual subjects of studies of violence)? By what reasoning and necessity is the "violence" of the poor in the ghettoes more worthy of our attention than the military bootcamps which numb recruits from the horrors of killing the "enemy" ("Oriental human beings," as we learned during the Calley trial)? But because these acts are not labelled "deviant," because they are covert, institutional, and normal, their "deviant" qualities are overlooked and they do not become part of the province of the sociology of deviance. Despite their best liberal intentions, these sociologists seem to perpetuate the very notions they think they debunk, and others of which they are unaware.

II.

As a result of the fascination with "nuts, sluts, and preverts," and their identities and subcultures, little attention has been paid to the unethical illegal, and destructive actions of powerful individuals, groups, and institutions in our society. Because these actions are carried out quietly in the normal course of events, the sociology of deviance does not consider them as part of its subject matter. This bias is rooted in the very conception and definition of the field. It is obvious when one examines the treatment, or, just as often, lack of it, of the issues of violence, crime, and white-collar crime.

Discussions of violence treat only one type: the "dramatic and predatory" violence committed by individuals (usually the poor and minorities) against persons and property. For example, we read, "crimes involving violence, such as criminal homicide, assault, and forcible rape, are concentrated in the slums" (Clinard, 1968:123). Wolfgang, an expert on violence, has developed a whole theory on the "subculture of violence" found among the lower classes (e.g., in Rushing, 1969:233–40). And Douglas (1970a:part 4, on violence) includes readings on street gangs and the Hell's Angels. Thompson (1966), in his book on the Hell's Angels, devotes many pages to an exploration of the Angels' social background. In addition, throughout the book, and especially in his concluding chapter, he places the Angels' violence in the perspective of a violent, raping, and destructive society, which refuses to confront the reality of the Angels by distorting, exaggerating, and romanticizing their actions. But Douglas reprints none of these pages; rather, he offers us the chapter where, during a July 4 weekend, the Angels were restricted by the police within a lakeside area, had a drunken weekend, and became a tourist sideshow and circus.

In short, violence is presented as the exclusive property of the poor in the slums, the minorities, street gangs, and motorcycle beasts. But if we take the concept *violence* seriously, we see that much of our political and economic system thrives on it. In violence, a person is *violated*—there is harm done to his person, his psyche, his body, his dignity, his ability to govern himself (Garver, in Rose, 1969:6). Seen in this way, a person can be violated in many ways; physical force is only one of them. As the readings in Rose (1969) show, a person can be violated by a system that denies him a decent job, or consigns him to a slum, or causes him brain damage by near-starvation during childhood, or manipulates him through the mass media, and so on endlessly.

Moreover, we must see that *covert institutional violence* is much more destructive than overt individual violence. We must recognize that people's lives are violated by the very normal and everyday workings of institutions. We do not see such events and situations as violent because they are not dramatic and predatory; they do not make for fascinating reading on the lives of preverts; but they kill, maim, and destroy many more lives than do violent individuals.

Here are some examples. Carmichael and Hamilton (1967:4), in distinguishing between *individual* and *institutional* racism, offer examples of each:

When white terrorists bomb a black church and kill five black children, that is an act of individual racism, widely deplored by most segments of the society. But when in that same city—Birmingham, Alabama—five hundred black babies die each year because of lack of proper food, shelter, and medical facilities, and thousands more are destroyed and maimed physically, emotionally and intellectually because of conditions of poverty and discrimination in the black community, that is a function of institutional racism.

Surely this is violence; it is caused by the normal, quiet workings of institutions run by respectable members of the community. Many whites also suffer from the institutional workings of a profit-oriented society and economy; poor health, dead-end jobs, slum housing, hunger in rural areas, and so on, are daily realities in their lives. This is surely much worse violence than any committed by the Hell's Angels or street gangs. Only these groups get stigmatized and analyzed by sociologists of deviance, however, while those good people who live in luxurious homes (fixing tax laws for their benefit) off profits derived from

an exploitative economic system—they are the pillars of their community.

Violence is committed daily by the government, very often by lack of action. The same system that enriches businessmen farmers with billions of dollars through farm subsidies cannot be bothered to appropriate a few millions to deal with lead poisoning in the slums. Young children

. . .get it by eating the sweet-tasting chips of peeling tenement walls, painted a generation ago with leaded paint.

According to the Department of Health, Education, and Welfare, 400,000 children are poisoned each year, about 30,000 in New York City alone. About 3,200 suffer permanent brain damage, 800 go blind or become so mentally retarded that they require hospitalization for the rest of their lives, and approximately 200 die.

The tragedy is that lead poisoning is totally man-made and totally preventable. It is caused by slum housing. And there are now blood tests that can detect the disease, and medicines to cure it. Only a lack of purpose sentences 200 black children to die each year (Newfield, 1971).[5]

Newfield goes on to report that on May 20, 1971, a Senate-House conference eliminated $5 million from an appropriations budget. In fact, 200 children had been sentenced to death and thousands more to maiming and suffering.

Similar actions of violence are committed daily by the government and corporations; but in these days of misplaced emphasis, ignorance, and manipulation we do not see the destruction inherent in these actions. Instead, we get fascinated, angry, and misled by the violence of the poor and the powerless. We see the violence committed during political rebellions in the ghettoes (called "riots" in order to dismiss them), but all along we ignored the daily violence committed against the ghetto residents by the institutions of the society: schools, hospitals, corporations, the government. Check any of these books on deviance, and see how much of this type of

---

[5] As Gittlin and Hollander (1970) show, the children of poor whites also suffer from lead poisoning.

violence is even mentioned, much less explored and described.

It may be argued that some of this violence is (implicitly) recognized in discussions of "white-collar" crime. This is not the case, however. Of the 16 books under considerations, only three pay some attention to white-collar crime (Cohen, 1966; Clinard, 1968; Dinitz, et al., 1969); and of these, only the last covers the issue at some length. Even in these few discussions, however, the focus remains on the *individuals* who commit the actions (on their greediness, lack of morality, etc.), not on the economic and political institutions within which they operate. The selection in Dinitz, et al. (1969:99–109), from the President's Commission on Law Enforcement and the Administration of Justice, at least three times (pp. 101, 103, 108) argues that white-collar crime is "pervasive," causes "financial burdens" ("probably far greater than those produced by traditional common law theft offenses"), and is generally harmful. At least in these pages, however, there is no investigation of the social, political, and economic conditions which make the pervasiveness, and lenient treatment, of white-collar crime possible.

The bias against examining the structural conditions behind white-collar crime is further revealed in Clinard's suggestions on how to deal with it (in his chapter on "The Prevention of Deviant Behavior"). The only recommendation in three pages of discussion (704–7) is to teach everyone more "respect" for the law. This is a purely moralistic device; it pays no attention to the structural aspects of the problem, to the fact that even deeper than white-collar crime is ingrained a whole network of laws, especially tax laws, administrative policies, and institutions which systematically favor a small minority. More generally, discussions on the prevention of "deviance" and crime do not deal with institutional violence, and what we need to do to stop it.[6]

But there is an obvious explanation for this oversight. The people committing serious white-collar crimes and executing the policies of violent institutions are respectable and responsible individuals, not "deviants;" this is the view of the President's Commission on Law Enforcement and the Administration of Justice.

Significantly, the Antitrust Division does not feel that lengthy prison sentences are ordinarily called for [for white-collar crimes]. It "rarely recommends jail sentences greater than 6 months—recommendations of 30-day imprisonment are most frequent" (Dinitz, et al., 1969:105).

Persons who have standing and roots in a community, and are prepared for and engaged in legitimate occupations, can be expected to be particularly susceptible to the threat of criminal prosecution. Criminal proceedings and the imposition of sanctions have a much sharper impact upon those who have not been hardened by previous contact with the criminal justice system (in Dinitz, et al., 1969:104).

At the same time, we are told elsewhere by the Commission that white-collar crime is pervasive and widespread; "criminal proceedings and the imposition of sanctions" do not appear to deter it much.

The executives convicted in the Electrical Equipment case were respectable citizens. "Several were deacons or vestrymen of their churches." The rest also held prestigious positions: president of the Chamber of Commerce, bank director, little-league organizer, and so on (Dinitz, et al., 1969:107). Moreover, "generally. . .in cases of white-collar crime, neither the corporations as entities nor their responsible officers are invested with deviant characters. . ." (Cohen, 1966:30). Once more, there is quiet acquiescence to this state of affairs. There is no attempt to find out why those who steal millions and whose actions violate lives are not "invested with deviant

---

[6]Investigation of the causes and prevention of institutional violence would probably be biting the hand that feeds the sociologist, for we read that the government and foundations (whose money comes from corporate profits) have supported research on "deviant behavior," especially its prevention.

"This has meant particularly that the application of sociological theory to research has increased markedly in such areas as delinquency, crime, mental disorder, alcoholism, drug addiction, and discrimination" (Clinard, 1968:742). That's where the action is, not on white-collar crime, nor on the covert institutional violence of the government and economy.

characters." There is no consideration given to the possibility that, as responsible intellectuals, it is our duty to explore and expose the structural causes for corporate and other serious crimes, which make for much more suffering than does armed robbery. We seem satisfied merely to observe what is, and leave the causes unexamined.

In conclusion, let us look at another form of institutional "deviance." The partial publication of the Pentagon papers (June 1971) made public the conscious lying and manipulation by the government to quiet opposition to the Vietnam war. But lying pervades both government and economy. Deceptions and outright lies abound in advertising (see Henry, 1963). During the 1968 campaign, Presidential candidate Nixon blessed us with an ingenious form of deception. McGinniss (1969:149–50) is recording a discussion that took place before Nixon was to appear on live TV (to show spontaneity) the day before the election and answer, unrehearsed, questions phoned in by the viewing audience.

"I understand Paul Keyes has been sitting up for two days writing questions," Roger Ailes said.

"Well, not quite," Jack Rourke said. He seemed a little embarrassed.

"What is going to happen?"

"Oh. . ."

"It's sort of semiforgery, isn't it?" Ailes said. "Keyes has a bunch of questions Nixon wants to answer. He's written them in advance to make sure they're properly worded. When someone calls in with something similar, they'll use Keyes' question and attribute it to the person who called. Isn't that it?"

"More or less," Jack Rourke said.

In short, despite the supposedly central position of *social structure* in the sociological enterprise, there is general neglect of it in the field of "deviance." Larger questions, especially if they deal with political and economic issues, are either passed over briefly or overlooked completely. The focus on the actions of "nuts, sluts, and preverts" and the related slight of the criminal and destructive actions of the powerful, are instances of this avoidance.

III.

Most of the authors under discussion mention the importance of *power* in labelling people "deviant." They state that those who label (the victimizers) are more powerful than those they label (the victims). Writers of the labelling school make this point explicitly. According to Becker (1963:17), "who can. . .force others to accept their rules and what are the causes of their success? This is, of course, a question of political and economic power." Simmons (1969:131) comments that historically, "those in power have used their positions largely to perpetuate and enhance their own advantages through coercing and manipulating the rest of the populace." And Lofland (1969:19) makes the same observation in his opening pages:

It is in the situation of a very powerful party opposing a very weak one that the powerful party sponsors the *idea* that the weak party is breaking the rules of society. The very concepts of "society" and its "rules" are appropriated by powerful parties and made synonymous with their interests (and, of course, believed in by the naive, e.g., the undergraduate penchant for the phrases "society says. . .," "society expects. . .," "society does. . .").

But this insight is not developed. In none of the 16 books is there an extensive discussion of how power operates in the designation of deviance. Instead of a study of power, of its concrete uses in modern, corporate America, we are offered rather fascinating explorations into the identities and subcultures of "deviants," and misplaced emphasis on the middle-level agents of social control. Only Szasz (1961, 1963, and notably 1970) has shown consistently the role of power in one area of "deviance," "mental illness." Through historical and contemporary studies, he has shown that those labelled "mentally ill" (crazy, insane, mad, lunatic) and institutionalized have always been the powerless: women, the poor, peasants, the aged, and others. Moreover, he has exposed repeatedly the means used by powerful individuals and institutions in employing the "mental illness" label to discredit, persecute, and eliminate opponents. In short, he has shown the political element in the "mental illness" game.

In addition, except for Szasz, none of the authors seems to realize that the stigma of prostitution, abortion, and other "deviant" acts unique to women comes about in large part from the powerlessness of women and their status in society. Moreover, to my knowledge, no one has bothered to ask why there have always been women prostitutes for men to satisfy their sexual desires, but very few men prostitutes for women to patronize. The very word *prostitute* we associate with women only, not men. Both men and women have been involved in this "immoral" act, but the stigma has been carried by the women alone.

All 16 books, some more extensively than others, discuss the ideology, modes of operation, and views of *agents of social control,* the people who designate what is to be "deviant" and those who handle the people so designated. As Gouldner (1968) has shown, however, these are the lower and middle level officials, not those who make basic policy and decisions. This bias becomes obvious when we look at the specific agents discussed.

For example, Simmons (1969:18) tells us that some of "those in charge at every level" are the following: "university administrators, patrolmen, schoolmasters, and similar public employees. . . ." Do university administrators and teachers run the schools alone? Are they teaching and enforcing their own unique values? Do teachers alone create the horrible schools in the slums? Are the uniformity, punctuality, and conformity teachers inculcate their own psychological hang-ups, or do they represent the interests of an industrial-technological-corporate order? In another sphere, do the police enforce their own laws?

Becker (1963:14) has shown consistent interest in agents of social control. However, a close examination reveals limitations. He discusses "moral crusaders" like those who passed the laws against marijuana. The moral crusader, "the prototype of the rule creator," finds that "the existing rules do not satisfy him because there is some evil which profoundly disturbs him." But the only type of rule creator

Becker discusses is the moral crusader, no other. The political manipulators who pass laws to defend their interests and persecute dissenters are not studied. The "unconventional sentimentality," the debunking motif Becker (1964:4–5) sees in the "new deviance" is directed toward the police, the prison officials, the mental hospital personnel, the "average" person and his prejudices. The basic social, political, and economic structure, and those commanding it who guide the labelling and persecution, are left untouched. We have become so accustomed to debunking these low-level agents that we do not even know how to begin to direct our attention to the ruling institutions and groups (for an attempt at such an analysis, see Liazos, 1970).

In a later paper, Becker (1967) poses an apparently insoluble dilemma. He argues that, in studying agents of social control, we are always forced to study subordinates. We can never really get to the top, to those who "really" run the show, for if we study X's superior Y, we find Z above him, and so on endlessly. Everyone has somebody over him, so there is no one at the top. But this is a clever point without substance. In this hierarchy some have more power than others and some are at the top; they may disclaim their position, of course, but it is our job to show otherwise. Some people in this society do have more power than others: parents over children, men over women; some have considerable power over others: top administrators of institutions, for one; and some have a great deal of power, those Domhoff (1967) and others have shown to be the ruling class. It should be our task to explore and describe this hierarchy, its bases of strength, its uses of the "deviant" label to discredit its opponents in order to silence them, and to find ways to eliminate this hierarchy.

Discussions of the police reveal the same misplaced emphasis on lower and middle level agents of social control. In three of the books (Matza, 1969:182–95; Rubington and Weinberg, 1968:ch. 7; Dinitz, et al., 1969:40–47), we are presented with the biases and prejudices of policemen; their modes of operation in confronting delinquents and others; the pressures on them from various quarters; etc. In short, the focus is on the role and psychology of the policeman.

All these issues about the policeman's situation need to be discussed, of course; but there is an even more important issue which these authors avoid. We must ask, who passes the laws the police enforce? Whose agents are they? Why do the police exist? Three excellent papers (Cook, 1968; A. Silver, in Bordua, 1967; T. Hayden, in Rose, 1969) offer some answers to these questions. They show, through a historical description of the origins of police forces, that they have always been used to defend the status quo, the interests of the ruling powers. When the police force was created in England in the early 1800's, it was meant to defend the propertied classes from the "dangerous classes" and the "mob."[7] With the rise of capitalism and industrialism, there was much unrest from the suffering underclass; the professional police were meant to act as a buffer zone for the capitalist elite. Similarly, in America during the early part of this century, especially in the 1930's, police were used repeatedly to attack striking workers and break their strikes. During the Chicago "police riot" of 1968, the police were not merely acting out their aggressions and frustrations; as Hayden shows, they acted with the consent, direction, and blessing of Mayor Daley and the Democratic party (which party represents the "liberal" wing of the American upper class).

It must be stressed that the police, like all agents of social control, are doing someone else's work. Sometimes they enforce laws and prejudices of "society," the much maligned middle class (on sex, marijuana, etc.); but at other times it is not "society" which gives them their directives, but specific interested groups, even though, often, "society" is manipulated to express its approval of such actions. Above all, we must remember that *"in a fundamentally unjust society, even the most impartial, professional, efficient enforcement of the laws by the police cannot result in justice"* (Cook, 1968:2). More generally, in an unjust and exploitative society, no matter how "humane" agents of social control are, their actions necessarily result in repression.

Broad generalization is another device used by some of these authors to avoid concrete examination of the uses of power in the creation and labelling of "deviance." Clairborne (1971) has called such generalization "*schlock*." The following are some of the tactics he thinks are commonly used in writing popular *schlock* sociology (some sociologists of deviance use similar tactics, as we shall see).

The Plausible Passive:
"New scientific discoveries are being made every day. . . . These new ideas are being put to work more quickly. . ." [Toffler, in *Future Shock*, is] thereby rather neatly obscuring the fact that scientists and engineers (mostly paid by industry) are making the discoveries and industrialists (often with the aid of public funds) are putting them to work. An alternative to the Plausible Passive is the Elusive Impersonal: 'Buildings in New York literally disappear overnight.' What Toffler is trying to avoid saying is that contractors and real estate speculators *destroy* buildings overnight (Clairborne, 1971:118).

Rampant Reification, by which "conceptual abstractions are transformed into causal realities," also abounds. Toffler

speaks of the "roaring current of change" as "an elemental force" and of "that great, growling engine of change—technology." Which of course completely begs the question of what fuels the engine and whose hand is on the throttle. One does not cross-examine an elemental force, let alone suggest that it may have been engendered by monopoly profits (especially in defense and aerospace) or accelerated by government incentives (e.g., open or concealed subsidies, low capital gains tax, accelerated depreciation—which Nixon is now seeking to reinstitute) (Clairborne, 1971:118).

There are parallels in the sociology of deviance. Clinard (1968:ch. 4) argues that urbanization and the slum are breeding grounds for "deviant behavior." But these conditions are reified, not examined concretely. He says about urbanization and social change:

Rapid social and cultural change, disregard for the importance of stability of generations, and untempered loyalties also generally characterize urban life. New

---

[7]See Rude (1966) on the role of mobs of poor workers and peasants in 18th and 19th century England and France.

ideas are generally welcome, inventions and mechanical gadgets are encouraged, and new styles in such arts as painting, literature, and music are often approved (1968:90).

But the slum, urbanization, and change are not reified entities working out their independent wills. For example, competition, capitalism, and the profit motive—all encouraged by a government controlled by the upper classes—have had something to do with the rise of slums. There is a general process of urbanization, but at given points in history it is fed by, and gives profits to, specific groups. The following are a few historical examples: the land enclosure policies and practices of the English ruling classes in the 17th and 18th centuries; the building of cheap housing in the 19th century by the owners of factory towns; and the profits derived from "urban renewal" (which has destroyed neighborhoods, created even more crowded slums, etc.) by the building of highways, luxury apartments, and stores.

Another favorite theme of *schlock* sociology is that "All Men Are Guilty." That means nothing can be done to change things. There is a variation of this theme in the sociology of deviance when we are told that a) all of us are deviant in some way, b) all of us label some others deviant, and c) "society" labels. Such statements preclude asking concrete questions: does the "deviance" of each of us have equal consequences for others? Does the labelling of each of us stick, and with what results?

For example, Simmons (1969:124) says:

. . .I strongly suspect that officials now further alienate more culprits than they recruit back into conventional society, and I think they imprison at least as many people in deviance as they rehabilitate. We must remember that, with a sprinkling of exceptions, officials come from, are hired by, and belong to the dominant majority.

Who is that dominant majority? Are they always the numerical majority? Do they control the labelling and correctional process all by themselves? These questions are not raised.

Another case of *schlock* is found in Matza's discussion (lack of it, really) of "Leviathan" (1969,

especially ch. 7). It is mentioned as a potent force in the labelling and handling of "deviance." But, vainly, one keeps looking for some exploration into the workings of "Leviathan." It remains a reified, aloof creature. What is it? Who controls it? How does it label? Why? Matza seems content to try to mesmerize us by mentioning it constantly (Leviathan is capitalized throughout); but we are never shown how it operates. It hovers in the background, it punishes, and its presence somehow cowers us into submission. But it remains a reified force whose presence is accepted without close examination.

The preceding examples typify much of what is wrong with the sociology of deviance: the lack of specific analysis of the role of power in the labelling process; the generalizations which, even when true, explain little; the fascination with "deviants;" the reluctance to study the "deviance" of the powerful.

IV.

I want to start my concluding comments with two disclaimers.

a. I have tried to provide some balance and perspective in the field of "deviance," and in doing so I have argued against the exclusive emphasis on *nuts, sluts,* and *preverts* and their identities and subcultures. I do not mean, however, that the usually considered forms of "deviance" are unworthy of our attention. Suicide, prostitution, madness, juvenile delinquency, and others *are* with us; we cannot ignore them. People do suffer when labelled and treated as "deviant" (in *this* sense, "deviants" *are* different from conformists). Rather, I want to draw attention to phenomena which also belong to the field of "deviance."[8]

---

[8]The question of "what deviance is to the deviant" (Gordon Fellman, private communication), not what the labelling, anomie, and other schools, or the present radical viewpoint say *about* such a person, is not dealt with here. I avoid this issue not because I think it unimportant, rather because I want to concentrate on the political, moral, and social issues raised by the biases of those presently writing about the "deviant."

b. It is because the sociology of deviance, especially the labelling approach, contains important, exciting, and revealing insights, because it tries to humanize the "deviant," and because it is popular, that it is easy to overlook some of the basic ideological biases still pervading the field. For this reason, I have tried to explore and detail some of these biases. At the same time, however, I do not mean to dismiss the contributions of the field as totally negative and useless. In fact, in my teaching I have been using two of the books discussed here, Simmons (1969) and Rubington and Weinberg (1968).

The argument can be summarized briefly. (1) We should not study only, or predominantly, the popular and dramatic forms of "deviance." Indeed, we should banish the concept of "deviance" and speak of oppression, conflict, persecution, and suffering. By focusing on the dramatic forms, as we do now, we perpetuate most people's beliefs and impressions that such "deviance" is the basic cause of many of our troubles, that these people (criminals, drug addicts, political dissenters, and others) are the real "troublemakers;" and, necessarily, we neglect conditions of inequality, powerlessness, institutional violence, and so on, which lie at the bases of our tortured society. (2) Even when we do study the popular forms of "deviance," we do not avoid blaming the victim for his fate; the continued use of the term "deviant" is one clue to this blame. Nor have we succeeded in normalizing him; the focus on the "deviant" himself, on his identity and subculture, has tended to confirm the popular prejudice that he is different.

REFERENCES

Becker, Howard S.
*1963   Outsiders. New York: Free Press.
*1964   (ed.) The Other Side. New York: Free Press.
 1967   "Whose side are we on?" Social Problems 14: 239–247 (reprinted in Douglas, 1970a, 99–111; references to this reprint).

Bell, Robert R.
*1971   Social Deviance: A Substantive Analysis. Homewood, Illinois: Dorsey.

Bend, Emil and Martin Vogenfanger
 1964   "A new look at Mills' critique," in Mass Society in Crisis. Bernard Rosenberg, Israel Gerver, F. William Howton (eds.). New York: Macmillan, 111–122.

Bordua, David (ed.)
 1967   The Police. New York: Wiley.

Carmichael, Stokeley and Charles V. Hamilton
 1967   Black Power. New York: Random House.

Clairborne, Robert
 1971   "Future schlock." The Nation, Jan. 25, 117–120.

Cleaver, Eldridge
 1968   Soul On Ice. New York: MacGraw-Hill.

Clinard, Marshall B.
*1968   Sociology of Deviant Behavior. (3rd ed.) New York: Holt, Rinehart, and Winston.

Cohen, Albert K.
*1966   Deviance and Control. Englewood Cliffs, N.J.: Prentice-Hall.

Cook, Robert M.
 1968   "The police." The Bulletin of the American Independent Movement (New Haven, Conn.), 3:6, 1–6.

Dinitz, Simon, Russell R. Dynes, and Alfred C. Clarke (eds.)
*1969   Deviance. New York: Oxford University Press.

Domhoff, William G.
 1967   Who Rules America? Englewood Cliffs, N.J.: Prentice-Hall.

Douglas, Jack D.
*1970a   (ed.) Observations of Deviance. New York: Random House.
*1970b   (ed.) Deviance and Respectability: The Social Construction of Moral Meanings. New York: Basic Books.

Fraser, C. Gerald
 1971   "Black prisoners finding new view of themselves as political prisoners." New York Times, Sept. 16.

Gittlin, Todd and Nanci Hollander
 1970   Uptown: Poor Whites in Chicago. New York: Harper and Row.

Gouldner, Alvin W.
 1968   "The sociologist as partisan: Sociology and the welfare state." American Sociologist 3:2, 103–116.

Henry, Jules
 1963   Culture Against Man. New York: Random House.

Jackson, George
1970   Soledad Brother. New York: Bantam Books.

Lefton, Mark, J. K. Skipper, and C. H. McCaghy (eds.)
*1968   Approaches to Deviance. New York: Appleton-Century-Crofts.

Lemert, Edwin M.
*1967   Human Deviance, Social Problems, and Social Control. Englewood Cliffs, N.J.: Prentice-Hall.

Liazos, Alexander
1970   Processing for Unfitness: Socialization of "emotionally disturbed" lower-class boys into the mass society. Ph.D. dissertation, Brandeis University.

Lofland, John
*1969   Deviance and Identity. Englewood Cliffs, N.J.: Prentice-Hall.

McCaghy, Charles H., J. K. Skipper, and M. Lefton (eds.)
*1968   In Their Own Behalf: Voices from the Margin. New York: Appleton-Century-Crofts.

McGinniss, Joe
1969   The Selling of the President, 1968. New York: Trident.

Malcolm X
1965   The Autobiography of Malcolm X. New York: Grove.

Matza, David
*1969   Becoming Deviant. Englewood Cliffs, N.J.: Prentice-Hall.

Mills, C. Wright
1943   "The professional ideology of social path-

ologists." American Journal of Sociology 49: 165–180.

Newfield, Jack
1971   "Let them eat lead." New York Times, June 16, p. 45.

Quinn, Olive W.
1954   "The transmission of racial attitudes among white southerners." Social Forces 33:1, 41–47 (reprinted in E. Schuler, et al., eds., Readings in Sociology, 2nd ed., New York: Crowell, 1960, 140–150).

Rose, Thomas (ed.)
1969   Violence in America. New York: Random House.

Rubington, Earl and M. S. Weinberg (eds.)
*1968   Deviance: The Interactionist Perspective. New York: Macmillan.

Rude, George
1966   The Crowd in History. New York: Wiley.

Rushing, William A. (ed.)
*1969   Deviant Behavior and Social Processes. Chicago: Rand McNally.

Simmons, J. L.
*1969   Deviants. Berkeley, Cal.: Glendessary.

Szasz, Thomas S.
1961   The Myth of Mental Illness. New York: Harper and Row.
1963   Law, Liberty, and Psychiatry. New York: Macmillan.
1970   The Manufacture of Madness. New York: Harper and Row.

Thompson, Hunter S.
1966   Hell's Angels. New York: Ballantine.

CLASS BIAS IN THE SOCIOLOGY OF DEVIANCE

Alex Thio
Ohio University, Athens

In the history of deviance studies, sociologists in the United States have developed three major perspectives. The earliest one, popular till about the forties, is that of the social pathologists. In the fifties this perspective was all but superseded by the value-free behavioral perspective, which in turn has been challenged during the sixties by the value-engaged labeling perspective. The labeling perspective appears to be becoming predominant in the present decade.

This paper is intended to show that the differences among these three perspectives on deviance are largely superficial because they share the same undercurrent of class bias. The class bias reveals itself through either one, or, more frequently, both of the following modi operandi: (1) In research strategy, students of deviance tend to follow the conventional, stereotyped lead in tracking down deviance, focusing on the deviance of the powerless class but relatively neglecting the deviance of the powerful. As a result, they either explicitly or implicitly suggest that the powerless are generally more deviant than the powerful. (2) In explaining the etiology of the deviance, they tend to concentrate on the individual deviant or his immediate milieu and thus avoid analysis of the established power structure in their society. The sociologists of deviance may be said to tacitly support the power

elite because both their research and analysis imply that the powerful are not only morally superior but should not be held responsible for *causing* deviance within their society.[1]

It may be noted that supporting the power elite of one's own country is not necessarily unique to American sociologists of deviance. Russian sociologists, for example, are heavily influenced by their support of the power elite in their society. Deeply committed to their Marxist-Leninist ideology that Soviet socialism is the "good society," they apparently cannot consider their power elite, the mainstay of Soviet socialism, as responsible for causing social deviance. Instead, they are likely to impute deviance-causation to the individual's immediate environment, involving such factors as his educa-

---

[1]This observation, however, is less relevant to the essentially power- or conflict-oriented works of Chambliss and Seidman (1971), Quinney (1970), Turk (1969), and other sociologists. The perspective of these works is in fact very similar to the one advocated here, but only in a general sense. For, more specifically, while they tend to consider deviance as "caused" by mere legal *definition,* we see deviance as *caused* by the powerful through their influential role in shaping the character of the social-cultural conditions of society which then directly generate deviance. Also see Liazos's (1972) critique on the sociology of deviance, which is even more similar to the intended thrust of the present paper. Again, there are some concrete differences between the two. E.g., for the current neglect of the powerful's deviance, Liazos blames the concept of deviance while I blame the users of the concept; he continues to advocate "exploration of the role of power in the *designation* of deviance," while I treat power as a crucial *cause* of both powerless and powerful persons' deviance.

Alex Thio (1973) "Class Bias in the Sociology of Deviance." *The American Sociologist* Vol. 8 (February): 1–12. Reprinted by permission of the American Sociological Association.

tion, occupation, residence, and family back-ground (Connor, 1972). A significant difference between Russian and American sociologists, however, is that the former may unabashedly avow their allegiance to Soviet socialism and its power elite, whereas the latter tend to betray their support of American democracy and its power elite in a covert and perhaps unconscious manner.

Before plumbing the ideological undercurrent in each of the three perspectives of American deviance sociology, let us propose a fourth perspective on deviance with which to assess later the other three.

One may begin by defining deviance as conduct that is in violation of rules made largely by the power elite of a given society or group. The most important component in this definition is the concept of a power elite. It is based on the assumption that all societies, including the United States, are founded upon unequal relations between powerful and powerless classes. The former consists of a small group of people with a disproportionately large quantum of power for protecting and enhancing their own interests more than, or at the expense of, those of the other class. Willfully or unwillfully or both, the powerful are inclined to exercise their power in the following ways:

(1) They rely upon various massive ideological apparatuses, such as the mass media and educational institutions, to insure their cultural hegemony over, and hence their support by, the powerless. (2) They use their scarce resources, such as prestige, wealth, and political clout, to help legislate (or prevent from being legislated) social policies which differentially affect their own and the powerless' life chances and social conditions. And (3) they resort to social control mechanisms predicated on the use or threat of coercive force, such as the law-making and law-enforcing agencies, to secure the established social order and thus the perpetuation of the social structure of inequality. For these reasons the power elite may be considered to be primarily responsible for creating and shaping the social and cultural structure of the society.

To be sure, the power elite is not necessarily a monolithic, conspiratorial entity. In the United States it has acquired a pluralistic quality by containing some antagonistic and competitive elements. But as such it is no less superordinate with respect to the powerless. It is also true that there may be historical, technological, and even biological forces that are beyond the control of the powerful (cf., e.g., Durant and Durant, 1968). Yet it is plain that the powerful contribute *immensely more* than the powerless to the character of a society and its culture. One may note, for instance, that whatever the differences between the two classes in subcultural traits and life-styles, it is the powerless who in addition to their own values also accept the values of the powerful class (cf. Rodman, 1963; Matza, 1963:33–67). Similarly, the legal structure of society is determined considerably more by the powerful than by the powerless so as to serve principally the vested interests of the former (cf. Quinney, 1970; Chambliss and Seidman, 1971).[2]

In sum, the power elite is largely responsible for the character of the social-cultural structure of society. On the other hand, many sociologists (e.g., Merton, 1957:131–160; Taft, 1966) suggest that social-cultural structure plays a significant part in causing deviance. We may thus combine these two ideas and propose that sociologists explore the possible ways the power elite influences the social-cultural structure so as to generate deviance. One line of argument as to how this may occur will be merely adumbrated at this point.

Since the power elite is more likely to make rules against both potential and actual deviants from among the powerless than the powerful, it is likely to create or reinforce the prevailing idea that the powerless are more potentially deviant than the powerful. Such prejudice against the powerless or in favor of the powerful tends to strengthen and be strengthened by various other forces of social control, ideological apparatus, and political influence that are largely in the hands of the powerful. All this helps to create,

---

[2]But see Friedman (1959) for an example of the opposite view that law is simply a reflection of public opinion. One may, however, observe that public opinion is largely determined by the power elite (Durant and Durant, 1968:77–78; Harris, 1971:406–409; Mankoff, 1970:428).

preserve, or buttress the existing social structure of unequal power that inevitably gives rise to deviance. More concretely, all this tends to cause a powerless person to conceive himself as a potential deviant and thereby lead him to commit acts of deviance (e.g., homicide, robbery, and so-called "street crimes") that he himself is likely to define as deviant. On the other hand, the same social, cultural, and political process tends to induce a powerful person to conceive himself as a respectable citizen without any deviant potential, and thereby encourage him to commit acts of deviance (e.g., corporate price-fixing, political bribery and deception, and unconstitutionally waging wars) that he himself is *not* likely to define as deviant. Thus, insofar as one is dealing with the etiological problems of deviation, one may say that the powerless are more sinned against than ready for sinning, while the powerful are more enticed to sin than ready for sinning. This is a crucial point that the other perspectives of deviance fail to grasp, with, as we shall see, determinable ideological consequences.

THE PERSPECTIVE OF SOCIAL PATHOLOGY

Around the turn of this century, Lester Ward and others were determined to establish American sociology as a scientific enterprise. Such determination was heralded by the publication of the official *American Journal of Sociology.* In the first issue, Ward (1895:21) declared à la Comte that sociology is "the last and highest of the sciences." Not long after that, Small (1916:857) urged sociologists to maintain strict scientific objectivity because "to betray an emotional attitude with reference to human facts is as compromising as an exchange of mysticism for literalness would be in astronomy or physiology."

During the first four decades, a number of sociologists whom Mills (1943) called "social pathologists" became interested in studying a variety of social deviants such as criminals, juvenile delinquents, prostitutes, drug addicts, the physically defective, the mentally ill, and the poor. These deviants' activities were all subsumed under the rubric of social disorganization or social pathology. Apparently driven by the reformist spirit stemming from their rural, Bible-reading, or social-work background, the social pathologists occasionally expressed their bias against the powerless in explicitly moralistic language (cf., e.g., Mangold, 1932:38, 59–61). For the most part, however, their sentiments against the powerless were—under the influence of the legacy of scientific objectivity—camouflaged by their dispassionate style of writing, as Mills (1943:168) recognized.

The conceptual arsenal deployed by the social pathologists in their texts includes "practical problems," "disorganization," "abnormality," "pathology," and "maladjustment." These are complemented by "W. I. Thomas's situational approach," "Cooley's organic concept of society or social interaction," "Ogburn's concept of cultural lag," "the evolutionary model of social change," and such ever-present standbys as "stability," "order," and "solidarity." To support these concepts, facts are marshaled from studying the pathological centers of urban areas populated by such maladjusted denizens as the immigrants, the poor, the irreligious, and the antisocial, along with dopefiends, hoboes, prostitutes, and the like (Mills, 1943).

A reexamination of all these suggests that the social pathologists adopted a fragmentary, individualistic perspective from which tacitly to condemn individual deviants as undesirable and blameworthy. In other words, the social pathologists failed to show even the slightest awareness of the deviance-causing role played by the powerful class. Their class bias is more unmistakably clear in that they directed attention exclusively to the deviant acts of the powerless. Ineluctably, their writings imply and reinforce the general public's stereotyped notion that the powerless are considerably more immoral than the powerful.

The same point is applicable to those sociologists who studied crime and delinquency per se during the same period. They turned their attention to first the biological, then psychological, and finally sociological explanations of why certain individuals or classes of individuals become criminals or delinquents. Yet their class bias is perceptible in that they all tended to view the powerless, but never the powerful, as criminals or delinquents who are biologically defective, psychologically abnormal, or socially maladjusted. As a result, Thrasher, Shaw, and other Chicago pioneers in this field (cf., e.g., Shaw and McKay, 1942) patently failed to suggest the possible influence of the powers-that-be on the criminal and delinquency problems in their society.

THE VALUE-FREE BEHAVIORAL PERSPECTIVE

Despite the underlying obstacle of their class bias, American sociologists continue to proclaim their discipline an objective science. In the fifties such advocacy reached its pinnacle with the banner of "value-free sociology." In the forefront of these self-styled "value-free" students are Parsons and Merton. Since Parsons has been abundantly discussed (cf., e.g., Gouldner, 1970:167–338), let us turn our attention to Merton—and others with the same perspective.

First, Merton apparently fails to come to grips with the power structure as a significant cause of deviance. Although Merton (1957:131–160) explicitly considers the "social and cultural structure" of American society as responsible for its high rates of deviance, he in no way suggests that the causal factor here could largely be the power structure. On the contrary, his "social-cultural structure" appears equivalent to the whole collectivity of American citizens. This inevitably implies that all of these citizens contribute equally to the high deviance rates of their society. It seems clear that Merton is under the heavy sway of American democratic ideology of equality, for its derivative logic is that if all citizens are equal they should all equally share the responsibility for whatever social problems are produced by their society. Such ideological undercurrent runs through Merton's analysis. But this bias is often masked by such claims of value-neutrality as: "It should be apparent [my] discussion is not pitched on a moralistic plane. . .[and my] concepts of social deviation and social dysfunction do not harbor concealed ethical premises" (Merton, 1957:159, 184).

Secondly, Merton's bias against the powerless class is particularly transparent with respect to his definition of "deviant behavior." He focuses on "deviant behavior" as an act with some intrinsic qualities: as such the concept is a priori accepted as having an ontological reality. But this presumptive reality is derived from the general public's stereotyped notion or law-enforcers' official definition and not from Merton's supposedly independent, value-free, scientific criterion for defining the phenomenon under investigation. Perhaps aware of this epistemological problem, he uses the outwardly value-neutral word, "innovation," to refer to a large category of deviance traditionally called "crime and delinquency." In fact, he describes "innovation" as an "affectively and ethically neutral concept" (Merton, 1957:181). Yet, his pronouncement of value-neutrality notwithstanding, his empirical referents of "innovation" still remain the types of crime and delinquency defined as such by governmental agencies such as the F.B.I. Since the official statistics, which show the criminals and delinquents as predominantly from the lower classes, are clearly biased against these classes, Merton's basically class-biased "anomie theory" (that deviance is the greatest among lower-class people) can be considered as only speciously supported.[3]

One may, however, point out that Merton does take into account the imperfection of the official statistics and the relative lack of class differentials in criminality shown by *un*official statistics and studies. Nevertheless, his acknowledgement of the empirical problem is merely a ritualistic obeisance to, rather than a genuine observance of, the scientific canon of objectivity. Thus his pro forma "balanced view" is obviously destined to incline toward de facto acceptance of official statistics:

But whatever the differential rates of deviant behavior in the several social strata, and we know from many sources that the official crime statistics uniformly showing higher rates in the lower strata are far from complete or reliable, it appears from our analysis that the

---

[3]As for the untenability of Merton's anomie theory qua theory, see Thio (1972).

greatest pressures toward deviation are exerted upon the lower strata (Merton, 1957:144).

In some ways, Merton's reliance on the seriously class-biased data resembles the early psychologists' reliance on the seriously race-biased I.Q. tests which were widely used during the First World War.[4] Compare, for example, Merton's argumentative style with that of Yerkes, a renowned psychologist of the time:

[The I.Q. tests] are to some extent influenced by educational acquirement, but in the main the soldier's inborn intelligence and not the accidents of environment determine his mental rating or grade in the Army . . . [And] the negro soldier is of relatively low grade intelligence (quoted by Gossett, 1963:368).

Not all sociologists who use the value-free behavioral perspective, however, employ the official statistics on criminality. Obviously, students of white-collar crime (cf., e.g., Sutherland, 1949; Geis, 1968) have seriously questioned the validity of these statistics. Since these sociologists attempt to show the prevalence of "respectable" crimes, they may appear to be free from any class bias. But in terms of explaining the *etiology* of crimes, their class bias remains nonetheless real, though driven deeper under the surface than is Merton's.

Sutherland and his followers, for example, tend to focus on deviants as individuals, losing sight of the causal nexus between deviance and the power elite. Consider, as a case in point, Sutherland's well-known theory of differential association along with his followers' revised and extended versions of it (cf., e.g, Burgess and Akers, 1966). The cores of their theoretical assertion is that offenders learn definitions favoring law-violation through their associations, while non-offenders acquire their law-abiding sentiments from a different set of social experiences. The focus is upon the social interaction among *individual* actors. This focus recalls the social pathologists' reliance on such interactionist perspectives as W. I. Thomas' situational approach, or Cooley's organic theory of social interaction.

They are all bound by a shared perspective that is tethered too closely to the individual's immediate milieu, and are therefore unable to see the importance of the far-reaching perspective of power structure.

THE VALUE-ENGAGED LABELING PERSPECTIVE

In the 1960's the labeling perspective, designed principally as an opposition to the value-free behavioral perspective, emerged with the aim of taking the side of the powerless class. But the actual application and consequence of the perspective ironically implies its subsurface support of the power elite. Gouldner (1968) has exposed this irony, which we shall use as the springboard for our exegesis of the perspective.

Gouldner's exposition suggests that the sentiments of the self-proclaimed underdog sociologists tend to accommodate to the interests of the overdog power elite. Such accommodation is made possible because their pragmatic needs dovetail: the sociologists need "large supplies of research funds," which are controlled by the powerful, while the powerful need information about underdogs from the sociologists "for much the same political reason that colonial governments supported similar researchers in anthropology."

However, Gouldner may have gone overboard in suggesting that cupidity for research largess is the prime mover of the underdog sociology of deviance. We may argue that the hankering for research funds is *both* cause and effect of the ascendancy of the labeling perspective. One need look beyond the Shylock explanation so as to disclose the ideological kinship between the value-engaged labeling perspective on the one hand, and the value-free behavioral and the earlier social-pathological perspectives on the other. In the light of this, we shall see why the labeling perspective inevitably lends its support to the powers that be.

1. As has been discussed previously, those who hew to the social-pathological and the value-free behavioral perspectives tend to focus on powerless deviants, thereby blurring the devi-

---

[4]Merton is not the only sociologist given to this indefensible argument; cf., e.g., Cohen (1955:42) and DeFleur et al. (1971:393–394).

ance of the powerful. Those who embrace the value-engaged labeling perspective do the same thing. They have in effect produced an extensive ethnographic catalogue of powerless persons' deviant behavior. Thus Gouldner (1968:111) characterizes the labeling theorists as liberal rather than radical sociologists in that "radical sociologists want to study 'power elite,' the leaders, or masters, of men; liberal sociologists focus their efforts upon underdogs and victims and their immediate bureaucratic caretakers."

A significant source of this focus can be traced to the way the labeling theorists define deviant behavior. To them, deviant behavior is not intrinsic to the act but merely a consequence of labeling by superordinate parties. In practical terms, this definition means, to use Glaser's (1971:33) paraphrase of Becker's thesis, that "crime is not a quality of the act one commits, but a consequence of one's arrest and punishment." As research has amply shown, the experience of arrest and punishment happens much more frequently to powerless than to powerful people, even when both have committed the same crime. It is thus plain that the prevailing prejudice against the powerless indirectly leads the labeling theorists to concentrate on the types of deviance commonly committed by the powerless and thereby deflects their research efforts from the deviance typically committed by the powerful. Indeed, labeling theory actually equates deviance with powerlessness. For example, in his manifesto, "Whose Side Are We On?" Becker (1967) identifies deviants with what he calls "subordinate parties." This unavoidably implies that the powerless are necessarily deviants but the powerful not deviants at all! The class bias in such an implication appears all the more unmistakable in the *patronizing* attitude toward powerless deviants reflected throughout the labeling theorists' substantive works.

2. Closely related to the foregoing is the labeling theorists' preponderant interest in "secondary deviation," to the virtual neglect of "primary deviation." (For the meanings of these two terms, see Lemert, 1967:40–64.) On the face of it, this seems explicable by the logical character of the labeling perspective as presently used by

Becker, Erikson, Lemert, and others. Since the theory sees deviance not as a quality of an act but instead a production of the audience's reaction to the act, it cannot possibly explain why the act itself has arisen *in the first place* (Akers, 1968). That is to say, the deviance *label itself* can create secondary deviation (such as the robbery committed by an ex-convict) but *not* primary deviation (such as his very first robbery before he gets convicted for it).

But a deeper analysis suggests that this kind of limitation does not necessarily inhere in the concept of labeling itself but rather in the underdog sociologists' unjustifiable implicit assumptions. (a) They assume that rules are made against *actual* deviants only (i.e., against those who have actually committed an act labeled as deviant). They also assume (b) that the impact of being successfully labeled as deviant affects *actual* deviants only; and (c) that such actual deviants are always from the *powerless* class. From our proposed perspective introduced earlier, we shall see why these three assumptions have prevented the labeling theorists from explaining the etiology of the powerless' *primary* deviation and of the *powerful's* primary and secondary deviation.

a. Rules are made not only against actual deviants (i.e., for punitive purposes) but against potential deviants (i.e., for deterrent purposes). As a society or an age becomes more "enlightened," the emphasis in rule-making tends to shift to the latter, as can be observed from comparing the legal and moral temper of the present period against that of the past. The deterrent aspect of rule-making is especially relevant to the etiology of *primary* deviation.

In possibly all societies past and present, the power elite tends to make rules more against powerless than against powerful potential deviants.[5] This may lead the society as a whole to

---

[5] One should be forewarned that it does not necessarily follow that the powerless are more likely to break rules simply because there are more rules made against them than against the powerful. For the rules are usually, if not always, sufficiently abstract and vague to be applicable to the powerful as well, disregarding the original intent of the rule-makers.

label the powerless as *more potentially* deviant or criminal in comparison with the powerful, which in turn tends to support the existing rules or to produce new rules of the same type. In view of this, we may say that the powerless (*non*deviants) are more sinned against than ready for sinning, rather than that "*deviants* are more sinned against than sinning" as Becker avers. In the manner of a self-fulfilling prophecy, the labeling, in creating or supporting various social, cultural, and political processes mentioned previously, may subtly and indirectly but nonetheless efficaciously affect the powerless: it helps to generate disadvantaged social conditions for the powerless and, consequently, leads the powerless to develop self-concepts as potential deviants. The disadvantaged social conditions include relatively inadequate housing, unsatisfactory medical care, lack of educational and occupational opportunity, high risk of being suspected, arrested, convicted, or imprisoned by the law-enforcers, and lack of respect by others and by oneself; all this may compel the powerless to conceive themselves as potential deviants. Both social conditions and self-concepts are likely to lead powerless persons to perform those acts condemned by the rules, particularly such *primary* deviations as homicide, robbery, and burglary, which Becker and his associates have failed to explain through their brand of labeling perspective. The subtle labeling process described here is what Lao-tse, the Chinese scholar who propounded the philosophy of *creative quietism* in about 500 B.C., meant: "The more laws and order are made prominent, the more thieves and robbers there will be" (Chan, 1963:57).

On the other hand, the same labeling process against the powerless tends to provide a contrast effect that sets off powerful persons as morally and legally unimpeachable. This in turn may subtly and indirectly but nonetheless efficaciously help (1) to create advantageous social conditions for the powerful and consequently (2) to lead powerful persons to see themselves as without deviant potential. It is a fundamental dilemma of human life that in terms of (1), the powerful have access to a greater number of and more varied *opportunities for deviance* when compared with the

powerless, precisely because the former enjoy a greater number of and more varied *legitimate opportunities* in life.[6] And with respect to (2), since the powerful do not conceive themselves to be potentially deviant in the same way as the powerless would (i.e., as a potential murderer, robber, or burglar), they are unlikely to commit these deviant acts. Instead, their self-concept is likely to encourage them to take advantage of the illegitimate opportunities open to them, because it enables them to consider the resulting acts of deviance, say, indirectly and impersonally killing and maiming thousands of motorists every year through the manufacturing of defective cars, as *non*deviant (i.e., *not* the same as the act of murder, which is more directly and personally performed by a powerless person). In the light of this, we may say that the powerful (*non*deviants) are more enticed to sin than ready for sinning, rather than that "*deviants* are more sinned against than sinning" as Becker claims.

b. Contrary to the labeling theorists' assumption, the impact of being labeled as deviant does not seem to affect *only actual* deviants labeled as such. Rather, it tends also to exert a kind of penumbra effect upon *non*deviants (who are not labeled as deviants). More specifically, when a small minority of powerless people are successfully labeled as deviants (i.e., arrested or convicted) by the law-enforcers, the majority of powerless people are likely to be labeled by the general public as potentially deviant when compared with the powerful. This is because the successful labeling of the small minority of powerless people as actual deviants is often widely publicized, thus consolidating the already pervasive stereotyped notion that powerless nondeviants are potentially more deviant than powerful nondeviants. All this in turn helps to hasten the social, cultural, and political processes that ultimately cause both the powerful and the powerless to peform primary deviant acts in the manner discussed in (a) above.

---

[6]This is partly inferred from Cohen's (1966:110) observation that "there are not *some* things that are legitimate opportunities and *other* things that are illegitimate opportunities, but the *same* things are typically, and perhaps always, both" (emphasis in the original).

c. The labeling theorists assume that when powerless persons are successfully labeled as deviants, *only* these powerless deviants are likely to commit *secondary* deviation. This assumption misses the fact that the same labeling (i.e., of the *powerless* as deviants) also induces the *powerful* deviants to commit *secondary* deviation. It is well known that the labeling of powerless persons as deviants occurs much more frequently and hence is much more often publicized, when compared with the labeling of powerful persons as deviants. The greater publicity about powerless deviants then may *directly* reinforce the public's demand that the law-enforcers increase their surveillance on *powerless* deviants, but *indirectly* deflect the concern and attention of the public and law-enforcers from *powerful* deviants. Consequently, powerful deviants are likely to be encouraged to commit secondary deviation. In other words, the labeling of the powerless as deviants not only leads these powerless deviants to commit secondary deviation, as the labeling theorists suggest, but also subtly and indirectly induces powerful deviants to commit secondary deviation.[7]

3. Without a clear view of the causal relations between power structure and deviance, the labeling theorists seem fated to consign themselves to the study of deviance in its immediate environment. It is historically significant, though not surprising, that today they heavily rely on symbolic interactionism, an essentially nonstructural approach. This approach is akin to such earlier ideas as W. I. Thomas' situational emphasis. Cooley's organic model of social interaction, and Sutherland's theory of differential association. All these theories are fundamentally nonstructural in their neglect of the concept of power structure; hence, they are readily applicable to the study of deviance that is confined to the immediate environment where the interaction between the individual actor and others can be observed. One can thus say that the emphasis on social interaction in these earlier theories is clearly carried into the latter-day perspective of labeling. Becker (1963:163), as a case in point, focuses on "*the process of interaction between people,* some of whom in the service of their interests make and enforce rules which catch others who, in the service of their own interests, have committed acts which are labeled as deviant" (emphasis added).

4. Intimately connected to the preceding argument is a fourth major critical point: If the production of deviance is assumed to occur within the immediate matrix of social interaction, the acts labeled as deviant are presumed to be *observable* directly or indirectly by the persons who are doing the labeling (Gibbs, 1966:13). If the acts were not observable at all, it would be extremely difficult, if not impossible, for the potential labelers to react to them. In fact, the labeling perspective specifically defines deviant behavior in terms of *reactions to it*. As Erikson (1964:11) explicitly states: "Deviance is not a property inherent in certain forms of behavior; it is a property conferred upon these forms by the audiences which directly or indirectly witness them" (emphasis added).

Such a conception of deviant behavior as observable would explain in part what has previously been discussed in regard to both the labeling perspective itself and its antecedents, the social-pathological and the value-free behavioral perspectives. It tends to incline sociologists toward focusing on deviance committed by the powerless rather than deviance committed by the powerful. This is simply because the former, as compared with the latter, is *appreciably easier to observe* and thus more amenable to description and quantification.

Overemphasis on observability may also provide sociologists with the methodological rationalization for eschewing such "vague and unoperationalizable" concepts as power distribution and power structure and their causal link to deviance. But the underlying reason that the concepts remain vague and unoperationalized may be sociologists' tacit support of the power elite. This has led sociologists to develop an ar-

---

[7]The proposed ideas in (b) and (c) may be referred to as "*inverted* Durkheimianism," for it is the Durkheimian dictum that deviance is functional rather than dysfunctional (e.g., Durkheim (1947:102): "Crime brings together upright consciences and concentrates them").

ray of sophisticated research methods primarily suitable for studying the behavior of the powerless. It has failed, however, to stimulate development of research methods that could enable sociologists to wrangle in the fashion of Nader's Raiders or, in the fashion of Jack Anderson, to wangle the necessary information from powerful persons who are understandably unwilling or "unable" to divulge their deviant activities.

CONCLUSION AND IMPLICATIONS

For the last seventy years an undercurrent of class bias has led sociologists in the United States to concentrate on deviance of the powerless class while preventing them from recognizing the prospect of viewing the power structure as a causal factor of deviance. This bias operates whether they work with the social pathological, value-free behavioral, or value-engaged labeling perspective. The power perspective proposed here promises to contribute more to the enhancement of sociological knowledge of deviance than any of the other three perspectives. It seems particularly promising in regard to helping sociologists to minimize bias against the powerless class. This would require sociologists to explore and explain a hitherto largely neglected area of deviant behavior—that of the powerful.

This is obviously not so simple an endeavor as it may appear on the surface. Perhaps by re-examining some of the fundamental problems that beset general sociology, students of deviance would then be able to decide for themselves whether they could take on the challenge presented by the perspective of power structure.

The problem of ideological bias has plagued sociology from its infancy to its present age, and yet American sociologists' efforts to cope with the problem have not slackened. As Sibley (1971: 13, 15) observes:

Positivism, frequently of a naive kind, has been a perennial leitmotif. Often attacked, it has more often received lip service from sociologists whose prejudiced normative preconceptions were more or less apparent to their unsympathetic contemporaries and became more visible in retrospect . . . [But as] the history of

American sociology down to the last few years [shows], despite the elusiveness of the goal of unbiased, objective, and rational understanding of society, its structures, and its functions, the continuing pursuit of this goal has been generally acknowledged to be the proper vocation of sociologists.

This observation may conjure up an image of sociology as the proverbial donkey that continuously toils at the treadmill while hopefully braying at the ever-elusive carrot dangling before it. The "master" responsible for the continuing elusiveness of sociologists' goal seems to be the power elite of the society. But American sociologists, apparently under the pervasive influence of their democratic ideology of equality, often ignore the power elite by using such amorphous terms as "society," "social structure," or "general culture." (For an example of this, see Denzin, 1970.)

Why is the power elite the master and sociology the servant?

1. The sociologist tends to unconsciously slip his citizenship role into his supposedly independent, intellectual work. This is primarily due to the fact that he "does give a damn whether his society lives or dies" (Killian, 1971:284). As a result, the sociologist is very likely to willy-nilly ally himself with members of the power elite, who have even a bigger stake in the survival of the society as it presently exists. For example, when faced with the powerless' violent expression of their opposition to the Vietnam War, the sociologist tended to adopt the official stance by regarding the violence of the powerless, but not the violence committed by the government against these people (and the Indo-chinese), as a "social problem," "deviance," or "crime" (Quinney, 1971).

2. There is a related and overtly expressed desire on the part of sociologists to turn their field into a profession instead of considering it simply as a scholarly or intellectual discipline. It is common knowledge from the sociology of occupations and professions that any profession tends to have a vested interest in either promoting itself or keeping itself from extinction, even though it may in fact be inutile or inimical to humanity.

Such a conscious interest in its own survival and promotion can hardly make sociology an objective discipline. For it causes sociologists to seek clients who have both access to research grants and support for the power elite. Under such circumstances, a sociologist is likely to lose his intellectual freedom because his clients would largely define the types of problems for him to study (see Denzin, 1970:126).

In consequence, the master-servant relations seem to have exacted a huge price, particularly from the sociology of deviance. First, there has been no breakthrough in this field, because the master-servant relations have seriously delimited the phenomenon of deviance to be studied by professional sociologists. Only an infinitesimal portion of the phenomenon has been accumulatively subjected to sociological investigation while the enormously greater portion of it, especially those hidden, elusive, and protean forms perpetrated by the powerful,[8] has remained all but undefined and unstudied. Professional sociologists could hardly hope to have a Galileo, a Newton, or an Einstein emerging from their midst if they are fated to prostitute, in exchange for professional survival and success, their *intellectual* freedom to define in their own way, the phenomenon under investigation.

Secondly, pinioned by their professionalism and their subtle and indirect alliance with the power elite, sociologists can hardly be objective in the sense of being able to soar over the conventional, stereotyped way of looking at the world. This is why sociologists lag behind serious writers and artists in imagination and creativity. It is within this context that Gouldner (1968: 11) appreciates what has been absent from sociology—the display of "objective partisanship" by great works of art that are able to take the perspectives of *both* the powerful and the powerless *simultaneously*. In a similar vein, Killian

(1971) perceives that, unlike modern novelists and playwrights, sociologists are incapable of studying human sufferings with genuine realism.

Thirdly, driven to serve their master in furtherance of their professional survival and prosperity, sociologists may have produced a considerable amount of fictitious "facts" concerning those social phenomena which those in power and the indoctrinated public consider as "extremely important" social problems. Take juvenile delinquency, for example. Millions of dollars have been spent on researching its various aspects such as its etiology, its prevention, and its rehabilitation, as if delinquency were a most serious social problem. Yet anywhere from 60 to 85 percent of those publicly or sociologically defined delinquents apparently do not become adult violators (Matza, 1964:22). Perhaps the remaining 15 to 40 percent tend to become adult offenders because of the labeling process that they are repeatedly subjected to by sociological researchers, social workers, policemen, judges, reform school personnel, and the general public. Admittedly, the sociological industry that specializes in manufacturing data on delinquency not only insures its own prosperity but aids the political fortune of the power elite and the earnings of such auxiliaries as the law-enforcement agents. Yet it can hardly be intellectually rewarding to be told, for example, of such cliched attributes of delinquency as lack of achievement, multifaceted strain, and peer identification (Empey et al., 1971), for this kind of study fails to show how both the sociological industry and its supporting companies may have already subtly and indirectly helped the power elite to create and perpetuate those attributes.

The preceding discussion would suggest that if sociologists of deviance are seriously interested in minimizing, though not completely eliminating, "the elusiveness of the goal of unbiased, objective, and rational understanding of [their subject matter]" (Sibley, 1971:15), they may need the courage to rebel against the power elite and become masters of their own intellectual pursuits. To do so will require at least two major interrelated actions. One entails the pursuance of the goal of liberated intellectual scholarship rather than professionalism in the sense discussed

---

[8]These may include corporate malfeasance, political skulduggery, wanton militarism or illegal warmaking, and misuse of policy-making power by top governmental leaders. True, sociologists who study white-collar crimes have dealt with some of these, but they have discovered only "the tip of the iceberg" regarding corporate crimes while having neglected the other three types.

above. Such a goal is implied by the Confucian model of a scholar: "The scholar who cherishes the love of comfort is not fit to be deemed a scholar" (Legge, 1960:276). This is not far from the more positive fashion in which C. Wright Mills has carved out the intellectual task for sociology. Flacks (1972:8) expresses it thus: "A genuinely liberative sociology would continuously seek ways *to enable all people to do sociology,* to put itself out of business as a specialty, as a profession" (emphasis in the original).

If the antiprofessional goal is conscientiously sought, then another action involving the sociologist as a rebel would be possible. The sociologist-as-rebel may seek his exemplar from Camus' (1956:23, 281) vision of the rebel slave: "The slave who opposes his master is not concerned, let us note, with repudiating his master as a human being. He repudiates him as a master. . . . Logically, murder and rebellion are contradictory. If a single master should, in fact, be killed, the rebel, in a certain way, is no longer justified in using the term *community of men* from which he derived his justification" (emphasis in the original). In a more positive fashion, Gouldner (1968:111) designates the rebel-sociologist's stance as "objective partisanship":

There are works of art that manifest this objective partisanship. The dramas of the great classical tragedians are a magnificent case in point. What makes them great is their objectivity; and what makes them objective is their capacity to understand even the nobility of their Persian enemies, even the dignity of their "barbarian" slaves, even the bumbling of their own wise men. They do indeed express a viewpoint which in some sense does take the standpoint of both sides, and does so simultaneously. If great art can do this, why should this be forbidden to great social science?

However, objective partisanship might require the rebel-sociologist to have the courage to confront the ironical triumph in the achievement of a truly independent consciousness, namely, the experiencing of the paradoxical tension between ecstasy and desperation. (For a discussion on this irony, see Berger, 1971:3.) Such an experience may in some way be compared to the tremendous agony which Prometheus, the archetypical rebel, had to suffer as

a consequence of having stolen fire and given it to humankind. If, despite or because of all this, sociologists are determined to pursue a rebel's career that would lead up to Mount Caucasus, they should first of all struggle against their own Panglossian spirit. For this spirit has prevented them from seeing the "stark reality" of human sufferings:

In the modern novel, play, or movie, there is little escape from the oppressive dilemma of mass society and the nuclear age. Human frailties are mercilessly, almost gleefully, exposed; the heroes are at the same time villains; there are no happy endings. In contrast, the typical sociological treatise is like a late, late movie produced in the forties. The problems are complex, the situation grows desperate, but there is hope at the end. If the cavalry does not arrive before the end of the story, there is at least the implication that it is just around a bend in the road (Killian, 1971:283).

In implementing the rebel vision of the intellectual, sociologists of deviance may need to start devoting far more energy to the development of "conflict methodology" than to that of currently popular "consensus methodology." (For the meanings of these two terms, see Young, 1971.) The latter has served professional sociology and its master well in mapping out the behavioral terrain of the *powerless* but has patently failed to explore the vast expanses of *terra incognita* of the *powerful.* Before this immense area of human behavior is known, the validity of any general theory of deviance inevitably remains suspect. To broaden sociological knowledge in this field, sociologists may have to resort to conflict methodology. Young (1971) has suggested the use of lawsuits. But sociologists may also investigate the possibility of employing various (genuine and/or quasi) intelligence and counterintelligence techniques. In this regard, sociologists have much to learn not only from such antiestablishment figures as Ralph Nader, Daniel Ellsberg, and Jack Anderson, but from such establishment bulwarks as the FBI and the CIA. But, would sociologists of deviance dare take up the challenge of this Promethean task? If they dare not, they might be expected to remain securely at the treadmill, toiling with the everelusive carrot before them—and braying at it.

REFERENCES

Akers, R. L.
1968 "Problems in the sociology of deviance: Social definitions and behavior." Social Forces 46 (June): 455–465.

Becker, H. S.
1963 Outsiders: Studies in the Sociology of Deviance. New York: Free Press.
1967 "Whose side are we on?" Social Problems 14 (Winter): 239–247.

Berger, P. L.
1971 "Sociology and freedom." American Sociologist 6 (February): 1–5.

Burgess, R. L. and R. L. Akers
1966 "A differential association-reinforcement theory of criminal behavior." Social Problems 14 (Fall): 128–147.

Camus, A.
1956 The Rebel: An Essay on Man in Revolt. New York: Vintage Books.

Chambliss, W. J. and R. B. Seidman
1971 Law, Order, and Power. Reading, Mass.: Addison-Wesley.

Chan, W. (tr.)
1963 The Way of Lao Tzu. Indianapolis: Bobbs-Merrill.

Cohen, A. K.
1955 Delinquent Boys: The Culture of the Gang. Glencoe, Ill.: Free Press.
1966 Deviance and Control. Englewood Cliffs, N.J.: Prentice-Hall.

Connor, W. D.
1972 Deviance in Soviet Society: Crime, Delinquency, and Alcoholism. New York: Columbia University Press.

DeFleur, M. L., W. V. D'Antonio, and L. B. DeFleur
1971 Sociology: Man in Society. Glenview: Scott, Foresman.

Denzin, N. K.
1970 "Who leads: Sociology or society?" American Sociologist 5 (May): 125–127.

Durant, W. and A. Durant
1968 The Lessons of History. New York: Simon and Schuster.

Durkheim, E.
1947 The Division of Labor in Society. New York: Free Press.

Empey, L. T., S. G. Lubeck, and R. L. LaPorte
1971 Explaining Delinquency: Construction, Test, and Reformulation of a Sociological Theory. Lexington, Mass.: D.C. Heath & Co.

Erikson, K. T.
1964 "Notes on the sociology of deviance." Pp. 9–21 in H. S. Becker (ed.), The Other Side. New York: Free Press.

Flacks, R.
1972 "Notes on the 'crisis of sociology.' " Social Policy (March–April): 4–12.

Friedman, L. M.
1959 Law in a Changing Society. Berkeley: California Press.

Geis, G. (ed.)
1968 White-Collar Criminal. New York: Atherton.

Gibbs, J. P.
1966 "Conceptions of deviant behavior: The old and the new." Pacific Sociological Review 9 (Spring): 9–14.

Glaser, D.
1971 "Criminology and public policy." American Sociologist 6 (June): 30–37.

Gossett, T. F.
1963 Race: The History of an Idea in America. Dallas: Southern Methodist University Press.

Gouldner, A. W.
1968 "The sociologist as partisan: Sociology and the welfare state." American Sociologist 3 (May): 103–116.
1970 The Coming Crisis of Western Sociology. New York: Basic Books.

Harris, M.
1971 Culture, Man, and Nature: An Introduction to General Anthropology. New York: Thomas Y. Crowell.

Killian, L. M.
1971 "Optimism and pessimism in sociological analysis." American Sociologist 6 (November): 281–286.

Legge, J. (tr.)
1960 The Chinese Classics, Vol. I: The Confucian Analects. Hong Kong: Hong Kong University Press.

Lemert, E. M.
1967 Human Deviance, Social Problems and Social Control. Englewood Cliffs, N.J.: Prentice-Hall.

Liazos, A.
1972 "The poverty of the sociology of deviance: Nuts, sluts, and preverts." Social Problems 20 (Summer): 103–120.

Mangold, G. B.
1932   Social Pathology. New York: Macmillan.

Mankoff, M.
1970   "Power in advanced capitalist society: A review essay on recent elitist and marxist criticism of pluralist theory." Social Problems 17 (Winter): 418-430.

Matza, D.
1964   Delinquency and Drift. New York: John Wiley & Sons.

Merton, R. K.
1957   Social Theory and Social Structure. New York: Free Press.

Mills, C. W.
1943   "The professional ideology of social pathologists." American Journal of Sociology 49 (September): 165-180.

Quinney, R.
1970   The Social Reality of Crime. Boston: Little, Brown.
1971   "Review essay." American Sociological Review 36 (August): 724-727.

Rodman, H.
1963   "The lower class value stretch." Social Forces 42 (December): 205-215.

Shaw, C. and H. D. McKay
1942   Juvenile Delinquency in Urban Areas. Chicago: University of Chicago Press.

Small, A. W.
1971   "Scientific sociology at bay?" American Sociologist 6 (June): 13-17.

Sibley, E.
1916   "Fifty years of sociology in the United States (1868-1915)." American Journal of Sociology 21 (May): 721-864.

Sutherland, E. H.
1949   White Collar Crime. New York: Holt, Rinehart and Winston.

Taft, D. R.
1966   "Influence of the general culture on crime." Federal Probation 30 (September): 16-23.

Thio, A.
1972   "A reexamination of Merton's anomie theory." Unpublished manuscript, Ohio University, Athens.

Turk, A. T.
1969   Criminality and Legal Order. Chicago: Rand McNally.

Ward, L. F.
1895   "The place of sociology among the sciences." American Journal of Sociology 1 (July): 16-27.

Young, T. R.
1971   "The politics of sociology: Gouldner, Goffman, and Garfinkle." American Sociologist 6 (November): 276-281.

THE LABELING PERSPECTIVE

Its Bias and Potential in the Study
of Political Deviance*

Paul G. Schervish
Jesuit School of Theology at Berkeley

THE BIAS

The most popular perspective on deviant behavior at the present time is commonly called the labeling approach. This approach, first enunciated in Tannenbaum's (1938) comments on "The Dramatization of Evil" and in Edwin M. Lemert's (1951) *Social Pathology* is most baldly stated by Becker (1963:9): "The deviant is one to whom that label has successfully been applied; deviant behavior is behavior that people so label."

Sociologists who describe deviance as a process of labeling draw upon the symbolic interactionism of George Herbert Mead. Mead (1964:209–46 passim) provides the social-psychological framework for understanding how the individual comes to be labeled deviant in the first place and then, as the consequence of this labeling, to manifest the various subjective orientations and conduct that Lemert (1967:40–64) refers to as "secondary deviation." The Meadian perspective enables sociologists to designate

the process of becoming deviant (cf. Matza, 1969) rather than merely to assert that "mind" or "personality" or some other intervening unknown or "black box" acts as a deterministic transmitter of forces, impinging upon the actor and making him deviant.

Ideally, then, the labeling approach to deviance studies organizational and social-psychological conditions and consequences not as separate issues but as related in an ongoing dialectic. Organizational factors do not deterministically force individuals into deviant patterns of behavior. Rather, the labeling approach provides the framework for a refined qualitative analysis of how an individual or group, with at least some degree of willful compliance, comes to internalize the normative expectations which are expressed in and communicated through particular labels.

With such an emphasis upon the creative yet social character of man, it is strikingly ironic that labeling theorists often neglect their Meadian heritage by speaking of man in a rhetoric more evocative of the determinism Mead sought to deny.

Although the labeling approach has generated numerous insightful studies of the processes of identification and deviance, the (unfortuitous) methodological and ideological thrust of this approach has been, with a few noteworthy exceptions, towards a philosophical bias or sentimentalism. Although my notion of philosophical bias is akin to Gouldner's (1955)

Paul G. Schervish (1973) "The Labeling Perspective: Its Bias and Potential in the Study of Political Deviance." *The American Sociologist* Vol. 8 (May): 47–57. Reprinted by permission of the American Sociological Association.

*An earlier version of this article comprised a section of a paper presented at the Twenty-first Annual Meeting of the Society for the Study of Social Problems in Denver, 1971. I wish to thank especially Howard S. Becker and John I. Kitsuse for their incisive and helpful comments on earlier versions of this paper.

72

concept of metaphysical pathos,[1] I am using the former term to denote the somewhat different pessimistic and fatalistic assumptions that an imputed labelee is both *passive* and stands alone as an *individual*.

This paper seeks to explore some of the reasons for this philosophical bias, to document how it has led sociologists within the labeling perspective to examine the passive and individualistic aspects of deviance, and finally to point to some hopeful signs that interactionists may be moving toward a balancing perspective, emphasizing aggressive, political, group resistance to and counter-application of labels.

There are two principal reasons why the labeling approach to deviance has fallen into the philosophical bias of viewing the imputed deviant in passive and individualistic terms. The first reason is methodological, the second is ideological.

METHODOLOGICAL SOURCE

The methodological orientation of labeling theorists is rooted in the emphasis on quantification and verification of data that arose in the late 1930's and is only now being seriously challenged. Until recently, sociologists dealing with qualitative data assumed the goals, rhetoric, norms of validity and reliability, and methodological procedures of the more positivistic, supposedly more scientific, wing of sociology. As a result, labeling theorists' efforts to develop and apply their perspective often became directed toward gathering verifiable data rather than

generating theory. In turn, these sociologists tended to concentrate on smaller scale studies of individual labelees where data was more reliable and more readily verified (even if not necessarily more valid).

Instances of sociology's flirtation with the canons of extreme quantification and positivism are well known. The work of George Lundberg (1939, 1947, 1955, 1956) is a case in point. Less familiar, perhaps, is how this natural science model specifically affected symbolic interactionists and thus the emergence of labeling theory. The labeling theorists, rightly understanding the subtlety and complexity of their framework, felt vulnerable to the pressures of positivistic methodology. As a result, they required that the context or field of their empirical studies be both fairly highly ordered and microcosmic in order to attain an adequate degree of validity within the limitations of their relatively low-powered methodology. In order to develop valid theoretical statements about the internalization of norms and identity, these labeling theorists naturally searched out those settings in which they could clearly explicate the process of interaction. Consequently, labeling theorists sought to study the most obvious and clearcut examples of the phenomenon of deviant-formation by labeling. Their modest methodological tools (as compared to the rigorous expectations of quantification)[2] compelled them to examine those situations in which the labelee is brought into contact with such highly formalized agencies as the school, mental hospital, prison, or novitiate. Only in these and comparable situa-

---

[1] In the middle fifties Gouldner (1955) criticized the *metaphysical pathos* of researchers who fatalistically and pessimistically (498) assumed the natural passivity of man and decried the impending spread of bureaucracy and its effects into every aspect of modern life. Debunking such pathos, Gouldner countered that the condition for Michel's concern about the "iron law of oligarchy" is an "iron law of democracy" according to which men "doggedly rebuild" the bridges of democracy after each inundation of oligarchy has washed them away (506). Although I am indebted to Gouldner for the notions of passisvity, pessimism, and fatalism (which I have incorporated in my notion of philosophical bias), a discussion of the bias of labeling studies must also emphasize how these studies focus on situations in which *individuals* rather than aggressive groups are engaged in the dynamics of labeling and counter-labeling.

[2] To their credit, Glaser and Strauss (1967) anticipated the direction of the criticism presented here. They proffer a clear analysis of how sociologists failed to appreciate the value of their qualitative methodology for generating grounded theory and focused instead on conforming and subordinating those qualitative aspects of their research to the seemingly more legitimate enterprise of developing and verifying logico-deductive theory. Glaser and Strauss point out two phases in the history of American sociology as the foundation for what I would consider a kind of inferiority complex among sociologists working with qualitative data. The first phase resulted in putting "the generation of grounded theory into second place, and made verification the dominant orientation in virtually all sociological work" (12). The second phase, closely linked to the first, was "the clash between advocates of quantitative and qualitative data" (15).

tions could the researcher ever hope to document the process by which the labelee becomes assimilated into the role patterns designated by the systematic application of label. Unfortunately for the long-range development of the labeling perspective, those situations that imposed the fewest methodological problems for research were, not surprisingly, the ones in which individuals become formed rather passively into secondary deviants.

With a few important exceptions, such as Becker and Geer[3] (1957, 1960; Becker, 1958), methodologists treating qualitative data have been rather apologetic in their efforts to make their approach respectable according to the criteria of quantitative research. This interpretation of the methodological source of the philosophical bias of labeling studies is confirmed by the methodological reflections of some of those directly connected with the labeling perspective. Even Blumer, in his "Appraisal of Thomas and Znaniecki's *The Polish Peasant in Europe and America*" (1939), threw the weight of his analysis "toward an examination of verification, rather than toward the question of how to generate rounded theory" (Glaser and Strauss, 1967: 14). But this stress on objective research and verification goes back even further. Mead (1964) took pains to enunciate the philosophical bases of scientific knowledge (45–61), and to establish the social act as the objective index of a person's subjective orientation (65–82). This emphasis has continued to the present, leaving its mark on almost all works dealing with methods of qualitative research (cf., for instance, Dean, et al., 1967; Hammond, 1964, especially Udy; Barton and Lazarsfeld, 1961; Adams and Preiss, 1960).

The most instructive examples of the bias toward verification and how this contributes to an individualistic bias in labeling studies are the methodological works of Cicourel (1964) and Bruyn (1966). Although Cicourel mentions the function of qualitative research for the development of theory (71), he focuses on the up-grading of qualitative methods to insure systematic verification of theories and hypotheses. He also reveals a lower esteem for the function of theory generation than Glaser and Strauss in his remark that participant observation should focus on "testing hypotheses. . . . Otherwise this method amounts to a continual 'pilot study' " (67). Similarly, the dominant concern of Bruyn's monograph exploring the historical and philosophical foundations of participant observation and its methodology is to encourage the field researcher "to be systematic in his work and obtain verifiable data" (252). Bruyn maintains that qualitative participant-observation research comprises a "new empiricism" to be distinguished from the more behavioristic "traditional empiricism" of social science (4–6). While Bruyn makes an impressive case for the role of participant-observation research and verification techniques (198–254, 255–270), he reveals strong attachment to verification in his approach to qualitative research.

Of course there is nothing inherently wrong with any attempt to bring rigor to the sociological enterprise. An exclusive focus on theory generation to the neglect of data-gathering and verification is just as inadequate as the opposite alternative and would return us to the disjunction between theory and research so well criticized by Merton (1945) over twenty-five years ago. But the point remains: an excessive emphasis on verification in quantitative research seems to have constrained the theoretical scope of this perspective. In practice, labeling theorists tend to apply their perspective to the more formal and structured settings in which individuals are labeled. A passive characterization of labelees readily follows. A single *individual* in a well organized situation is seldom able to accomplish a viable political denial of the validity of a label. At most he might occasionally resist the application of a label to himself or to an associate.

IDEOLOGICAL SOURCE

A second reason why the labeling approach has tended to focus on the passive aspects of the individual labeled deviant derives from the liberal perspective espoused by many contemporary

---

[3]Becker and Geer take pains to differentiate the distinctive methods, types of data, and theory-generating function of participant observation and to resist the subordination of this approach to models of quantitative research.

sociologists. Whenever someone engages in cutting through a society's ideological understanding of its institutions he becomes more aware of the coercive effect these institutions have on their members or clients (cf. Berger, 1963:25–53; 1971). This realization, I believe, has led sociologists to study those situations and aspects of so called "deviant" behavior where agents of social control coercively apply labels to individuals. Becker's (1967:243–46) classic essay, "Whose Side Are We On?", summarizes the sympathies of contemporary practitioners of the interactionist perspective and frankly admits the perspective's ideological bias. According to Becker, in the past sociologists all too frequently assumed that "the man at the top knows best." Consequently, sociologists failed to realize that they were actually taking a side when analyzing conflict or deviance within levels of a hierarchy. When students of deviance came to the awareness that they must inevitably "take a side" and that the side they had usually taken in the past was the side of the super-ordinate, they developed—by choice and out of reaction— a counter perspective to the earlier pro-establishment bias. The result, notes Becker (1964), has been the development of an "unconventional sentimentality." Consequently, says Becker (1964:5), the proestablishment bias

assumes, and refuses to examine the assumption, that things are in fact "worse" than they might be, . . . (the unconventional sentimentalist) assumes. . .that the underdog is always right and those in authority always wrong. . . . The same kind of sentimentality is sometimes found in studies of deviance, manifesting itself in a tendency to refuse to admit that the deviants under study have done wrong.

As we will exemplify below, this unconventional sentimentality, while clearly a necessary balance to the pro-establishment bias, too often blinded those working within the labeling perspective to the study of *political deviance:* those cases where aggressive, activist groups present ideologies and/or perform actions that radically challenge an established hierarchy of values and norms. Further—and what is important for our considerations in this paper—this political deviance' invariably involves negotiation or struggle between agents of social control and political deviants in which various favorable and unfavorable labels are exchanged, accepted, resisted and countered.

THE IRONY OF LABELING STUDIES

Obviously, identifying the reasons for the contemporary emphasis on the passive individual does not refute the theoretical or empirical findings of existent labeling studies. It is not so much that these studies have been wrong but that labeling theorists, more often than not, failed to appreciate the power of their new perspective for studying political deviance.

Moreover, what is more ironic (and unfortunate) about this failure is that precisely because labeling studies have been so stimulating and provocative, they have spurred further research which, instead of expanding the scope of interactionist analysis to study the negotiation of labels by aggressive groups, has merely repeated documentation of the successful labeling of helpless individuals.

DOCUMENTATION OF THE BIAS: VIEWING THE LABELEE AS PASSIVE

As we have said, the philosophical bias of studies of deviance has two components: first, an emphasis on the passivity of the labelee; second, a focus on the individual rather than on the group as the unit being labeled. This dual bias of individuality and passivity pervades the literature of the labeling approach.[4] First, we will document the bias toward studying settings in which individuals remain passive within the labeling process.

---

[4]For example, both biases can be seen in this quotation from Denzin's (1968) study, "The Self-Fulfilling Prophecy and Patient-Therapist Interaction":

In order for the therapist to enact his own role as medical practitioner, it is necessary for the patient to publicly accept his status in the hospital and to develop a view of self which is in accordance with the therapist's. In short, the patient must learn to view the hospital as a legitimate treatment source. In addition, he must learn to view himself as mentally ill and in need of treatment. . . . The therapist forms an initial definition on the basis of this presentation and proceeds to act toward the patient in a manner which tends to support and validate his initial definitions (349–50).

Thomas Scheff (1964; 1966), Thomas Szasz (1961), R. D. Laing (1962; 1967), and Erving Goffman (1961) all study how powerless individuals come to be treated as mentally ill according to the will and perspective of their families, friends and psychiatrists rather than according to some inherent or objective mental disability. In the legal sphere, Duster (1970) and Schur (1965) report the secondary consequences of labeling for drug users, homosexuals, and women having abortions. Sudnow (1965) and Chevigny (1969) unveil the dynamics and underlying rationale behind the seemingly arbitrary plea and charge negotiations by which police and courts allocate particular individuals to specific categories of crime or guilt. Similarly, Matza (1969), Cicourel (1968), and Tannenbaum (1938) describe how various imputations or labels imposed upon people lead to the emergence of delinquent and criminal behavior. Erikson (1964; 1966) and Currie (1968) describe how legal systems cull out and certify certain quotas of persons as deviant in order to identify the normative boundaries of the society. Studying less dramatic expressions of many of the same processes, Goffman (1963), Freidson (1965), and Kitsuse (1964) examine the dynamics of stigmatization whereby various negative characteristics are imputed to a person who subsequently faces such reactions as the retrospective reinterpretation of his previous actions and words. Another striking use of the labeling approach to study imputations of labels to individuals is Cicourel and Kitsuse's (1963) investigation of how the designation of students as either ''college-qualified'' or ''non-college qualified'' (and, by implication, the designation of their occupational choices) are determined not so much by the student's ability, motivation or peer-group but by practices of the high school administrative organization, especially the routine decisions of guidance and counseling personnel.

DOCUMENTATION OF THE BIAS: THE INDIVIDUAL AS THE UNIT OF ANALYSIS

Freidson (1965:98) suggests that sociologists might profit from paying more attention to the aggressive aspects of the labelee's role in the process of label designation:

Individuals do come to define themselves in a particular way and to seek out the agencies at which they present themselves. In this sense, the deviant population defined by agencies may not be that which the agency has picked out so much as that which has picked itself out—''professional deviants,'' as it were, of special characteristics.[5]

While Freidson's comment seems to suggest the balance we are advocating, his caveat falls short. Apart from the general tendency of labeling studies to concentrate on the passive rather than the aggressive aspects of the labelee, on the *coerced imputation* of a label rather than the *chosen internalization* of a label, we have also noted the focus on the individual rather than the group. Returning to Freidson's statement, it is significant that even when he does discuss the value of studying the defensive or aggressive moves of the imputed recipient, he still speaks of individuals.

Several studies have been made on the process of defensive label-resistance or aggressive counter-labeling by particular individuals. But, because these studies continue to focus on the individual, they fail to come to grips with the politics of power that groups use when seeking to resist and counter an ''enemy's'' label.[6]

For instance, Goffman in *Stigma* (1963) and *Asylums* (1961) speaks of the processes, respectively, of ''stigma management'' and ''secondary adjustment'' by which an individual appears to follow the rules while secretly resisting an expected routine. Sykes and Matza (1957) investigate four neutralization techniques by which an

[5]However, Freidson admits that in his own study of the disabled he speaks of the labelee ''as a pawn'' (1965:98).

[6]Alex Thio (1973) in the most recent issue of this journal suggested a closely related argument. Thio would presumably agree with the thesis of this paper that labeling theorists have focused on powerless individuals and that this bias expresses itself in the methodological, conceptual, and theoretical formulations of the labeling perspective. The critical difference between our arguments is that while Thio maintains that the cause of this bias is the labeling sociologists' ''tacit support of the power elite'' (8), I include methodological sources as well. Also, somewhat more optimistically, I discern signs of hope within the labeling perspective for a response to this bias.

individual may resist the internalization of the socially derogatory label of criminal. Sobel and Ingalls (1968) examine the efforts of psychiatric patients to resist the self-help role their psychiatrists insist upon, and to substitute what the patients consider the more pleasing medical-patient role that allows for greater passivity, dependency, and submission.

Kai T. Erikson (1968:337–38), seeking to stress the active character of the medical patient, distinguishes two aspects of the labeling process, role-validation and role-commitment:

Role validation takes place where a community "gives" a person certain expectations to live up to . . . Role commitment is the complementary process whereby a person adopts certain styles of behavior as his own, committing himself to role themes that best represent the kind of person he assumes himself to be, and best reflect the social position he considers himself to occupy.

According to Erikson (1968) sociologists have been more concerned with the processes of validation than personal commitment. In so doing, "sociologists have largely overlooked the extent to which a person can *engineer* a change in the role expectation held in his behalf, rather than passively waiting for others to 'allocate' or 'assign' roles to him" (338). Applying the corrective he advocates (but still focusing on the individual), Erikson documents the "long and delicate negotiations" between the individual patient and the hospital staff during which a compromise emerges between the individual's personal sense of identity and the functional needs of the institution.

Orrin E. Klapp (1972:3) is also concerned with the dynamics of self-typing as opposed to typing by others; but again the individual is the unit of analysis. Klapp maintains the premise that "everyone in modern society is vitally interested in creating a type for himself, the deviant no less than the Philistine. Self-typing gives psychological content to the quest of status." Going further, efforts at self-typing are basically attempts at "finding oneself"; thus personality-typing is "less a matter of measuring 'traits' than of finding out how people type themselves" (4). Finally, correctly pointing out the usually im-

plicit attempts at counter-labeling, Klapp maintains that the effort to type oneself "includes the effort to type others."

Also examining the negotiation of labels by individuals, Austin T. Turk (1966:339–40) holds that deviance measured by the violation of laws often results from the response of nonpathological, "essentially normal persons" to realistic conflicts of interest. Scheff's (1968:4) discussion of the negotiation of labels in the psychotherapeutic and criminal (plea-bargaining) settings corroborates Turk's point:

My purpose is to argue that responsibility is at least partly a product of social structure. The alternative to the doctrine of absolute responsibility is that of relative responsibility: the assessment of responsibility always includes a process of negotiation. In this process, responsibility is in part constructed by the negotiating parties.

Happily, these studies stress that an individual is not determinately fixed in a particular role merely because a group attempts to impute that role. However, even though some labeling theorists manifest an appreciation for the aspects of conflict whereby labels are negotiated, neutralized, resisted, or countered, they still fail to consider cases where the negotiation of labels occurs between two groups rather than between two individuals or an individual and a group.

In summary, four points can be made. First, these studies consistently consider the individual as the unit of analysis. In almost every instance the sociologist examines the imputation by an organization or group of people of a label to an individual. There is virtually no consideration of two or more organizations or groups vying for a particular label or seeking to impute a label to one another. Second, there is a persistent overtone of deterministic language and imagery. The labelee is spoken of as "victimized"; he is "imputed" a label; he is under "compulsion." For example, while bowing to the fact that "reality is not wholly like that," Friedson (1965:98) explicitly maintains a perspective that "sees the individual as a pawn or victim of others' conceptions of him, and of the structure of agencies into which he happens to get pushed." Third, it is precisely these characteristics of labeling studies—their emphasis on the individuality and passivity of the labelee—that betray their pathos of pessimism and fatalism. Fourth, this bias, as we have said is directly opposed to what we would expect from analysts who are committed to Mead's insistence that individuals are in constant reflective dialogue with reality rather than simply determined by it.

BREAKING AWAY FROM PHILOSOPHICAL BIAS

Is there any possibility that sociologists who use the labeling perspective will overcome their philosophical bias? In view of the theoretical resources implicit in Mead's concept of social interaction, labeling theory should be able to cope with aggressive group negotiations. Moreover, the recent increase in the visibility of political deviance may spur sociologists to a more encompassing use of the labeling perspective.

The Meadian Framework

On the theoretical level as we have pointed out, the Meadian stance from which the labeling perspective emerged insists that the formation of identity involves more than the result of externally imposed patterns of behavior and thought. It also stresses an opposite aspect: what Strauss (1964:xv) calls "emergent evolution." Based on Mead's notion of the creative, unpredictable "I" dimension of the "self," the notion of "emergent evolution" implies, says Strauss (xv), "that persons are somewhat freer agents than is allowed in the more usual sociological view: freer not only to find ways to circumvent norms and rules, but also freer to help change the social structures within which they find themselves."

Although seldom treated explicitly, this inherent potential of symbolic interactionism to study the voluntaristic aspects of interaction and to extend its framework to the group level never has remained too far beneath the surface and has begun to be treated more directly. Thus a return to this original Meadian affirmation is not so

much a new insight as a fuller explication and application of a neglected theme.

For example, in one recent study, Becker and Horowitz (1970) take note of the aggressive approach of various groups ordinarily labeled deviant. The authors point out that in San Francisco a "culture of civility" has emerged which allows for a toleration of and accommodation to the "minor forms of deviance encompassed in sex, dope, and cheap thrills." . . . Thus "deviants find it possible to live somewhat more openly in San Francisco than elsewhere" (1970:17, 14).

Earlier, Lemert (1967:14) suggested the need, in studies of deviance, "for a theory of associational groups as agencies which fix and alter the order of value satisfaction, as well as shape means to ends." Suggesting that forms of aggressive group deviance (even if not political in the strict sense of radically new value assertions) have been around for a long time, Lemert points out that

A vast amount of case evidence that illegal price-fixing, misrepresentation, adulteration, collusive bidding, abetting extortion by labor racketeers, tax evasion, restrictive covenants, as well as a modicum of more traditional crimes, including even behavior chargeable as treason, follow from informal, clandestine, political decisions of associations (15).

Going back even further, although Goffman (1961:215) consistently focuses on the individuals as his unit of analysis (because "collective means of working the system seem not too common in mental hospitals"), he does speak of the character and function of "secondary adjustment" (189) by which "the individual (or group) stands apart from the role and the self that were taken for granted for him by the institution." He also speaks of the "underlife" of an institution (199) as comprised of the "full set of such adjustments that all the members of the organization severely and collectively sustain."

In sum, it seems that although the labeling approach has not followed them up, it theoretically does leave a place for the analysis of forms of aggressive political deviance.

Visibility of Political Deviance

Some would hold that the neglect of the political aspects of the labeling process is due simply to the scarcity of political deviance during the late 1950's and early 1960's when the labeling perspective was emerging. Along this line, Horowitz and Liebowitz (1968:282) contend that "Deviance has been studied by employing a consensus welfare model rather than a conflict model because, for the most part . . . the subordinate parties, the deviants themselves, have not entered the political arena." In the words of Becker (1967:240-1):

It is a situation in which, while conflict and tension exist in the hierarchy, the conflict has not become openly political. The conflict segments or ranks are now organized for conflict; no one attempts to alter the shape of the hierarchy. While subordinates may complain about the treatment they receive from those above them, they do not propose to move to a position of equality with them, or to reverse positions in the hierarchy. Thus, no one proposes that addicts should make and enforce laws for policemen, that patients should prescribe for doctors, or that adolescents should give orders to adults. We call this a political case.

While it would not be difficult to make the case that the incidence and visibility of political deviance have increased during the past few years, it does not seem valid to maintain that such deviance is a recent phenomenon. Examples abound of individuals and groups undercutting existing value orientations by aggressively seeking to win acceptance for their views of reality as expressed in the labels they attempt to legitimate: colonists who dumped tea into Boston Harbor, failed to pay taxes, and asserted their independence; slaves who conspired to rebel and flee and the whites who sheltered them; the Confederacy that sought to dissolve the Union; the early years of labor organizing and conflict; pacifists throughout American history who were brought to trial and jailed; the numerous phases of the black struggle for civil rights; women's efforts to win suffrage; the battle by Communists to gain the right to free speech and the right to hold public office; the conflicts surrounding atheists who refused to pray and science teachers who neglected Genesis.

Nevertheless, the recent increase in the incidence and visibility of political deviance may provide an objective context within which labeling theorists may counteract their philosophical bias.

At an early date, Becker (1965:78) suggested that such activities as homosexual defense organizations, self-help organizations of heroin addicts, and the LSD movement headed by Timothy Leary and Richard Alpert "exemplify the increasing militancy, organization, and self-consciousness of deviant worlds and their growing unwillingness to let respectable society have its own way with them unchallenged." More dramatically, perhaps, groups of radicals and revolutionaries, such as the Black Panthers, the Chicago 7, the Catonsville 9, and American Indian and Chicano defense leagues have challenged the legitimacy of existing norms, values, and behavior. They have explicitly and aggressively confronted dominant American culture and authority in the press, in the courts, on the streets, and in the countryside. Regrettably, among sociologists using the labeling perspective, this data goes begging for analysis.

Other Sources of Transition

Surely the increased amount and visibility of political deviance and the inherent emphasis of Meadian interactionism are factors contributing to the new consciousness of political deviance evidenced in Becker's statement quoted above. But other factors more directly involved in the relations of labeling theorists to political deviance provide a fuller explanation of this transition. Although a detailed examination of these factors is beyond the scope of this paper, some speculation is possible.

First, it is hardly a secret that social scientists (and especially sociologists) are a liberal lot (cf. Lipset and Ladd, 1970). Likewise, sociologists, as well as their graduate students and undergraduate majors, tend to be overrepresented in the moral radical activities on the campuses and in many change-oriented groups and movements. Within this framework it is not difficult to suppose that labeling theorists who already make their living by close analysis of contemporary social phenomena would be doubly interested in the more radical instances of labeling and counterlabeling which are sociologically exciting and to which they, their students, and their friends are related.[7] Consequently, labeling theorists, who are already sensitive to emergent social patterns, are now becoming even more aware of the forms of political resistance present today. It would not be surprising then to find that they will increasingly transfer their methodology for participant observation to the study of macro-level, political cases of resistance to labels and counter-labeling.

Finally, new attitudes towards qualitative research might legitimize more macroscopic studies of political labeling among groups. Labeling theorists (among other sociologists using qualitative data) are ceasing to be embarrassed by their concern for generating rather than verifying theory, or by their use of qualitative rather than quantitative data. Recent methodological treatises (Glaser and Strauss, 1967; Blumer, 1969; Becker, 1970; Lofland, 1971) have enhanced the sophistication of the methods of qualitative research, and have legitimated theory generation from qualitative data as a valuable enterprise distinct from logico-deductive theory and verification.[8] Labeling theorists are no longer quite so defensive or apologetic about their methodology, and may even boast that its creativity and accuracy surpasses that of the logico-deductive approach. Moreover, labeling theorists now should be able to move beyond their carefully drawn social-psychological studies of individuals and begin to explore group, organizational, and societal levels of labeling conflict.[9]

CONCLUSION

In conclusion, it is hoped that this treatment of the conceptual, ideological, and methodological shortcomings of the labeling approach may encourage labeling theorists to confront the limitations that pose a perennial problem for studies in the interaction framework. As sociologists begin to examine the various forms of political "deviance" (as staged in and around the courtroom, for instance) they may come to shed light upon other significant theoretical issues such as Lemert's (1967:3) call for a "suitable way of integrating the notion of deviation into a theory of social change." In this way, labeling theorists will be able to break out of the dilemma that now disposes them either to limit their investigations to microcosmic social-psychological settings (where existent norms and values are seldom significantly challenged), or to study rather amorphous macrocosmic situations where it is difficult to document much more than the platitude that social life is a matter of symbolic interaction.

---

[7]In my own case, for example, my political views about the Vietnam war, coupled with my personal concern for a friend who was on trial for destroying draft files, provided the impetus for my application of the labeling perspective to the dynamics of the political trial of the Chicago 15 (Schervish, 1971).

[8]A number of implications follow from the methodological stance taken in the works cited just above: 1) most significantly, an emphasis upon the generation of grounded theory as the signal goal and raison d'etre of qualitative methods (cf. Glaser and Strauss, 1967:6–7); 2) a functional classification of qualitative methods according to how field research actually proceeds rather than according to some analytic scheme which seeks to reduce methodology "to a defensible set of rules and procedure" (Becker, 1970:8; cf. also Lofland, 1971:13–58); 3) the evolution of methodological procedures such as "exploration" and "inspection" to ensure "the direct naturalistic examination of the empirical social world (Blumer, 1969:42 ff.); 4) the abandoning of current methodology which give preference "to theoretical schemes, to preconceived models, to arrays of vague concepts, to sophisticated techniques of research, and to an almost slavish adherence to what passes as the proper protocol of research inquiry" (Blumer, 1969:33); and 5) the realizations that "there is no fundamental clash between the purposes and capacities of qualitative methods of data," and that "accurate description and verification are not so crucial when one's purpose is to generate theory" (Glaser and Strauss, 1967:7, 28).

[9]The trial courtroom, because it is an increasingly popular forum of political "deviants" for confrontation, offers a fertile opportunity for theory generation, and is sufficiently structured to satisfy those concerned about quantitative rigor, may provide a starting point for the application of the labeling perspective to political "deviance." The legal framework of the American courtroom provides a relatively uncomplicated forum within which conflict parties debate the validity of labels before a jury that ultimately determines which one of the opposing labels may become operant in its consequences. Further, the courtroom is a highly visible yet formalized platform from which conflicting groups can execute the politics of communication and constituency building.

REFERENCES

Adams, Richard N. and Jack J. Preiss (eds.)
1960 Human Organization Research: Field Relations and Techniques. Homewood, Ill.: Dorsey.

Barton, A. H. and P. F. Lazarsfeld
1961 "Qualitative analysis in social research." Pp. 95–122 in S. M. Lipset and N. J. Smelser (eds.), Sociology: The Progress of a Decade. Englewood Cliffs, N.J.: Prentice-Hall.

Becker, Howard S.
1958 "Problems of inference and proof in participant observation." American Sociological Review 23 (December): 652–660.
1963 Outsiders: Studies in the Sociology of Deviance. New York: Free Press.
1964 "Introduction." Pp. 1–6 in Howard S. Becker (ed.), The Other Side: Perspectives on Deviance. New York: The Free Press.
1965 "Deviance and deviates." Pp. 73–82 in David Boroff (ed.) The State of the Nation. Englewood Cliffs, N.J.: Prentice-Hall.
1967 "Whose side are we on?" Social Problems 14 (Winter): 239–47.
1970 Sociological Work: Method and Substance. Chicago: Aldine.

Becker, H. S. and B. Geer
1957 "Participant observation and interviewing: A comparison." Human Organization 16 (Fall): 28–32.
1960 "Participant observation: The analysis of qualitative field data." Pp. 267–289 in Richard N. Adams and Jack J. Preiss (eds.), Human Organization Research: Field Relations and Techniques. Homewood, Ill.: Dorsey.

Becker, H. S. and I. L. Horowitz
1970 "The culture of civility." Trans-action 7 (April): 12–19.

Berger, Peter L.
1963 Invitation to Sociology: A Humanistic Perspective. Garden City, N.Y.: Doubleday Anchor Books.
1971 "Sociology and freedom." The American Sociologist 6 (February): 1–5.

Blumer, Herbert
1939 Appraisal of Thomas and Znaniecki's The Polish Peasant in Europe and America. New York: Social Science Research Council.
1969 Symbolic Interactionism: Perspective and Method. Englewood Cliffs, N.J.: Prentice-Hall.

Bruyn, Severyn T.
1966 The Human Perspective in Sociology: The Methodology of Participant Observation. Englewood Cliffs, N.J.: Prentice-Hall.

Chevigny, Paul
1969 Police Power: Police Abuses in New York City. New York: Vintage Books.

Cicourel, Aaron V.
1964 Method and Measurement in Sociology. New York: Free Press.
1968 The Social Organization of Juvenile Justice. New York: John Wiley.

Cicourel, Aaron V. and John I. Kitsuse
1963 The Educational Decision-Makers. Indianapolis: Bobbs-Merrill.

Currie, E. P.
1968 "Crimes without criminals: Witchcraft and its control in renaissance Europe." Law and Society Review 3 (August): 7–32.

Dean, J. P., R. L. Eichhorn, L. R. Dean
1967 "Observation and interviewing." Pp. 274–304 in John T. Doby (ed.), An Introduction to Social Research. Second edition. New York: Appleton-Century-Crofts.

Denzin, N. K.
1968 "The self-fulfilling prophecy and patient-therapist interaction." Pp. 349–358 in Stephen P. Spitzer and Norman K. Denzin (eds.), The Mental Patient: Studies in the Sociology of Deviance. New York: McGraw-Hill.

Duster, Troy
1970 The Legislation of Morality: Law, Drugs, and Moral Judgment. New York: Free Press.

Erikson, Kai T.
1968 "Patient role and social uncertainty." Pp. 337–42 in Earl Rubington and Martin S. Weinberg (eds.), Deviance: The Interactionist Perspective. London: Macmillan.
1964 "Notes on the sociology of deviance." Pp. 9–21 in Howard S. Becker (ed.), The Other Side: Perspectives on Deviance. New York: Free Press.
1966 Wayward Puritans: A Study in the Sociology of Deviance. New York: John Wiley.

Freidson, E.
1965 "Disability as social deviance." Pp. 71–99 in Marvin B. Sussman (ed.), Sociology

and Rehabilitation. Washington, D.C. American Sociological Association.

Glaser, Barney G. and Anselm L. Strauss
1967 The Discovery of Grounded Theory: Strategies for Qualitative Research. Chicago: Aldine.

Goffman, Erving
1961 Asylums: Essays on the Social Situation of Mental Patients and Other Inmates. Garden City, N.Y.: Doubleday Anchor Books.
1963 Stigma: Note on the Management of Spoiled Identity. Englewood Cliffs, N.J.: Prentice-Hall.

Gouldner, A. W.
1955 "Metaphysical pathos and the theory of bureaucracy." American Political Science Review 49 (June): 496–507.

Hammond, Phillip E. (ed.)
1964 Sociologists at Work: Essays on the Craft of Social Research. New York: Basic Books.

Horowitz, I. L. and M. Liebowitz
1968 "Societal deviance and political marginality: Toward a redefinition of the relation between sociology and politics." Social Problems 15 (Winter): 280–96.

Kitsuse, J. I.
1964 "Societal reaction to deviant behavior: Problems of theory and method." Pp. 87–102 in Howard S. Becker (ed.), The Other Side: Perspectives on Deviance. New York: Free Press.

Klapp, Orrin E.
1972 Heroes, Villains and Fools: Reflections of the American Character. San Diego: Aegis.

Laing, R. D.
1962 The Self and Others. Chicago: Quadrangle Press.
1967 The Politics of Experience. New York: Ballantine.

Lemert, Edwin M.
1951 Social Pathology. New York: McGraw-Hill.
1967 Human Deviance, Social Problems, and Social Control. Englewood Cliffs, N.J.: Prentice-Hall.

Lipset, S. M. and E. C. Ladd Jr.
1970 ". . .And what professors think." Psychology Today 4 (November): 49ff.

Lofland, John
1971 Analyzing Social Settings: A Guide to Qualitative Observation and Analysis. Belmont, Cal.: Wadsworth.

Lundberg, George A.
1939 Foundations of Sociology. New York: Macmillan.
1947 Can Science Save Us? New York: Longmans, Green.
1955 "The natural science trend in sociology." American Journal of Sociology 61 (November): 191–202.
1956 "Some convergence in sociological theory." American Journal of Sociology 62 (July): 21–27.

Matza, David
1969 Becoming Deviant. Englewood Cliffs, N.J.: Prentice-Hall.

Mead, George Herbert
1964 George Herbert Mead on Social Psychology: Selected Papers. Anselm Strauss (ed.). Chicago: University of Chicago Press.

Merton, R. K.
1945 "Sociological theory." American Journal of Sociology 50 (May): 462–473.

Scheff, Thomas J.
1966 Being Mentally Ill: A Sociological Theory. Chicago: Aldine.
1968 "Negotiating reality: Notes on power in the assessment of responsibility." Social Problems 16 (Summer): 3–17.

Scheff, T. J. with the assistance of D. M. Culver
1964 "The societal reaction to deviance: Ascriptive elements in the psychiatric screening of mental patients in a midwestern state." Social Problems 11 (Spring): 401–13.

Schervish, P. G.
1971 "Deviance as a political strategy: The trial of the Chicago 15." Paper read at the Twenty-first Annual Meeting of the Society for the Study of Social Problems, Denver, Colo.

Schur, Edwin M.
1965 Crimes Without Victims. Englewood Cliffs, N.J.: Prentice-Hall.

Sobel, R. and A. Ingalls
1968 "Resistance to treatment: Explorations of the patient's sick role." Pp. 324–34 in Stephan P. Spitzer and Norman K. Denzin (eds.), The Mental Patient: Studies in

the Sociology of Deviance. New York: McGraw-Hill.

Strauss, A.
1964 "Introduction." Pp. vii–xxv in George Herbert Mead on Social Psychology: Selected Papers. Anselm Strauss (ed.). Chicago: University of Chicago Press.

Sykes, G. and D. Matza
1957 "Techniques of neutralization: A theory of delinquency." American Sociological Review 22 (December): 664–70.

Sudnow, D.
1965 "Normal crimes: Sociological features of the penal code." Social Problems 12 (Winter): 255–76.

Szasz, Thomas S.
1961 The Myth of Mental Illness. New York: Hoeber-Harper.

Tannenbaum, Frank
1938 Crime and the Community. New York: Columbia University Press.

Thio, A.
1973 "Class bias in the sociology of deviance." The American Sociologist 8 (February): 1–12.

Turk, A. T.
1966 "Conflict and criminality." American Sociological Review 31 (June): 338–52.

Udy, S. H., Jr.
1964 "Cross-cultural analysis: A case study." Pp. 161–183 in Philip E. Hammond (ed.), Sociologists at Work. New York: Basic Books.

PRINCIPLE AND RATIONALIZATION IN RACE RELATIONS

Everett C. Hughes

One of the most distressing and dangerous of the symptoms of our sick world is the distortion of people's minds and sentiments, and of our social practices and institutions along the axis of racial and cultural (ethnic) differences. It is right and proper that students of society should direct their attention to these symptoms and to their underlying causes. This social scientists have been and are doing. Much valuable work has been and is being done. More power to the people who are doing it; to those anthropologists who have not merely accelerated their investigations into the nature of racial differences but have also launched programs of popular education to clear up misapprehensions. All credit also to those sociologists, political scientists and other specialists who have turned their scientific effort in this direction; and to those people, of various professions, who have undertaken, by bold experiment, to bring more justice into the relations between people of different racial and ethnic backgrounds. And if scholars and other persons who are themselves members of the disadvantaged groups of our society show a special penchant for studying problems of this order, no less credit is due them. It is not only their right,

but also their special duty, to undertake research and action which will benefit society at large none the less for being directed especially at injustices done to the group to which they themselves belong. The others of us in social science might, however, search our professional consciences to see whether we do not passively conspire to confine Negro social scientists to study of Negro problems, women to study of the problems of women and children, and so on (for this is one of the subtler forms of discrimination—"Go up higher, brother, to the head of your own table").

The main business of this paper is, however, not to praise, but to criticize the way in which we have gone about the business of improving the relations between races and ethnic groups.

Our main fault has been opportunism, and especially an opportunism of logic, a fault common enough in American social science and social action. I do not mean that there is necessarily any opportunism in the turning of our attention to the problems of our own time and country. On that point we should not yield an inch to those who would have us choose our objects of study purely on the basis of something called "the state of knowledge" without reference to what is currently going on in the world. There has undoubtedly been some opportunism in choice of problems for investigation by American social scientists; we may have respected sacred cows and may have run after the

Published by permission of Transaction Publishers, from *The Sociological Eye: Selected Papers,* by Everett C. Hughes. Copyright © 1984 by Transaction Publishers.

Presented at the Eighth Annual Convention of the American Catholic Sociological Society, Dec. 28, 1946.

problems for whose investigation funds are easy to get. An opportunism of logic is, however, much more serious.

The main evidence of the kind of opportunism to which I refer is that we allow the direction of our research and educational effort to be dictated by the enemy, the defenders of racial and ethnic injustice. It is common for people to defend their sentiments and actions by rationalizations. In some societies a given set of rationalizations may last so long as to become traditional. In our society, we are quick to change them. We actively seek new ones; this is one of the functions of annual conventions—to find more up-to-date reasons for our old policies, interests and sentiments. Being scientifically minded, we Americans dress our new rationalizations in the sheep's clothing of science. The inequality of the position of the races in this country was once defended by scriptural quotation; now it is defended by what are called "facts" of biology and psychology. And those of us who are interested in getting new light on and more just action in the relations between peoples, take up the chase. If someone says Negroes have such poor jobs because they are biologically incapable of learning complicated skills, we set about to prove that Negroes can learn to do anything anyone else can learn to do. If then the "fact" of incapacity to learn is modified to say that Negroes are good with their hands, but not with their heads, we get busy to prove that that isn't so, either. Then someone comes along with the defense that although they can learn as well, or almost as well, as other people, Negroes lack sexual or other controls necessary to the nicer positions in our society; we chase that one. Or perhaps Negroes don't smell nice; so we start counting sweat glands. We store the sweat of people of various races in bottles and have it smelt by noses of several shapes, sizes and colors, just as advertising agencies say they do with cigarettes in their "scientific" blind-fold tests— and note with glee that women have more sweat-glands than men and that while the smellers couldn't tell what race the samples came from, a Chinese man picked as worst of all the sweat of an Anglo-Saxon. Someone will no doubt soon analyze the oil from the skin and hair of some

group unfortunately dubbed "greasers." Perhaps someday a broad-minded East Indian will be disturbed by the disgust his fellow-countrymen are said to feel at the sight of lobster-red sunburned English skin. Desirous of eliminating this unwarranted prejudice against Europeans, he will have chemists make tests; if all goes well, they will find no chemical difference between the beautiful bronze skin of Hindu vegetarians and the parboiled hide of a beef-eating Colonel Blimp.

Now I have no basic objection to the making of such tests, and none to the dissemination, to as many people as possible, of whatever findings result from them. Truth is better than error, and should be spread with the more vigor when the error is one that does great damage. What I do object to is giving the terms of the game into the hands of the enemy, who, by inventing a new rationalization every day, leads us a merry and endless chase. We attack the devil's changing disguises instead of the devil himself.

Each of these rationalizations brought up in defense of racial and ethnic injustices is part of a syllogism. The minor premise, stating an alleged fact, is expressed; the major premise, a principle, is left out. Instead of driving our opponents and ourselves back to the major premise, we are content to question and disprove the minor premise, the allegation of fact.

Suppose we take a couple of the common statements: "Jim Crow practices are justified because Negroes smell bad," and "Jews should not be admitted to medical schools because they are aggressive." The first, completed, would read something like this:

There should be separate public facilities for people who smell bad.

Negroes smell bad.

Therefore, Negroes should have separate facilities.

The second would read like this:

People who are aggressive beyond some determined degree should not be admitted to medical schools.

Jews are aggressive beyond this degree.

Therefore, Jews should not be admitted to medical schools.

The orders of fact alleged in these two examples are quite different. But they serve equally well for our purpose. The major premise is ordinarily not stated in either case by the persons who use the statement; nor is it often stated or answered by those who oppose racial and ethnic discrimination of the kinds they refer to.

I suspect—though it might be hard to prove—that the suppression of the major premise in these and similar cases is not a psychological accident. There is said to be a kind of shrewdness in the fevered reasoning of the neurotic, as well as in that of the devil. The shrewdness in these rationalizations lies in the use of implied major premises that people of our culture, those who believe in racial and ethnic equality, as well as those who use these rationalizations, do not care to bring out into the open.

Let us look again at the syllogism about odors. We are a people who can be frightened by advertisements which tell us that we will not be promoted to be superintendents of factories and sales-managers of businesses unless we smell nice; and the American woman can be frightened by the threat that she will not get her man or that she may lose him over a matter of a little unpleasant odor of which her best friend can't bring herself to speak. We are not told at what point in his rise to authority and higher income the man must begin to make himself pleasant. Nor do we learn whether the man who is about to be lost had so sensitive a nose when he got the girl, or whether he picked up this nicety later. But the reference to the great—and legitimate—American dream of getting ahead is obvious enough. And it is perhaps not difficult to understand why we do not question the main premise behind the alleged fact of Negro odor.

Or let us take the defense of restrictive covenants by the statement that the presence of Negroes in a neighborhood destroys property values. The major premise would be something like this: People are justified in preventing property in their neighborhood from being occupied by people whose presence reduces property values. Now it is true that residential property values respond in some degree, under certain circumstances, to a change in the kind of people who live in the area. This may be due to the way

of living of the new people, or it may be due to an attitude toward them, or to both. It is also true that Americans in great numbers try to turn an improvement in their economic condition into an improvement in their social standing by moving to a new neighborhood. This is a perfectly natural and generally proper thing for them to do. But the trouble is that there is always some later comer treading on one's heels. So that it is, in a sense, the great American game to break in where one is not wanted. It is a game that is successful just to the extent that one seems not to be playing it: to seem to play it is to be aggressive, and one gets punished for that although he may not necessarily be rewarded for not being aggressive. Herein lies the great American dilemma, although I do not mean to belittle Mr. Myrdal's statement of it. The thought that I may be one of those whose presence in a neighborhood might—through other people's attitudes toward me—reduce its desirability to them is not a pleasant one to face, especially when combined with my own concern lest some group of people from whom I wish to be dissociated may some day threaten the neighborhood in which I have achieved a social footing and perhaps a dearly bought family house.

The preceding paragraph contains a clue to the effectiveness of the use of alleged Jewish aggressiveness as justification for limiting their entry to the professions. We Americans do not like to talk about just what degree of aggressiveness is proper; we might find that the amount of this virtue necessary to realize our ambitions is greater than the amount which turns it into a punishable vice. I am tempted to pursue a like analysis of what is hidden in the question, "How would you like your sister to marry a nigger?" I will spare you—and myself—that ordeal. To those of you who are still college students, I recommend it as an exercise for the brain and the spine.

Let me repeat that I do not pretend to prove that the enemies of interracial and interethnic justice exercise conscious slyness in the choice of their defensive rationalizations. Nor can I prove that it is the discomfort of facing major premises about which we are fearfully ambivalent, rather than mere logical carelessness and the love of empiricism at all costs, that prevents us from filling out these syllogisms. But certainly we are ambivalent about the principles hidden in these statements. We, like those who defend the racial and ethnic inequalities of our society, are all Americans. They and we share the same aspirations; the hidden fundament of our minds is the same as theirs. I only suggest that that gives them a certain advantage over us, and that we have allowed them full benefit of it.[1]

Whatever causes it, the failure to ferret out major premises has other consequences than merely leading us on to a merry chase for facts. It leads to too much protestation as well. We counter the exaggerated statements of our opponents with exaggerations in another direction. Nearly all of the statements in favor of racial and ethnic discrimination allege faults in the minority groups in question. These faults range from serious moral defect to slight departures from the canons of good taste. In our counter-arguments, the members of the racial or ethnic groups involved appear as paragons of virtue, delightful in their manners—better, in fact, than it is common for human creatures to be.

This brings up the whole problem of the differences between people of different racial and ethnic categories. Those opposed to racial prejudices and inequalities have shown a tendency to slight, or even to deny, the existence of any differences at all. Fishberg's book on the Jews has long served as a text to prove that no one can tell a Jew when he sees him—a very dubious compliment to Jewish parents who have put forth great effort so to bring up their children that they will respect and practice conduct which the parents consider rooted in their Jewish faith and culture. All that Fishberg says about the physical characteristics of Jews may be true; and there are occasions when statement of his or other such findings is called for. But to use them to try to prove that there are no discernible or significant differences between one ethnic, or religious, group and another can lead to no good.

In the first place, overuse of such argument

implies that the only basis for social, political and economic equality is the lack of differences between the groups concerned. That would put our faith in the rightness of social equality on a very dubious foundation, both because it might some day turn out that there are some differences we don't know about and because it would imply that the price of equality is the elimination of peculiar traits which some group of people may properly cultivate and cherish. Heaven knows that in our prejudiced world members of some groups are given plenty of temptation to deny that they belong to the groups in which they were born and bred, and in so doing to eliminate all identifying marks. That is a matter for their own consciences. We can only have sympathy for such victims of racial, ethnic and religious injustice. Our sympathy should not lead us to engage in counter-propaganda which expressly or implicitly denies or tones down the differences which really exist between groups.

There is, further, the danger—so cogently stated by David Reisman in an article entitled "Equality and Social Structure"—that common people will consider the whole propaganda for tolerance a fake intended to obfuscate them. For, as Riesman says—speaking of the way into which the democratic world played into the hands of the Nazis:

That (democratic) world denied that there was any difference between races. . . .[Anthroplogists] insisted. . .that only the ignorant and the prejudiced could find any differences between Jews and non-Jews, and sociologists supplemented this with statistics to show that, in all tangible ways, Jews were just like everybody else. . . .One can see now that it would have been better strategy to admit the differences while denying that they justified political and economic stratification in most cases. . . .For the differences *are* there, no less so for being subtle and impalpable, or being mostly culturally conditioned, not biological in origin. . . .

At any rate, in the eyes of the ordinary man, there were differences between races and between the sexes and between men in general. He could not always put his finger on them, but he could feel them, and feel that there was something fishy in the liberal denials.[2]

---

[1]For a penetrating analysis of hidden factors in interethnic sentiment, see Ichheiser, Guslav, "Diagnosis of Anti-Semitism," Sociometry Monographs, No. 8.

[2]*Journal of Legal and Political Sociology,* Vol. I, 1943, pp. 79–80.

Riesman's warning applies not only to those differences which merely distinguish, or are supposed to, one group from another; it applies as well to those real or alleged differences which imply faults. For if groups of people maintain somewhat different virtues in their peculiar cultures, is it not likely that they will differ somewhat in their vices also? A record of the problems with which practical theologians have had to deal in different times and places, and of the special questions of conscience which have turned up in the confessional in various periods and countries, and among people of different ethnic background and social position, would—I am sure—give ample evidence of differences in the sins for which people have a predilection. In this matter, it would probably be more effective to gloss over nothing; and especially not to gloss over our own sins. The doctrine of original sin, which rests equally on all, is a sounder starting point than protestation that the groups which are the special objects of prejudice do not have any special vices. For, again speaking of our logical opportunism, the use of the denial of special faults as an argument against racial or ethnic prejudices and injustices implies somehow that we who are not discriminated against are in that blessed state because at some time or other we were without special disqualifying faults or vices, and were therefore elevated to our privileged position. It further implies the right of those who consider themselves without special faults or vices to give or withhold full equality from others.

In this kind of argument, incidentally, we again play into the hands of the enemy, for in arguing so hard that groups of people whose rights we have limited are without fault we encourage the idea—implicit in the "fault" justification of prejudice and limited rights—that justice and equality are something to be earned, and that the wage is to be paid by and at the discretion of the more privileged group. This argument turns up in the statement that Negroes are not ready for full political rights and for access to all kinds of jobs, supported by a false use of evolutionary ideas—"the Negroes are only yesterday out of the jungle." "It will take another hundred years," etc.

I do not mean to suggest that the problem of the relation between faults and access to full privileges in a society is an easy one, either in theory or in practice. There are circumstances in which society withdraws full freedom from an individual because of a weakness betrayed in his actions towards others. But the principle on which this is done is not that the other members of society have the right to do this because they are virtuous. They do it not in the name of and by right of their own virtue, but in the name of the good of the community and through functionaries of the law who—although they should certainly be people of uprightness and as far above reproach as possible—act with an authority delegated by society. The principles involved are far from those implied in any rationalization which justifies one group of people, supposedly free of faults, in limiting the social privileges of another whole category of persons because of the latter's alleged faults. It is some such principle that we give consent to if we answer the "fault" argument for discrimination by protesting that the minority concerned is not different in any way from other groups. It makes us parties to a revolting self-righteousness.

Allow me to mention briefly one more consequence of the denial or glossing over of differences, and especially of faults. It has already led to a feeling, in this country, that no one not a member of a certain group may express any but the most laudatory sentiments or judgments concerning it. Even those who are members of the group are enjoined to say nothing critical in such a way that it may reach ears outside the group. Again, the abuses and misunderstandings have been so flagrant that one can understand the effort to enforce a certain censorship upon criticism of one group by members of another. But that kind of tolerance which prevents statement of honest opinion and conviction is a false tolerance. It is the kind of tolerance which requires us to look about the room, and ask of our neighbor in a whisper, "Is there a Lower Slobbovian present?" before we open our mouths to speak. Granting that a careful tongue is an organ of great virtue, it does not follow that an honest one is less to be valued.

I have made but one point, or sung but one theme, with some variations: that it is worse than of no avail to gather and disseminate the true facts which refute the alleged facts offered in defense of racial and ethnic inequality of social rights, unless at the same time we dig out and bring to our own view, as well as to that of our opponents, the major premises, or principles, which lie hidden beneath the disguise of rationalizations.

DEFENDERS OF ORDER
OR GUARDIANS
OF HUMAN RIGHTS?*

Herman Schwendinger

Julia Schwendinger

Crime, most modern sociologists agree, is behavior which is defined by the legal codes and sanctioned by the institutions of criminal justice. It is generally agreed, moreover, the legal definitions of crime and the criminal are ultimate standards for deciding whether a scholarly work should be considered criminological.[1] Because of this, the contention that imperialist war and racism are crimes is not only considered an unjustifiable imposition of values, but also an incompetent use of the notion of crime. In order to challenge this prevailing judgment, it is necessary to critically review some of the complex issues involved in a thirty year old controversy about the definition of crime.

I: THE THIRTY YEAR OLD CONTROVERSY

Toward the end of the great depression, sociologists became involved in a controversy about

legal definitions of crime and criminals. At least two developments stimulated the issue raised at the time: the rapid growth of a corporate liberal, sociological empiricism and the socially critical interest in white collar crime. The former gave rise to what was primarily a scientific, methodological critique of the traditional legal definition. The second generated a substantive and ethical criticism. The positivist, reformist and traditionalist aspects of this controversy will be selectively reviewed, as they were represented by three of the chief participants: Thorsten Sellin (1938), Edwin Sutherland (1945), and Paul Tappan (1947).

A. Positivism and the Definition of Crime

In the controversy, American sociologists and lawyers argued furiously about definitions which would distinguish crimes from other types of behavior and criminals from other types of persons. It was observed that traditionally, criminologists used definitions provided by the *criminal law* and, as a result, the domain of criminology was restricted to the study of behavior encompassed by that law. However, one sociologist, Thorsten Sellin, declared in 1937 that if the criminologist is interested in developing a science of criminal behavior, he must rid himself of the shackles forged by criminal law. Criminologists,

Herman Schwendinger and Julia Schwendinger (1970) "Defenders of Order or Guardians of Human Rights?" *Issues in Criminology* Vol. 5 (Summer): 123–157. Reprinted by permission of Social Justice.

*The authors wish to express their appreciation to Sheldon Messinger, Anthony Platt, Paul Takagi and Joseph Weis for their advice and criticism. We would like to thank, in particular, Menachem Amir and Anatole Shaffer for their detailed suggestions which helped clarify this paper.

[1]Criminology studies, therefore, provide knowledge which is diachronically or synchronically related to *legally* defined crimes and criminals.

Sellin added, should not permit nonscientists (e.g. lawyers or legislators) to fix the terms and boundaries of the scientific study of crime. Scientists have their own unique goals which include the achievement of causal theories of criminal behavior. In evaluating the usefulness of legal definitions for scientific purposes, Sellin noted that such definitions merely denote "external similarities" rather than "natural properties" of criminal behavior. The legal definitions, therefore, do not arise from the "intrinsic nature" of the subject matter at hand. They are, in Sellin's view, inappropriate as *scientific* definitions of crime (1938:20–21).

How can scientific definitions be developed? In an effort to answer this, Sellin pointed out that scientists are interested in universal relationships. Since "conduct norms" represent such relationships (they "are found wherever groups are found"), studies of conduct norms "afford a sounder basis for the development of scientific categories than a study of crime as defined by the criminal law." "Such a study," Sellin added, "would involve the isolation and classification of norms into *universal categories,* transcending political and other boundaries, a necessity imposed by the logic of science." Conduct norms transcend any concrete group or institution such as the State, in Sellin's opinion, because "they are not the creation of any normative group; they are not confined within political boundaries; they are not necessarily embodied in the law" (1937:30).

Sellin's argument, it should be noted, was organized around the assumption that scientific definitions are determined by the goals and methods of the scientist qua scientist. The limits of Sellin's critique, consequently, focused primarily on the achievement of *scientific* explanations. Moreover, his scientific *standards* for constructing definitions of crime, including his preference for universal, and obviously formal categories and generalizations, are apparently devoid of any moral content: they coldly reflect allegedly intrinsic "natural properties" of human behavior and the "necessity imposed by the logic of science." Sellin's approach to the definition of crime is therefore ostensibly *value-free.*

B. A Reformist Definition in Which the State Still Reigns Supreme

For many years European and American sociologists incorporated specific references to the ethical properties of criminal behavior in their definitions of crime. William A. Bonger (1936:5), for example, referred to crime as "a serious antisocial act to which the State reacts consciously by inflicting pain. . . ." Other terms such as "social injury" were also used for this purpose (in the sense that crime involved socially injurious behavior). In some cases these ethical defining criteria provided an implicit warrant for defining unethical practices as crimes, even though these practices might not have been covered by the criminal law. Because these ethical defining criteria have implications for social policy, we shall regard statements embodying their usage as *reformist* definitions.

In 1945, another sociologist, Edwin Sutherland, added fuel to the controversy over the legal definition of crime. His research (1940, 1941) into unethical practices among businessmen and corporation managers produced evidence that, even though very injurious to the public, these practices were considered violations of the civil rather than criminal law. (Consequently, penalties for petty thieves resulted in imprisonment while businessmen who defrauded the public of large sums of money were given insignificant fines.) Sutherland asserted that some of these unethical business practices, while unlawful, were being classified as civil violations because legislators were subservient to powerful interest groups who wanted to avoid the social stigma and penal sanctions imposed under criminal law.

Other consequences followed official subservience. Since criminologists were traditionally limited to behavior prescribed and proscribed by the criminal law, it followed that they were not assured of finding direct legal precedents[2] for the

---

[2]Because of this, Sutherland's discussions on this topic attempted to demonstrate the connection between criminal and civil violations via analogy, historical parallels, and certain similarities between civil and criminal procedures, etc. (e.g. He wrote, ". . .although many laws have been enacted for the regulation of occupations other than business, such as

study of the unethical practices by groups powerful enough to fashion the law to their own advantage *no matter how socially injurious their practices might be.* In order to rectify this arbitrary
restriction, Sutherland justifiably brushed aside
the criteria used by legal scholars to differentiate
between criminal and civil violations. He suggested (1945) that social scientists define crime
on the basis of the more abstract notions of
"social injury" and "legal sanctions." The legal
sanctions he had in mind were not restricted to
criminal law but were to include those in civil
law. And although legal scholars traditionally
contended that civil violations were viewed as injuries to individual persons, Sutherland's definition of "white collar" *crime* obviously designated
some civil violations as crimes because they were
social injuries rather than private wrongs.
Sutherland's use of the terms "social injury" and
"legal sanctions" for defining crime was understandably not wholly endorsed by legal scholars.

Sutherland's argument, it should be noted,
made no reference to scientific goals and standards. Unlike Sellin's ostensibly value-free approach, moreover, Sutherland's solution to the
problem assumed that there exist *moral* criteria
of social injury which can be used to formulate
definitions of crime. However, when Sutherland
insisted that the abstract notion of "sanctions"
be interpreted to mean legal sanctions, his conception of the relevant laws conjoined both
criminal and civil laws. The domain of criminological inquiry, therefore, was extended
beyond the limits of criminal law.

On the other hand, this domain still continued
to reside within the limits of whatever was
deemed socially injurious and sanctionable by
the *State.* Although Sutherland never delineated
his criteria of social injury in any organized manner, it can be inferred from comparisons between
his different definitional statements that these
criteria cannot exceed those legitimated by
agents[3] of the State. In a definition, therefore,

Sutherland (1949:31) stated, "The essential
characteristic of crime is that it is behavior which
is prohibited by *the State* as an injury to *the State*
and against which *the State* may react, at least as
a last resort, by punishment" (our emphasis).

C. The Traditionalist Approach to the Definition of Crime

In 1947, Paul Tappan indignantly exclaimed
that the criminal law contained the only
justifiable definition of crime. Those who wanted
to abandon this definition were saying, in his
opinion: "Off with the old criminology, on with
the new orientation . . ." (1947:96). Since these
laws also referred to procedural rules, Tappan
added that a person could not be considered
criminal until he was adjudicated and found
guilty of a crime by the State. Were the new
trends allowed to triumph, he foresaw potential
hazards in that "the rebel may enjoy a veritable
orgy of delight in damning as criminal most anyone he pleases; one imagines that some experts
would thus consign to the criminal classes any
successful capitalistic businessman. . . ." Such
an approach to the definition of crime, Tappan
explained, "is not criminology. It is not social
science." Sutherland's approach, therefore,
received methodological denunciation because
the "terms 'unfair,' 'discrimination,' 'injury to
society,' and so on, employed by the white collar criminologist cannot, taken alone, differentiate criminal and noncriminal. Until re-
defined to mean certain actions they are merely
epithets" (1947:99).

Tappan criticized Sellin's and Sutherland's
universal concepts for the absence of criteria defining such terms as "injurious." Furthermore,
he felt these concepts served to delude the sociologist into assuming that "there is an ab-
soluteness and permanence in this undefined
category, lacking in the law." "It is unwise,"
Tappan added, "for the social scientist ever to
forget that all standards of social normation are
relative, impermanent, variable. And they do
not, certainly the law does not, arise out of mere
fortuity or artifice." As a consequence, he con-

---

agriculture or plumbing, the procedures used in the enforcement of these other laws *are more nearly the same* as the conventional criminal procedures. . .") (1945:139 our emphasis).

[3]The term "agents" is used in the broad sense. It includes,
for example, legislators, judiciary and police because the

definition and operative interpretation of crime are not
restricted to lawmakers.

demned Sellin's and Sutherland's "vague omnibus concepts defining crime" as "a blight upon either a legal system or a system of sociology that strives to be objective" (1947:99). Indeed, he suspected subversive motives and attacked the critics of the legal definition for attempting to "revolutionize" its concepts and infiltrate it with terms of "propaganda." He expressed fears that in the end "the result may be fine indoctrination . . ." (1947:99).

Also, carrying his logic to an extreme, Tappan flatly stated that the only persons who could be *specifically* studied as criminals were those found guilty by the judicial system. He recommended that sociologists study prison inmates because these persons were truly representative of the total population of criminal offenders. By this logic, persons who had committed a robbery, rape or murder but had not been adjudicated were not criminals; therefore, they could not be part of a representative sample of criminals. Although there were, without question, more persons who had violated laws and had not been adjudicated for their violations, Tappan stubbornly argued that the traditional legal definitions of crime were more precise and objective than other definitions. Tappan's argument is obviously unjustified. However, it verges on the absurd when we add to the roster of criminals at large, those who have been falsely imprisoned. In the case of these guiltless victims, Tappan's argument, in its practical effects, is also pernicious: according to this argument Dreyfus and other less celebrated individuals should have been counted and considered among the criminal population merely because they had been adjudicated and found guilty by the institutions of criminal justice, for the duration of their lives or at least until the State admits that it has allowed a miscarriage of justice.

Although Tappan also characterized crime as social injury, he made no explicit attempt to follow up his criticism of others by indicating the nature of its defining criteria. He merely deferred to the officials of the State as the only persons who could legitimately decide this question and write it into law. Their decisions, therefore, in addition to determining the specific populations of criminals to be studied by criminologists, also

determined the scientific definitions of crime and criminals. Any scientific convention contradictory to this rule was considered illegitimate.

D. The Legalistic Compromise Between Traditionalists and Reformists

The definition of crime and the criminal cannot be wholly separated on an abstract level because the criminal cannot be defined without a definition of crime. The sharp differentiation between definitions of crime and criminals has arisen because of the objections to the legal operational criteria which are part of the traditionalist definition of crime. Sutherland, as we have seen, objected to these operational criteria. He suggested that researchers can consider persons as criminals even though they have not been found guilty of a crime by legal procedures.[4]

It has been indicated recently (Quinney, 1970:4) that Sutherland's definition of crime as a violation of the *criminal law* has been the most acceptable to sociologists in this country. But Sutherland proposed more than one definition of crime. In various places he suggested that crime encompasses the concepts of "social injury," "injury to the State," and both the civil and criminal law. If his reformist preference is distinguished by the insistence that criteria such as "social injury" be explicitly used to define crime, then it is more accurate to say that traditionalist definitions of crime are generally used by sociologists today. In regard to the definition of *crime*, therefore, Tappan has won the day.[5] On

---

[4]Sutherland (1960:19) stated, "However, for scientific purposes it is not necessary that every decision be made in court; the criminologist must only know that a certain class of acts is defined as crime and that a particular person has committed an act of this class. Just as there is justification for writing of 'crimes known to the police' and 'unsolved crimes,' there is justification for writing of 'unapprehended criminals' and 'criminals at large.' "

[5]Gresham Sykes' evaluation of Tappan's criticism of the use of ethical criteria is one example. Sykes (1956:20) states, in regard to the attempts by sociologists to equate "criminal" with "anti-social" that ". . .Paul Tappan, as a lawyer-sociologist, has carefully indicated the hazards surrounding this position: it invites subjective value judgements; it substitutes the rather vague category of anti-social behavior for the more precise category of crime; and what is perhaps more important, it is apt to make the social scientist forget that all social rules are 'relative, impermanent, variable.' "

the other hand, as we shall see, Sutherland's less restrictive definition of the individual *criminal* prevails over the traditionalist approach. In a sense, sociologists have made an ambiguous compromise between the traditionalist and reformist solutions to the definitional problem.

Nevertheless, although phrased differently, almost all American criminologists today define crime and the criminal by specific or abstract references to definitions and/or sanctions administered by *the State*.[6] Because of this, the term "legalistic" will be used to refer to the variety of legal definitions; and "legalists" refers to those social scientists assuming the legal definition, however reformist or traditional it may be. It has been observed that definitions of crime are ultimate standards for deciding whether a scholarly work should be considered criminological. By extension, therefore, it can be claimed that the domain of the science of criminology is still, in spite of Sellin and the reformist approaches, determined by the agents of the political state because legalistic definitions of crime are formulated by these agents.

II. SCIENTIFIC STANDARDS FOR EVALUATING LEGALISTC DEFINITIONS

Each one of the scholars involved in the thirty year old controversy preferred particular defining criteria. Sellin, for example, indicated that "universal" or "causal" relationships should be signified by the definition of crime. Sutherland noted that criteria based on the notion of "social injury" and "sanction" were adequate. Tappan argued for procedural criteria which included reference to the rules by which the criminal law is instituted. He also contended that the legal definition is more precise than others. In order to evaluate these different critical attributes of the definition of crime, it will be shown that it is necessary to distinguish standards held useful by philosphers of science for scientific concept formation.[7] Since criminology is above all, the *scientific* study of the causes, characteristics, prevention and control of the incidence of criminal behavior, it is necessary to further note why scientific standards must take precedence over legal standards in evaluating the definition of crime.

A. Scientists Have Many Definitions of Crime

When their definitional usages are examined, it is found that social scientists are not bound by a single definition of crime; whatever definition is employed depends upon the types of activity the scientist is engaged in, or the kinds of relationships he is interested in.[8] Some of these activities require replication by other scientists and the definitions produced for this purpose operate like a manual of instructions which specifies the procedures for measuring phenomena. When a scientist is concerned with choosing among procedures for measuring crime, whether based on personal observation, self-report questionnaires, interview responses, or administrative processes involving police, judges and juries, he becomes involved in making a choice of an *operational* definition of crime.[9]

Operational definitions, however, do not exhaust the kinds of definitions used by scientists. There are times when it is helpful to explicate the meaning of categories such as "social control," "anomie," "predatory crimes," or

---

[6]No better example can be given than Richard Quinney's meticulous definition of crime. Quinney (1970:6-7) writes, ". . .conduct is not regarded as criminal unless these conditions are present. . . 1) the label of crime has been officially imposed on conduct 2) by *authorized persons and agencies* 3) of a *politically organized society.* Crime is therefore a legal category that is assigned to conduct by authorized agents of a politically organized society. The criminal is, it follows, a person who is assigned the status of criminal on the basis of the official judgment that his conduct constitutes a crime" (our emphasis).

[7]For an insightful discussion of the relation between definitions of crime and scientific concepts, see H. Bianchi (1956:90-111).

[8]For the meanings of such terms as "operational," "analytic," "nominal," and "real" definitions as well as the "explication," see Carl G. Hempel (1952).

[9]It should be noted in passing that Tappan's defense of the precision of the legal definition is inconsistent because he had been a foremost critic of the "imprecision" of the legal codes defining criminal behavior among juveniles (Tappan, 1947).

"crimes against property." In this case, a second or *analytic* definition might be in order.

In formulating useful, parsimonious and workable theories of empirical relationships, scientists have also found it necessary to use abbreviated forms of already understood meanings or to single out a particular property, relationship or function for convenient reference. Definitions of this type are called *nominal* definitions, and are even used in textbooks where crime is abstractly but not causally defined by reference to such properties or relations as "social injury," "sanction" or the "actor's relation to the State."

Finally, among the very most important definitions used by scientists are the *real* definitions which signify diachronic and synchronic relationships between variables.[10] Only one member of this class, causal definitions, which signify the necessary and sufficient conditions for the existence of a phenomenon, are real definitions. Causal definitions may be very complex and actually consist of a general theory of the phenomena in question. This may not be apparent in such statements as "anomy is the contradiction of all morality" (Durkheim, 1933:431), "crime is a symptom of social disorganization" (Sutherland and Cressey, 1960:23), or delinquency is an expression of "unsocialized aggression" (Jenkins and Hewitt, 1944). However, these statements are actually abbreviated expressions of general theories of criminal behavior such as social disorganization theories or psychoanalytic theories.

The operational, analytic, nominal and real definitions by no means exhaust the variety of definitional statements which characterize the work of scientists but they do indicate that the problem of selecting an appropriate definition of crime is not as simple as the legal scholars might suggest in their desire to achieve a universal definition of crime.

Historically, scholars involved in the study of theoretical explanations of human relationships have justifiably developed new modes of thought which depart greatly from customary ways of thinking in other professions. Perhaps the single most important feature of this perspective is the requirement that scientific categories must lead directly or indirectly to the formulation of empirically testable relationships. In light of this injunction, analytic or nominal categories may not be arbitrary; they must be heuristic and accurately descriptive and ultimately refer to accurate assumptions about the nature of the real world.

Sellin apparently challenged the notion that the *real* definition of crime must be derived from legal statutes however narrowly or loosely this mandate is defined. To our knowledge, however, no modern sociologist has fully considered the degree to which the empirical thrust of his challenge resides most importantly within the principle of the *autonomy of scientific inquiry*.[11] This principle was first raised and named by John Dewey (1938) as the "autonomy of inquiry." In developing this principle, Dewey was primarily concerned with encroachments by logicians and philosophers of science in the "logic in use" developed by scientists (Kaplan, 1964:3–11). However, as Abraham Kaplan (1964:3–6) has indicated the act of encroachment can have its sources in other professions as well. For example, the insistence by members of the legal profession that the law provides the only possible definitions of crime is an unjustifiable encroachment by lawyers on the autonomy of science. But this disregards the fact that legal definitions do not meet standards of scientific inquiry. Legal definitions have questionable heuristic value when used nominally or analytically. Operationally, these definitions are unreliable and invalid. Legalistic real definitions are sheerly descriptive; they play a trivial and common-sensical role in advancing theories of criminal behavior. To demonstrate the validity of these evaluations, we will systematically compare defining criteria based on the notions of "precision," "procedural law," and "sanctions," with the standards regulating the proper use of operational, real, analytic and nominal definitions.

---

[10]Our interpretation of the real definition is broader than Hempel's. He generally restricts real definitions to causal definitions.

[11]Sellin's criticism of the legal definition, as we will note later, represents an unsuccessful and incomplete attempt to question this definition on the basis of the autonomy of science.

B. What Is Precision? Or. . . "Is There a Lawyer in the House?"

In light of the variation in types of scientific definitions, it is difficult to comprehend from a scientific point of view what is meant when lawyers or sociologists claim that the legal definition of crime is the only "precise" or appropriately "technical" term available for defining crime.[12] What definitional usage is being referred to? If crime is to be defined in terms of its causal relationships, then it is important to reiterate that these real definitions which may consist of such abbreviated terms as "anomie" or "maladjustment" are actually theories of crime or criminals. The notion of "precision" in relation to this kind of definition has little meaning because in a causal inquiry, sensitizing concepts and hypothetical constructs[13] are not only permissible but are often absolutely necessary for achievement of explanations with high systematic (theoretical) import.

Legal scholars may agree on the importance of standardizing a *single* legal definition for every type of crime and criminal, but it can be flatly stated that the standardization of causal defini-

tions in this manner would destroy the free marketplace of scientific ideas and the ability of scientists to advance the state of knowledge in the field.[14]

C. Are the Legalists Referring to Precise, Operational Definitions?

For purposes of scientific inquiry, the legal definition is a curious formulation which mixes normative, descriptive and operational meanings without regard to their very different functions. But the plain fact is that even if we differentiated these meanings and employed them separately, they would still be inadequate for scientific purposes. To illustrate this, let us assume, for example, that legalists are actually talking about the use of the legal definition for operational purposes when they insist on its "precise" characteristics.[15] If used for operational purposes, then the key meaning of the legal definition would be the stipulation that administrative rules (i.e. procedural law), supply the procedures by which the amount of crime is to be measured. It should be noted that the only possible measurements which are permitted by these rules take the form of official enumerations of adjudicated cases. When criminologists derive their statistical rates from these enumerations, they operationalize criminal behavior in the *only way made possible by the law.*

Although the legality of a proposed definition of crime may be determined by a majority in a parliamentary situation (and, therefore, as we shall see later, subsuming the activity of social scientists under the prevailing dominant ideology), operational definitions cannot be con-

---

[12]Michael and Adler (1932:22) stated "The most *precise* and least ambiguous definition of crime is that which defines it as behavior which is prohibited by the criminal code" (our emphasis). Tappan also used the term precision in criticizing definitions of crime not grounded in the criminal law. In 1967, Leonard Savitz (1967:46–47) indicated that "if the defendant is not convicted, or the conviction is not upheld by appellate courts, he is not a criminal." Savitz added that "it is disconcerting to note that often, even in serious research projects, the terms crime and criminals are used with considerable lack of *precision*. It seems to be often assumed that anyone who is arrested is necessarily a criminal. As these are basic concepts upon which the field of criminology is based, such casual indifference is somewhat difficult to understand" (our emphasis).

[13]These sensitizing concepts and hypothetical constructs appear vague because their meanings often vary depending upon the usages to which they are put by different theorists and researchers. Furthermore, these categories are often reformulated in light of additional knowledge. But this very property of impermanence, and the rich connotations which are characteristic of these ideas, make them useful to scientists interested in the discovery of heretofore unknown empirical relationships. The fact that there are a number of these definitions at any one time cannot be taken as a sign of the inability of scientists to formulate "precise" notions of criminal behavior.

[14]If Tappan's insistence that scientists use the legal definition instead of their own causal definitions is pushed to its logical limit, then it means that no other definitions of crime are warranted. The insistence, for example, means that there should exist no competing causal definitions of crime in general or of any type of criminal behavior.

[15]For example, Michael and Adler state (1932:23), "However inadequate conviction of crime may be as a test of criminality, in no other way can criminality be established with sufficient certainty for either practical or scientific purposes. The criminologist is therefore quite justified in making the convict population the subject of his studies, as he does." This reference obviously utilizes the legal definition to operationally define criminals.

sidered appropriate by a majority vote from an empiricist's point of view. Instead, standards based on the concepts of scientific reliability and validity are used to evaluate their worthiness. On the basis of these standards, social scientists have for decades[16] criticized the use of officially adjudicated data as invalid and unreliable measures of criminal behavior. As a result, some research scientists have, in practice, abandoned the operative meanings contained in the legalistic definitions of crime irrespective of their own explicit commitments to these definitions. Even the substantive contents of these categories, which are stipulated in the legal code, are not used in the operational definitions in present practice. All that remains of legalistic definitions is the *formal* acquiescence, on the part of researchers, to such conceptual categories as robbery, rape or homicide.[17]

D. Political Power as a Determinant of Precision

Recent works on "crimes without victims" (Schur, 1965) or "crimes of consumption" (Glaser, 1970:138) are good indicators of the considerable disagreement regarding *ethical* standards to be used in the definition of crime and criminals. (These standards are usually subsumed under such categories as "social injury.") As an outcome, in practice, administrative procedures and sanctions preempt "social injury" by default. In comparison with this ethical category, these standards are allegedly *relatively* more precise because they are operationally more reliable. (At least scholars *know* what is meant by the terms procedures and sanctions, but there may exist little understanding of "social injury.") But even though this is undoubtedly the case, it should not obscure the fact that the degree of linguistic precision (i.e. social determinacy and usage) of the meanings of "procedures" and "sanctions" in this case, is actually dependent upon political processes. Ultimately, legal definitions assume certain political conditions for optimum operational precision. These conditions can be *best* fulfilled by a *totally* controlled society such as Orwell's "Oceania" in *1984.* The "reliability" of the measurements or descriptive relationships which are directly or indirectly defined by reference to administrative procedures and sanctions is dependent upon administrative purpose and expertise; but the completeness of its execution is dependent on political power. This is why it can be assumed that with regard to the legal definition: political power determines the precision of the definition and the measurement of the phenomena.

E. The Real Definitions of Legal Definitions and Legal Definitions as Real Definitions

Toward the beginning of criminology textbooks, a legalistic-nominal definition is usually offered. In this statement the authors single out certain ethical properties of criminal behavior and/or limit themselves to consideration of the relationships between criminal behavior and sanctioning agencies. Although these nominal definitions are sometimes treated as real or causal definitions, there are a number of reasons why they are merely nominal. Behavior which is legally defined as crime, according to the views of most persons trained in an empiricist tradition, had existed *before* its legal definition was formulated.[18] The *behavior*[19] can, therefore, be justifiably regarded as a determinant and as such, it is not the law which determines crime,

---

[16]In recent years, in particular, criminologists engaged in delinquency research have begun to systematically reject the use of official data altogether as measures of the actual distribution of delinquency in a community. By constructing measures of delinquency other than those prescribed by criminal law, they have suggested that the official, political procedures are invalid for scientific purposes (Cicourel, 1968; Nye, Short, and Olsen, 1958; Dentler and Monroe, 1961; Empey and Erickson, 1966; Gold, 1966).

[17]As an illustration of this discrepancy between formal and substantive contents, compare the instructions on any self-report deliquency questionnaire with the substantive contents of the statutes defining these same offenses in the criminal law.

---

[18]Although not sufficient, the behavior is obviously necessary for the existence of the social processes which lead to a definition of crime.

[19]Even with the possibility that "labeling" theories of crime (Werthman, 1969; Becker, 1963; Kitsuse, 1963) are proven valid for some types of crime, it is doubtful that most crimes will ever be explained on this basis. (This point will be expanded in our forthcoming book tentatively entitled, *Ideology and Adolescence.*)

but *crime which determines the law.*[20] In light of this, it is again highly misleading to use legalistic definitions (which refer, for example, to sanctions) as real definitions, in spite of the fact that sanctioning processes feed back and influence this behavior over time.

Sociologists are explicating and redefining the legal definition for purposes that are quite foreign to its original, legalistic usage. One reason for this is that, once formed, legally established sanctioning processes do influence criminal behavior. And the nature of this influence is being inquired into by sociologists today. The reworking of the definition is necessary because complex, and often discretionary, operational processes, which influence ongoing characteristics of criminal behavior, are very inadequately symbolized in the original legal statement.[21]

Are legal definitions real, i.e. causal definitions? In the process of ascertaining the effects of the institutions of criminal justice on criminals, it has become imperative to differentiate criminals who have been sanctioned by law from those who have avoided sanctions. But this is not the only reason why this differentiation is important. The certain knowledge that there are vast numbers of criminals "at large" has long generated serious questions about the adequacy of those theories which have only been confirmed by the use of official statistics. In light of this, scientists are fully justified in rejecting the logic of the argument that a criminal's status can only be defined legalistically. They are justified in viewing this matter as an *empirical* question in order to settle outstanding issues in their field. In the view of these scientists, the efficacy of calling "criminal" those who have acted as such but

who have not been adjudicated and found guilty of their violations can be substantiated by empirical test. Canons of logic cannot be substituted for empirical criteria in making this assessment.[22]

Criminologists interested in the study of the *institutions of criminal justice* often use the notion of sanction to define crime. This notion is particularly plausible as a defining criterion because it is easily related to everyday experiences. One illustration of this is Austin T. Turk's explication of "the sanctioning process" as "generic"[23] to the word *criminal.* Turk (1969:22) indicates that the sanctioning process is observed when "Somebody asserts a right-wrong; someone fails to conform; and some mode of coercion is used in the course of defining a violator and depriving him of something, even if it is little more than a few minutes spent in sending a lawyer to bat." It is suggested here, however, that if social scientists are interested in real definitions of the institutions of criminal justice, that they organize their defining criteria with reference to a *general theory* of the State (particularly in capitalist and socialist societies) rather than simple properties of microscopic and often contractually governed interpersonal relationships.

In constructing real definitions of the causes or control of crime, therefore, there is no absolute

---

[20]The determining relation between crime and the law has been noted by many criminologists, including, for example, H. Bianchi (1956:97), and it is particularly apparent in the analysis of "white collar crime."

[21]Again we note the irony in Tappan's remarks to the effect that his orientation is an "objective" one, and that sociologists are engaged in some sort of immoral or subversive enterprise when they do not use the traditional legal definition of crime. It is now a matter of record that modern research in delinquency (which is not dependent on official statistics) has produced clear evidence of class and racial bias in the administration of the law. It is curious how morally appropriate these "immoral" sociologists can be.

[22]From this empiricist point of view, the legal argument that criminal status is, by definition, necessarily determined by the criminal justice system leads to an empirically *unfalsifiable* corollary. It logically implies that *all* persons who actually violate a statute but are not adjudicated by these institutions are *not* criminals. (Such persons include, for example, those who have committed unsolved crimes.) This corollary, however, is scientifically unacceptable because its truth value is determined solely on logical grounds. If a scientific definition is meant to signify relations in the real world, there must be some empirical criteria by which it can be ultimately evaluated. In order to utilize these criteria, the definition of criminal behavior itself must be formulated so that it can be empirically tested. This formulation, it is argued, cannot be made without operationally defining criminal behavior *independently* of legal sanctions or procedures which are commonly used to identify crime.

[23]Turk (1969:22) states, "Thus, anyone who is defined officially as a violator. . .is criminal in the *generic* sense, whatever he may be called in accord with the terminologies and assumptions currently in vogue. That there are differences in the ways in which authorities perceive and process violators does not negate the fact that . . . our observations are of the *sanctioning processes*" (our emphasis).

necessity for utilizing the notion of sanction as a defining criterion. In light of this, a general definition which identifies crime as behavior which is sanctioned by the State is highly misleading. Just as misleading, however, is the notion that sanction is intrinsically necessary for *any* type of scientific definition of crime.

F. Are Sanctions Generic?

As we have quoted, neither positivistic nor legalistic arguments can provide adequate explanations for the existence of a generally accepted notion that sanction is generic for defining crime. This notion, as we have seen, is certainly not necessary for scientific operational definitions of criminals. Nor is it necessarily essential to real definitions. It may be useful for defining particular kinds of relationships between the criminal and the State but there are undoubtedly instances where sanctions are an incidental aspect of this relationship. If we think in terms of the general relationship between the State and crime, rather than the State and the individual criminal, sanctions may be even less significant than other kinds of relationships. To some extent this fact has been obscured by the unanalyzed, metaphorical use of the term sanction to symbolize the extremely complex relationships between crime and the State.

Regardless of this unsubstantiated claim, authors of most textbook definitions identify crime by singling out sanctioning processes. To argue that crime must be defined in terms of sanction, however, is to insist that sanctions are absolutely necessary for understanding, predicting, preventing and/or controlling crime. Studies in the sociology of law and criminal behavior indicate that this necessity may exist in some cases,[24] but it has never been demonstrated that it holds as a general rule.

Humanistic scholars, including scientists and nonscientists, have been tantalized by the possibility that behavior which is injurious to the

great majority of persons in society can be prevented or controlled by means other than punishment of individuals. Psychologists and psychiatrists have asked whether there are other reeducative or rehabilitative procedures which can replace sanctioning processes as we have traditionally come to understand them. Sociologists, from their perspective, have asked whether the radical restructuring of social institutions or systems can eliminate crime more effectively and fairly than traditional and repressive forms of social control. Whatever one may think of the efficacy of any one specific proposal in this respect, it is quite clear that most run counter to the legislative definitions regarding the treatment of crime. They, more often than not, also contradict standards which legislators currently employ in defining criminal behavior. By contending that sanctions are generic to the definition of crime, legalists discourage the possibility of viewing crime from very different points of view and limit the definitions of crime to those established by the current occupants of the houses of political power. Political power, as we have seen, makes procedural criteria allegedly more "precise" for scientific purposes than ethical criteria. As a parallel to this, power also seems to make sanctions generic to the definition of crime.

The differentiation of the empirical properties of social relationships is strongly dependent upon the theoretical intentions of the social scientist. Because of this, it can be said that just as the knowledge of the empirical properties of social phenomena does *not* arise (as Sellin contends) "intrinsically from the nature of the subject matter," sanctioning processes are not more intrinsic to the definition of crime than any other possible relationship. This does not mean that sanctions are extraneous to all theoretical purposes. *This will always depend upon the theoretical perspective involved.*

G. The Critical Role of Ethical Criteria in Relation to Sanctions

Sellin was concerned with developing a general strategy for explaining crime while Sutherland was interested in explaining a par-

---

[24]An outstanding example of the determining relationship between the law and crime includes the development of criminal syndicates involved in the illegal production and sale of alcoholic beverages during the prohibition era. Today a similar relationship exists with respect to narcotics.

ticular type of crime (i.e. white collar crime). When Sellin's proposals in the controversy over the definition of crime are compared with Sutherland's, therefore, it can be shown that the differences between these scholars are due less to their general orientation than to their different purposes; they were concerned with problems on disparate levels of specificity. In other writings, Sutherland did propose a general, "normative conflict"[25] theory of crime, which was derived from the same metatheoretical assumptions underlying Sellin's "culture conflict" theory. The similarities in orientation between these scholars also become salient when it is realized that Sutherland was not alone in singling out sanctions as an essential feature of the phenomena he was interested in. Sellin, it is true, was concerned with more inclusive normative phenomena than legally codified norms, but in turning his attention to the concrete problem of comparing legal and nonlegal norms, he suggested that the degree of *sanction* be used as a *universal* standard of comparison (1938:23–45).

Perhaps the most revealing part of the controversy about the legal definition is the degree to which theoretical sociologists like Sellin and Sutherland avoided the confrontation with standards which could have been used in fully evaluating *the moral justifications* of legal codes. Even Sutherland, who did most to question the justification for the separation between civil and criminal codes, went to great pains to show that his interpretation of white collar crime was in *accord* with established legal precedents. However, if ruling classes and powerful interest groups are able to manipulate legislators to their own advantage, isn't it possible that there are instances of socially injurious behavior which have no legal precedents? Consider further the chance that there are practices by men of power which are highly injurious to most of mankind and which are neither defined nor sanctioned by civil or criminal laws, such as, for example, genocide and economic exploitation. Isn't it apparent, if Sutherland had consistently explored the use of ethical categories like social injury, that he would

have concluded that there are, on one hand, socially non-injurious acts which are defined as crimes and, on the other, socially injurious acts which are nevertheless not defined as either civil or criminal violations?

It is in relation to these logical possibilities that the ideological function of legal sanctions (as a defining criterion) is fully exposed. If the *ethical* criteria of "social injury," "public wrong," or "antisocial behavior" are not explicated, then the existent *ethical standpoint of the State is taken as a given* when the criterion of sanctions by the State is also used in the definitions of crime. This is why the meanings of such categories as social injury are so critical for the definition of crime.

In light of this, it can be concluded that, in the controversy over the definition of crime, the only argument which transcended the State was ostensibly value-free,[26] while, in addition, the only argument which admitted moral criteria, considered these criteria applicable solely if they were embodied in the law. What explains the extreme selectivity which is manifest in the controversy over the definition of crime? Why hasn't any American sociologist proposed that these definitions of crime are *not* the only possible definitions? The answers to these questions and those raised at the conclusion of the previous section will be suggested in the form of a very terse review of the historical development of the *ideological* perspective which has unduly dampened the controversy over the legal definition of crime.

III. IDEOLOGICAL ASPECTS OF THE CONTROVERSY OVER THE DEFINITION OF CRIME

A. Ideological Influences on the Usage of Categories

It can be readily understood that, in the desire to examine and utilize apparently more precise categories, scholars might overlook the degree to which their own scientific behavior is deter-

---

[25]The term "differential social organization" was also used to refer to this general theory of crime (Cressey, 1960).

[26]The concept of "value-free" sociology has been under sharp attack in recent years. For references to this controversy, see John Horton (1966) and Alvin Gouldner (1968).

mined by the same political conditions which gave rise to legal definitions in use. But this is insufficient for explaining why conventional political categories have succeeded in superseding all other ethical, as well as professional, criteria for defining the nature of crime. Nor can inertia supply the reason for the supremacy of conventional political standards. These political standards are more than an encroachment on the autonomy of science. They are also in contradiction to the truly scientific and humanistic mandate that it is not the professional's function to be a mere technician who complies, wittingly or unwittingly, with established authorities. According to this mandate every professional is morally responsible for his own actions: this responsibility can not be justifiably delegated to agents of the State.

B. Corporate Liberalism and Metatheoretical Categories

Are non-legal definitions of crime currently in use among sociologists? At one point in his argument, Sellin (1938:8) declared that "Innumerable definitions of crime have been offered which if not read *in their context* would appear to go beyond the legal definition. Upon examination, however, almost all of them prove to be the legal norms clothed in sociological language" (our emphasis). This observation is as accurate and observable today[27] as it was in 1937. Less clear, however, is the degree to which highly formal and nominal definitions of crime have per-

sisted even in cases where scholars have explicitly repudiated their use.

American sociology abounds in formal and nominalist categories which are metatheoretical in nature. It is often not realized that the most influential categories of this type have been generated only after scholars have reflected on the meanings of previous theoretical works and singled out properties or relationships which seem to have been used time and time again by different theorists. Therefore, although these properties or relationships are nominally defined, they are not to be considered arbitrary distinctions. Instead, they refer, indirectly, to the theories of human behavior which have claimed the attention of sociological interest for some time. Such categories as "conduct norms" or "normative conflict" are the outcomes of this process. For purposes of analysis they can be termed "metatheoretical categories" because they are derived by abstracting relationships designated by theories.[28]

The metatheoretical categories which maintain legalistic definitions of crime were generated during the formative years of sociology. Works which mark the beginning and end of this period were Lester Ward's *Dynamic Sociology* (1883) and William F. Ogburn's *Social Change* (1922). During this time, traditional liberal assumptions as to the nature of man and society were substantially altered by leading scholars, not only in sociology and criminology but in every other discipline and professional field. As a consequence, a new variant of the liberal ideology, corporate liberalism, came into being.[29] In sociology, the leading American scholars[30] in-

---

[27]In 1968, for example, Irving L. Horowitz and Martin Liebowitz (1968:282) offered this "radical" definition of deviancy: "Deviancy is a conflict between at least two parties: *superordinates* who make and *enforce* rules, and subordinates whose behavior violates these rules" (our emphasis). The authors indicate that their definition is based on a "conflict model." When the context of this definition is examined, it is found that, in most cases, the authors refer to behavior defined by law, involving prostitutes, homosexuals, drug addicts, illegal forms of civil disobedience, etc. The "superordinates" in this case are therefore agents of the State and the reference to rule enforcement involves State sanctions. Finally, when the principles underlying Horowitz and Liebowitz's "conflict model" are examined, they turn out to be old fashioned, pluralist principles regarding the nature of social conflict and conflict resolution.

[28]The prefix, *meta,* in this case symbolizes a process of abstracting relationships contained in theories. (The outcome of this process is a collection of formal categories, axioms and mechanisms which may or may not be systematically related in a general orientation or strategy of theory construction in specific types of inquiry.) The suffix, *theory,* indicates that the object of study is not the real world but theories of that world.

[29]European scholars were also involved in this task, including Emile Durkheim and Sigmund Freud.

[30]For discussions of the complex relations between the development of corporate liberalism and the social, political and economic changes during the period, see, for example, Williams (1961), Kolko (1963), and Weinstein (1968).

volved in the modern reconstruction of liberalism included besides the above mentioned, Albion Small, Frank Giddings, Edward A. Ross, W. I. Thomas, Robert E. Park and Ernest W. Burgess, among others.

Particularly after the publication of a series of essays by Ross beginning in 1895,[31] scholars urged the study of every conceivable type of social relationship from within the framework of a liberal functionalist metatheory of *social control.* These essays accelerated an intellectual development which culminated in the systematic combination of corporate liberal concepts of social control with those derived from the classical liberal notion of the harmony of interests.[32] This combination was utilized in order to solve what sociologists call the "problem of social integration" or synonymously, "the problem of *order.*"[33]

In formulating solutions to the problem of integration, American and European scholars were spurred by the extraordinary social instabilities which accompanied the rise of monopoly capitalism. During the last quarter of the nineteenth century, the United States, for example, sporadically experienced sixteen years of depressions and recessions (Mitchell, 1927). From the turn of the century until the First World War, the United States was still economically unstable (Kolko, 1967); it was characterized by extensive immigration and rapid industrial change. There was no diminution of industrial violence (Adamic, 1931), and the very foundations of American capitalism appeared to be threatened by the emergence of progressive movements, labor unions and socialist parties (Weinstein, 1968). Some, but not all members of these movements, were also militantly opposed to the new and aggressive foreign policies which were instituted by the American government (Preston, 1963). These policies vigorously supported the penetration of economic markets overseas with every means possible including armed forces (Williams, 1961).

American sociologists from Ward onwards utilized their theoretical ideas to criticize socialist doctrines, as well as the "effete minds" (i.e. intellectuals)[34] who opposed American imperialist wars. They also attacked the laissez-faire capitalist ("the Robber Barons") and the older laissez-faire liberal theorists like Herbert Spencer, because they opposed political regulation of the economy. The new liberal sociologists proposed that the State should actively rationalize and stabilize the economy. This proposal was substantiated by their new conceptions of man and society. These conceptions admitted the existence of "the perpetual clash of interest groups" but suggested ways of stabilizing and restraining this conflict. The expanded powers of the State, it was claimed, would enable it to perform an effective role in reconciling or regulating conflicts between "interest groups" within the framework of capitalism.

The American scholars also turned their attention toward ways of maintaining established institutions such as the family. In the process, they developed theories and metatheories focusing on solutions to the problem of integration from their new ideological point of view. In time, their efforts produced categories and generalizations which led directly to the modern liberal functionalist orientations called pluralism and structural-functionalism.

Space limitations preclude an adequate discussion of these general developments or consid-

---

[31]These essays appeared later in a single volume entitled *Social Control* (1901).

[32]For an extended discussion of corporate liberal concepts of social control, see the forthcoming work, tentatively entitled, *Sociology: The Formative Years: 1883-1922* by the Schwendingers, Herman and Julia.

[33]Scholars grapple with this problem when they are concerned with explaining the persistent features of social systems. How do social systems remain stable? What is at stake in achieving a stable social order in the midst of great conflicts or accelerated change? These are the kinds of questions which pose the problem of integration.

[34]Long before Vice President Spiro Agnew's reference to "effete snobs," Ward (1903:240) stated that most "peace agitation is characterized by total blindness to all the broader cosmic factors and principles and this explains its complete impotence." Identifying individuals who agitate for peace as "effete minds" he noted that "it is the mark of the effete mind to exaggerate small things while ignoring great things" and reminiscent of contemporary references to "silent majorities," he added, "the crude instincts of the general public" are far safer guides to the evaluation of war than "maudlin sentimentality and . . . certain minds which, from culture or advantage, gain the credit of constituting the cream of the most advanced intelligence."

eration of the role they played in contributing to Sellin's interpretation of the concept of norms. It can be demonstrated, however, that his concept was derived from a very general functionalist orientation which implicitly assumed that certain "optimum" social relationships were functionally imperative to the associated life of man. These relationships were called "natural" or "normal" states. And the functional prerequisites for these states were utilized as criteria for evaluating all behavior which was considered inimical to optimum functioning (i.e. a gradually changing but stable order). In theory, these prerequisites were usually hypostatized as "norms"; and unnatural or *abnormal* conduct was perceived as a *normative* departure or deviation from "normative expectations."[35] Within this general perspective, normal societies were actually depicted as being repressive. They repressed and channeled the anarchic, egotistic tendencies allegedly inherent in the nature of man by the "judicious" application of rewards and sanctions.

C. Technocratic Doctrines

Side by side with the development of basic corporate liberal orientations, the early American sociologists also professed and greatly elaborated the *technocratic doctrines* which were expressed in rudimentary form by Henri Saint-Simon.[36] These doctrines can be regarded as an independent system of ideas[37] but they were developed in conjunction with an intellectual tradition which can be called "liberal syndicalism."[38]

Basic to the definition of technology is the vision of a society managed not by common people but by experts or enlightened leaders who are highly informed by expert advisors.[39] Another hallmark of technocratic doctrine is the implicit use of the norms of established institutions as standards for identifying "abnormal," "pathological," or "deviant" behavior. A further indicator of the use of technocratic doctrines is the contention that sociologists are involved in a *value-free* or ideologically neutral enterprise in the very shadow of their simultaneous subscription to established norms.[40]

What was the state of criminology almost two decades after the formative period? At the time when Sellin challenged the legal definition of crime, sociology had long been rooted in corporate liberal theories of human relationships. In addition, crime was perceived as but one instance of the structural relationships within the larger and more general culture. Criminal personalities were seen as little more than simple homologues of these social relationships.[41] Solutions to the problem of integration also encompassed the concepts of criminal behavior.

---

[35]Sellin (1938:6) states, for example, "It would seem best, in order to avoid misunderstanding to speak . . . of normal and abnormal conduct, i.e. conduct in accord with or deviating from a conduct norm."

[36]American sociologists have generally mistakenly attributed the origins of technocracy and positivism to Comte. Although Comte insisted on the originality of his conceptions, most of them were plagiarized from Saint-Simon. In addition, technocratic doctrines were developed further by the disciples of Saint-Simon, such as Bazard, Laurent and Engantin (who were called the Saint-Simonians); although as Georg Iggers (1958) points out, these doctrines were made subservient to theocratic standards and principles.

[37]The independence of technocratic doctrines from corporate liberalism is testified by the fact that socialist scholars have also subscribed to them.

[38]In the United States, corporate liberal syndicalists included Small and Weatherly. In Europe, De Greef, Tarde and Durkheim were numbered along the outstanding liberal syndicalists. It is important to note that this type of syndicalist thought is most responsible for the later development of modern pluralism. For a discussion of some of the salient characteristics of this form of syndicalist thought, see Williams' (1961:356–60, 384–86) description of the development of "American syndicalism."

[39]For a classic criticism of this approach, see Mills (1942) and Mills (1959: 84–99).

[40]Although Ward insisted on the doctrine of a value-free social science as early as 1883 (and symbolized this in his distinction between "pure" and "applied" sociology in a two volume work in 1903), it was not until the early twenties that this doctrine took firm hold among the Americans. At that time, the scholarly academics opposing this doctrine were chiefy represented by the "Christian sociologists." Their influence on the way in which professionals defined the field disappeared after President Wilson's administration.

[41]In this view, the "abnormal" conditions which produced criminal behavior and criminals were, on the level of social relationships, culture *conflict* and social *disorganization;* on the level of personality relationships: personal *conflict* and personality *disorganization* (Blumer, 1937).

These stressed the creation and maintenance of normative consensus. (Conflict was to be minimized, reconciled, or regulated; consensus was to be maximized because of its role as a functional imperative to the maintenance of a stable and socially integrated order.) Conflict and disorganization! These key words signified the preconditions for crime. Consensus, harmony and equilibrium! These terms referred to stability and order.

D. Value-Free Sociology

In light of these developments it is possible to understand the essence of Sellin's seemingly radical proposal, as well as his *complementary,* rather than contradictory, relation with Sutherland's legalistic position. Sellin proposed, in essence, that the organizing principles for examining and explaining the nature of criminal behavior be derived from the highly general propositions and categories which were being used by sociologists at the time. By proposing that the concept ''conduct norm'' be used instead of the legal definition, Sellin was simply advising sociologists that they would not get far with the highly descriptive contents of the legal definitions. If they wanted to explain crime, the notion of conduct norms was a key to unlocking a whole stockpile of axioms, mechanisms and categories derived from the theories which corporate liberal scholars had found useful for solving the problem of integration.

Armed with this strategy, Sellin did *not* advocate the elimination of the legal definition. To the contrary, he (1938:367) specifically suggested that this definition be used to indicate *criminal* departures from the conduct norms of ''political groups.'' (These norms, he observed, were different from other norms because they are legally codified.) But Sellin also suggested that the scientific explanation of these departures would have to take into account theoretical concepts which emerged from the study of both legal *and* non-legal norms. He proposed further that, since the relation between the criminal and civil law is ambiguous from this larger point of view, the criminologist's ''concern with *crime norms* and their violations may well be *broadened to include*

legal conduct norms embodied in *the civil law''* (1938:39). Thus, even though Sellin began his journey from a more abstract starting point, he arrived at the same destination as Sutherland.[42] This is not surprising, considering that both scholars were using similar metatheoretical assumptions in approaching the subject of criminal behavior.

At bottom, therefore, Sellin's argument reinforced rather than challenged the broader legalistic approach which had been developed by Sutherland. It did not challenge this approach because it was woven from the same corporate liberal and technocratic ideologies which had emerged among the founders of American sociology. These founders constructed a view of the world which was of service to the new corporate liberal state and implicitly justified the use of criteria which favored the maintenance of established institutions. In the metatheory of social control, departures from norms of established institutions were ''abnormal'' and conducive to social instability. Normative sanctions, therefore, were considered an important mode of social integration. Individual behavior had to be controlled by these sanctions if the established institutions were to survive.

Guided by the metatheory of social control, many American criminologists functioned as technocratic ''consultants'' who spent their lives gathering information which would be of use to the men who managed existing institutions, whether they were aware of this or not. The profession of ideological neutrality on their part was by no means a guarantee of this neutrality. Instead, it was one of the great myths which prevented principled scholars from being aware of the ideological character of their basic theoretical assumptions.[43]

---

[42]The differences between Sellin and Sutherland disappear altogether when Sutherland considers the definition of the ''nature of crime from a *social* point of view'' (our emphasis). In the discussion of the ''social'' nature of crime, Sutherland (1960:14–15) uses three criteria to distinguish crime: 1) values of a political group, 2) isolation or culture conflict, and 3) sanctions. If the term ''conduct norms'' was substituted for ''values'' then this interpretation would be identical with Sellin's.

[43]To a great extent, the ostensibly value-free character of criminology in the United States is derived from the fact that

IV. A MODERN HUMANISTIC ALTERNATIVE

Because of space limitations, the final section of this paper will not attempt a definitive alternative to the legal definition. Instead, there will be suggested, in desperate brevity, what is hoped will be useful points of departure for those interested in exploring new approaches to this problem. It is felt that this discussion will have served a useful purpose if it stimulates the development of a number of alternative approaches at this time,[44] when so many received doctrines are being called into question.[45]

---

it developed historically under the aegis of sociology rather than law (as was the case in Europe). It is interesting to note in passing, however, that Tappan's argument supported a definition of crime which was actually posed by Michael and Adler, who edited a 1932 report by a committee under the auspices of the School of Law of Columbia University on the feasibility of an Institute of Criminology and Criminal Justice. Sutherland and Sellin were members of the committee's staff, and obviously objected to the narrowly stated legal definition of crime in the report. Their objections, emerging in 1937 and 1940, as noted, reflected a broader sociological approach to the statement.

[44]There are scholars today who analyze legally defined relationships from a socially critical standpoint. It is not the purpose of this section to deny their humanitarian outlook. The logic of our previous argument, however, suggests that the humanistic content of their theories are not derived from their use of a value-free methodological perspective nor the use of a legal definition "in-itself." Instead, the humanistic content is derived from a concept of rights which tacitly regulates their scholarly activity. Because of this, it is felt that a definition of crime which is squarely based on conceptions of human rights will make explicit what is now inchoate, inconsistent and implicit. The charge will be made that our alternative to the legal definition will "taint" the objective, scholarly character of criminology by bringing each scholar's political biases to the fore. The answer to this objection, is that a scrupulous inspection of theories in the field will indicate that the individual ideological biases have always existed although the mystique of a value-free methodology has obscured their inexorable influence.

[45]One cannot overestimate the degree to which even doctrinnaire interpretations of the more humanitarian legal definitions of crime, which were originally extended as a result of the Second World War, are being rejected as a result of contemporary events. One example is the insistence of George Wald (Nobel Laureate in Physiology and Medicine) that the directors and managers of the Dow Chemical Corporation be held responsible for participating in a "crime against humanity" by their production of napalm. A similar case against Dow is made with regard to herbicides and defoliants. (Wald, 1970)

A. Moral Criteria for Definitions of Crime

No scholar involved in the controversy about the definitions of crime has been able to avoid direct or indirect use of moral standards in a solution to this problem. In spite of this, the choices of defining criteria have been accompanied by a technocratic incapacity to confront the moral implications of this selection. It is not clear, for example, that the acceptance of procedural law as a defining criterion delegates personal responsibility to agents of the State. But this delegation is no less a moral act and therefore cannot avoid complicity in the actual definitions made by official agents. Just as moral is the explicit use of sanctions or the implicit use of other defining criteria,[46] derived from functional imperatives of established institutions or political economies. In light of this, the claim that value judgments have no place in the formulation of the definition of crime is without foundation.

An alternative solution to the definition of crime should openly face the moral issues presented by this definitional dilemma. Traditionally, these issues have been inadequately represented by such unanalyzed terms as "social injury," "anti-social act," or "public wrongs." But how does one confront the problem of explicating "social injury" or "public wrongs"? Is this done by reference to the functional imperatives of social institutions or by the historically determined rights of individuals? In our opinion, the latter is the only humanistic criterion which can be used for this purpose.

There has been an expansion of the concept of human rights throughout history. And political events have made it possible, at this time, to insist on the inclusion of standards clustered around modern egalitarian principles, as well as enduring standards such as the right to be secure in one's own person, the right to speak one's mind, and the right to assemble freely. We refer to these ideas as modern because they are to be

---

[46]These other criteria usually define crime as a departure from "normal" states, which may be vaguely signified by such exceedingly formal terms as "the mores," "the group," "the political group," "superordinates," "the public," or "society."

distinguished from those fashioned in the eighteenth century when a rising middle class formulated a challenge to the economic prerogatives of feudal aristocracies. At that time, the functional imperatives of the patriarchal family, price-making market, and political state were reified, by recourse to natural law, as basic human needs. In this reified form, equality was primarily perceived as the immutable right to compete *equally* with others for a position in social, economic and political spheres of life. In the context of our modern political and economic institutions, however, competitive equality has not had, as an empirical outcome, the furtherance of human equality. Instead, it has been used to justify inequalities between the sexes, classes, races and nations.

Life in industrialized nations over the last two hundred years has clearly indicated that rhetoric regarding the equality of opportunities cannot preserve the spirit of the egalitarian credo. Nor can liberalism, the ideology which, above all others, has laid claim to the concept of equality of opportunity, be used in defense of egalitarianism. Liberalism is, at bottom, a highly elitist ideology. It has justifed and helped perpetuate social inequality in the name of equality. It was in the name of free competition and laissez-faire liberalism, for example, that Western nations converted the people and natural resources in South America, Asia and Africa into sources of cheap labor and raw materials during the nineteenth and twentieth centuries.[47] Because of the use of the concept of equality of opportunity by liberals, ostensibly egalitarian notions cannot be taken for granted. They must be subjected to careful scrutiny.

When the concept of equality of opportunity is analyzed, it is found that it does not refer to egalitarian principles at all. Instead, it refers to principles of equity or fairness which should govern the ways in which social *inequality* is instituted in our society. In its most defensible form it stipulates that meritarian standards rather than lineage, race or other "natural" criteria should regulate the unequal distribution of the goods of life. But there is no society on the face of this earth which actually distributes the goods of life on the basis of differences in *natural* talents of individuals. The differences which actually determine the distribution of rewards are for the most part socially determined. As a consequence, even in democratic societies, the notion of equality of opportunity serves more as a justification for gross inequalities established on the basis of class, race, sex, ethnicity and other grounds. Within the framework of liberalism, moreover, equality of opportunity is merely one among many standards which justifies an elitist morality. This morality can rightfully claim that each individual should be treated equally, but in practice, some preferred criterion is always inserted to guarantee that some men are treated more equally than others.[48]

In opposition to the ever increasing demand for equalitarianism, elitist social scientists have formulated theoretical justifications for social inequality.[49] We deny the ethical and empirical validity of these theoretical justifications! Irrespective of claims to the contrary (Warner, 1949; Moore, 1963), there is no universal moral rule or empirical property which is inherent to man or society which makes social inequality a functional necessity. Above all, there is no valid moral or empirical justification for the outstand-

[47]The inequality inherent in the relation between the colonial and colonizer was, and still is, among the most profound of human inequalities. Nevertheless, during the second half of the nineteenth and the beginning of this century, social Darwinism, propounded first and foremost by the famous liberal scholar, Herbert Spencer, was used to justify the subjugation of peoples of color on the grounds that they were genetically inferior; and the exploitation of domestic labor in the name of equality of competition between nations and equality of opportunity between individuals.

[48]As Stanley I. Benn (1967:68) has succinctly stated: "Although the elitist would allow that ordinary men have interests deserving some consideration, the interests of the super-man, super-class, or super-race would always be preferred. Some men, it might be said, are simply worth more than others, in the sense that any claim of theirs, whatever it might be and whatever its specific ground, would always take precedent. Such a morality would maintain that there was some criterion, some qualifying condition of race, sex, intellect, or personality, such that a person once recognized as satisfying it would automatically have prior claim in every field over others."

[49]For a classic debate on this issue, see the discussion between Davis (1953), Moore (1953) and Tumin (1953a, 1953b).

ing forms of social inequality in existence today including economic, racial and sexual inequality. If the traditional egalitarian principle that *all* human beings are to be provided the opportunity for the free development of their potentialities is to be achieved in modern industrial societies, then persons must be regarded as more than objects who are to be "treated equally" by institutions of social control. All persons must be guaranteed the fundamental prerequisites for well-being, including food, shelter, clothing, medical services, challenging work and recreational experiences, as well as security from predatory individuals or repressive and imperialistic social elites. These material requirements, basic services and enjoyable relationships are not to be regarded as rewards or privileges.[50] They are rights!

In formulating a conception of human rights which can be useful to criminologists, it is important to recognize the political *limits* of the ethical doctrine of *equal intrinsic value* when applied to human beings. This doctrine asserts generally that all men are to be regarded not as means but as *ends* in themselves. This doctrine has been found useful by philosophers and other scholars in formulating a logically consistent defense of egalitarian principles which subordinates criteria based on social expedience and utilitarian logic, to those based on some kind of "ultimate," irreducible "natural" equality of men. However, although philosophers of ethics and legal scholars may require logically consistent and persuasive justifications for equality (and common sense may contend that men are born free and equal), the plain fact is that throughout all history, equality has been decisively defended, not on the basis of formal logic but on *political* grounds. Most of the inhabitants of this earth, furthermore, have never been born

free and equal. The achievement of freedom and equality has been won at great cost to individuals and their families.

By delineating the naturally intrinsic qualities of men, philosophers have attempted to transcend the politically controversial issues posed by the abrogation of human rights. Their natural law principles, however, cannot be substituted for a substantive and historically relevant interpretation of human rights which takes into account the political ideals men have, as well as the kinds of social institutions which can nullify or realize these ideals. It is not enough to provide good reasons for the achievement of broader human rights or to catalogue these rights. Criminologists must be able to identify those forms of individuals' behavior and social institutions which should be engaged in order to defend human rights. To defend human rights, criminologists must be able to sufficiently identify the violations of these rights—by whom and against whom; how and why.

This reconstruction of the definition of crime will entail the problem of priorities regarding different rights. This problem may be uniquely posed in varying types of political economies. In the Soviet Union, for example, the right to those basic conditions which allow for the fullest possible democratic participation in political life, such as free speech and asembly, would be given high priority. Likewise, in the United States, the right to economic well-being for all men should be considered crucial. This priority will come into conflict with the prerogatives of governing social classes, economic strata or political elites. But this must be expected by humanistic criminologists. Also to be expected is the opposition from the legal interpreters of crime. If the right to be secure in one's own person is to have greater value than social inequalities based on the ownership of property, for example, then one should be prepared to define the use of deadly force on the part of police officers as unjustifiable homicide when this force is used in defense of property. (This would be the case, for example, were a thief to be slain by an officer while refusing to halt when ordered to do so.) There is no doubt that significant portions of the existing criminal law would overlap with the definition of crime

---

[50]The degree to which the fulfillment of basic human needs is equated with dollars in our society is revealed in the American Medical Association's persistent denial of the right of all persons to medical services. As John H. Knowles (1970:74) states ". . .a significant group of doctors has the attitude as stated by a past AMA president, that health is a privilege, not a right. I think that health is as much a right as the right to schooling or decent housing or food, and the people have begun to perceive it as a right."

on the basis of human rights. But on the other hand, it is also true that many forms of behavior including those now defined as crimes without victims or crimes of consumption would not be defined as crimes within this new perspective.

B. There Are Criminal Social Systems

Perhaps there are no statements more repugnant to traditional legal scholars than those which define social systems as criminal. But this repugnance reflects the antiquarian psychologistic and technocratic character of the legal tradition. This tradition is blind to the fact that extensive social planning makes it possible to evaluate, mitigate or eliminate the *social* conditions which generate criminal behavior. It is no longer sufficient to justify the restriction of criminology to the study of those institutions which define, adjudicate and sanction *individual* criminals. It has become evident that any group which attempts to control or prevent criminal behavior by the activity of the traditional institutions of criminal justice alone is incapable of accomplishing this end.

As a rule, criminal behavior *does* involve individual moral responsibility and the assessment of psychological relationships, such as the motivated character of the criminal act. However, the science of crime has gone beyond the centuries old notion that crime can be conceived as a function of the properties of atomistic individuals alone.[51] Social scientists today are intensely involved in scrutinizing social relationships which generate criminal behavior. This activity is reflected in the *real definitions* of crime which have been and are being developed by sociologists,

economists, anthropologists and political scientists.

The logical strictures on the definition of social systems or relationships as criminal are removed when it is realized that real definitions by social scientists establish a diachronic relationship between the notion of criminal rates, for example, and the *socially* necessary and sufficient conditions for these rates.

If crime is defined by scientists in terms of the *socially* necessary and sufficient conditions for its existence, what would be more logical than to call these social conditions criminal? After all, crime has been traditionally defined by legalists on the basis of nominalist definitions or descriptive definitions which refer to the ways in which agents of the State react to criminal behavior. To be sure, some legalists have used ethical terms such as "public wrongs" or "social injury" in earmarking criminal behavior. But isn't a real definition of crime vastly superior to a nominalist definition or a definition which does not even define crime but merely refers to how the State reacts to it? And isn't a scientist justified in making a logically implied, normative evaluation of what he considers to be the cause of crime? And given the acceptance of criminal institutions and social-economic relationships as real definers of crime, what more ultimate claim can social scientists use to justify their unique role as criminologists, than to use the term crime to identify social systems which can be regulated or eliminated in order to control or prevent crime? What better term than crime can be used to express their *normative* judgments of the conditions which generate criminal behavior?

It can be argued that the term "criminogenic" be used to designate the social conditions which cause crime. But this term obfuscates the main point being made here; namely, that the *social conditions* themselves must become the *object* of social policy and that it is not an individual or a loose collection of atomistic individuals which is to be controlled, but rather the social relationships between individuals which give rise to criminal behavior. (Even if we put everybody involved in criminal behavior at any one time behind bars, there is no guarantee that a new generation of criminals would not emerge given

---

[51]The science of crime has gone beyond this even though the legalists may not have progressed this far. It is vital, however, that legalists be informed that social scientists are not merely interested in isolated criminal acts but in personality relationships, social relationships and systems of social relationships which generate a succession of criminal acts on the part of distinct individuals, on one hand, and socially distributed instances of criminal acts by many individuals on the other hand. The psychiatrist or psychologist, for example, interested in the moral careers of individuals, has moved beyond the empirical issues which were traditionally addressed by legal scholars and which are still reflected in the way in which the criminal law is fashioned today.

the maintenance of social conditions which originally made these individuals criminal.) In this context, the term crime as a label for social systems becomes a warrant, not for controlling atomistic individuals, or preventing an atomistic act, but rather the regulation or elimination of social relationships, properties of social systems, or social systems taken as a whole.

C. Are Imperialistic War, Racism, Sexism and Poverty Crimes?

Once human rights rather than legally operative definitions are used to earmark criminal behavior, then it is possible to ask whether there are violations of human rights which are more basic than others and to designate these rights as most relevant to the domain of criminology.[52] Basic rights are differentiated because their fulfillment is absolutely essential to the realization of a great number of values. Although the lower boundary of this number is not specified here, the sense of what is meant can be ascertained by considering security to one's person as a basic right. Obviously a danger to one's health or life itself endangers all other claims: A dead man can hardly realize *any* of his human potentialities.

Similar assessments can be made of the right to racial, sexual and economic equality. The abrogation of these rights certainly limits the individual's chance to fulfill himself in many spheres of life. These rights therefore are basic because there is so much at stake in their fulfillment. It can be stated, in light of the previous argument, that individuals who deny these rights

to others are criminal. Likewise, social relationships and social systems which regularly cause the abrogation of these rights are also criminal. If the terms imperialism, racism, sexism and poverty are abbreviated signs for theories of social relationships or social systems which cause the systematic abrogation of basic rights, then imperialism, racism, sexism, and poverty can be called crimes according to the logic of our argument.

It is totally irrelevant, in this light, to consider whether leaders of imperialist nations are war criminals by virtue of legal precedent or decisions by war tribunals.[53] Nor is it relevant to make

---

[52]The basic human rights, it should be reiterated, that are not being referred to here are those alleged rights which are intrinsic to the nature of man, or which are functionally imperative for social stability and order. A prime example of the reification of social imperatives is Garafolo's depiction of "natural crimes" on the basis of basic moral sentiments of *pity* (involving empathic feelings) and *probity* (involving respect for rights of private property). These "basic moral sentiments" are functionally necessary for the maintenance of "modern societies." Garafolo's theory was in the *reform* Darwinist tradition initiated by early corporate liberals. This tradition was used to justify the expansion of the political power of the State in order to regulate the uncontrolled competitive processes represented by laissez-faire capitalism.

[53]It is rather incredible to find sociologists publishing what appear to be poorly written legal briefs criticizing the war in Indo-China. We suggest that they spend their time explaining the imperialist nature of this war and leave the legal criticisms to lawyers who also recognize the unjust character of the war. Generally, sociologists have used legalistic justifications where the status of the behavior in question is equivocally defined from the standpoint of the criminal law and, in practice, are usually concerned with the analysis of business and political crimes. But certain assumptions underly this legalistic mode of justifying the definition of behavior as criminal. For example, when to call genocide a crime is justified on the basis of legal precedents, it is assumed that agreements arising out of a contractual relationship, "freely" entered into by a group of nation states, provide the essential criterion for defining such a crime. As a result, the *procedural conventions* existing between these states are imposed as necessary conditions for deciding whether an indisputably grave injury to mankind has taken place in any specific case. Isn't this an absurd and arbitrary basis on which to identify a crime of such magnitude as genocide? This decision to use a procedural convention is an *ethical decision*. And the fact that contractual or other agreements are necessary to establish precedents for these conventions does not, by any means, make these agreements necessary for recognizing that genocide is a heinous crime or, on the other hand, that men are able to commit genocide without ever being charged with their crimes by the State.

The reliance on legal precedent elevates the importance of procedural standards in spite of the fact that in following this approach, one can just as easily contend (by tautological reference to these standards) that genocide did not exist before the Nuremberg trials; that the act of dropping one hundred thousand tons of bombs on a Vietnamese city is not sufficient proof of complicity in a war crime on the part of American military personnel; that the Biafran people were not victims of genocidal acts; and that political leaders of powerful imperialistic nations cannot be considered war criminals after ordering the devastation of smaller nations unless they are brought before an international tribunal and found guilty.

note of the fact that property rights which underlie racist practices are guaranteed by law. It is likewise unimportant that sexual inequality in such professions as sociology is maintained by references to the weight of tradition. Neither can persistent unemployment be excused because it is ostensibly beyond the control of the State. What is important is that hundreds of thousands of Indo-Chinese persons are being denied their right to live; millions of black people are subjected to inhuman conditions which, on the average, deny them ten years of life, the majority of the human beings of this planet are subjugated because of their sex, and an even greater number throughout the world are deprived of the commodities and services which are theirs by right. And no social system which systematically abrogates these rights is justifiable.

Is there wonder why we have raised questions about the legalistic definitions of crime when the magnitude of "social injury" caused by imperialism, racism, sexism and poverty is compared to that wrought by individual acts which the State legally defines as crimes? Isn't it time to raise serious questions about the assumptions underlying the definition of the field of criminology when a man who steals a paltry sum can be called a criminal while agents of the State can, with impunity, legally reward men who destroy food so that price levels can be maintained while a sizable portion of the population suffers from malnutrition. Our nation is confronted with a grave moral crisis which is reflected above all in the technocratic "benign neglect" shown in the unwillingness to recognize the criminal character of great social injuries inflicted on heretofore powerless people, merely because these injuries are not defined in the legal codes.

D. Modern Libertarian Standards

The limits of this paper do not permit the detailing of operating standards[54] which might be useful for earmarking the kinds of behavior which should be of central interest to criminologists, but neither these standards, nor the

notion of basic human rights itself, are more difficult to define than the operating standards and notions underlying legal conceptions of "social injury" or "public wrong." The solution to this problem is also no less political. Indeed, it is time to recognize that all of the above concepts are brought to light and operationalized by the political struggles of our time.

It is not claimed that a satisfactory solution to the problem of defining crime has been offered in this paper. What is sure, is that the legalistic definitions cannot be justified as long as they make the activity of criminologists subservient to the State. It is suggested that an alternative solution can be developed which is based on some of the traditional notions of crime as well as notions organized around the concept of egalitarianism. In this process of redefining crime, criminologists will redefine themselves, no longer to be the defenders of order but rather the guardians of human rights. In reconstructing their standards, they should make man, not institutions, the measure of all things.

REFERENCES

Adamic, Louis
  1931   Dynamite, the Story of Class Violence in America. New York: Harper and Row.
Becker, Howard
  1963   Outsiders, Studies in the Sociology of Deviance. New York: The Free Press.
Benn, Stanley I.
  1967   "Egalitarianism and the Equal Consideration of Interests." Equality, J. Roland Pennock and John Chapman, eds. New York: Atherton Press: 61–78.
Bianchi, H.
  1956   Position and Subject-Matter of Criminology: Inquiry Concerning Theoretical Criminology. Amsterdam: North Holland Publishing Co.
Blumer, Herbert
  1937   "Social Disorganization and Individual Disorganization." American Journal of Sociology 42:871–77.
Bonger, W. A.
  1936   An Introduction to Criminology. London: Methuen and Co.

---

[54]Such as infant mortality, length of life, quality of food diets, medical and recreational services, employment opportunities, etc.

Cressey, Donald R.
1960 "Epidemiology and Individual Conduct: A Case from Criminology." Pacific Sociological Review 3 (Fall): 47–58.

Cicourel, Aaren V.
1968 The Social Organization of Juvenile Justice. New York: Wiley.

Davis, Kingsley
1953 "Reply to Tumin." American Sociological Review 18: 394–97.

Davis, Kingsley and Wilbert E. Moore
1945 "Some Principles of Stratification." American Sociological Review 10:242–49.

Dentler, Robert and Lawrence J. Monroe
1961 "Early Adolescent Theft." American Sociological Review 26 (October): 733–43.

Dewey, John
1938 Logic: The Theory of Inquiry. New York: Henry Holt and Co.

Durkheim, Emile
1933 The Division of Labor in Society. Glencoe, Ill.: The Free Press (Originally published in 1893).

Empey, LaMar and Maynard L. Erickson
1966 "Hidden Delinquency and Social Status." Social Forces 44 (June): 546–54.

Freud, Sigmund
1957 Civilization and Its Discontents. London: The Hogarth Press, Ltd. (Originally published in 1930).

Garofolo, Raffaele
1885 Criminology. English Transl. Boston: Little, Brown and Co.

Glaser, Daniel
1970 "Victim Survey Research: Theoretical Implications." Criminal Behavior and Social Systems, Anthony L. Guenther, ed. Chicago: Rand McNally and Co.: 136–48.

Gold, Martin
1966 "Undetected Delinquent Behavior." Journal of Research in Crime and Delinquency 3 (January): 27–46.

Gouldner, Alvin W.
1968 "The Sociologist as Partisan: Sociology and the Welfare State." American Sociologist 3 (May): 103–16.
1962 "Anti Minotaur: The Myth of a Value-Free Sociology." Social Problems 9 (Winter): 199–213.

Hempel, Carl G.
1952 Fundamentals of Concept Formation in Empirical Science. International Encyclopedia of Unified Science, Vol. II, No. 7. Chicago: University of Chicago Press.

Horowitz, Irving H. and Martin Liebowitz
1968 "Social Deviance and Political Marginality: Toward a Redefinition of the Relation Between Sociology and Politics." Social Problems 16 (Winter): 280–96.

Horton, John
1966 "Order and Conflict Theories of Social Problems as Competing Ideologies." American Journal of Sociology 71:701–13.

Iggers, Georg C.
1958 The Doctrine of Saint-Simon: An Exposition. First Year, 1828–1829. Transl. with notes and an introduction by Georg C. Iggers, Boston: Beacon Press.

Jenkins, R. L. and Lester Hewitt
1944 "Types of Personality Structure Encountered in Child Guidance Clinics." American Journal of Orthopsychiatry (January): 84–94.

Kaplan, Abraham
1964 The Conduct of Inquiry. San Francisco: Chandler Publishing Co.

Kitsuse, John I.
1963 "Societal Reactions to Deviant Behavior: Problems of Theory and Method." Social Problems 9 (Winter): 247–56.

Knowles, John
1970 "U.S. Health: Do We Face a Catastrophe?" Look Magazine (June 2): 74, 78.

Kolko, Gabriel
1967 The Triumph of Conservatism. Chicago: Quadrangle Paperbacks.

Lemert, Edwin M.
1951 Social Pathology. New York: McGraw-Hill, Inc.

Michael, Jerome and Mortimer J. Adler
1932 An Institute of Criminology and of Criminal Justice. (The Report of a Survey Conducted for the Bureau of Social Hygiene under the Auspices of the School of Law of Columbia University) New York: Bureau of Social Hygiene, Inc.

Mills, C. Wright
1959 Sociological Imagination. New York: Oxford University Press.
1942 The Professional Idealogy of Social Pathologists. American Journal of Sociology 49 (September).

Mitchell, Wesley C.
  1927   Business Cycles. New York: National Bureau of Economic Research, Inc.

Moore, Wilber
  1963   "But Some Are More Equal Than Others." American Sociological Review 28: 13–18.

Ogburn, William F.
  1922   Social Change. New York: The Viking Press.

Nye, F. Ivan, James F. Short, Jr., and V. J. Olsen
  1958   "Socio-Economic Status and Delinquent Behavior." American Journal of Sociology 23 (January): 318–29.

Preston, William Jr.
  1963   Aliens and Dissenters. Cambridge, Mass.: Harvard University Press.

Quinney, Richard
  1970   The Problem of Crime. New York: Dodd, Mead and Co.

Ross, Edward A.
  1901   Social Control. New York: The Macmillan Co.

Savitz, Leonard
  1970   "Crime and the Criminal." Criminal Behavior and Social Systems. Anthony L. Guenther, ed. Chicago: Rand McNally and Co.: 42–47. (Originally published in Leonard Savitz, Dilemmas in Criminology. New York: McGraw-Hill, 1967: 9–16.)

Schur, Edwin M.
  1965   Crime Without Victims. Englewood Cliffs, N.J.: Prentice-Hall.

Sellin, Thorsten
  1938   Culture Conflict and Crime. New York: Social Science Research Council Bulletin No. 41.

Sutherland, Edwin H., and Donald R. Cressey
  1960   Criminology. New York: J. B. Lippincott Co.

Sutherland, Edwin H.
  1945   "Is 'White Collar Crime' Crime?" American Sociological Review 10: 132–39.
  1941   "Crime and Business." Annals of the American Academy of Political and Social Science 217: 112–18.

  1940   'White Collar Criminality." American Sociological Review 5: 1–12.

Sykes, Gresham M.
  1961   Crime and Society. New York: Random House.

Tappan, Paul R.
  1947   "Who Is the Criminal?" American Sociological Review 12: 96–102.

Tumin, Melvin
  1953a "Some Principles of Stratification: A Critical Analysis." American Sociological Review 18: 387–94.
  1953b "Reply to Kingsley Davis." American Sociological Review 18: 394–97, 18: 672–673.

Turk, Austin T.
  1969   Criminality and the Legal Order. Chicago: Rand McNally and Co.

Wald, George
  1970   "Corporate Responsibility for War Crimes." The New York Review of Books 25 (July 2): 4–6.

Ward, Lester L.
  1906   Applied Sociology. New York: Macmillan Co.
  1903   Pure Sociology. New York: Macmillan Co. (Citations from this work are derived from the second edition, published in 1911).
  1883   Dynamic Sociology. New York: D. Appleton and Co.

Weinstein, James A.
  1968   The Corporate Ideal in the Liberal State: 1900–1918. Boston: Beacon Press.

Werthman, Carl
  1969   "Delinquency and Moral Character." Delinquency, Crime and Social Process, Donald R. Cressey and David A. Ward, eds. New York: Harper and Row: 613–32.

Williams, William Appleman
  1961   Contours of American History. New York: World Publishing Co.

2

INSTITUTIONS, INTERESTS, AND THE CREATION OF DEVIANCE

The papers in this section demonstrate how political, economic, and social institutions can directly influence specific definitions of deviance and its punishment. The Chambliss paper isolates the institutional basis for changing legal structures whereby even personal freedom of movement can be outlawed. Griffin demonstrates that rape is widely supported by American social institutions as a means of female oppression. The Hall paper analyzes the volatile combination of racism, sexism, and lynching. In a parallel expression of racism, the United States stands alone among Western industrialized democracies in using the death penalty. The article by Greenberg and Himmelstein discusses the racism inherent in American use of capital punishment. In the last selection of this section Hughes shows that in an extreme case Jews were the victims of genocide in Nazi Germany for imaginary crimes, a persecution that nonetheless had institutional and legal support.

A SOCIOLOGICAL ANALYSIS
OF THE LAW OF VAGRANCY

William J. Chambliss

With the outstanding exception of Jerome Hall's analysis of theft[1] there has been a severe shortage of sociologically relevant analyses of the relationship between particular laws and the social setting in which these laws emerge, are interpreted, and take form. The paucity of such studies is somewhat surprising in view of widespread agreement that such studies are not only desirable but absolutely essential to the development of a mature sociology of law.[2] A fruitful method of establishing the direction and pattern of this mutual influence is to systematically analyze particular legal categories, to observe the changes which take place in the categories and to explain how these changes are themselves related to and stimulate changes in the society. This paper is an attempt to provide such an analysis of the law of vagrancy in Anglo-American Law.

---

[1]Hall, J., *Theft, Law and Society,* Bobbs-Merrill, 1939. See also Alfred R. Lindesmith, "Federal Law and Drug Addiction," *Social Problems* Vol. 7, No. 1, 1959, p. 48.

[2]See, for example, Rose, A., "Some Suggestions for Research in the Sociology of Law," *Social Problems* Vol. 9, No. 3, 1962, pp. 281–283, and Geis, G., "Sociology, Criminology, and Criminal Law," *Social Problems* Vol. 7, No. 1, 1959, pp. 40–47.

LEGAL INNOVATION: THE EMERGENCE OF THE LAW OF VAGRANCY IN ENGLAND

There is general agreement among legal scholars that the first full fledged vagrancy statute was passed in England in 1349. As is generally the case with legislative innovations, however, this statute was preceded by earlier laws which established a climate favorable to such change. The most significant forerunner to the 1349 vagrancy statute was in 1274 when it was provided:

Because that abbies and houses of religion have been overcharged and sore grieved, by the resort of great men and other, so that their goods have not been sufficient for themselves, whereby they have been greatly hindered and impoverished, that they cannot maintain themselves, nor such charity as they have been accustomed to do; it is provided, that none shall come to eat or lodge in any house of religion, or any other's foundation than of his own, at the costs of the house, unless he be required by the governor of the house before his coming hither.[3]

Unlike the vagrancy statutes this statute does not intend to curtail the movement of persons from

---

[3]3 Ed. 1. c. 1.

one place to another, but is solely designed to provide the religious houses with some financial relief from the burden of providing food and shelter to travelers.

The philosophy that the religious houses were to give alms to the poor and to the sick and feeble was, however, to undergo drastic change in the next fifty years. The result of this changed attitude was the establishment of the first vagrancy statute in 1349 which made it a crime to give alms to any who were unemployed while being of sound mind and body. To wit:

Because that many valiant beggars, as long as they may live of begging, do refuse to labor, giving themselves to idleness and vice, and sometimes to theft and other abominations; it is ordained, that none, upon pain of imprisonment shall, under the colour of pity or alms, give anything to such which may labour, or presume to favour them towards their desires; so that thereby they may be compelled to labour for their necessary living.[4]

It was further provided by this statute that:

. . .every man and woman, of what condition he be, free or bond, able in body, and within the age of threescore years, not living in merchandize nor exercising any craft, nor having of his own whereon to live, nor proper land whereon to occupy himself, and not serving any other, if he in convenient service (his estate considered) be required to serve, shall be bounded to serve him which shall him require. . . . And if any refuse, he shall on conviction by two true men,. . .be commited to gaol till he find surety to serve.

And if any workman or servant, of what estate or condition he be, retained in any man's service, do depart from the said service without reasonable cause or license, before the term agreed on, he shall have pain of imprisonment.[5]

There was also in this statute the stipulation that the workers should receive a standard wage. In 1351 this statute was strengthened by the stipulation:

An none shall go out of the town where he dwelled in winter, to serve the summer, if he may serve in the same town.[6]

By 34 Ed. 3 (1360) the punishment for these acts became imprisonment for fifteen days and if they "do not justify themselves by the end of that time, to be sent to gaol till they do."

A change in official policy so drastic as this did not, of course, occur simply as a matter of whim. The vagrancy statutes emerged as a result of changes in other parts of the social structure. The prime-mover for this legislative innovation was the Black Death which struck England about 1348. Among the many disastrous consequences this had upon the social structure was the fact that it decimated the labor force. It is estimated that by the time the pestilence had run its course at least fifty per cent of the population of England had died from the plague. This decimation of the labor force would necessitate rather drastic innovations in any society but its impact was heightened in England where, at this time, the economy was highly dependent upon a ready supply of cheap labor.

Even before the pestilence, however, the availability of an adequate supply of cheap labor was becoming a problem for the landowners. The crusades and various wars had made money necessary to the lords and, as a result, the lord frequently agreed to sell the serfs their freedom in order to obtain the needed funds. The serfs, for their part, were desirous of obtaining their freedom (by "fair means" or "foul") because the larger towns which were becoming more industrialized during this period could offer the serf greater personal freedom as well as a higher standard of living. This process is nicely summarized by Bradshaw:

By the middle of the 14th century the outward uniformity of the manorial system had become in practice considerably varied. . .for the peasant had begun to drift to the towns and it was unlikely that the old village life in its unpleasant aspects should not be resented. Moreover the constant wars against France and Scotland were fought mainly with mercenaries after

---

[4]35 Ed. 1. c. 1.
[5]23 Ed. 3.

[6]25 Ed. 3 (1351).

Henry III's time and most villages contributed to the new armies. The bolder serfs either joined the armies or fled to the towns, and even in the villages the free men who held by villein tenure were as eager to commute their services as the serfs were to escape. Only the amount of 'free' labor available enabled the lord to work his demense in many places.[7]

And he says regarding the effect of the Black Death:

. . .in 1348 the Black Death reached England and the vast mortality that ensued destroyed that reserve of labour which alone had made the manorial system even nominally possible.[8]

The immediate result of these events was of course no surprise: Wages for the "free" man rose considerably and this increased, on the one hand, the landowners problems and, on the other hand, the plight of the unfree tenant. For although wages increased for the personally free laborers, it of course did not necessarily add to the standard of living of the serf, if anything it made his position worse because the landowner would be hard pressed to pay for the personally free labor which he needed and would thus find it more and more difficult to maintain the standard of living for the serf which he had heretofore supplied. Thus the serf had no alternative but flight if he chose to better his position. Furthermore, flight generally meant both freedom and better conditions since the possibility of work in the new weaving industry was great and the chance of being caught small.[9]

It was under these conditions that we find the first vagrancy statutes emerging. There is little question but that these statutes were designed for one express purpose: to force laborers (whether personally free or unfree) to accept employment at a low wage in order to insure the landowner an adequate supply of labor at a price he could afford to pay. Caleb Foote concurs with this interpretation when he notes:

The anti-migratory policy behind vagrancy legislation began as an essential complement of the wage stabiliza-

tion legislation which accompanied the breakup of feudalism and the depopulation caused by the Black Death. By the Statutes of Labourers in 1349–1351, every ablebodied person without other means of support was required to work for wages fixed at the level preceding the Black Death; it was unlawful to accept more, or to refuse an offer to work, or to flee from one county to another to avoid offers of work or to seek higher wages, or go give alms to able-bodied beggars who refused to work.[10]

In short, as Foote says in another place, this was an "attempt to make the vagrancy statutes a substitute for serfdom."[11] This same conclusion is equally apparent from the wording of the statute where it is stated:

Because great part of the people, and especially of workmen and servants, late died in pestilence; many seeing the necessity of masters, and great scarcity of servants, will not serve without excessive wages, and some rather willing to beg in idleness than by labour to get their living: it is ordained, that every man and woman, of what condition he be, free or bond, able in body and within the age of threescore years, not living in merchandize, (etc.) be required to serve. . . .

The innovation in the law, then, was a direct result of the afore-mentioned changes which had occurred in the social setting. In this case these changes were located for the most part in the economic institution of the society. The vagrancy laws were designed to alleviate a condition defined by the lawmakers as undesirable. The solution was to attempt to force a reversal, as it were, of a social process which was well underway; that is, to curtail mobility of laborers in such a way that labor would not become a commodity for which the landowners would have to compete.

Statutory Dormancy: A Legal Vestige

In time, of course, the curtailment of the geographical mobility of laborers was no longer requisite. One might well expect that when the function served by the statute was no longer an important one for the society, the statutes would

---

[7]Bradshaw, F., *A Social History of England,* p. 54.
[8]Ibid.
[9]Ibid., p. 57.

[10]Foote, C., "Vagrancy Type Law and Its Administration," *Univ. of Pennsylvania Law Review* (104), 1956, p. 615.
[11]Ibid.

be eliminated from the law. In fact, this has not occurred. The vagrancy statutes have remained in effect since 1349. Furthermore, as we shall see in some detail later, they were taken over by the colonies and have remained in effect in the United States as well.

The substance of the vagrancy statutes changed very little for some time after the first ones in 1349–1351 although there was a tendency to make punishments more harsh than originally. For example, in 1360 it was provided that violators of the statute should be imprisoned for fifteen days[12] and in 1388 the punishment was to put the offender in the stocks and to keep him there until "he find surety to return to his service."[13] That there was still, at this time, the intention of providing the landowner with labor is apparent from the fact that this statute provides:

and he or she which use to labour at the plough and cart, or other labour and service of husbandry, till they be of the age of 12 years, from thenceforth shall abide at the same labour without being put to any mistery or handicraft: and any covenant of apprenticeship to the contrary shall be void.[14]

The next alteration in the statutes occurs in 1495 and is restricted to an increase in punishment. Here it is provided that vagrants shall be "set in stocks, there to remain by the space of three days and three nights, and there to have none other sustenance but bread and water; and after the said three days and nights, to be had out and set at large, and then to be commanded to avoid the town."[15]

The tendency to increase the severity of punishment during this period seems to be the result of a general tendency to make finer distinctions in the criminal law. During this period the vagrancy statutes appear to have been fairly inconsequential in either their effect as a control mechanism or as a generally enforced statute.[16]

The processes of social change in the culture generally and the trend away from serfdom and into a "free" economy obviated the utility of these statutes. The result was not unexpected. The judiciary did not apply the law and the legislators did not take it upon themselves to change the law. In short, we have here a period of dormancy in which the statute is neither applied nor altered significantly.

A SHIFT IN FOCAL CONCERN

Following the squelching of the Peasants' Revolt in 1381, the services of the serfs to the lord ". . . tended to become less and less exacted, although in certain forms they lingered on till the seventeenth cenutry. . . . By the sixteenth century few knew that there were any bondmen in England . . . and in 1575 Queen Elizabeth listened to the prayers of almost the last serfs in England . . . and granted them manumission."[17]

In view of this change we would expect corresponding changes in the vagrancy laws. Beginning with the lessening of punishment in the statute of 1503 we find these changes. However, instead of remaining dormant (or becoming more so) or being negated altogether, the vagrancy statutes experienced a shift in focal concern. With this shift the statutes served a new and equally important function for the social order of England. The first statute which indicates this change was in 1530. In this statute (22 H.8.c. 12 1530) it was stated:

If any person, being whole and mighty in body, and able to labour, be taken in begging, or be vagrant and can give no reckoning how he lawfully gets his living; . . . and all other idle persons going about, some of them using divers and subtle crafty and unlawful games and plays, and some of them feigning themselves to have knowledge of . . . crafty sciences . . . shall be punished as provided.

What is most significant about this statute is the shift from an earlier concern with laborers to a concern with *criminal* activities. To be sure, the

---

[12]34 Ed. 3 (1360).

[13]12 R. 2 (1388).

[14]Ibid.

[15]11 H. & C. 2 (1495).

[16] As evidenced for this note the expectation that " . . . the common gaols of every shire are likely to be greatly pestered

with more numbers of prisoners than heretofore . . ." when the statutes were changed by the statute of 14 Ed.c.5 (1571).

[17]Bradshaw, op. cit., p. 61.

stipulation of persons "being whole and mighty in body, and able to labour, be taken in begging, or be vagrant" sounds very much like the concerns of the earlier statutes. Some important differences are apparent however when the rest of the statute includes those who ". . . can give no reckoning how he lawfully gets his living"; "some of them using divers subtil and unlawful games and plays." This is the first statute which specifically focuses upon these kinds of criteria for adjudging someone a vagrant.

It is significant that in this statute the severity of punishment is increased so as to be greater not only than provided by the 1503 statute but the punishment is more severe than that which had been provided by *any* of the pre-1503 statutes as well. For someone who is merely idle and gives no reckoning of how he makes his living the offender shall be:

. . . had to the next market town, or other place where they [the constables] shall think most convenient, and there to be tied to the end of a cart naked, and to be beaten with whips throughout the same market town or other place, till his body be bloody by reason of such whipping.[18]

But, for those who use "divers and subtil crafty and unlawful games and plays," etc., the punishment is ". . . whipping at two days together in manner aforesaid."[19] For the second offense, such persons are:

. . . scourged two days, and the third day to be put upon the pillory from nine of the clock till eleven before noon of the same day and to have one of his ears cut off.[20]

And if he offend the third time ". . . to have like punishment with whipping, standing on the pillory and to have his other ear cut off."

This statute (1) makes a distinction between types of offenders and applies the more severe punishment to those who are clearly engaged in "criminal" activities, (2) mentions a specific concern with categories of "unlawful" behavior,

and (3) applies a type of punishment (cutting off the ear) which is generally reserved for offenders who are defined as likely to be a fairly serious criminal.

Only five years later we find for the first time that the punishment of death is applied to the crime of vagrancy. We also note a change in terminology in the statute:

and if any ruffians . . . after having been once apprehended . . . shall wander, loiter, or idle use themselves and play the vagabonds . . . shall be eftsoons not only whipped again, but shall have the gristle of his right ear clean cut off. And if he shall again offend, he shall be committed to gaol till the next sessions; and being there convicted upon indictment, he shall have judgment to suffer pains and execution of death, as a felon, as an enemy of the commonwealth.[21]

It is significant that the statute now makes persons who repeat the crime of vagrancy a felon. During this period then, the focal concern of the vagrancy statutes becomes a concern for the control of felons and is no longer primarily concerned with the movement of laborers.

These statutory changes were a direct response to changes taking place in England's social structure during this period. We have already pointed out that feudalism was decaying rapidly. Concomitant with the breakup of feudalism was an increased emphasis upon commerce and industry. The commercial emphasis in England at the turn of the sixteenth century is of particular importance in the development of vagrancy laws. With commercialism came considerable traffic bearing valuable items. Where there were 169 important merchants in the middle of the fourteenth century there were 3,000 merchants engaged in foreign trade alone at the beginning of the sixteenth century.[22] England became highly dependent upon commerce for its economic support. Italians conducted a great deal of the commerce of England during this early period and were held in low repute by the populace. As a result, they were subject to attacks by citizens and, more important, were frequently robbed of their goods while

[18]22 H. 8. c. 12 (1530).
[19]Ibid.
[20]Ibid.

[21]27 H. 8. c. 25 (1535).
[22]Hall, op. cit., p. 21.

transporting them. "The general insecurity of the times made any transportation hazardous. The special risks to which the alien merchant was subjected gave rise to the royal practice of issuing formally executed covenants of safe conduct through the realm."[23]

Such a situation not only called for the enforcement of existing laws but also called for the creation of new laws which would facilitate the control of persons preying upon merchants transporting goods. The vagrancy statutes were revived in order to fulfill just such a purpose. Persons who had committed no serious felony but who were suspected of being capable of doing so could be apprehended and incapacitated through the application of vagrancy laws once these laws were refocused so as to include ". . . any ruffians . . . [who] shall wander, loiter, or idle use themselves and play the vagabonds . . ."[24]

The new focal concern is continued in 1 Ed. 6. c. 3 (1547) and in fact is made more general so as to include:

Whoever man or woman, being not lame, impotent, or so aged or diseased that he or she cannot work, not having whereon to live, shall be lurking in any house, or loitering or idle wandering by the highway side, or in streets, cities, towns, or villages, not applying themselves to some honest labour, and so continuing for three days; or running away from their work; every such person shall be taken for a vagabond. And . . . upon conviction of two witnesses . . . the same loiterer (shall) be marked with a hot iron in the breast with the letter V, and adjudged him to the person bringing him, to be his slave for two years. . . .

Should the vagabond run away, upon conviction, he was to be branded by a hot iron with the letter S on the forehead and to be thenceforth declared a slave forever. And in 1571 there is modification of the punishment to be inflicted, whereby the offender is to be "branded on the chest with the letter V" (for vagabond). And, if he is convicted the second time, the brand is to be made on the forehead. It is worth noting here that this method of punishment, which first

appeared in 1530 and is repeated here with somewhat more force, is also an indication of a change in the type of person to whom the law is intended to apply. For it is likely that nothing so permanent as branding would be applied to someone who was wandering but looking for work, or at worst merely idle and not particularly dangerous *per se*. On the other hand, it could well be applied to someone who was likely to be engaged in other criminal activities in connection with being "vagrant."

By 1571 in the statute of 14 E1. C. 5 the shift in focal concern is fully developed:

All rogues, vagabonds, and sturdy beggars shall . . . be committed to the common gaol . . . he shall be grievously whipped, and burnt thro' the gristle of the right ear with a hot iron of the compass of an inch about; . . . And for the second offense, he shall be adjudged a felon, unless some person will take him for two years in to his service. And for the third offense, he shall be adjudged guilty of felony without benefit of clergy.

And there is included a long list of persons who fall within the statute: "proctors, procurators, idle persons going about using subtil, crafty and unlawful games or plays; and some of them feigning themselves to have knowledge of . . . absurd sciences . . . and all fencers, bearwards, common players in interludes, and minstrels . . . all juglers, pedlars, tinkers, petty chapmen . . . and all counterfeiters of licenses, passports and users of the same." The major significance of this statute is that it includes all the previously defined offenders and adds some more. Significantly, those added are more clearly criminal types, counterfeiters, for example. It is also significant that there is the following qualification of this statute: "Provided also, that this act shall not extend to cookers, or harvest folks, that travel for harvest work, corn or hay."

That the changes in this statute were seen as significant is indicated by the following statement which appears in the statute:

And whereas by reason of this act, the common gaols of every shire are like to be greatly pestered with more number of prisoners than heretofore hath been, for that the said vagabonds and other lewd persons before

---

[23]Ibid., p. 23.
[24]27 H. 8. c. 25 (1535).

recited shall upon their apprehension be committed to the said gaols; it is enacted. . . .[25]

And a provision is made for giving more money for maintaining the gaols. This seems to add credence to the notion that this statute was seen as being significantly more general than those previously.

It is also of importance to note that this is the first time the term *rogue* has been used to refer to persons included in the vagrancy statutes. It seems, *a priori*, that a "rogue" is a different social type than is a "vagrant" or a "vagabond"; the latter terms implying something more equivalent to the idea of a "tramp" whereas the former (rogue) seems to imply a more disorderly and potentially dangerous person.

The emphasis upon the criminalistic aspect of vagrants continues in Chapter 17 of the same statute:

Whereas divers *licentious* persons wander up and down in all parts of the realm, to countenance their *wicked behavior;* and do continually assemble themselves armed in the highways, and elsewhere in troops, *to the great terror* of her majesty's true subjects, *the impeachment of her laws*, and the disturbance of the peace and tranquility of the realm; and whereas many outrages are daily committed by these dissolute persons, and more are likely to ensue if speedy remedy be not provided. (Italics added.)

With minor variations (*e.g.,* offering a reward for the capture of a vagrant) the statutes remain essentially of this nature until 1743. In 1743 there was once more an expansion of the types of persons included such that "all persons going about as patent gatherers, or gatherers of alms, under pretense of loss by fire or other casualty; or going about as collectors for prisons, gaols, or hospitals; all persons playing of betting at any unlawful games; and all persons who run away and leave their wives or children . . . all persons wandering abroad, and lodging in ale-houses, barns, outhouses, or in the open air, not giving good account of themselves," were types of offenders added to those already included.

By 1743 the vagrancy statutes had apparently been sufficiently reconstructed by the shifts of

concern so as to be once more a useful instrument in the creation of social solidarity. This function has apparently continued down to the present day in England and the changes from 1743 to the present have been all in the direction of clarifying or expanding the categories covered but little has been introduced to change either the meaning or the impact of this branch of the law.

We can summarize this shift in focal concern by quoting from Halsbury. He has noted that in the vagrancy statutes:

". . . elaborate provision is made for the relief and incidental control of destitute wayfarers. These latter, however, form but a small portion of the offenders aimed at by what are known as the Vagrancy Laws, . . . many offenders who are in no ordinary sense of the word vagrants, have been brought under the laws relating to vagrancy, and the great number of the offenses coming within the operation of these laws have little or no relation to the subject of poor relief, but are more properly directed towards the prevention of crime, the preservation of good order, and the promotion of social economy."[26]

Before leaving this section it is perhaps pertinent to make a qualifying remark. We have emphasized throughout this section how the vagrancy statutes underwent a shift in focal concern as the social setting changed. The shift in focal concern is not meant to imply that the later focus of the statutes represents a completely new law. It will be recalled that even in the first vagrancy statute there was reference to those who "do refuse labor, giving themselves to idleness and vice and sometimes to theft and other abominations." Thus the possibility of criminal activities resulting from persons who refuse to labor was recognized even in the earliest statute. The fact remains, however, that the major emphasis in this statute and in the statutes which followed the first one was always upon the "refusal to labor" or "begging." The "criminalistic" aspect of such persons was relatively unimportant. Later, as we have shown, the criminalistic potential becomes of paramount importance. The thread runs back to the earliest

---

[25] 14 Ed. c. 5. (1571).

[26] Earl of Halsbury, *The Laws of England*, Butterworth & Co., Bell Yard, Temple Bar, 1912, pp. 606–607.

statute but the reason for the statutes' existence as well as the focal concern of the statutes is quite different in 1743 than it was in 1349.

VAGRANCY LAWS IN THE UNITED STATES

In general, the vagrancy laws of England, as they stood in the middle eighteenth century, were simply adopted by the states. There were some exceptions to this general trend. For example, Maryland restricted the application of vagrancy laws to "free" Negroes. In addition, for *all* states the vagrancy laws were even more explicitly concerned with the control of criminals and undesirables than had been the case in England. New York, for example, explicitly defines prostitutes as being a category of vagrants during this period. These exceptions do not, however, change the general picture significantly and it is quite appropriate to consider the U.S. vagrancy laws as following from England's of the middle eighteenth century with relatively minor changes. The control of criminals and undesirables was the *raison de etre* of the vagrancy laws in the U.S. This is as true today as it was in 1750. As Caleb Foote's analysis of the application of vagrancy statutes in the Philadelphia court shows, these laws are presently applied indiscriminately to persons considered a "nuisance." Foote suggests that ". . . the chief significance of this branch of the criminal law lies in its quantitative impact and administrative usefulness."[27] Thus it appears that in America the trend begun in England in the sixteenth, seventeenth and eighteenth centuries has been carried to its logical extreme and the laws are now used principally as a mechanism for "clearing the streets" of the derelicts who inhabit the "skid roads" and "Bowerys" of our large urban areas.

Since the 1800's there has been an abundant source of prospects to which the vagrancy laws have been applied. These have been primarily those persons deemed by the police and the courts to be either actively involved in criminal activities or at least peripherally involved. In this context, then, the statutes have changed very little. The functions served by the statutes in England of the late eighteenth century are still being served today in both England and the United States. The locale has changed somewhat and it appears that the present day application of vagrancy statutes is focused upon the arrest and confinement of the "down and outers" who inhabit certain sections of our larger cities but the impact has remained constant. The lack of change in the vagrancy statutes, then, can be seen as a reflection of the society's perception of a continuing need to control some of its "suspicious" or "undesirable" members.[28]

A word of caution is in order lest we leave the impression that this administrative purpose is the sole function of vagrancy laws in the U.S. today. Although it is our contention that this is generally true it is worth remembering that during certain periods of our recent history, and to some extent today, these laws have also been used to control the movement of workers. This was particularly the case during the depression years and California is of course infamous for its use of vagrancy laws to restrict the admission of migrants from other states.[29] The vagrancy statutes, because of their history, still contain germs within them which makes such effects possible. Their main purpose, however, is clearly no longer the control of laborers but rather the control of the undesirable, the criminal and the "nuisance."

DISCUSSION

The foregoing analysis of the vagrancy laws has demonstrated that these laws were a legislative innovation which reflected the socially perceived necessity of providing an abundance of cheap labor to landowners during a period when serfdom was breaking down and when the pool of

---

[27]Foote, op. cit., p. 613. Also see in this connection, Irwin Deutscher, "The Petty Offender," *Federal Probation*, XIX, June, 1955.

[28]It is on this point that the vagrancy statutes have been subject to criticism. See for example, Lacey, Forrest W., "Vagrancy and Other Crimes of Personal Condition," *Harvard Law Review* (66), p. 1203.

[29]Edwards *vs* California. 314 S: 160 (1941).

available labor was depleted. With the eventual breakup of feudalism the need for such laws eventually disappeared and the increased dependence of the economy upon industry and commerce rendered the former use of the vagrancy statutes unnecessary. As a result, for a substantial period the vagrancy statutes were dormant, undergoing only minor changes and, presumably, being applied infrequently. Finally, the vagrancy laws were subjected to considerable alteration through a shift in the focal concern of the statutes. Whereas in their inception the laws focused upon the "idle" and "those refusing to labor" after the turn of the sixteenth century and emphasis came to be upon "rogues," "vagabonds," and others who were suspected of being engaged in criminal activities. During this period the focus was particularly upon "roadmen" who preyed upon citizens who transported goods from one place to another. The increased importance of commerce to England during this period made it necessary that some protection be given persons engaged in this enterprise and the vagrancy statutes provided one source for such protection by refocusing the acts to be included under these statutes.

Comparing the results of this analysis with the findings of Hall's study of theft we see a good deal of correspondence. Of major importance is the fact that both analyses demonstrate the truth of Hall's assertion that "The functioning of courts is significantly related to concomitant cultural needs, and this applies to the law of procedure as well as to substantive law."[30]

Our analysis of the vagrancy laws also indicates that when changed social conditions create a perceived need for legal changes that these alterations will be effected through the revision and refocusing of existing statutes. This process was demonstrated in Hall's analysis of theft as well as in our analysis of vagrancy. In the case of vagrancy, the laws were dormant when the focal concern of the laws was shifted so as to provide control over potential criminals. In the case of theft the laws were re-interpreted (interestingly, by the courts and not by the

legislature) so as to include persons who were transporting goods for a merchant but who absconded with the contents of the packages transported.

It also seems probable that when the social conditions change and previously useful laws are no longer useful there will be long periods when these laws will remain dormant. It is less likely that they will be officially negated. During this period of dormancy it is the judiciary which has principal responsibility for *not* applying the statutes. It is possible that one finds statutes being negated only when the judiciary stubbornly applies laws which do not have substantial public support. An example of such laws in contemporary times would be the "Blue Laws." Most states still have laws prohibiting the sale of retail goods on Sunday yet these laws are rarely applied. The laws are very likely to remain but to be dormant unless a recalcitrant judge or a vocal minority of the population insist that the laws be applied. When this happens we can anticipate that the statutes will be negated.[31] Should there arise a perceived need to curtail retail selling under some special circumstances, then it is likely that these laws will undergo a shift in focal concern much like the shift which characterized the vagrancy laws. Lacking such application the laws will simply remain dormant except for rare instances where they will be negated.

This analysis of the vagrancy statutes (and Hall's analysis of theft as well) has demonstrated the importance of "vested interest" groups in the emergence and/or alteration of laws. The vagrancy laws emerged in order to provide the powerful landowners with a ready supply of cheap labor. When this was no longer seen as necessary and particularly when the landowners were no longer dependent upon cheap labor nor were they a powerful interest group in the society the laws became dormant. Finally a new interest group emerged and was seen as being of great

---

[30]Hall, op. cit., p. XII.

[31]Negation, in this instance, is most likely to come about by the repeal of the statute. More generally, however, negation may occur in several ways including the declaration of a statute as unconstitutional. This later mechanism has been used even for laws which have been "on the books" for long periods of time. Repeal is probably the most common, although not the only, procedure by which a law is negated.

importance to the society and the laws were then altered so as to afford some protection to this group. These findings are thus in agreement with Weber's contention that "status groups" determine the content of the law.[32] The findings are inconsistent, on the other hand, with the perception of the law as simply a reflection of "public opinion" as is sometimes found in the literature.[33] We should be cautious in concluding, however, that either of these positions are necessarily correct. The careful analysis of

[32]M. Rheinstein, *Max Weber on Law in Economy and Society*, Harvard University Press, 1954.

[33]Friedman, N. *Law in a Changing Society*, Berkeley and Los Angeles: University of California Press, 1959.

other laws, and especially of laws which do not focus so specifically upon the "criminal," are necessary before this question can be finally answered.

In conclusion, it is hoped that future analyses of changes within the legal structure will be able to benefit from this study by virtue of (1) the data provided and (2) the utilization of a set of concepts (innovation, dormancy, concern and negation) which have proved useful in the analysis of the vagrancy law. Such analyses should provide us with more substantial grounds for rejecting or accepting as generally valid the description of some of the processes which appear to characterize changes in the legal system.

RAPE

The All-American Crime

Susan Griffin

I have never been free of the fear of rape. From a very early age I, like most women, have thought of rape as part of my natural environment—something to be feared and prayed against like fire or lightning. I never asked why men raped; I simply thought it one of the many mysteries of human nature.

I was, however, curious enough about the violent side of humanity to read every crime magazine I was able to ferret away from my grandfather. Each issue featured at least one "sex crime," with pictures of a victim, usually in a pearl necklace, and of the ditch or the orchard where her body was found. I was never certain why the victims were always women, nor what the motives of the murderer were, but I did guess that the world was not a safe place for women. I observed that my grandmother was meticulous about locks and quick to draw the shades before anyone removed so much as a shoe. I sensed that danger lurked outside.

At the age of eight, my suspicions were confirmed. My grandmother took me to the back of the house where the men wouldn't hear, and told me that strange men wanted to do harm to little girls. I learned not to walk on dark streets, not to talk to strangers or get into strange cars, to lock doors, and to be modest. She never explained why a man would want to harm a little girl, and I never asked.

If I thought for a while that my grandmother's fears were imaginary, the illusion was brief. That year, on the way home from school, a schoolmate a few years older than I tried to rape me. Later, in an obscure aisle of the local library (while I was reading *Freddy the Pig*) I turned to discover a man exposing himself. Then, the friendly man around the corner was arrested for child molesting.

My initiation to sexuality was typical. Every woman has similar stories to tell—the first man who attacked her may have been a neighbor, a family friend, an uncle, her doctor, or perhaps her own father. And women who grow up in New York City always have tales about the subway.

But though rape and the fear of rape are a daily part of every woman's consciousness, the subject is so rarely discussed by that unofficial staff of male intellectuals (who write the books which study seemingly every other form of male activity) that one begins to suspect a conspiracy of silence. And indeed, the obscurity of rape in print exists in marked contrast to the frequency of rape in reality, for *forcible rape is the most frequently committed violent crime in America today*. The Federal Bureau of Investigation classes three crimes as violent: murder, aggravated assault and forcible rape. In 1968, 31,060 rapes were

Susan Griffin (1975) "Rape: The All-American Crime," in *Women: A Feminist Perspective*, ed. Jo Freeman, Palo Alto, Calif.: Mayfield Publishing Company. © 1975, Mayfield Publishing Company.

reported. According to the FBI and independent criminologists, however, to approach accuracy this figure must be multiplied by at least a factor of ten to compensate for the fact that most rapes are not reported; when these compensatory mathematics are used, there are more rapes committed than aggravated assaults and homicides.

When I asked Berkeley, California's Police Inspector in charge of rape investigation if he knew why men rape women, he replied that he had not spoken with "these people and delved into what really makes them tick, because that really isn't my job." However, when I asked him how a woman might prevent being raped, he was not so reticent. "I wouldn't advise any female to go walking around alone at night . . . and she should lock her car at all times." The Inspector illustrated his warning with a grisly story about a man who lay in wait for women in the back seats of their cars, while they were shopping in a local supermarket. This man eventually murdered one of his rape victims. "Always lock your car," the Inspector repeated, and then added, without a hint of irony, "Of course, you don't have to be paranoid about this type of thing."

The Inspector wondered why I wanted to write about rape. Like most men he did not understand the urgency of the topic, for, after all, men are not raped. But like most women I had spent considerable time speculating on the true nature of the rapist. When I was very young, my image of the "sexual offender" was a nightmarish amalgamation of the bogey man and Captain Hook: he wore a black cape, and he cackled. As I matured, so did my image of the rapist. Born into the psychoanalytic age, I tried to "understand" the rapist. Rape, I came to believe, was only one of many unfortunate evils produced by sexual repression. Reasoning by tautology, I concluded that any man who would rape a woman must be out of his mind.

Yet, though the theory that rapists are insane is a popular one, this belief has no basis in fact. According to Professor Menachem Amir's study of 646 rape cases in Philadelphia, *Patterns in Forcible Rape*, men who rape are not abnormal. Amir writes, "Studies indicate that sex offenders do not constitute a unique or psychopathological type; nor are they as a group invariably more disturbed than the control groups to which they are compared." Alan Taylor, a parole officer who has worked with rapists in the prison facilities at San Luis Obispo, California, stated the question in plainer language: "Those men were the most normal men there. They had a lot of hang-ups, but they were the same hang-ups as men walking out on the street."

Another canon in the apologetics of rape is that, if it were not for learned social controls, all men would rape. Rape is held to be natural behavior, and not to rape must be learned. But in truth rape is not universal to the human species. Moreover, studies of rape in our culture reveal that, far from being impulsive behavior, most rape is planned. Professor Amir's study reveals that in cases of group rape (the "gangbang" of masculine slang) 90 percent . . . were planned; in pair rapes, 83 percent . . . were planned; and in single rapes, 58 percent were planned. These figures should significantly discredit the image of the rapist as a man who is suddenly overcome by sexual needs society does not allow him to fulfill.

Far from the social control of rape being learned, comparisons with other cultures lead one to suspect that, in our society, it is rape itself that is learned. (The fact that rape is against the law should not be considered proof that rape is not in fact encouraged as part of our culture.)

This culture's concept of rape as an illegal, but still understandable, form of behavior is not a universal one. In her study *Sex and Temperament*, Margaret Mead describes a society that does not share our views. The Arapesh do not ". . . have any conception of the male nature that might make rape understandable to them." Indeed our interpretation of rape is a product of our conception of the nature of male sexuality. A common retort to the question, why don't women rape men, is the myth that men have greater sexual needs, that their sexuality is more urgent than women's. And it is the nature of human beings to want to live up to what is expected of them.

And this same culture which expects aggression from the male expects passivity from the female. Conveniently, the companion myth about the nature of female sexuality is that all women secretly want to be raped. Lurking beneath her modest female exterior is a subconscious desire to be ravished. The following description of a stag movie, written by Brenda Starr in Los Angeles' underground paper, *Everywoman*, typifies this male fantasy. The movie "showed a woman in her underclothes reading on her bed. She is interrupted by a rapist with a knife. He immediately wins her over with his charm and they get busy sucking and fucking." An advertisement in the *Berkeley Barb* reads, "Now as all women know from their daydreams, rape has a lot of advantages. Best of all it's so simple. No preparation necessary, no planning ahead of time, no wondering if you should or shouldn't; just whang! bang!" Thanks to Masters and Johnson even the scientific canon recognizes that for the female, "whang! bang!" can scarcely be described as pleasurable.

Still the male psyche persists in believing that, protestations and struggles to the contrary, deep inside her mysterious feminine soul, the female victim has wished for her own fate. A young woman who was raped by the husband of a friend said that days after the incident the man returned to her home, pounded on the door and screamed at her, "Jane, Jane. You loved it. You know you loved it."

The theory that women like being raped extends itself by deduction into the proposition that most or much of rape is provoked by the victim. But this too is only myth. Though provocation, considered a mitigating factor in a court of law, may consist of only "a gesture," according to the Federal Commission on Crimes of Violence, only 4 percent of reported rapes involved any precipitative behavior by the woman.

The notion that rape is enjoyed by the victim is also convenient for the man who, though he would not commit forcible rape, enjoys the idea of its existence, as if rape confirms that enormous sexual potency which he secretly knows to be his own. It is for the pleasure of the armchair rapist that detailed accounts of violent rapes exist in the media. Indeed, many men appear to take sexual pleasure from nearly all forms of violence. Whatever the motivation, male sexuality and violence in our culture seem to be inseparable.

James Bond alternately whips out his revolver and his cock, and though there is no known connection between the skills of gunfighting and love-making, pacifism seems suspiciously effeminate.

In a recent fictional treatment of the Manson case, Frank Conroy writes of his vicarious titillation when describing the murders to his wife:

"Every single person there was killed." She didn't move.

"It sounds like there was torture," I said. As the words left my mouth I knew there was no need to say them to frighten her into believing that she needed me for protection.

The pleasure he feels as his wife's protector is inextricably mixed with pleasure in the violence itself. Conroy writes, "I was excited by the killings, as one is excited by catastrophe on a grand scale, as one is alert to pre-echoes of unknown changes, hints of unrevealed secrets, rumblings of chaos. . . ."

The attraction of the male is our culture to violence and death is a tradition Manson and his admirers are carrying on with tireless avidity (even presuming Manson's innocence, he dreams of the purification of fire and destruction). It was Malraux in his *Anti-Memoirs* who said that, for the male, facing death was *the* illuminating experience analogous to childbirth for the female. Certainly our culture does glorify war and shroud the agonies of the gun-fighter in veils of mystery.

And in the spectrum of male behavior, rape, the perfect combination of sex and violence, is the penultimate act. Erotic pleasure cannot be separated from culture, and in our culture male eroticism is wedded to power. Not only should a man be taller and stronger than a female in the perfect love-match, but he must also demonstrate his superior strength in gestures of dominance which are perceived as amorous. Though the law attempts to make a clear division between rape and sexual intercourse, in fact the courts find it difficult to distinguish between a case where the decision to copulate was mutual and one where a man forced himself upon his partner.

The scenario is even further complicated by the expectation that, not only does a woman mean "yes" when she says "no," but that a really decent woman ought to begin by saying "no," and then be led down the primrose path to acquiescence. Ovid, the author of Western Civilization's most celebrated sex manual, makes this expectation perfectly clear: "and when I beg you to say "yes," say "no." Then let me lie outside your bolted door. . . . So Love grows strong."

That the basic elements of rape are involved in all heterosexual relationships may explain why men often identify with the offender in this crime. But to regard the rapist as the victim, a man driven by his inherent sexual needs to take what will not be given him, reveals a basic ignorance of sexual politics. For in our culture heterosexual love finds an erotic expression through male dominance and female submission. A man who derives pleasure from raping a woman clearly must enjoy force and dominance as much as or more than the simple pleasures of the flesh. Coitus cannot be experienced in isolation. The weather, the state of the nation, the level of sugar in the blood—all will affect a man's ability to achieve orgasm. If a man can achieve sexual pleasure after terrorizing and humiliating the object of his passion, and in fact while inflicting pain upon her, one must assume he derives pleasure directly from terrorizing, humiliating and harming a woman. According to Amir's study of forcible rape, on a statistical average the man who has been convicted of rape was found to have a normal sexual personality, tending to be different from the normal, well-adjusted male only in having a greater tendency to express violence and rage.

And if the professional rapist is to be separated from the average dominant heterosexual, it may be mainly a quantitative difference. For the existence of rape as an index to masculinity is not entirely metaphorical. Though this measure of masculinity seems to be more publicly exhibited among "bad boys" or aging bikers who practice sexual initiation through group rape, in fact "good boys" engage in the same rites to prove their manhood. In Stockton, a small town in California which epitomizes silent-majority America, a bachelor party was given [in the early 1970's] for a young man about to be married. A woman was hired to dance "topless" for the amusement of the guests. At the high point of the evening the bridegroom-to-be dragged the woman into a bedroom. No move was made by any of his companions to stop what was clearly going to be an attempted rape. Far from it. As the woman described, "I tried to keep him away—told him of my Herpes Genitalis, et cetera, but he couldn't face the guys if he didn't screw me." After the bridegroom had finished raping the woman and returned with her to the party, far from chastising him, his friends heckled the woman and covered her with wine.

It was fortunate for the dancer that the bridegroom's friends did not follow him into the bedroom for, though one might suppose that in group rape, since the victim is outnumbered, less force would be inflicted on her, in fact, Amir's studies indicate, "the most excessive degrees of violence occurred in group rape." Far from discouraging violence, the presence of other men may in fact encourage sadism, and even cause the behavior. In an unpublished study of group rape by Gilbert Geis and Duncan Chappell, the authors refer to a study by W. H. Blanchard which relates, "The leader of the male group . . . apparently precipitated and maintained the activity, despite misgivings, because of a need to fulfill the role that the other two men had assigned to him. 'I was scared when it began to happen,' he says. 'I wanted to leave but I didn't want to say it to the other guys—you know—that I was scared.' "

Thus it becomes clear that not only does our culture teach men the rudiments of rape, but society, or more specifically other men, encourage the practice of it.

II

Every man I meet wants to protect me. Can't figure out what from.

—Mae West

If a male society rewards aggressive, domineering sexual behavior, it contains within itself a sexual schizophrenia. For the masculine man is also expected to prove his mettle as a protector of women. To the naive eye, this dichotomy implies that men fall into one of two categories: those who rape and those who protect. In fact, life does not prove so simple. In a study euphemistically entitled "Sex Aggression by College Men," it was discovered that men who believe in a double standard of morality for men and women, who in fact believe most fervently in the ultimate value of virginity, are more liable to commit "this aggressive variety of sexual exploitation."

(At this point in our narrative it should come as no surprise that Sir Thomas Malory, creator of that classic tale of chivalry [La morte d'Artur], was himself arrested and found guilty for repeated incidents of rape.)

In the system of chivalry, men protect women against men. This is not unlike the protection relationship which the Mafia established with small businesses in the early part of this century. Indeed, chivalry is an age-old protection racket which depends for its existence on rape.

According to the male mythology which defines and perpetuates rape, [the desire to rape] is an animal instinct inherent in the male. The story goes that sometime in our pre-historical past, the male, more hirsute and burly than today's counterpart, roamed about an uncivilized landscape until he found a desirable female. (Oddly enough, this female is *not* pictured as more muscular than the modern woman.) Her mate does not bother with courtship. He simply grabs her by the hair and drags her to the closest cave. Presumably, one of the major advantages of modern civilization for the female has been the civilizing of the male. We call it chivalry.

But women do not get chivalry for free. According to the logic of sexual politics, we too have to civilize our behavior. (Enter chastity. Enter virginity. Enter monogamy.) For the female, civilized behavior means chastity before marriage and faithfulness within it. Chivalrous behavior in the male is supposed to protect that chastity from involuntary defilement. The fly in the ointment of this otherwise peaceful system is the fallen woman. She does not behave. And therefore she does not deserve protection. Or,

to use another argument, a major tenet of the same value system, what has once been defiled cannot again be violated. One begins to suspect that it is the behavior of the fallen woman and not that of the male, that civilization aims to control.

The assumption that a woman who does not respect this double standard deserves whatever she gets (or at the very least "asks for it") operates in the courts today. While in some states a man's previous rape convictions are not considered admissible evidence, the sexual reputation of the rape victim is considered a crucial element of the facts upon which the court must decide innocence or guilt.

The court's respect for the double standard manifested itself particularly clearly in the case of the People v. Jerry Plotkin. Mr. Plotkin, a 36-year-old jeweler, was tried for rape [in 1971] in a San Francisco Superior Court. According to the woman who brought the charges, Plotkin, along with three other men, forced her at gunpoint to enter a car one night in October 1970. She was taken to Mr. Plotkin's fashionable apartment where he and the three other men first raped her and then, in the delicate language of the *San Francisco Chronicle*, "subjected her to perverted sex acts." She was, she said, set free in the morning with the warning that she would be killed if she spoke to anyone about the event. She did report the incident to the police, who then searched Plotkin's apartment and discovered a long list of names of women. Her name was on the list and had been crossed out.

In addition to the woman's account of her abduction and rape, the prosecution submitted four of Plotkin's address books containing the names of hundreds of women. Plotkin claimed he did not know all of the women since some of the names had been given to him by friends and he had not yet called on them. Several women, however, did testify in court that Plotkin had, to cite the *Chronicle*, "lured them up to his apartment under one pretext or another, and forced his sexual attentions on them."

Plotkin's defense rested on two premises. First, through his own testimony Plotkin established a reputation for himself as a sexual libertine who frequently picked up girls in bars and took them to his house where sexual relations often took place. He was the Playboy. He claimed that the accusation of rape, therefore, was false—this incident had simply been one of many casual sexual relationships, the victim one of many playmates. The second premise of the defense was that his accuser was also a sexual libertine. However, the picture created of the young woman (fully thirteen years younger than Plotkin) was not akin to the lighthearted, gay-bachelor image projected by the defendant. On the contrary, the day after the defense cross-examined the woman, the *Chronicle* printed a story headlined, "Grueling Day For Rape Case Victim." (A leaflet passed out by women in front of the courtroom was more succinct, "rape was committed by four men in a private apartment in October; on Thursday, it was done by a judge and a lawyer in a public courtroom.")

Through skillful questioning fraught with innuendo, Plotkin's defense attorney James Martin MacInnis portrayed the young woman as a licentious opportunist and unfit mother. MacInnis began by asking the young woman (then employed as a secretary) whether or not it was true that she was "familiar with liquor" and had worked as a "cocktail waitress." The young woman replied (the *Chronicle* wrote "admitted") that she had worked once or twice as a cocktail waitress. The attorney then asked if she had worked as a secretary in the financial district but had "left that employment after it was discovered that you had sexual intercourse on a couch in the office." The woman replied, "That is a lie. I left because I didn't like working in a one-girl office. It was too lonely." Then the defense asked if, while working as an attendant at a health club, "you were accused of having a sexual affair with a man?" Again the woman denied the story: "I was never accused of that."

Plotkin's attorney then sought to establish that his client's accuser was living with a married man. She responded that the man was separated from his wife. Finally he told the court that she had "spent the night" with another man who lived in the same building.

At this point in the testimony the woman asked Plotkin's defense attorney, "Am I on trial? . . . It is embarrassing and personal to admit these things to all these people. . . . I did not commit a crime. I am a human being." The lawyer, true to the chivalry of his class, apologized and immediately resumed questioning her, turning his attention to her children. (She is divorced, and the children at the time of the trial were in a foster home.) "Isn't it true that your two children have a sex game in which one gets on top of another and they—" "That is a lie!" the young woman interrupted him. She ended her testimony by explaining, "They are wonderful children. They are not perverted."

The jury, divided in favor of acquittal ten to two, asked the court stenographer to read the woman's testimony back to them. After this reading, the Superior Court acquitted the defendant of both the charges of rape and kidnapping.

According to the double standard a woman who has had sexual intercourse out of wedlock cannot be raped. Rape is not only a crime of aggression against the body; it is a transgression against chastity as defined by men. When a woman is forced into a sexual relationship, she has, according to the male ethos, been violated. But she is also defiled if she does not behave according to the double standard, by maintaining her chastity, or confining her sexual activities to a monogamous relationship.

One should not assume, however, that a woman can avoid the possibility of rape simply by behaving. Though myth would have it that mainly "bad girls" are raped, this theory has no basis in fact. Available statistics would lead one to believe that a safer course is promiscuity. In a study of rape done in the District of Columbia, it was found that 82 percent of the rape victims had a "good reputation." Even the Police Inspector's advice to stay off the streets is rather useless, for almost half of reported rapes occur in the home of the victim and are committed by a man she has never before seen. Like indiscriminate terrorism, rape can happen to any woman, and few women are ever without this knowledge.

But the courts and the police, both dominated by the white males, continue to suspect the rape victim, *sui generis*, of provoking or asking for her own assault. According to Amir's study, the police tend to believe that a woman without a good reputation cannot be raped. The rape victim is usually submitted to countless questions about her own sexual mores and behavior by the police investigator. This preoccupation is partially justified by the legal requirements for prosecution in a rape case. The rape victim must have been penetrated, and she must have made it clear to her assailant that she did not want penetration (unless of course she is unconscious). A [woman's] refusal to accompany a man to some isolated place to allow him to touch her does not in the eyes of the court [make the subsequent act a] rape. She must have said "no" at the crucial genital moment. And the rape victim, to qualify as such, must also have put up a physical struggle—unless she can prove that to do so would have been to endanger her life.

But the zealous interest the police frequently exhibit in the physical details of a rape case is only partially explained by the requirements of the court. A woman who was raped in Berkeley was asked to tell the story of her rape four different times "right out in the street," while her assailant was escaping. She was then required to submit to a pelvic examination to prove that penetration had taken place. Later, she was taken to the police station where she was asked the same questions again: "Were you forced?" "Did he penetrate?" "Are you sure your life was in danger and you had no other choice?" This woman had been pulled off the street by a man who held a 10-inch knife at her throat and forcibly raped her. She was raped at midnight and was not able to return to her home until five in the morning. Police contacted her twice again in the next week, once by telephone at two in the morning and once at four in the morning. In her words, "The rape was probably the least traumatic incident of the whole evening. If I'm ever raped again . . . I wouldn't report it to the police because of all the degradation. . . ."

If white women are subjected to unnecessary and often hostile questioning after having been raped, third world women are often not believed at all. According to the white male ethos (which is not only sexist but racist), third world women are defined from birth as "impure." Thus the white male is provided with a pool of women who

are fair game for sexual imperialism. Third world women frequently do not report rape and for good reason. When blues singer Billie Holliday was ten years old, she was taken off to a local house by a neighbor and raped. Her mother brought the police to rescue her, and she was taken to the local police station crying and bleeding:

When we got there, instead of treating me and Mom like somebody who called the cops for help, they treated me like I'd killed somebody . . . I guess they had me figured for having enticed this old goat into the whorehouse. . . . All I know for sure is they threw me into a cell . . . a fat white matron . . . saw I was still bleeding, she felt sorry for me and gave me a couple glasses of milk. But nobody else did anything for me except give me filthy looks and snicker to themselves.

After a couple of days in a cell they dragged me into a court. Mr. Dick got sentenced to five years. They sentenced me to a Catholic institution.

Clearly the white man's chivalry is aimed only to protect the chastity of "his" women.

As a final irony, that same system of sexual values from which chivalry is derived has also provided womankind with an unwritten code of behavior, called femininity, which makes a feminine woman the perfect victim of sexual aggression. If being chaste does not ward off the possibility of assault, being feminine certainly increases the chances that it will succeed. To be submissive is to defer to masculine strength; is to lack muscular development or any interest in defending oneself; is to let doors be opened, to have one's arm held when crossing the street. To be feminine is to wear shoes which make it difficult to run; skirts which inhibit one's stride; underclothes which inhibit the circulation. Is it not an intriguing observation that those very clothes which are thought to be flattering to the female and attractive to the male are those which make it impossible for a woman to defend herself against aggression?

Each girl as she grows into womanhood is taught fear. Fear is the form in which the female internalizes both chivalry and the double standard. Since, biologically speaking, women in fact have the same if not greater potential for sexual expression as do men, the woman who is taught that she must behave differently from a man must also learn to distrust her own carnality. She must deny her own feelings and learn not to act from them. She fears herself. This is the essence of passivity, and of course, a woman's passivity is not simply sexual but functions to cripple her from self-expression in every area of her life.

Passivity itself prevents a woman from ever considering her own potential for self-defense and forces her to look to men for protection. The woman is taught fear, but this time fear of the other; and yet her only relief from this fear is to seek out the other. Moreover, the passive woman is taught to regard herself as impotent, unable to act, unable even to perceive, in no way self-sufficient, and, finally, as the object and not the subject of human behavior. It is in this sense that a woman is deprived of the status of a human being. She is not free to be.

III

Since Ibsen's Nora slammed the door on her patriarchical husband, woman's attempt to be free has been more or less fashionable. In this nineteenth-century portrait of a woman leaving her marriage, Nora tells her husband, "Our home has been nothing but a playroom. I have been your doll-wife just as at home I was papa's doll-child." And, at least on the stage, "The Doll's House" crumbled, leaving audiences with hope for the fate of the modern woman. And today, as in the past, womankind has not lacked examples of liberated women to emulate: Emma Goldman, Greta Garbo and Isadora Duncan all denounced marriage and the double standard, and believed their right to freedom included sexual independence; but still their example has not affected the lives of millions of women who continue to marry, divorce and remarry, living out their lives dependent on the status and economic power of men. Patriarchy still holds the average woman prisoner not because she lacks the courage of an Isadora Duncan, but because the material conditions of her life prevent her from being anything but an object.

In the *Elementary Structures of Kinship*, Claude Levi-Strauss gives to marriage this universal description, "It is always a system of exchange that we find at the origin of the rules of marriage." In this system of exchange, a woman is the "most precious possession." Levi-Strauss continues that the custom of including women as booty in the marketplace is still so general that "a whole volume would not be sufficient to enumerate instances of it." Levi-Strauss makes it clear that he does not exclude Western Civilization from his definition of "universal" and cites examples from modern wedding ceremonies. (The marriage ceremony is still one in which the husband and wife become one, and "that one is the husband.")

The legal proscription against rape reflects this possessory view of women. An article in the 1952–53 *Yale Law Journal* describes the legal rationale behind laws against rape: "In our society sexual taboos, often enacted into law, buttress a system of monogamy based upon the law of 'free bargaining' of the potential spouses. Within this process the woman's power to withhold or grant sexual access is an important bargaining weapon." Presumably then, laws against rape are intended to protect the right of a woman, not for physical self-determination, but for physical "bargaining." The article goes on to explain explicitly why the preservation of the bodies of women is important to men:

The consent standard in our society does more than protect a significant item of social currency for women; it fosters, and is in turn bolstered by, a masculine pride in the exclusive possession of a sexual object. The consent of a woman to sexual intercourse awards the man a privilege of bodily access, a personal "prize" whose value is enhanced by sole ownership. An additional reason for the man's condemnation of rape may be found in the threat to his status from a decrease in the "value" of his sexual possession which would result from forcible violation.

The passage concludes by making clear whose interest the law is designed to protect. "The man responds to this undercutting of his status as *possessor* of the girl with hostility toward the rapist; no other restitution device is available. The law of rape provides an orderly outlet for his vengeance.'' Presumably the female victim in any case will have been sufficiently socialized so as not to consciously feel any strong need for vengeance. If she does feel this need, society does not speak to it.

The laws against rape exist to protect rights of the male as possessor of the female body, and not the right of the female over her own body. Even without this enlightening passage from the *Yale Law Review*, the laws themselves are clear: in no state can a man be accused of raping his wife. How can any man steal what already belongs to him? It is in the sense of rape as theft of another man's property that Kate Millett writes, ''Traditionally rape has been viewed as an offense one male commits against another—a matter of abusing his women.'' In raping another man's woman, a man may aggrandize his own manhood and concurrently reduce that of another man. Thus a man's honor is not subject directly to rape, but only indirectly, through ''his'' woman.

If the basic social unit is the family, in which the woman is a possession of her husband, the super-structure of society is a male hierarchy, in which men dominate other men (or patriarchal families dominate other patriarchal families). And it is no small irony that, while the very social fabric of our male-dominated culture denies women equal access to political, economic and legal power, the literature, myth and humor of our culture depict women not only as the power behind the throne, but the real source of the oppression of men. The religious version of this fairy tale blames Eve for both carnality and eating of the tree of knowledge, at the same time making her gullible to the obvious devices of a serpent. Adam of course, is merely the trusting victim of love. Certainly this is a biased story. But no more biased than the one television audiences receive today from the latest slick comedians. Through a medium which is owned by men, censored by a State dominated by men, all the evils of this social system which make a man's life unpleasant are blamed upon ''the wife.'' The theory is: were it not for the female who waits and plots to ''trap'' the male into marriage, modern man would be able to achieve Olympian freedom. She is made the scapegoat for a system which is in fact run by men.

Nowhere is this more clear than in the white racist use of the concept of white womanhood. The white male's open rape of black women, coupled with his overweening concern for the chastity and protection of his wife and daughters, represents an extreme of sexist and racist hypocrisy. While on the one hand she was held up as the standard for purity and virtue, on the other the Southern white woman was never asked if she wanted to be on a pedestal, and in fact any deviance from the male-defined standards for white womanhood was treated severely. (It is a powerful commentary on American racism that the historical role of Blacks as slaves, and thus possessions without power, has robbed black women of legal and economic protection through marriage. Thus black women in Southern society and in the ghettoes of the North have long been easy game for white rapists.) The fear that black men would rape white women was, and is, classic paranoia. Quoting from Ann Breen's unpublished study of racism and sexism in the South, *''The New South: White Man's Country,''* Frederick Douglass legitimately points out that had the black man wished to rape white women, he had ample opportunity to do so during the Civil War when white women, the wives, sisters, daughters and mothers of the rebels, were left in the care of Blacks. But yet not a single act of rape was committed during this time. The Ku Klux Klan, who tarred and feathered black men and lynched them in the honor of the purity of white womanhood, also applied tar and feathers to a Southern white woman accused of bigamy, which leads one to suspect that Southern white men were not so much outraged at the violation of the woman as a person, in the few instances where rape was actually committed by black men, but at the violation of his property rights. In the situation where a black man was found to be having sexual relations with a white woman, the white woman could exercise skin-privilege, and claim that she had been raped, in which case the black man was lynched. But if she did not claim rape, she herself was subject to lynching.

In constructing the myth of white womanhood so as to justify the lynching and oppression of black men and women, the white male has created a convenient symbol of his own power which has resulted in black hostility toward the white "bitch," accompanied by an unreasonable fear on the part of many white women of the black rapist. Moreover, it is not surprising that after being told for two centuries that he wants to rape white women, occasionally a black man does actually commit that act. But it is crucial to note that the frequency of this practice is outrageously exaggerated in the white mythos. Ninety percent of reported rape is intra- not inter-racial.

In *Soul on Ice*, Eldridge Cleaver has described the mixing of a rage against white power with the internalized sexism of a black man raping a white woman. "Somehow I arrived at the conclusion that, as a matter of principle, it was of paramount importance for me to have an antagonistic, ruthless attitude toward white women. . . . Rape was an insurrectionary act. It delighted me that I was defying and trampling upon the white man's law, upon his system of values and that I was defiling his women—and this point, I believe, was the most satisfying to me because I was very resentful over the historical fact of how the white man had used the black woman." Thus a black man uses white women to take out his rage against white men. But in fact, whenever a rape of a white woman by a black man does take place, it is again the white man who benefits. First, the act itself terrorizes the white woman and makes her more dependent on the white male for protection. Then, if the woman prosecutes her attacker, the white man is afforded legal opportunity to exercise overt racism. Of course, the knowledge of the rape helps to perpetuate two myths which are beneficial to white male rule—the bestiality of the black man and the desirability of white women. Finally, the white man surely benefits because he himself is not the object of attack—he has been allowed to stay in power.

Indeed, the existence of rape in any form is beneficial to the ruling class of white males. For rape is a kind of terrorism which severely limits the freedom of women and makes women dependent on men. Moreover, in the act of rape, the rage that one man may harbor toward another higher in the male hierarchy can be deflected toward a female scapegoat. For every man there is always someone lower on the social scale on whom he can take out his aggressions. And that is any woman alive.

This oppressive attitude toward women finds its institutionalization in the traditional family. For it is assumed that a man "wears the pants" in his family—he exercises the option of rule whenever he so chooses. Not that he makes all the decisions—clearly women make most of the important day-to-day decisions in a family. But when a conflict of interest arises, it is the man's interest which will prevail. His word, in itself, is more powerful. He lords it over his wife in the same way his boss lords it over him, so that the very process of exercising his power becomes as important an act as obtaining whatever it is his power can get for him. This notion of power is key to the male ego in this culture, for the two acceptable measures of masculinity are a man's power over women and his power over other men. A man may boast to his friends that "I have 20 men working for me." It is also aggrandizement of his ego if he has the financial power to clothe his wife in furs and jewels. And, if a man lacks the wherewithal to acquire such power, he can always express his rage through equally masculine activities—rape and theft. Since male society defines the female as a possession, it is not surprising that the felony most often committed together with rape is theft. . . .

Rape is an act of aggression in which the victim is denied her self-determination. It is an act of violence which, if not actually followed by beatings or murder, nevertheless always carries with it the threat of death. And finally, rape is a form of mass terrorism, for the victims of rape are chosen indiscriminately, but the propagandists for male supremacy broadcast that it is women who cause rape by being unchaste or in the wrong place at the wrong time—in essence, by behaving as though they were free. . . .

But rape is not an isolated act that can be rooted out from patriarchy without ending patriarchy itself. The same men and power structure who victimize women are engaged in the act of raping Vietnam, raping Black people and the very earth we live upon. Rape is a classic act of domination where, in the words of Kate Millett, ''the emotions of hatred, contempt, and the desire to break or violate personality'' take place. This breaking of the personality characterizes modern life itself. No simple reforms can eliminate rape. As the symbolic expression of the white male hierarchy, rape is the quintessential act of our civilization, one which, Valerie Solanis warns, is in danger of ''humping itself to death.''

"THE MIND THAT BURNS IN EACH BODY"
Women, Rape, and Racial Violence

Jacquelyn Dowd Hall

I
HOSTILITY FOCUSED ON HUMAN FLESH

FLORIDA TO BURN NEGRO AT STAKE: SEX CRIMINAL SEIZED FROM JAIL, WILL BE MUTILATED, SET AFIRE IN EXTRA-LEGAL VENGEANCE FOR DEED
—Dothan (Alabama)
Eagle, October 26, 1934

After taking the nigger to the woods . . . they cut off his penis. He was made to eat it. Then they cut off his testicles and made him eat them and say he liked it.
—Member of a lynch mob, 1934[1]

In *Powers of Desire: The Politics of Sexuality*, 1983. Copyright © by Ann Snitow, Christine Stansell, and Sharon Thompson. Reprinted by permission of Monthly Review Foundation.

My title comes from Adrienne Rich, "Disloyal to Civilization: Feminism, Racism, Gynephobia," in Rich, *On Lies, Secrets and Silences: Selected Prose, 1966–1978* (New York: W. W. Norton, 1979), p. 299. Parts of this essay are taken from Jacquelyn Dowd Hall, *Revolt Against Chivalry: Jessie Daniel Ames and the Women's Campaign Against Chivalry* (New York: Columbia University Press, 1979), and full documentation can be found in that work. See also Hall, " 'A Truly Subversive Affair': Women Against Lynching in the Twentieth-Century South," in *Women of America: A History*, ed. Carol Berkin and Mary Beth Norton (Boston: Houghton Mifflin, 1979). Thanks to Rosemarie Hester, Walter Dellinger,Loretta Ross, Nkenge Toure, Janet Colm, Kathleen Dowdy, and Nell Painter for their help and encouragement.

[1]Quoted in Howard Kester, *The Lynching of Claude Neal* (New York: National Association for the Advancement of Colored People, 1934).

Lynching, like rape, has not yet been given its history. Perhaps it has been too easily relegated to the shadows where "poor white" stereotypes dwell. Perhaps the image of absolute victimization it evokes has been too difficult to reconcile with what we know about black resilience and resistance. Yet the impact of lynching, both as practice and as symbol, can hardly be underestimated. Between 1882 and 1946 almost 5,000 people died by lynching. The lynching of Emmett Till in 1955 for whistling at a white woman, the killing of three civil rights workers in Mississippi in the 1960s, and the hanging of a black youth in Alabama in 1981 all illustrate the persistence of this tradition of ritual violence in the service of racial control, a tradition intimately bound up with the politics of sexuality.

Vigilantism originated on the eighteenth-century frontier where it filled a vacuum in law enforcement. Rather than passing with the frontier, however, lynching was incorporated into the distinctive legal system of southern slave society.[2] In the nineteenth century, the industrializing North moved toward a modern criminal justice system in which police, courts, and prisons administered an impersonal, bureaucratic rule of law designed to uphold property rights and discipline unruly workers. The South,

[2]Michael Stephen Hindus, *Prison and Plantation: Crime, Justice, and Authority in Massachusetts and South Carolina, 1767–1878* (Chapel Hill: University of North Carolina Press, 1980), pp. xix, 31, 124, 253.

in contrast, maintained order through a system of deference and customary authority in which all whites had informal police power over all blacks, slave owners meted out plantation justice undisturbed by any generalized rule of law, and the state encouraged vigilantism as part of its overall reluctance to maintain a strong system of formal authority that would have undermined the planter's prerogatives. The purpose of one system was class control, of the other, control over a slave population. And each tradition continued into the period after the Civil War. In the North, factory-like penitentiaries warehoused displaced members of the industrial proletariat. The South maintained higher rates of personal violence than any other region in the country and lynching crossed over the line from informal law enforcement into outright political terrorism.

White supremacy, of course, did not rest on force alone. Routine institutional arrangements denied to the freedmen and women the opportunity to own land, the right to vote, access to education, and participation in the administration of the law. Lynching reached its height during the battles of Reconstruction and the Populist revolt; once a new system of disfranchisement, debt peonage, and segregation was firmly in place, mob violence gradually declined. Yet until World War I, the average number of lynchings never fell below two or three a week. Through the twenties and thirties, mob violence reinforced white dominance by providing planters with a quasi-official way of enforcing labor contracts and crop lien laws and local officials with a means of extracting deference, regardless of the letter of the law. Individuals may have lynched for their own twisted reasons, but the practice continued only with tacit official consent.[3]

Most importantly, lynching served as a tool of psychological intimidation aimed at blacks as a group. Unlike official authority, the lynch mob was unlimited in its capriciousness. With care and vigilance, an individual might avoid situations that landed him in the hands of the law.

But a lynch mob could strike anywhere, any time. Once the brush fire of rumor began, a manhunt was organized, and the local paper began putting out special editions announcing a lynching in progress, there could be few effective reprieves. If the intended victim could not be found, an innocent bystander might serve as well.

It was not simply the threat of death that gave lynching its repressive power. Even as outbreaks of mob violence declined in frequency, they were increasingly accompanied by torture and sexual mutilation. Descriptions of the first phase of Hitler's death sweep are chillingly applicable to lynching: "Killing was ad hoc, inventive, and in its dependence on imagination, peculiarly expressive . . . this was murder uncanny in its anonymous intimacy, a hostility so personally focused on human flesh that the abstract fact of death was not enough."[4]

At the same time, the expansion of communications and the development of photography in the late nineteenth and early twentieth centuries gave reporting a vividness it had never had before. The lurid evocation of human suffering implicated white readers in each act of aggression and drove home to blacks the consequences of powerlessness. Like whipping under slavery, lynching was an instrument of coercion intended to impress not only the immediate victim but all who saw or heard about the event. And the mass media spread the imagery of rope and faggot far beyond the community in which each lynching took place. Writing about his youth in the rural South in the 1920s, Richard Wright describes the terrible climate of fear:.

The things that influenced my conduct as a Negro did not have to happen to me directly; I needed but to hear of them to feel their full effects in the deepest layers of my consciousness. Indeed, the white brutality that I had not seen was a more effective control of my behavior than that which I knew. The actual experience would have let me see the realistic outlines of what was really happening, but as long as it remained something terrible and yet remote, something whose horror and blood might descend upon me at

---

[3]For recent overviews of lynching, see Robert L. Zangrando, *The NAACP Crusade Against Lynching, 1909–1950* (Philadelphia: Temple University Press, 1980); McGovern, *Anatomy of a Lynching*; and Hall, *Revolt Against Chivalry*.

[4]Terrence Des Pres, "The Struggle of Memory," *The Nation*, 10 April 1982, p. 433.

any moment, I was compelled to give my entire imagination over to it.[5]

A penis cut off and stuffed in a victim's mouth. A crowd of thousands watching a black man scream in pain. Such incidents did not have to occur very often, or be witnessed directly, to be burned indelibly into the mind.

II
NEVER AGAINST HER WILL

White men have said over and over—and we have believed it because it was repeated so often—that not only was there no such thing as a chaste Negro woman—but that a Negro woman could not be assaulted, that it was never against her will.

—Jessie Daniel Ames (1936)

Schooled in the struggle against sexual rather than racial violence, contemporary feminists may nevertheless find familiar this account of lynching's political function, for analogies between rape and lynching have often surfaced in the literature of the anti-rape movement. To carry such analogies too far would be to fall into the error of radical feminist writing that misconstrues the realities of racism in the effort to illuminate sexual subordination.[6] It is the suggestion of this essay, however, that there is a significant resonance between these two forms of violence. We are only beginning to understand the web of connections among racism, attitudes toward women, and sexual ideologies. The purpose of looking more closely at the dynamics of repressive violence is not to reduce sexual assault and mob murder to static equivalents but to illuminate some of the strands of that tangled web.

The association between lynching and rape emerges most clearly in their parallel use in racial subordination. As Diane K. Lewis has pointed out, in a patriarchal society, black men, as men, constituted a potential challenge to the estab-

lished order.[7] Laws were formulated primarily to exclude black men from adult male prerogatives in the public sphere, and lynching meshed with these legal mechanisms of exclusion. Black women represented a more ambiguous threat. They too were denied access to the politico-jural domain, but since they shared this exclusion with women in general, its maintenance engendered less anxiety and required less force. Lynching served primarily to dramatize hierarchies among men. In contrast, the violence directed at black women illustrates the double jeopardy of race and sex. The records of the Freedmen's Bureau and the oral histories collected by the Federal Writers' Project testify to the sexual atrocities endured by black women as whites sought to reassert their command over the newly freed slaves. Black women were sometimes executed by lynch mobs, but more routinely they served as targets of sexual assault.

Like vigilantism, the sexual exploitation of black women had been institutionalized under slavery. Whether seized through outright force or voluntarily granted within the master-slave relation, the sexual access of white men to black women was a cornerstone of patriarchal power in the South. It was used as a punishment or demanded in exchange for leniency. Like other forms of deference and conspicuous consumption, it buttressed planter hegemony. And it served the practical economic purpose of replenishing the slave labor supply.

After the Civil War, the informal sexual arrangements of slavery shaded into the use of rape as a political weapon, and the special vulnerability of black women helped shape the ex-slaves' struggle for the prerequisites of freedom. Strong family bonds had survived the adversities of slavery; after freedom, the black family served as a bulwark against a racist society. Indeed, the sharecropping system that replaced slavery as the South's chief mode of production grew in part from the desire of blacks to withdraw from gang labor and gain control over their own work, family lives, and bodily integrity. The sharecropping family enabled

---

[5]Quoted in William H. Chafe, *Women and Equality: Changing Patterns in American Culture* (New York: Oxford University Press, 1977), p. 60.

[6]Margaret A. Simons, "Racism and Feminism: A Schism in the Sisterhood," *Feminist Studies* 5 (Summer 1979): 384–401.

[7]Diane K. Lewis, "A Response to Inequality: Black Women, Racism, and Sexism," *Signs* 3 (Winter 1977): 341–42.

women to escape white male supervision, devote their productive and reproductive powers to their own families, and protect themselves from sexual assault.[8]

Most studies of racial violence have paid little attention to the particular suffering of women.[9] Even rape has been seen less as an aspect of sexual oppression than as a transaction between white and black men. Certainly Claude Lévi-Strauss's insight that men use women as verbs with which to communicate with one another (rape being a means of communicating defeat to the men of a conquered tribe) helps explain the extreme viciousness of sexual violence in the post-emancipation era.[10] Rape *was* in part a reaction to the effort of the freedmen to assume the role of patriarch, able to provide for and protect his family. Nevertheless, as writers like Susan Griffin and Susan Brownmiller and others have made clear, rape is first and foremost a crime against women.[11] Rape sent a message to black men, but more centrally, it expressed male sexual attitudes in a culture both racist and patriarchal.

Recent historians of Victorian sexuality have traced the process by which a belief in female "passionlessness" replaced an older notion of women's dangerous sexual power.[12] Even at the height of the "cult of true womanhood" in the nineteenth century, however, views of women's sexuality remained ambivalent and double-edged. The association between women and nature, the dread of women's treacherous carnality, persisted, rooted, as Dorothy Dinnerstein persuasively argues, in the earliest experiences of infancy.

In the United States, the fear and fascination of female sexuality was projected onto black women; the passionless lady arose in symbiosis with the primitively sexual slave. House slaves often served as substitute mothers; at a black woman's breast white men experienced absolute dependence on a being who was both a source of wish-fulfilling joy and of grief-producing disappointment. In adulthood, such men could find in this black woman a ready object for the mixture of rage and desire that so often underlies male heterosexuality. The black woman, already in chains, was sexually available, unable to make claims for support or concern; by dominating her, men could replay the infant's dream of unlimited access to the mother.[13] The economic and political challenge posed by the black patriarch might be met with death by lynching, but when the black woman seized the opportunity to turn her maternal and sexual resources to the benefit of her own family, sexual violence met her assertion of will. Thus rape reasserted white dominance and control in the private arena as lynching reasserted hierarchical arrangements in the public transactions of men.

III
LYNCHING'S DOUBLE MESSAGE

The crowds from here that went over to see [Lola Cannidy, the alleged rape victim in the Claude Neal lynching of 1934] said he was so large he could not assault her until he took his knife and cut her, and also had either cut or bit one of her breast [sic] off.

> —Letter to Mrs. W. P. Cornell, October 29, 1934, Association of Southern Women for the Prevention of Lynching Papers

[8]Jacqueline Jones, *Freed Women? Black Women, Work, and the Family During the Civil War and Reconstruction*, Working Paper No. 61, Wellesley College, 1980; Roger L. Ransom and Richard Sutch, *One Kind of Freedom: The Economic Consequences of Emancipation* (New York: Cambridge University Press, 1977), pp. 87–103.

[9]Gerda Lerner, *Black Women in White America: A Documentary History* (New York: Random House, 1972), is an early and important exception.

[10]Robin Morgan, "Theory and Practice: Pornography and Rape," *Take Back the Night: Women on Pornography*, ed. Laura Lederer (New York: William Morrow, 1980), p. 140.

[11]Susan Griffin, "Rape: The All-American Crime," *Ramparts* (September 1971): 26–35; Susan Brownmiller, *Against Our Will: Men, Women, and Rape* (New York: Simon and Schuster, 1975). See also Kate Millet, *Sexual Politics* (Garden City, N.Y.: Doubleday & Co., 1970).

[12]Nancy F. Cott, "Passionlessness: An Interpretation of Victorian Sexual Ideology, 1790–1850," *Signs* 4 (Winter 1978): 219–36.

[13]Dorothy Dinnerstein, *The Mermaid and the Minotaur: Sexual Arrangements and Human Malaise* (New York: Harper and Row, 1977). See also Phyllis Marynick Palmer, "White Women/Black Women: The Dualism of Female Identity and Experience," unpublished paper presented at the American Studies Association, September 1979, pp. 15–17 Similarly, British Victorian eroticism was structured by class relations

. . . more than rape itself, the fear of rape permeates our lives. . . . and the best defense against this is not to be, to deny being in the body, as a self, to . . . avert your gaze, make yourself, as a presence in the world, less felt.

—Susan Griffin, *Rape: The Power of Consciousness* (1979)

In the 1920s and 1930s, the industrial revolution spread through the South, bringing a demand for more orderly forms of law enforcement. Men in authority, anxious to create a favorable business climate, began to withdraw their tacit approval of extralegal violence. Yet lynching continued, particularly in rural areas, and even as white moderates criticized lynching in the abstract, they continued to justify outbreaks of mob violence for the one special crime of sexual assault. For most white Americans, the association between lynching and rape called to mind not twin forms of white violence against black men and women, but a very different image: the black rapist, "a monstrous beast, crazed with lust";[14] the white victim—young, blond, virginal; her manly Anglo-Saxon avengers. Despite the pull of modernity, the emotional logic of lynching remained: only swift, sure violence, unhampered by legalities, could protect white women from sexual assault.

The "protection of white womanhood" was a pervasive fixture of racist ideology. In 1839, for example, a well-known historian offered this commonly accepted rationale for lynching: black men find "something strangely alluring and seductive . . . in the appearance of the white woman; they are aroused and stimulated by its foreignness to their experience of sexual pleasures, and it moves them to gratify their lust at any cost and in spite of every obstacle." In

1937, echoing an attitude that characterized most local newspapers, the Jackson, Mississippi, *Daily News* published what it felt was the *coup de grace* to anti-lynching critics: "What would you do if your wife, daughter, or one of your loved ones was ravished? You'd probably be right there with the mob." Two years later, 65 percent of the white respondents in an anthropological survey believed that lynching was justified in cases of sexual assault.[15] Despite its tenacity, however, the myth of the black rapist was never founded on objective reality. Less than a quarter of lynch victims were even accused of rape or attempted rape. Down to the present, almost every study has underlined the fact that rape is overwhelmingly an intraracial crime, and the victims are more often black than white.[16]

A major strategy of anti-lynching reformers, beginning with Ida B. Wells in the 1880s and continuing with Walter White of the NAACP and Jessie Daniel Ames of the Association of Southern Women for the Prevention of Lynching, was to use such facts to undermine the rationalizations for mob violence. But the emotional circuit between interracial rape and lynching lay beyond the reach of factual refutation. A black man did not literally have to attempt sexual assault for whites to perceive some transgression of caste mores as a sexual threat. White women were the forbidden fruit, the untouchable property, the ultimate symbol of white male power. To break the racial rules was to conjure up an image of black over white, of a world turned upside down.

Again, women were a means of communication and, on one level, the rhetoric of protection, like the rape of black women, reflected a power

---

in which upper-class men were nursed by lower-class country women. See Ellen Ross and Rayna Rapp in this volume.

[14]A statement made in 1901 by George T. Winston, president of the University of North Carolina, typifies these persistent images: "The southern woman with her helpless little children in a solitary farm house no longer sleeps secure. . . . The black brute is lurking in the dark, a monstrous beast, crazed with lust. His ferocity is almost demoniacal. A mad bull or a tiger could scarcely be more brutal" (quoted in Charles Herbert Stember, *Sexual Racism: The Emotional Barrier to an Integrated Society* [New York: Elsevier, 1976], p. 23).

[15]Philip Alexander Bruce, *The Plantation Negro as a Freeman* (New York: Putnam's, 1889), pp. 83–84; Jackson *Daily News*, 27 May 1937; Hortense Powdermaker, *After Freedom: A Cultural Study in the Deep South* (1939; New York: Atheneum, 1969), pp. 54–55, 389.

[16]For a contradictory view, see, for example, S. Nelson and M. Amir, "The Hitchhike Victim of Rape: A Research Report," in *Victimology: A New Focus. Vol. 5: Exploiters and Exploited*, ed. M. Agopian, D. Chappell, and G. Geis, and I. Drapkin and E. Viano (1975), p. 47; and "Black Offender and White Victim: A Study of Forcible Rape in Oakland, California," in *Forcible Rape: The Crime, the Victim, and the Offender* (New York: Columbia University Press, 1977).

struggle among men. But impulses toward women as well as toward blacks were played out in the drama of racial violence. The fear of rape was more than a hypocritical excuse for lynching; rather, the two phenomena were intimately intertwined. The "southern rape complex" functioned as a means of both sexual and racial suppression.[17]

For whites, the archetypal lynching for rape can be seen as a dramatization of cultural themes, a story they told themselves about the social arrangements and psychological strivings that lay beneath the surface of everyday life. The story such rituals told about the place of white women in southern society was subtle, contradictory, and demeaning. The frail victim, leaning on the arms of her male relatives, might be brought to the scene of the crime, there to identify her assailant and witness his execution. This was a moment of humiliation. A woman who had just been raped, or who had been apprehended in a clandestine interracial affair, or whose male relatives were pretending that she had been raped, stood on display before the whole community. Here was the quintessential Woman as Victim: polluted, "ruined for life," the object of fantasy and secret contempt. Humiliation, however, mingled with heightened worth as she played for a moment the role of the Fair Maiden violated and avenged. For this privilege—if the alleged assault had in fact taken place—she might pay with suffering in the extreme. In any case, she would pay with a lifetime of subjugation to the men gathered in her behalf.

Only a small percentage of lynchings, then, revolved around charges of sexual assault; but those that did received by far the most attention and publicity—indeed, they gripped the white imagination far out of proportion to their statistical significance. Rape and rumors of rape became the folk pornography of the Bible Belt. As stories spread the rapist became not just a black man but a ravenous brute, the victim a beautiful young virgin. The experience of the woman was described in minute and progressively embellished detail, a public fantasy that implied a group participation in the rape as cathartic as the subsequent lynching. White men might see in "lynch law" their ideal selves: patriarchs, avengers, righteous protectors. But, being men themselves, and sometimes even rapists, they must also have seen themselves in the lynch mob's prey.

The lynch mob in pursuit of the black rapist represented the trade-off implicit in the code of chivalry: for the right of the southern lady to protection presupposed her obligation to obey. The connotations of wealth and family background attached to the position of the lady in the antebellum South faded in the twentieth century, but the power of "ladyhood" as a value construct remained. The term denoted chastity, frailty, graciousness. "A lady," noted one social-psychologist, "is always in a state of becoming: one acts like a lady, one attempts to be a lady, but one never *is* a lady." Internalized by the individual, this ideal regulated behavior and restricted interaction with the world.[18] If a woman passed the tests of ladyhood, she could tap into the reservoir of protectiveness and shelter known as southern chivalry. Women who abandoned secure, if circumscribed, social roles forfeited the claim to personal security. Together the practice of ladyhood and the etiquette of chivalry controlled white women's behavior even as they guarded caste lines.

Proslavery theorist Thomas R. Dew spelled out this dialectic. The "essence of manhood," he wrote, is "predation." The essence of womanhood is "allure." Only the rise of gallantry and the patriarchal family offered a haven from male aggression. Stripped to its bare essentials, then, the difference between the sexes was the opposition between the potential rapist and the potential victim of sexual assault, and the family metaphor that justified slavery offered the

[17]Winthrop Jordan, *White over Black: American Attitudes Toward the Negro, 1550–1812* (Baltimore: Penguin Books, 1969); W. J. Cash, *The Mind of the South* (New York: Knopf, 1941), p. 117.

[18]This reading of lynching as a "cultural text" is modeled on Clifford Geertz, "Deep Play: Notes on the Balinese Cockfight," in *The Interpretation of Cultures: Selected Essays by Clifford Geertz* (New York: Basic Books, 1973), pp. 412–53. For "ladyhood," see Greer Litton Fox, " 'Nice Girl': Social Control of Women Through a Value Construct," *Signs* 2 (Summer 1977): 805–17.

exchange of dependence for protection to the mistress as well as to the slaves. Dew's notion of female sexuality, however, did not deny her passions of her own. On the contrary, because her role was not to seek, "but to be sought . . . not to woo, but to be wooed," she was forced to suppress her "most violent feelings . . . her most ardent desires."[19] In general, the law of rape expressed profound distrust of women, demanding evidence of "utmost resistance," corroboration by other witnesses in addition to the victim's word, and proof of the victim's chastity—all contrary to the rules of evidence in other forms of violent crime. In sharp contrast, however, when a black man and a white woman were concerned intercourse was prima facie evidence of rape. The presiding judge in the 1931 Scottsboro trial, in which nine black youths were accused of rape, had this to say:

Where the woman charged to have been raped, as in this case is a white woman, there is a very strong presumption under the law that she would not and did not yield voluntarily to intercourse with the defendant, a Negro; and this is true, whatever the station in life the prosecutrix may occupy, whether she be the most despised, ignorant and abandoned woman of the community, or the spotless virgin and daughter of a prominent home of luxury and learning.[20]

Lynching, then, like laws against intermarriage, masked uneasiness over the nature of white women's desires. It aimed not only to engender fear of sexual assault but also to prevent voluntary unions. It upheld the comforting fiction that at least in relation to black men, white women were always objects and never agents of sexual desire.

Although the nineteenth-century women's movement for the most part advocated higher moral standards for men, not sexual liberation for women, opponents insisted that it threatened the family and painted feminists as spinsters or libertines, sexual deviants in either case. It may be no accident, then, that the vision of the black

man as a threatening beast flourished during the first phase of the southern women's rights movement, a fantasy of aggression against boundary-transgressing women as well as a weapon of terror against blacks. Certainly the rebelliousness of that feminist generation was circumscribed by the feeling that women were hedged about by a "nameless horror." The South, wrote one turn-of-the-century woman, had become "a smoldering volcano, the dark of its quivering night . . . pierced through by the cry of some outraged woman."[21]

When women in the 1920s and 1930s did begin to assert their right to sexual expression and to challenge the double standard Thomas Dew's injunctions implied, inheritors of the plantation legend responded with explicit attacks that revealed the sanctions at the heart of the chivalric ideal. William Faulkner's *The Sanctuary*, published in 1931, typified a common literary reaction to the fall of the lady. The corncob rape of Temple Drake—a "new woman" of the 1920s—was the ultimate revenge against the abdicating white virgin. Her fate represented the "desecration of cult object," the implicit counterpoint to the idealization of women in a patriarchal society.[22]

IV
LADY INSURRECTIONISTS

The lady insurrectionists gathered together in one of our southern cities. . . . They said calmly that they were not afraid of being raped; as for their sacredness, they would take care of it themselves; they did not need the chivalry of lynching to protect them and did not want it.

—Lillian Smith, *Killers of the Dream* (1949)

On November 1, 1930, twenty-six white women from six southern states met in Atlanta to form

---

[19]Quoted in William R. Taylor, *Cavalier and Yankee: The Old South and American National Character* (Garden City, N.Y.: Doubleday/Anchor, 1963), pp. 148–51.

[20]Dan T. Carter, *Scottsboro: An American Tragedy* (Baton Rouge: Louisiana State University Press, 1969), p. 36.

[21]Belle Kearney, *A Slaveholder's Daughter* (New York: Abbey Press, 1900), p. 96; Myrta Lockett Avary, *Dixie after the War* (1906; New York: Negro Universities Press, 1969), pp. 377–90. See also John E. Talmadge, *Rebecca Latimer Felton: Nine Stormy Decades* (Athens: University of Georgia Press, 1960), pp. 98–124.

[22]Leslie Fiedler, *Love and Death in the American Novel* (New York: Delta, 1966), pp. 320–24.

the Association of Southern Women for the Prevention of Lynching. Organized by Texas suffragist Jessie Daniel Ames, the association had a central, ideological goal: to break the circuit between the tradition of chivalry and the practice of mob murder. The association was part of a broader interracial movement; its contribution to the decline of lynching must be put in the perspective of the leadership role played by blacks in the national anti-lynching campaign. But it would be a mistake to view the association simply as a white women's auxiliary to black-led struggles. Rather, it represented an acceptance of accountability for a racist mythology that white women had not created but that they nevertheless served, a point hammered home by black women's admonitions that "when Southern white women get ready to stop lynching, it will be stopped and not before."[23]

Jessie Ames, the association's leader, stood on the brink between two worlds. Born in 1883 in a small town in East Texas, a regional hotbed of mob violence, she directed the anti-lynching campaign from Atlanta, capital of the New South. She drew eclectically on the nineteenth-century female reform tradition and advocated an implicitly feminist anti-racism that looked backward to the abolitionist movement as well as forward to feminists of our own times.

Ames had come to maturity in a transitional phase of the women's movement, when female reformers used the group consciousness and Victorian sense of themselves as especially moral beings to justify a great wave of female institution building. When Jessie Ames turned from suffrage to the reform of race relations, she looked naturally to this heritage for her constituency and tactics. The association drew its members from among small-town church women, schooled for decades in running their own affairs within YMCAs, women's clubs, and missionary societies and sensitized by the temperance and suffrage movements to a politics that simultaneously stressed domestic order and women's rights.[24] Ames's strategy for change called for enfranchised women to exercise moral influence over the would-be lynchers in their own homes, political influence over the public officials who collaborated with them, and cultural influence over the editors and politicians who created an atmosphere where mob violence flourished. Like Frances Willard and the temperance campaign, she sought to extend women's moral guardianship into the most quintessentially masculine affairs.

Ames's tenacity and the emotional energy of her campaign derived from her perception that lynching was a women's issue: not only an obstacle to regional development and an injustice to blacks, but also an insult to white women. Along with black women leaders before her, who had perceived that the same sexual stereotyping that allowed black women to be exploited caused black men to be feared, she challenged both racist and patriarchal ideas.[25] Disputing the notion that blacks provoked mob action by raping white women, association members traced lynching to its roots in white supremacy.[26] More central to their campaign was an effort to dissociate the image of the lady from its connotations of sexual vulnerability and retaliatory violence. If lynching held a covert message for white women as well as an overt one for blacks, then the

---

[23]Rich, "Disloyal to Civilization"; Jessie Daniel Ames to Mary McLeod Bethune, 9 March 1938, Association of Southern Women for the Prevention of Lynching (ASWPL) Papers, Atlanta University, Atlanta, Georgia (henceforth cited as ASWPL Papers). For black women's prior activities, see Ida B. Wells, *Crusade for Justice: The Autobiography of Ida B. Wells* (Chicago: University of Chicago Press, 1970); Lerner, *Black Women*, pp. 194–215; Bettina Aptheker, *Lynching and Rape: An Exchange of Views*, Occasional Paper No. 25, American Institute of Marxist Studies (1977); and Angela Y. Davis, *Women, Race, and Class* (New York: Random House, 1982), pp. 169–98.

[24]For this reform tradition, see Estelle Freedman, "Separatism as Strategy: Female Institution Building and American Feminism, 1870–1930," *Feminist Studies* 5 (Fall 1979): 512–29; Mari Jo Buhle, *Women and American Socialism, 1780–1920* (Urbana: University of Illinois Press, 1981); and Barbara Leslie Epstein, *The Politics of Domesticity: Women, Evangelism, and Temperance in Nineteenth-Century America* (Middletown, Conn.: Wesleyan University Press, 1981).

[25]Deb Friedman, "Rape, Racism—and Reality," *Aegis* (July/August, 1978); 17–26.

[26]Jessie Daniel Ames to Miss Doris Loraine, 5 March 1935, ASWPL Papers.

anti-lynching association represented a woman-centered reply. Lynching, it proclaimed, far from offering a shield against sexual assault, served as a weapon of both racial and sexual terror, planting fear in women's minds and dependency in their hearts. It thrust them in the role of personal property or sexual objects, ever threatened by black men's lust, ever in need of white men's protection. Asserting their identity as autonomous citizens, requiring not the paternalism of chivalry but the equal protection of the law, association members resisted the part assigned to them.

If, as Susan Brownmiller claims, the larger anti-lynching movement paid little attention to lynching's counterpart, the rape of black women, the women's association could not ignore the issue. For one thing, black women in the interracial movement continually brought it to their attention, prodding them to take responsibility for stopping both lynching and sexual exploitation. For another, from slavery on, interracial sex had been a chronic source of white women's discontent.[27] In 1920, for example, a white interracialist and women's rights leader, who had come to her understanding of racial issues through pioneering meetings with black women, warned a white male audience:

The race problem can never be solved as long as the white man goes unpunished [for interracial sex], while the Negro is burned at the stake. I shall say no more, for I am sure you need not have anything more said. When the white men of the South have come to that position, a single standard for both men and women, then you will accomplish something in this great problem.[28]

In the winter of 1931, Jessie Daniel Ames called a meeting of black and white women for an explicit discussion of the split female image and the sexual double standard. The women, she thought, should gather in closed session with no men present "because there are some vices of Southern life which contribute subtly to [lynching] that we want to face by ourselves." The black leader Nannie Burroughs agreed: "All meetings with white and colored women on this question should be held behind closed doors and men should not be admitted." White male attitudes, the group concluded, originated in a slave system where black women "did not belong to themselves but were in effect the property of white men." They went on to explore the myths of black women's promiscuity and white women's purity, and noted how this split image created a society that "considers an assault by a white man as a moral lapse upon his part, better ignored and forgotten, while an assault by a Negro against a white woman is a hideous crime punishable with death by law or lynching." Relationships among women interracialists were far from egalitarian, nor could they always overcome the impediments to what Ames called "free and frank" discussion.[29] Yet on occasions like this one the shared experience of gender opened the way for consciousness-raising communication across the color line.

If such discussions of male behavior had to be held behind closed doors, even more treacherous was the question of sex between black men and white women. In 1892, Memphis anti-lynching reformer and black women's club leader Ida B. Wells was threatened with death and run out of town for proclaiming that behind many lynchings lay consensual interracial affairs. Over sixty years later, in the wake of the famous Scottsboro case, Jessie Daniel Ames began delving beneath the surface of lynchings in which white women were involved. Like Barnett, she found that black men were sometimes executed not for rape but for interracial sex. And she used that information to disabuse association members of one of the white South's central fictions:

---

[27] Anne Firor Scott, "Women's Perspective on the Patriarchy in the 1850's," *Journal of American History* 6 (June 1974): 52–64.

[28] Carrie Parks Johnson Address, Commission on Interracial Cooperation (CIC), CIC Papers, Atlanta University, Atlanta, Georgia.

[29] Jessie Daniel Ames to Nannie Burroughs, 24 October 1931; Burroughs to Ames, 30 October 1931, ASWPL Papers; "Appendix F, Digest of Discussion," n.d. [November 20, 1931], Jessie Daniel Ames Papers, University of North Carolina at Chapel Hill.

that, as a Mississippi editor put it, there had never been a southern white woman so depraved as to "bestow her favors on a black man."[30]

But what of lynching cases in which rape actually had occurred? Here association leaders could only fall back on a call for law and order, for they knew from their own experience that the fear engendered in their constituency by what some could bring themselves to call only "the unspeakable crime" was all too real. "Whether their own minds perceive danger where none exists, or whether the fears have been put in their minds by men's fears," Ames commented, women could not but see themselves as potential victims of black assault.[31] It would be left to a future generation to point out that the chief danger to white women came from white men and to see rape in general as a feminist concern. Association leaders could only exorcise their own fears of male aggression by transferring the means of violence from mobs to the state and debunking the myth of the black rapist.

In the civil rights movement of the 1960s, white women would confront the sexual dimension of racism and racial violence by asserting their right to sleep with black men. Anti-lynching reformers of the 1930s obviously took a very different approach. They abhorred male violence and lynching's eroticism of death, and asserted against them a feminine standard of personal and public morality. They portrayed themselves as moral beings and independent citizens rather than vulnerable sexual objects. And the core of their message lay more in what they were than in what they said: southern ladies who needed only their own rectitude to protect them from interracial sex and the law to guard them from sexual assault. When Jessie Ames referred to "the crown of chivalry that has been pressed like a crown of thorns on our heads," she issued a cry of protest that belongs to the struggle for both racial and sexual emancipation.[32]

V
THE DECLINE OF CHIVALRY

As male supremacy becomes ideologically untenable, incapable of justifying itself as protection, men assert their domination more directly, in fantasies and occasionally in acts of raw violence.

—Christopher Lasch,
Marxist Perspectives (1978)

In the 1970s, for the second time in the nation's history, rape again attracted widespread public attention. The obsession with interracial rape, which peaked at the turn of the nineteenth century but lingered from the close of the Civil War into the 1930s, became a magnet for racial and sexual oppression. Today the issue of rape has crystallized important feminist concerns.

Rape emerged as a feminist issue as women developed an independent politics that made sexuality and personal life a central arena of struggle. First in consciousness-raising groups, where autobiography became a politicizing technique, then in public "speakouts," women broke what in retrospect seems a remarkable silence about a pervasive aspect of female experience. From that beginning flowed both an analysis that held rape to be a political act by which men affirm their power over women and strategies for change that ranged from the feminist self-help methods of rape crisis centers to institutional reform of the criminal justice and medical care systems. After 1976, the movement broadened to include wife-battering, sexual harassment, and, following the lead of Robin Morgan's claim that "pornography is the theory, rape the practice," media images of women.[33]

By the time Susan Brownmiller's *Against Our Will: Men, Women and Rape* gained national attention in 1975, she could speak to and for a feminist constituency already sensitized to the issue by years of practical, action-oriented work. Her book can be faulted for supporting a notion of universal patriarchy and timeless sexual victimization; it leaves no room for understanding the reasons for women's collaboration, their own sources of power (both self-generated and

---

[30]Jackson (Mississippi) *Daily News*, February 1931, ASWPL Papers.

[31]Jessie Daniel Ames, "Lynchers' View on Lynching," ASWPL Papers.

[32]Quoted in Wilma Dykeman and James Stokely, *Seeds of Southern Change: The Life of Will Alexander* (Chicago: University of Chicago Press, 1962), p. 143.

[33]Noreen Connell and Cassandra Wilsen, eds., *Rape: The First Sourcebook for Women* (New York: New American Library, 1974); Morgan, "Theory and Practice."

derived), the class and racial differences in their experience of discrimination and sexual danger. But it was an important milestone, pointing the way for research into a subject that has consistently been trivialized and ignored. Many grassroots activists would demur from Brownmiller's assertion that all men are potential rapists, but they share her understanding of the continuum between sexism and sexual assault.[34]

The demand for control over one's own body—control over whether, when, and with whom one has children, control over how one's sexuality is expressed—is central to the feminist project because, as Rosalind Petchesky persuasively argues, it is essential to "a sense of being a person, with personal and bodily integrity," able to engage in conscious activity and to participate in social life.[35] It is this right to bodily integrity and self-determination that rape, and the fear of rape, so thoroughly undermines. Rape's devastating effect on individuals derives not so much from the sexual nature of the crime (and anti-rape activists have been concerned to revise the idea that rape is a "fate worse than death" whose victims, if no longer "ruined for life," are at least so traumatized that they must rely for recovery on therapeutic help rather than on their own resources) as from the experience of helplessness and loss of control, the sense of one's self as an object of rage. And women who may never be raped share, by chronic attrition, in the same helplessness, "otherness," lack of control. The struggle against rape, like the anti-lynching movement, addresses not only external dangers but also internal consequences: the bodily muting, the self-censorship that limits one's capacity to "walk freely in the world."[36]

The focus on rape, then, emerged from the internal dynamics of feminist thought and practice. But it was also a response to an objective increase in the crime. From 1969 to 1974, the number of rapes rose 49 percent, a greater increase than for any other violent crime. Undoubtedly rape statistics reflect general demographic and criminal trends, as well as a greater willingness of victims to report sexual attacks (although observers agree that rape is still the most underreported of crimes).[37] But there can be no doubt that rape is a serious threat and that it plays a prominent role in women's subordination. Using recent high-quality survey data, Allan Griswold Johnson has estimated that, at a minimum, 20 to 30 percent of girls now twelve years old will suffer a violent attack sometime in their lives. A woman is as likely to be raped as she is to experience a divorce or to be diagnosed as having cancer.[38]

In a recent anthology on women and pornography, Tracey A. Gardner has drawn a parallel between the wave of lynching that followed Reconstruction and the increase in rapes in an era of anti-feminist backlash.[39] Certainly, as women enter the workforce, postpone marriage, live alone or as single heads of households, they become easier targets for sexual assault. But observations like Gardner's go further, linking the intensification of sexual violence directly to the feminist challenge. Such arguments come dangerously close to blaming the victim for the crime. But they may also contain a core of truth. Sociological research on rape has only recently begun, and we do not have studies explaining the function and frequency of the crime under various historical conditions; until that work is done we cannot with certainty assess the current situation. Yet it seems clear that just as lynching ebbed and flowed with new modes of racial control, rape—both as act and idea—cannot be divorced from changes in the sexual terrain.

---

[34]Interview with Janet Colm, director of the Chapel Hill-Carrboro (North Carolina) Rape Crisis Center, April 1981. Two of the best recent analyses of rape are Ann Wolbert Burgess and Lynda Lytle Holmstrom, *Rape: Crisis and Recovery* (Bowie, Md.: Robert J. Brady Co., 1979) and Lorenne M. G. Clark and Debra J. Lewis, *Rape: The Price of Coercive Sexuality* (Toronto: Canadian Women's Educational Press, 1977).

[35]Rosalind Pollack Petchesky, "Reproductive Freedom: Beyond 'A Woman's Right to Choose,'" *Signs* 5 (Summer 1980): 661–85.

[36]Adrienne Rich, "Taking Women Students Seriously," in *Lies, Secrets and Silences*, p. 242.

[37]Vivian Berger, "Man's Trial, Women's Tribulation: Rape Cases in the Courtroom," *Columbia Law Review* 1 (1977): 3–12. Thanks to Walter Dellinger for this reference.

[38]Allan Griswold Johnson, "On the Prevalence of Rape in the United States," *Signs* 6 (Fall 1980): 136–46.

[39]Tracey A. Gardner, "Racism in Pornography and the Women's Movement," in *Take Back the Night*, p. 111.

In 1940, Jessie Ames released to the press a statement that, for the first time in her career, the South could claim a "lynchless year," and in 1942, convinced that lynching was no longer widely condoned in the name of white womanhood, she allowed the Association of Southern Women for the Prevention of Lynching to pass quietly from the scene. The women's efforts, the larger, black-led anti-lynching campaign, black migration from the rural South, the spread of industry—these and other developments contributed to the decline of vigilante justice. Blacks continued to be victimized by covert violence and routinized court procedures that amounted to "legal lynchings." But after World War II, public lynchings, announced in the papers, openly accomplished, and tacitly condoned, no longer haunted the land, and the black rapist ceased to be a fixture of political campaigns and newspaper prose.

This change in the rhetoric and form of racial violence reflected new attitudes toward women as well as toward blacks. By the 1940s few southern leaders were willing, as Jessie Ames put it, to "lay themselves open to ridicule" by defending lynching on the grounds of gallantry, in part because gallantry itself had lost conviction.[40] The same process of economic development and national integration that encouraged the South to adopt northern norms of authority and control undermined the chivalric ideal. Industrial capitalism on the one hand and women's assertion of independence on the other weakened paternalism and with it the conventions of protective deference.[41] This is not to say that the link between racism and sexism was broken; relations between white women and black men continued to be severely sanctioned, and black men, to the present, have drawn disproportionate punishment for sexual assault. The figures speak for themselves: of the 455 men executed for rape since 1930, 405 were black, and almost all the complainants were white.[42] Nevertheless, "the protection of white womanhood" rang more hollow in the postwar New South and the fear of interracial rape became a subdued theme in the nation at large rather than an openly articulated regional obsession.

The social feminist mainstream, of which Jessie Ames and the anti-lynching association were a part, thus chipped away at a politics of gallantry that locked white ladies in the home under the guise of protecting them from the world. But because such reformers held to the genteel trappings of their role even as they asserted their autonomous citizenship, they offered reassurance that women's influence could be expanded without mortal danger to male prerogatives and power. Contemporary feminists have eschewed some of the comforting assumptions of their nineteenth-century predecessors: women's passionlessness, their limitation to social housekeeping, their exclusive responsibility for childrearing and housekeeping. They have couched their revolt in explicit ideology and unladylike behavior. Meanwhile, as Barbara Ehrenreich has argued, Madison Avenue has perverted the feminist message into the threatening image of the sexually and economically liberated woman. The result is a shift toward the rapaciousness that has always mixed unstably with sentimental exaltation and concern. Rape has emerged more clearly into the sexual domain, a crime against women most often committed by men of their own race rather than a right of the powerful over women of a subordinate group or a blow by black men against white women's possessors.[43]

---

[40]Jessie Daniel Ames, "Editorial Treatment of Lynching," *Public Opinion Quarterly* 2 (January 1938): 77–84.

[41]For a statement of this theme, see Christopher Lasch, "The Flight from Feeling: Sociopsychology of Sexual Conflict," *Marxist Perspectives* 1 (Spring 1978): 74–95.

[42]Berger, "Man's Trial, Woman's Tribulation," p. 4. For a recent study indicating that the harsher treatment accorded black men convicted of raping white women is not limited to the South and has persisted to the present, see Gary D. LaFree, "The Effect of Sexual Stratification by Race on Official Reactions to Rape," *American Sociological Review* 45 (October 1980): 842–54. Thanks to Darnell Hawkins for this reference.

[43]Barbara Ehrenrich, "The Women's Movement: Feminist and Antifeminist," *Radical America* 15 (Spring 1981): 93–101; Lasch, "Flight from Feeling." Because violence against women is so inadequately documented, it is impossible to make accurate racial comparisons in the incidence of the crime. Studies conducted by Menachen Amir in the late 1950s

It should be emphasized, however, that the connection between feminism and the upsurge of rape lies not so much in women's gains but in their assertion of rights within a context of economic vulnerability and relative powerlessness. In a perceptive article published in 1901, Jane Addams traced lynching in part to "the feeling of the former slave owner to his former slave, whom he is now bidden to regard as his fellow citizen."[44] Blacks in the post-Reconstruction era were able to express will and individuality, to wrest from their former masters certain concessions and build for themselves supporting institutions. Yet they lacked the resources to protect themselves from economic exploitation and mob violence. Similarly, contemporary feminist efforts have not yet succeeded in overcoming women's isolation, their economic and emotional dependence on men, their cultural training toward submission. There are few restraints against sexual aggression, since up to 90 percent of rapes go unreported, 50 percent of assailants who are reported are never caught, and seven out of ten prosecutions end in acquittal.[45] Provoked by the commercialization of sex, cut loose from traditional community restraints, and "bidden to regard as his fellow citizen" a female being whose subordination has deep roots in the psyches of both sexes, men turn with impunity to the use of sexuality as a means of asserting dominance and control. Such fear and rage are condoned when channeled into right-wing attacks on women's claim to a share in public power and control over their bodies. Inevitably they also find expression in less acceptable behavior. Rape, like lynching, flourishes in an atmosphere in which official policies toward members of a subordinate group give individuals tacit permission to hurt and maim.

In 1972 Anne Braden, a southern white woman and long-time activist in civil rights struggles, expressed her fear that the new anti-rape movement might find itself "objectively on the side of the most reactionary social forces" unless it heeded a lesson from history. In a pamphlet entitled *Open Letter to Southern White Women*—much circulated in regional women's liberation circles at the time—she urged anti-rape activists to remember the long pattern of racist manipulation of rape fears. She called on white women, "for their own liberation, to refuse any longer to be used, to act in the tradition of Jessie Daniel Ames and the white women who fought in an earlier period to end lynching," and she went on to discuss her own politicization through left-led protests against the prosecution of black men on false rape charges. Four years later, she joined the chorus of black feminist criticism of *Against Our Will*, seeing Brownmiller's book as a realization of her worst fears.[46]

Since this confrontation between the Old Left and the New, between a white woman who placed herself in a southern tradition of feminist anti-racism and a radical feminist from the North, a black women's movement has emerged, bringing its own perspectives to bear. White activists at the earliest "speakouts" had acknowledged "the racist image of black men as rapists," pointed out the large number of black women among assault victims, and debated the contradictions involved in looking for solutions to a race and class-biased court system. But not until black women had developed their own autonomous organizations and strategies were true alliances possible across racial lines.

---

indicated that rape was primarily intraracial, with 77 percent of rapes involving black victims and black defendants and 18 percent involving whites. More recent investigations claim a somewhat higher percentage of interracial assaults. Statistics on reported rapes show that black women are more vulnerable to assault than white women. However, since black women are more likely than white women to report assaults, and since acquaintance rape, most likely to involve higher status white men, is the most underreported of crimes, the vulnerability of white women is undoubtedly much greater than statistics indicate (Berger, "Man's Trial, Woman's Tribulation," p. 3, n. 16; LaFree, "Effect of Sexual Stratification," p. 845, n. 3; Johnson, "On the Prevalence of Rape," p. 145).

[44]Quoted in Aptheker, *Lynching and Rape*, pp. 10–11.

[45]Berger, "Woman's Trial, Man's Tribulation," p. 6; Johnson, "On the Prevalence of Rape," p. 138.

[46]Anne Braden, "A Second Open Letter to Southern White Women," *Generations: Women in the South*, a special issue of *Southern Exposure* 4 (Winter 1977), edited by Susan Angell, Jacquelyn Dowd Hall, and Candace Waid.

A striking example of this development is the Washington, D.C., Rape Crisis Center. One of the first and largest such groups in the country, the center has evolved from a primarily white self-help project to an aggressive interracial organization with a multifaceted program of support services, advocacy, and community education. In a city with an 80 percent black population and more than four times as many women as men, the center has recruited black leadership by channeling its resources into staff salaries and steering clear of the pitfalls of middle-class voluntarism on the one hand and professionalism on the other. It has challenged the perception of the anti-rape movement as a "white woman's thing" by stressing not only rape's devastating effect on women but also its impact on social relations in the black community. Just as racism undermined working-class unity and lynching sometimes pitted poor whites against blacks, sexual aggression now divides the black community against itself. In a society that defines manhood in terms of power and possessions, black men are denied the resources to fulfill their expected roles. Inevitably, they turn to domination of women, the one means of manhood within their control. From consciousness-raising groups for convicted rapists to an intensive educational campaign funded by the city's public school system and aimed at both boys and girls from elementary through high school, the center has tried to alter the cultural plan for both sexes that makes men potential rapists and women potential victims.[47]

As the anti-rape movement broadens to include Third World women, analogies between lynching and rape and the models of women like Ida B. Wells and Jessie Daniel Ames may become increasingly useful. Neither lynching nor rape is the "aberrant behavior of a lunatic fringe."[48] Rather, both grow out of everyday modes of interaction. The view of women as objects to be possessed, conquered, or defiled fueled racial hostility; conversely, racism has continued to distort and confuse the struggle against sexual violence. Black men receive harsher punishment for raping white women, black rape victims are especially demeaned and ignored, and, until recently, the different historical experience of black and white women has hindered them from making common cause. Taking a cue from the women's anti-lynching campaign of the 1930s as well as from the innovative tactics of black feminists, the anti-rape movement must not limit itself to training women to avoid rape or depending on imprisonment as a deterrent, but must aim its attention at changing the behavior and attitudes of men. Mindful of the historical connection between rape and lynching, it must make clear its stand against *all* uses of violence in oppression.

---

[48]Johnson, "On the Prevalence of Rape," p. 137.

---

[47]Interview with Loretta Ross and Nkenge Toure, Washington, D.C., May 12, 1981. See also Rape Crisis Center of Washington, D.C., *How to Start a Rape Crisis Center* (1972, 1977).

VARIETIES OF ATTACK
ON THE DEATH PENALTY*

Jack Greenberg
*Director-Counsel, NAACP Legal Defense
and Educational Fund, Inc.
A.B., 1945, LL.B., 1948, Columbia University*

Jack Himmelstein
*Assistant Counsel, NAACP Legal Defense
and Educational Fund, Inc.
A.B., 1962, Cornell University; LL.B., 1965, Harvard University*

Any organization that concerns itself with America's racial problems and their relation to the law soon confronts the grim fact of capital punishment. This has been the continuous experience of the Legal Defense Fund. Early cases in criminal law involving Negroes, such as the Scottsboro cases,[1] posed issues of right to counsel,[2] jury discrimination,[3] and forced confession,[4] among others. But lurking in the background of each case was the awareness that what was at stake was not merely justice, not just the legal standards that evolve out of new situations, not simply the number of individuals affected, but the irreversible fact of death.

THE GROVELAND CASE

From 1950 to 1954 a great part of the time of the Legal Defense Fund staff was spent on the investigation, trial, appeals, and post-conviction proceedings[5] in the Groveland, Fla., case,[6] in which four Negroes were charged with the rape of a white woman. One of the four was killed, while asleep in a wood, by a sheriff's posse. Another received life imprisonment, most likely because he was only sixteen at the time of the crime or because the jury had misgivings about his guilt. The two other defendants were sentenced to death. After reversal of their convictions by the Supreme Court of the United States, one was killed by a sheriff on the way to the courthouse for the retrial, and the other was re-sentenced to death. After several more years of litigation, the prosecutor, asserting that he had serious doubts about the man's guilt, joined in the defendant's plea to the governor for commutation. The death penalty was commuted and, after approximately eighteen years of imprisonment, that defendant is now on parole. What is most significant, however, is that the sixteen-year-old refused to appeal his life sentence (which, in the case of his co-defendants, was reversed by the U.S. Supreme Court[7]) for

---

Jack Greenberg and Jack Himmelstein (1969) "Varieties of Attack on the Death Penalty." *Crime and Delinquency* Vol. 15 (January): 112–120, copyright © 1969 by Sage Publications, Inc. Reprinted by permission of Sage Publications, Inc.

*Based on an address delivered by Jack Greenberg at the NAACP Legal Defense Fund National Conference on Capital Punishment, New York City, May 3, 1968.

[1]Powell v. Alabama, 287 U.S. 45 (1932).

[2]E.g., Powell v. Alabama, *supra* note 1; Hamilton v. Alabama, 368 U.S. 52 (1961).

[3]Patton v. Mississippi, 332 U.S. 463 (1947); Shepherd v. Florida, 341 U.S. 50 (1951).

[4]Fikes v. Alabama, 352 U.S. 191 (1957).

[5]Under the direction of Thurgood Marshall, chief counsel of the Legal Defense Fund from its formation in 1949 until his appointment in 1961 to the United States Court of Appeals for the Second Circuit.

[6]Shepherd v. State, 46 So. 2d 880 (Fla. 1950), *rev'd*, Shepherd v. Florida, 341 U.S. 50 (1951), *appeal from second conviction*, Irvin v. State, 66 So. 2d 288 (Fla. 1953), *cert. denied*, 346 U.S. 927 (1954), *habeas denied*, Irvin v. Chapman, 75 So. 2d 591 (Fla. 1954), *cert. denied*, 348 U.S. 915 (1955).

[7]See *supra* note 6.

fear that on the second trial he might be sentenced to death. The death penalty had worked its injustice.

OTHER RAPE CASES

Another case we dealt with at that time was that of a Negro convicted of rape who was electrocuted even though his lawyer confessed publicly that, at the start of the trial, he was not in possession of what was perhaps the most important fact in the case—that the victim was white.[8] In the early fifties, the courts were not as receptive as they are today to a variety of arguments, and it was often impossible to obtain a stay and a hearing before a defendant was executed. In the case of the Martinsville (Va.) Seven, seven Negroes, convicted of raping a white woman, were electrocuted.[9]

In such cases, the issue of the validity of capital punishment imposed discriminatorily was occasionally raised. The reply of the courts was, ''How could one prove that race was a factor?'' Each case, they said, is different; each jury is different. Some defendants have criminal records; some are more vicious; some have good lawyers and others have bad ones; some victims were innocent, and some may have invited the assault.[10] The courts were not impressed by the fact that, of 455 men executed since 1930 for rape, 405 (90 per cent) were Negroes.[11] In these and many other cases, therefore, we relied principally on other constitutional defenses, often with success. The issues of discrimination in selection of the jury, the right to counsel, illegal search and

seizure, and coerced confession were taken to the Supreme Court many times. And many defendants had their convictions reversed.[12]

DISCRIMINATION IN APPLICATION OF THE DEATH PENALTY

As the courts became more sensitive to the issue of racial discrimination as well as discrimination against the poor, we began to think of attacking capital punishment as such, and particularly racial discrimination in imposition of the capital penalty.

The race statistics for all capital crimes are somewhat less extreme than for rape cases, but they are significant. Of the nearly 4,000 persons executed since 1930, 55 percent were Negroes.[13] And, if we relate executions to poverty, we approach 100 percent.

These facts were brought home vividly to us when, in connection with pending litigation in Florida, discussed below, we were authorized to interview the inmates of death row. Of the thirty-four condemned men interviewed whose state appeal had been denied at that time, all were indigent. Half were without counsel; most of the others were represented by volunteer counsel. The mean intelligence level was considerably below normal. The mean number of years of schooling (not necessarily grades attained) was eight. Most were unskilled farm or industrial laborers.[14]

These facts form the basis of one of our legal claims. We argue that the state is required to appoint counsel to represent these men even after their appeal to the state courts. Too often an illiterate man about to be executed attempts to write to appropriate courts and lawyers across the country to secure a stay of execution.

The case which triggered our campaign was *Hamilton v. Alabama*.[15] Hamilton, a Negro,

---

[8]Jones v. State, 209 Ga. 685, 75 S.E.2d 429 (1953); *habeas denied*, 210 Ga. 262, 79 S.E. 2d 1 (1953), *cert. denied*, 347 U.S. 956 (1954).

[9]Hampton v. Commonwealth, 190 Va. 531, 58 S.E.2d 288 (1950), *cert. denied*, 339 U.S. 989 (1950).

[10]Hampton v. Commonwealth, *supra* note 9; see also Florida *ex rel*. Copeland v. Mayo, 87 So. 2d 501 (Fla. 1956); Thomas v. State, 92 So. 2d 621 (Fla. 1957), *cert. denied*, 354 U.S. 925 (1957); Florida *ex rel*. Thomas v. Culver, 253 F.2d 507 (5th Cir. 1958); Maxwell v. Stephens, 229 F. Supp. 205 (1964), *aff'd*, 348 F.2d 325 (8th Cir. 1965), *cert. denied*, 382 U.S. 944 (1965) (see notes 21 and 23 *infra*).

[11]Bureau of Prisons, United States Department of Justice, National Prisoner Statistics, Executions, 1930–67, No. 42, June 1968, at 10–11.

[12]E.g., *supra* notes 2–4.

[13]National Prisoner Statistics, *supra* note 11, at 11–12.

[14]Petitioners Report on Prisoner Interviews and Memorandum in Support of Maintaining Class Action, Adderly v. Wainwright, No. 67-298-Civ.-J. (M.D. Fla.).

[15]Hamilton v. State, 270 Ala. 184, 116 So. 2d 906 (1960), *cert. denied*, 363 U.S. 852 (1960); see also note 16 *infra*.

entered the apartment of an elderly white woman near Birmingham, Ala., where he was arrested. Though there is considerable doubt about what actually happened, no claim was made at the trial that he had touched her. Nevertheless, he was sentenced to death for burglary with intent to commit rape. We took the case to the United States Supreme Court, maintaining that he had been denied counsel at his arraignment, and on this ground his conviction was reversed.[16] Hamilton's new trial, we felt, would be an appropriate case in which to raise two issues— (1) racial discrimination in the imposition of the death penalty and (2) cruel and unusual punishment, because capital punishment was grossly unfair when imposed in a case where no life had been taken and no bodily harm had been inflicted. At his second trial, however, Hamilton received a life term.

PROVING RACIAL DISCRIMINATION

Soon thereafter, Justice Goldberg wrote a brief dissent from the denial of certiorari in *Rudolph v. Alabama*,[17] where a Negro had been sentenced to death for the rape of a white woman, questioning whether capital punishment where no life had been taken or endangered was not cruel and unusual punishment.[18]

To develop the claims of cruel and unusual punishment and the denial of equal protection, we began to search for statistics that might isolate the racial factor. Professors Anthony Amsterdam[19] and Marvin Wolfgang,[20] to whom we presented the problem, designed a study which inquired into every possible ground that a jury might take into account in deciding whether to impose life imprisonment or death for the crime of rape. These grounds included such things as the viciousness of the crime, the prior relationship between the defendant and the victim, the time of the attack, the place of the attack, the number of attackers, whether a simultaneous crime occurred, whether the defendant testified at the trial, and every other conceivable factor that might influence sentencing. A team of thirty-five law students searched the records of 2,500 cases and the results were subjected to rigorous statistical analysis.[21] The likelihood that any factor other than race accounted for the disproportionality in sentencing proved insignificant. Race alone stood out as the constant factor in distinguishing cases in which the death penalty was imposed from those in which some lesser penalty was chosen. If the defendant was Negro and the victim was white, the chance of a death penalty proved high; in all other rape cases, the chance of a death penalty was remote. The results of this study have been introduced in several cases,[22] and we are taking

---

[16]Hamilton v. Alabama, 368 U.S. 52 (1961).

[17]375 U.S. 889 (1963).

[18]"The following questions, *inter alia*, seem relevant and worthy of argument and consideration:

"1. In light of the trend both in this country and throughout the world against punishing rape by death, does the imposition of the death penalty by those States which retain it for rape violate 'evolving standards of decency that mark the progress of [our] maturing society,' or 'standards of decency more or less universally accepted'?

"2. Is the taking of human life to protect a value other than human life consistent with the constitutional proscription against 'punishments which by their excessive . . . severity are greatly disproportioned to the offenses charged'?

"3. Can the permissible aims of punishment (e.g., deterrence, isolation, rehabilitation) be achieved as effectively by punishing rape less severely than by death—e.g., by life imprisonment; if so, does the imposition of the death penalty for rape constitute 'unnecessary cruelty'?" 375 U.S. 889.

[19]Professor of law and co-director of the Center for Studies in Criminology and Criminal Law, University of Pennsylvania.

[20]Chairman of the Department of Sociology and co-director of the Center for Studies in Criminology and Criminal Law, University of Pennsylvania.

[21]A description of the Georgia aspect of the study appears in the opinion of the Court of Appeals for the Fifth Circuit in Matter of Sims and Abrams, 389 F.2d 148 (5th Cir. 1967), and its South Carolina counterpart described in the memorandum order of the Court of Appeals for the Fourth Circuit in Moorer v. South Carolina, 368 F.2d 458 (4th Cir. 1966); see also for Arkansas, Maxwell v. Bishop, 257 F. Supp. 710 (E.D. Ark. 1966); Maxwell v. Bishop, 398 F.2d 138 (8th Cir. 1968).

[22]Aaron v. Simpson, Civ. No. 2170-N (N.D. Ala.); Alabama v. Wheeler Billingsley, Jr., Etowah County Cir. Ct., No. 1159; Alabama v. Robert Butler, Etowah County Cir. Ct., No. 1160; Alabama v. Liddell, Etowah County Cir. Ct., No. 1161; Alabama v. Robert Swain, 7th Div. No. 796; Craig

a petition this term to the Supreme Court of the United States.[23]

Once having raised these claims, however, it was not adequate to assert them on behalf of some defendants and ignore other defendants in the hope that they would receive the benefit of a new rule announced at a later date. And one cannot ignore the prejudices, not merely racial, that bring a jury to select this man and not another for death—indeed, to select any man for death for any crime. The attack quickly became one against capital punishment as such.

THE LEGAL ISSUES

It was not difficult to find solid legal arguments for an all-out attack on the death penalty. An institution as irrational and archaic as capital punishment is bound to be surrounded by procedure whose irrationality is readily assailable and whose only claim to validity is the length of time it has been used.

First, selecting a jury for a capital trial has often lasted several days. The prime reason was that all persons who had religious or moral scruples against the death penalty were systematically excluded from jury service. A capital jury was, therefore, made up entirely of that part of the population which approves of the death penalty as a sanction. This procedure was challenged as a denial of the defendant's right to a jury that is representative of a cross-section of the community and as a denial of a fair trial. The demand for a true cross-section is no theoretical abstraction. It insures the accused an equal opportunity to benefit from all the attitudes people may have so as to prevent any one group from dominating the delicate jury process.

On June 3, 1968, the Supreme Court of the United States reversed the death sentence of William C. Witherspoon, who, on his own and with the assistance of court-appointed attorneys, had been staying alive and challenging his death

sentence in Illinois and federal courts for nine years. (Again, the need for all states to provide counsel for condemned men becomes obvious.) In *Witherspoon v. Illinois*,[24] the Court held that a sentence of death cannot be carried out if the jury which imposed or recommended it excluded persons who were generally opposed to the death penalty. That decision, however, left unresolved the question of whether a state could validly exclude a prospective juror who made clear (1) that his attitude was so fixed that he would automatically vote against the death penalty in every conceivable case or (2) that he would not be able to make an impartial decision on the defendant's guilt. Thus, states have continued to seek and secure death sentences by procedures designed to fall outside the condemnation of *Witherspoon*. And although *Witherspoon* would seem to invalidate the death sentences of many of the five hundred men on the nation's death rows, some state courts have given the Supreme Court's opinion a hostile reception.[25] By reading *Witherspoon* narrowly, limiting the interpretation to the particular facts of the Illinois case, these courts have affirmed death sentences imposed by death-qualified juries in other states. Thus, we are still litigating the issue of whether any form of moral or religious opposition to the death penalty can constitutionally disqualify a person from sitting on a jury which determines whether a man is fit to live, and particularly whether the exclusion of this segment of the population makes for a jury more prone to convict.

Second, in capital trials the jury decides punishment—whether or not death will be the penalty—in addition to its regular task of determining the issue of guilt. In making this decision between life and death, the jurors are left completely without guidance. They receive instruction that they must follow on every aspect of the case except the question of the death penalty; there they are told simply to do as they see fit. Such total discretion compels the kind of ar-

---

v. Wainwright, No. 66-595-Civ.-J. (M.D. Fla.); Drumwright and Gilley v. Wainwright, No. 67-110-Orl. Civ. (M.D. Fla.); Arkwright v. Kelly, No. 5283, Super. Ct., Tatnall County, Ga.; Williams v. Kelly, No. 5284, Super. Ct., Tatnall County, Ga. See also cases cited *supra* note 21.

[23]Maxwell v. Bishop, O.T. 1968, No. 622.

[24]391 U.S. 510 (1968).

[25]See Forcella v. New Jersey, 52 N.J. 263, 245 A.2d 181 (1968), *petition for cert. pending*, Misc. No. 947 (O.T. 1968), see *infra* note 33; Pittman v. State, Tex. Crim. App. No. 41393 (decided July 29, 1968); Bell v. Patterson, ——F.2d——, 10096 (Oct. 18, 1968).

bitrariness that is illustrated by the prevalence of racial discrimination in sentencing for rape. On appeal, courts cannot review such a decision in any meaningful way because the law has never established any set of criteria for the death penalty. This process of undefined responsibility carries all the way down to the execution. At some hangings, three men tripped releases, only one of which actually sprung the trap. That way, no one person could be identified as responsible; but the man was dead.

The vice of the jury's limitless discretion in sentencing is compounded by the fact that, in most states, the jury decides the issues of guilt and capital punishment at the same sitting.[26] In noncapital sentencing, the judge usually receives a presentence report and the defense can address the court on the issue. In capital cases, however, the defendant (unless he gives up his privilege against self-incrimination) cannot introduce evidence relevant to sentencing. In determining whether the defendant shall live or die, the jurors have only the evidence about the crime and their own standards about the death penalty.

Finally, the death penalty is challenged as cruel and unusual punishment within the prohibition of the Eighth Amendment. Among those who are condemned, many are winnowed out by postlitigation procedures, in courts and before the governors, based on legal issues, appeals of mercy, or evidence of insanity. Following this grisly lottery, a few are chosen to be executed. Death in such cases is truly "unusual," as it is cruel. The arbitrariness and the irrationality of the death penalty are thrown into sharp relief in a case currently being considered by the Supreme Court of the United States—a case in which the death penalty was imposed for the crime of robbery.[27]

These issues have been raised in differing forms for years by lawyers struggling to keep condemned men alive. But developments in the law have given new form and currency to the arguments. Developments in the social sciences have given new evidentiary support. The temper of the times seems to be turning against capital punishment, with executions in the last seven years falling from 47 to 21 to 15 to 7 to 1 to 2 to 0.[28] Of course, the smaller the number, the greater the anomaly and the irony.

These arguments do not all necessarily mean, on their face, that capital punishment is unconstitutional. Instead, much of the attack is focused on the unfair and irrational procedures that inhere in the administration of the death penalty. But the result may well be the same. If rational decision-making processes are required, reason and responsibility will focus on an institution where reason does not exist and where responsibility has become diffuse.

COLLECTIVE SUITS

These several assertions, while first made on behalf of Negroes in several of our cases, are equally applicable to all defendants.

In the first Legal Defense Fund collective suit, raising these claims common to all men under sentence of death, Tobias Simon, of Miami, Fla., went into the United States District Court in Jacksonville, claiming that constitutional rights were denied all those on Florida's death row. As a result, on April 13, 1967, the court granted a stay of all executions[29] so that none of the fifty condemned men could be executed while the several claims were being litigated. (During the gubernatorial campaign, Claude Kirk vowed that he would end the stays of execution given by his predecessor. After taking office, he visited death row to appraise the situation, shook the hands of the condemned men, and then sought to schedule the execution of fourteen during the spring.)

The scene then shifted to California, where Governor Brown's reluctance to execute had produced a backlog of about seventy condemned men at the change of administration. Following the inauguration of Ronald Reagan, Aaron Mitchell was executed on April 12, 1967, and

---

[26]California, Connecticut, New York, Pennsylvania, and Texas now provide for bifurcated trials (separate hearings on guilt and punishment).

[27]Boykin v. Alabama, O.T. 1968, No. 642, *cert. granted* Oct. 14, 1968.

[28]National Prisoner Statistics, *supra* note 11, p. 8.

[29]Adderly v. Wainwright, M.D. Fla. No. 67-298-Civ.-J.

eleven gassings were scheduled for the summer months. As the result of a Legal Defense Fund suit, a similar class stay was granted by the federal District Court on July 5, 1967.[30] Since then, in one of our cases, argued by lead counsel, Professor Anthony Amsterdam, claims have been brought before the Supreme Court of California (which similarly granted a class stay of all executions).[31] By the fall of 1968, Florida had fifty-four men on death row; California, eighty-three men and one woman.

In other states, where the number of condemned men is so much smaller, resort to class actions has been deemed inappropriate. But the same arguments have been and are being presented on behalf of the majority of the approximately five hundred inmates of the nation's death rows. Stays have always been secured.[32]

---

[30]Hill v. Nelson, Cal., No. 47318 (Order of July 5, 1967).

[31]Application of Anderson, Cal. Sup. Ct., Crim. No. 11572; Application of Saterfield, Cal. Sup. Ct., Crim. No. 11573, order of Nov. 14, 1967. See transcript of oral argument, March 28, 1967, on file with the Supreme Court of California. On Nov. 18, 1968, the Supreme Court of California reversed the death sentences of petitioners Anderson and Saterfield on *Witherspoon* grounds; it rejected the constitutional challenge to the death penalty as administered in California (Justices Tobriner, Traynor, and Peters dissenting); and it held that counsel would be appointed at the post-appeal stage.

[32]Stays of execution of condemned men have been issued by numerous state and federal courts in post-conviction proceedings raising *inter alia* the capital punishment issues together with, in some cases, the contention of racial discrimination in capital sentencing. E.g., Spencer v. Beto, 5th Cir. No. 25548, order of Nov. 16, 1967 (death penalty later reversed on *Witherspoon* grounds, 398 F.2d 500 [5th Cir. 1968]); Brent v. White, 5th Cir. No. 25496, order of Nov. 28, 1967 (remanded for exhaustion of state remedies), 398 F.2d 503 (5th Cir. 1968); Shinall v. Breazeale, 5th Cir., No. 25807, order of Feb. 21, 1968; Bell v. Patterson, No. 67-C-458, order of Sept. 14, 1967 (U.S.D.C., D. Colo.), *death sentence affirmed*, Bell v. Patterson,——F.2d—— (10th Cir. Oct. 18, 1968); Segura v. Patterson, No. 67-C-497, order of Oct. 13, 1967 (U.S.D.C., D. Colo.), *death sentence affirmed*, Segura v. Patterson,——F.2d——(10th Cir. Oct. 1, 1968); Brown v. Lane, No. 4129, order of Dec. 29, 1967 (U.S.D.C., N.D. Ind.); Childs v. Turner, No. 2663, order of May 12, 1967. (U.S.D.C.,W.D.N.C.); Chevallier v. Beto, No. 68-H-57, order of Jan. 24, 1968 (U.S.D.C., S.D. Tex.); Arkwright v. Kelly, *supra* note 22, order of Dec. 1, 1967; Williams v. Kelly, *supra* note 22, order of Dec. 1, 1967. State v. Davis, Indictment No. 185-J-62, order of March 5, 1968 (Union Cty. Ct., N.J.).

There has been no execution in the United States since June 2, 1967, when a Colorado man was executed after refusing the assistance of counsel. (The phenomenon of "judicial suicide"—men who kill in order to be killed—is, incidentally, not uncommon, and it is an interesting commentary on the death penalty as a deterrent.) There is, thus, ample legal authority to prevent any executions before resolution of these issues, which have now been brought to the Supreme Court of the United States.[33]

THE DEATH PENALTY

I have mentioned what we are doing as lawyers, but the consequences of capital punishment go beyond these limited legal arguments. The very existence of the death penalty distorts the legal system. Many men have been known to plead guilty to crimes they did not commit when the prosecutor threatened them with the death penalty if they pleaded not guilty. The Supreme Court of the United States recognized the coercive impact of capital punishment in *United States v. Jackson.*[34] There the Court struck down a provision of the federal kidnaping statute, which reserved the death penalty for those who pleaded not guilty and demanded trial by jury but authorized a maximum of life imprisonment for those who pleaded guilty or waived jury trial.[35] Also, as in the Groveland case,[36] men have often refused to appeal a conviction for which they were sentenced to life imprisonment for fear that a new trial would again present the possibility of the death penalty. The judicial process has also been distorted when judges, reluctant to send a

---

[33]The issues are now pending before the Court in petitions for writ of certiorari in Forcella v. New Jersey, O.T. 1968, Misc. No. 947, presenting the several capital punishment issues; Maxwell v. Bishop, O.T. 1968, No. 622, presenting *inter alia* the issue of racial discrimination in capital sentencing for rape; and Boykin v. Alabama, *supra* note 27, in which certiorari has been granted.

[34]390 U.S. 570 (1968).

[35]Forcella v. New Jersey, *supra* note 33, includes a challenge to the New Jersey procedure, common to other states, which, in capital crimes, provides for a maximum of life imprisonment to one sentenced pursuant to a guilty plea.

[36]See *supra* note 6.

man to his death, have strained a rule of law to save him. Finally, the mockery of a man executed and later found to be innocent is self-evident.

Today, deterrence is the only argument we hear in support of the death penalty, and there is simply no evidence that the threat of the death penalty is a better deterrent than the threat of imprisonment.[37] On this uncertainty, society sends men to death. Rather than providing the solution, the death penalty diverts attention from a reasoned approach to crime and contributes to the irrationality underlying most criminal behavior. For the death penalty is no less than a resort to and legitimization of extreme violence.

The battle over capital punishment may be seen as a microcosm of the conflict between those in authority who believe in violence as a means of coping with society's problems and those who oppose the use of violence. We have seen it in war. We have heard it in political promises to "get tough with crime in the streets." Reasonable force may sometimes be the only possible way to cope with violence. However, violent force, employed after the fact, legitimizes a method of coping with issues that is the antithesis of the right procedures of a just society. Capital punishment is the supreme example of this irrational response.

Either explicitly or implicitly, as Justice Cardozo said, the courts assert the moral sense of the times.[38] Things are in a state of uncertainty at the moment, with executions stayed all over the country while numerous courts consider the issues. As the reassessment continues, we think that consideration of these cases will persuade the courts, the legislatures, and the public that we owe ourselves a commitment to reason. We do not know how to solve all of society's ills, and particularly all of the problems of crime. But we do know that one way not to do it is to kill needlessly. If the goal of this litigation is achieved, we will have spared a few lives that, thereafter, will be spent in prisons. We will perhaps' make it possible, in some cases, for men whose innocence is established years from now to go free. Most important of all, we may make a small contribution to advancing the day when man's problems are dealt with by reason and persuasion and not by brute force.

---

[37]See, e.g., Sellin, The Death Penalty (1959), published as an appendix to Model Penal Code (Tent. Draft No. 9, May 8, 1959).

[38]Cardozo, The Nature of the Judicial Process (1921).

GOOD PEOPLE AND DIRTY WORK

Everett C. Hughes

". . . une secte est le *noyau* et le *levain* de toute foule. . . . Etudier la foule c'est juger un drame d'après ce qu'on voit sur la scène; étudier la secte c'est le juger d'après ce qu'on voit dans les coulisses."
—Sighele, S. *Psychologie des sectes*. Paris, 1898. Pp. 62, 63, 65.[1]

The National Socialist Government of Germany, with the arm of its fanatical inner sect, the S.S., commonly known as the Black Shirts or Elite Guard, perpetrated and boasted of the most colossal and dramatic piece of social dirty work the world has ever known. Perhaps there are other claimants to the title, but they could not match this one's combination of mass, speed and perverse pride in the deed. Nearly all peoples have plenty of cruelty and death to account for. How many Negro Americans have died by the hands of lynching mobs? How many more from unnecessary disease and lack of food or of knowledge of nutrition? How many Russians died to bring about collectivization of land? And who is to blame if there be starving millions in some parts of the world while wheat molds in the fields of other parts?

I do not revive the case of the Nazi *Endloesung* (final solution) of the Jewish problem in order to condemn the Germans, or make them look worse than other peoples, but to recall to our attention dangers which lurk in our midst always. Most of what follows was written after my first postwar visit to Germany in 1948. The impressions were vivid. The facts have not diminished and disappeared with time, as did the stories of alleged German atrocities in Belgium in the first World War. The fuller the record, the worse it gets.[2]

[1]". . . a sect is the nucleus and the yeast of every crowd. . . . To study a crowd is to judge by what one sees on the stage; to study the sect is to judge by what one sees backstage." These are among the many passages underlined by Robert E. Park in his copy, now in my possession, of Sighele's classic work on political sects. There are a number of references to this work in the Park and Burgess *Introduction to the Science of Sociology*, Chicago, 1921. In fact, there is more attention paid to fanatical political and religious behavior in Park and Burgess than in any later sociological work in this country. Sighele's discussion relates chiefly to the anarchist movement of his time. There have been fanatical movements since. The Secret Army Organization in Algeria is but the latest.

[2]The best source easily available at that time was Eugen Kogon's *Der SS-Staat. Das System der Deutschen Konzentrationslager*, Berlin, 1946. Many of my data are from his book. Some years later H. G. Adler, after several years of research, wrote *Theresianstadt, 1941–1945. Das Antlitz einer Zwangsgemeinschaft* (Tuebingen, 1955), and still later published *Die Verheimlichte Wahrheit, Theresienstaedter Dokumente* (Tuebingen, 1958), a book of documents concerning that camp in which Czech and other Jews were concentrated, demoralized and destroyed. Kogon, a Catholic intellectual, and Adler, a Bohemian Jew, both wrote out of personal experience in the concentration camps. Both considered it their duty to present the phenomenon objectively to the public. None of their statements has ever been challenged.

Several millions of people were delivered to the concentration camps, operated under the leadership of Heinrich Himmler with the help of Adolf Eichmann. A few hundred thousand survived in some fashion. Still fewer came out sound of mind and body. A pair of examples, well attested, will show the extreme of perverse cruelty reached by the S.S. guards in charge of the camps. Prisoners were ordered to climb trees; guards whipped them to make them climb faster. Once they were out of reach, other prisoners, also urged by the whip, were put to shaking the trees. When the victims fell, they were kicked to see whether they could rise to their feet. Those too badly injured to get up were shot to death, as useless for work. A not inconsiderable number of prisoners were drowned in pits full of human excrement. These examples are so horrible that your minds will run away from them. You will not, as when you read a slightly salacious novel, imagine the rest. I therefore thrust these examples upon you and insist that the people who thought them up could, and did, improvise others like them, and even worse, from day to day over several years. Many of the victims of the camps gave up the ghost (this Biblical phrase is the most apt) from a combination of humiliation, starvation, fatigue and physical abuse. In due time, a policy of mass liquidation in the gas chamber was added to individual virtuosity in cruelty.

This program—for it was a program—of cruelty and murder was carried out in the name of racial superiority and racial purity. It was directed mainly, although by no means exclusively, against Jews, Slavs and Gypsies. It was thorough. There are few Jews in the territories which were under the control of the Third German Reich—the two Germanies, Holland, Czechoslavakia, Poland, Austria, Hungary. Many Jewish Frenchmen were destroyed. There were concentration camps even in Tunisia and Algiers under the German occupation.

When, during my 1948 visit to Germany, I became more aware of the reactions of ordinary Germans to the horrors of the concentration camps, I found myself asking not the usual question, "How did racial hatred rise to such a high level?", but this one, "How could such dirty work be done among and, in a sense, *by* the millions of ordinary, civilized German people?'' Along with this came related questions. How could these millions of ordinary people live in the midst of such cruelty and murder without a general uprising against it and against the people who did it? How, once freed from the regime that did it, could they be apparently so little concerned about it, so toughly silent about it, not only in talking with outsiders—which is easy to understand—but among themselves? How and where could there be found in a modern civilized country the several hundred thousand men and women capable of such work? How were these people so far released from the inhibitions of civilized life as to be able to imagine, let alone perform, the ferocious, obscene and perverse actions which they did imagine and perform? How could they be kept at such a height of fury through years of having to see daily at close range the human wrecks they made and being often literally spattered with the filth produced and accumulated by their own actions?

You will see that there are here two orders of questions. One set concerns the good people who did not themselves do this work. The other concerns those who did do it. But the two sets are not really separate; for the crucial question concerning the good people is their relation to the people who did the dirty work, with a related one which asks under what circumstances good people let the others get away with such actions.

An easy answer concerning the Germans is that they were not so good after all. We can attribute to them some special inborn or ingrained race consciousness, combined with a penchant for sadistic cruelty and unquestioning acceptance of whatever is done by those who happen to be in authority. Pushed to its extreme, this answer simply makes us, rather than the Germans, the superior race. It is the Nazi tune, put to words of our own.

Now there are deep and stubborn differences between peoples. Their history and culture may make the Germans especially susceptible to the doctrine of their own racial superiority and especially acquiescent to the actions of whoever is in power over them. These are matters deserving of the best study that can be given them. But to say that these things could happen in Germany simply because Germans are different—from us—buttresses their own excuses and lets us off too easily from blame for what happened there and from the question whether it could happen here.

Certainly in their daily practice and expression before the Hitler regime, the Germans showed no more, if as much, hatred of other racial or cultural groups than we did and do. Residential segregation was not marked. Intermarriage was common, and the families of such marriages had an easier social existence than they generally have in America. The racially exclusive club, school and hotel were much less in evidence than here. And I well remember an evening in 1933 when a Montreal business man—a very nice man, too—said in our living room, "Why don't we admit that Hitler is doing to the Jews just what we ought to be doing?" That was not an uncommon sentiment, although it may be said in defense of the people who expressed it, that they probably did not know and would not have believed the full truth about the Nazi program of destroying Jews. The essential underlying sentiments on racial matters in Germany were not different in kind from those prevailing throughout the western, and especially the Anglo-Saxon, countries. But I do not wish to over-emphasize this point. I only want to close one easy way out of serious consideration of the problem of good people and dirty work, by demonstrating that the Germans were and are about as good and about as bad as the rest of us on this matter of racial sentiments and, let us add, their notions of decent human behaviour.

But what was the reaction of ordinary Germans to the persecution of the Jews and to the concentration camp mass torture and murder? A conversation between a German school-teacher, a German architect and myself gives the essentials in a vivid form. It was in the studio of the architect, and the occasion was a rather casual visit, in Frankfurt am Main in 1948.

The architect: "I am ashamed for my people whenever I think of it. But we didn't know about it. We only learned about all that later. You must remember the pressure we were under; we had to join the party.

We had to keep our mouths shut and do as we were told. It was a terrible pressure. Still, I am ashamed. But you see, we had lost our colonies, and our national honour was hurt. And these Nazis exploited that feeling. And the Jews, they *were* a problem. They came from the east. You should see them in Poland; the lowest class of people, full of lice, dirty and poor, running about in their Ghettos in filthy caftans. They came here, and got rich by unbelievable methods after the first war. They occupied all the good places. Why, they were in the proportion of ten to one in medicine and law and government posts!"

At this point the architect hesitated and looked confused. He continued: "Where was I? It is the poor food. You see what misery we are in here, Herr Professor. It often happens that I forget what I was talking about. Where was I now? I have completely forgotten."

(His confusion was, I believe, not at all feigned. Many Germans said they suffered loss of memory such as this, and laid it to their lack of food.)

I said firmly: "You were talking about loss of national honour and how the Jews had got hold of everything."

The architect: "Oh, yes! That was it! Well, of course that was no way to settle the Jewish problem. But there *was* a problem and it had to be settled some way."

The school-teacher: "Of course, they have Palestine now."

I protested that Palestine would hardly hold them.

The architect: "The professor is right. Palestine can't hold all the Jews. And it was a terrible thing to murder people. But we didn't know it at the time. But I am glad I am alive now. It is an interesting time in men's history. You know, when the Americans came it was like a great release. I really want to see a new ideal in Germany. I like the freedom that lets me talk to you like this. But, unfortunately that is not the general opinion. Most of my friends really hang on to the old ideas. They can't see any hope, so they hang on to the old ideas."

This scrap of talk gives, I believe, the essential elements as well as the flavor of the German reaction. It checks well with formal studies which have been made, and it varies only in detail from other conversations which I myself recorded in 1948.

One of the most obvious points in it is unwillingness to think about the dirty work done. In this case—perhaps by chance, perhaps not—

the good man suffered an actual lapse of memory in the middle of this statement. This seems a simple point. But the psychiatrists have shown that it is less simple than it looks. They have done a good deal of work on the complicated mechanisms by which the individual mind keeps unpleasant or intolerable knowledge from consciousness, and have shown how great may, in some cases, be the consequent loss of effectiveness of the personality. But we have taken collective unwillingness to know unpleasant facts more or less for granted. That people can and do keep a silence about things whose open discussion would threaten the group's conception of itself, and hence its solidarity, is common knowledge. It is a mechanism that operates in every family and in every group which has a sense of group reputation. To break such a silence is considered an attack against the group; a sort of treason, if it be a member of the group who breaks the silence. This common silence allows group fictions to grow up; such as, that grandpa was less a scoundrel and more romantic than he really was. And I think it demonstrable that it operates especially against any expression, except in ritual, of collective guilt. The remarkable thing in present-day Germany is not that there is so little reference to something about which people do feel deeply guilty, but that it is talked about at all.

In order to understand this phenomenon we would have to find out who talks about the concentration camp atrocities, in what situations, in what mood, and with what stimulus. On these points I know only my own limited experiences. One of the most moving of these was my first post-war meeting with an elderly professor whom I had known before the Nazi time; he is an heroic soul who did not bow his head during the Nazi time and who keeps it erect now. His first words, spoken with tears in his eyes, were:

"How hard it is to believe that men will be as bad as they say they will. Hitler and his people said: 'Heads will roll,' but how many of us— even of his bitterest opponents—could really believe that they would do it."

This man could and did speak, in 1948, not only to the likes of me, but to his students, his colleagues and to the public which read his articles, in the most natural way about the Nazi atrocities whenever there was occasion to do it in the course of his tireless effort to reorganize and to bring new life into the German universities. He had neither the compulsion to speak, so that he might excuse and defend himself, nor a conscious or unconscious need to keep silent. Such people were rare; how many there were in Germany I do not know.

Occasions of another kind in which the silence was broken were those where, in class, public lecture or in informal meetings with students, I myself had talked frankly of race relations in other parts of the world, including the lynchings which sometimes occur in my country and the terrible cruelty visited upon natives in South Africa. This took off the lid of defensiveness, so that a few people would talk quite easily of what happened under the Nazi regime. More common were situations like that with the architect, where I threw in some remark about the atrocities in response to Germans' complaint that the world is abusing them. In such cases, there was usually an expression of shame, accompanied by a variety of excuses (including that of having been kept in ignorance), and followed by a quick turning away from the subject.

Somewhere in consideration of this problem of discussion versus silence we must ask what the good (that is, ordinary) people in Germany did know about these things. It is clear that the S.S. kept the more gory details of the concentration camps a close secret. Even high officials of the government, the army and the Nazi party itself were in some measure held in ignorance, although of course they kept the camps supplied with victims. The common people of Germany knew that the camps existed; most knew people who had disappeared into them; some saw the victims, walking skeletons in rags, being transported in trucks or trains, or being herded on the road from station to camp or to work in fields or factories near the camps. Many knew people who had been released from concentration camps; such released persons kept their counsel on pain of death. But secrecy was cultivated and supported by fear and terror. In the absence of a determined and heroic will to know and publish the truth, and in the absence of all the instruments of opposition, the degree of knowledge was undoubtedly low, in spite of the fact that all knew that something both stupendous and horrible was going on; and in spite of the fact that Hitler's *Mein Kampf* and the utterances of his aides said that no fate was too horrible for the Jews and other wrong-headed or inferior people. This must make us ask under what conditions the will to know and to discuss is strong, determined and effective; this, like most of the important questions I have raised, I leave unanswered except as answers may be contained in the statement of the case.

But to return to our moderately good man, the architect. He insisted over and over again that he did not know, and we may suppose that he knew as much and as little as most Germans. But he also made it quite clear that he wanted something done to the Jews. I have similar statements from people of whom I knew that they had had close Jewish friends before the Nazi time. This raises the whole problem of the extent to which those pariahs who do the dirty work of society are really acting as agents for the rest of us. To talk of this question one must note that, in building up his case, the architect pushed the Jews firmly into an out-group: they were dirty, lousy and unscrupulous (an odd statement from a resident of Frankfurt, the home of old Jewish merchants and intellectual families long identified with those aspects of culture of which Germans are most proud). Having dissociated himself clearly from these people, and having declared them a problem, he apparently was willing to let someone else do to them the dirty work which he himself would not do, and for which he expressed shame. The case is perhaps analogous to our attitude toward those convicted of crime. From time to time, we get wind of cruelty practiced upon the prisoners in penitentiaries or jails; or, it may be, merely a report that they are ill-fed or that hygienic conditions are not good. Perhaps we do not wish that the prisoners should be cruelly treated or badly fed, but our reaction is probably tempered by a notion that they deserve something, because of some dissociation of them from the in-group of good people. If what they get is worse than what we like to think about, it is a little bit too bad.

It is a point on which we are ambivalent. Campaigns for reform of prisons are often followed by counter-campaigns against a too high standard of living for prisoners and against having prisons run by softies. Now the people who run prisons are our agents. Just how far they do or could carry out our wishes is hard to say. The minor prison guard, in boastful justification of some of his more questionable practices, says, in effect: "If those reformers and those big shots upstairs had to live with these birds as I do, they would soon change their fool notions about running a prison." He is suggesting that the good people are either naive or hypocritical. Furthermore, he knows quite well that the wishes of his employers, the public, are by no means unmixed. They are quite as likely to put upon him for being too nice as for being too harsh. And if, as sometimes happens, he is a man disposed to cruelty, there may be some justice in his feeling that he is only doing what others would like to do, if they but dared; and what they would do, if they were in his place.

There are plenty of examples in our own world which I might have picked for comparison with the German attitude toward the concentration camps. For instance, a newspaper in Denver made a great scandal out of the allegation that our Japanese compatriots were too well fed in the camps where they were concentrated during the war. I might have mentioned some feature of the sorry history of the people of Japanese background in Canada. Or it might have been lynching, or some aspect of racial discrimination. But I purposely chose prisoners convicted of crime. For convicts are formally set aside for special handling. They constitute an out-group in all countries. This brings the issue clearly before us, since few people cherish the illusion that the problem of treating criminals can be settled by propaganda designed to prove that there aren't any criminals. Almost everyone agrees that something has to be done about them. The question concerns what is done, who does it, and the nature of the mandate given by the rest of us to those who do it. Perhaps we give them an unconscious mandate to go beyond anything we ourselves would care to do or even to acknowledge. I venture to suggest that the higher and more expert functionaries who act in our behalf represent something of a distillation of what we may consider our public wishes, while some of the others show a sort of concentrate of those impulses of which we are or wish to be less aware.

Now the choice of convicted prisoners brings up another crucial point in inter-group relations. All societies of any great size have in-groups and out-groups; in fact, one of the best ways of describing a society is to consider it a network of smaller and larger in-groups and out-groups. And an in-group is one only because there are out-groups. When I refer to *my* children I obviously imply that they are closer to me than other people's children and that I will make greater efforts to buy oranges and cod-liver oil for them than for others' children. In fact, it may mean that I will give them cod-liver oil if I have to choke them to get it down. We do our own dirty work on those closest to us. The very injunction that I love my neighbor as myself starts with me; if I don't love myself and my nearest, the phrase has a very sour meaning.

Each of us is a center of a network of in and out-groups. Now the distinctions between *in* and *out* may be drawn in various ways, and nothing is more important for both the student of society and the educator than to discover how these lines are made and how they may be redrawn in more just and sensible ways. But to believe that we can do away with the distinction between *in* and *out*, *us* and *them* in social life is complete nonsense. On the positive side, we generally feel a greater obligation to in-groups; hence less obligation to out-groups; and in the case of such groups as convicted criminals, the out-group is definitely given over to the hands of our agents for punishment. That is the extreme case. But there are other out-groups toward which we may have aggressive feelings and dislike, although we give no formal mandate to anyone to deal with them on our behalf, and although we profess to believe that they should not suffer restrictions or disadvantages. The greater their social distance from us, the more we leave in the hands of others a sort of mandate by default to deal with them on our behalf. Whatever effort we put on reconstructing the lines which divide in and out-

groups, there remains the eternal problem of our treatment, direct or delegated, of whatever groups are considered somewhat outside. And here it is that the whole matter of our professed and possible deeper unprofessed wishes comes up for consideration; and the related problem of what we know, can know and want to know about it. In Germany, the agents got out of hand and created such terror that it was best not to know. It is also clear that it was and is easier to the conscience of many Germans not to know. It is, finally, not unjust to say that the agents were at least working in the direction of the wishes of many people, although they may have gone beyond the wishes of most. The same questions can be asked about our own society, and with reference not only to prisoners but also to many other groups upon whom there is no legal or moral stigma. Again I have not the answers. I leave you to search for them.

In considering the question of dirty work we have eventually to think about the people who do it. In Germany, these were the members of the S.S. and of that inner group of the S.S. who operated the concentration camps. Many reports have been made on the social backgrounds and the personalities of these cruel fanatics. Those who have studied them say that a large proportion were "gescheiterte Existenzen," men or women with a history of failure, of poor adaptation to the demands of work and of the classes of society in which they had been bred. Germany between wars had large numbers of such people. Their adherence to a movement which proclaimed a doctrine of hatred was natural enough. The movement offered something more. It created an inner group which was to be superior to all others, even Germans, in their emancipation from the usual bourgeois morality; people above and beyond the ordinary morality. I dwell on this, not as a doctrine, but as an organizational device. For, as Eugen Kogon, author of the most penetrating analysis of the S.S. and their camps, has said, the Nazis came to power by creating a state within a state; a body with its own counter-morality, and its own counter-law, its courts and its own execution of sentence upon those who did not live up to its orders and standards. Even as a movement, it had inner circles within inner circles; each sworn to secrecy as against the next outer one. The struggle between these inner circles continued after Hitler came to power; Himmler eventually won the day. His S.S. became a state within the Nazi state, just as the Nazi movement had become a state within the Weimar state. One is reminded of the oft quoted but neglected statement of Sighele: "At the center of a crowd look for the sect." He referred, of course, to the political sect; the fanatical inner group of a movement seeking power by revolutionary methods. Once the Nazis were in power, this inner sect, while becoming now the recognized agent of the state and, hence, of the masses of the people, could at the same time dissociate itself more completely from them in action, because of the very fact of having a mandate. It was now beyond all danger of interference and investigation. For it had the instruments of interference and investigation in its own hands. These are also the instruments of secrecy. So the S.S. could and did build up a powerful system in which they had the resources of the state and of the economy of Germany and the conquered countries from which to steal all that was needed to carry out their orgy of cruelty luxuriously as well as with impunity.

Now let us ask, concerning the dirty workers, questions similar to those concerning the good people. Is there a supply of candidates for such work in other societies? It would be easy to say that only Germany could produce such a crop. The question is answered by being put. The problem of people who have run aground (gescheiterte Existenzen) is one of the most serious in our modern societies. Any psychiatrist will, I believe, testify that we have a sufficient pool or fund of personalities warped toward perverse punishment and cruelty to do any amount of dirty work that the good people may be inclined to countenance. It would not take a very great turn of events to increase the number of such people, and to bring their discontents to the surface. This is not to suggest that every movement based on discontent with the present state of things will be led by such people. That is obviously untrue; and I emphasize the point lest my remarks give comfort to those who would damn all who express militant discontent. But

I think study of militant social movements does show that these warped people seek a place in them. Specifically, they are likely to become the plotting, secret police of the group. It is one of the problems of militant social movements to keep such people out. It is of course easier to do this if the spirit of the movement is positive, its conception of humanity high and inclusive, and its aims sound. This was not the case of the Nazi movement. As Kogon puts it: "The SS were but the arch-type of the Nazis in general."[3] But such people are sometimes attracted for want of something better, to movements whose aims are contrary to the spirit of cruelty and punishment. I would suggest that all of us look well at the leadership and entourage of movements to which we attach ourselves for signs of a negativistic, punishing attitude. For once such a spirit develops in a movement, punishment of the nearest and easiest victim is likely to become more attractive than striving for the essential goals. And, if the Nazi movement teaches us anything at all, it is that if any shadow of a mandate be given to such people, they will—having compromised us—make it larger and larger. The processes by which they do so are the development of the power and inward discipline of their own group, a progressive dissociation of themselves from the rules of human decency prevalent in their culture, and an ever-growing contempt for the welfare of the masses of people.

The power and inward discipline of the S.S. became such that those who once became members could get out only by death; by suicide, murder or mental breakdown. Orders from the central offices of the S.S. were couched in equivocal terms as a hedge against a possible day of judgment. When it became clear that such a day of judgment would come, the hedging and intrigue became greater; the urge to murder also became greater, because every prisoner became a potential witness.

Again we are dealing with a phenomenon common in all societies. Almost every group which has a specialized social function to perform is in some measure a secret society, with a body of rules developed and enforced by the

---

[3]Op. cit. p. 316.

members and with some power to save its members from outside punishment. And here is one of the paradoxes of social order. A society without smaller, rule-making and disciplining powers would be no society at all. There would be nothing but law and police; and this is what the Nazis strove for, at the expense of family, church, professional groups, parties and other such nuclei of spontaneous control. But apparently the only way to do this, for good as well as for evil ends, is to give power into the hands of some fanatical small group which will have a far greater power of self-discipline and a far greater immunity from outside control than the traditional groups. The problem is, then, not of trying to get rid of all the self-disciplining, pro-

tecting groups within society, but one of keeping them integrated with one another and as sensitive as can be to a public opinion which transcends them all. It is a matter of checks and balances, of what we might call the social and moral constitution of society.

Those who are especially devoted to efforts to eradicate from good people, as individuals, all those sentiments which seem to bring about the great and small dirty work of the world, may think that my remarks are something of an attack on their methods. They are right to this extent; that I am insisting that we give a share of our effort to the social mechanisms involved as well as to the individual and those of his sentiments which concern people of other kinds.

3

INSTITUTIONALIZED CORPORATE CRIME AND DEVIANT BEHAVIOR

Many of the papers in this section reflect the massive problems of theft, and even destruction of human life, that are caused by giant corporations. Social scientists and others have often misconceived of the real problems of large-scale crime as being synonymous with the Mafia, as Smith and Alba and Chambliss show. Smith and Alba discuss the false notions of the Mafia and organized crime as a secret Italian-American conspiracy, and Chambliss shows how organized crime is, indeed, a part of government and business.

Leonard and Weber found that bogus auto repairs are literally forced upon dealers by manufacturers. And, according to Farberman, bribery and tax evasion are forced on auto dealers by auto manufacturers. Vaughan found less compulsion in the Revco Drug Company techniques of massive computer theft that she analyzes. The long history of Johns-Manville asbestos abuses is presented in the research of Calhoun and Hiller. The irresponsible promotion of the Dalkon Shield IUD by A.H. Robins Company is described by Mintz. During the past two decades transnational corporations have expanded operations in Third World nations where, as the research by Michalowski and Kramer found, legal controls on corporate depredations are nonexistent. The United Nations has begun to attempt to fill this gap through efforts to develop an international Code of Conduct based on universal human rights for evaluating the activities of such corporations.

ORGANIZED CRIME
AND AMERICAN LIFE

Dwight C. Smith, Jr.,

Richard D. Alba

For the past two decades the specter of "Mafia" has haunted America. The criminologist Donald Cressey has expressed fears that the Mafia might some day control the occupant of the White House. *New York Times* columnist William Safire fears it nearly succeeded in the case of John F. Kennedy; and journalist Robert Sam Anson even suggests that the Mafia was involved in Kennedy's assassination. Nicholas Gage adds, "If the Mafia were a legitimate corporation, it would top the list of *Fortune* magazine's Five Hundred largest corporations."

Most Americans now take for granted that a secret criminal society of Sicilian origins, variously called the "Mafia" or "Cosa Nostra," lies at the heart of American organized crime. While belief in the Mafia was once derided, its acceptance has grown steadily since the sensational testimony of Joseph Valachi in the early 1960s. Today it is a journalist's cliché, the basis for numberless exposes and essays, and the cornerstone of public policy against organized crime.

The image of Mafia is ominous but hazy. Its label is joined to a core of fearful but unproven assumptions endorsed by many criminologists, lawmen, and journalists and expounded in such places as the President's Crime Commission Report and Donald Cressey's *Theft of the Nation*. In this view, the Mafia is a secret society of 5,000 to 10,000 men, all of Italian ancestry and organized into at least 24 "families" throughout the United States. It is a highly structured organization, with clearly delineated lines of authority and responsibility. Held together by bonds rooted in kinship and cemented by ritual, the Mafia is imagined to be a cohesive force, ruling over the domain of American organized crime and overwhelming any who resist its hegemony, whether competitor or victim. Estimates of its wealth make it seem a nation within a nation: billions of dollars a year in licit and illicit earnings are attributed to it.

But behind these assumptions lies a more fundamental conception, which hangs from a single, crucial premise: that organized crime is essentially alien to American life. In the now common Mafia view of organized crime, its roots lie in values derived from the culture of a specific ethnic group—values antithetical to those of mainstream America. Consequently, organized crime appears as the parasitic burrowing of traditional man—with his irrational emphases on kinship and rootedness, hierarchical relations and face—into the body of a modern, industrialized society. Inevitably, Americans are led by this conception to see organized crime as a dangerous ethnic conspiracy arising from a sense of particularistic loyalty that is linked to an ancient tradition of criminality.

Published by permission of Transaction Publishers, from *Society*, Vol. 16, No. 3. Copyright © 1979 by Transaction Publishers.

Also from this conception have sprung the major outlines of the ''story'' of organized crime in America. That story traces the movement of a cultural ethos (or the seeds of an organization, according to the sophistication of the teller) from its origins in Sicilian society to its entry into American society, along with Italian immigrants, in the late nineteenth century. It describes as well the evolution of a small, secret criminal group into the fully developed organization that emerged at the end of Prohibition, prepared to make a netherworld in its own image.

This conception colors the glass through which many observe the face of organized crime. As a result, they are able to see only the Italian features of contemporary organized crime and, even worse, to see them divorced from the American social contexts which make them comprehensible. These ethnic shades have encouraged a descriptive emphasis on conspirational attributes and allegedly Sicilian-derived organizational features as the keys to an understanding of organized crime. Thereby, the reality of entrepreneurial activity and the structural necessities of illicit marketplaces are ignored.

We need an alternative view of organized crime, one that places it within the spectrum of American enterprise and relates its conspiratorial features and frequent violence to the conditions under which it operates and the marketplaces where it is active. Such a view need not altogether dispense with the evidence accumulated under the rubric of ''Mafia.'' But it must free that evidence from the contaminated assumptions with which it is currently confounded and reinterpret it from the perspective that illicit enterprise has been a continuing and prevalent feature of American life. Such a view will lead us to see far beyond the Sicilians in today's headlines.

SOME PROBLEMATIC HISTORY

Any change in the American view of organized crime must begin by confronting the powerful influence of its present, underlying alien assumptions. As a beginning, the inner necessities which logically shape the present view—which guide,

for example, its selection and interpretation of historical and contemporary material—must be laid bare.

The contemporary Mafia view began to emerge during the Kefauver hearings of the 1950s, although it did not become a force in American public opinion until the mid-1960s. Its development and promulgation rested in part on a revision of the history of organized crime in American life. Previously, images of the gangster and racketeer found their referents in Prohibition and the decade that followed, with a cast of characters that reflected the American melting pot. Names like O'Banion, Schultz, Buchalter, and Capone testified in earlier times that organized crime was the product of no one group, and seemed to root it in American soil and circumstances. But the need to see organized crime as the creature of an alien force in the light of the Mafia view required a different narrative: one which itemized the links in a chain of continuous development connecting contemporary American organized crime to a Sicilian past. So a suitable narrative took shape, which diminished earlier images of the gangster in order to elevate an Italian-dominated history, rooted in a sequence of events in Sicily centuries before and leading to the emergence of a nationwide criminal organization in the United States.

This revision proves a strange concoction on close inspection. Events which had previously seemed important—like the ''fall'' of Abe Reles from a Brooklyn hotel window, abruptly ending the investigations of Murder, Inc.—receded into the background. Other events were subject to inexplicable twists of interpretation—as when the older view that Lepke Buchalter ordered the murder of Salvatore Maranzano as a result of a labor dispute simply vanished only to be replaced by an interpretation which saw that murder as part of Lucky Luciano's attempt to Americanize the Mafia. Still other events which had never before attracted attention, possibly because they had never happened—like the supposedly nationwide ''purge of the greasers''—suddenly loomed into prominence.

The Italianization of organized crime history required two parts, each necessary for the creation of a coherent narrative. The first was the creation of a plausible Sicilian ancestor for American organized crime. Such an ancestor required an ominous antiquity in order to justify the claim of its persistence in and stranglehold over American life. As a result, the Mafia literature abounds in assertions that its subject is a criminal society of ancient origins in Sicily, one of the most popular being a belief that the Mafia was born during the Sicilian Vespers, a Sicilian revolt in 1282. Frequently added to these fabulous tales of Mafia origins is the notion that its original purpose, the protection of peasants from the predations of lords and invaders alike, was perverted by successive generations into a wholly criminal enterprise. The Sicilian experience was also required to supply a suitable prototype for an American criminal organization. Thus, the American Mafia literature has generally described the Mafia in Sicily as a single island-wide society or organization with a hierarchical structure analogous to the nation-wide structure attributed to the American Mafia.

Contemporary scholarship—most especially, the writings of Joseph Albini, Anton Blok, and Henner Hess—has demolished the Sicilian foundation constructed to support the official and popular theory of American organized crime. The legendary material which had been pressed into that foundation has been exposed as lacking any historic sense. As one example, the legend that the Mafia was born during the thirteenth-century Sicilian Vespers rests on the claim that "Mafia" was the acronym for a slogan supposedly used during the Vespers ("Morte Alla Francia Italia Anela"—"Death to the French is Italy's cry"). But the slogan—in its nationalism, for example—makes sense only in nineteenth-century Italy, not in thirteenth-century Sicily (just as, one might add, much of the story of Sicily as told in the American literature makes sense only in twentieth-century America). In any event, there is substantial evidence that the term "Mafia," whose meaning often forms the fulcrum of legendary accounts of the Mafia's birth, did not acquire its contemporary meaning until first used in that way by a dialect play of the 1860s.

Even more importantly, contemporary scholarship has demonstrated how closely tuned the Sicilian Mafia has been to Sicilian circumstances, where it emerged as a mode of social organization, not as a specific criminal society. Adapting to the absence of effective state power, the classical Mafioso was a rural power broker who gathered others around him to form a clique within a village. Mafiosi achieved power partly through intimidation and violence and partly through the careful cultivation of relationships involving reciprocal obligations. An "understanding" and a degree of cooperation sometimes existed between different cliques in the same region, but often they remained independent of or in conflict with each other. In sum, the secret of Mafia power lay not in a criminal society but in the Mafioso's central location in a complex web of obligations and kinship relations, as well as in his ability to call his debts to achieve specific ends.

The second part of the revision making the Mafia the essential principle of American criminal history was required to explain the arrival of a unified organization in the United States and its growth on American soil. Here, a few scattered incidents have been used to prove an American presence by the end of the nineteenth century. Though some tale-bearers have identified earlier events (as when Nicholas Gage found that "the first recorded Mafia killing in the United States," occurred "on January 24, 1889, when a man named Vincenzo Ottumvo was murdered in New Orleans during a card game") most authors have been content to start with the famous Hennessy murder in 1890.

David Hennessy, the New Orleans police chief, was struck down by persons who remain unknown but, while dying, was said to have attributed his murder to "dagos." A number of Italians subsequently were charged with Hennessy's murder, but a jury failed to convict any of them. In response to this apparent miscarriage of justice, a mob led by several prominent New Orleans citizens stormed the local jail the following day and lynched 11 Italians held in connection with the case—though some of them had not even been on trial.

While there is reason to think that Hennessy's murder may have been connected with a struggle between two Italian groups for stevedore rights on certain New Orleans docks, not even that much is certain and there is no substantial reason to implicate a Mafia. The widespread belief at the time that Hennessy's murder was committed by the Mafia must be seen against the background of American xenophobia, particularly in reaction to sudden waves of immigration from southern and eastern Europe. Americans often uncritically accepted claims about the Mafia and used them as interpretive guides to events among the Italians. Thus, the lynching in New Orleans was fueled by the raising of Italian flags in celebration of King Umberto's birthday, the day following the verdict. The American community, ignorant of royal birthdays, immediately concluded that the court victory of the Mafia was the cause of rejoicing among the foreigners.

Relatively little has been advanced as Mafia history during the period between the Hennessy murder and Prohibition. A few scattered hints are offered, concerning isolated events. There is usually some mention in Mafia histories of "Black Hand," the name given by a New York journalist to extortionist gangs which flourished in Italian ghettoes in the first decades of the twentieth century, and of the still unexplained murder of a New York police officer in Palermo in 1909.

But it is Prohibition and its aftermath which generally claim the greatest attention in the Mafia narrative. From them emerged the phenomenon of syndicated crime, with Prohibition-enriched groups diversifying their rackets and extending the geographical area under their control, while entering into agreements among each other to forestall violent conflicts over turf. It is impossible for any narrative to wholly ignore the attention that these syndicates attracted during the sensational Murder, Inc. trials of the 1940s. Some of our most compelling images of the gangster and racketeer come from that period. But the multiethnic coloration of those images is troubling for those who want to understand contemporary organized crime as a simple descendant of a Sicilian criminal society, and equally troubling to the more sophisticated observer who wants to believe that organized crime is the product of a unique cultural ethos.

In meeting the challenge posed by Prohibition and its aftermath, the contemporary Italian-American narrative resorts to some peculiar twists. It begins by acknowledging that many groups entered organized crime because of the artificial stimulus of Prohibition but then argues that only the Italians had the organizational strength to continue to flourish once that stimulus was ended. It does so in part by excluding from clear focus most of the complex events and developments which characterize organized crime in the post-Prohibition period in order to dwell single-mindedly on a few events associated with the Italians, like the so-called "Castellammarese War," which supposedly led to the emergence of a nationwide Americanized Mafia in the early 1930s.

There is ample reason to suspect the truth and significance this narrative offers. The climax of the "Castellammarese War," to take an instance, was September 11, 1931. It has been known since Joseph Valachi's 1963 testimony as "Purge Day," when scores of the oldtime greasers were supposedly killed in the nationwide purge by which Lucky Luciano completed the Americanization of the Mafia. No Mafia text documents the accuracy of this story, and perhaps for good reason: there is little or no evidence to support it. The historians Alan Block and Humbert Nelli, independently sifting through newspaper reports in major American cities, have been able to turn up no more than a few murders possibly attributable to such a purge, nearly all of them occurring in the area around New York.

Even more important than the distortions of the Mafia narrative are its omissions. It underplays or omits entirely the late- and post-Prohibition events that reveal the continuing multiethnic character of organized crime and the crucial roles played by non-Italians in its development. To take New York as an example, Murder, Inc.—the focal point of organized crime news in the 1940s—is now scarcely mentioned because its leadership by Jewish racketeers like Lepke Buchalter calls into question the mafiologist's emphasis on Italians. So, too, current accounts usually ignore Dutch Schultz's conquest of the black numbers bankers in

Harlem in the early 1930s, despite its significance in consolidating and strengthening a new market which would compensate for the ending of Prohibition. While the importance of Meyer Lansky in current accounts might seem an important exception to this general pattern of omission, his place in the new narrative actually underlines the predominant Italian focus. Lansky is held to be important in organized crime only because he possesses specialized knowledge and skills lacking among the Italians.

All these tactical problems of Mafia history reflect its underlying theoretical deficiency: an inability to comprehend the importance of non-Italian organized crime. Even as the President's Crime Commission formally endorsed a unique role for the Mafia in the official view of organized crime in 1967, it was impossible objectively to ignore the presence of non-Italians. The principal solution of the Crime Commission and its chief consultant, Donald Cressey, was to relegate non-Italians to the lowest echelons of a single organizational structure, where they would be controlled by Italians. When the record was too strong to ignore—as with Meyer Lansky—specialized roles were created. For times when neither subordination nor the exception principle could be maintained—when, for example, John Gardiner's study of "Wincanton" and the "Stern syndicate" was published with no Italians on the scene at all—other, more convoluted solutions were needed. Thus, when pressed to explain why the Italians allow non-Italians to operate even though they "could within 24 hours dispose of all the non-Italian operators in the United States," Cressey advances such reasons as gratitude for past favors and a desire not to kill the "goose that laid the golden eggs," while ignoring the obvious answer: Italians have lacked the power to control all organized crime.

Our purpose in pointing to deficiencies in the Mafia narrative should not be misunderstood. To suggest that organized crime is multiethnic rather than predominately or exclusively Italian is not to deny the importance of ethnic dynamics in organized crime, or that ethnically identifiable groups do come to dominate important spheres of criminal activity at particular times and in particular places. Italians have come to dominate some spheres of organized criminal activity, such as gambling and loan sharking, in many American cities, just as those spheres were dominated in previous generations by Jews, Irish, and others. While the notion of "ethnic succession" is sometimes taken too simply, especially when it is used to imply that the degree of access to legitimate avenues of social mobility is the *only* variable governing ethnic participation in organized crime, it is still broadly true as a major thread in the development of American organized crime.

So, too, our rejection of the Mafia narrative's insistence on the unilinear development from the Mafia in Sicily to Cosa Nostra in America does not mean that we reject the proposition that an ethnic group's cultural traits influence its success at organized criminal activity. But the role of culture cannot be understood, nor can the crucial cultural traits even be identified, until organized crime is recognized as a part of American society, nurtured and shaped by American circumstances, not simply as an alien, parasitic force.

THE SOCIAL ORGANIZATION OF ORGANIZED CRIME

Historical narrative is not the only tool by which Mafia theory seeks to attribute a unique character to Italian-American organized crime in order to demonstrate that organized crime is essentially a cultural, and alien, phenomenon. A parallel skewing occurs in interpretations of the social organization of Italian-American criminal groups.

The most terrifying aspect of the Mafia, as it is presented to the public by journalists and law-enforcement officials, is its organization: rigidly structured and highly centralized, with clearly recognizable positions like "soldier" and "underboss" and a national governing body, the "Commission." This image promotes the illusion of an organization able to overwhelm any who resist its hegemony—able, for example, to seek out its enemies no matter where they run—and thereby insure its domination. This image also fosters the illusion of an organization capable of being rationally directed toward the goal of maximum profits.

The dominant model in the American Mafia literature is one of formal or bureaucratic organization. The social organization of Italian-American organized crime is viewed as a series of positions (soldier, underboss, capo, etc.) linked together in a hierarchy of authority and responsibility. The behavior of men in those positions is said to be governed by rules and procedures which are standard throughout the organization and which imply that membership is a 24-hour proposition. The Mafia thus appears as something like a corporation—an IBM of crime, as it were—or a military organization, parallels which are explicitly drawn throughout the literature. This degree of organization is represented as unique in the history of organized crime, and it is presumed to be possible only on the basis of a prior cultural blueprint: the Sicilian Mafia.

But this organizational model is difficult to believe, both on empirical grounds and for reasons that emerge from a serious theoretical examination of criminal organization. Indeed, difficulties seem to fly at this monolithic structure from everywhere once criminal organization is considered as problematic, not given. Two such difficulties emerge immediately from the commonly accepted lore of organized crime. The Federal Bureau of Investigation list of Mafia "families" shows that they are highly concentrated in the industrial cities of the Northeast, paralleling—not surprisingly—the pattern of settlement of Italian-Americans. Most major cities outside the Northeast are without a Mafia "family." This distribution makes the nationwide extent of Italian-American organized crime seem highly questionable, as it does the premise that the Mafia is rationally arranged from above toward the goal of maximum profits. Equally troubling is the fact that the organization name used by insiders varies from place to place, from "the office" in New England to "the outfit" in Chicago. It is difficult to reconcile the absence of a uniform name—or, indeed, the absence of an accepted name for some larger entity—with

the view that local criminal groups are just component parts of a single organization. And it is indicative of much in the Mafia literature that the commonly accepted names of a supposedly nationwide organization—"Cosa Nostra" or "Mafia"—are, in their generality, labels imposed by outside observers.

Similarly, variations in local structure challenge the assumption that organized crime is dominated by a national organization. Despite the official portrayal of a uniform structure, as in the Crime Commission's 1967 report, local circumstances vary even in Italian-American organized crime in ways that have never been fully described or acknowledged by those adhering to the Mafia view. Francis Ianni, in his study of one New York crime group, did not find the structure described in the Mafia literature, nor any which could be reconciled with a bureaucratic model of organization. Vincent Teresa's reminiscences, now part of the standard Mafia literature, describe the New England "family" of Raymond Patriarca as differing in many respects from the prototype described in the Crime Commission report. And even Joseph Valachi's original testimony, from which most theories of Mafia organization are drawn, did not describe a single structure for the five families of New York City.

Finally, the major problem with this organizational model is that it reifies structure, giving it more stability and rigidity than is possible in the conditions under which criminals operate. This is nowhere more visible than in official interpretations of the DeCarlo and DeCavalcante tapes. Their full-length transcripts comprise an important segment of the publicly available data by which the social organization of Italian-American criminals can be assessed. The major actors in these conversations talk *at times* in ways that appear to substantiate official assumptions. They use the standard terms for positions in a "family" (it should be noted that both sets of tapes are from the same area of New Jersey in the early 1960s) and they speak of the "Commission." But to interpret these terms as equivalents to the standard language of bureaucracy ignores fundamental constraints on criminal organization, particularly those associated with the problem of trust.

Whatever the ethnic origins of organized criminals, one must recognize that the basic mortar of their relationships is trust. Individuals who join together in the commission of crime are uniquely vulnerable. Their lives and welfare are jeopardized not only by the police but also by each other, and even so simple a matter as the division of their proceeds rests essentially upon trust. Prior agreements cannot, for obvious reasons, be written down; nor can the courts be used to enforce them. Thus, whether to trust a particular individual must be the first question confronting anyone involved in organized crime. In the case of Italian-American criminal groups, trust is based frequently upon natural or ritual kinship (the ''godparent'' relationship), fortified in many cases by childhood friendship. Such trust is not generalized to a formal organizational structure; an individual cannot easily extend trust beyond a small circle of others whose roots are close to his own.

Necessarily, crime appears more organized at the local level, because the relationships of mutual trust and cooperation which develop over a long period of time within small groups of individuals generate standard patterns of behavior. But those patterns cannot be generalized easily beyond or apart from the specific individuals involved in them. Trust and cooperation exist between people; when one of them dies or departs, another cannot simply take his place as one might succeed to a bureaucratic role such as vice-president in General Electric or major in the army. By its identification with the individuals who are a part of it, the organization of crime is basically different from that of a corporate or bureaucratic organization, where personnel changes are frequent within a relatively constant structure.

The DeCarlo and DeCavalcante tapes reflect this distinction. More important than their references to a Commission, underbosses, and *caporegime* is the view they offer of a world dominated by personal ''connections.'' The essential outlines of that world are quite unlike those of a corporation, where the relationships an individual has to others—his rights and duties, his patterns of communication—stem largely from the position he occupies. Rather, an individual's position in the world of organized crime is determined by his relationships to others, especially those relationships arising from kinship and common origins. By virtue of birth and experience he occupies a unique place within a complex web of particularistic ties and is able to derive advantage from privileged relationships to specific others—his ''connections.'' When someone in the DeCarlo or DeCavalcante tape asks the question, ''Who is X?,'' he generally does not want the title of an organizational position as an answer. Rather, he wants to know to whom X is connected. A typical answer is therefore something like, ''He's Carlo's man,'' or ''He's Joe's cousin.''

This is not to deny that there is a tendency toward impersonality, toward the creation of standardized rules and procedures, evident in these conversations. The protagonists talk at times, especially during periods of stress and conflict, as if the world should move in rational, rule-following ways. Often rules are invoked when one person is attempting to persuade another to behave in a certain way. But the very nature of these conversations undercuts any interpretation of the world of organized crime in terms simply of standardized rules and procedures. Their most common features are disagreement over the existence of the rules to be invoked and contention over the meaning of the ones identified.

The reification of criminal organization found in conventional Mafia theory has been abetted by the preoccupation with Italian-American organized crime which has accompanied it. Because of that preoccupation, a major methodological chasm underlies organized crime theory: comparative analysis of organized criminal groups. A serious test of the assertion that Italian-American organized crime is unique is virtually impossible because the Mafia fixation of the past 15 years has precluded study of non-Italian organized crime in the United States. The focus on Mafia has led law-enforcement agencies to concentrate their energies on Italians with the result that much is known about them and little about anyone else. And little note has been taken of the existence of organized criminal groups in other societies, like the *Yakuza* in Japan.

What little is known of non-Italian criminal organization should make anyone suspicious of a single ethnic theory. The occurrence of assemblies like that at Joseph Barbara's Apalachin home in 1957, for example, attended by individuals from different parts of the country, has been seized upon to lend credence to the claim of uniqueness. But such meetings, whether conducted by Italians or non-Italians, have probably been a feature of syndicated crime since the 1920s. Thus, there were probably two major conferences preceding the formation of the syndicate later known as Murder, Inc.'' in which both Italians and non-Italians were involved. Like members of any legitimate profession, organized criminals undoubtedly feel the need to confer about matters of common concern.

ORGANIZED CRIME AND AMERICAN SOCIETY

What is especially misrepresented in Mafia theory is the link between organized crime and a much wider range of activities that are inherently American and fundamentally linked to a market economy. The activities labeled "organized crime" are not simply vice crimes, as they have traditionally been viewed. Though law violations are integral to their existence, more important is their entrepreneurial character. When viewed apart from traditional assumptions about lower-class crime and immigrant groups, the events described as "organized crime" become part of a much wider problem that includes major segments of white-collar crime as well.

Organized crime represents an extension of entrepreneurial activities into areas normally proscribed, for the pursuit of profit and usually in response to latent illicit demand. It is, in other words, "illicit enterprise." In this view, the loan shark is a banker; the drug or cigarette smuggler is a wholesaler and the fence a retailer; and the bribe taker is a power broker. Mafia theory has generally turned away from these concep-

tual connections, preferring to see the loan shark, smuggler, fence, and briber as members of a criminal conspiracy that can be explained in its own terms, without reference to banking, wholesaling, retailing, or power brokering.

Important aspects of organized crime are clarified when similarities with the American marketplace replace assumptions of an alien intrusion. It then necessarily shares one fundamental motivating force with legitimate entrepreneurial activity: the need to maintain and extend its share of the market. In consequence, the behavior patterns that have generally focused attention on criminality rather then entrepreneurship—including even the use of violence—can be understood as the products of marketplace dynamics rather than as the outgrowth of cultural values which support criminal behavior. The illicit marketplace is precluded by definition from the stabilizing mechanisms available to legitimate business such as the use of the courts and, ultimately, the police power of the state to maintain property rights. Thus the loan shark may have to resort to violence when the debtor defaults because he cannot, as the banker may, use the courts to compel payment. At the same time, the illicit entrepreneur must avoid the imposition of regulatory power, and his extralegal efforts to evade it—often paralleling the legitimate businessman's use of lobbies and other political devices—form the basis of corruption.

Adherents of the Mafia view have spent so long mapping the presumed organizational details of a single national conspiracy that they are frequently unable to observe the actual coalitions of men and women which form (and occasionally reform) to exploit specific entrepreneurial possibilities. Many features of their coalitional structures can be understood better as responses to particular marketplaces. After all, one cannot do business in such areas as narcotics, numbers, and bookmaking without some degree of organization or coordination of the activities functionally necessary for successful operation.

The narcotics industry, as an example, requires links among individuals and groups who can carry out a variety of specialized activities, such as purchasing the raw materials where they are produced, smuggling them across national borders, processing the raw materials into usable form, and finishing and distributing the final product. Any one of these activities is likely to require organization—i.e., regular cooperation and recognition of a common enterprise—among more than a few individuals; and a group which spans several activities will require organization of a fairly large number of individuals into a coordinated network. Thus, one recent series of New York City indictments named 30 people connected with the operation of one heroin ring, which linked the procurement of opium in the "Golden Triangle" of southeast Asia to the sale of heroin on the streets of New York. And as is frequently true in Italian-American organized crime, most of those 30 black men and women were related to each other and shared geographical origins in North Carolina.

Once criminal organization is understood to be rooted in the structure and dynamics of illicit marketplaces rather than in a particular cultural ethos, then similarities among a wide range of events, currently seen as distinct by Mafia theory, can be recognized. Recent investigations of Medicaid abuses, particularly those in the nursing-home industry; the electrical-industry price-fixing case of the early 1960s; the collapse of Equity Funding: all these reflect varieties of "organized" crime that are equal in their entrepreneurial foundations and in their significance for American society to bookmaking, drug smuggling, and loan sharking. They reveal a degree of organized, concerted action among a large number of individuals engaged in illicit endeavor similar, in behavioral terms, to that of traditional organized crime.

ETHNICITY AND ORGANIZED CRIME

By this line of argument alone it would seem that the basic imperative in organized crime is economic. Historical development and cultural influences are also important, however; and as these three forces meet on the American crime scene we can see how appealing, and yet how terribly misleading, the convential Mafia

explanation has been. Organized crime has flourished of late with a predominantly Italian cast, but the explanation lies not in a secret criminal conspiracy but in processes of ethnic mobility and in ethnic variations in the cultural mechanisms for the creation of relationships of trust and mutual support.

The most problematic aspect of criminal organization is trust. In this sense, cultures which stress the importance of kinship, especially kinship beyond the limited confines of the nuclear family, provide advantages to the groups which possess them in the establishment of stable criminal organization. Kinship provides an especially durable foundation for a criminal relationship. Not only are there usually strong norms against injury to a kinsman, but betrayal—one of the most disruptive forces in criminal organization—is made all the more difficult because the betrayer cannot easily use the kin network to hide from retribution. In addition, extended kinship provides a relatively large pool of potential participants for an enterprise, one which is continually refreshed by younger relatives who enable the enterprise to survive beyond the lifetimes of a single generation. In contrast, groups formed solely on such bases as childhood friendship or shared prison experience are usually limited in their potential membership and in their ability to make the transition to a new generation.

In this respect, some individuals of southern Italian ancestry were superbly equipped for careers in crime. The single most important fact about the *Mezzogiorno* was the weakness of the state, even in the elemental provision of police protection for the individual. The consequence has been a culture that stressed family ties above all else as the source of mutual aid and protection. This cultural advantage at least partly explains the present importance of Italian-Americans in organized crime.

But historically specific processes of ethnic mobility and change also have accounted for the ethnic complexion of organized crime. Daniel Bell's well-known phrase, "crime as the queer ladder of social mobility," and Francis Ianni's "ethnic succession" point to the important role of a group's status in the evolving American social structure. Organized criminal enterprise generally has been a point of economic entry for groups near the bottom of society, whose members experience great difficulty in obtaining social mobility by legitimate routes.

At an early stage in the process of ethnic mobility, illicit upward movement is aided by residential segregation, allowing criminal networks to flourish in ghettoes. The ghetto limits the visibility of the illicit network to those outside of the group (except for consumers who seek them out); and it fosters an ethos that emphasizes the social boundary between members of the group and the world beyond, thus encouraging members to protect their criminal "brothers" from the occasional investigations of outsiders. Paradoxically, criminal networks display a tendency to expand beyond their ethnic neighborhood base at precisely the moment when legitimate avenues of mobility also begin to open. This expansion is promoted, as John Landesco pointed out in one of the earliest works on organized crime, by bonds resulting from common social origins among gangsters, politicians, police officials, and businessmen.

In the Mafia view, these dynamics corresponded to the stages of importation and development of an ethnic conspiracy, culminating in the establishment of an all-powerful nationwide criminal organization. By contrast, when organized crime is recognized as an American institution, through which some groups pass along paths determined by aspects of their culture and place in American society, then far more complex dynamics become visible. For contemporary policy, the most important implications of this process concern the factors governing transition from one group to another. Inevitably, the dominant criminal group's hold over the world of vice crime weakens as its ghettoes dissolve and the protection they afforded from police intrusion disappears. As its members experience more open access to legitimate, and hence less risky, avenues of mobility and cease to be the pool of continuing talent, its grip on vice enterprises wanes. In the end, it is forced out by other groups pushing upward from below. This pro-

cess of ethnic succession is already visible in contemporary vice crime. Blacks and Latins have begun to replace European groups in some types of criminal enterprise, most notably, narcotics and gambling. Just as organized crime existed before the Italians gained entry, so it will continue after they depart.

REASSESSMENT

The time is ripe for a reassessment of the Mafia concept. Its history is little more than a collection of fables; an air of unreality seeps through its view of criminal organization; and the Italian domination it presumes flies in the face of increasingly visible ethnic shifts in organized crime, to say nothing of the past history of American organized crime.

But the need for reassessment is not based solely on scholarly arguments. More importantly, we need something better as the basis for public policy. The Mafia view of organized crime has led to an insatiable public fascination with the trappings and ritual of a secret criminal conspiracy, a fascination stimulated by romantic concoctions like *The Godfather*. The consequences would be serious enough if they ended with a simplistic equation in the public mind between Italians and organized crime. But official attempts to understand and control organized crime have become victims of the same fascination. Millions of dollars are spent on research to reiterate the same flawed view of organized crime. More millions are spent in pursuit of criminals with Italian names. Yet organized crime flourishes. It should be obvious by now that current strategies for its control are bankrupt. They are so because the concept on which they are founded, that of a "Mafia," is bankrupt. It is time for a new view that focuses on the dynamics of American life rather than romantic imaginings about Italians.

READINGS SUGGESTED BY THE AUTHORS

Blok, Anton. *The Mafia of a Sicilian Village, 1860–1890.* New York: Harper Torchbooks, 1975.

Hess, Henner. *Mafia and Mafiosi: The Structure of Power.* Lexington, Mass.: Lexington Books, 1973.

Ianni, Francis A. J. *Black Mafia.* New York: Simon and Schuster, 1974.

Nelli, Humbert S. *The Business of Crime.* New York: Oxford University Press, 1976.

Smith, Dwight C., Jr. *The Mafia Mystique.* New York: Basic Books, 1975.

VICE, CORRUPTION, BUREAUCRACY, AND POWER

William J. Chambliss

I. INTRODUCTION

At the turn of the century Lincoln Steffens made a career and helped elect a president by exposing corruption in American cities.[1] In more recent years the task of exposure has fallen into the generally less daring hands of social scientists who, unlike their journalistic predecessors, have gathered their information from police departments, attorney generals' offices, and grand jury records.[2] Unfortunately, this difference in source of information has probably distorted the descriptions of organized crime and may well have led to premature acceptance of the Justice Department's long-espoused view regarding the existence of a national criminal organization.[3]

It almost certainly has led to an over-emphasis on the *criminal* in organized crime and a corresponding de-emphasis on *corruption* as an institutionalized component of America's legal-political system.[4] Concomitantly, it has obscured perception of the degree to which the structure of America's law and politics creates and perpetuates syndicates that supply the vices in our major cities.

Getting into the bowels of the city, rather than just the records and IBM cards of the bureaucracies, brings the role of corruption into sharp relief. Organized crime becomes not something that exists outside law and government but is instead a creation of them, or perhaps more accurately, a hidden but nonetheless integral part of the governmental structure. The people most likely to be exposed by public inquiries (whether conducted by the FBI, a

---

William J. Chambliss (1971) "Vice, Corruption, Bureaucracy, and Power." *Wisconsin Law Review* Vol. 1971 (no. 4): 1150–1173. Reprinted with permission.

I am grateful to W. G. O. Carson, Terence Morris, Paul Rock, Charles Michener, Patrick Douglas, Donald Cressey, and Robert Seidman for helpful comments on earlier versions of this paper.

[1]L. Steffens, *The Shame of the Cities* (1904). See *The Autobiography of Lincoln Steffens* (1931).

[2]D. Cressey, *Theft of the Nation* (1969); Gardiner, "Wincanton: The Politics of Corruption," Appendix B of *The President's Commission on Law Enforcement and Administration of Justice, Task Force Report: Organized Crime* (1967); in W. Chambliss, *Crime and the Legal Process* 103 (1969).

[3]The view of organized crime as controlled by a national syndicate appears in D. Cressey, *supra* note 2. For a criticism of this view see H. Morris & G. Hawkins, *The Honest Politician's Guide to Crime Control* (1970).

[4]Most recent examples of this are D. Cressey, *supra* note 2; H. Morris & G. Hawkins, *supra* note 3; King, "Wild Shots in the War on Crime," 20 *J. Pub. Law* 85 (1971); Lynch & Phillips, "Organized Crime-Violence and Corruption," 20 *J. Pub. Law* 59 (1971); McKeon, "The Incursion by Organized Crime into Legitimate Business," 20 *J. Pub. Law* 117 (1971); Schelling, "What Is the Business of Organized Crime?" 20 *J. Pub. Law* 71 (1971); Thrower, "Symposium: Organized Crime, Introduction," 20 *J. Pub. Law* 33 (1971); Tyler, "Sociodynamics of Organized Crime," 20 *J. Pub. Law* 41 (1971). For a discussion of the importance of studying corruption see W. Chambliss, *supra* note 2, at 89; W. Chambliss & R. Seidman, *Law, Order, and Power* (1971); McKitvick, "The Study of Corruption," 72 *Pol. Sci. Q.* 502 (1957).

grand jury, or the Internal Revenue Service) may officially be outside of government, but the cabal of which they are a part is organized around, run by, and created in the interests of economic, legal, and political elites.

Study of Rainfall West (a pseudonym), the focus of this analysis of the relationship between vice and the political and economic system, dramatically illustrates the interdependency. The cabal that manages the vices is composed of important businessmen, law enforcement officers, political leaders, and a member of a major trade union. Working for, and with, this cabal of respectable community members is a staff which coordinates the daily activities of prostitution, gambling, bookmaking, the sale and distribution of drugs, and other vices. Representatives from each of these groups, comprising the political and economic power centers of the community, meet regularly to distribute profits, discuss problems, and make the necessary organizational and policy decisions essential to the maintenance of a profitable, trouble-free business.

A. Data Collection

The data reported in this paper were gathered over a period of seven years, from 1962 to 1969. Most came from interviews with persons who were members of either the vice syndicate, law enforcement agencies, or both. The interviews ranged in intensity from casual conversations to extended interviewing, complete with tape recording, at frequent intervals over the full seven years of the study. In addition, I participated in many, though not all, of the vices that comprise the cornerstone upon which corruption of the law enforcement agencies is laid.

There is, of course, considerable latitude for discretion on my part as to what I believe ultimately characterizes the situation. Obviously not everyone told the same story, nor did I give equal credibility to all information acquired. The story that does emerge, however, most closely coincides with my own observations and with otherwise inexplicable facts. I am confident that the data are accurate, valid, and reliable; but this cannot be demonstrated by pointing to unbiased sampling, objective measures, and the like for, alas, in this type of research such procedures are impossible.

B. The Setting: Rainfall West

Rainfall West is practically indistinguishable from any other city of a million population. The conspicuous bulk of the population—the middle class—shares with its contemporaries everywhere a smug complacency and a firm belief in the intrinsic worth of the area and the city. Their particular smugness may be exaggerated due to relative freedom from the urban blight that is so often the fate of larger cities and to the fact that Rainfall West's natural surroundings attract tourists, thereby providing the citizenry with confirmation of their faith that this is, indeed, a "chosen land!"[5]

However, an invisible, although fairly large minority of the population, do not believe they live in the promised land. These are the inhabitants of the slums and ghettos that make up the center of the city. Camouflaging the discontent of the center are urban renewal programs which ring the slums with brick buildings and skyscrapers. But satisfaction is illusory; it requires only a slight effort to get past this brick and mortar and into the not-so-enthusiastic city center—a marked contrast to the wildly bubbling civic center located less than a mile away. Despite the ease of access, few of those living in the suburbs and working in the area surrounding the slums take the time to go where the action is. Those who do go for specific reasons: to bet on a football game, to find a prostitute, to see a dirty movie, or to obtain a personal loan that would be unavailable from conventional financial institutions.

---

[5]Thinking of one's own residence as a "chosen land" need not of course be connected with any objectively verifiable evidence. A small Indian farm town where the standard of living is scarcely ever above the poverty level has painted signs on sidewalks which read "Isn't God good to Indians?" Any outside observer knowing something of the hardships and disadvantages that derive from living in this town might well answer an unequivocal no. Most members of this community nevertheless answer affirmatively.

II. BUREAUCRATIC CORRUPTION AND ORGANIZED CRIME: A STUDY IN SYMBIOSIS

Laws prohibiting gambling, prostitution, pornography, drug use, and high interest rates on personal loans are laws about which there is a conspicuous lack of consensus. Even persons who agree that such behavior is improper and should be controlled by law disagree on the proper legal response. Should persons found guilty of committing such acts be imprisoned, or counseled? Reflecting this dissension, large groups of people, some with considerable political power, insist on their right to enjoy the pleasures of vice without interference from the law.

In Rainfall West, those involved in providing gambling and other vices enjoy pointing out that their services are profitable because of the demand for them by members of the respectable community. Prostitutes work in apartments which are on the fringes of the lower-class area of the city, rather than in the heart of the slums, precisely because they must maintain an appearance of ecological respectability so that their clients will not feel contaminated by poverty. While professional pride may stimulate exaggeration on the part of the prostitutes, their verbal reports are always to the effect that "all" of their clients are "very important people." My own observations of the comings and goings in several apartment houses where prostitutes work generally verified the girls' claims. Of some fifty persons seen going to prostitutes' rooms in apartment houses, only one was dressed in anything less casual than a business suit.

Observations of panorama—pornographic films shown in the back rooms of restaurants and game rooms—also confirmed the impression that the principal users of vice are middle and upper class clientele. During several weeks of observations, over 70 percent of the consumers of these pornographic vignettes were well dressed, single-minded visitors to the slums, who came for fifteen or twenty minutes of viewing and left as inconspicuously as possible. The remaining thirty percent were poorly dressed, older men who lived in the area.

Information on gambling and bookmaking in the permanently established or floating games is less readily available. Bookmakers report that the bulk of their "real business" comes from "doctors, lawyers, and dentists" in the city:

It's the big boys—your professionals—who do the betting down here. Of course, they don't come down themselves; they either send someone or they call up. Most of them call up, 'cause I know them or they know Mr. _____ [one of the key figures in the gambling operation].

Q. How 'bout the guys who walk off the street and bet?

A. Yeh; well, they're important. They do place bets and they sit around here and wait for the results. But that's mostly small stuff. I'd be out of business if I had to depend on them guys.

The poker and card games held throughout the city are of two types: (1) the small, daily game that caters almost exclusively to local residents of the area or working-class men who drop in for a hand or two while they are driving their delivery route or on their lunch hour; (2) and the action game which takes place twenty-four hours a day, and is located in more obscure places such as a suite in a downtown hotel. Like the prostitutes, these games are located on the edges of the lower-class areas. The action games are the playground of well-dressed men who were by manner, finances, and dress clearly well-to-do businessmen.

Then, of course, there are the games, movies, and gambling nights at private clubs—country clubs, Elks, Lions, and Masons clubs—where gambling is a mainstay. Gambling nights at the different clubs vary in frequency. The largest and most exclusive country club in Rainfall West has a funtime once a month at which one can find every conceivable variety of gambling and a limited, but fairly sophisticated, selection of pornography. Although admission is presumably limited to members of the club, it is relatively easy to gain entrance simply by joining with a temporary membership, paying a two dollar fee at the door. Other clubs, such as the local fraternal organizations, have pinball machines present at all times; some also provide slot machines.

Many of these clubs have ongoing poker and other gambling card games, run by people who work for the crime cabal. In all of these cases, the vices cater exclusively to middle and upper class clients.

Not all the business and professional men in Rainfall West partake of the vices. Indeed, some of the leading citizens sincerely oppose the presence of vice in their city. Even larger members of the middle and working classes are adamant in their opposition to vice of all kinds. On occasion, they make their views forcefully known to the politicians and law enforcement officers, thus requiring these public officials to express their own opposition and appear to be snuffing out vice by enforcing the law.

The law enforcement system is thus placed squarely in the middle of two essentially conflicting demands. On the one hand, their job obligates them to enforce the law, albeit with discretion; at the same time, considerable disagreement rages over whether or not some acts should be subject to legal sanction. This conflict is heightened by the fact that some influential persons in the community insist that all laws be rigorously enforced while others demand that some laws not be enforced, at least not against themselves.

Faced with such a dilemma and such an ambivalent situation, the law enforcers do what any well-managed bureaucracy would do under similar circumstances—they follow the line of least resistance. Using the discretion inherent in their positions, they resolve the problem by establishing procedures which minimize organizational strains and which provide the greatest promise of rewards for the organization and the individuals involved. Typically, this means that law enforcers adopt a tolerance policy toward the vices, selectively enforcing these laws only when it is to their advantage to do so. Since the persons demanding enforcement are generally middle-class persons who rarely venture into the less prosperous sections of the city, the enforcers can control visibility and minimize complaints by merely regulating the ecological location of the vices. Limiting the visibility of such activity as sexual deviance, gambling, and prostitution appeases those persons who demand the enforcement of applicable laws. At the same time, since controlling visibility does not eliminate access for persons sufficiently interested to ferret out the tolerated vice areas, those demanding such services are also satisfied.

This policy is also advantageous because it renders the legal system capable of exercising considerable control over potential sources of real trouble. For example, since gambling and prostitution are profitable, competition among persons desiring to provide these services is likely. Understandably, this competition is prone to become violent. If the legal system cannot control those running these vices, competing groups may well go to war to obtain dominance over the rackets. If, however, the legal system cooperates with one group, there will be a sufficient concentration of power to avoid these uprisings. Similarly, prostitution can be kept clean if the law enforcers cooperate with the prostitutes; the law can thus minimize the chance, for instance, that a prostitute will steal money from a customer. In this and many other ways, the law enforcement system maximizes its visible effectiveness by creating and supporting a shadow government that manages the vices.

Initially this may require bringing in people from other cities to help set up the necessary organizational structure. Or it may mean recruiting and training local talent or simply coopting, coercing, or purchasing the knowledge and skills of entrepreneurs who are at the moment engaged in vice operations. When made, this move often involves considerable strain, since some of those brought in may be uncooperative. Whatever the particulars, the ultimate result is the same: a syndicate emerges—composed of politicians, law enforcers, and citizens—capable of supplying and controlling the vices in the city. The most efficient cabal is invariably one that contains representatives of all the leading centers of power. Businessmen must be involved because of their political influence and their ability to control the mass media. This prerequisite is illustrated by the case of a fledgling magazine which published an article intimating that several leading politicians were corrupt. Immediately major advertisers canceled their advertisements in the magazine. One large chain store refused to sell that issue of the magazine in any of its stores. And when one of the leading cabal members was accused of accepting bribes, a number of the community's most prominent businessmen sponsored a large advertisement declaring their unfailing support for and confidence in the integrity of this "outstanding public servant."

The cabal must also have the cooperation of businessmen in procuring the loans which enable them individually and collectively to purchase legitimate businesses, as well as to expand the vice enterprises. A member of the banking community is therefore a considerable asset. In Rainfall West the vice president of one of the local banks (who was an investigator for a federal law enforcement agency before he entered banking) is a willing and knowledgeable participant in business relations with cabal members. He not only serves on the board of directors of a loan agency controlled by the cabal, but also advises cabal members on how to keep their earnings a secret. Further he sometimes serves as a go-between, passing investment tips from the cabal on to other businessmen in the community. In this way the cabal serves the economic interests of businessmen indirectly as well as directly.

The political influence of the cabal is more directly obtained. Huge, tax-free profits make it possible for the cabal to generously support political candidates of its choice. Often the cabal assists both candidates in an election, thus assuring itself of influence regardless of who wins. While usually there is a favorite, ultracooperative candidate who receives the greater proportion of the contributions, everyone is likely to receive something.

III. THE BUREAUCRACY

Contrary to the prevailing myth that universal rules govern bureaucracies, the fact is that in day-to-day operations rules can and must—be selectively applied. As a consequence, some degree of corruption is not merely a possibility, but rather is a virtual certainty which is built into the very structure of bureaucratic organizations.

The starting point for understanding this structural invitation to corruption is the observation that application of all the rules and procedures comprising the foundation of an organization inevitably admits of a high degree of discretion. Rules can only specify what should be done when the actions being considered fall clearly into unambiguously specifiable categories, about which there can be no reasonable grounds of disagreement or conflicting interpretation. But such categories are a virtual impossibility, given the inherently ambiguous nature of language. Instead, most events fall within the penumbra of the bureaucratic rules where the discretion of office-holders must hold sway.

Since discretionary decisionmaking is recognized as inevitable in effect, all bureaucratic decisions become subject to the discretionary will of the office-holder. Moreover, if one has a reason to look, vagueness and ambiguity can be found in any rule, no matter how carefully stipulated. And if ambiguity and vagueness are not sufficient to justify particularistic criteria being applied, contradictory rules or implications of rules can be readily located which have the same effect of justifying the decisions which, for whatever reason the office-holder wishes, can be used to enforce his position. Finally, since organizations characteristically develop their own set of common practices which take on the status of rules (whether written or unwritten), the entire process of applying rules becomes totally dependent on the discretion of the office-holder. The bureaucracy thus has its own set of precedents which can be invoked in cases where the articulated rules do not provide precisely the decision desired by the office-holder.

Ultimately, the office-holder has license to apply rules derived from a practically bottomless set of choices. Individual self-interest then depends on one's ability to ingratiate himself to office-holders at all levels in order to ensure that the rules most useful to him are applied. The bureaucracy therefore is not a rational institution with universal standards, but is instead, irrational and particularistic. It is a type of organization in which the organization's reason for being is displaced by a set of goals that often conflict with the organization's presumed purposes. This is precisely the consequence of the organizational response to the dilemma created by laws prohibiting the vices. Hence, the bureaucratic nature of law enforcement and political organization makes possible the corruption of the legal-political bureaucracy.

In the case of Rainfall West the goal of maintaining a smooth functioning organization takes precedence over all other institutional goals. Where conflict arises between the long-range goals of the law and the short-range goal of sustaining the organization, the former lose out, even at the expense of undermining the socially agreed-upon purposes for which the organization presumably exists.

Yet, the law enforcement agency's tendency to follow the line of least resistance of maintaining organizational goals in the face of conflicting demands necessarily embodies a choice as to whose demands will be followed. For bureaucracies are not equally susceptible to all interests in the society. They do not fear the castigation, interference, and disruptive potential of the alcoholics on skid row or the cafe-owners in the slums. In fact, some residents of the black ghetto in Rainfall West and of other lower-class areas of the city have been campaigning for years to rid their communities of the gambling casinos, whorehouses, pornography stalls, and bookmaking operations. But these pleas fall on deaf ears. The letters they write and the committees they form receive no publicity and create no stir in the smoothly functioning organizations that occupy the political and legal offices of the city. On the other hand, when the president of a large corporation in the city objected to the "slanderous lies" being spread about one of the leading members of the crime cabal in Rainfall West, the magazine carrying the "lies" was removed from newstand sale, and the editors lost many of their most profitable advertisers. Similarly, when any question of the honesty or integrity of policemen, prosecuting attorneys, or judges involved in the cabal is raised publicly, it is either squelched before aired (the editor of the leading daily newspaper in Rainfall West is a long-time friend of one of the cabal's leading members) or it arouses the denial of influential members of the banking community (especially those bankers whose institutions loan money to cabal members), as well as leading politicians, law enforcement officers, and the like.

In short, bureaucracies are susceptible to differential influence, according to the economic and political power of the groups attempting to exert influence. Since every facet of politics and the mass media is subject to reprisals by cabal members and friends, exposition of the ongoing relationship between the cabal and the most powerful economic groups in the city is practically impossible.

The fact that the bureaucrats must listen to the economic elites of the city and not the have-nots is then one important element that stimulates the growth and maintenance of a crime cabal. But the links between the elites and the cabal are more than merely spiritual. The economic elite of the city does not simply play golf with the political and legal elite. There are in fact significant economic ties between the two groups.

The most obvious nexus is manifested by the campaign contributions from the economic elite to the political and legal elites. We need not dwell on this observation here; it has been well documented in innumerable other studies.[6] However, what is not well recognized is that the crime cabal is itself an important source of economic revenue for the economic elite. In at least one instance, the leading bankers and industrialists of the city were part of a multi-million dollar stock swindle engineered and manipulated by the crime cabal with the assistance of confidence-men from another state. This entire case was shrouded in such secrecy that eastern newspapers were calling people at the University of Rainfall West to find out why news about the scandal was not forthcoming from local wire services. When the scandal was finally exposed, the fact that industrialists and cabal members heavily financed the operation (and correspondingly reaped the profits) was conveniently ignored in the newspapers and the courts; the evil-doers were

[6]See generally W. Domhoff, *Who Rules America?* (1969); Overa, *Presidential Campaign Funds* (1946); J. Shannon, *Money and Politics* (1959); Overa, *Money in Elections* (1932); Bernstein, "Private Wealth and Public Office: The High Cost of Campaigning," 22 *The Nation* 77 (1966).

limited to the outsiders who were in reality the front men for the entire confidence operation.

In a broader sense, key members of the economic elite in the community are also members of the cabal. While the day-to-day, week-to-week operations of the cabal are determined by the criminal-political-legal elite, the economic elite benefits mightily from the cabal. Not surprisingly, any threat to the cabal is quickly squelched by the economic elite under the name of "concerned citizens," which indeed they are.

The crime cabal is thus an inevitable outgrowth of the political economy of American cities. The ruling elites from every sphere benefit economically and socially from the presence of a smoothly running cabal. Law enforcement and government bureaucracies function best when a cabal is part of the governmental structure. And the general public is satisfied when control of the vices gives an appearance of respectability, but a reality of availability.

IV. VICE IN RAINFALL WEST

The vices available in Rainfall West are varied and tantalizing. Gambling ranges from bookmaking (at practically every street corner in the center of the city) to open poker games, bingo parlors, off-track betting, casinos, roulette and dice games (concentrated in a few locations and also floating out into the suburban country clubs and fraternal organizations), and innumerable two and five dollar stud-poker games scattered liberally throughout the city.

The most conspicuous card games take place from about ten in the morning—varying slightly from one fun house to the next—until midnight. A number of other twenty-four hour games run constantly. In the more public games, the limit ranges from one to five dollars for each bet; in the more select twenty-four hours a day games, there is a pot limit or no limit rule. These games are reported to have betting as high as twenty and thirty thousand dollars. I saw a bet made and called for a thousand dollars in one of these games. During this game, the highest stakes game I witnessed in the six years of the

study, the police lieutenant in charge of the vice squad was called in to supervise the game—not, need I add, to break up the game or make any arrests, but only to insure against violence.

Prostitution covers the usual range of ethnic group, age, shape, and size of female. It is found in houses with madams *à la* the New Orleans stereotype, on the street through pimps, or in suburban apartment buildings and hotels. Prices range from five dollars for a short time with a streetwalker to two hundred dollars for a night with a lady who has her own apartment (which she usually shares with her boyfriend who is discreetly gone during business operations).

High interest loans are easy to arrange through stores that advertise, "your signature is worth $5,000." It is really worth considerably more; it may in fact to be worth your life. The interest rates vary from a low of 20 percent for three months to as high as 100 percent for varying periods. Repayment is demanded not through the courts, but through the help of "The Gaspipe Gang," who call on recalcitrant debtors and use physical force to bring about payment. "Interest only" repayment is the most popular alternative practiced by borrowers and is preferred by the loan sharks as well. The longer repayment can be prolonged, the more advantageous the loan is to the agent.

Pinball machines are readily available throughout the city, most of them paying off in cash.

The gambling, prostitution, drug distribution, pornography, and usury which flourish in the lower-class center of the city do so with the compliance, encouragement, and cooperation of the major political and law enforcement officials in the city. There is in fact a symbiotic relationship between the law enforcement-political organizations of the city and a group of *local*, as distinct from national, men who control the distribution of vices.

V. CORRUPTION IN RAINFALL WEST

In the spring of 19— a businessman whom I shall call Mr. Van Meter sold his restaurant and began looking for a new investment when he noticed an advertisement in the paper which read:

Excellent investment opportunity for someone with $30,000 cash to purchase the good will and equipment of a long established restaurant in down town area. . . .

After making the necessary inquiries, inspecting the business, and evaluating its potential, Mr. Van Meter purchased it. In addition to the restaurant, the business consisted of a card room which was legally licensed by the city, operating under a publicly acknowledged tolerance policy which allowed card games, including poker, to be played. These games were limited by the tolerance policy to a maximum $1.00 limit for each bet.

Thus, Mr. Van Meter had purchased a restaurant with a built-in criminal enterprise. It was never clear whether he was, at the time of purchasing the business, fully aware of the criminal nature of the card room. Certainly the official tolerance policy was bound to create confusion over the illegality of gambling in the licensed card rooms. The full extent to which this purchase involved Mr. Van Meter in illegal activities crystallized immediately upon purchase of the property.[7]

[W]e had just completed taking the inventory of [the restaurant]. I was then handed the $60,000 keys of the premises by Mr. Bataglia, and he approached me and said, "Up until now, I have never discussed with you the fact that we run a bookmaking operation here, and that we did not sell this to you; however if you wish to have this operation continue here, you must place another $5,000 to us, and we will count you in. Now, if you do not buy it, we will put out this bookmaking operation, and you will go broke." "In other words," Mr. Bataglia continued, "we will use you, and you need us." I told Mr. Bataglia that I did not come to this town to bookmake or to operate any form of rackets, and I assumed that I had purchased a legitimate business. Mr. Bataglia said, "You have purchased a legitimate business; however, you must have the bookmaking operation in order to survive." I promptly kicked him out of the place.

The question of how "legitimate" the business Mr. Van Meter had purchased was is not so simple as he thought. It was, to be sure, a licensed operation; there was a license to operate the restaurant, a license to operate the card room attached to the restaurant, and a license to operate the cigar stand (where much of the bookmaking operation had taken place before Mr. Van Meter purchased the place). These licenses, although providing a "legitimate business," also had the effect of making the owner of the business constantly in violation of the law, for the laws were so constructed that no one could possibly operate a "legitimate" business "legally." Thus, anyone operating the business was vulnerable to constant harassment and even closure by the authorities if he failed to cooperate with law enforcement personnel.

The card room attached to the business was the most flagrant example of a legitimate enterprise that was necessarily run illegally. The city of Rainfall West had adopted by ordinance a tolerance policy toward gambling. This tolerance policy consisted of permitting card rooms, which were then licensed by the city, pinball machines that paid off money to winners, and panorama shows. The city ordinance allowed a maximum one dollar bet at the card table in rooms such as those in Mr. Van Meter's restaurant.

This ordinance was in clear and open violation of state law. The State Attorney General had publicly stated that the tolerance policy of the city was illegal and that the only policy for the state was that all gambling was illegal. Despite these rulings from higher state officials, the tolerance policy continued and flourished in the city, although it did so illegally.

This general illegality of the card room was not, however, easily enforceable against any one person running a card room without enforcement against all persons running card rooms. There were, however, wrinkles in the tolerance policy ordinance which made it possible discriminately to close down one card room without being forced to take action against all of them. This was accomplished in part by the limit of one dollar on a bet. The card room was allowed to take a certain percentage of the pot from each game, but the number of people playing

---

[7]All quotations are from taped interviews. The names of persons and places are fictitious.

and the amount of percentage permitted did not allow one to make a profit if the table limit remained at one dollar. Furthermore, since most people gambling wanted to bet more, they would not patronize a card room that insisted on the one dollar limit. Mr. Van Meter, like all other card room operators, allowed a two to five dollar limit. The ordinance was written in such a way that, in reality, everyone would be in violation of it. It was therefore possible for the police to harass or close down whatever card rooms they chose at their own discretion.

The health and fire regulations of the city were also written in such a way that no one could comply with all the ordinances. It was impossible to serve meals and still avoid violation of the health standards required. Thus, when the health or fire department chose to enforce the rules, they could do so selectively against whatever business they chose.

The same set of circumstances governed the cabaret licenses in the city. The city ordinances required that every cabaret have a restaurant attached; the restaurant, the ordinance stated, had to comprise at least seventy-five per cent of the total floor space of the cabaret and restaurant combined. Since there was a much higher demand for cabarets than restaurants in the central section of the city, this meant that cabaret owners were bound by law to have restaurants attached, some of which would necessarily lose money. Moreover, these restaurants had to be extremely large in order to constitute seventy-five percent of the total floor space. For a one-hundred square foot cabaret, an attached three-hundred square foot restaurant was required. The cabaret owner's burden was further increased by an ordinance governing the use of entertainers in the cabaret, requiring that any entertainer be at least twenty-five feet from the nearest customer during her act. Plainly, the cabaret had to be absolutely gigantic to accommodate any customers after a twenty-five foot buffer zone encircled the entertainer. Combined with the requirement that this now very large cabaret had to have attached to it a restaurant three times as large, the regulatory scheme simply made it impossible to run a cabaret legally.

The effect of such ordinances was to give the police and the prosecuting attorney complete discretion in choosing who should operate gambling rooms, cabarets, and restaurants. This discretion was used to force pay-offs to the police and cooperation with the criminal syndicate.

Mr. Van Meter discovered the pay off system fairly early in his venture:

I found shortages that were occurring in the bar, and asked an employee to explain them, which he did, in this manner: "The money is saved to pay the 'juice' of the place." I asked him what was the "juice." He said in this city you must "pay to stay." Mr. Davis said, "You pay for the beat-man [from the police department] $250.00 per month. That takes care of the various shifts, and you must pay the upper brass, also $200.00 each month. A beat-man collects around the first of each month, and another man collects for the upper brass. You get the privilege to stay in business. That is true; however, you must remember that it is not what they will do for you, but what they will do *to* you, if you don't make these pay-offs as are ordered. "If I refuse, what then?" I asked. "The *least* that could happen to you is you will lose your business."

During the next three months, Mr. Van Meter made the pay-offs required. He refused, however, to allow the bookmaking operation back into the building or to hire persons to run the card room and bar whom members of the organized crime syndicate and the police recommended to him for the job. He also fired one employee who he found was taking bets while tending bar.

In August of the same year, a man whom Mr. Van Meter had known prior to buying the restaurant met him in his office:

Mr. Danielski met with me in my office and he came prepared to offer me $500 per month—in cash deductions—of my remaining balance of the contract owing against [the restaurant] if I would give him the bookmaking operation, and he would guarantee me another $800 a month more business. He warned that if he wanted to give my establishment trouble, he would go to a certain faction of the police department; if he wanted me open, he would go to another faction. "So do some thinking on the subject, and I will be in on Monday for your answer." Monday, I gave Mr. Danielski his answer. The answer was no.

In June of 19—, a man by the name of Joe Link, who I found later was a second-string gang member of Mr. Bataglia's, made application to me to operate my card room. I did give him the opportunity to operate the card room because I had known him some 20 years ago when he was attending the same high school that I was. After I had refused the offer of Mr. Danielski, Mr. Joe Link had received orders from Mr. Danielski and Mr. Bataglia to run my customers out and in any way he could, cripple my operation to bring me to terms. I terminated Mr. Link on November 6, 19—, and shortly after, after I had removed Mr. Link, Police Officer Herb C. conferred with me in my office, and Officer Herb C. said that I had better reappoint Mr. Link in my card room; that his superiors were not happy with me. If I did not return Mr. Link to his former position, then it would be necessary to clear anyone that I wanted to replace Mr. Link with. Officer C. felt that no one else would be acceptable. He further stated I had better make a decision soon, because he would not allow the card room to run without an approved boss. I informed Officer C. that I would employ anyone I chose in my card room or in any other department. Officer C. said, "Mr. Van Meter, you, I think, do not realize how powerful a force you will be fighting or how deep in City Hall this reaches. Even I am not let know all the bosses or where the money goes." I did not return Mr. Link, as I was ordered by Officer C., and I did select my own card room bosses.

On November 7, 19—, I received a phone call stating that I soon would have a visitor who was going to shoot me between the eyes if I did not comply with the demands to return Mr. Link to his former position.

The crime cabal in Rainfall West (including police officers, politicians, and members of the organized criminal syndicate), like the criminal law which underpins it, relies on the threat of coercion to maintain order. That threat, however, is not an empty one. Although Mr. Van Meter was not "shot between the eyes" as threatened, others who defied the cabal were less fortunate. Although it has never been established that any of the suspicious deaths that have taken place involving members of the crime cabal were murder, the evidence, nonetheless, points rather strongly in that direction. Eric Tandlin, former county auditor for Rainfall West, is but one of thirteen similar cases which occurred from 1955–1969.

Tandlin had been county auditor for seventeen years. He kept his nose clean, did the bidding of the right politicians, and received a special gift every Christmas for his cooperation. In the course of doing business with the politicians and criminals, he also developed extensive knowledge of the operations. Suddenly, without warning or expectation on his part, Eric was not supported by his party, for re-election as auditor, losing the nomination to the brother-in-law of the chief of police. It was a shock from which Eric did not soon recover. He began drinking heavily and frequenting the gambling houses; he also began talking a great deal. One Friday evening, he made friends with a reporter who promised to put him in touch with someone from the attorney general's office. Saturday night at 6:30, just as the card rooms were being prepared for the evening, word spread through the grapevine along First Street that Eric had been done in: "Danielski took Eric for a walk down by the bay."

The Sunday morning paper carried a small front page story:

Eric Tandlin aged forty-seven was found drowned in back bay yesterday at around 5:00 P.M. The Coroner's office listed the cause of death as possible suicide. Friends said Mr. Tandlin who had been county auditor for many years until his defeat in the primaries last fall had been despondent over his failure to be re-elected.

The coroner, who was the brother-in-law of the chief of police, described the probable cause of death as "suicide." The people of Miriam Street knew better. They also knew that this was a warning not to talk to reporters, sociologists, or anyone else "nosing around." In the last few years the cabal has been responsible for the deaths of several of its members. Drowning is a favorite method of eliminating troublemakers, because it is difficult to ascertain whether or not the person fell from a boat by accident, was held under water by someone else, or committed suicide.[8] L.S., who was in charge of a portion

---

[8] According to one informant: "Murder is the easiest crime of all to get away with. There are 101 ways to commit murder that are guaranteed to let you get away with it." He might

of the pinball operations, but who came into disfavor with the cabal, was found drowned at the edge of a lake near his home. J.B., an assistant police chief who had been a minor member of the cabal for years, drowned while on a fishing trip aboard one of the yachts owned by a leading member of the cabal. In both instances the coroner, who was the brother-in-law of one of the leading cabal members, diagnosed the deaths as "accidental drownings." Over the years, he has often made that diagnosis when cabal members or workers in the organization have met with misfortune.

Other deaths have been arranged in more traditional ways. At least one man, for example, was shot in an argument in a bar. The offender was tried before a judge who has consistently shown great compassion for any crimes committed by members of the cabal (although he has compensated for this leniency with cabal members by being unusually harsh in cases against blacks who appear before him), and the case was dismissed for lack of evidence.

However, murder is not the preferred method of handling uncooperative people. Far better, in the strategy of the crime cabal, is the time honored technique of blackmail and co-optation. The easiest and safest tactic is to purchase the individual for a reasonable amount, as was attempted with Mr. Van Meter. If this fails, then some form of blackmail or relatively minor coercion may be in order.

For instance, Sheriff McCallister was strongly supported by the cabal in his bid for office. Campaign contributions were generously provided since McCallister was running against a local lawyer who was familiar with the goings-on of the cabal and had vowed to attack its operations. McCallister won the election—cabal candidates almost never lose local elections—but underwent a dramatic change-of-heart shortly thereafter. He announced in no uncertain terms that he would not permit the operation of gambling houses in the county, although he did not intend to do anything about the operations within the city

limits since that was not his jurisdiction. Nevertheless, the county, he insisted, would be kept clean.

The cabal was as annoyed as it was surprised. The county operations were only a small portion of the total enterprise, but they were nonetheless important, and no one wanted to give up the territory. Further, the prospect of closing down the lay-off center operating in the county was no small matter. The center is crucial to the entire enterprise, because it is here that the results of horse races and other sports events come directly to the bookmakers. The center also enables the cabal to protect itself against potential bankruptcy. When the betting is particularly heavy in one direction, bets are laid off by wiring Las Vegas where the national betting pattern always takes care of local variations. Clearly, something had to be done about McCallister.

No man is entirely pure, and McCallister was less pure than many. He had two major weaknesses: gambling and young girls. One weekend shortly after he took office a good friend of his asked if he would like to go to Las Vegas for the weekend. He jumped at the opportunity. While the weekend went well in some respects, McCallister was unlucky at cards. When he flew back to Rainfall West Sunday night, he left $14,000 worth of I.O.U.'s in Las Vegas.

Monday morning one of the cabal chiefs visited McCallister in his office. The conversation went like this:

Say, Mac, I understand you was down in Vegas over the weekend.

Yeah.

Hear you lost a little bit at the tables, Mac.

Uuh-huh.

Well the boys wanted me to tell you not to worry about those pieces of paper you left. We got them back for you.

I don't. . . .

Also, Mac, we thought you might like to have a momento of your trip; so we brought you these pictures. . . .

The "momentos" were pictures of McCallister in a hotel room with several young girls. Thereafter things in the county returned to normal.

---

have added that this was especially true when the coroner, the prosecuting attorney, and key police officials were cooperating with the murderers.

Lest one think the cabal exploitative, it should be noted that McCallister was not kept in line by the threat of exposure alone. He was, in fact, subsequently placed on the payroll in the amount of one thousand dollars a month. When his term as sheriff was over, an appointment was arranged for him to the state parole board. He was thus able to continue serving the cabal in a variety of ways for the rest of his life. Cooperation paid off much better than would have exposure.

Threats from outside the organization are more rare than are threats from within. Nevertheless, they occur and must be dealt with in the best possible way. Since no set strategy exists, each incident is handled in its own way. During Robert Kennedy's days as attorney general, the federal attorney for the state began a campaign to rid the state of the members of the cabal. People who held political office were generally immune, but some of the higher-ups in the operational section of the cabal were indicted. Ultimately five members of the cabal, including a high ranking member of the local Teamsters' Union, were sentenced to prison. The entire affair was scandalous; politicians whose lives depended on the cabal fought the nasty business with all their power. They were able to protect the major leaders of the cabal and to avert exposure of the cabal politicians. However, some blood ran, and it was a sad day for the five sentenced to prison terms. Yet the organization remained intact and, indeed, the five men who went to prison continued to receive their full share of profits from the cabal enterprises. Corruption continued unabated, and the net effect on organized crime in the state was nil.

One reason that Mr. Van Meter was not "shot between the eyes" was that, although not fully cooperative, he was nonetheless paying into the cabal four hundred and fifty dollars a month in "juice." Eventually he cut down on these payments. When this happened Mr. Van Meter became a serious problem for the cabal, and something more than mere threats was necessary:

No extortion was paid by me directly to them, but it involved a third party. Some time shortly after the first of each month, the sum of $250.00 was paid to [the above mentioned] Officer C., which he presumably divided up with other patrolmen on the beat. Two hundred dollars each month was given to [another bagman] for what the boys termed as "It was going to the upper braid." The $200.00 per month was paid each month from June 19— with payment of $200.00 being made in January 19—. After that I refused to make further payments. . . . After some wrangling back and forth, I just told them that I would not pay any more. They said, "Well, we will take $100.00 per month on a temporary basis. I paid $100.00 per month for the next twelve months. Early the next year I had planned to cut off all payments to the patrolmen. . . . About the 8th of July the explosion occurred. Police officers Merrill and Lynch conducted a scare program; jerked patrons off stools, ran others out of my establishment; Patrolman Lynch ordered my card room floorman into the rest room; and ordered my card room closed. When my floorman came out of the rest room, he left white and shaking and never to be seen in the city again.

Following this incident, Mr. Van Meter met with his attorney, the chief of police, and a former mayor. Although the meeting was cordial, he was told they could do nothing unless he could produce affidavits substantiating his claims. He did so, but quickly became enmeshed in requests and demands for more affidavits, while the prosecuting attorney's office resisted cooperating.

The refusal of cooperation from the prosecuting attorney was not surprising. What Mr. Van Meter did not realize was that the prosecuting attorney was the key political figure behind the corruption of the legal and political machinery. He was also the political boss of the county and had great influence on state politics, coming as he did from the most populous area of the state. Over the years his influence had been used to place men in key positions throughout the various government bureaucracies, including the police department, the judiciary, the city council, and relevant governmental agencies such as the tax office and the licensing bureau.

There was, however, a shift in emphasis for a short time in the cabal's dealings with Mr. Van Meter. They offered to buy his business at the price he had paid for it. But when he refused, the pace of harassment increased. Longshoremen came into his restaurant and started fights. Police stood around the card room day and night observing. City health officials would come to inspect the cooking area during mealtimes, thereby delaying the food being served to customers; the fire department made frequent visits to inspect fire precautions. On several occasions, Mr. Van Meter was cited for violating health and safety standards.

Finally, he was called to the city council to answer an adverse police report stating that he allowed drunks and brawling in his establishment. At the hearing, he was warned that he would lose all of his licenses if a drunk were ever again found in his restaurant.

During the next six months, the pressure on Mr. Van Meter continued at an ever-increasing rate. Longshoremen came into the restaurant and card room and picked fights with customers, employees, and Mr. Van Meter himself. The health department chose five o'clock in the evening several days running to inspect the health facilities of the establishment. The fire inspector came at the lunch hour to inspect the fire equipment, writing up every minor defect detectable. Toward the end of Mr. Van Meter's attempt to fight the combine of the government, the police force, and the criminal syndicate, he received innumerable threats to his life. Bricks and stones were thrown through the windows of his building. Ultimately, he sold his business back to the man from whom he had purchased it at a loss of thirty thousand dollars and left the city.

The affair caused considerable consternation among the legal-political-criminal cabal which controlled and profited from the rackets in Rainfall West. In the "good old days" the problem would have been quickly solved, one informant remarked, "by a bullet through the fat slob's head." But ready resort to murder as a solution to problems was clearly frowned upon by the powers that operated organized crime in Rainfall West. Although the syndicate had been responsible for many murders over the past ten years, these murders were limited to troublesome persons *within* the syndicate. As nearly as could be determined, no outsider had been murdered for a number of years.

Overall the gambling, bookmaking, pinball, and usury operations grossed at least twenty-five million dollars a year in the city alone. It was literally the case that drunks were arrested on the street for public intoxication while gamblers made thousands of dollars and policemen accepted bribes five feet away.

Payoffs, bribes, and associated corruption were not limited solely to illegal activities. To obtain a license for tow-truck operations one had to pay ten thousand dollars to the licensing bureau; a license for a taxi franchise cost fifteen thousand dollars. In addition, taxi drivers who sold bootleg liquor (standard brand liquors sold after hours or on Sunday) or who would steer customers to prostitutes or gambling places, paid the beat policeman and the sergeant of the vice squad. Tow-truck operators also paid the policeman who called the company when an accident occurred.

As one informant commented:

When I would go out on a call from a policeman I would always carry matchbooks with three dollars tucked behind the covers. I would hand this to the cops when I came to the scene of the accident.

Q. Did every policeman accept these bribes?

A. No. Once in a while you would run into a cop who would say he wasn't interested. But that was rare. Almost all of them would take it.

Most of the cabarets, topless bars, and taverns were owned either directly or indirectly by members of the organized crime syndicate. Thus, the syndicate not only controlled the gambling enterprises, but also "legitimate" businesses associated with night life as well. In addition, several of the hotels and restaurants were also owned by the syndicate. Ownership of these establishments was disguised in several ways, such as placing them formally in the name of a corporation with a board of directors who were really front-men for the syndicate or placing them in the names of relatives of syndicate members. It should further be underlined that the official ownership by the syndicate must be interpreted to mean by all of the members who were in the political and legal bureaucracies and simultaneously members of the syndicate, as well as those who were solely involved in the day-to-day operations of the vice syndicate.

The governing board of the syndicate consisted of seven men, four of whom held high positions in the government and three of whom were responsible for the operation of the various enterprises. The profits were split among these seven men. We are *not* then talking about a syndicate that paid off officials, but about a syndicate that is part and parcel of the government, although not subject to election.

VI. CONCLUSION

There is abundant data indicating that what is true in Rainfall West is true in virtually every city in the United States and has been true since at least the early 1900's. Writing at the turn of the century, Lincoln Steffens observed that "the spirit of graft and of lawlessness is the American spirit." He went on to describe the results of his inquiries:

in the very first study—St. Louis—the startling truth lay bare that corruption was not merely political; it was financial, commercial, social; the ramifications of boodle were so complex, various and far-reaching, that our mind could hardly grasp them. . . . St. Louis exemplified boodle; Minneapolis Police graft; Pittsburgh a political and industrial machine; Philadelphia general civil corruption. . . .[9]

In 1931, after completing an inquiry into the police, the National Commission on Law Observance and Enforcement concluded:

Nearly all of the large cities suffer from an alliance between politicians and criminals. For example, Los Angeles was controlled by a few gamblers for a number of years. San Francisco suffered similarly some years ago and at one period in its history was so completely dominated by the gamblers that three prominent gamblers who were in control of the politics of the city and who quarrelled about the appointment of the police chief settled their quarrel by shaking dice to determine who would name the chief for the first two years, who for the second two years, and who for the third.

Recently the gamblers were driven out of Detroit by the commissioner. These gamblers were strong enough politically to oust this commissioner from office despite the fact that he was recognized by police chiefs as one of the strongest and ablest police executives in America. For a number of years Kansas City, Mo., was controlled by a vice ring and no interference with their enterprises was tolerated. Chicago, *despite its unenviable reputation*, is but one of numerous cities where the people have frequently been betrayed by their elected officials.[10]

Frank Tannenbaum once noted:

It is clear from the evidence at hand—that a considerable measure of the crime in the community is made possible and perhaps inevitable by the peculiar connection that exists between the political organizations of our large cities and the criminal activities of various gangs that are permitted and even encouraged to operate.[11]

Similarly, the Kefauver Commission summarized the results of its extensive investigation into organized crime in 1951:

1. There is a nationwide crime syndicate known as the Mafia, whose tentacles are found in many large cities. It has international ramifications which appear most clearly in connection with the narcotics traffic.
2. Its leaders are usually found in control of the most lucrative rackets in their cities.
3. There are indications of centralized direction and control of these rackets, but leadership appears to be in a group rather than in a single individual.[12]

And in 1969, Donald R. Cressey, using data gathered from the attorney general of the United States and local crime commissions, capsulized the state of organized crime in the United States:

In the United States, criminals have managed to put together an organization which is at once a nation-

---

[10]Garrett & Monroe, "Police Conditions in the United States," 14 *National Commission on Law Observance and Enforcement Report on Police* 45 (1931).

[11]F. Tannenbaum, *Crime and the Community* 128 (1938).

[12]President's Commission on Law Enforcement and Administration of Justice, *The Challenge of Crime in a Free Society* 7 (1967).

---

[9]See L. Steffens, *The Shame of the Cities* 151 (1904).

wide illicit cartel and a nationwide confederation. This organization is dedicated to amassing millions of dollars by means of extortion, and from usury, the illicit sale of lottery tickets, chances on the outcome of horse races and athletic events, narcotics and untaxed liquor.[13]

The frequency of major scandals linking organized criminals with leading political and legal figures suggests the same general conclusion. Detroit, Chicago, Denver, Reading, Pennsylvania, Columbus and Cleveland, Ohio, Miami, New York, Boston, and a horde of other cities have been scandalized and cleansed innumerable times.[14] Yet organized crime persists and, in fact, thrives. Despite periodic forays, exposures, and reform movements prompted by journalists, sociologists, and politicians, organized crime has become an institution in the United States and in many other parts of the world as well.[15]

Once established, the effect of a syndicate on the entire legal and political system is profound. Maintenance of order in such an organization requires the use of extra-legal procedures since, obviously, the law cannot always be relied on to serve the interests of the crime cabal. The law can harass uncooperative people; it can even be used to send persons to prison on real or faked charges. But to make discipline and obedience certain, it is often necessary to enforce the rules of the syndicate in extra-legal ways. To avoid detection of these procedures, the police, prosecuting attorney's office, and judiciary must be organized in ways that make them incapable of discovering events that the cabal does not want disclosed. In actual practice, policemen, prosecutors, and judges who are *not* members of the cabal must not be in a position to investigate those things that the syndicate does not want investigated. The military chain of command of the police is, of course, well-suited to such a purpose. So, in fact, is the availability of such subtle but nonetheless important sanctions as relegating uncooperative policemen to undesirable positions in the department. Conversely, cooperative policemen are rewarded with promotions, prestigious positions on the force, and of course a piece of the action.

Another consequence is widespread acceptance of petty graft. The matchbox fee for accident officers is but one illustration. Free meals and cigarettes, bottles of whiskey at Christmas, and the like are practically universal in the police department. Television sets, cases of expensive whiskey, and on occasion new automobiles or inside information on investments are commonplace in the prosecuting attorney's office.

Significantly, the symbiotic relationship between organized crime and the legal system not only negates the law enforcement function of the law vis-à-vis these types of crimes but actually increases crime in a number of ways. Perhaps most important, gradual commitment to maintaining the secrecy of the relationship in turn necessitates the commission of crimes other than those involved in the vices per se. At times, it becomes necessary to intimidate through physical punishment and even to murder recalcitrant members of the syndicate. Calculating the extent of such activities is risky business. From 1955 to 1969 in Rainfall West, a conservative estimate of the number of persons killed by the syndicate is fifteen. However, estimates range as high as "hundreds." Although such information is impossible to verify in a manner that creates confidence, it is virtually certain that some murders have been perpetrated by the syndicate in order to protect the secrecy of its operations. It is also certain that the local law enforcement officials, politicians and businessmen involved with the syndicate have cooperated in these murders.

The location of the vices in the ghettos and slums of the city may well contribute to a host of other types of criminality as well. The disdain which ghetto residents have for the law and law enforcers is likely derived from more than simply their own experiences with injustice and police harassment. Their day-to-day observations that criminal syndicates operate openly and freely in their areas with complete immunity from punishment, while persons standing on a corner or

---

[13]D. Cressey, *supra* note 2. For a discussion of similar phenomena in Great Britain see N. Lucas, *Britain's Gangland* (1969). See also D. Bell, *End of Ideology* (1960).

[14]Wilson, "The Police and Their Problems: A Theory," 12 *Pub. Policy* 189 (1963).

[15]See McMullen, "A Theory of Corruption," 9 *Soc. Rev.* 181 (1961).

playing cards in an apartment are subject to arrest, cannot help but affect their perception of the legal system. We do not know that such observations undermine respect for and willingness to comply with the law, but that conclusion would not seem unreasonable.

It is no accident that whenever the presence of vice and organizations that provide the vices is exposed to public view by politicians, exposure is always couched in terms of organized crime. The question of corruption is conveniently left in the shadows. Similarly, it is no accident that organized crime is inevitably seen as consisting of an organization of criminals with names like Valachi, Genovese, and Joe Bonanno. Yet the data from the study of Rainfall West, as well as that of earlier studies of vice, make it abundantly clear that this analysis is fundamentally misleading.

I have argued, and I think the data demonstrate quite convincingly, that the people who run the organizations which supply the vices in American cities are members of the business, political, and law enforcement communities—not simply members of a criminal society. Furthermore, it is also clear from this study that corruption of political-legal organizations is a critical part of the life-blood of the crime cabal. The study of organized crime is thus a misnomer; the study should consider corruption, bureaucracy, and power. By relying on governmental agencies for their information on vice and the rackets, social scientists and lawyers have inadvertently contributed to the miscasting of the issue in terms that are descriptively biased and theoretically sterile. Further, they have been diverted from sociologically interesting and important issues raised by the persistence of crime cabals. As a consequence, the real significance of the existence of syndicates has been overlooked; for instead of seeing these social entities as intimately tied to, and in symbiosis with, the legal and political bureaucracies of the state, they have emphasized the criminality of only a portion of those involved. Such a view contributes little to our knowledge of crime and even less to attempts at crime control.

AUTOMAKERS AND DEALERS
A Study of Criminogenic Market Forces

William N. Leonard
Hofstra University

Marvin Glenn Weber
Mount Marty College

MARKET STRUCTURE AND OCCUPATIONAL CRIMES

That the American culture contains criminogenic elements leading to blue-collar crime, white-collar crime and noncriminal exploitation has been recognized by sociologists. Sutherland (1949:9) defined a white-collar crime as one "committed by a person of respectability and high social status in the course of his legitimate occupation." White-collar crime included such acts as false and deceptive advertising, mislabeling of goods, price fixing, selling adulterated goods, violating weights and measures statutes, performing illegal operations (by doctors), fee-splitting (by lawyers), and others. Thus crime could no longer be defined solely as the illegal activity of blue-collar, low-class and pathological persons, but extended to all classes, with the prestige group at the top setting a pattern of lawlessness reflected and emulated by subgroups.

The Theory of Occupational Crime

Other sociologists have advocated use of the term "occupational crime" to refer to illegal business activities. Newman (1958:737) noted that "farmers, repairmen, and others in essentially non-white-collar occupations, could

through such illegalities as watering milk for public consumption, making unnecessary 'repairs' on television sets and so forth, be classified as white collar violators." In his study of wartime black market operations, Clinard (1952) listed gasoline station operators as white-collar criminals. Following these studies, Quinney (1964) proposed an expansion of the concept of white-collar crime to include all violations which occur in the performance of occupational duties regardless of the social status of the offender. The essential point of the act, whether classed as white-collar crime or occupational crime, was that it occurred in a legitimate occupation but violated the legal and commercial codes established by statute.

A further refinement in occupational crime has been suggested by Bloch and Geis (1967)— the separation of such crime on the basis of the nature of the occupation. They recognize three categories of occupational crime:

1. Those committed by independent individuals and professionals, such as doctors and lawyers;
2. Those of employees against corporations (or government) such as embezzlements by bank employees (or welfare workers); and
3. Those committed by policy-making officers of corporations.

The latter class includes conspiracies to fix prices, misrepresentation of merchandise, labor exploitation, and other illegal activities.

William N. Leonard and Marvin Glenn Weber (1970) "Automakers and Dealers: A Study of Criminogenic Market Forces." *Law and Society Review* Vol. 4 (February): 407–424. Reprinted by permission of the Law and Society Association.

Failure to Analyze Market Structure

Insufficient attention has been focused by sociologists on the extent to which market structure—that is, the economic power available to certain corporations in concentrated industries—may generate criminal conduct. In the studies of the electrical industry conspiracy, for example, sociologists concentrated on the noncriminal backgrounds and the prestigious positions of the corporate officials who had engaged in the slippery conspiracy to violate the anti-trust laws. Other sociologists concerned themselves with the problems of individual versus corporate guilt, and the extent to which the officials involved were aware of the illegal character of their price-fixing activities. Geis (1967:145) and others have pointed out that "to meet with competition [had become] common and [had] gone on for so many years" that some individuals in the electrical corporations had lost sight of its illegality. Nonetheless, the gentlemen conspirators went to great lengths to avoid detection, using blank stationery, adopting assumed names, meeting secretly in motels to rig bids according to the phase of the moon, and using other cloak and dagger tactics.

What Geis and other commentators failed to recognize is that price fixing of an effective character (whereby an increase in industry price yields higher revenues and profits) could not succeed unless two economic conditions existed:

1. The industry was concentrated with the bulk of output in the hands of a few producers who could easily get together; and
2. Demand for the product or products was price inelastic, that is, the buyers of heavy electrical equipment (in this case utilities) would not reduce purchases if prices were increased.

These economic conditions made it possible for officers of a few electrical equipment manufacturers to conspire to fix industry price on a wide range of heavy electrical items and insured the effectiveness of their actions (Wolfgang and Savitz, 1962:361). The name of the game is profits, and unless illegal activity actually generates profits, it will not become accepted practice in any industry. Geis correctly noted that the price-fixing agreements flourished when market conditions deteriorated and antitrust enforcement abated, yet pressures for profits from each company division remained insistent.

Market structure can also illuminate the three classes of crime cited by Bloch and Geis, particularly since it delimits the freedom of action of the individuals concerned and the impact of their crime on others. Policy-making officers of corporations have a wide range of discretionary action, and their decisions affect thousands of persons. Large corporations can increase profits not merely by fixing prices (illegal) or raising prices in concentrated industries (legal), but by such steps as improving products, shifting investments, increasing advertising and sales promotion, merging, branching, or better cost control. A second Bloch-Geis class, the independent individual, may possess considerable freedom of action if he is a professional—doctor, lawyer, certified public accountant, and the like—but if he operates a filling station or dealership as the agent of a large company, or is a small businessman competing against large firms, his range of discretion is severely restricted, and the impact of his behavior circumscribed. Last, those employees who commit crimes against corporations or government—e.g., embezzlement—have the least freedom of action and criminal impact. Nonetheless, the laws determining the legality of employee behavior are the most definitive. Laws or codes which seek to define the ethics of the professional person, small businessman, or big businessman are vague, or if statutory (like the antitrust laws) can often be circumvented (Wolfgang and Savitz, 1962:20–24). In general, the standards of ethics of the professional appear more likely to govern his behavior than the laws against deceptive practices or discriminatory pricing seem to affect the actions of businessmen, large or small. In the market place, it is still *caveat emptor*. One of the large problems of society is that policy-making businessmen who have a wide scope of discretion and whose choices affect millions of persons, have the least clearly defined standards of conduct. A competitive market system supposedly limits their opportunity for consumer deception, fraud, shoddy merchandise and poor service. In the absence of competition, no such limitations exist.

As a result of the failure to introduce analysis of market structure into sociological studies of occupational predatory crime, criticism is directed largely and excessively against the corporate ways of life and the profit system, while corrective action is sought (short of revolution) in public vigilance to detect and prosecute price fixing, discrimination, trying contracts, and other proscribed practices which means more personnel and resources for antitrust. Characteristically, the "more policemen" solution indicates a failure of social science to deal adequately with the basic causes of crime. With respect to occupational crime, the lack of analysis of market structure can easily mean that the criminal roots will never be touched, although the limbs continue to be cut. The need is for a market structure in each industry to allow competitive forces rather than government to do the regulating.[1] Such analysis, it is argued, can throw considerable light on the conditions which produce both white- and blue-collar crime, and lead to practical proposals for correction.

Concentrated market structure generates excessive power in the hands of a few corporations which can use it against suppliers, distributors, and customers and create conditions conducive to corporate profits which may, however, induce those with whom the corporations deal directly—e.g., distributors—to engage in unethical activity against the public. Rather than curb such actions, corporations wink at them.

MARKET STRUCTURE OF THE AUTOMOBILE INDUSTRY

In economic literature market structure involves these aspects:

1. Seller concentration, or market share of the leading producers;
2. Buyer concentration, or market share of principal buyers;
3. Product differentiation, or extent to which the product can be distinguished in the customer's mind through refinements, advertising, and so forth;
4. Entry barriers—e.g., costs of capital, patents, economies of scale, advertising expenses;
5. Price elasticity of demand; and
6. Growth rate of demand. (Most important are 1, 3, and 4.)

The automobile industry stands out both as to seller concentration and in the height of entry barriers to the industry. Use of the assembly line techniques makes it imperative to have a high sales volume (250,000 cars per year at a minimum) in order to attain scale economics. Emphasis on styling (the annual model change, a plethora of models, colors, gimmicks, and so forth) and extensive advertising make it difficult for small companies to compete. Many small manufacturers have gone out of business since 1921 when there were 81 car makers, and there has not been a successful entrant since Chrysler in 1925. The failure of Henry Kaiser, who entered the industry by merger with Fraser in 1947, and the chronic deficits of American Motors, which has three percent of the car output total, documents the difficulty of a new or small company in competing with the "Big Three." Thus the high concentration in the industry, plus entry barriers erected by capital costs, scale economics, and product differentiation, make the automobile industry one of the most solidly entrenched oligopolies among United States industries. This combination of factors also gives the Big Three abnormally high profit rates,[2] and great market power. The very large volume of sales associated with this industry and the concentration of sales in three companies afford the Big Three a market power without parallel in industry. That power can be exercised on suppliers, e.g., the rubber and steel industries from which the car makers purchase tires and metal at extremely low cost, or against dealers and distributors. The manufacturer-dealer rela-

---

[1]Chief Justice Warren has stated: "An industry that does not have a competitive structure will not have competitive behavior" (U.S. v. E.I. DuPont de Nemours and Co.).

[2]From 1960–1967, General Motors earned 20.5% return on investment; Ford obtained 14.3%; and Chrysler 11.8%. All industries averaged about 8–9% in this period (Federal Trade Commission, 1968:159).

tion in the marketing of automobiles illustrates how the superior market power of the manufacturer can be exercised to coerce dealers and cause criminal behavior on their part.

MANUFACTURER-DEALER RELATIONS

While only four domestic manufacturers of cars remain, their products are distributed through 30,000 dealers with facilities scattered throughout the United States. Technically, the dealer is an independent businessman. Rarely, however, does he have the capital to acquire more than a fraction of the value of property involved in the dealership. The rest is supplied by the manufacturer, and although the dealer may increase his ownership, rising costs of real estate, equipment and facilities, plus expansion of the dealership, may keep him dependent on the manufacturer for a long time. Further, he operates under restrictive agreement, terms of which are set by the manufacturer.

In the franchise agreement, often referred to as the selling agreement, a dealer contracts to sell and service the products of his manufacturer. The dealer does not receive an exclusive franchise for a given territory, but obtains a location for the sale and servicing of the products, often largely owned by the manufacturer. The dealer promises to display and advertise the manufacturer's cars and trucks. The dealer must also agree to stock parts, provide service to customers and make numerous reports on all phases of the business to the manufacturer. He promises to meet the minimum sales responsibility, or quota of sales established by the manufacturer and if he does not, his franchise is subject to cancellation. No franchise extends for more than five years, and many provide for cancellation within thirty to ninety days. Since the manufacturer's chief concern is the sales of the original product (ninety percent of his income is derived from new cars sales and only ten percent from the sale of parts in connection with service to the product), he often cancels dealers for failure to meet sales quotas. However, manufacturers reported to the Federal Trade Commission that they had never

cancelled a dealer for failure to have adequate service facilities or for poor service performance (Federal Trade Commission, 1968:118–119).

Dealers are therefore pressured to be sales-oriented and to adopt the manufacturer's position that service is "a necessary evil." The manufacturer normally selects as dealer—(note that dealers cannot choose their successors in the business)—a person who is a salesman, has some capital to invest, and a good reputation in the community. He soon learns that new car sales represent his bread and butter. The manufacturer's sales representatives place unremitting pressure on the dealer to increase sales, and all sorts of contests are initiated to induce higher sales. While the manufacturer has service representatives in the area, they have a status inferior to that of the sales people. The dealer and his sales people may receive bonuses for superior sales performance, but there are no financial rewards for good service. What use is a good reputation for service to a dealer whose franchise is terminated because of a poor sales record? In such a case, the manufacturer, as required by law, pays the dealer a sum equal to his investment in the establishment—the unlucky franchise-holder receives nothing for good will in the community. The direction in which the incentives operate is clear: enhance sales and downgrade service.

One may ask why dealers choose to burden themselves with such franchises. The answer is that if a man wishes to sell and service cars, he has only four domestic manufacturers who can provide this opportunity, and they offer similar franchises. On the other hand, there appear to be numerous persons in the factory and in the field from the ranks of whom the manufacturer may select a dealer. If the prospect lacks sufficient capital, this will be supplied by the manufacturer, but on the latter's terms. Consequently, the manufacturer enjoys a superior bargaining position which is reflected in the franchise.

Between 1954 and 1968 the numbers of franchised dealers of domestic manufacturers declined 35%, from 43,000 to 27,800. Even though the average size of establishment increased and service sales per dealer doubled, the dealer's share of the automobile service market dropped from 43 to 32%. This trend (controlled by the manufacturer) has enabled the manufacturer to concentrate sales in fewer dealerships and to improve supervision over dealers, but has reduced the number of dealer outlets available to those seeking service on their motor vehicles. With the rapid increase in cars on the road over this period, dealers have been hard-pressed to afford service to customers and have lost business to other outlets, principally independent shops and garages, also to service stations and to individuals who prefer to buy parts and make their own repairs. A general shortage of mechanics has plagued the industry, a shortage which has grown steadily worse. In the 1950s, there was one mechanic for every eighty cars on the road, but by 1968 the ratio had risen to one for every one hundred thirty cars. During this period cars have become more complicated, with a large proportion of new cars having power steering, power brakes, air conditioning, push-button windows, and other mechanisms. The heavy pressure of repair work, arising from the growing number of car registrations, the increased complexity of cars and the demand of the public for quick repair service, combined with the shortage of automobile mechanics, produced a situation in which sharp and deceptive practices developed and flourished. The average car operator understands little about the functioning of an automobile, and the multiplication of car mechanisms and parts has increased his ignorance. He is fair game to be plucked by the unscrupulous repair outlets, and evidence exists that plucking is widespread (Federal Trade Commission, 1968:109). It is not confined to dealers and their mechanics, although sociological analysis here presented relates primarily to the automobile service performed by dealers.

EVIDENCE OF CRIMINAL BEHAVIOR

Several years ago, Dr. George Gallup made a nationwide survey to determine the public image for seven occupational groups; new car dealers, bankers, druggists, supermarket managers, undertakers, service station managers, and plumbers. Gallup's interviewers asked respondents: "Rank these businessmen in terms of how honest and trustworthy you think they are." New car dealers trailed every other occupation; only 3% of the public surveyed considered new car dealers "most honest and truthworthy." Plumbers outscored the dealers three to one, undertakers five to one and druggists nearly twenty to one.[3] When the question was turned around and those surveyed were asked whom they considered "least honest and trustworthy," 57% picked the dealer. Undertakers and plumbers were tied for second place, with 29% of the vote.

In a second survey, David Ogilvy (1965:4–6) found that 54% of the public preferred to take their car to the dealer for service (only 29% preferred to go to the service station), giving as reasons that the dealers specialized in that make of car, had well-trained mechanics, and a good stock of parts. However, a majority of those surveyed went elsewhere for service. Only 38% patronized the dealer; they considered his prices high, they had to wait for service, and they did not trust him. Ogilvy told the dealers that their general reputation was "awful."

Specific instances of unethical and illegal conduct by dealers and their mechanics may be found in a number of places. In 1966, two authors published a book entitled *Highway Robbery* (Crowther and Winehouse, 1966), which examined numerous cases taken from the files of the district attorney's office in Queens County, New York, from the Better Business Bureaus of New York City and St. Louis, Missouri, from FBI files and from hearings before a subcommittee of the Senate Banking and Currency Committee which investigated car-finance rackets. Dozens of cases were reported involving fraud in sales of new cars, accessories not ordered but "forced" on buyers, used cars sold for new, engines switched in cars, excessive finance charges, automotive repair overcharges, "fake"

---

[3]Respondents ranked as honest and trustworthy: bankers—74%; druggists—56%; supermarket managers—14%; undertakers—16%; service station managers—14%; plumbers—8%; and new car dealers—3% (Ogilvy, 1965).

repair diagnoses, and many other abusive practices. In the vast majority of these cases, dealers and their mechanics were involved.

Since 1965, thousands of letters of complaint concerning automobile warranties and automobile repairs have poured into the Federal Trade Commission and now constitute the thickest consumer file in the commission's 55-year history. Nearly all the letters cite new cars delivered in defective condition, dealers who failed to perform under the warranty, and improper repairs. A report on automobile warranties prepared by the commission's staff late in 1968 summarized the nature of these complaints and sought to find reasons for the failure of motorists to receive proper service from dealers under the warranty. The report strongly emphasized the role of manufacturer-dealer relations, particularly the superior market power exercised by the manufacturer vis-à-vis the dealer.

In December 1968, the Subcommittee on Antitrust and Monopoly of the United States Senate opened a series of hearings on automobile repairs; the series received national newspaper and television coverage. Witnesses who spoke on the high cost of automobile repairs cited as a reason the deterioration in automobile service of dealers brought about by the excessive concern of manufacturers for car sales and the treatment of car repairs as a necessary evil. One witness (Leonard, 1968) listed a series of "rackets" which characterized some dealerships, specifically:

1. *Forcing accessories.* For example, new cars arrive with accessories which the buyer did not order but must pay for in order to get delivery.
2. *Used car markups.* Since dealers make only $150-$200 per unit on new car sales, they endeavor to compensate for this by large markups on used cars (dealers often make $400 on a $2,000 used car, compared to $150 on a $3,200 new car).
3. *Service gouging.* Dealers also make up for their low returns in the sale of new cars by overcharging for service. This can be managed in many ways: by putting down more labor time than that actually consumed in repairs, by charging for repairs not actually made (or charging for a major tune-up when a minor tune-up is performed), by finding

things wrong with the car that do not actually need repair, by replacing parts unnecessarily, and so on.
4. *High finance.* Dealers will often finance cars themselves, borrowing money from a bank or credit agency and lending at a higher rate of interest. Sometimes the dealer will recommend a poor credit risk to a loan shark and receive a commission in return.
5. *Parts pushing.* This involves overcharging for parts, or use of a rebuilt part while charging for a new one. Sometimes the dealer and his mechanics will use a new part when the old one could be repaired at less expense to the customer, or will find a part defective which is not actually so.
6. *Other practices.* Dealers also will sell cars used by fleets for six months or a year as "executive" cars, will turn odometers back to make cars appear less used and engage in other practices which deceive customers.

The witness made it clear that he did not attribute such practices to the majority of dealers and cited Better Business Bureau data indicating other repair outlets engaged in the same or similar practices.

Despite disclaimers, such practices are sufficiently widespread among dealers as to produce the "awful" public image of dealers reported by David Ogilvy, and to generate thousands of letters of complaint which have poured into the files of the Federal Trade Commission, Senate and House committees, and the President's Counsel on Consumer Affairs.

MARKET STRUCTURE
AND CRIMINAL BEHAVIOR
IN AUTOMOBILE REPAIRS

It is argued here that what appears to the public as unethical or criminal behavior on the part of dealers and mechanics represents "conditioned" crime, or crime stimulated by conditions over which the dealer or mechanic has but little control. Perhaps a better phrase would be "coerced" crime, since it results from the coercion of strong corporations whose officers can utilize the concentrated market power of their companies to bend dealer and mechanic to serve company objectives. Following Donald Taft, we can term automobile manufacturers "socially dangerous people" since they function as "causers of the causes" of crime. Taft defines "socially dangerous people" as those "who, not technically criminal themselves, nevertheless create conditions which result in crime" (Taft, 1966:15–23). Dealers and mechanics operate within systems controlled by outsiders, specifically by a few large automobile manufacturers.

Some description has been given of the franchise system under which the dealer sells and services cars. Terms are set by the manufacturer, and if the dealer does not sell up to quota, he incurs the risk of cancellation. In 1939, a study by the Federal Trade Commission (1939:1076) found that under the franchise system:

motor vehicle manufacturers . . . especially General Motors Corporation, Chrysler Corporation and Ford Motor Company, have been, and still are, imposing on their respective dealers unfair and inequitable conditions of trade.

The commission described the Big Three manufacturers as ruthless in pressing their dealers for volume. Since that time, little improvement in the situation has occurred. Complaints by dealers and public hearings led to passage in 1956 of the Automobile Dealers Franchise Act, which required the manufacturer to act in good faith in terminating the dealer. However, the dealer must prove that the manufacturer did not act in good faith in the cancellation, and this is rarely possible. Consequently, the franchise still conveys excessive power to the manufacturer and makes the dealer not an independent businessman, but an agent or pawn of his manufacturer.[4]

In recent years, the pressure on dealers to sell new cars, always intense, has been heightened by the establishment of "factory stores." These are dealerships, located in urban areas, entirely or almost entirely owned by the manufacturer, where the dealer in charge is a compliant cap-

tive of the factory. These outlets retail cars below the prices offered by other dealers in the area, which means the markup runs considerably below $200 per car. Though they lose money on new cars, these outlets win substantial cash prizes at the end of the year for sales leadership, and the manufacturer can point to such outlets in talking over sales with other dealers, and ask, "Why can't you sell like Mr. Giveaway?" (See Leonard, 1968:18.) The major impact of the factory store is to push sales in the area, particularly by stimulating regular dealers to shave prices and profits in order to match sales quotas. Chrysler and Ford, always trying to stay in the competition with General Motors, have backed the factory store as a means of spurring sales.

What is the impact of the system of forcing new car sales upon dealers' service operations? Simply this. If the dealer loses money in new car sales, he will endeavor to make it up somewhere else, and this often means charging excessive prices for service. Lanzilotti (1961:350–351) puts the case this way:

The dealer finds himself in the uncomfortable position between the powerful manufacturer on the one hand, and a demanding and not too understanding public on the other. The public appears to gain from automobile forcing through lower prices more closely related to the dealer's actual cost, but may lose as much from parts and accessory forcing and from high repair charges dealers use to offset margins on new car sales.

But the dealer's reaction to high sales pressure and low margins on new cars does not stop with overcharging on repairs or wide margins on used cars. It induces him to perform phony repairs, to charge for new parts when used parts were employed, and to engage in other illicit repair practices. For these, he is not held accountable by the manufacturer, who, in fact, condones this illicit behavior and never terminates a dealer for poor service.

As for the mechanic, if he is employed by a dealership where abusive practices exist, he becomes part of the system whereby the customer is cheated. He can adapt himself to the unethical climate by learning and practicing the tricks by which customers are parted from their

---

[4]A district court in New Jersey recently termed Chrysler's system of sales quotas "unfair," one which would allow the corporation to terminate half of its dealers at any given time (Swartz Motors v. Chrysler). Chrysler's sales agreement does not differ markedly from that of other domestic manufacturers.

money, or he may rebel and leave the dealership, as one mechanic (Leonard, 1969) reported in a newspaper article:

An Amarillo, Texas man drove his car into a shop for a small repair. The mechanic turned in a ticket for 80 cents, with no charge for labor. Next day the mechanic spied the car still in the shop and found that his original ticket had been replaced by one for $60. When he asked why, the shop foreman told him that the shop could not make money on 80-cent items, that the owner had been called and ''expected'' to pay for the service to his car, and that was the reason for keeping the car an extra day and for padding the repair bill. The mechanic phoned the man, told him the true story and quit his job.

Some observers may consider this story unusual, for it would appear more likely that a mechanic under these circumstances would keep his silence and his share of the loot. A further probability is that, having learned how to charge for repairs—and for no repairs—an enterprising mechanic could then establish his own repair shop and select his customers—or victims—for himself. In fact, many do just this. Certainly, unethical repair practices are not the monopoly of dealerships.

But another system operates to induce improper repairs and repair charges by mechanics, no matter where they may be employed. This is the prevailing flat-rate system. Designed as an incentive system for mechanics, it consists of standard times set by automobile manufacturers for repair jobs performed by dealers which, when multiplied by the dealer's flat rate—usually about twice the mechanic's wage in order to cover overhead and profit—indicates what the customer should be charged for a particular operation. For example, if changing a fuel pump is timed at one-half hour, and the labor rate is $8 an hour, the mechanic receives $2 for his labor, the dealer gets $2, and the customer pays $4 for the labor, plus the cost of a new fuel pump. If the mechanic does the job in 15 minutes, he gets paid the same amount, but he can go on to a new job that much more quickly. Of course, he can exceed the time also, but he receives the same sum. The system induces the mechanic to try to beat the time, and this often means a quick

and superficial repair. It can also mean the use of a new part rather than fixing an old part which might still be usable but would take more time to repair. Since very little time is allowed by the manufacturer for diagnosis—and rattles, short circuits, and other problems often require considerable time to locate—cursory diagnosis of an automotive problem often results. Also, the mechanic will ordinarily not take the time to test-drive the car when this ought to be done to check a particular repair. As a result, the flat-rate system encourages rapid and often inadequate repair work. Mechanics in independent garages, service stations, and other repair outlets use *Chilton's Motors* and other manuals which follow closely the times set by manufacturers, and the system operates in these outlets in similar fashion to that found in dealerships. Over the years, the times set for many jobs in these manuals have declined, requiring mechanics to strive even harder to beat the time by whatever method of skill or subtlety they can employ. With a nationwide shortage of skilled mechanics and a rising tide of demand for service, it is no wonder that both technically and ethically improper repairs have increased in frequency.[5]

THE WARRANTY SHAM

In recent years, motorists by the thousands have complained about the failure of dealers to honor new car warranties. Here again, the responsibility for the wholesale disregard of warranties appears to lie with manufacturers.

At one time, the warranty ran from manufacturer to dealer, and from dealer to car owner. Today the warranty runs directly from manufacturer to owner, and warrants him against defects in material or workmanship for a stated period of time or distance traveled. However, it is the dealer's responsibility to service the car and to be reimbursed by the factory—under terms set unilaterally by the manufacturer.

[5]See statements of Mr. Harold Halfpenny, Independent Garage Owners of America (U.S. Senate, 1969:309) and Mr. James W. Hall, independent garage owner (U.S. Senate, 1969:334).

The trouble began late in 1962 when Chrysler extended the warranty—which covered defects for twelve months or 12,000 miles, whichever came first—to five years or 50,000 miles on the power train—i.e., engine, transmission, steering, suspension and wheels—and all the car makers moved up to a two-year/24,000 mile warranty on the rest of the car.

For Chrysler, whose share of car output had dropped to ten percent, the extended warranty was chiefly a sales gimmick. A company official admitted as much to service managers gathered in Detroit in 1964, adding:

When you think of it, selling cars is not only the reason for 5/50 and Certified Car Care . . . it's also the one prime reason for any dealership's existence! The other dealership activities—including our service department—are all planned to support our new-car sales operation. So, in a very real sense, we're all involved in selling new cars. [Federal Trade Commission, 1968:35]

Rarely have so many cats been let out of the bag at one time. Chrysler advertised the warranty liberally as proof of engineering leadership, doubled its sales in a few years, and the other manufacturers all adopted the extended warranty.

But the extended warranty, instead of affording more protection and value to the motorist, actually conveyed less. An increasing number of buyers began to complain of cars delivered new with defects, and many could not get their cars serviced. Apparently Detroit found it expedient to rush the cars off the assembly line and rely on dealers for predelivery inspection to catch flaws, but dealers felt that the allowance provided for inspection was inadequate, and did little more than a carwash. The Federal Trade Commission's Investigation (1968:93) of automobile warranties disclosed:

There is inadequate inspection and quality control at the factory. This overburdens the dealer's predelivery inspection and service facilities and substantially increases the dealer's costs without compensation, other than an allowance in the retail price suggested by the manufacturer. Consequently, the consumer often is delivered a car in unsatisfactory condition.

Further, the manufacturer's labor rate set for dealer's warranty work failed to reimburse them for warranty work (they were paid by Detroit at about two-thirds the rate charged to regular customers), on top of which dealers had to tag, store, and return to the factory parts replaced under the warranty.[6] Making out warranty repair claims involved a great deal of paper work, and frequently these were denied by the factory after the dealer had performed the work.

In view of the cumbersome procedures established for its operation and the extra costs and burden of paperwork with which the dealer was saddled, it is no wonder that car owners encountered difficulty in obtaining warranty repairs. Dealers could—and had to—earn more in servicing cash customers and tried to avoid warranty work. Typical ploys included telling owners that a repair falling under the warranty was not covered by it, that they could not schedule the car in the shop for a week or more, or that the owner would have to leave it for several days. And often, after the owner had brought the car in, it was not serviced at all.

Despite all the problems, many dealers tried to give good service under the warranty. Yet Consumers Union reported that one-fifth of all new car owners who attempted to have their cars repaired under the warranty found service unsatisfactory. In view of the conditions established by manufacturers for the performance of dealers under the warranty, it is amazing that the proportion of car owners encountering poor service was not several times as large (Leonard, 1968:45–47).

But the manufacturers played still one more game with dealers and car buyers. At least one of the Big Three introduced a system of competition among its regions on the basis of which it could award promotions, bonuses, and prizes, part of the competition being to determine which region could underspend its warranty budget (set at so many dollars per car over a given period) by the largest possible percentage. To win out, a region had to hold down its warranty costs by

---

[6]Manufacturers were obviously suspicious that their dealers might cheat them by authorizing repairs not covered under the warranty and set up this system of checks.

every means possible, including the denial of borderline claims, refusing service, and various tactics. Obviously such a system vitiated the spirit of the warranty and established an additional incentive for unethical behavior on the part of dealers.

SUMMARY

Coerced occupational crime, whether performed by white- or blue-collar personnel, can be better understood when the conditions affecting the performance of occupational duties are known. In many industries and trades, criminal behavior in an occupation is conditioned by concentrated market power of producers capable of establishing terms of employment and rewards for the occupation. The analysis of market power also has utility in assessing the corporate and individual responsibility of persons who violate the antitrust laws by fixing prices, as in the conspiracy involving manufacturers of heavy electrical equipment successfully prosecuted in 1961. Unless the industry is highly concentrated, a few producers cannot effectively conspire to fix prices and boost profits.

This market power concept as used in regard to the car dealers tends to support three of Taft's explanations that the general culture can be a cause of crime.

1. Our society involves the relative tolerance, acceptance, and even the approval of exploitative behavior either of the white-collar crime type or that of the noncriminal exploiter (Taft and England, 1964:276).
2. Organized businessmen are not inclined to be specific in defining the right ways to conduct business. How truthful should advertisers and sellers feel obligated to be in telling of the merits of their goods, and should they tell the whole truth about their products? (Taft and England, 1964:38–39).
3. Socially dangerous people (causers of the causes)— these dangerous people are those who, not necessarily technically criminal themselves, nevertheless create conditions which result in crime or serve as examples consciously or unconsciously imitated by the potential criminal (Taft, 1966:17).

Taft feels that the social system compels the business institution to be exploitative. It is our opinion that additional economic factors must be taken into account. In automobile retailing and repairs, the franchise system controlled by the factory sets the terms of daily operation for dealers. It enables the manufacturer to place pressure on the dealer to sell cars and demotes service to the status of a "necessary evil" (Leonard, 1968:41). The manufacturers' motivation is twofold:

1. he makes nearly ten times as much in selling new cars as in selling parts involved in repairs; and
2. if repair service deteriorates in quality, and/or increases in cost, motorists will be more likely to buy new cars rather than keep the old ones in repair.

Considerable evidence—from Consumers Union, the Better Business Bureau, files of local district attorneys, the Federal Trade Commission, and the President's Consumer Counsel— exists to show unethical behavior on the part of automobile dealers (coerced occupational crime). A Gallup-Ogilvy poll revealed that only three percent of the American public considers the new car dealer honest and trustworthy. Yet the dealer's actions can be readily understood— though not necessarily justified—by examination of his weak position under the selling agreement made with the manufacturer (the socially dangerous person). He is compelled by this agreement, and by constant pressures from the manufacturer to meet a sales quota set for him, with risk of losing his franchise if he fails. No dealer is ever terminated for failure to provide good service to his customers. Further, some dealers who enjoy high sales volumes but poor reputations for service within their communities are rewarded by manufacturers with additional franchises in other areas. Reports of the Federal Trade Commission and statements by federal judges furnish proof that the franchise enables the manufacturer to exert "unfair," even "ruthless" pressure on dealers to increase sales.

Because of the intense emphasis on sales, heightened in recent years by manufacturers' development of factory stores which stimulate sales in an area by aggressive methods, dealers often sell cars for low margins, then endeavor to recoup by higher margins on used cars and by overcharging for repairs. Another consequence of this effort by the dealer to earn a living under conditions controlled from outside is the tolerance of repair practices which deceive and defraud the motorist. Mechanics working both in and outside of dealerships also become involved as defrauders. Most mechanics operate within a flat rate system controlled from Detroit which induces quick and superficial repairs by encouraging the mechanic to "beat the time" set by the factory (or other) manual for particular repair jobs. Inadequate diagnosis, rapid repairs, spurious repairs, and insubstantial testing of repairs made, all result from this system.

In recent years, thousands of complaints have been received from new car buyers who found their cars delivered in defective condition and could not obtain service under the warranty. On examination, the warranty turned out to be a "sales gimmick" of the manufacturer, not an assurance of mechanical reliability. Manufacturers used the warranty to limit their liability under the law and further limited the effectiveness of the warranty by establishing cumbersome paperwork and procedures for dealers and by compensating the dealers in labor and parts below the levels charged for regular repairs. As a result, dealers tended to avoid warranty work, or provided poor service to new car owners. Dealers made motorists wait for service, often failed to work on cars brought into the shop or told owners they could not fix them, sometimes "discovered" additional repairs which could be charged, and padded bills. The improper behavior of dealers encountered by motorists who sought to have the warranties honored reflects the market power of manufacturers, who unilaterally drafted the warranties and made the representation to car buyers—but then undermined warranty service by creating conditions which induced dealers to operate unethically in providing repairs.

In sum, the frequent unethical actions of dealers and mechanics in furnishing repair service to the public must largely be regarded as coerced occupational crime resulting from a market structure in the automotive industry which provides the auto-maker with potential, and applied, criminogenic power.

CASES

U.S. v. E. I. DuPont de Nemours and Co. (1956) U.S. 351: 377.

Swartz Motors v. Chrysler (1969) New Jersey District Ct. Civil Action 1230-68. March 11.

REFERENCES

Bloch, H. A. and G. Geis
    1967   Man, Crime, and Society, New York: Random House.

Clinard, M. B.
    1968   Sociology of Deviant Behavior, New York: Holt, Rinehart & Winston.
    1952   The Black Market: A Study of White Collar Crime. New York: Holt, Rinehart & Winston.

Consumer Reports
    1969   "Warranties . . . and what should be done about them." 34 (April): 179.

Crowther, S. and I. Winehouse
    1966   Highway Robbery. New York: Stein & Day.

Federal Trade Commission
    1939   Report on the Motor Vehicle Industry. Washington, D.C.: Government Printing Office.
    1968   Staff Report on Automobile Warranties. Washington, D.C.: Government Printing Office.

Geis, G.
    1967   "White collar crime: the heavy electrical equipment antitrust cases of 1961," in M. B. Clinard and R. Quinney (eds.) Criminal Behavior Systems: A Typology. New York: Holt, Rinehart & Winston.

Lanzilotti, R. F.
    1961   "The automobile industry," in W. Adams (ed.) The Structure of American Industry. New York: Macmillan.

Leonard, W. N.
    1968   Statement before the Senate Subcommittee on Antitrust and Monopoly, Washington, D.C.: December 3.
    1969   "The auto-repair jungle." Newsday (January 11): 6W.

Newman, D. J.
  1958 "White collar crime." Law and Contemporary Problems 23 (Autumn): 735–753.

Ogilvy, D.
  1965 "What's Wrong with Your Image—and What You Can Do About It." Speech to Annual Convention of National Automobile Dealers Association in Las Vegas, Nevada. February 3.

Quinney, R.
  1964 "The study of white collar crime: toward a reorientation in theory and research." J. of Criminal Law, Criminology and Police Sci. 55 (June): 208–214.

Quinney, R. and M. B. Clinard
  1967 Criminal Behavior Systems: A Typology. New York: Holt, Rinehart & Winston.

Sutherland, E. H.
  1949 White Collar Crime. New York: Dryden.

Taft, D.
  1966 "Influence on the general culture on crime." Federal Probation 30 (September): 16–24.

Taft, D. and R. W. England
  1964 Criminology. New York: Macmillan.

U.S. Senate
  1969 Subcommittee on Antitrust and Monopoly of the Committee on the Judiciary. Automotive Repair Industry. Washington, D.C.: Government Printing Office.

Wolfgang, M. and L. Savitz
  1962 The Sociology of Crime and Delinquency. New York: John Wiley.

A CRIMINOGENIC MARKET STRUCTURE
The Automobile Industry*

Harvey A. Farberman
Health Sciences Center,
State University of New York at Stony Brook

Sociologists have come under attack for ignoring the role powerful elites play in controlling society's central master institutions by establishing political and economic policies which set the structural conditions that cause other (lower level) people to commit crimes[1] (Gouldner, 1968, 1970; Quinney, 1970; Liazos, 1972; Taylor et al., 1974). My aim here is to suggest how one elite, namely, automobile manufacturers, creates a "criminogenic market structure"[2] by impos-

Harvey A. Farberman (1975) "A Criminogenic Market Structure: The Automobile Industry." *The Sociological Quarterly* Vol. 16 (Autumn): 438–457. Reprinted with permission.

*I presented working notes for this paper at the Minnesota Symposium on Symbolic Interaction in June, 1974, and at the annual meetings of the American Sociological Association in August, 1974. I wish to thank Herbert Blumer, Norman K. Denzin, Erich Goode, Peter M. Hall, David R. Maines, Carolyn and Martin Needleman, Harold Orbach, and Gregory P. Stone for helpful comments.

[1]Typical explanations for this neglect include the observation that sociologists of deviance often work out of a symbolic interactionist perspective, and that this perspective has an ideological-theoretical bias which offers tacit support to power elites (Thio, 1973); that it has a philosophical-methodological bias which focuses attention on the passive, powerless individual and thus cannot conceptualize transcendent, unobservable, active groups (Schervish, 1973); and, finally, that it tends toward a grounded-emergent rather than a logico-theroretic style of theory construction and thus is vulnerable to the unequal power distribution embodied in everyday life and, consequently, has a conservative bias (Huber, 1973). For a reply to some of these points, see Stone et al. (1974).

[2]I borrow the term "criminogenic market" from Leonard and Weber (1970), who contend that the most useful con-

ceptual approach to occupational crime is to see it as a *direct consequence of legally established market structure*. In the present study, by "criminogenic market structure" I mean the deliberate and lawful enactment of policies by those who manage economically concentrated and vertically integrated corporations and/or industries which coerce lower level (dependent) participants into unlawful acts. Those who set the conditions which cause others to commit unlawful acts remain non-culpable, while those who perform under these conditions remain eminently culpable. A micro illustration suggestive of this approach was played out in the heavy electric industry where the U.S. government was able to show that a cartel existed among corporations which resulted in a price-fixing conspiracy. Nevertheless, the actual corporate officials who were indicted and convicted came from the second and third echelon of the corporate hierarchy and, upon exposure, were legally and morally disavowed by the first level echelon. Division heads and vice presidents were censured and repudiated by presidents and directors for contravening corporate policy. Those indicted and convicted, however, never for a moment thought of themselves as contravening corporate policy, nor of having done anything but what was expected of them—their jobs (Smith, 1961). Although this case describes activity *within* a corporation, I wish to extrapolate it to an entire industry. Thus, at the pinnacle of the economically concentrated auto industry sit four groups of manufacturers who control 92 percent of the new car market and who, on the distribution side of the industry alone, set economic conditions which control approximately 31,000 franchised new car dealers, approximately 4,000 used car wholesalers, and approximately 65,000 "independent" used car retailers. Despite the fact that those on the top cause the conditions which compel others into untoward patterns of action, they do not reap the public's wrath. At the same time that new car and used car dealers consistently trail far behind every other occupational grouping in terms of public esteem, there never has been a presidential administration—beginning with Franklin Roosevelt—without an automobile *manufacturing executive* in a cabinet or sub-cabinet position!

ing upon their new car dealers a pricing policy which requires high volume and low per unit profit. While this strategy gives the *manufacturer* increased total net aggregate profit (by achieving economies of scale and by minimizing direct competition among oligopolist "rivals"), it places the new car dealer in a financial squeeze by forcing him to constantly free-up and continuously re-cycle capital into fixed margin new car inventory. This squeeze sets in motion a downward spiral of illegal activities which (1) inclines the new car dealer to engage in compensatory profit taking through fraudulent service operations, (2) under certain conditions, generates a "kickback" system which enables used car managers of new car dealerships to exact graft from independent used car wholesalers, and (3) forces the independent used car wholesaler into illegal "short-sales" in order to generate unrecorded cash for kickback payments. I shall present the evidence which provides the grounding for this model as I came upon it in the research process. What follows, then, is a natural history which reconstructs the stages of my investigation.[3]

THE BASE SITE

My principal research site was a medium-sized used car wholesale operation located in an eastern metropolitan area.[4] There are approximately forty other wholesale operations in this area,[5] the top three of which sell between 6,000

and 8,000 cars per year.[6] My base operation, which sold 1,501 cars in 1971 and 2,124 in 1972,[7] carried a 125-car wholesale inventory and a repair shop at one location and a 25-car retail inventory at another location. There were 16 employees altogether, including three partners (an older one who runs the office and two younger ones who function as buyers), three additional buyers (who also sell wholesale when not on the road), a retail manager, a retail salesman, two shop workers, a bookkeeper, and two-to-five drivers. The firm also retains the services of a lawyer and an accountant.[8]

Entry into my principal research site and later into other operations was relatively easy, for during my high school and college days I had made pin money selling used cars on a lot owned by the older partner. Later I came across two old acquaintances from high school days who hustled cars when I did; one is now a new car agency general sales manager, and the other a partner in a "family-owned" new car dealership.

Although I was always more an observer than a participant, I increasingly was expected to answer phone calls, take messages, move cars around the wholesale lot, and deliver cars as part

---

[3]For a discussion of this presentation format see H. Becker (1970:37).

[4]For a breezy, journalistic description of the used car wholesaling scene see Levine (1968:26–29). For sociological insight into various levels of the auto industry see: Brown (1973) for independent used car retailing; Vanderwicken (1972) for franchised new car dealing; and Robbins (1971) for manufacturing.

[5]This figure derives from enumeration by wholesalers themselves. I was forced to rely on this source for three reasons. First, the appropriate State Departments of Motor Vehicles informed me that their statistical information does not distinguish between new and used and wholesale and retail dealers. Nevertheless, they intend to introduce such breakdowns within the next few years. Second, the *U.S. Bureau of the Census, County Business Patterns, 1970* places fundamentally different *kinds* of wholesale automobile establishments

into the same reporting category. Thus, wholesale body and fender shops, junk yards, auction sales, freelance wholesalers, and regular wholesalers appear in the same category. Moreover, the census also includes businesses that are legally chartered in a state but not actually doing business there. Consequently, for my purposes the census was not helpful. Third, the various county *Yellow Pages* phone books in which used car wholesalers advertise did not allow me to distinguish "cut-book" wholesalers, who free lance and work out of their home addresses, from regular wholesalers, who have substantial business premises, a staff of employees, and sizable inventories.

[6]This figure also comes from wholesalers themselves.

[7]I compiled these figures from the dealers' "Police Book." For each car in stock, dealers must enter 23 items of descriptive information. Detectives from the Motor Vehicle squad routinely inspect this book.

[8]Subsequent to the completion of my study, three more operations were opened: a retail lot with a thirty-car capacity, a wholesale lot with a forty-car capacity, and a twelve-stall body and fender shop. Each of these operations was situated on land or in buildings purchased by the corporation. The staff also increased with the addition of three more buyers, two retail salesmen, seven body and fender men, one mechanic, and a pool of part-time drivers which fluctuates from three to ten on any given day.

of a "caravan" with the regular drivers.[9] Eventually, I gained access to all files. At about the same time the firm offered me a gasoline credit card, reimbursement for my private telephone bill, maintenance work on my own car, and drivers to pick me up at the airport when I returned from out-of-town trips. I did not decline the maintenance work or the airport service[10]; however, I did break off field appearances—but maintained social contact—when the firm adopted one of my opinions as the basis for its expansion policy, and it became clear that my role as an investigator had somehow given way to that of an advisor or consultant.

From December 1971 to August 1973, I spent an average of one day a week including evenings and weekends at my principal site, on the road, and at the homes of or out socializing with various members of my base organization and their families. Sometimes, though, I would hang around the lot for two or three consecutive days in order to get some sense of the continuity and rhythm of the operation. I always carried a notebook and, when necessary, made entries in full view of all present. I also tape-recorded extensive in-depth interviews with the consent of participants, but only when I knew more or less what I wanted information about, thus not abusing the privilege. These "formal" interviews allowed me to nail down—for the record—what I had observed, participated in, or been told during the course of everyday activity or conversation over the course of nearly two years. The insight and information gleaned from these informal conversations were the basis for the "formal" interviews, the first of which I held during the sixth month of my field appearances.

SERENDIPITY

I should note here that I did not start out to study a criminogenic market structure. Rather, I wanted to follow up on a speculative hypothesis which grew out of some previous research on low income consumers (Farberman, 1968; Farberman and Weinstein, 1970). As a result of the latter study in particular, I had hypothesized that low income consumers strengthened their bargaining position vis-à-vis high status or expert sales or service people by changing the normative ground of the transaction from universalism to particularism, and thereby were able to coerce the expert other to respond as a concerned friend rather than as a mercenary stranger. Consequently, I began the present investigation to see if I could discover if people who bought used cars employed (wittingly or unwittingly) a set of bargaining tactics. I therefore observed over 50 transactions between retail customers and used car salesmen and, indeed, have been able to identify several bargaining tactics, associate them with distinct types of customers, and provide a theoretical interpretation.[11]

My interest in the systemic nature of occupational crime developed without my realizing it for sometimes, while I wrote up notes in the office after watching a sales transaction, I would vaguely overhear or observe the sales manager and customer "write-up" the deal. I began to notice that occasionally the customer would make out a check *as well as* hand over some cash. This was accompanied by the customer's saying how "taxes were killing the little man" and "if you didn't watch out, the Governor would bleed you to death." Out of simple curiosity I began *deliberately to observe* the "write-ups"—something I had originally paid no attention to since I

---

[9]For a discussion of the ratio of observation to participation see Gold (1958:217–233).

[10]During one of these trips, I parked my car—a small 1965 Buick Special—on the wholesale lot. As a gag, and in addition to whatever prudential motives may have been involved,

the firm sold my car and with the proceeds put me into a large 1970 Oldsmobile. The firm, at considerable expense to itself, and, in the words of one of the partners, "felt that a Professor, who you also call Doctor, should drive around in a better car." At one and the same time the "gag" shows deference to my status, takes liberty with my property (albeit improves it) and coerces me into a more conventional status appearance. This gambit smacks of something approaching a hazing ritual. It is fun, yet it prepares the initiate for further entree into the club by manipulating him into club conventions. I imagine field workers often run this sort of gamut before they gain entrance into the secret place. Unhappily, these experiences usually remain unrecorded.

[11]See my forthcoming article "Coming-To-Terms: The Reconciliation of Divergent Meanings and Values in the Sale of Used Cars."

thought the transaction was actually over after the bargain had been made and the salesman had "closed" the deal. It was at the "write-up," however, that a new research problem emerged, because what I had witnessed—and what, in fact, led me off in a new direction—was an instance of "selling short," or "a short-sale," an illegal act which constitutes the first link in a chain of activity that goes back to Detroit.[12] In the section which follows, I will describe (a) what a "short-sale" is; (b) how it benefits and costs both the retail customer and the dealer; and (c) why the dealer feels compelled to engage in it.

THE SHORT-SALE

A "short-sale" begins to develop when a retail customer observes the sales manager compute and add on to the selling price of the car the state sales tax—a hefty eight percent. Often, the customer expresses some resentment at the tax bite and asks if there is any way to eliminate or reduce it. The sales manager responds in a sympathetic fashion and allies himself with the customer in a scheme to "cut down on the Governor's share of the deal" by suggesting that the customer might make out a check for less than the actual selling price of the car. In turn, the manager will make out a bill of sale for the lesser amount. The customer then will pay the difference between the *recorded* selling price and the *actual* selling price in cash. A car which normally costs $2,000 would carry an additional 8 percent (or $160) state sales tax, thus actually costing the customer $2,160. If a bill of sale which records the selling price as $1,500 is made out, however, then at 8 percent the taxes would be $120, for an apparent total of $1,620. Although the customer still pays $2,000 for the car ($1,500 by check and $500 in cash), he "saves" $40 in taxes.

Almost as important as saving the $40 is the obvious delight the customer typically takes at finally discovering himself in a situation where he can "even the odds," "give the big guys what for," and "make sure the little guy gets his two cents too." The attitude and mood which washes through the short-sale suggests a welcome, if minor, triumph in the back-stepping of everyday life. As an observer witnessing this "petty" collusion between little Davids against remote Goliath, I had a rather difficult time identifying it pursuant to the criminal code—as a conspiracy to defraud the government through tax evasion. Obviously, the meaning, value, and sentiment attached to the act by at least one of the participants (the customer) is totally incongruous with the meaning, value, and sentiment attached to it by the criminal code. Thus does a minor victory in everyday life co-exist in the same act with a punishable transgression of law. The victory is often more symbolic than material, however, since, if the customer at any future time has an accident or theft, his insurance company, in part, will initiate compensation calculations based on the selling price recorded in the bill of sale—a sum which understates the actual price paid.

But, if the customer derives both a small material savings and a large measure of delight, what does the dealer derive? For one thing, a lot of money; more precisely, a lot of *unrecorded* cash. At the moment the customer "saves" $40 in taxes the dealer gains $500 in cash. The "short sale" to the customer allows the dealer to "steal-from-the-top." In any given year an accumulation of these short sales can total to tens of thousands of dollars. In an effort to determine if "stealing from the top" was anything other than rank venality, I questioned one of the partners in my principal site.

Q: You've just said that it's [stealing-from-the-top] O.K. for the customer but bad for you. I don't understand that. Jeez, look at the money!

A: Yeah, sure, but who the hell wants to live with any of the retail customers. You see

---

[12]Although my initial research problem situated me so that I luckily tripped over and recognized a new problem, the new problem actually links to the old problem so that my understanding of the dynamics of customer/salesman interaction is enlarged by my understanding of the systemic dynamics of "short sales." In fact, deliberate—as opposed to accidental—problem transformation may be integral to the methodologic of contextual, vertical analysis.

what goes on. They don't know shit about a car. They look at the interior, turn on the radio, check the odometer, kick the tire, push the windshield wiper button, turn on the air conditioner, open up the trunk, look at the paint. What the fuck has any of that got to do with the *condition* of the car? I mean, the way the fucker runs. If I put money into all this crap, I can't put it into improving the mechanical condition. Three weeks later the fucking car falls apart and they're on my ass to fix it. Then I got to live with them. They drive me off the wall. Then that broad down the consumer affairs office wants to know why I don't give the customer a fair shake. Shit, why the hell don't she educate the customers? It would make things a lot easier.

Q: Listen, if they're such a pain, why do you put up with them?

A: What do you mean?

Q: I don't know what I mean, but there is usually a bottom line and it's usually money!

A: Well, if you mean that they bail me out every now and then, sure.

Q: What do you mean?

A: Well, you know those creeps [buyers] I got on the road buying for me, you know what their philosophy is? "If you don't buy, you don't earn." They pay big numbers; what do they care; it's my money. If they get in too high on a package [group of cars] or a piece [one car], and I can't blow [wholesale] it out, then I look for a retail shot [sale]. But that means I can't turn over my money quickly, I got to lay with it out on the lot and hope some yo-yo [retail customer] comes along. Believe me, it's a pain in the ass. This whole business is in and out, in and out. Anything that slows the turnover costs money.

Q: O.K., so retail customers generally are a pain, but you put up with them because they bail you out on bad buys, but that still doesn't get to it. What about those retail sales that are "short" sales, that's where the bread is. That's what I'm trying to get at.

A: All right, listen: A wholesaler runs a big grocery store; if it's not on the shelves, you can't buy it. Without cars to sell, I can't sell cars. Look, we make enough legit, but you can't pay graft by check. Those bums get you coming and going.

Q: What bums?

A: You ever wanta meet a crook, go see a used car manager [of a new car dealership]. They clip a quarter [$25], a half [$50], a yard [$100], maybe more [on each car]. Put a package together and take it out [buy it from them] and they'll zing you for a week's pay. They steal their bosses blind.

Q: So, you have to pay them to get cars. You mean something under the table?

A: Yeah, the "vig."

Q: The what?

A: The grease, the commission, the kickbacks. How I'm gonna stay in business with no cars? You tell me.

Q: Incidentally, how many of your retail sales do you figure are "short"?

A: Maybe 70–75 per cent. I can't be sure.[13]

Q: Tell me, do you ever wind up with more than you need for the kickbacks?

A: Sure, am I gonna lie to you? So I put a little away [in safety deposit boxes]. You think I'm the only one? But if it's buried, you can't use it. Better it should be in the business; I could use it—besides, who needs the aggravation?

Q: Are you ever able to get it [buried money] back into the business?

A: Yeah.

Q: How?

A: Aw, you know.

---

[13]Since the operation in question is primarily a *wholesale* not a retail house, the proportion of retail sales typically do not exceed 25 percent of total sales. Of these, however, about 75 percent are "short" sales. Thus, of 2,124 total sales, 398 are short. At a minimum of $100 stolen from the top per short sale, approximately $39,000 is generated in unrecorded cash. Used car *wholesalers* may well engage in retail selling for cash and, therefore, are clearly different from used and new car *retailers* who *avoid* cash sales in favor of "credit" or "installment" sales. This latter point was vividly disclosed at a hearing before California's Corporations Commissioner when Sears, Roebuck and Company requested a license to make low cost automobile loans *directly* to customers, thus by-passing

Apparently, the dealer's reasons for engaging in "short-sales" include, but are not confined to, rank venality. After all, most, but not all, of the unrecorded money is passed along in the form of "kickbacks"; only the residual excess actually finds its way directly into his own hands, and even this excess must be buried or occasionally laundered.[14] The principal reason the dealer engages in short sales is to come up with kickback cash in order to keep his sources of supply open, and this imperative is more than enough to keep him involved with "short-sales,"

---

dealers. Direct loans, in effect, would turn consumers into cash customers. This the dealers emphatically did not want as the following testimony reveals:

> Q: . . . Do you want to sell cars for cash?
> A: I do not want to sell them for cash if I can avoid it.
> Q: You would not want to sell the cars you do for a cash price, then?
> A: No, sir.
> Q: Does this mean that you are not really in the business of selling automobiles?
> A: It does not mean that at all.
> Q: But you don't want to sell automobiles for cash?
> A: It means that I want to sell cars for the most profit that I can per car. Finance reserve (dealer's share of the carrying charges) and insurance commissions are part of the profit derived from selling a car on time.

Moreover, these dealers have no qualms about extending credit to poor risk customers; the car always can be repossessed and resold (Quoted in Macaulay, 1966:186).

[14]*"Burying money"* means putting it in a safety deposit box. Ironically, this money becomes a source of long-term anxiety instead of long-term security. First, it remains a concrete symbol of criminality and is at odds with the dealer's self-image. Second, it also always is the target of potential investigatory disclosure although known instances of such activity are virtually unheard of. Third, the dealer resents the accumulation of "idle" cash and is frustrated by his inability to "turn it over" easily and make it productive. *Laundering* occurs in tight money situations when capital *must* be made available. It invokes a symbiotic relationship between the dealer and a "bookie." The bookie is hired on as a "commissioned agent" of the dealership. The dealer "pays" him a weekly salary using a legitimate business check; in return, the bookie gives the dealer an equal amount in cash. The dealer provides the bookie with a W2 form and the bookie declares and pays taxes on this "income." The dealer then "declares" the income brought in by the bookie. Since this income derives from nonexistent buying or selling it is subtly apportioned and spread over actual transactions. The dealer also periodically writes a letter to the bookie's probation officer testifying to the bookie's reliable and gainful contribution to the business.

even though it means he has to deal with retail customers—the very bane of his existence.

The antagonism the dealer holds toward the retail customer is incredibly intense and appears to have two sources. First, it stems from the dealer's apparent inability to sell the customer what the dealer considers to be the *essential* element of a car—namely, its *mechanical condition*. Instead, he is compelled to sell what to him is non-essential—*physical appearance*. If he is to improve the car's physical appearance, then he must skimp on improving its mechanical condition. This, in the long run, works to his own disadvantage since he must "live with the customer" and, in some measure, make good on repairs affecting mechanical condition. Put another way, the wholesaler's *conceptualization* of the car and the retail customer's *conceptualization* of the car do not overlap. Where the wholesaler wishes to sell such *unobservables* as a good transmission, a tight front end, a solid chassis, and an engine without knocks in it, the typical retail customer wishes to buy such *observables* as a nice paint job, a clean interior, etc. The wholesaler and the retail customer basically have a hard time "coming-to-terms," that is, abstracting out of the vehicle the same set of concrete elements to invest with meaning and value. The vehicle literally *means* different things to each of them and the establishment of a shared meaning which is *mutually* valued is extremely problematic.[15]

The second source of the dealer's antagonism stems from his overwhelming dependence on these ignorant customers. This dependence heightens dramatically when the dealer's own professional "house" buyers make bad buys; that is, pay too high a "number," or price for the car, which makes it impossible for the car to be quickly re-wholesaled. If the car is in basically sound mechanical condition, it will be "shaped" out in hopes of "bailing out" through a "retail shot." Though a bad buy can be redeemed through a retail sale, this route of redemption bodes ill for the house buyer since it reflects on his competence. It bodes ill for the

---

[15]See my already cited forthcoming article for an elaboration of this.

TABLE 1　Units* Within, and Vehicles Generated by, Various Sources of Supply

	1971		1972	
Source of Supply	Units	Vehicles	Units	Vehicles
1. Used car depts. of new car agencies	72	1134	94	1472
2. Rental, lease or fleet companies	9	145	18	104
3. Off-the-street customers	116	116	172	172
4. Dealers auctions	2	38	1	38
5. Body and fender shops	6	35	6	105
6. Retail used car dealers	11	27	17	193
7. Wholesale used car dealers	3	6	4	40
	219	1501	312	2124

*The generic term "units" encompasses "establishments" as in categories 1–2 and 4–7, and customers as in category 3.
Source: Dealer's Police Books.

dealer as well since he must tie up money, men, and space waiting for a fickle retail customer to get everyone off the hook. Thus, the dealer's antagonism toward the retail customer stems from his own dependence, for short-sales and bailouts, on ignorant yo-yo's who don't know anything about cars. The dealer's redemption, then, lies in the hands of "idiot saviors," an unhappy situation at best.

KICKBACKS AND SUPPLY

In any event, based on what I had seen, heard, and been told, I concluded that the wholesale used car dealer engaged in "short-sales" principally to insure his supply of used cars. Since this conclusion was derived exclusively from observation and interview, I wanted to check it out against the dealer's inventory files. In the following section, I seek evidence of two things: (a) that the predominant source of the wholesaler's inventory, in fact, is the used car department of new car agencies; and (b) that used car managers in new car agencies universally receive kickbacks.

Accordingly, I classified all vehicles in my base site for the years 1971 and 1972 by their source of origin. Table 1 indicates that, of the 1,501 vehicles bought in 1971, 1,134 or 75.5 percent came from used car departments of new car dealers; of the 2,124 bought in 1972, 1,472, or 69.3 percent came from the same source. These figures corroborate the used car wholesaler's overwhelming dependence on the used car

department of the new car agency for supply. They also suggest that there may well be a decreasing supply in the number of used cars available on the market altogether. From 1971 to 1972 there was a 6.2 percent decrease (75.5 to 69.3) in the proportion of cars from used car departments of new car dealers even though the number of new car agencies dealt with increased from 72 to 94.[16]

---

[16]These figures are consistent with national trend figures provided to me by Thomas C. Webb, research assistant. National Automobile Dealers Association (personal communication, March 11, 1974). Estimations of the number of used cars sold "on" and "off" the market in 1960 and 1973 indicate that, of the 20.7 million used cars sold in 1960, 14.9 million or 71.6 percent were sold "on" the market, whereas of the 31.4 million used cars sold in 1973, 18.7 million or 59.6 percent were sold "on" the market. Thus, there was a net decrease of 12.0 percent. A possible explanation for the decreasing supply of used cars on the market may be the consequence of an already established social-economic trend toward the multiple car family. Whereas a decade ago only 15 percent of the total population owned more than one car, today 30 percent do. Indeed, one out of every three families whose head of household is between the ages of 35–44 owns two cars and one out of ten whose head of household is between 45–54 owns three cars (MVMA, 1974:38–39). What this probably means is that cars are *handed down* from husband to wife to children and literally "run-into-the-ground." In other words, we may well be seeing the reemergence of "second-hand" cars. Cars change hands but outside the commercial nexus i.e., "off-the-market." An additional factor which may be contributing to this trend is declining public confidence in auto dealers. Not too long ago a poster showed a picture of former President Nixon with a caption which asked, "Would you buy a used car from this man?" The credibility of the new and used car dealer apparently has never been lower. Confirmation of this comes from several different polls which seek to determine the public image of new

TABLE 2 Kickbacks by Vehicle, Agency, and Franchise

Franchise	No. of Agencies		No. of Vehicles		Kickback Agencies		No. of Kickback Vehicles	
	1971	*1972*	*1971*	*1972*	*1971*	*1972*	*1971*	*1972*
Giant Motors	35	51	571	976	7	7	304	614
Fore	10	16	159	209	—	—	—	—
Crisis	15	16	256	191	—	—	—	—
U.S.	1	2	1	5	—	—	—	—
Foreign	8	6	143	62	—	—	—	—
Unknown	3	3	4	29	—	—	—	—
	72	94	1,134	1,472	7	7	304	614

Given an overall paucity of used cars on the market, it would seem that used car managers of new car agencies are in a perfect position to exact tribute from the independent used car wholesaler whose major source of supply is in their hand. I thus proceeded to check out the universality of kickbacks. I classified all inventory by the *specific* new car agency it came from, and then asked the older partner of my base operation to indicate at which agencies kickbacks were paid. As shown in column 4 of Table 2, kickbacks were paid on 304 (out of 1,134) vehicles in 1971 and on 614 (out of 1,472) vehicles in 1972. Moreover, column 3—much to my surprise—shows that *all* of these cars come from only *seven* (7) agencies in both 1971 and 1972 and each of these agencies carried a Giant Motors franchise. Note, however, that these seven constitute only a small proportion of the total number of G.M. agencies dealt with, which is 35 in 1971 and 51 in 1972. Moreover, only 10 percent of *all* agencies in 1971 and less than 7 percent in 1972 required kickbacks. Nevertheless, in 1971 these agencies did, in fact, provide nearly 27 percent of all supply coming from used car departments of new car agencies and 20 percent of total supply. Similarly, in 1972 they

provided 56 percent of supply from used car departments and 31 percent of all supply.

A closer examination of these seven G.M. agencies, however, discloses some common characteristics. First, an inspection of their zip codes and street addresses reveals that all seven are located in the same high density, urban area. Second, a rank ordering of all new car agencies by the number of cars they supply, as shown in Table 3, reveals that these seven are the top supply sources and, by agreement among house buyers, are large agencies. Third, the remaining eight agencies among the top 15 supply sources all are located in suburban areas and are described by house buyers as medium sized.

With this information in hand, I again questioned the older partner of my base operation.

Q: Listen, didn't you know that you only paid kickbacks at large, urban, G.M. agencies? Why did you guys give me the impression that you paid kickbacks to *all* used car managers?

A: Really?

Q: Really, what!?

---

and used car dealers compared to other occupational groups. Auto dealers uniformly trail way behind others in terms of the trust they inspire in the buying public (Leonard and Weber, 1970). Still another compatible and contemporary factor is the deteriorating condition of our national economy where the combination of rising prices and decreasing purchasing power inhibit overall consumer demand and thus retard new car sales and accompanying trade-ins.

TABLE 3 Number of Dealerships by Number of Vehicles Supplied: 1972

Number of Dealerships	*Number of Vehicles Supplied*
2	100 +
1	75 +
4	50 +
8	25 +
79	1 +

A: Really, you thought we paid off all the managers? Well, I guess these are the big houses for us—it seems like a lot. I'll tell ya, the hicks are O.K. They don't know from conniving. The city is full of crooks.

Q: Really? Don't you think it has anything to do with these particular agencies, maybe the way they're set up or maybe with G.M.? After all, the other manufacturers have agencies there too.

A: No, it's a freak thing! It just means that seven crooks work at these places.

Q: Aw, come on. I don't believe that.

A: Listen, your barking up the wrong tree if you think it has anything to do with G.M.

Q: But why only at G.M.? and why only at G.M. agencies in the city?

A: Look, there's more G.M. agencies than [Fore] and [Crisis]. G.M. sells more cars, they get more trade-ins, they have solid used cars operations. These crooks go where the action is. They're good used car men, they get the best jobs. But they're crooks. I'm telling you, believe me!

Q: But if they're crooks, and you know it, why don't their bosses know it?

A: Look, the bosses aren't stupid. They know what's going on. If the used car man pushes the cars out, and turns over capital, and doesn't beat the boss too bad—they're happy.

Q: I guess I must be thick, I'm still not convinced.

A: All right. The boss is busy running the new car operation. He brings in a sharp used car man and bank rolls him. The used car man pays rent to the boss for the premises and splits profits with him depending on the deal they work out. O.K.? The used car man takes the trade-ins, he keeps the good stuff and wholesales the bad. He wholesales me an off-model, say, for two grand. He tells his boss, the car brought $1,875.00. I send a check for $1,875.00, and grease him a buck and a quarter. At $1,875.00, he still made a legitimate fifty or a hundred on the car—the boss gets half of that. As long as the used car man doesn't get too greedy,

there's no problem. The boss takes a short profit but frees up his capital. Believe me, that's crucial, especially if he's paying one percent a month interest on his bank roll to begin with.

Q: So, what you're saying, is that the best agencies are in the city, that they're G.M., the G.M. dealers know their used car men are beating them, but that they don't get uptight as long as they make something and can free-up their capital.

A: Yeah.

Q: Listen, you've got a point, but isn't there another way to look at this? Isn't it possible that the boss does more than just tolerate being ripped off a little by his used car man? Isn't it possible that he's working with the used car man and beating his own business. In other words, he's splitting the kickbacks or something like that?

A: Look, anything's possible, but all I know is that the used car managers are a bunch of crooks. The bosses, I can't say; as for [Giant Motors], forget it, they're a legit concern.

Q: Maybe you're right but it sure would make sense if the bosses [G.M. dealers] did both—you know, turn over money and beat their own business. Hell, you do it and you're the boss, why shouldn't they?

A: Well, I have to. I don't know about them. Just don't go off half-cocked. Be careful before you lean on anybody.

This interview material has two intriguing aspects. Despite the dealer's strenuous insistence that kickbacks are the artifact of corrupt and venal individual used car managers, there is also the suggestion that such venality can take place precisely because large, urban G.M. agencies sell a lot of cars and therefore have an abundance of trade-ins, the best of which are recycled back into the agencies' used car retail line while the surplus is wholesaled out. The power to determine how this surplus is dispersed into the wholesale market places the used car managers of the involved agencies in the position to demand and receive "kickbacks." Moreover, the new car dealer himself, who is under pressure to free up capital in order to avoid paying excess interest on money borrowed to purchase new car inventory, may have an incentive to "look-the-other-way," and perhaps even split "kickbacks" as long as his used car manager keeps moving cars and freeing capital.

THE FINANCIAL SQUEEZE

In the section which follows, I seek to check out (a) the existence of a financial squeeze on dealers, and (b) whether this squeeze inclines dealers to tolerate or even participate in kickbacks. By way of checking these points, I contemplated interviewing some people in the "kickback" agencies. The more I thought about how to guide myself in such interviews, the more I realized I was facing an interesting dilemma. I wanted to do the interviews precisely because I had discovered that the agencies were paid kickbacks by the wholesalers. Yet, in each case the kickback was being paid specifically to the manager of the used car department of the agency and I was not sure if the manager was acting on his own or was acting with the knowledge of his principal. If he was acting on his own, and I disclosed this, I might then put him in jeopardy. If he was acting with the knowledge of his principal, it was certain I would have an unreliable interview since in these cases I did not have personal bonds strong enough to insure truthful responses. Since I did not wish to deceive or jeopardize any of the respondents, and since I did not feel I could be truthful—as no doubt I would have had to disclose just how I had discovered the "kickback" arrangement, and thus transgress the truth that I had established with the wholesalers and run the risk of jeopardizing their ongoing business relationships with the new car dealers—I developed another approach. I decided to interview G.M. dealers in "non-kickback" agencies and try to elicit information which would allow me to pinpoint the key differences between kickback and non-kickback agencies, thereby nailing down an interpretation of the "kickback" phenomenon.

I managed to arrange interviews with three different dealers. The following quoted interview lasted five hours, was granted on the basis of a personal tie, and therefore is most reliable and valid. In addition, the elicited material is highly representative of the other interviews. The general thrust of my questioning was first to ask the dealer to talk about issues which are problematic in the running of his own business, and then to comment on the "kickback" phenomenon at the urban agencies. I was interested mainly in knowing if the pressure to turn over capital and avoid interest payments would encourage a dealer to "look-the-other-way" on "kickbacks" or even split them.

Q: How long have you been a dealer?
A: A dealer? About 20 years. About five or six years after [I finished] college, my dad and I went in as partners. It's mine now.
Q: Have you enjoyed it?
A: Well, it's been good to me for a goodly number of years, but frankly, during these past three to four years the business has changed markedly. It's a tougher, tighter business. I'm more tied down to it now than ever before. I can't be as active in the community as I would like. You know, that's important to me.
Q: Why is that the case? Is the business expanding?
A: Not really, well it depends on how you measure it. I work harder, have a larger sales and service staff than ever, I've expanded the facilities twice and refurbished the fixtures and touched up several times, and yes, I'm selling more new cars than before, but is the business expanding? Well, I suppose, yes, but not the way I'd like it to.
Q: Could you elaborate on that?
A: Well, the point is—and I know this will sound anomalous, well, maybe not to you—but I wish I could ease off on the number of new cars and pick up somewhere else, maybe on used cars.
Q: Why is that?
A: It boils down to investment—return ratios. The factory [manufacturer] has us on a very

narrow per unit profit margin [on new car sales]. But if I had the money and the cars, I could use my capital more effectively in used cars.[17]

Q: In other words, G.M. establishes how much profit you can make on each new car you sell?

A: Just about. And more than that, they more or less determine how much [new car] inventory I have to carry, and the composition of that inventory.

Q: So, you have to take what they give you—even if you don't want or need it. How do you pay for the inventory?

A: I borrow money at prevailing interest rates to finance the inventory. And, sometimes it gets tight. Believe me, if I am unable to sell off that inventory relatively quickly, I'm pressed. I have got to keep that money turning or that interest begins to pinch.

Q: Is it fair to say that you compensate for narrow margins on new cars by making wider margins on used cars?

A: Not really, not in practice, at least not out here [in the suburbs]. Used cars, good used cars, are hard to come by. I imagine the city dealers have an easier time getting trade-ins. We get a lot of repeat customers, but I don't believe they trade up. They just buy new cars. Actually, we tend to pick up additional revenue from our service repair operation. I'm not particularly proud about it, but there is a lot of skimping going on. It's quite complicated. The factory has a terrible attitude toward service repair generally, and the [mechanics] union is overly demanding and inflexible. It's rather demoralizing and, frankly, I'm looking out for myself, too.

Q: Could you expand on that?

A: I prefer you not press me on that.

Q: If you had a choice, how would you prefer to set up your operation?

A: Well, if I had a choice—which I don't—I would rather have a low volume, high margin operation. I could get by with smaller facilities, a smaller staff, put less time into the business, and not constantly face the money squeeze.

Q: Do you think the really large city dealers would prefer the same kind of alternative?

A: I guess so, but it's hard to say. Their situation is somewhat different from mine.

Q: In what way?

A: Well, first of all, some of them, especially if they're located in [megalopolis] have even less control over their operation than I do. Some of them really run factory stores. That is, G.M. directly owns or controls the agency. Those outfits are really high-volume houses. I don't see how they can make a go of it. The factory really absorbs the costs.[18]

Q: You did say that they probably had strong used car operations or, at least, had a lot of trade-ins. Do you think that helps?

A: Possibly.

Q: Do you think a really sharp used car man could do well in that kind of operation?

A: Well, he would do well in any operation in which he had used cars to work with.

Q: He could both retail and wholesale?

A: Oh, yes, if he had the cars to work with.

Q: Is it likely, in the wholesale end, he could demand and receive "kickbacks" from wholesalers?

A: Well, it's been known to happen. You know, those wholesalers, they're always willing to accommodate a friend. But it would only pay them to do that in relatively

---

[17]Leonard and Weber (1970:4) estimate that a dealer can make a gross profit margin of $400 on a $2,000 used car but only $150–200 on a $3,200 new car. Indeed the new car dealers I interviewed all indicated a desire to be able to sell more used cars.

[18]According to White (1971), Detroit manufacturers generally avoid owning their own retail outlets or "factory" stores since a network of financially independent but exclusively franchised dealers helps to spread the risk of doing business, defrays cost, and provides local management with entrepreneurial incentive. Edwards (1965) also suggests that a franchise dealer system establishes local identity for products as well as provides facilities which handle trade-ins and repairs. Nevertheless, as a matter of prestige and because no individual dealer can afford the extremely high cost of land in this particular megalopolis, manufacturers usually own retail outlets directly.

large operations where they could anticipate a fairly steady flow of cars.

Q: So, it would certainly make sense for them to accommodate friends in large, high volume, urban G.M. agencies?

A: Sure.

Q: Do you suppose the used car managers split kickbacks with their bosses?

A: Well, it's possible, but more than likely, the boss is more interested in moving those cars out quickly any way he can, so he can turn over that money and place it back into new car inventory.

Although this material does not permit any educated guess as to whether the dealers might split kickbacks with their used car managers, it does provide some assurance that new car dealers are under pressure to sell off cars relatively quickly in order to turn over capital and thus reduce interest payments. This pressure may be enough of a stimulus to, at least, incline the dealer to "look-the-other-way" if and when his used car man partakes in graft. As long as the used car man doesn't become too greedy and cut into the boss's pocket, his activity will be tolerated. Of course, we may still speculate, but not conclude, that if a "boss" is merely managing or only controlling a minimal share in a new car agency which is principally owned directly by G.M., he may be inclined to collude with his used car manager against "his own" agency. In any event, it is safe to presume that dealers feel under constant pressure to continuously recycle capital back into new car inventory and to get out from under interest payments. Corroboration of this comes from Vanderwicken (1972:128) who did a financial analysis of a medium-sized Fore agency located in a suburb of Cleveland, Ohio, and reported that:

The average car is in inventory thirty days before it is sold. Quick turnover is important to a dealer, the instant a car leaves the factory, he is billed for it and must begin paying interest on it. This interest is one of [the dealer's] biggest single expenses.

Additional support also comes from Fendell (1975:11) who asked a New Jersey [Fore] dealer how he was coping with decreasing consumer demand and received the following response:

I'm making deals I lose money on just to get the interest costs off my back. Those cars sit out there, costing me money every second. [Fore] has been paid in full for them a long time ago.

The dealer went on to say that his interest rates run between 10.25 percent to 11 percent per year.

MANUFACTURERS' PRICING POLICY

The constant and unremitting emphasis on new car inventory and the capital squeeze it places dealers in apparently is no accident. To the contrary, it is the calculated outcome of the manufacturers' pricing policy. According to Stewart Macaulay (1966:8), manufacturers and dealers enter into relationships for the mutual goal of making profit; however, their strategies for making that profit may differ.

For example, a . . . dealer might be able to make a hundred dollars profit on the sale of one car or a ten dollar profit on each sale of ten cars . . . [it makes a great deal of difference to the manufacturer] because in one case it sells only one car while in the other it sells ten. . . . It must sell many units of all the various models it makes. . . .

This imperative to sell *many* cars stems from the manufacturers' effort to achieve economies of scale, that is, savings in production and other costs as a result of massive, integrated, and coordinated plant organization. George Romney, when President of American Motors, testified before a Senate Judiciary Subcommittee on Antitrust and Monopoly and reported that:

A company that can build between 180,000 and 220,000 cars a year on a one-shift basis can make a very good profit and not take a back seat to anyone in the industry in production efficiency. On a two-shift basis, annual production of 360,000 to 440,000 cars will achieve additional small economies . . . (quoted in Lanzillotti, 1968:266).

An economist, Joe S. Bain (quoted in Edwards, 1966:162) estimates that an even higher minimal production volume is needed for savings.

In general, 300,000 units per annum is a low estimate of what is needed for productive efficiency in any one line.

Thus, in order to cut costs to a minimum, the manufacturers—as in days gone by—must continue to engage in mass production,[19] which leads to mass distribution and the need for a dealer network into which the manufacturer can pump massive doses of new cars in a *controlled* fashion. According to economist Lawrence J. White (1971:139), this translates into a "forcing model," which may be defined as "the requirement that the retailer sell a specified number of units as a condition of holding his franchise."[20] In effect, this allows the manufacturer to manipulate dealer inventories in a way that serves the oligopolist interests of an economically concentrated industry. Oligopolist "rivals" recognize their interdependence and avoid direct competition. Placing new dealerships in each others' territory would only call forth counter placements which, rather than expanding total auto sales, would perhaps cut into one's own already established dealerships. Thus,

it would be better to concentrate on lowering the [profit] margins of existing dealers, which could only be met by equal actions . . . by one's rivals and which . . . has the effect of expanding the overall demand for the product (White, 1971:142.)

All the manufacturer need do then to reduce per unit margins, which increases total net aggregate profit for the manufacturer, is to increase dealer inventory volume. This puts pressure on the dealer to free up capital from alternative investment possibilities such as used cars or to borrow capital at prevailing interest rates. Either way the dealer faces a financial squeeze and has a powerful incentive to sell off his inventory as quickly as possible, which industry trend statistics bear out. Despite the fact that new car dealers can achieve more efficient investment–return ratios from used car inventory—that is, if it is available—the ratio of new to used car sales from 1958 to 1972 per franchised new car dealer reflects an increasing preoccupation with new car sales. Examination of Table 4, column 3, indicates that over the last decade and a half new car dealers have been forced away from used cars and into new cars. In 1958, the ratio of used to new car sales was 1.77, but steadily declined until it reached 1.00 in 1970. And after 1970 it actually reversed itself so that in 1972 it was .81.[21]

This pressure to slant one's operation overwhelmingly in the direction of new car sales places the dealer in a tight margin operation. Vanderwicken (1972:121) observes that ". . . most people have a vastly exaggerated notion of a car dealer's profits . . . the average car dealer earns less than 1 percent on his volume, a miniscule margin far below that of most other retailers." He also provides a breakdown for the

---

[19]In principle, much the same strategy was used in the early 1900s when Henry Ford introduced mass production techniques and reduced the price of the Model "T" from $950.00 in 1909 to under $300.00 in the early 1920s and, as a result, boosted sales from 12,000 to two million and captured 50 percent of the market (Lanzillotti, 1968). Rothchild (1973) undoubtedly is correct when she observes that the auto industry continues to rely on ancient and probably obsolete formulas.

[20]For a further mathematical articulation of this model, see Pashigan (1961:33–34, 52–56) and White (1971:137–145).

[21]Interestingly enough, the decreasing ratio of used to new car sales more or less parallels the increasing market penetration of foreign auto makers. In 1963 foreign auto makers held 6.0 percent of the American market; that percentage increased to 14.6 percent by 1972. And the very year the ratio of used to new car sales declined to 1:00 or parity in 1970, G.M. lost nearly 7.1 percent of its previous market share (NADA, 1973:5). Put another way, increasing market penetration by foreign firms may have placed greater pressure on American auto makers to push harder on new car sales. One plausible way to accomplish this would be to require the dealer distribution network to put still more capital into new car inventory thus enabling the manufacturer to increase the volume of sales and thereby hold its market share. There is another compatible interpretation for the dramatic and unprecedented 7.1 percent market loss sustained by G.M. in a one year period. This interpretation is held widely by dealers themselves, namely, that G.M. was attempting to prevent rumored anti-trust action by the justice department and was inclined to show itself under competitive siege. In the following year, 1971, G.M. recouped all but 1.6 percent of its previous loss and has held subsequently at about 45.4 percent of the total market.

Ford agency he studied. Thus, on a car that the customer paid the dealer $3,337.00, the dealer paid the manufacturer $3,025.00. The dealer's gross margin was therefore $312.00 or 9 percent. (Average gross margin for retailers in other industries runs between 20–25 percent.) Nevertheless, of this $312.00 the dealer paid $90.00 in salesman's commission, $43.00 in wages and salaries, $30.00 in advertising, $28.00 in interest, $27.00 miscellaneous, $24.00 in taxes, $22.00 in rent and maintenance, $16.00 in preparation and pre-delivery work, $9.00 in free customer service, and $7.00 in employee benefits—giving him a net profit of $16.00 per unit. As the boss of the Ford agency remarked, "Our low margins reflect the manufacturer's constant clamor for volume . . . the manufacturer sure as hell gets his . . ." (Vanderwicken, 1972:124).[22]

Should the dealer seek to protest this situation because it locks his time, effort, and money exclusively into fixed margin new car sales, he finds himself under subtle coercion. Quick delivery from the factory becomes problematic and so does a substantial supply of "hot" models (Macauley, 1966:173). Moreover, unfavorable sales comparison with "factory" stores, which sell cars below average retail price, raises questions of effective management (Leonard and Weber, 1970:416). And should such subtle coercion fail to reach home, there is always the threat of franchise termination—a threat which cannot be dismissed as idle given the elimination of over 3,300 dealerships between 1961 when there were 33,500 and 1970 when there were 30,200[23] (NADA, 1973:30). If a franchise is cancelled, it is unlikely that another manufacturer will step in and offer a new franchise or that a new dealer will offer to buy one's premises, equipment, stock, and reputation. Consequently, new car

---

[22]The per unit net of $16.00 does not reflect per unit revenue from financing or insurance which can boost that figure by 200 percent. Little wonder retail dealers want to avoid cash customers.

[23]It is difficult to know what percentage of these 3,300 was the result of attrition, voluntary termination, bankruptcy, or direct and indirect franchise cancellation. It is probably safe to assume, however, that the existing network of franchises reflect manufacturers' preferences relative to location and pricing strategy.

TABLE 4 Cars Sold per Franchised New Car Dealer: 1958–1972

Year	New	Used	Ratio Used to New
1958	125	221	1.77
1959	168	272	1.62
1960	191	285	1.49
1961	175	271	1.55
1962	208	302	1.45
1963	225	317	1.41
1964	239	311	1.30
1965	283	354	1.25
1966	285	336	1.18
1967	269	328	1.22
1968	302	326	1.08
1969	309	389	1.26
1970	281	292	1.00
1971	331	—	—
1972	354	275	.81

Sources: Compiled from *The Franchised New Car and Truck Dealer Story*, Washington, D.C., National Automobile Dealers Association, 1973, p. 32, and *Automobile Facts and Figures*, Detroit: Automobile Manufacturers Association, 1971, p. 33.

dealers apparently accommodate to this "forcing" procedure and avoid direct reaction. Nevertheless, it appears that they do undertake a form of indirect reaction.

DEALER REACTION

An expert witness who testified before the Senate Judiciary Subcommittee on Antitrust and Monopoly in December 1968 reported on a series of "rackets" which dealers perpetrate on the public in order to supplement their short new car profits. These "rackets" include charging for labor time not actually expended, billing for repairs not actually done, replacing parts unnecessarily, and using rebuilt parts but charging for new parts (Leonard and Weber, 1970). In addition to fleecing customers, they also attempt to retaliate against manufacturers whom they accuse of having a hypocritical attitude on service work. Virginia Knauer (Sheppard, 1972:14), special assistant to the President for consumer affairs, reports that complaints about auto service repair lead the list of all complaints. According to Knauer, local car dealers themselves complain that the manufacturers simply do not care about service repairs because if they did, they would adequately compensate dealers for pre-delivery inspection and for warranty work and they certainly would not set up—as one of the Big Three did—a regional competition in which prizes were awarded to regions that *underspent* their warranty budgets (Leonard and Weber, 1970). Indeed, the resentment held by the dealers toward the factory on the issue of service work, as well as the manner and magnitude of retribution engaged in by the dealers against the factory, has been of such proportion that one manufacturer, General Motors, recently fired its entire Chevrolet Eastern Zone office, which has jurisdiction over no less than 60 Chevrolet dealers, for colluding with those dealers against the factory, in the cause of more just compensation for dealer's service work (Farber, 1975).

It would seem, then, that the forcing of fixed margin new car inventory works to the manufacturers' advantage by increasing total net aggregate profit without risking direct competition. This high volume low per unit profit strategy, however, precipitates a criminogenic market structure. It forces new car dealers to free up money by minimizing their investment in more profitable used car inventory as well as by borrowing capital at prevailing interest rates. The pressure of interest payments provides a powerful incentive for the dealer to move his inventory quickly. The need to turn money over and the comparatively narrow margins available to the dealer on new car sales alone precipitate several lines of illegal activity: First, it forces dealers to compensate for short new car profit margins by submitting fraudulent warrantee statements to the manufacturers, often with the collusion of the manufacturers' own representatives. Second, it forces dealers to engage in service repair rackets which milk the public of untold sums of money. Third, it permits the development of a kickback system, especially in large volume dealerships, whereby independent used car wholesalers are constrained to pay graft for supply. Fourth, the wholesalers, in turn, in order to generate unrecorded cash, collude with retail customers in "short-sales." Fifth, to the extent that short-sales spawn excess cash, the wholesaler is drawn into burying and laundering money. In sum, a limited number of

oligopolist manufacturers who sit at the pinnacle of an economically concentrated industry can establish economic policy which creates a market structure that causes lower level dependent industry participants to engage in patterns of illegal activity. Thus, criminal activity, in this instance, is a direct consequence of legally established market structure.

REFERENCES

Becker, Howard S.
  1970   Sociological Work: Method and Substance. Chicago: Aldine Publishing Company.

Brown, Joy
  1973   The Used Car Game: A Sociology of the Bargain. Lexington, Mass.: Lexington Books.

Edwards, Charles E.
  1965   Dynamics of the United States Automobile Industry. Columbia: University of South Carolina Press.

Farber, M. A.
  1975   "Chevrolet, citing 'policy violations,' ousts most zone aids here." The New York Times, Sunday, January 12, Section L.

Farberman, Harvey A.
  1968   A Study of Personalization in Low Income Consumer Interactions and Its Relationship to Identification with Residential Community, unpublished Ph.D. thesis, Department of Sociology, University of Minnesota.

Farberman, H. A., and E. A. Weinstein
  1970   "Personalization in lower class consumer interaction." Social Problems 17 (Spring): 449–457.

Fendell, B.
  1975   "Dealers struggle for survival." The New York Times, Sunday, February 2, Section A.

Gouldner, Alvin
  1970   The Coming Crisis of Western Sociology. New York: Basic Books.
  1968   "The sociologist as partisan: sociology and the welfare state." American Sociologist 3 (May): 103–116.

Huber, Joan
  1973   "Symbolic interaction as a pragmatic perspective: the bias of emergent theory."

American Sociological Review 38 (April): 274–284.

Lanzillotti, Robert F.
1971 "The automobile industry." Pp. 256–301 in W. Adams (ed.), The Structure of American Industry, 4th edition. New York: The Macmillan Company.

Leonard, W. N. and N. G. Weber
1970 "Automakers and dealers: a study of criminogenic market forces." Law and Society 4 (February): 407–424.

Levine, L.
1968 "Jerome Avenue." Motor Trend 20 (December): 26–29.

Liazos, A.
1972 "The poverty of the sociology of deviance: nuts, sluts, and perverts." Social Problems 20 (Summer): 103–120.

Macaulay, Stewart
1966 Law and the Balance of Power: The Automobile Manufacturers and Their Dealers. New York: Russell Sage Foundation.

Motor Vehicle Manufacturing Association
1972 1972 Automobile Facts and Figures. Detroit: MVMA.

National Automobile Dealers Association
1973 The Franchised New Car and Truck Dealer Story. Washington, D.C.: NADA, Table 6, p. 30.

Pashigan, Bedros P.
1961 The Distribution of Automobiles, An Economic Analysis of the Franchise System. Englewood Cliffs, N.J.: Prentice Hall.

Quinney, Richard
1970 The Social Reality of Crime. Boston: Little, Brown and Company.

Robbins, Harold
1971 The Betsy. New York: Trident Press.

Rothchild, Emma
1973 Paradise Lost: The Decline of the Auto-Industrial Age. New York: Random House.

Schervish, P. G.
1973 "The labeling perspective: its bias and potential in the study of political deviance." The American Sociologist 8 (May): 47–57.

Sheppard, Jeffrey M.
1972 The New York Times, Sunday, November 5. Section A.

Smith, R. A.
1961 "The incredible electrical conspiracy." Parts I and II, Fortune (April–May).

Stone, G. P., D. Maines, H. A. Farberman, G. I. Stone, and N. K. Denzin
1974 "On methodology and craftsmanship in the criticism of sociological perspectives." American Sociological Review 39 (June): 456–463.

Taylor, I., P. Walton, and J. Young
1974 "Advances towards a critical criminology." Theory and Society 1 (Winter): 441–476.

Thio, A.
1973 "Class bias in the sociology of deviance." The American Sociologist 8 (February): 1–12.

Vanderwicken, Peter
1972 "How Sam Marshall makes out with his 'deal.'" Fortune 86 (December): 121–130.

White, Lawrence J.
1971 The Automobile Industry Since 1945. Cambridge: Harvard University Press.

TRANSACTION SYSTEMS AND UNLAWFUL ORGANIZATIONAL BEHAVIOR *

Diane Vaughan
Yale University

Coleman (1974) points out that the rise and increase of complex organizations have changed the nature of the social structure over time. New sets of interaction patterns have resulted. In addition to individuals interacting with individuals through roles, individuals now interact with organizations, and organizations interact with other organizations. These new sets of relationships have natural consequences for unlawful behavior. Where once both victim and offender were individuals, increasingly both roles have been played by complex organizations (Vaughan, 1980; 1983). Though inter-organizational relations are receiving intense sociological scrutiny (Aldrich, 1979; Evan, 1978; Pfeffer and Salancik, 1978), unlawful conduct between organizations has seldom been analyzed from an inter-organizational perspective (Vaughan, 1980; citation deleted). To do so draws attention to a neglected but critical element of inter-organizational relations: the nature of transactions and the transaction systems of complex organizations. Transactions, transaction systems, and the way in which they facilitate and in some cases *generate* unlawful organizational behavior are the subject of this paper.

© 1982 by the Society for the Study of Social Problems. Reprinted from *Social Problems*, Vol. 29, No. 4, April 1982, pp. 373–379, by permission.

*This research was partially supported by grant number 2 T32 MH15123, National Institute of Mental Health. Correspondence to: Department of Sociology, Yale University, Box 1965 Yale Station, New Haven, Connecticut 06520.

THE NATURE OF TRANSACTIONS

Though interaction between organizations may be both formal and informal, exchange has become increasingly formal, complex, and impersonal as organizations themselves have become more formal, complex, and impersonal. The massive volume and diversity of daily transactions between organizations have made rules and procedures necessary for the routinization of exchange. In the same manner that formalization develops to coordinate and control intraorganizational activities, formalization emerges as a mechanism by which organizations attempt to cope with the variety and multiplicity of interactions with other organizations in their sets. Accompanying this development has been the growth of technology necessary for recording and processing these complex transactions—accounting procedures and computer systems. Transactions are coded in special languages created for processing, storing and retrieving masses of information. Because of specialization, both the rules and procedures governing exchange and the accounting procedures and computer systems created to keep track of transactions vary between organizations. However, though sub-units within a specific organization differ in many respects, the language, transaction processing and recording strategies, and rules and procedures governing intra-organizational transactions are usually internally consistent—if not in substance, at least in form. This is not likely to be the case between organizations. Monitoring exchange under these circumstances is understandably difficult. Moreover, the ability of one organization to effectively monitor its numerous transactions with other organizations is also constrained by considerations of efficiency.

. . . Modern society, with all its complexities, presupposes business transactions based upon a considerable amount of trust. No matter what the degree of supervisorial restriction imposed on modern employees, an element of trust must remain. If strict controls were imposed on all corporate personnel, then embezzlement, management fraud, and other illegal conduct would be greatly reduced, but very little business would be done (Cressey and Moore, 1980:85).

Thus, because of organizational constraints to monitoring, trust becomes a concomitant of interorganizational exchange almost by default. Monitoring becomes a matter of observation based on sampling, tapping selected indicators, and spot checks, rather than intensive transaction-by-transaction analysis.

Transactions between complex organizations have four distinguishing characteristics: (1) formalization; (2) intricate and highly specialized processing and recording methods; (3) reliance on trust; and (4) general, rather than specific, monitoring procedures. Considered separately, the four factors commonly associated with transactions between complex organizations may each present opportunities for unlawful behavior. However, it is reasonable to assume that the potential for violations increases when the factors combine. For example, complex methods for recording and processing transactions present opportunities for violation. Sorensen et al. (1980:235) note how highly diversified companies with numerous businesses have complex accounting procedures which allow "creative accounting"—and thus fraud. The tendency of accounting procedures to facilitate unlawful behavior has been exacerbated by the advent of computer and other electronic equipment, which have come to dominate the daily operation of nearly all large organizations. While these new technologies complete and record transactions with increased speed and efficien-

cy, they simultaneously offer faster and more efficient ways to gain resources unlawfully.

Computers are a direct link to organizational resources. Theft can be accomplished without breaking and entering. Records, secret information, funds, and programs can be stolen. Assets can be shifted from one location to another. Large amounts can be taken in minutes, or resources can be slowly drained away over long periods. The presence of the offender is not required at the scene of the offense: electronic action can happen in the future, separated by time as well as space from the action of the individual. Nonetheless, offenders weigh the risks of detection when using computers or complex accounting procedures to secure desired resources unlawfully. Hence, trust and general monitoring procedures also precipitate the unlawful conduct.

The factors that characterize transactions between organizations may combine in many forms to provide opportunities for unlawful behavior. However, when the four factors in combination repeatedly generate violations, then the *transaction system* of an organization may be said to be at fault. A transaction system may encourage unlawful behavior between organizations in two ways. First, it may *directly* encourage misconduct by providing convenient access to resources with little risk of detection by the other party to the exchange. Spence's (1974) notion of market signaling illustrates this possibility. Second, a transaction system may *indirectly* encourage the choice of unlawful behavior to attain organizational goals because the system itself blocks completion of the exchange, thus creating an impetus to search for alternative and, perhaps, unlawful methods. The Revco case illustrates this system interface problem.

MARKET SIGNALING AND UNLAWFUL ORGANIZATIONAL BEHAVIOR

Spence (1974:6) notes that the nature of transactions inhibits an organization's ability to discriminate in decision-making. Organizations make decisions in a world of incomplete information-gathering. Because of the number and complexity of transactions in which they engage, and the amount of information necessary to complete each one, organizations are unable to thoroughly know each individual case. As a result, signals and indexes are used as criteria to make decisions when the organization considers a transaction about which product uncertainty exists.

Spence uses transactions in the job market as an example. An employer, confronted with a pool of potential employees, is unable to gather complete information on each one in order to assess the competence of the applicant. Though the information is obtainable, in most cases the employer is unwilling to conduct a thorough search because of cost. Instead, the organization relies on readily observable characteristics to make the decision. Of those characteristics that are observable to the employer, some are subject to manipulation by the individual applicant and some are not. *Signals* are observable, alterable characteristics, such as years of education, or performance, as measured by grades. In sociological terms, signals are achieved characteristics, and therefore capable of manipulation. *Indexes*, on the other hand, are observable, unalterable characteristics, such as race. In a competitive situation, applicants make those adjustments which will make them appear more favorable to an employer. This is called "signaling" (1974:10). Herein lies an opportunity for fraud: some signals can be falsified, and incomplete information-gathering and broad monitoring procedures may permit false signals to pass unnoticed.

Though Spence's examples are limited to individual signaling, the model is appropriate for organizations. The key elements are: (1) a transaction between organizations; (2) a decision-maker and a pool of applicants (organizations); (3) product uncertainty; and (4) high observation costs, necessitating reliance on signals and indexes. The delivery of Medicaid benefits illustrates the model. Medicaid services are provided to recipients through contractual arrangements between federal, state, or local government agencies and third parties (providers) for specialized goods and services to be delivered from the private sector. Organizations under contract as providers to recipients include pharmacies, dental clinics, hospitals, ambulance services, and nursing homes. To become and remain eligible to participate in the program, providers submit eligibility data (signals) on their own behalf. Due to excessive red tape, burdensome paperwork, inadequate verification of data, and poor quality control, some providers manipulate the system to their advantage. Lange and Bowers provide three examples of willful misrepresentation of eligibility signals by providers:

Major fraud and abuse occurred in the summer food service program where prime sponsors claimed to establish several feeding sites within the inner-city and these sites subsequently were shown to be duplicative. Since feeding sites are created on the basis of demographic data on potential eligible children to be served, providers would create sites on paper, never serve meals at some of the sites, and yet fraudulently collect reimbursement for each meal claimed to have been served (1979:25).

Misrepresentation of service abilities may occur separately or in conjunction with misrepresented eligibility data for those whom third parties intend to serve. For example, some providers serving the Rural Housing Program for the USDA have misrepresented the eligibility of recipients. Program regulations allow providers of large housing developments or tenant housing to submit the applications of potentially eligible borrowers in a single package, thereby presenting a number of applications to USDA county offices at a time. As the program is currently structured, high volume offices have come to rely on "packaged applications" to speed the benefit delivery process. The problem is that falsified and misrepresented eligibility information which is submitted without verification is frequently taken at face value by administrative personnel (1979:26).

Third parties submit eligibility data for non-existent clients they claim to serve. They then collect benefits for "ghost" eligibles. Bogus eligibility data to create a "ghost" client may be drawn from identification from the living or deceased. Duplicate social security numbers, forged obituary data, abandoned residence addresses, or falsified wage reports illustrate ways of establishing "ghosts". The Unemployment Insurance, CETA, SBA 8(a) and Vocational Education programs have documented incidences of this pattern of provider offense (1979:26).

Thus, to enter and remain in an exchange agreement with the welfare department, providers (organizations and individuals) may falsify market signals concerning service abilities, client eligibility, and even the existence of clients. Of course, the misrepresentation of market signals by recipients in order to obtain benefits is well-known (Lange and Bowers, 1979). However, we are primarily concerned with signaling by organizations. When legitimate avenues to resources are blocked or appear uncertain, an organization in a market signaling situation may falsify signals in order to obtain strategic resources. Hence, the opportunities for unlawful behavior by organizations in a market signaling situation may be extended to other examples: organizations competing for government defense contracts, private firms negotiating a merger or sale, or organizations seeking accreditation (Wiley and Zald, 1968) or approval of a product (Vandiver, 1978).

The Medicaid examples raise another point: false signaling may regularly occur in transactions with certain organizations. The degree to which the focal organization defines it as a chronic rather than infrequent problem might be estimated by the amount of resources the organization allocates to detect false signaling. When a focal organization is repeatedly the victim of false signaling as other organizations in its set attempt to gain resources fraudulently, the factors associated with transactions may, in combination, create a *criminogenic transaction system* in which violations are regularly produced in the course of organizational exchange.

THE SYSTEM INTERFACE PROBLEM AND UNLAWFUL ORGANIZATIONAL BEHAVIOR

A system interface problem occurs when the language, rules, procedures, and recording and processing systems of two organizations fail to mesh, so that a transaction is inhibited rather than facilitated. Resource exchange may stall and become difficult to complete to the satisfaction of both parties. One or both of the organizations concerned may have to adjust their system.

Negotiations may often flounder in a between-system lag induced by formalized communications. The problem may be short- or long-term, depending on the two organizations, the nature of their interdependence, their frequency of interaction, the task around which the specific exchange revolves, and the resources each can devote to correcting the difficulty. Should one of the organizations be unwilling or unable to devote resources to legitimate resolution, or require immediate completion of the exchange in order to gain resources, the transaction system itself may be the chosen mechanism for bypassing the system interface problem. The result may be unlawful behavior, as the Revco case illustrates (Vaughan, 1980; 1983).

In 1977, Revco Drug Stores, Inc., one of the largest discount drug chains in the United States, was found guilty of Medicaid-provider fraud: specifically, a computer-generated double-billing scheme that resulted in the loss of over half a million dollars in Medicaid funds to the Ohio Department of Public Welfare. Revco was engaged in exchange on a contractual basis with the welfare department, as a provider of pharmacy goods and services to Medicaid recipients. Prescriptions were given to recipients by Revco pharmacists, then submitted to the welfare department for reimbursement. That a system interface problem existed is indicated by the history of high rejection rates for Revco claims submitted to the welfare department for reimbursement. Documents and memos showed that Revco had experienced reimbursement problems since the welfare department first began processing and paying claims by computer in 1972.

According to representatives of both organizations, Revco's high rejection rates were a function of welfare department rules for allowable Medicaid recipient claims and procedures for claim-filing on the part of providers. The number of rules and procedures was overwhelming; they changed frequently, and providers received periodic notification of how computer claims submission procedures should be altered to suit new criteria. The modifications could be costly and time-consuming, and, in addition to the computer changes, required assimilation by pharmacists in each store. Errors were common, and computer modifications either lagged behind or were not made. Claims were rejected for all three reasons. As a consequence, Revco was not reimbursed for filling the prescriptions which had been dispensed to recipients in the belief that the reimbursement would be forthcoming. When a claim is rejected, reimbursement is withheld until the error is corrected, and the claim successfully resubmitted. In Revco's case, rather than correct the rejected claims for resubmission, rejected claims accumulated. Over 50,000 claims, rejected by welfare department computers and representing more than half a million dollars in accounts receivable, accumulated at Revco headquarters.

Two Revco officials initiated a plan to bring the company's outstanding accounts receivable back into balance. A temporary clerical staff of six was hired to alter the rejected claims to make them acceptable to the welfare department computer. According to Revco officials, the decision to falsify prescription claims was influenced by four factors. (1) They had faced this situation before. Revco had a history of stalled negotiations with the welfare department which impeded reimbursement for provider services. Revco executives believed the corporation had repeatedly been victimized in this same manner by the welfare department (Vaughan, 1980). (2) The two executives believed that the rejected claims represented resources legitimately owed to Revco. (3) They calculated that the cost of legitimate correction and resubmission would be more than the average amount of the claims. (4) They believed that the funds could be retrieved without being detected by the department's screening system. This belief was based on the skills possessed by the two executives. One was a licensed pharmacist and the other a computer specialist who knew the welfare department's computer system well. They thoroughly understood the intermesh between the two organizations' transaction systems. To take back resources they believed belonged to the corporation, the executives falsified prescriptions equal in number to those rejected, and submitted them through the transaction system.

The Revco case suggests that when a system interface problem ties up resources or inhibits resource delivery, unlawful attainment of resources may be a function of: (1) demand for the resources; (2) legitimate access blocked by cost and delay; (3) structured opportunity to secure the resources through the transaction system; (4) low probability of detection and sanctioning (Vaughan, 1983); and (5) redefinition of property rights concerning possession of organizational resources (Dynes and Quarantelli, 1974).

Because the Revco incident is a case study, no conclusions can be drawn about the extensiveness of the system interface problem. In exchange between Medicaid providers and the welfare department in Ohio, all providers routinely had claims rejected. This fact might indicate that in this particular welfare department, the system interface problem runs rampant. However, the department monitors the rate of provider rejection for two reasons: to work out system interface problems, and to detect fraud. If a provider's rejection rate is higher than the average for all providers, or from its own rejection history, either system interface difficulties or intentional fraud could be the explanation. The Revco case is an example of a system interface problem which led to fraud. System interface difficulties can exist without fraud, or as in the market signaling example, fraud may be the principle purpose of a transaction, rather than the solution to a bureaucratic snag.

Without examining rejection rates of other providers and identifying the facts of each case, generalizations cannot be made about system interface problems in the Ohio Medicaid system. In this case, a system interface problem did occur, and unlawful behavior was used to resolve it. System interface problems occasionally occur for nearly all organizations, demanding varying amounts of resources to complete transactions that stall. With transactions encumbered by formalization, complex processing methods and mechanisms, and general rather than specific monitoring practices, some organizations may resolve their difficulties unlawfully. For some organizations, system interface problems may be the rule, rather than the exception, increasing the likelihood of fraudulent resolution. When this is the case, the transaction system itself may be labelled criminogenic.

SUMMARY AND IMPLICATIONS

Transaction systems which develop to cope with the complex legitimate exchanges between complex organizations can also be used to secure gains unlawfully. Because transactions of complex organizations are characterized by high degrees of formalization, intricate processing and recording methods, exchange based on trust, and general monitoring procedures, illegal conduct can be carried out with little risk of detection. Not only are opportunities for unlawful behavior present in each of these four characteristics, but also in the ways they combine in a transaction system. Indeed, the transaction systems of some organizations may be criminogenic, repeatedly generating violations between organizations. Unlawful conduct may occur regularly when exchange between organizations relies upon market signals as the basis for decision-making. Signals can be falsified, and transaction systems with incomplete information gathering and broad monitoring procedures facilitate the fraudulent attainment of resources. Transaction systems may also systematically generate illegality by creating system interface problems. Unlawful conduct may occur because the transaction system itself blocks legitimate access to resources.

Opportunities for violations multiply as transaction system complexity increases. While not all organizations in a market signaling situation or confronting system interface problems will resort to unlawful behavior,[1] some organizations may be more likely to become offenders, depending upon the complexity of their transaction systems and those of the various organizations in their set. This variability across organizations is important, for the Medicaid system examined here is highly-complex: a criminogenic transaction plagued by violations as a result of the four factors functioning individually to generate illegal behavior, as well as acting in combination to present opportunities for violations both through a market signaling situation and system interface problems.

Of the organizational characteristics believed to be associated with unlawful organizational behavior (Gross, 1980; Needleman and Needleman, 1979; Stone, 1975; Vaughan, 1980; 1983), the transaction systems of organizations have been least addressed by scholars and activists, and yet are perhaps the most vulnerable to manipulation. Because the complexity of inter-organizational exchange appears to have systematic consequences for illegality, reducing the complexity of transactions may also reduce rates of violations. To realize this possibility, organizations must assume a social responsibility to recognize the relationship between transaction complexity and unlawful conduct and, hence, to monitor and adjust their own transaction systems to minimize the possibility that they are the source of violations. Reducing transaction complexity between organizations may result in fewer violations by decreasing opportunities for illegality, improving the risk of detection, and/or decreasing the probability of system interface problems, thus eliminating a source of motivation to pursue resources unlawfully.

What could motivate organizations to reduce the complexity of their own transaction systems? System complexity not only increases the potential for an organization to engage in unlawful behavior, but also promotes the possibility that an organization will be victimized—by other organizations or by its own members. Changes that decrease the possibility that an organization will commit an offense also decrease the possibility that the organization will be victimized; resources lost to an organization in this manner can be conserved. Though revamping transaction systems may create a strain on the organization, in the long run savings from forestalled victimization can be applied to the legitimate pursuit of organizational goals. Thus, self-surveillance and modification of transaction systems is in an organization's best interest. Furthermore, reducing the complexity of inter-organizational exchange is socially responsible because it may reduce the costs of unlawful

---

[1] For an analysis of the variation in patterns of organizational behavior under circumstances conducive to illegality, see Vaughan, 1983.

organizational behavior and its control, which ultimately fall upon the public.

REFERENCES

Aldrich, Howard E.
1979   Organizations and Environments. Englewood Cliffs, N.J.: Prentice-Hall.

Coleman, James S.
1974   Power and the Structure of Society. Philadelphia: University of Pennsylvania Press.

Cressey, Donald R. and Charles A. Moore
1980   Corporation Codes of Ethical Conduct: Report to the Peat, Marwick, and Mitchell Foundation. New York: Peat, Marwick, and Mitchell.

Dynes, Russell R. and E. L. Quarantelli
1974   "Organizations as victims in mass civil disturbances." Pp. 67–77 in Israel Drapkin and Emilio Viano (eds.), Victimology: A New Focus. Lexington, Mass.: D. C. Heath.

Evan, William M. (ed.)
1978   Interorganizational Relations. Philadelphia: University of Pennsylvania Press.

Gross, Edward
1980   "Organizational structure and organizational crime." Pp. 52–76 in Gilbert Geis and Ezra Stotland (eds.), White-Collar Crime: Theory and Research. Beverly Hills: Sage.

Lange, Andrea G. and Robert A. Bowers
1979   Fraud and Abuse in Government Benefit Programs. Washington, D.C.: U.S. Government Printing Office.

Needleman, Martin L. and Carolyn Needleman
1979   "Organizational crime: Two models of criminogenesis." Sociological Quarterly 20: 517–528.

Parker, Donn B.
1980   "Computer-related white-collar crime." Pp. 199–220 in Gilbert Geis and Ezra Stotland (eds.), White-Collar Crime: Theory and Research. Beverly Hills: Sage.

Pfeffer, Jeffrey and Gerald Salancik
1978   The External Control of Organizations: A Resource Dependence Perspective. New York: Harper and Row.

Reiss, Albert J., Jr.
1981   "Towards a revitalization of theory and research on victimization by crime." Journal of Criminal Law and Criminology 72: 704–713.

Sorensen, James E., Hugh D. Grove, and Thomas L. Sorensen
1980   "Detecting management fraud: The role of the independent auditor." Pp. 221–251 in Gilbert Geis and Ezra Stotland (eds.), White-Collar Crime: Theory and Research. Beverly Hills: Sage.

Spence, Michael
1974   Market Signaling. Cambridge: Harvard University Press.

Stone, Christopher D.
1975   Where the Law Ends: The Social Control of Corporate Behavior. New York: Harper and Row.

Vandiver, Kermit
1978   "Why should my conscience bother me?" Pp. 80–101 in M. David Ermann and Richard J. Lundman (eds.), Corporate and Governmental Deviance: Problems of Organizational Behavior in Contemporary Society. New York: Oxford University Press.

Vaughan, Diane
1980   "Crime between organizations: Implications for victimology." Pp. 77–97 in Gilbert Geis and Ezra Stotland (eds.), White-Collar Crime: Theory and Research. Beverly Hills: Sage.
1983   On the Social Control of Organizations. Chicago: The University of Chicago Press.

Wiley, M. G. and Mayer N. Zald
1968   "The growth and transformation of educational accrediting agencies: An exploratory study of the social control of institutions." Sociology of Education 41: 36–56.

COPING WITH INSIDIOUS INJURIES

The Case of Johns-Manville Corporation and Asbestos Exposure*

Craig Calhoun
University of North Carolina, Chapel Hill

Henryk Hiller
University of North Carolina, Chapel Hill

The new technologies and large scale markets that have proliferated since the industrial revolution have been mechanisms of new kinds of injuries on a growing and often extraordinarily large scale. The progression of coal mine accidents, collapsing bridges, railway and airplane crashes, and factory explosions forms a frightening counterpoint to industrial progress. A new legal field, "mass torts," has emerged to deal with liability stemming from public hazards, dangerous workplaces, and injurious consumer products. Some of these injuries are not only massive, they are insidious in the way they strike and are thus much harder for existing legal and regulatory institutions to deal with. In this paper we conceptualize such insidious injuries and suggest why they raise difficult issues about legal responsibility. Then we examine litigation over asbestos related injuries, especially those involving the Johns-Manville Corporation, to show how these issues arose in a concrete historical context. We relate this specific case history to the more general transformation of tort law, which

is our society's main means to deter or punish injurers and compensate victims. Last, we discuss some issues underlying the formation of public policies to deal with insidious injuries.

INSIDIOUS INJURIES AND LEGAL RESPONSIBILITY

Injuries are "insidious" when the links between their causes and manifest symptoms are obscure. This is particularly common where the symptoms are those of a general disease rather than a specific trauma, for example, lung cancer rather than a broken bone. Identifying such diseases as injuries is often difficult. Insidious injuries (a) appear only after a period of latency, like asbestosis and silicosis; (b) strike only a segment of the exposed population, either randomly or patterned by varying individual vulnerabilities, like diseases caused by pollution; (c) manifest themselves by raising rates of risk for diseases that also have other causes, as occupational exposure to various toxins may multiply cancer risks, and/or (d) affect victims widely dispersed through the population, like the results of faulty pharmaceutical products. Some injuries, like those stemming from exposure to asbestos dust, are insidious in all four senses.

Insidious injuries are associated with increased scale of social organization and with introduction of complex and dangerous new technologies, but they are not simply reducible

©1988 by the Society for the Study of Social Problems. Reprinted from *Social Problems*, Vol. 35, No. 2, April 1988, pp. 162–181, by permission.

*The authors are grateful for advice and discussion from Andrew W. Couch, Cynthia Greenleaf, Michael Powell, Lee Schlesinger, Barbara Stenross, and audiences at Harvard University, the State University of New York at Stony Brook, and the University of North Carolina at Chapel Hill. Correspondence to: Calhoun, Department of Sociology, University of North Carolina, Chapel Hill, NC 27514.

to such impersonal forces. They are injuries caused by people and often by corporate "persons." For this reason, attempts to seek redress for insidious injuries fall into the province of tort law. In the United States, the absence of any national health care or universal health insurance system means that victims are often led to file tort suits simply as a way of coping with extraordinary medical costs. Litigation is, however, generally a slow and difficult means of securing compensation, which is further complicated by the pursuit of deterrence and/or punishment.

Social scientists have paid little attention to the nature and development of insidious injuries. Lawyers are more generally aware of the issues, but their work has focused more on technical matters of litigation in mass and/or insidious tort cases than on understanding the problem in its social context and considering possible responses to it. Questions about how to reduce insidious injuries and how to compensate and/or pay for the care of victims are inextricably bound up with questions about corporate versus individual responsibility, the choice of legal doctrines in tort cases, the asymmetry of corporate and individual litigants, and the appropriate role for government.

Asbestos related diseases offer an advantageous starting point for analysis of the changing nature of insidious injuries and their implications for tort law and public policy. First, asbestos related litigation combines several dimensions of insidiousness in a very large scale mass tort. Second, it raises interesting questions about what it means to treat corporations as responsible actors, both because asymmetry distorts suits between corporations and natural persons and because of the anthropomorphism of arguments that corporations ought to be punished and made to feel pain for their misdeeds. Third, largely because of the tort and bankruptcy litigation involving Johns-Manville,[1] it offers a wealth of documentary evidence. A particularly interesting feature of the Manville case is the unusual strategy the firm adopted to protect its assets from the millions of dollars of claims produced by tort

litigation. It sought protection in the bankruptcy courts while still clearly solvent and profitable. Manville was not the first firm to employ this defense against tort liability, but it was the first *Fortune* 500 firm to do so.

Manville's action provoked strong responses. Paul Brodeur (1986:231, 350), a widely read journalist who covered the litigation from the point of view of plaintiff lawyers, suggested that the corporation was simply using legal complexities to escape its true responsibility. One plaintiff lawyer told him that it was "the greatest corporate mass murderer in history" (quoted in Brodeur, 1986:231). *The New York Times* (1982), by contrast, published an editorial on the day after the company filed for bankruptcy protection, arguing that, "Asbestos is a tragedy, most of all for the victims and their families, but also for the companies which are being made to pay the price for decisions made long ago." Angry plaintiff lawyers wondered how anyone could worry about the companies rather than the human victims (e.g., Robert Steinberg, quoted in Brodeur, 1986:287).

Indeed, those sympathetic to the victims very commonly urged that the company be punished. It is unclear, however, whether they wished to hurt employees, current managers, the retired and/or deceased managers who made the decisions leading to the injury, or stockholders, which in this as in most other large companies were mostly institutions (including pension funds and others) representing people only loosely linked to the company. Expiation seemed as important as compensation to many; they would have liked to see Manville "killed."

THE MANVILLE CORPORATION AND ASBESTOS RELATED DISEASE

Asbestos is a fibrous material useful primarily as a fire retardant. The resilient fibers are removed from mined rock and are flexible enough to be woven, sprayed, or packed. End-products include fireproof textiles, construction materials, brake linings, and other surfaces for coping with high friction.

Henry W. Johns pioneered commerical applications for asbestos in the late 1860s. In 1901,

---

[1] Hereafter referred to as Manville, in accord with its 1982 change of name.

Johns's successors merged his firm with the Manville Covering Company, an insulation firm. The newly-formed Johns-Manville Corporation rapidly increased its annual sales to some forty million dollars by 1925. The business concentrated on asbestos roofing and pipe insulation and operated a huge asbestos mine in Quebec. By 1934, the company was manufacturing 1,400 products (most with asbestos); as of 1981, asbestos had thousands of commercial applications (U.S. Congress: House Committee on Education and Labor [HCEL], 1981:9).

Throughout the twentieth century, Manville dominated many of its markets and expanded rapidly abroad, gaining a two-thirds share of total U.S. sales for insulation material composed partly of asbestos. Manville claimed as recently as 1982 to be the largest asbestos processor and the largest asbestos-cement manufacturer in the free world (Moody's, 1982:3995). Raw asbestos fiber, insulation, pipe, and roofing constituted the largest portion of its sales. Asbestos remained a major ingredient in most of these products even after litigation concerning its health effects was well under way; a rapid decline began in the middle 1980s (Goodwyn, 1972:12–13; Johns-Manville Annual Report, 1978 et seq.). The company has been on *Fortune* magazine's list of the 500 largest corporations in the United States from its inception and was for many years among the 200 largest. Its sales peaked at $2.2 billion in 1979, and in 1981 its assets totaled $2.3 billion.

In the early years of the asbestos industry, the mineral seemed an unalloyed good. Gradually, however, the picture darkened. Shortly after 1900, evidence began to show dangers associated with asbestos use. Mining, milling, weaving, transportation, and other uses all create asbestos dust. This dust is composed of tiny asbestos fibers that are easily inhaled by exposed individuals. The very properties that render asbestos strong and fire-retardant make it very difficult for the body's defense mechanisms to dispose of it; up to one-half of the inhaled fibers become lodged in the lungs (U.S. Congress: HCEL, 1979:49). These fibers and the body's reaction to them can result in various asbestos related diseases. The three most common are

asbestosis, lung cancer, and mesothelioma. Precise specification of each disease and its relation to asbestos exposure is still a matter of some dispute.

Asbestosis is a breathing difficulty resulting from the formation of fibrous, scarlike tissue around asbestos fibers lodged in the alveolar tissue of the lung. It generally progresses over a period of 10 to 30 years. Symptoms are slow to develop, and the fibrous tissue growth can be detected by X-ray only in advanced stages. Asbestosis itself is seldom fatal, but the decreased lung efficiency it causes often contributes to fatal respiratory disease such as pneumonia or to heart failure. It has been estimated that ten percent of those working with asbestos die from these and other complications associated with asbestosis (U.S. Congress: HCEL, 1978:134). Asbestosis is dose-related; that is, lower levels of exposure produce lesser problems. Contrary to earlier belief, however, no "safe" exposure levels exist (see U.S. Congress: HCEL, 1979:51).

Lung cancer and, less often, gastro-intestinal cancer are also related to asbestos exposure. Though the statistical connection has appeared since the 1930s, the precise mechanism by which asbestos exposure contributes to malignant formations is unclear. The coupling of cigarette smoking and asbestos exposure greatly increases cancer risks, though exposed non-smokers are also apparently at risk. In most cases, the cancer will be latent for 20 to 30 years after first exposure and upon manifestation will quickly result in the victim's death. Of those heavily exposed to asbestos dust (including factory workers and those installing asbestos products), 20 to 25 percent are estimated to die of lung cancer (U.S. Congress: HCEL, 1978:134).

Mesothelioma is a cancer of the mesothelial cells in the pleura (which lines the chest cavity) or the peritoneum (which lines the abdominal cavity). The tumor remains latent for 20 to 40 years and then quickly spreads throughout the chest or abdomen. Breathlessness and severe pain occur, vital organ function is affected, and death results very quickly. Mesothelioma occurs almost exclusively among those exposed to asbestos and was not recognized in the medical literature until the 1940s. The incidence of this cancer appears to be increasing, and it is estimated that 7 to 10 percent of heavily exposed workers die from it (U.S. Congress: HCEL, 1978:134).

Approximately eleven million people in the United States have been exposed to asbestos dust at work. Most of the intensive exposures occurred in shipyards during the Second World War. Dust exposure levels varied over time and work area in the shipyards and other places where asbestos was used. It is estimated that asbestos related diseases will claim the lives of 40 percent of the four million workers heavily exposed to asbestos dust and 15 percent of the four to seven million with less exposure (U.S. Congress: HCEL, 1978:135; see also Vermeulen and Berman, 1982:21). Because of the long latency periods, however, the connection between diseases and asbestos exposure was slow to be discovered, remaining both disputable in court and unclear to the general public for many years.

Corporate Responses to Asbestos Related Disease

Since awareness of asbestos related health hazards developed slowly, Manville and other firms in the asbestos industry had the opportunity to develop a four-stage strategic response.

Controlling the Spread of Information. The first phase began in the early 1930s with the initial medical evidence linking asbestos exposure to disease and lasted until conclusive independent research from Mt. Sinai School of Medicine in New York began appearing in the mid-1960s. During this period the dangers of asbestos exposure became increasingly clear to Manville executives. Their response was two-fold: to limit the dissemination of information on potential health dangers and to challenge unfavorable research findings through industry-sponsored research.

The first case of asbestosis was reported in England in 1906; subsequently, a report of this was published in a 1918 Bulletin of the U.S. Department of Labor Statistics with a call for fur-

ther research (U.S. Congress: House Committee on the Judiciary [HCJ], 1980:42). By 1930, studies in the United Kingdom had strongly suggested a link between asbestos exposure and pulmonary disease (U.S. Congress: HCEL, 1978:26, 1979:97; U.S. Congress: HCJ, 1980:42). Indeed, early studies in the United States, including those sponsored by Manville and the asbestos industry, supported the existence of such a link (U.S. Congress: HCJ, 1980:492, 493).

Executives at Manville and other industry firms interpreted adverse research findings so as to minimize their importance, arguing that the English findings did not bear on the U.S. situation and that the problem was one of "individual susceptibilities" (U.S. Congress: HCEL, 1978:152; U.S. Congress: Senate Committee of Labor and Human Resources [SCLHR], 1980:206). In addition, they repeatedly and successfully prevented publication of those findings in the trade journal *Asbestos*, read by those in the industry as well as by users of asbestos products (e.g., U.S. Congress: HCJ, 1980:103). The company's general counsel (and later, secretary) Vandiver Brown stated in a 1935 letter to Sumner Simpson, president of the second largest asbestos producer, Raybestos Manhattan: "Our interests are best served by having asbestosis receive the minimum of publicity" (printed in U.S. Congress: HCEL, 1978:152). Consequently, most compensation claims were settled out of court; only one suit reached the appellate level before 1970 (*Vogel v. Johns-Manville Products Corp.*, 1936).

Manville also limited the information reaching its workers as to their own physical condition. There is evidence indicating that as late as the 1960s employees were not being warned of dust dangers (U.S. Congress: HCEL, 1979:151; see also U.S. Congress: HCJ, 1980:533). Medical indications of disease were not revealed to affected workers, and even the outside physician for one Manville plant was reportedly not aware asbestos was used there until 1972 (*Johns-Manville Products Corp. v. Superior Court*, 1980; U.S. Congress: HCEL, 1979:151; U.S. Congress: HCJ, 1980:508–10, 533, 538; Berman, 1978:3).

Company executives realized as early as the 1930s that minimizing public awareness of the hazards of asbestos exposure was an inadequate strategy by itself, given the steadily increasing flow of non-industry research (notably Hueper, 1956, printed in U.S. Congress: HCEL, 1979:153). Manville began to sponsor its own research in 1928 with a small study using only non-human subjects and examining only possible links to cancer (i.e., not to asbestosis). The explicit aim of the industry-sponsored research was to provide scientific evidence to combat the negative non-industry findings as well as to defend against workers' compensation claims and tort suits (Brown, 1934; Hobart, 1934). In 1936, Brown and Simpson proposed a joint research program to an industry group which they dominated. As Simpson (1936) wrote,

We could determine from time to time after the findings are made whether we wish any publication or not. My own idea is that it would be a good thing to distribute the information among the medical fraternity, providing it is of the right type and would not injure our companies.

The resulting research agreement with the Saranac Laboratories in New York State stipulated that the funders:

will determine whether, to what extent and in what manner they [results] should be made public. In the event it is deemed desirable that the results be made public, the manuscript of your study will be submitted to us for approval prior to publication (quoted in Brown, 1939).

The medical professionals involved were clearly willing to cooperate with the asbestos industry. Funding requests by these professionals to asbestos trade associations in the 1950s suggested that research be undertaken to defend against claims or to counter negative nonindustry studies. In 1955, for example, the Saranac director requested funds from an industry trade association, suggesting the relationship between asbestos and cancer be studied in animals in order to provide facts "to combat unjust compensation claims" (*Dishner v. Johns-Manville Corp.*, 1978:850). The next year, Manville's

medical director recommended that the association fund a study on the cancer link "in order that we could procure information which would combat current derogatory literature now being circulated throughout the United States and Canada" (quoted from U.S. Congress: HCEL, 1979:153). Results of industry-sponsored research were submitted to Manville and other firms for review and withheld from publication if they did not satisfactorily advance these goals (e.g., U.S. Congress: HCJ, 1980:52–53). Moreover, the results that were published were sometimes carefully misleading. For example, studies published in the 1950s emphasized that *asbestosis* did not cause cancer. This obscured the very real relationship found between the substance asbestos and cancer (U.S. Congress: HCJ, 1980:52, 53; Smith, 1955:202–03).

By the mid-1960s, managing information was no longer a viable strategy. Many of those exposed to asbestos in the past were manifesting disease. Most importantly, research first published in 1964, principally by Dr. Irving Selikoff of the Mt. Sinai School of Medicine, clearly established the widespread and long-term danger of asbestos exposure (e.g., Selikoff et al., 1964). Manville was forced to deal with this public knowledge, reversing in 1964 its long-standing policy against attaching health warnings to its asbestos products. Moreover, union concern for health and safety issues increased, combining with the new scientific evidence to dramatically increase the number and size of compensation claims. Selikoff joined the unions in lobbying for federal dust regulations, and the 1972 standards were among the first to be established under the Occupational Safety and Health Act (Brodeur, 1973:29–31; Ashford, 1976:5–6).

Confronting the Litigation Explosion. The second phase in Manville's response was to confront the explosion of asbestos related litigation. In 1973, an appellate court first held that asbestos manufacturers could be liable to those using asbestos products for failing to warn of or test for dangers that were reasonably foreseeable (*Borel v. Fibreboard Paper Products*, 1973). This touched off an avalanche of product liability suits. Manville, as the major manufacturer, was named as a defendant in perhaps 13,000 of 20,000 suits industry-wide between 1968 and 1982 (Lublin, 1982; Johns-Manville Debtor's Petition, 1982), although fewer than one hundred reached the trial stage.

By the late 1970s, these suits had become a significant financial threat. In 1976, 159 new lawsuits were filed against the corporation; in 1978, the number reached 792. Crucially, in 1977, a plaintiff attorney discovered the existence of the "Sumner Simpson Papers" (several of which are cited above), which included correspondence among industry executives from as far back as the 1930s coordinating action to limit the spread of information concerning the health hazards of asbestos products and production processes. These letters undermined Manville's argument that there was insufficient medical evidence of health dangers until 1964 to warrant warnings and testing beyond what was done. The tide turned against the company; jury awards ran as high as $750,000 (Soloman, 1979:198), and legal costs mounted. Nonetheless, Manville continued to fight every case vigorously, exhausting every legal option open to it—an approach that plaintiff attorneys regarded as stalling and attempting to fight not on the merit of cases but on relative financial capacity to continue litigation.

Perhaps the most critical threat to the firm came in 1976 when Manville's insurers refused to renew their policies, claiming they were unable to estimate future liability expenses adequately to arrive at an appropriate fee (see U.S. Congress: HCJ, 1980:59, 1982:208). Manville was forced into self-insurance. This not only removed its buffer against liability payments, it made the company immediately responsible for all defense costs. Insurance and asbestos companies entered into litigation to determine whether an asbestos "injury" arose at initial exposure to asbestos (rendering those insuring Manville in the 1930s and 1940s liable) or at manifestation of disease (rendering those insuring at time of manifestation liable). No court decision was forthcoming until 1980; in the late 1970s, the company faced the possibility that a manifestation theory would be accepted, which would leave it liable as self-insurer for all diseases manifested after 1976, and thus for the majority of claims.

Impending Disaster and Protective Legislation. In the third phase of its response to the developing awareness of the health hazards of asbestos, the company sought relief from its severe immediate and long-term problems by helping to draft federal legislation that would create a fund for the settlement of claims from victims of asbestos related disease. Representative Millicent Fenwick of New Jersey sponsored the 1977 Asbestos Health Hazards Compensation Act (H.R. 2740), and Senator Gary Hart of Colorado sponsored its 1980 successor (S. 2847). Manville was a principal drafter of both these bills, as Fenwick and Hart readily acknowledged (U.S. Congress: HCEL, 1979:2; U.S. Congress: SCLHR, 1980:172). Neither bill reached the legislative floor. Manville viewed them as legitimate efforts to share the burden created by changing social standards as to what constitutes reasonable business practices as well as changing medical knowledge about the dangers of asbestos. To many critics, however, including legislators, the bills were mere attempts to avoid responsibility for the costs of past corporate practices.

Manville and other supporters of the compensation bills argued that workers' compensation programs and product liability litigation were inadequate to compensate victims. They attempted to show that victims sued manufacturers of products they had used rather than their employers because workers' compensation benefited only a fraction of those with legitimate claims and provided severely limited benefits even in those few cases (U.S. Congress: SCLHR, 1980:169, 207, 227). They similarly faulted tort litigation for failing to provide adequate compensation for victims (U.S. Congress: SCLHR, 1980:205). Since legal expenses (including attorneys fees and court costs) exceeded the compensation received by victims by 66 percent, litigation seemed to them an ineffective and inefficient means of providing compensation (U.S. Congress: HCEL, 1982:202; Kakalik et al., 1983, 1984; see also *Harvard Law Review*, 1980).

The Fenwick and Hart bills similarly called for standardized payments to confirmed victims of asbestos related disease. Each contained a clause prohibiting all persons eligible for compensation under the proposed statute from bringing suits against employers, manufacturers, insurers, unions, or the government; in other words, the bills proposed to create an exclusive remedy. Each bill provided for some means by which payments would be rendered predictable as well as adequate. This predictability was crucial; it would allow the company to plan its business activities with some clear notion of future liabilities and probably allow it to reinsure itself.

The Fenwick bill proposed to provide compensation by means of a federally administered fund; companies would pay in a fixed percentage of their sales from fifteen years before. Under the Hart bill, payments would be made by companies into state administered workers' compensation programs in amounts corresponding to nationally standardized "percentage rates of liability" for current and expected future claims. The Fenwick bill would have been preferable for Manville because past sales are a more certain indicator of liability than future claims, but each would have provided the needed level of predictability.

Under the Fenwick bill, Manville had no incentive to reduce asbestos dust levels because the corporation's financial contribution to victims would be based directly on its level of sales, not its workers' health. Similarly, under the Hart bill, firms would pay a percentage of total liability which, though not necessarily based on market share, would at least provide for insurance at something close to an industry-wide rate.

Each bill included an attempt to make tobacco companies share some of the cost of asbestos related disease, primarily on the basis of research showing that cigarette smoking greatly increases the risk of lung cancer for those exposed to asbestos. However, the proposals evaded two key issues. First, were tobacco companies responsible for workers' smoking (an individual choice) in the same sense in which asbestos companies were responsible for spreading asbestos dust?

Second, should the asbestos industry share in this liability because it had systematically minimized the chances that workers had to find out about the combined risks of asbestos exposure and smoking?

Finally, the bills sought to have the federal government contribute to the compensation fund. About one-half of all workers occupationally exposed in any intense way to asbestos dust worked in shipyards owned or controlled by the government, especially during the Second World War (Hart, 1983). The government, moreover, had done some early research and failed to do much to implement recommendations that greater precautions be taken (U.S. Congress: HCEL, 1978:38–39). The government would acknowledge liability only for victims directly employed at federal facilities, that is, not for employees of contractors. In the absence of any relevant court decisions, the extent of government liability remained unclear.

Bankruptcy. Manville's failure to secure financial protection by legislation forced the corporation to try a final and more drastic action. In August 1982, the company filed for protection from its creditors while it reorganized under Chapter 11 of the Federal Bankruptcy Code. At about the same time, the company changed its name from Johns-Manville to the Manville Corporation in an attempt to symbolically distance the corporate identity from the asbestos litigation. This was newsworthy because it was a highly unusual move for a company far from bankrupt in current account terms. In December 1981, as noted, Manville's assets totaled $2.3 billion.

Filing for protection under bankruptcy statutes was an extreme measure but, at least in the short term, an effective one. It immediately froze action on all creditors' claims, including pending and future tort claims. The corporation's longer-term goal was to keep its main operating assets from possible seizure to pay claim settlements. The bankruptcy proceeding, in short, saved the corporation from more or less rapid dissolution as litigation costs and settlements cut increasingly into capital. It was not a painless solution, however, and Manville chose it pretty much as a last resort.

By 1981 the company faced prosecution in some 9,300 cases brought by 12,800 separate plaintiffs. The average award was $16,000 per claim. Total costs were more than twice that, however, as defense costs reached the level of $23,400 per claim (Johns-Manville Debtor's Petition, 1982:5, 6; see also Kakalik et al., 1983, 1984). Moreover, the award ceiling kept rising. In 1981, a Los Angeles County jury awarded a plaintiff $1.2 million in compensatory damages alone (U.S. Congress: HCEL, 1982:204). Much more importantly, in 1981 Manville was first found liable for punitive damages at the trial court level. If the awards were upheld on appeal, Manville would be responsible for full payment no matter when the injury took place because punitive damages generally are not insurable (Stone, 1975:56; though this question is often litigated).

For somewhat more technical legal reasons, four judicial decisions between 1980 and 1982 also added greatly to the uncertainty of Manville's future. First, the *Flatt v. Johns-Manville Sales Corp.* (1980) decision used the *Borel* case to bar Manville from denying liability when a diseased plaintiff established Manville's asbestos as the source of exposure. A second case, *Johns-Manville Products Corp. v. Superior Court* (1980), found that a California workers' compensation law barred suit only for the initial injury sustained in an occupational setting. The court ruled that an employee could recover for subsequent aggravation of injury occurring due to employer's fraudulent concealment of the employee's condition and its cause. A third case, *White v. Johns-Manville Corp.* (1981), established that seamen and shipyard workers may file claims under admiralty law, thus avoiding state statutes of limitations. Finally, in *Beshada v. Johns-Manville Products Corp.* (1982), strict liability was imposed and state-of-the-art defense tactics were barred.

These four decisions effectively meant that Manville would face more suits with less ability to defend itself. To make disaster complete, by 1982 there were four appellate rulings on the insurance issue; only one would force the cor-

poration's insurers to assume the full cost of litigation and settlements even for early disease claims.[2] The overall result of the conflicting rulings was that insurance companies generally refused to make any payments in asbestos cases, asserting the theory they found most advantageous and inviting litigation (see *Harvard Law Review*, 1984). Manville brought suit against 27 insurance companies but until resolution of the matter was forced to bear all litigation costs itself (Metz, 1982).

Use of the bankruptcy proceeding as a defense was made possible in part by 1978 reforms in the Federal Bankruptcy Code. The new code provides that a reorganization plan may include estimated future liabilities, rather than only considering liabilities already outstanding (11 U.S.C. Sec. 101[4], 1982; 11 U.S.C. Sec. 1123, 1982). Moreover, the new code omitted its predecessor's explicit injunction against the "bad faith" use of the law for inappropriate ends—i.e., simply to evade creditors or litigants (11 U.S.C. Sec. 546, 1977; 11 U.S.C. Table 1, 1982 [Sec. 546 repealed]; see also Gaffney, 1980:210). Prior to 1978, under the good faith requirement, a company would have been required to demonstrate that the court's aid was necessary to regain solvency, not merely financially helpful (Cater, 1982:2029). Chapter 11 of the Bankruptcy Reform Act of 1978, by contrast, pointedly does not require that a debtor be insolvent before filing for reorganization.

The question of when the financial burden of a debtor is sufficiently heavy to legitimate filing for reorganization is an open one. Plaintiff's attorneys asked the bankruptcy court to set aside Manville's petition for reorganization on grounds of "abusing" the bankruptcy process, in effect asking the court to treat the good faith requirement as implicit and regard the company's filing as in bad faith (Lewin, 1982). Their appeal was rejected and Manville was allowed to proceed with reorganization. In the words of

---

[2]These four cases are: *Insurance Company of North America v. Forty-Eight Insulations*, 1980; *Porter v. American Optical Corp.*, 1981; *Keene v. Insurance Company of North America*, 1981; *Eagle-Picher v. Liberty Mutual*, 1982.

U.S. Bankruptcy Judge Lifland, "Manville must not be required to wait until its economic picture has deteriorated beyond salvation to file for reorganization" (Lewin, 1984). Roe (1984:848) has argued at length and on varied grounds that "when future claims are large in relation to firm value there should be an early reorganization that resolves those claims" (see also Jackson, 1986:47–54).

Through reorganization Manville will achieve two key goals: predictable costs and protection of sufficient operating capital. The appointed representative of future claimants joined with attorneys representing current claimants (both victims and commercial creditors) in negotiating a single comprehensive settlement, though some future litigation of the issue of comprehensiveness seems likely. The advance settlement does shield the corporation from further future direct liability. It does so, however, by transferring majority ownership of the company to a trust designed to fund and manage such liability. Protection of the corporation against future liability has taken place only through a fundamental restructuring of corporate ownership. Nonetheless, Manville is being provided with an estimate of the maximum amount of all present and future asbestos health claims, on which basis it can presumably purchase insurance to cover such claims (or otherwise amortize them over an extended period). Punitive damage awards may also be ended by this compensation scheme. While crucial gains for the corporation, they have not been painless for management nor are they likely to please equity investors. In sum, the court required Manville to adopt a much more costly plan than the firm originally proposed.

The court held that epidemiological and other statistical indicators should be the basis for determining the potential total liability and that Manville should provide for most of this liability immediately rather than gradually as cases mature. Claims are to be evaluated by medical experts and adjusted up or down from court-determined standards. The trust is expected to pay out $2.5 to $3 billion. It will be funded by insurance proceeds estimated at $615 million, a bond issue for $1.8 billion, $200 million in cash, 20 percent of future profits (starting four years

after emergence from bankruptcy), and 72 million shares of Manville common stock. With the trust comes an immediate 94 percent dilution in the value of common stock, to be accomplished through a reverse stock split and issuance of new shares. Eleven million of these new shares will be transferred to commercial creditors to compensate them for lost interest on their loans. The largest proportion (from 50 to 80 percent of total Manville common stock) will go to the victims' trust. The stock transferred to the trust will have voting rights only after four years. At that point, however, the trust will become the majority owner of Manville. The company itself will be immune from further suits over asbestos related disease, but claimants dissatisfied with proposed settlements could sue the trust. The trust, to be administered by a court-approved board of trustees, will remain in operation as long as claims are filed.

Manville potentially is liable not only for health related claims, but for property damage claims filed by the owners of buildings from which asbestos must be removed. The reorganization agreement sets aside $125 million in a separate trust to pay property damage claims; this trust will also receive any insurance payments over the $615 million allocated to disease victims and any part of the 20 percent of profits paid to the victims' trust that the trust does not need (Lewin, 1986).

The court officially accepted Manville's reorganization proposal on December 18, 1986. Though various legal challenges were mounted (notably by lawyers for one group of victims and by a common stockholders group), they met with little success (Mitchell, 1986). The company indicated that it expects to emerge from bankruptcy protection in early 1988 (*Wall Street Journal*, 1987).

For over 30 years, Manville executives resisted many paths of action that might have prevented or alleviated the suffering of the victims of asbestos related diseases. Because the diseases have long latency periods, the impact of these corporate decisions continued well beyond that 30-year period. It is important to note that since the mid-1960s, no decisions with regard to ordinary company operations could have undone the bulk of the damage for which the corporation now faces liability. Any change in operating procedures, such as the phasing out of asbestos use or the adoption of higher safety standards, could only have reduced the incidence of disease years in the future.

The most important point is not that Manville or its executives were distinctively bad, but that the scale of the company's operations and the danger of its products made the bad actions of its executives distinctively efficacious. The case history indicates that the increasing size, complexity, and impact of corporate actors, and the resulting rise of new and widespread injuries, pose fundamental challenges to the legal system and, particularly, tort law.

TORT LAW AND CORPORATE RESPONSIBILITY

Part of the interest in the cases of asbestos related diseases is that they bring to the fore a competition between admonitory and compensatory uses of tort law. Modern tort law has taken shape over the past two hundred years largely as a private law analog to criminal law, holding individuals accountable for injuries they could reasonably have been expected to foresee. The English common law had allowed tort claims only under fairly narrow criteria of willful injury and forms of strict liability where certain injuries demanded compensation regardless of their causes or even their avoidability. The right to do certain forms of business thus entailed the responsibility for certain forms of injury.

Modern tort law, however, has relied increasingly on the concept of negligence, or failure to take due precautions. These changes were driven in part by the requirements of expanding commerce, especially the need simultaneously to encourage firms to provide public amenities and consumer goods and to admonish them to do so carefully. Negligence defined the nature of the wrong and the rights of victims to legal remedies, but it focused on the underlying fault that made defendants blameworthy. Punishment was intended to admonish and/or deter. Negligence was gradually stretched to provide for compensa-

tion in cases where its determination was not always obvious. However appropriate to direct, immediate, and obvious injuries, the negligence doctrine was challenged by injuries remote in time or space or whose manifestations were mediated by statistical chance in large populations.

The negligence doctrine was stretched because jurists wanted to see innocent victims compensated. This was partly a simple change in attitudes as egalitarian ideas of justice gained support. It was partly due to growing reliance on the law as substitute for more personal relationships and for welfare institutions to care for those who suffered. Tort law remains a branch of private law, but increasingly it is used to decide cases similar to those of public law, intimately concerned with matters of general public welfare (Calabresi and Bobbitt, 1978; Calabresi, 1985). These changes in tort law and tort decisions were also driven by material changes in social and economic arrangements.

Tort law was not developed to deal with contractual arrangements, family life, or other established relationships. Rather, it focused on injurious contacts among parties with no prior legal relationship (Friedman, 1973:261–64, 409–27; Horowitz, 1977:85–99; White, 1980). Earlier, injuries and accidents took place primarily in direct, face-to-face contacts. Who the parties were was usually readily evident; often they knew each other. As the scale of social organization grew, and new technologies were introduced, "personal injuries" became less personal. More and more social and economic relationships were indirect, mediated by markets, communication technology, and complex organizations. Injuries came before the courts that were very difficult to trace back to individual actions or events. Technological and social changes thus contributed to innumerable hard cases which led jurists and scholars to stretch the doctrine of negligence or suggest its abandonment in favor of strict liability. One problem was establishing the causal agency and thus responsibility for injuries where such actions were taken by or on behalf of complex organizations. Another was how to apportion liability among firms supplying a market for dangerous products when it could not be established which firm's products caused which specific injury (Thompson, 1986: chs. 12, 13).

Tort lawyers and judges also faced more cases in which causation was remote and/or probabilistic. Many insidious injuries, including those related to asbestos exposure, come from actions that affect the statistical distribution of risk rather than from actions that directly cause such injury or disease. A key stumbling block in contemporary insidious injury cases is the difficulty of establishing how much knowledge different parties may reasonably be expected to have about remote and probabilistic causes. From the victim's perspective, it is often difficult both to know the nature and source of one's own injury and to identify other victims. While the perpetrators of such torts are in a better position to understand these causal links, they are not always apparent even to them.

The older tradition of tort law focused on admonishment, with linked subsidiary goals of punishment and deterrence. Prior to 1900, compensation was a consequence of successful tort action, but the major legal purpose was to punish or deter blameworthy conduct (White, 1980:62). Today, tort law focuses more on compensation or restitution than on punishment or retribution. Nonetheless, the two goals coexist, each organizing different areas of tort law (or life), and on occasion competing and sometimes informing and bolstering each other:

Compensation became a primary concern in products liability cases in the 1970s. An admonitory view of the function of tort law assumed that there was nothing unjust about the costs of injuries being borne by injured parties themselves unless the injurer had done something blameworthy. The injustice of no compensation for tort victims lay in the fact that blameworthy injurers were not admonished rather than that injured people were not being compensated. Once the situations where a blameworthy (contributorily negligent) person was deprived of compensation for his injuries came to be regarded as "unjust," a new primary purpose for tort law could be assumed. "Injustice" could not be equated with the absence of compensation for injuries rather than with the failure to admonish blameworthy conduct (White, 1980:164–65).

Tort law seems to be coming full circle in at least one sense: from a preponderance of strict liability to a focus on the doctrine of negligence to what appears to be the introduction of a new version of strict liability (White, 1980; Steiner, 1987). The first shift was accomplished largely by introducing the principle that all citizens owe a duty of care in any of their actions that might affect others; negligence was the failure to exercise this universally required care. The second shift stems centrally from making compensation the primary goal of tort law. It rests on the notion that those who share even to a limited extent in responsibility for an injury should be required to make amends.

A crucial further support for this second shift has been jurists' conviction that insurance was an effective means of distributing the costs of routine risks across a large population. In the influential first edition of his famous text on torts, for example, Prosser (1941:689; see also White, 1980:197–207) argued that the producer was "best able to distribute the risk to the general public by means of prices and insurance." According to this prominent theory of tort law, insurance was a means to allow risky but socially desirable ventures to be undertaken. If such ventures occasionally produce accidents, these costs should not be borne fully by individual victims. Moreover, such costs should be borne by all those venturers who created *risks*, not just by those whose activities produced the actual injury. Just as automobile insurance spread the costs of accidents (some rate of which is an unavoidable by-product of automobile transportation) among all drivers, so product liability insurance was to spread the costs of occasional unforeseen injuries among the wide range of businesses creating consumer products. Insurance also provided a means for individual firms to spread liability across time, making it a predictable cost.

The Corporation as Defendant

Insurance made the compensatory focus of modern tort law possible; the large corporation made it especially important. First, large corporations helped to transform the scale of social organization. Single production facilities grew to employ thousands of people, single companies hundreds of thousands. Organizational and technological complexities helped to make accidents likely; structural rigidity in bureaucratic hierarchies often inhibited efforts to prevent them (Sherman, 1978; Clinard, 1983; Ermann and Lundman, 1987). The very scale of operations in any case was such that even seemingly low probabilities of accidents might produce large absolute numbers of injuries; it was necessary to think in terms of statistical risk rather than only particular cases (Perrow, 1984; Huber, 1985). As the NASA space shuttle disaster recently showed, public bureaucracies can have problems similar to those of private industry.

Beyond this, the corporate form of organization created a basic asymmetry between the two sorts of "persons" who faced each other in litigation. On the one hand were the "natural persons" and on the other were legally created corporations. Each sort of person had the same basic status in tort litigation, but strict liability doctrine came to be invoked to secure compensation precisely when "the typical tort claim arose out of an interaction between persons with unequal power, no previous contractual relations or customary dealings, and imperfect information about risks" (White, 1980:219). Coleman (1982) treats such extreme disparities in wealth, power, and longevity between corporations and human individuals as a defining characteristic of modern society. They also create obvious problems for natural persons who must challenge large corporations in the courts.

One of the crucial ways in which corporations and individuals are asymmetrical is in their ability to control and/or gain access to information. In the asbestos related cases, individuals faced difficulties in finding out about the nature and causation of injuries done to them and in pursuing legal remedies (Schroeder and Shapiro, 1984). Even without the sort of manipulation and bad faith practiced by Manville executives, individuals are unlikely to be able to gather sufficient knowledge to inform their own decision-making adequately without creating still other large-scale collective actors. Unions and "disinterested" medical research organizations were thus instrumental in bringing an effective challenge to Manville's practices. Potential victims of asbestos related diseases are widely dispersed and knit together only loosely. In the ordinary course of events, information—to the extent it is available at all—will spread only slowly and unevenly among potential victims (see Stone, 1975: ch. 18). The exposed population has little social organization through which to undertake collective action.

Even when individuals learn of the possible consequences of exposure, they face substantial costs in any effort to challenge the corporation. They may succeed in obtaining counsel from attorneys willing to take their cases on a contingency basis (something that is easy to do only after a fairly considerable momentum has built up), but they are unlikely to be able to match the financial resources a large corporation can use in litigation. Plaintiff lawyers do have a certain interest in taking on some early cases they will likely lose, because this enables them to prepare better for (and advertise their availability for) eventual winning cases. Nonetheless, plaintiffs are at a disadvantage, especially in the early years of litigation. In the Manville cases it took decades of preparation and trial work before the tide turned in favor of plaintiffs. Moreover, the legal system allows defendants almost unlimited opportunities to increase the costs of the proceedings for their opponents, while it simultaneously restricts the interests of plaintiffs' attorneys in their own work (Rosenberg, 1984: 904–05; see Galanter, 1975, on the advantages of corporations in such litigation).

Individuals also face difficulties in gathering and analyzing information. Major personal injury cases can involve millions of documents and computerized records: statistics on production, distribution and use of hazardous substances, statistics on the health of thousands of workers, testimony or written evidence from hundreds of sources. Gathering such information requires substantial resources and/or enormous time and dedication. A RAND Corporation study indicates that between the early 1970s and the Manville bankruptcy filing in August 1982, the industry and its insurers had spent $606 million to defend asbestos related cases; plantiffs' litigation expenses amounted to $164 million (Kakalik et al., 1983:39; net compensation was $236 million with some cases still pending).

Longevity is another relevant asymmetry between corporations and individuals. Individual life spans are limited while corporations may "live" indefinitely. A corporation may choose to drag litigation on for years, regarding the additional legal costs it pays as negligible compared to its potential liability. Its liability, after all, must be understood not in terms of the single case but as magnified by the thousands of others to which it might lead (Galanter, 1975). Corporate executives, moreover, have little incentive to see a potentially expensive case settled during their tenure of office. Since corporate executives often move from one position to another within a company, or among firms, this can be a major issue. No official wants the extraordinary costs of a disadvantageous settlement to threaten his reputation. Each would rather leave the case pending, as he found it (see Stone, 1980; Roe, 1984:9–10). This is an issue of particular force in the case of long-latent diseases. In the Manville case, no senior actors in the original plan of concealment and manipulation of information are alive to face the consequences of their actions.

This bears on one major argument about how to make corporations more responsible. Simply fining corporations and/or making them pay damages to victims does not produce the intended deterrent effect, this argument goes, because such expenses do not translate into direct financial liability for the individuals who made the blameworthy decisions. Critics of corporations have generally viewed corporate status as a shield illegitimately deflecting punishment from culpable individuals and simultaneously depriving deserving victims of compensation (Nader and Green, 1973; Nader, Green, and Seligman, 1976). Many have called for a legal apparatus (e.g., for Nader, a charter) that affirms the right of government to reach inside the corporations to enforce its own standards of good behavior.

Some defenders of corporations have claimed that they should be exempt from this level of government interference because they are essentially creatures of private contract rather than public concession (Hessen, 1979). In this view, the corporation is neither an entity in itself nor a legal fiction in the sense of Justice Marshall's classic description (in *Dartmouth v. Woodward*) of "an artificial being, visible, intangible, and existing only in contemplation of law." Ironically, this "defense" of corporations harbors serious dangers for them. If the corporation is merely a private association of its members (by which is usually meant its shareholders), then doctrines of limited liability must be called into serious doubt. Either individual employees would be liable (perhaps following some version of the old common law of master and servant) or individual owners would be fully liable, that is, liable to the extent of their assets rather than merely the amount of their initial investment. Yet the modern large company presumably depends on limited liability for its shareholders, if not perhaps for its executives (see Orhnial, 1982).

Corporate charters might be used to build a variety of requirements into the very constitution of corporations. Nader's proposal to use them to reach inside to bring legal action against individuals has little bearing on cases of injuries involving long-latency periods, however, though pressing tort and/or criminal charges against corporate officers may be efficacious in some other cases. Charters might, however, be used to promote corporate social responsibility through internal structural reforms and to produce a more ethical corporate culture (Stone, 1975; Ackerman, 1975). The insidious injury cases lend some support to this idea. Charter provisions could be designed to promote structures that encourage corporations to monitor product and process safety and issue early warnings of potential dangers. But any such provisions would in many ways run counter to the tendency of the tort law to encourage corporations to treat all such information as a potential legal risk and thus minimize both its collection and its dissemination. Of course, it may be desirable that high moral standards rather than minimum criteria of legal acceptability be the goal for managerial (as for all other) behavior.

Punishment vs. Compensation

Whatever the desirability of such reform efforts, they are not likely to be the direct product of tort litigation against corporations. In insidious injuries cases, tort law is best suited to providing compensation to victims. What place, we now need to ask, is left for punishment?

Deciding that compensation should be provided to victims still leaves the question of who should pay? Conventional notions of justice would have blameworthy parties pay. In other words, payment would punish those who have caused injuries; publicizing this punishment would deter others. The Manville case, however, suggests that considerable complexities challenge attempts to apply this simple principle in concrete cases. Focusing solely on the company's blameworthiness leads some to propose dissolving it, thus limiting funds available to compensate future claimants.

Clearly, since the pursuit of profit produces the risk, it seems reasonable to argue that even the least blameworthy corporation is the appropriate source of compensation. It is one-sided for the *New York Times* (1982) to describe asbestos related diseases as a tragedy for "the companies, which are being made to pay the price for decisions made long ago." But those who speak of making the company "suffer" should be pressed to make clear what this means. A company is not a sensory agent capable of "feeling" punishment; any presumed punishment of a corporation must translate into the bad feelings of some set of individuals, whether owners, managers, or other employees. Even though investors might reasonably be held voluntarily to assume the risks associated with financial problems such as those now confronting Manville, punishing them would seem to be plausible primarily as an expiatory ritual, not as a deterrent or source of compensation. At best, the prospect of such "punishment" might encourage future investors to impose demands for clear information as to the "good practices" of firms, that is, to ask for a social audit or certification of due care to minimize actionable injuries. It is not clear that very many investors could conceivably enforce such demands unless they were aided by public monitoring and sanctions for failure to comply. The public information which Manville provided right up to the time of the bankruptcy filing was certainly misleading though apparently not to the point of illegal misrepresentation.

Indeed, insisting on using tort law to effect "punishments" of corporations might lead officers to further restrict or distort information and to resist prompt and just settlement of tort claims. This may include keeping certain top executives ignorant of such information so that they can honestly claim not to know of their own firm's practices or their consequences. "Digging in" of managerial heels is a major problem to be considered in any attempt to deal with insidious injuries. Businesses themselves will be in the best position to detect early signs of insidious diseases. Some form of government regulation may be required to get them to act positively on their knowledge.

There is good reason to think that corporations, unlike individual criminals, will discriminate effectively among severe penalties (see Clinard and Yeager, 1980; Ermann and Lundman, 1982); for instance, between dissolution and large financial costs. As Rosenberg (1984:855) has pointed out, "mass exposure" torts such as the ones at issue in asbestos litigation are "frequently products of the deliberate policies of businesses that tailor safety investments to profit margins." In principle, this should make threats of liability more effective in reducing corporate negligence. The key is for the liability to appear large enough to deter without being so large as to produce strategies of legal delay or manipulation of information.

For corporations confronted with massive tort liability, predictability of costs and hence the possibility of effective strategic planning is crucial. For corporate officers faced with mounting tort claims over long-latent diseases, the availability of a well-managed and eventually more predictable bankruptcy proceeding might provide a more palatable course of action than fighting on and risking dissolution. At that point, executives can no longer solve the corporation's problems by changing corporate practices; they can only choose strategically among responses to the corporation's legal liability.

In the Manville case, bankruptcy makes sense when considered as part of an effort to secure compensation to victims, even though some critics argue that it impeded punishment of Manville and deterrence of future tortfeasors.

Punishment and incentives for prevention were sacrificed to the achievement of compensation. Even under a negligence standard individuals had great difficulty getting a large corporation like Manville to redress (or even address) the wrongs it created; liability in individuals' suits was too ineffective to be considered a significant deterrent.

Making compensation the primary pursuit of the courts simply gives up the notion that tort law should seek to induce either corporate or individual responsibility. As both Posner (1973:214) and White (1980:235) point out, strict liability doctrines also remove some of the incentives for consumers to use products carefully, though possible financial compensation seems unlikely to make individual consumers extraordinarily careless. Whether there is any mechanism to translate potential costs into motivation for good actions in even more doubtful than in comparable cases decided on a "pure" negligence standard. The Manville case presents problems, thus, for an economic theory of tort law such as Posner's (1972) with its contention that proceedings in terms of negligence will effectively motivate prevention as well as punish wrong-doing and compensate victims. Manville's bankruptcy settlement may give pause to other corporate managers considering such a defense against tort liability. But nothing in the tort litigation itself suggests that such managers, in a situation similar to Manville's, would be poorly advised (on soley economic grounds) to hide the problem as long as possible and then fight all lawsuits vigorously. If compensation is the goal, the problems are to find and distribute funds. Corporations, their insurers, and/or the government must establish a fund; and the claims of current victims must be balanced against the rights of expected future claimants. Insurance ordinarily accomplishes this. The possibility of losing insurance coverage in cases of long-latent diseases shifts the burden back to the producer and victim with a minimal actuarial buffer. As in the Manville case, private insurers will often prudently refuse protection even where businesses still operate. Where long-latent disease is at issue the law is unclear as to which insurers are liable and in what proportions

(see also *Indiana Law Review*, 1982; *Harvard Law Review*, 1984). Until the law is clear, victims bear most of the burden of delayed compensation. Any attempt to "punish" the corporation by, for instance, liquidating its assets and dissolving it, will likely benefit current claimants and commercial creditors. This will be at the expense of future sufferers of asbestos related disease, as well as of management, employees, and possible investors.

A government-subsidized fund was one possibility to avoid this sort of fix in the asbestos cases. Manville and other firms only grudgingly gave up hope for this option. Those who hold that punishment and not merely compensation must be a central goal resisted such a scheme. Such resistance was reinforced by the fact that the legislative plans put forward were grossly favorable to the company. In most imaginable cases, an "after-the-fact" legislative solution would involve either shifting a large part of the burden to the general taxpaying public or developing an almost unprecedented mechanism for close government involvement in the running of a "private" business (though see discussion in *Texas Law Review*, 1983).

Failing insurance and government backing, the corporation itself becomes the best source of funds for compensation. Where only moderate amounts are at issue, it may be possible for corporations to handle such claims as self-insurers. Where amounts are much larger, some form of legally enforced protection and reorganization may be essential to secure compensation and to save the company. Bankruptcy reorganization may be the only effective procedure available to balance the claims of future claimants against current ones, and the only means of providing a sufficiently large source of funds to meet the claims of all. It should not be thought that the bankruptcy reorganization necessarily will lead to any very different form of corporate management. The trustees will be bound by a fiduciary responsibility to victims and other creditors much like what boards of directors ordinarily have towards stockholders. Presumably this will be interpreted in the same predominantly financial terms of prudent judgment, namely, a fairly narrow seeking of profit and perhaps growth by means of standard business practices. There is little in our knowledge of corporate boards to suggest that trustees acting by similar standards would implement dramatically new management practices (Herman, 1981).

DISCUSSION

Corporations have both caused insidious injuries and impeded individual and collective efforts to cope with them. At the same time, corporations may also be the only social actors able to compensate their victims. If the corporation did not endure and remain viable, there would often be no one to sue in a case of long-latent disease. There would be no "deep pocket" against which to make legal claims. The only remaining option would be a government-backed compensation scheme.

Similarly, just as individuals are shorter-lived than corporations, small firms are shorter-lived than large ones. Though Manville was the perpetrator (or at least the mechanism) of a large evil, its very size made it a practical source of compensation. The very corporate form and the particular size and power of Manville indeed allowed it and its agents to avoid responsibility for many actions over a long period of time. The structural asymmetry between Manville and those it wronged did contribute to the perpetuation and extension of the wrong. Ironically, however, that same asymmetry helps to provide an effective means of funding those very claims that the corporation ultimately was unable to deflect.

This irony does not rest well with everyone. Brodeur (1986:350) would rather rely more exclusively on tort litigation and see a more punitive justice: "The asbestos litigation was a triumph of justice which is now being betrayed by the thickets of the Bankruptcy Code." Many plaintiff lawyers agreed, at least initially, and they rankled at the suggestions that the tort system "failed," became "clogged" or operated so as best to serve greedy attorneys. Representatives of the asbestos industry have helped to promote such a view, but they have been joined by some powerful shapers of public opinion, including editorial writers for the *New York Times*

(1982), *Wall Street Journal* (1985a), and the then chief justice of the United States (see *Wall Street Journal*, 1985b). The argument is primarily that tort litigation is inefficient and expensive. It also results in a variety of inequities which a uniform claims facility might minimize. While these arguments have some merit, proponents tend to forget the crucial role played by tort litigation in getting Manville to face any responsibility or pay any compensation for its role in the occurrence of asbestos related disease.

But, as we have seen, to praise tort law as a sole and satisfactory solution overlooks some very basic problems. Only a preeminent desire for punishment seems to sustain the demand for exclusive and extreme reliance on tort law. Even those plaintiff attorneys who place compensation ahead of punishment find less "betrayal" than does Brodeur. As Robert Rosenberg (cited in Dahl, 1985), an attorney with the Bankruptcy Court's Committee of Plaintiffs, put it: "If there's enough money for the victims, what difference does it make who pays it?"

Given the difficulties of using the tort law system for effective punishment or admonishment in cases of insidious injuries, we should turn elsewhere for our primary preventive measures. Central to any of these must be recognition that injuries of this sort are inevitable. We show little inclination to give up the technologies or the scale of social organization characteristic of modern production processes and commodity circulation. As a result, some significant rate of insidious injuries will continue. New products that appear benign will prove fatal; diseases will be linked to environmental or occupational exposure to toxins now unrecognized. Traditions of free business and consumer decision-making only accentuate this. In sum, with even the highest possible standards of good business behavior, insidious injuries will be discovered years after they have been caused.

It is, of course, socially desirable both to compensate the victims of these injuries and to minimize their extent. The legal system presently offers few alternatives to the use of tort law as a means of securing compensation, even where long latency periods inhibit its effectiveness. Mandatory participation in government-backed compensation insurance schemes would speed the process of providing for victims, though tort law will no doubt remain a crucial backup and goad. But tort litigation needs to be used sparingly enough to encourage corporations to act responsibly in monitoring the safety of their products and production processes. Epidemiological data needs to be collected continuously to aid in the identification of potential insidious health problems and much relevant information will have to come from firms involved in manufacturing and marketing. It is important to recognize that business corporations are fundamentally public, not private, actors. Their creation partly by contract should not be taken to impede such regulation as is needed to ensure that they gather and disseminate information on product and process safety.

Regulatory apparatuses also need to be in place to coordinate action to minimize further risks when such problems are recognized. But such efforts will be severely impeded if firms' actions are oriented substantially toward defense against future tort liability. And in the absence of an alternative compensation scheme, and especially in the presence of the possibility of claims large enough to bankrupt the country's wealthiest firms, managers are apt to follow in the footsteps of those at Manville who manipulated information then dragged out legal defenses as long as they could. In the end, the Manville reorganization was a fair settlement, but it came much too late. We should hope that procedures for corporate reorganization will be established which are sufficiently well understood and appropriately administered that they can be used as other than a last ditch defense. Whether handled in bankruptcy court or by other agencies, such reorganizations provide an effective way of funding both present and future claims.

REFERENCES

Ackerman, Robin W.
    1975   The Social Challenge to Business. Cambridge, MA: Harvard University Press.

Ashford, Nicholas A.
    1976   Crisis in the Workplace: Occupational Disease and Injury. Cambridge, MA: Masachusetts Institute of Technology Press.

Berman, Daniel M.
    1978   Death on the Job: Occupational Health and Safety Struggles in the United States. New York: Monthly Review Press.

Brodeur, Paul
    1973   Expendable Americans. New York: Viking.
    1986   Outrageous Misconduct: The Asbestos Industry on Trial. New York: Pantheon.

Brown, Vandiver
    1934   Letter to A. J. Lanza, December 10.
    1939   Letter to S. Simpson, May 3.

Calabresi, Guido
    1985   Ideals, Beliefs, Attitudes, and the Law. Syracuse, NY: Syracuse University Press.

Calabresi, Guido and Philip Bobbit
    1978   Tragic Choices. New Haven: Yale University Press.

Cater, Morrow
    1982   "Manville bankruptcy case may prompt Congress to close loophole in law." National Journal November 27: 2029–30.

Chen, E.
    1984   "Asbestos litigation is a growth industry." Atlantic July: 24–32.

Clinard, Marshall
    1983   Corporate Ethics and Crime: The Role of Middle Management. Beverly Hills: Sage.

Clinard, Marshall and Peter C. Yeager
    1980   Corporate Crime. New York: Free Press.

Coleman, James S.
    1982   The Asymmetric Society. Syracuse, NY: Syracuse University Press.

Ermann, M. David and Richard J. Lundman
    1982   Corporate Deviance. New York: Holt, Rinehart, and Winston

Ermann, M. David and Richard J. Lundman, eds.
    1987   Corporate and Governmental Deviance Problems of Organizational Behavior in Contemporary Society. New York: Oxford University Press.

Friedman, Lawrence M.
    1973   A History of American Law. New York: Simon and Schuster.

Galanter, Marc
    1975   "Why the 'haves' come out ahead: Speculations on the limits of legal change." Law and Society Review 9: 95–160.

Goodwyn, W. Richard
1972 The Johns-Manville Story. New York: The Newcomen Society of North America.

Harvard Law Review
1980 "Compensating victims of occupational disease." Harvard Law Review 93: 916-28.
1984 "Adjudicating asbestos insurance liability: Alternatives to contract analysis." Harvard Law Review 97: 739-58.

Hart, Gary
1983 "Let government bear its share." New York Times November 5, Sec. 3: 2.

Herman, Edward S.
1981 Corporate Control, Corporate Power. New York: Cambridge University Press.

Hessen, Robert
1979 In Defense of the Corporation. Stanford, CA: The Hoover Institution.

Hobart, George
1934 Letter to V. Brown.

Horwitz, Morton J.
1977 The Transformation of American Law, 1780-1860. Cambridge, MA: Harvard University Press.

Huber, Peter
1985 "Safety and the second best: The hazards of public risk management in the courts." Columbia Law Review 85: 277-337.

Indiana Law Review
1982 "Asbestos litigation: The insurance coverage question." Indiana Law Review 15: 851.

Jackson, Thomas H.
1986 The Logic and Limits of Bankruptcy Law. Cambridge, MA: Harvard University Press.

Johns-Manville Corporation
1978 Johns-Manville Corporation Annual Report.
et seq.
1982 Debtor's Petition Under Chapter 11.

Kakalik, James S., P. A. Ebener, W.L.F. Felstiner, and M. G. Shanley
1983 Costs of Asbestos Litigation. Santa Monica, CA: RAND Corporation.

Kakalik, James S., P. A. Ebener, W.L.S. Felstiner, G. W. Haggstrom, and M. G. Shanley
1984 Variation in Asbestos Litigation Compensation and Expenses. Santa Monica, CA: RAND Corporation.

Lewin, Tamar
1982 "Asbestos lawyers ask court to curb Manville." New York Times November 9: 29.
1984 "Manville bankruptcy is upheld: Future claims remain issue." New York Times January 24: 27, 32
1986 "A new set of hurdles for Manville." New York Times February 17: 19, 21.

Lublin, Joann
1982 "Occupational diseases receive more scrutiny since the Manville case." Wall Street Journal December 20: 12.

Metz, Robert
1982 "The attraction of Manville." New York Times November 2: 36.

Mitchell, Cynthia F.
1986 "Manville, its bankruptcy plan in hand, girds for the long haul to pay its debts." Wall Street Journal December 8: 8.

Moody's Investors' Service, Inc.
1982 Moody's Industrial Manual Vol. 2. R. P. Hansen (ed.), New York: Moody's Investor's Services.

Nader, Ralph and Mark Green, eds.
1973 Corporate Power in America. New York: Grossman.

Nader, Ralph, Mark Green, and Joel Seligman
1976 Taming the Giant Corporation. New York: W. W. Norton & Co.

Orhnial, T., ed.
1982 Limited Liability and the Corporation. London: Croom Helm.

Perrow, Charles
1984 Normal Accidents. New York: Basic Books.

Posner, Richard A.
1972 "A theory of negligence." Journal of Legal Studies 1: 29-96.
1973 "The theory of strict liability: A comment." Journal of Legal Studies 2.

Prosser, William V.
1941 The Law of Torts. Minneapolis, MN: West.

Roe, Mark J.
1984 "Bankruptcy and mass tort." Columbia Law Review 84: 846-922.

Rosenberg, David
1984 "The causal connection in mass exposure cases: A 'public law' vision of the tort system." Harvard Law Review 97: 851-929.

Schroeder, Elinor P. and Sidney A. Shapiro
    1984   "Responses to occupational disease: The role of markets, regulation and information." The Georgetown Law Journal 72: 1231–1309.

Selikoff, Irving J., J. Chrug, and E. C. Hammond
    1964   "Asbestos exposure and neoplasia." Journal of the American Medical Association 188: 22–26.

Sherman, Lawrence W.
    1978   Scandal and Reform: Controlling Police Corruption. Berkeley, CA: University of California Press.

Simpson, Sumner
    1936   Letter to F. H. Schluter, November 13.
    1939a   Letter to A. S. Rossiter, March 22.
    1939b   Letter to V. Brown, May 4.

Steiner, Henry J.
    1987   Moral Argument and Social Vision in the Courts: A Study of Tort Accident Law. Madison, WI: University of Wisconsin Press.

Stone, Christopher D.
    1975   Where the Law Ends: The Social Control of Corporate Behavior. New York: Harper and Row.
    1980   "The place of enterprise accountability in the control of corporate conduct." Yale Law Journal 90: 1–15.

Texas Law Review
    1983   "Mass tort claims and the corporate tortfeasor: Bankruptcy reorganization and legislative compensation versus the common-law tort system." Texas Law Review 61: 1297–1355.

Thompson, Judith Jarvis
    1986   Rights, Restitution, and Risk: Essays in Moral Theory. W. Parent (ed.), Cambridge, MA: Harvard University Press.

U.S. Congress, House of Representatives, Committee on Education and Labor (HCEL)
    1978   "Asbestos related occupational diseases." Hearings before the Subcommittee on Labor Standards, 95th Congress, 2d session.
    1979   "Occupational diseases and their compensation, part I: Asbestos related diseases." Hearings before the Subcommittee on Labor Standards on H.R. 2740, 96th Congress, 1st session.

    1981   "The attorney general's asbestos liability report to the Congress." 97th Congress, 1st session.
    1982   "Occupational health hazards compensation act of 1982." Hearings before the Subcommittee on Labor Standards on H.R. 5735, 97th Congress, 2d session.

U.S. Congress, House of Representatives, Committee on the Judiciary (HCJ)
    1980   "Corporate criminal liability." Hearings before a subcommittee of the House Committee on the Judiciary on H.R. 4973, 96th Congress, 1st and 2d sessions.

U.S. Congress, Senate, Committee of Labor and Human Resources (SCLHR)
    1980   "Asbestos health hazards compensation act of 1980." Hearings before the Senate Committee on Labor and Human Resources on S. 2847, 96th Congress, 2d session.

Vermeulen, James E. and Daniel M. Berman
    1982   "Asbestos companies under fire." Business and Society Review 42: 21–25.

Wall Street Journal
    1985a   "Bhopal's best hope." August 12: 18.
    1985b   "Manville reorganization delayed by appeal of plan." August 17: 4.

White, G. Edward
    1980   Tort Law in America: An Intellectual History. New York: Oxford.

Cases Cited

Beshada v. Johns-Manville Prods. Corp., 90 N.J. 191,447 A.2d 539 (1982)

Borel v. Fibreboard Paper Prods. Corp., 493 F.2d 1076 (5th Cir. 1973)

Dartmouth v. Woodward, 17 U.S. (4 Wheat.) 518 (1819)

Dishner v. Johns-Manville Corp., No.77–518 (E.D. Va. 1978)

Eagle-Picher Indus. v. Liberty Mut. Ins. Co., 682 F.2d 12 (1st. Cir. 1982)

Flatt v. Johns-Manville Sales Corp., 488 F. Supp. 836 (E.D. Tex. 1980)

Insurance Co. of N. Am. v. Forty-Eight Insulations, Inc., 633 F.2d 1212 (6th Cir. 1980)

Johns-Manville Prods. Corp. v. Super. Ct., 27 Cal.3d 465, 612 P.2d 948, 165 Ca. Rptr. 858 (1980)

In re Johns-Manville Corp., 3 Bankr. L. Rep. (CCH) Para 69 (Bankr. S.D.N.Y. January 23, 1984)

In re Johns-Manville Corp., (Bankr. S.D.N.Y. 1983–5, various dates)

Keene Corp. v. Johns-Manville Prods. Corp., 667 F.2d 1034 (D.C. Cir. 1981)

Porter v. American Optical Corp., 641 F.2d 1128 (5th Cir. 1981)

Vogel v. Johns-Manville Prods. Corp., 363 Ill. 473, 2 N.E.2d 716 (1936)

White v. Johns-Manville Corp., 662 F.2d 234 (4th. Cir. 1981)

AT ANY COST
Corporate Greed, Women, and the Dalkon Shield

Morton Mintz

In January 1971, the A. H. Robins Company began to sell the Dalkon Shield, promoting it as the "modern, superior," "second generation," and, most important, "safe" intrauterine device for birth control. Robins, a major pharmaceutical manufacturer in Richmond, Virginia, distributed 4.5 million of the IUDs in eighty countries before halting sales in the mid-1970s. There followed a catastrophe without precedent in the annals of medicine and law.

The story of the Dalkon Shield lays bare the perils inherent in contemporary business practices and in corporate law, in a system that allows corporations to profit even if they put human beings at risk. The Shield created a disaster of global proportions because a few men with little on their minds except the pursuit of megabucks made decisions, in the interest of profit, that exposed millions of women to serious infection, sterility, and even death. To be sure, the same pursuit finally led Robins, in August 1985, to seek reorganization under Chapter 11 of the Bankruptcy Code. For the uncompensated victims, this may be yet another blow because, critics fear, reorganization could let the company put them at the end of a line of lenders, suppliers, and other creditors.

The problem at the core of such conduct is not simply that corporations have no conscience, but that they are endowed by law with rights beyond those allowed to individuals. Corporations too often act without compassion and, no matter what damage they cause, without remorse. Even worse, they cannot be held accountable, as people can be. You cannot lock up a corporation, or sentence it to hard labor or to the electric chair. And too often the law fails to look behind the corporate veil, to prosecute the individuals who make decisions and act in the name of the corporation.

A human being who would not harm you on an individual face-to-face basis, who is charitable, civic-minded, loving, and devout, will wound or kill you from behind the corporate veil. He may do this without qualm because he has been conditioned to drop a curtain between his private moral and religious self and his corporate immoral and irreligious self. Society at large accepts and, if only by its silence, *validates* such compartmentalization.

Worldwide, the seriously injured victims of the Dalkon Shield could number in the tens of thousands. Nearly all suffered life-threatening forms of the infections known as pelvic inflammatory disease (PID). In the United States alone, PID killed at least eighteen women who had been wearing Shields. Most of the infections impaired or destroyed the women's ability to bear children.

Morton Mintz (1985) "At Any Cost: Corporate Greed, Women, and the Dalkon Shield." *The Progressive* Vol. 49 (November): 20–25.

Not only was the Shield unsafe, it was surprisingly ineffective. The number of wearers who became pregnant with the devices in place was on the order of 110,000, or 5 per cent, a rate nearly five times the one falsely claimed in advertising and promotion to physicians and women, and a rate sharply higher than that for many other IUDs. The exaggerated and bogus claim led women to reject more effective birth control in favor of the Shield, and this led directly to consequences far worse than unwanted pregnancies.

An estimated 60 per cent of the U.S. women who conceived with Shields in place lost their unborn, or about 10,000 more than would have done so had they been wearing other IUDs. Some of these women had elective abortions. Others suffered the previously rare miscarriages called *spontaneous abortions*. Others, in the fourth to sixth months of pregnancy, experienced the still rarer infected miscarriages, or *septic spontaneous abortions*. By the count of the Food and Drug Administration (FDA), 248 women, just in this country, endured this dangerous, Shield-related complication. For fifteen of them, these septic abortions were fatal.

Hundreds of women throughout the world who conceived while wearing the Shield gave birth prematurely, in the final trimester, to children with grave congenital defects, including blindness, cerebral palsy, and mental retardation. No one can pinpoint the exact number of such women, partly because no one knows how many times women or their doctors failed to make a proper connection between the Shield and the premature birth of a defective baby.

Robins distributed about 2.86 million Shields in the United States, and doctors implanted them, by the company's estimate, in 2.2 million women. Abroad, Robins distributed about 1.71 million Shields, and in June 1974 it estimated that 800,000 to one million were implanted.

In 1974, increasing and alarming numbers of Shield-related spontaneous septic abortions became known to the FDA, and the agency asked Robins to suspend Shield sales in the United States. It did so on June 28, 1974.

In 1975, a year after the suspension of Shield sales here, Martina Langley was a volunteer at a family-planning clinic in El Salvador. Now a lawyer in Austin, Texas, she recalls that the only IUD the clinic's doctors were inserting was the Shield, and that some clinics in El Salvador continued to implant Shields until 1980.

"Sometimes the doctor would say to the patient, 'This is from the United States and it's very good,' " Langley told David Phelps, a Washington correspondent for the *Minneapolis Star and Tribune*. Then, she said, the doctor would motion toward her and tell the woman, "She is from the United States and people [there] use it." Figures are simply unavailable from most of the countries where the Shield was used. My guess is that Shield-related PID killed hundreds—possibly thousands—of women outside of the United States.

Dr. Richard P. Dickey, a former member of the Food and Drug Administration's obstetrical and gynecological devices advisory panel, has seen first-hand the conditions faced by a woman who suffers PID. An infected Shield wearer "where there are no doctors, no antibiotics, she's going to die," he told me.

Today, more than a decade after Shield sales officially ended in the United States, its legacies of death, disease, injury, and pain persist. Even women who have had the Shield removed are not out of danger. Because PID is commonly not an affliction that is simply treated and is then over and done with, large numbers of Dalkon Shield wearers suffer chronic pain and illness, sometimes requiring repeated hospitalization and surgery. Many have waged desperate battles to bear children despite severe damage to their reproductive systems.

More cheerless news came last April from two studies funded by the National Institutes of Health. They showed that childless IUD wearers who have had PID run a far higher risk of infertility if their devices were Shields than if they were other makes. Not even women who still wear the Shield with no apparent problem are safe: They run the risk of suddenly being stricken by life-threatening PID. In the words of Miles W. Lord, who retired recently as Chief District Judge for Minnesota, they are wearing "a deadly depth charge in their wombs, ready to explode at any time."

The exact number of women still wearing the Shield is unknown. By early 1983, some FDA officials and gynecologists were confident that few American women, probably only hundreds, still used it. Other qualified observers, however, were estimating the figure to be much higher, anywhere from 80,000 to more than half a million.

Certainly the response to Robins's own call-back campaign of October 1984 suggests the higher figures are closer to the mark. By February 1, 1985, a $4 million advertising drive, which urged women still wearing the Shields to have them removed at Robins's expense, had drawn more than 16,000 telephone calls on toll-free hotlines; by the end of March, 4,437 women had filed claims for Shield removals. The claims were flowing in at the dramatic rate of more than 100 a week.

Mary Beth Kornhauser, a screenwriter in West Hollywood, California, was thirty-one when I interviewed her last December. In its essentials, her story is similar to that of countless other women whose quest for safe and effective birth control led them to trust their physicians, who in turn trusted the manufacturer.

Mary was first fitted with a Shield when she was eighteen. She began having dangerous, extremely painful, and recurring pelvic infections. From the start, her misfortune was compounded by physicians whose incompetent diagnoses, such as that she was experiencing a nervous breakdown, destroyed her chances for a full and swift recovery.

In October 1972, one physician pronounced her seriously infected and removed her Shield; he did not properly treat the infection and intimated that she had gotten it because of a promiscuous life style. After seven terrible years of misdiagnosis and illness she was finally deprived of her ability to bear a child. Here is her description of the events directly preceding the "total hysterectomy" she suffered at age twenty-five:

"In 1978, I started getting sick cramps, vomiting, high fever, the same spells that had come up periodically. I went to a doctor, and he gave me oral antibiotics, which didn't work.

So I went back to the University of California at Los Angeles Medical Center, where a doctor recommended me to . . . Dr. Charles E. Hamrell in Santa Monica, and he immediately put me in the hospital.

"I was very infected with tubo-ovarian abscesses, one the size of a grapefruit, one the size of an orange. I was apparently about ready to explode. To try to control the infection to prevent it from spilling into the abdominal cavity, Dr. Hamrell put me in Santa Monica Hospital for serious intravenous antibiotic therapy, by which I mean that three different antibiotics were pumped into me, one each hour."

After eight days in the hospital, Mary returned to her apartment, sensing that she was only having a reprieve: Hamrell had prepared her for the possibility of a radical hysterectomy. She took antibiotics orally and was cared for by her sister, who flew in from the Midwest, and her mother, who came from Maryland. Two weeks later, Hamrell had to operate. It was February 15, 1979—one day less than seven years after her Dalkon Shield had been inserted.

Mary filed suit against Robins in November 1979. When her lawyer, John T. Baker, prepared a "statement of facts," she said, "it read like Watergate, except that this was my life. You know, charges such as reckless disregard of truth, fraud. The reality of seeing this in print, it was staggering. But the real truth was that what they did was criminal, and that criminal charges should have been brought against the persons responsible.

"That there was a conspiracy by Robins executives to hide the truth is what got me. The fact that Americans, especially in pharmaceutical companies, would so knowingly ravage women, and get away with it, was staggering. . . . You'd think that when people deal in pharmaceutical medicine, they'd be honorable people. . . .

"It's worse than abortion. They took away the right of someone to decide to have children. Losing the ability to choose whether I wanted a family—that was the hardest thing for me to get over."

Robins sent her pretrial interrogatories, but did not move to take her deposition. "They went right to trying to settle, because, I believe, I had a strong case," she said. At the same time, Mary said she did not want to go to trial. She found herself unable to bear the prospect of litigating for two to five more years, "never able to put the pain behind me, wondering when I would have to completely relive the experience in a trial situation. . . . I had had enough pain caused by them. . . .

"A lot of things had been blown apart by the hysterectomy; it was an intensely painful period in my life. I was not emotionally stable because of it and its ramifications. I had lost ten pounds in two days. I wanted to heal myself and I knew I couldn't if I had to dredge everything up. I had already waited two years for the setting of a trial date. Money's fine, but were they going to give me my ovaries back? Like, yes, Your Honor, ladies and gentlemen of the jury, are you going to give me a boy child and a girl child? Maybe for that I would have waited for trial."

In February 1982, Mary settled out of court.

Peggy J. Mample, thirty-two years old when I interviewed her in February, is one of several hundred mothers who conceived while wearing a Dalkon Shield and gave birth prematurely, in the third trimester, to a child with a grave birth defect. She was nineteen when she had Melissa, who has cerebral palsy and will be in a wheelchair for life. "Melissa is very intelligent," she told me. "Her only disability is that she can't walk." At home, the child moves about by crawling, but she attends regular classes in a public elementary school.

Peggy Mample is also among the hundreds of mothers who were themselves physically unharmed or not seriously harmed, by the Shield while, unknown to them, it attacked their unborn children.

She learned she was pregnant in February 1972. At the time, the medical profession was divided as to the wisdom of removing an IUD from a pregnant woman, and her obstetrician was among the physicians who believed the odds were fifty-fifty that removal of the Shield would induce a miscarriage.

The Robins Company, which had made no studies at the time of the IUD's potential to induce premature births or of the possible consequences of such births, was making a soothing promotional claim that it would abandon two years later. As the fetus grew, Robins claimed, the Dalkon Shield would be "pushed gently aside" and no harm would befall either the fetus or the mother. The obstetrician's advice was to leave the Shield in place and go to term, and Peggy agreed. She then gave birth prematurely to Melissa on July 22, 1972.

She had no basis for implicating the Shield until almost nine years later. On April 19, 1981, when she was living in Seattle, the CBS investigative news program "60 Minutes" included a scorching segment on "the disaster of the Dalkon Shield." A friend who saw the television program called to tell her about it and to ask if the IUD she had worn was a Shield. This led her to consult a lawyer and, shortly after, to sue Robins.

Peggy Mample's lawyers, Jane I. Fantel and John J. Davids, argued to the jury that the cerebral palsy was the ultimate result of Robin's false effectiveness claims, of its failure to do studies on the Shield's potential to cause premature births, and of its related failure to investigate the consequences of such births.

Checking around the country before and during the trial, Fantel and Davids found thirty more children of Shield wearers who had been born prematurely in the third trimester with major congenital defects. They told me that Robins initially resisted their demands for data on such children but finally confirmed the number.

Actually, according to trial testimony by Dr. David A. Eschenbach of the University of Washington, an expert on the adverse effects of IUDs, the total number of such children in the United States was 200 to 300.

The jury awarded $125,000 to Mrs. Mample, but nothing to Melissa, holding that a causal relation had not been established between the Shield and her premature birth and cerebral palsy. Mample then filed a new lawsuit for damages for Melissa. In June 1984, when Melisa was almost twelve, a second jury returned a verdict for her. Although the sum is secret, it was well above an initial offer by Robins to settle for $1.4 million.

Mample now lives in Boise, Idaho. She is still

The paradox by which immersion in the corporation washes away personal responsibility is perfectly captured in the figure of E. Claiborne Robins, builder and chairman of the *Fortune* 500 company that bears his name. A towering presence in American philanthropy, he has given away truly astonishing sums in gifts to a broad array of worthy causes.

In 1969, he gave $50 million to the University of Richmond, an unrestricted gift said by the university to have been the largest by a living person ever made to an institution of higher education. Since then, Robins and his family have given at least $50 million more to the university and to various other causes. In December 1983, *Town and Country* magazine listed him among the top five of "The Most Generous Americans."

A Baptist, Robins was nominated by the Richmond chapter of B'nai B'rith International for the Jewish service organization's Great American Tradition Award. At the presentation banquet in June 1982, E. Bruce Heilman, president of the University of Richmond, was the principal speaker. "Truly the Lord has chosen you as one of His most essential instruments," he told Robins. "We applaud you for the high accomplishment of always exhibiting a steadfast and devoted concern for your fellow man. . . . Your example will cast its shadows into eternity, as the sands of time carry the indelible footprints of your good works."

—M.M.

enraged when speaking about the company. "I just think it's absolutely incredible that a large corporation can do this to the American public, using us as guinea pigs," she says. "Needless to say, I don't buy Robin's products any more. . . . I just experienced so many emotions—the anger, the shock, of knowing what large corporations, what *this* corporation, did to my child. . . .It's absolutely incredible that the American public puts up with it, that they don't do something about it."

The anger of the Shield's victims has been fueled by Robins's consistent stonewalling and professions of innocence and ignorance. In the face of several thousand settlements, multimillion-dollar court awards of punitive damages, and its own Shield removal campaign, the claims of innocent ignorance seem incredible, but persist. At a series of depositions taken in 1984 by plaintiff's lawyer Dale Larson, E. Claiborne Robins swore that he was unable to recall ever having discussed the Shield with his son, E. Claiborne Robins Jr., the company's chief executive officer and president.

"You certainly knew, when you started marketing this device, that pelvic inflammatory disease was a life-threatening disease, did you not?" Larson asked. "I don't know that," Robins testified. "I have never thought of it as life-threatening." Did he know it could destroy fertility? "Maybe I should, but I don't know that," he swore. "I have heard that," he added. "I am not sure where."

Larson drew similar answers from Carl Lunsford. Since 1978, when he became senior vice president for research and development, Lunsford has been in charge of the company's medical department and thus the highest-ranking executive with specific jurisdiction over the Shield's safety. He is a chemist whose involvements with the Shield date back to the premarketing year of 1970.

Lunsford swore he recalled no "expressions of concern" by any company official about PID, and did not remember having "personally wondered" about the toll it was taking. He had not tried to find out how many users died. He had not "personally reviewed" any studies of the Shield's safety or effectiveness in preventing conception. Did he have "any curiosity" about why the company, a few months before, had paid $4.6 million, mostly in punitive damages, to settle seven Shield lawsuits? The answer was "no."

In February 1977, extremely few of the more than 800,000 American women believed to be wearing the Shield had the faintest notion that the devices were becoming more hazardous with each passing day. But Bradley Post, a leading plaintiff's lawyer, did know of the danger, and so he wrote a letter to the company. He asked that Robins mail a corrective "Dear Doctor" letter, partly to urge "immediate removal of devices in use."

Upon receiving no response, Post sent a second letter. He wrote that he had just learned of deaths of two young women, that the circumstances were clearly causally related to their Shields, and that he was concerned about how many more fatalities and serious injuries would have to occur before Robins would take preventive action. No response came to this plea, either.

Four years later, a sequence of deaths began to be reported among long-time Shield users who were not pregnant. The first, in November 1981, was a Los Angeles woman; the second, in April 1983, was Eugenie Standeford, thirty-four of New Orleans. Ten months later, on February 29, 1984, Judge Lord pleaded for a recall in an instantly famous courtroom reprimand to three senior company officers. He told E. Claiborne Robins Jr., the company's chief executive officer, Carl Lunsford, the senior vice president, and William A. Forrest Jr., the vice president and general counsel:

"The only conceivable reasons you have not recalled this product are that it would hurt your balance sheet and alert women who already have been harmed that you may be liable for their injuries. . . .If this were a case in equity, I would order that your company make an effort to locate each and every person who still wears this device and recall your product. But this court does not have the power to do so. I must therefore resort to moral persuasion and a personal appeal to each of you. . . . You are the corporate conscience. Please, in the name of humanity, lift your eyes above the bottom line. . . . Please, gentlemen, give consideration to tracing down the victims and sparing them the agony that will surely be theirs."

Robins contended, however, that no campaign was needed, because the Shield was no more hazardous than rival IUDs.

Eighteen days after Judge Lord's appeal, Christa Berlin, forty-one, was admitted to Los Angeles County–University of Southern California Medical Center with lower abdominal pain and fever. The diagnosis was a pelvic abscess. Antibiotics in high doses were injected into her, but the condition worsened, requiring drastic surgery including a hysterectomy. After the operation her condition improved for a time, only to deteriorate again.

"Despite intensive care and cardiorespiratory support," said Dr. Charles M. March, the chief gynecologist, in a letter to the company, "she expired on the eighteenth postoperative day." He pointed out that Berlin had worn a Shield for many years. In October 1984, six months after she died, Robins finally announced a recall campaign. It is reasonable to suggest that Eugenie Standeford, Christa Berlin, and other women might not have died, and that thousands of other women would not have suffered pain and agony, if Robins had acted earlier. But Robins consistently claimed—and continues to claim—that the Dalkon Shield was safe and effective when "properly used." Robins executives insist that they did not know of any special hazard. But they did know, and they chose to do nothing—until it was much too late.

What does the Dalkon Shield catastrophe teach us? Not that the A. H. Robins Company was a renegade in the pharmaceutical industry. Yes, Robins knowingly and willfully put corporate greed before human welfare; suppressed scientific studies that would ascertain safety and effectiveness; concealed hazards from consumers, the medical profession, and government; assigned a lower value to foreign lives than to American lives; behaved ruthlessly toward victims who sued, and hired outside experts who would give accommodating testimony. Yet almost every other major drug company has done one or more of these things, some have done them repeatedly or routinely, and some still continue to do so.

Nor does the Shield catastrophe teach us that the pharmaceutical industry is unique. Cigarette companies profit from smoking, the single greatest cause of preventable disease and death. Knowingly and willfully, automobile manufacturers have sold cars that would become rolling incinerators in rear-end collisions; chemical companies have sold abroad carcinogenic pesticides that are banned here; makers of infant formula have, in impoverished Third World countries, deprived babies of breast milk, the nearly perfect food; assorted industries have dumped poisonous wastes into the environment; coal companies have falsified records showing the exposure of miners to the particles that cause black lung disease; military contractors have supplied defective weapons to the armed services.

No, the lesson of the Dalkon Shield catastrophe is not that Robins alone behaved in an immoral or unexpected fashion, but that, first, the corporate structure itself—oriented as it is toward profit and away from liability—is a standing invitation to such conduct; second, the global scale of contemporary marketing has made hazardous corporate activities more perilous to ever larger numbers of people, and, third, all the deterrents and restraints that normally govern our lives—religion, conscience, criminal codes, economic competition, press exposure, social ostracism—have been overwhelmed.

Government provides insufficient and erratic protection, in part because it is subject to political pressure from both Congress and the corporations themselves, and in part because of the lethargy of entrenched bureaucracy. Thus, despite evidence produced by trial lawyers that rotting tail strings put large numbers of women at risk, the Food and Drug Administration did nothing to protect Shield wearers for nine yers, from the time the Shield went off the market in 1974 until 1983, when a study by the Centers for Disease Control incriminated the device.

The FDA never acted on a petition filed by the National Women's Health Network in April 1983 for a recall, to be paid for by Robins, to ensure retrieval of the Shield "from all women who currently wear it" and for imposition of criminal penalties. I am not suggesting that we

should abandon Government regulation, but only that we must recognize its limitations. As it stands now, it often provides the illusion, but not the substance, of adequate protection.

Modern society cannot function without the large organization. It manages our great endeavors; it brings us great good. The need today is to stop the individuals who run corporations from inflicting harm. This will not be done by weakening or eliminating existing deterrents and restraints, such as Federal regulators; our hopes lie in strengthening them and adding new ones.

For the foreseeable future, there is no prospect of enacting legislation embodying the powerful moral command in Leviticus 19:16: "Neither shalt thou stand idly by the blood of thy neighbor." Not so long as Ronald Reagan is President. Not so long as the likes of George Bush may succeed him. Not so long as Congress allows special interests to control election financing. And not so long as Americans remain content to live with the paradoxical proposition that harm knowingly and willfully inflicted on them is to be punished, even by death, if done for personal reasons, but is to be unpunished, not even by a day in jail, if done for corporate reasons.

But even in today's political climate, growing numbers of Americans have awakened to the paradox. They have become aware, in part through the repercussions of the Shield disaster, of the impossibility of reconciling personal responsibility with corporate immunity; they know that the proposition is fraudulent. As the public mood becomes more receptive to efforts to hold individuals accountable for corporate actions, we can expect prosecutors, governors, and legislators in many states to make such efforts, and to earn public approval for doing so.

Only last summer in Illinois, three former executives of Film Recovery Systems, Inc., in Elk Grove Village were successfully prosecuted for murdering a sixty-one-year-old Polish immigrant who had inhaled cyanide used to recover silver from used X-ray film. The murder charges, brought by Cook Country prosecutors, were said to be the first in a work-related death. Circuit Judge Ronald J. P. Banks sentenced the executives to twenty-five years in prison and $10,000 fines. Such prosecutions must proliferate, and state office-holders and candidates must make passage of tougher laws an issue. The press and clergy, too, will have to take the stand that a person's criminal and immoral conduct is criminal, period, and that no ethical counter-argument exists.

Judge Lord saw the absurdity of condemning what a man did in a bedroom but not in a boardroom when he said: "We still haven't grasped that the man who assaults women from an office chair is as grave a sinner as the man who assaults a woman in an alley." Surely the time has come to extend the definition of immoral conduct into the boardroom and the corporate office.

THE SPACE BETWEEN LAWS
The Problem of Corporate Crime in a Transnational Context*

Raymond J. Michalowski
University of North Carolina at Charlotte

Ronald C. Kramer
Western Michigan University

Transnational corportions (TNCs)[1] engage in a wide variety of socially-injurious actions (Barnet and Muller, 1974; Simon and Eitzen, 1986). These harmful corporate acts raise a number of important sociological questions. One central set of questions concerns the conceptualization of these corporate harms for purposes of criminological research. Some have argued that the concept of crime only refers to criminal convictions and violations of criminal law (Shapiro, 1983; Tappan, 1947). Others have proposed that the traditional definition of crime be expanded to include violations of civil and regulatory law, as well as violations of specific criminal statutes (Blum-West and Carter, 1983; Clinard and Yeager, 1980; Schrager and Short, 1978; Sutherland, 1940, 1949). Still others claim that state definitions are too restrictive and unduly influenced by corporate power, and therefore, should be abandoned in favor of broader social definitions of crime based on concepts such as human rights (Schwendinger and Schwendinger, 1970; Tift and Sullivan, 1980).

The increasing global reach of modern transnational corporations aggravates the difficulties of arriving at a satisfactory conception of corporate crime. TNCs at times engage in practices which, while they would be illegal in their home nations, are legal in a number of host nations. The ability of TNCs to have a significant influence on the legal climate in host countries further renders the particular laws of these nations an inadequate basis for the study of corporate crime.

The purpose of this paper is to contribute to the resolution of this conceptual dilemma. The first step, following Blum-West and Carter (1983), is to separate the study of the organization and causation of socially-injurious corporate actions from a consideration of the socio-political definition of these acts. This distinction creates two "research domains" (Blum-West and Carter, 1983:552) or "paradigms" (Kramer, 1985:472). In the first paradigm, the objective

© 1987 by the Society for the Study of Social Problems. Reprinted from *Social Problems,* Vol. 34, No. 1, February 1987, pp. 34–53, by permission.

*We would like to thank David Ermann, David Kowalewski, Martha Huggins, Marjorie Zatz, and several anonymous reviewers for helpful comments on an earlier draft of this paper. Correspondence to: Michalowski, Department of Sociology and Anthropology, University of North Carolina at Charlotte, NC 28223.

[1]There is an ideological distinction and a political debate over whether the term "transnational corporation" or the designation "multinational corporation" should be used to name the modern world-company. The term *trans*/national implies an entity with an existence above and beyond the states in which it operates, while "multinational" suggests only a business with operations *in* more than one country. We use the term "transnational" here for two reasons. First, we agree with the theory that the corporations in question have an existence that *trans*/cends the nation state. Second, the designation "transnational corporations" or "TNCs" is consistent with the majority of the United Nations documents regarding business across borders.

is to explain (and eventually control) the harmful corporate actions of TNCs. Corporate crime researchers operating within this paradigm need to develop their own behavioral definitions to delimit the subject matter and identify cases for study. We will offer such a definition in this paper.

The definitional paradigm is concerned with the socio-political construction of legal definitions of corporate acts that cause social injury. The goal of this paradigm is to understand the historical origins and development of laws and political labels concerning harmful corporate behavior. This corporate criminalization process has been studied almost exclusively at the level of the nation state. However, we intend to show that the spread of TNCs requires that we broaden this focus in two ways: by examining the social construction of political labels in the international arena as exemplified by the development of United Nations codes of conduct for TNCs, and by incorporating what we term *analogous social injuries* within the scope of corporate crime research.

TNCS AND THE RELOCATION OF CORPORATE HAZARDS

Over the last quarter century, foreign investment by TNCs has expanded dramatically (United Nations, 1978:36). In the 20 years from 1960 to 1980, the revenues of TNCs grew tenfold—from 199 billion dollars to 2,155 billion dollars—with U.S. based corporations accounting for 50 percent of this growth (Cavanaugh and Clairmonte, 1983:17). By 1983, the worldwide profits of TNCs had reached a record high of 130 billion dollars (*Multinational Monitor*, 1984:11). This internationalization of corporate activity necessitates an expansion of corporate crime research beyond its dominant focus on offenses by corporations in their home countries.[2]

2For example see: Clinard (1946); Clinard and Yeager (1980); Conklin (1977); Denzin (1977); Edelhertz (1970); Farberman (1975); Geis (1967); Hartung (1950); Leonard and Weber (1970); Shapiro (1984); Shover (1980); Sutherland (1940, 1949); Vaughan (1983).

While, on a dollar basis, foreign investment in developed nations exceeds that in developing nations (Hamilton, 1983:3; United Nations, 1978:40; U.S. Department of Commerce, 1984:8), it is transnational investments *in developing nations* that pose the greatest likelihood of injurious corporate activity, and which raise the most perplexing problems for the definition and study of corporate crime. There are several reasons for this.

First, the most significant change in patterns of foreign investment since the Second World War has been the increased location of TNC industrial facilities in developing nations (United Nations, 1978:40–41). Three-fourths of all U.S. companies with sales over 100 million dollars had manufacturing facilities in other countries by 1975 (United Nations, 1978:222). By 1977, developing nations had surpassed developed ones in dollar value as locations for manufacturing by U.S. industries (U.S. Department of Commerce, 1981:159). Reimportation of overseas assembly by U.S. companies increased five-fold between 1969 and 1983, and in the textiles and electronics industries more than half of all current sales by U.S. corporations are now assembled abroad (Grunwald and Flamm, 1985:12–13). As TNCs export their industrial operations to developing nations, many of the hazards of industrial production and the associated possibilities for corporate crime are relocated from developed to developing countries. Moreover, as the fatal poisoning of over 2,000 residents of Bhopal, India dramatized (Hazarka, 1984:1), the settlement patterns, population density, and limited disaster preparedness of developing nations means that, when problems do occur, the human and environmental costs are likely to be greater than those resulting from similar incidents in developed countries.

Second, the growth in consumer exports to the Third World, as well as the increased local production of consumer goods by TNCs in developing nations, has generated significant consumer safety issues. Differences in marketing practices of TNCs in home versus host nations, variations in the provision of information by TNCs regarding product hazards, and variations in cultural practices regarding product usage has led to unnecessary injury, illness, and death for Third World consumers of TNC products (Mattelart, 1983).

Finally, in comparison to developed nations, developing nations frequently have fewer legal controls over workplace, environmental, and consumer hazards of industrial production (Braithwaite, 1984; Castleman, 1975; Dewar, 1978; Vieira, 1985). Therefore, the potential for corporations to behave in socially-injurious ways in developing nations is greater. For these reasons the growing internationalization of business points to developing nations as a significant emerging arena for injurious corporate activity.

TNCS AND CORPORATE DEVIANCE IN THE THIRD WORLD

In recent years corporate injuries to workers, physical environments, and consumers in developing nations have revealed significant problems with respect to the control of corporate activity in these countries. We will explore each of these arenas, with particular attention to injurious actions that arise in the space between legal systems—actions which were prohibited in home nations, but permissible in the host countries where they occurred.

Working Conditions

According to the International Labor Organization (1985:55), industrial workers in TNCs in developing nations "suffer from more safety and health problems than similar workers in the developed countries." While in some cases TNC manufacturing operations provide better working conditions than locally-owned factories (Blake, 1980; International Labor Organization, 1985:44), it is the comparison between TNC operations in home and host countries, rather than between TNCs and local conditions, that raises the most perplexing questions for the study of injurious corporate activities.

In a number of instances, occupational safety and other working conditions in TNC operations have been found to fall below those mandated by law in more developed countries. The ex-

posure of workers in electronics assembly plants to levels of carcinogens and other toxic materials beyond those allowed in the United States, for instance, has been one of the consequences of the exportation of this "clean" industry (LaDou, 1984). In the more obviously "dirty" industries such as asbestos and chemical production, foreign workers in U.S. subsidiaries have been knowingly exposed to toxic levels that were illegal in the United States. In 1972 for instance, Amatax, a Pennsylvania asbestos yarn mill, moved its entire production facility to Mexico to take advantage of the fact that Mexico had no laws regulating exposure of workers to asbestos fibers. Similarly, in 1974 Raybestos-Manhattan acquired 47 percent of the stock in a Venezuelan asbestos plant in order to take advantage of Venezuelan law which allows higher levels of airborne asbestos fibers than does the Occupational Safety and Health Administration (OSHA) in the United States (Castleman, 1979). In a similar case, Arasco, the only U.S. producer of arsenic, moved its entire operation to Mexico when OSHA lowered the U.S. limit for exposure to airborne arsenic from 500 to 4 micrograms per cubic meter of air (Mattelart, 1983:102). In the electronics industry, Third World workers in U.S. subsidiaries have been found to suffer eye strain and eye failure due to constant peering into microscopes without the benefit of rest breaks on company time required by law in the United States (Fuentes and Ehrenreich, 1983:6).

Industrial operations by some TNCs in developing host countries have used wage and employment practices prohibited in their more developed home nations. In some cases, work is contracted out to home workers at piece rates which require a level of effort comparable to nineteenth-century garment sweatshops. These contract workers enjoy no benefits in terms of holidays, health insurance, sick leave or pensions—all of which are legally-protected worker rights in more developed nations (Fernandez-Kelly, 1983:118). Likewise, the practice of using extended "probationary" periods during which workers (often women) are paid a lower wage rate and then "laid off" just prior to completing this period would be illegal under U.S. labor law (Fuentes and Ehrenreich,

1983:9-10). As Fernandez-Kelly (1983:114) found in the "maquiladoras" factories of the Mexican border, a variation of this theme is to bring prospective workers in for a "test" during which they spend a day or more sewing garments for no pay in the hopes of possible employment. Ong (1983:431) suggested that employers also deliberately keep workers on "temporary status" for prolonged periods to minimize the risks of unionization. This strategy makes it easy to fire workers who organize or join unions.

Environmental Pollution

In some instances TNCs have located and/or relocated high-pollution industries in less-developed countries in order to escape the pollution control costs imposed by environmental protection laws in their home nation. Blake and Walters (1976:159) have suggested that TNCs "will be very sensitive to disparities among various [national] pollution control standards which affect production costs and competitiveness in international trade" as a means of expanding or protecting profit margins. This sensitivity reflects the fact that pollution control costs in the United States are higher than in most other countries (Pearson and Pryor, 1978:170). Robert Strauss (1978:451), President Carter's chief trade negotiator, warned in 1978 of a developing "pattern of flight" as U.S. companies are drawn to developing nations with less costly pollution control laws. Castleman (1978:3) similarly noted that "hazard export is emerging as a driving force in new plant investment in many hazardous and polluting industries." In some cases entire industries involving highly toxic substances such as asbestos, arsenic, mercury, and benzidene dyes have been exported to rapidly developing nations such as Korea, Mexico, Brazil, India, and Ireland (Leonard and Duerksen, 1981:55). Even computer and electronics assembly, once through to be "clean" industries, often expose the environments of developing nations to a wide range of toxic substances that are more closely regulated in the United States (*Cultural Survival*, 1981; *Dollars and Sense*, 1984:6).

There has been some disagreement over whether pollution control costs actually play a significant role in location decisions (Flamm, 1985:77-78; Randall, 1977:v). However, the debate over the relative importance of pollution regulations for location decisions speaks only to the question of corporate motivation, not the consequences of corporate behavior. Even if they are not actively seeking "pollution havens," in many developing nations TNCs remain legally free to expose the water, air, soil, and bodies of workers to hazardous substances at rates higher than those allowed in their home countries (Vieira, 1985).

In addition to the problem of pollutants produced by TNCs operating in host countries, hazardous waste produced *in developed countries* has begun to find its way into developing nations. Some TNCs have sought to avoid the costs of mandated controls on hazardous waste storage in their home nation by transporting wastes to countries which have few or no legal controls on hazardous waste disposal (Centre on Transnational Corporations, 1985:59-60). In these cases, the TNCs involved are clearly acting to circumvent laws in their home nations rather than simply being passive beneficiaries of the difference in laws between home and host nations.

Consumer Safety

According to the U.N. Centre on Transnational Corporations (1985:58) "the one issue that has generated the greatest emotion and controversy in the 1980s regarding transnational corporations. . .is the exportation of products deemed to be harmful to health and the environment." Several cases in recent years have dramatized the kinds of hazards consumers in developing nations face when TNCs circumvent product regulations in their home nations.

The export of children's sleepwear treated with the carcinogenic flame retardant Tris, after the sale of such sleepwear was banned in the United States, was one of the first cases of knowingly-exported consumer hazards to receive widespread attention (*New York Times*, 1978:26). In the late 1970s, A. H. Robins Company arranged (with the help of United States Agency for International Development) for the distribution of the Dalkon Shield intrauterine device in a number of developing countries. This overseas market was sought after Robins already knew that the Shield was responsible for 20,000 cases of serious uterine infection, that it had resulted in several thousand hysterectomies among its users in the United States, and that the product would soon be banned at home (Dowie and Johnston, 1976; Mintz, 1985). In another case, Parke-Davis, a U.S. pharmaceutical comany, successfully promoted the drug chloramphenicol on a non-prescription basis in 39 nations but provided no information concerning its dangerous and sometimes fatal side effects—even though the drug was banned in the United States and Japan (Mattelart, 1983:100–101).

In addition to the hazards posed by consumer goods, it is estimated that annually 375,000 people in the developing world are poisoned—10,000 of them fatally—through the misuse of industrial and agricultural chemicals exported from developed nations. There is evidence that much of this poisoning results from the failure of TNCs to provide adequate information on the hazards of their chemical exports, and from their active attempts to find markets for chemicals banned at home (Bull, 1982; Weir and Schapiro, 1981). In one such instance, paraquat was successfully promoted for use as a marijuana defoliant in Latin America after it was banned for that purpose in the United States (del Olmo, 1986).

Most of the injurious corporate actions described above were not prosecutable as crimes or regulatory violations in the nations where they occurred. Yet to omit them from the study of corporate crime on this basis does little to help us understand either the organization and causation of injurious actions by TNCs, or the definitional process by which these actions have been rendered legal in host nations. Moreover, as we argue in the next section, the ability of TNCs to influence regulatory climates in host nations may play a crucial role in keeping injurious actions by TNCs from being defined and prosecuted as crimes.

TNCS AND REGULATORY CLIMATES

TNCs can influence the regulatory climates of developing host nations in indirect and direct ways. The logic of development in the free-market world necessitates that developing nations create hospitable environments for foreign investment. Simply by holding the economic keys to development, TNCs indirectly limit the political willingness of developing nations to establish strict controls over potential or actual corporate harms. At times, TNCs have also exerted pressure in more direct ways to forestall legislation contrary to their interests, and in some cases to subvert political movements or leaders deemed inhospitable to these interests. We now examine this relationship between TNCs and regulatory climates in closer detail, with a particular focus on labor policies.

Indirect Influences

Free-market nations that have followed a capitalist model of development based on foreign investment find their potentials for economic growth closely linked to their ability to attract TNCs. Domestic elites in developing nations frequently find that general economic improvement and political stability in their countries, as well as their own economic and political success, depend upon creating hospitable environments for investment by foreign TNCs. The deepening need for inflows of foreign investment in developing nations, and the pressures this places on domestic policy, have been extensively examined by a number of dependency theorists.[3] The specific regulatory adaptations that have been made to attract TNCs have been examined in less detail. However, there is some evidence that the existence of a profitable double-standard which allows TNCs in host countries to do what they are prohibited from doing in their home nations is related to the desire of host nations to attract foreign investment by creating regulatory climates hospitable to the interests of TNCs.

---

[3]See in particular Amin (1974); Chase-Dunn (1978); Frank (1975); Sunkle (1973); and Wallerstein (1979).

Controls over the rights of workers to organize for improved wage and working conditions is a good example of how TNCs become the passive beneficiaries of policies designed to attract them. Labor costs represent one of the most significant factors in the location of manufacturing plants (Burns, 1984). For instance, assembly line workers in the United States often earn per hour what assembly workers in developing nations earn per day (Fuentes and Ehrenreich, 1983:5). The desire to take advantage of significant differentials in national wage rates has been the primary stimulus for the location of TNC production facilities in developing nations (Grunwald and Flamm, 1985:3–9). Leaders in some developing nations have used limitations on worker rights as a strategy to convince foreign companies that, if they do invest, they will enjoy continued benefits from lower labor costs. The belief that this will attract foreign investment has received a degree of confirmation from investment practices of TNCs.[4] For instance, investment in Thailand by the U.S. semiconductor industry did not reach significant levels until 1977, the year following the installment of a military junta that ended a period of democratic government characterized by strikes and other movements for increased popular control over the economy. Similarly, foreign direct investment in semiconductor assembly in the Philippines entered a period of significant growth beginning in 1972, the year Marcos declared martial law (Grunwald and Flamm, 1985:77). In 1982, Marcos continued his efforts to create a profitable climate for these TNCs by issuing a decree banning all strikes in the semiconductor industry as being against the "national interest" (O'Connor and Wong, 1983).

Another strategy used in developing nations to attract foreign investment at the expense of

labor rights protected by law in developed nations is the creation of *economic free zones* (EFZs). In some cases these zones are little more than labor camps "where trade unions, strikes and freedom of movement are severely limited, if not forbidden" (Fuentes and Eherenrich, 1983:5). For example, advertisements for Caribbean Assemblies, a set of EFZs in Haiti and the Dominican Republic, promise foreign companies a "large, urbanized, low-cost labour pool" and "strict anti-strike and labour regulation laws" (Matellart, 1983:106). A promotional document by the South Korea government offers this description of its EFZ:

The zone has the characteristics of a reserved territory in which the application of laws or relevant regulations is partially or totally suppressed or attenuated. . . . It is an industrial territory in which a series of fiscal and legal privileges are offered to firms of foreign capital (Medawar, 1979:62).

Promotional materials such as these make it abundantly clear that limitations on the rights of workers are part of the bait that EFZs offer to foreign companies in some developing nations.

Lim (1983:14) has argued that locating TNC industrial facilities in developing countries is beneficial to workers in nations where unemployment and poverty are widespread, even if the rights of these workers are minimal. This perspective is manifest in the June 6, 1980 issue of *Fortune* magazine which asks, "Even though the people working on Castle and Cooke's banana plantations in Central America earn far less than the U.S. minimum wage, would they be better off if the company decided to move elsewhere?" However, the economic conditions that TNCs "improve" cannot be analyzed in isolation from the economic domination by foreign business interests that characterizes the history of many developing host nations. Moreover, while the factory work provided by TNCs may improve the incomes of some workers, the dependent development it represents generally results in a distorted economy, a split labor market, and exploitation of women who are the primary laborers in these factories (Amin, 1974; Frank, 1975; Nash, 1979; Wallerstein, 1979).

---

[4]From the point of view of TNCs there are limits to the attractiveness of strict controls over labor rights. Regimes that are so repressive as to loose legitimacy can incite significant popular unrest. If the regime is not able to control this opposition, the resulting political instability can negate the benefits of a strong anti-labor government (International Labor Organization, 1985:62–63). The 1986 ouster of Marcos, a strong anti-labor dictator, from the Philippines is a case in point.

Direct Influences

In addition to benefiting indirectly from restrictive labor climates, TNCs have at times actively used their economic power in developing nations to limit the rights of workers to organize into unions to protect and promote their interests. In some cases, TNCs have used the threat of the runaway shop to discipline workers. For instance, when the Malaysian government indicated in 1983 that it might permit the formation of a union for electronics workers, U.S. electronics firms in Malaysia indicated that, should this happen, they would consider moving their plants elsewhere. Subsequently, the Malaysian government shelved its plans for the union. In a similar case, Control Data Corporation closed a Korean production facility in response to attempts by workers to unionize (O'Connor and Wong, 1983). Such threats or actual incidents of capital flight can have a chilling effect on both labor activism and governmental support for labor rights in nations dependent on foreign investment.

Besides attempts to influence specific policies, some TNCs have used their economic and political power to alter the flow of broader political developments in host nations. In some cases, TNCs have contributed to the elimination of progressive or socialist governments in favor of conservative ones. Activities of this sort are often based on clandestine contacts between TNCs and governments in home or host nations. As a result, relatively little is known about their scope or frequency. However, cases such as ITT's contributions to the overthrow of Allende in Chile, the participation of United Fruit, International Railways of Central America, and Electric Bond and Share in bringing about the downfall of the progressive leader, Jacobs Arbenz, in Guatemala in 1954, and the more recent financial support provided by some U.S. corporations to the Nicaraguan *contras* in their efforts to overthrow the socialist government there, indicate that TNCs are not above using their power to alter the flow of political events in developing nations (Bonner, 1983; Jensen, 1973; Kenworthy, 1973; LaFeber, 1984; Langley, 1985:142–43).

Overall, the combined effects of economic pressures to create a favorable climate for foreign investment, and support by transnational corporate capital for governments or political parties hospitable to their interests, can create a set of structural/legal conditions which allow TNCs in host countries to do what would be illegal in their country of origin. We are not suggesting that all TNCs have taken full advantage of these favorable structural/legal climates, or that all actively engage in efforts to create these climates. We are suggesting that researchers must always be sensitive to the political influences of TNCs on the political climates and legal frameworks of host countries. Accordingly, the laws governing corporate behavior in these nations are a poor starting place for setting the scope of inquiry into corporate offenses in a transnational context. In the following sections, we consider an alternative definitional framework for research on injurious action by TNCs: the U.N. codes of corporate conduct.

THE U.N. CODE AS INTERNATIONAL POLITICS

Multinational business is now international politics. Multinational companies are increasingly being forced to operate in a framework not just determined by the laws of supply and demand. . .but also by a proliferating set of inter-governmental arrangements specifically targeted at them (Robinson, 1983:3).

Recognizing that the political power of TNCs is truly transnational and hegemonic, and that independent national action is limited, many developing countries have come to believe that the only way they can confront and control TNCs is through the creation of international standards. The two most far-reaching attempts to establish worldwide standards for TNCs have been undertaken by the United Nations with the Draft Codes of Conduct on Transnational Corporations and the Guidelines for Consumer Protection. The development of these codes is a unique and highly relevant empirical case for a theoretical examination of the political definition of harmful corporate actions.

The definitional process that created the U.N. codes supports Robinson's (1983) assertion that multinational business is now international politics. The code developmental process has brought into sharp focus the fundamental differences of perspectives and interests between developed and developing nations, and between free-market and centrally-planned economies. Charles Lindblom (1977:ix) succinctly characterized these differences when he wrote: "Aside from the difference between despotic and libertarian government, the greatest distinction between one government and another is in the degree to which market replaces government or government replaces market." The formation of the draft codes for consumer protection and transnational corporate behavior at the United Nations represents an attempt to replace markets with politics. That is, through the political mechanisms of the United Nations, non-aligned and less developed nations are seeking to implement a set of rules governing the market relations between TNCs, and the citizens and governments of the nations in which they operate. This process assumes the primacy of politics over markets, and in this way, transnational business has indeed become international politics.

Historical Background

The politicalization of international business, and the origins of the U.N. codes, have their roots in the "multinational debate" of the 1960s that reached its climax in the confrontation between developing and industrialized nations in the early 1970s (Robinson, 1983). The developing nations, many of them recently enfranchised, made claims concerning the harmful practices of TNCs and called for a New Economic Order and some form of binding control over TNCs. Throughout the 1970s, the United Nations led the crusade for a comprehensive, legally-binding international code of conduct for TNCs. Within the United Nations, this crusade was led by the developing countries—grouped together as the so-called

Group of 77—international trade unions, and some small, developed nations, such as the Scandinavian states (Hamilton, 1983).

The U.N. code of conduct on TNCs has its direct roots in a 1972 decision of the United Nations Economic and Social Council (ECOSOC) to establish a group of "eminent persons" to make recommendations for international action on TNCs (Robinson, 1983). Their report, "The Impact of Multinational Corporations on Development and International Relations," was published in May, 1974, and it provided the rationale for the subsequent development of the code. In December, 1974, ECOSOC created a Commission and Centre on Transnational Corporations. The Commission was charged with the job of drawing up a set of recommendations which could become the basis for a Code of Conduct dealing with TNCs.

The Commission on Transnational Corporations met annually from 1975 into the 1980s. However, the economic downturn associated with the 1974 oil crisis and the corresponding increased need of the developing nations for foreign investment tempered the Commission's work (Robinson, 1983). The multinational issue was no longer a debate—it had become a negotiation. The principal forum for the negotiations was the "Intergovernmental Working Group on a Code of Conduct" which first met in January, 1977, and its reports to the Commission on Transnational Corporations.

As the Intergovernmental Working Group began its task, several other international groups issued guidelines for TNCs. In 1976, the Organization for Economic Cooperation and Development (OECD) established its *Guidelines for Multinational Enterprises,* and, one year later, the International Labor Organization (ILO) approved the *Declaration of Principles Concerning Multinational Enterprises and Social Policy.* In 1980, the United Nations Conference on Trade and Development (UNCTAD) promulgated the *Set of Multilaterally Agreed Equitable Principles and Rules for the Control of Restrictive Business Practices,* and the World Health Organization's (WHO) International Code of Marketing of Breast Milk Substitutes was passed by the General Assembly in May of 1981.

The ILO, UNCTAD and WHO guidelines are all sectoral codes for international business within the United Nations. They were developed to deal with specific problems that may arise from TNC activity and must be understood in the context of the more general negotiations occurring within the United Nations concerning TNCs. The OECD guidelines were a preemptive Western strike at the general UN codes. As Robinson (1983:7) points out:

. . .the guidelines are a calculated compromise by Western governments between, on the one hand, the need to sensitize firms to their social, economic, and political responsibilities and, on the other, the need to make the rest of the world aware, and in particular the LDCs negotiating a UN code of conduct for transnational corporations, that the West is not prepared to see excessive constraints imposed on their major creators of wealth.

Despite the passage of these other international guidelines, the U.N. code of conduct remains in draft form. The Intergovernmental Working Group concluded its work on the code in May, 1982 at its seventeenth session. However, at this time the code has not yet been adopted by the General Assembly. On the other hand, the Consumer Code promulgated by the Economic and Social Council, was approved by the General Assembly in November, 1984.

Key Actors and Issues in the Definitional Process

The primary impulse behind the U.N. codes was the desire of the developing countries—the Group of 77—to establish a "New Economic Order" and some mechanism for legal control over TNCs. Their manifesto for a U.N. code, produced in 1976, included a 21-point list of grievances and criticisms concerning the behavior of TNCs (Robinson, 1983). Their position, to use Lindblom's (1977:ix) terms, was that international politics must replace markets. The economic crisis of the mid-1970s mellowed the ideological tenor of the Group of 77 and they increasingly came to realize that to have any chance of success they would need to compromise with the developed countries. The ma-

jor issue on which they compromised was the binding character of the code. They acknowledged that any code of conduct must be voluntary and not legally binding at this point in time.

The major ally of the developing countries was the international trade union movement centered in Western Europe. In fact, the unions and the TNCs were key interest group participants in the political struggle to shape the U.N. codes. As Robinson (1983:195) points out,

. . .there is no doubt that the war of influence that has engaged the trade unions and multinational business since the start of the TNC debate in the 1960s, has an often determining impact on the measures being drawn up in . . . the UN and its specialized agencies.

The trade unions favor increased regulation of big business and are supportive of attempts to increase public control of the international economy. In addition, the European unions generally bring to the debate over the codes an overt anti-capitalist ideology which broadens the framework of discussion. Furthermore, Robinson (1983) points out that the trade unions have a streamlined and interlocking organization that allows them to significantly influence international policy.

The industrialized or developed countries, including the United States, West Germany, and the United Kingdom, have generally taken a much more conservative stance toward the whole idea of a code of conduct for TNCs. As the home countries of the majority of TNCs, these states have a much more positive assessment of TNC behavior. They have been concerned with making the codes voluntary arrangements that provide stable conditions for international investment. They have argued that the code of conduct must include a statement about the general treatment of TNCs by the countries in which they operate. They have also been concerned about the issues of nationalization and compensation.

Of course, the TNCs themselves are significantly involved in trying to shape the U.N. codes. At the beginning of the definitional process, the TNCs appeared to be resigned to the prospect of international codes of conduct and their strategy was to try to shape codes that they could at least live with. More recently though, big business and its lobbies (the International Chamber of Commerce in particular) have stepped up the attack on the fundamental principles that lay behind the codes. The TNCs are more forcefully asserting the primacy of markets over politics in the debates on the code. The election of Ronald Reagan in 1980 may provide a partial explanation for the aggressive stance of the TNCs. The Reagan administration has been quite vociferous in its condemnation of the codes and its support of markets over politics. As Caplan and Malcomson (1986:108) note, ". . .it is clear that the international business community, alone and in partnership with the Reagan Administration, is engaged in an active and effective assault on U.N. initiatives that are perceived as threats to corporate profits."

Speaking before the American Enterprise Institute in December, 1983, Jeane Kirkpatrick, then U.S. Ambassador to the United Nations, stated that the "proliferation of activities aimed at the regulation of international business [is] a very big problem" (Kirkpatrick, 1983). These regulatory efforts, she said, arise not from hazards posed by TNCs, but from "ideological distortions," such as the view of poor nations that they are victims of exploitation by TNCs. She went on to say that such regulation would result in "global paternalism" by the United Nations, a view similar to that expressed by the Reagan Administration in its opposition to the Infant Formula Code (Kirkpatrick, 1983). Echoing Kirkpatrick's concern, Murray Weidenbaum (1983:1), former chairman of President Reagan's Council of Economic Advisors, has accused the United Nations of trying to become a "global nanny," and warned that "the United Nations is in a growth phase in its attempts to control private enterprise" (1984:13).

Advertising Age, the trade paper of the advertising industry, worried that the consumer codes could limit the free choice of consumers in Third World countries as well as the freedom of merchants to promote their wares in the way they deem most effective (1984:58). *Chemical Week,* the trade organ of the U.S. chemical industry, ex-pressed a similar concern (1981:15). In perhaps the most strident attack on the U.N. activities, the Heritage Foundation warned that "a new wave of extremist, anti-free enterprise consumer organizations" is using "distortions to undermine the multinational corporations and the private sector approach to development." This threat to free enterprise results, they say, from the fact that:

Various consumer, union and church organizations have been banding together and refining and sharing their techniques. . . . They are developing international networks that allow them to draw attention to targeted issues. . .forcing multinational firms to pay closer attention to their corporate activities (Heritage Foundation, 1983).

Emerging Political Definitions and Their Significance

Out of the sharp political and ideological conflicts within the United Nations, and despite the opposition of the international business community, a Draft Code of Conduct on Transnational Corporations has been produced. This code, along with the consumer code, constitutes a set of international norms for the conduct of transnational business—a new set of political definitions concerning the behavior of TNCs. While space does not permit a full description of the code of conduct, the outline in Table 1 highlights the major areas and topics covered by the code. The specific standards formulated under the topic headings in the draft code have one key notion running through them— accountability. As Robinson (1983:224) notes:

By accountability is meant the accountability of business to new constituencies—to governments, to the general public, and, above all, to the workforce. And being accountable to such new constituencies, the multinational company is forced into a new context of political and social responsibility.

Caplan and Malcomson (1986) offer another perspective on the code when they observe that it modestly seeks to universalize much of what we in the United States have already achieved in imperfect form—consumer protection,

TABLE 1 Activities of Transnational Corporations Covered by U.N. (Draft) Code of Conduct

A. General and Political
  1. Respect for national sovereignty and observance of domestic laws, regulations and administrative practices
  2. Adherence to economic goals and development objectives, policies and priorities
  3. Adherence to socio-cultural objectives and values
  4. Respect for human rights and fundamental freedom
  5. Non-interference in internal political affairs
  6. Non-interference in intergovernmental relations
  7. Abstention from corrupt practices
B. Economic, Financial and Social
  1. Ownership and control
  2. Balance of payments and financing
  3. Transfer pricing
  4. Taxation
  5. Competition and restrictive business practices
  6. Transfer of technology
  7. Consumer protection
  8. Environmental protection

Source: *CTC Reporter,* 1982:3–4, 23–24

safeguards against exposure to hazardous products, control over national resources, corporate accountability, and economic sovereignty.

It is important not to overestimate the significance of the codes. The code of conduct on TNCs has not yet been adopted by the General Assembly. Neither code is legally binding or enforceable. The code of conduct also sets standards for the treatment of TNCs by the countries in which they operate. Some observers believe that the impact of the codes has already been eviscerated by the international business community (Caplan and Malcomson, 1986). Another observer warns that the codes may actually benefit TNCs by securing a stable international business framework and, by placing them on an equal footing with government, legitimize their activities in the eyes of their critics (Hamilton, 1983).

Whatever the truth of these observations, the real significance of the U.N. codes is that they create transnational standards for evaluating the behavior of TNCs. A worldwide set of general principles has emerged out of the political definitional process within the uniquely distinctive setting of the United Nations. Just as broader con-

ceptions of human rights and corporate crime emerged in the United States through class struggle and the political mobilization of a wide range of interest groups (Coleman, 1983), the United Nations has provided a global arena for political struggles between developing and developed nations and between the trade union movement and the international business community over the dominance of politics or markets, and the appropriateness of specific actions by TNCs. Finally, even though we have noted the hegemonic process of legal definition in developing nations, the legitimacy of transnational standards in conjunction with the political power of the United Nations may allow the U.N. codes to serve as model legislation to be enacted within specific developing nations.

THE SEARCH FOR ALTERNATIVE FRAMEWORKS

The evolution of U.N. codes for the conduct of TNCs returns us to our central problematic—that the laws of nation-states represent theoretically inappropriate frameworks for the study of injurious actions by TNCs. The need for criminological researchers to derive behavioral standards independent of law is not a new concern for criminologists. Nearly a half-century ago Thorsten Sellin (1938:104–5) argued that criminologists should not limit their investigations to "categories set up by the criminal law," because these categories "do not arise intrinsically from the nature of the subject matter," but instead, reflect the "character and interests of those groups in the population which influence legislation." In recent years some criminologists have responded to this challenge by employing various concepts of "human rights" in constructing alternative definitions of crime (Schwendinger and Schwendinger 1970; Tift and Sullivan, 1980). These "human rights" definitions of crime, in turn, have generated their own set of criticisms.

The central critique of "human rights" definitions of crime has been that researchers who utilize them simply substitute their personal moral concerns for those contained in law.

Shapiro (1983:307) argues that corporate crime research that extends beyond the boundaries of what is illegal is inevitably flawed because it is suffused with the "moral agenda" of the observer. A more trenchant criticism is offered by John Braithwaite (1985:18) who suggests that:

Those who choose to study violations of "politically defined human rights," or some other imaginative definition of deviance, will deserve to be ignored for indulging their personal moralities in a social science that has no relevance for those who do not share that morality.

The typical rejoinder to criticisms of this type is that relying upon law to define the boundaries of criminological inquiry is no less suffused with moral choice than is choosing definitions based on concepts of human rights. For instance, Schwendinger and Schwendinger (1970:142) argue that:

No scholar involved in the controversy about the definitions of crime has been able to avoid direct or indirect use of moral standards in the solution to this problem. . . . In light of this, the claim that moral judgments have no place in the formulation of the definitions of crime is without foundation.

While the observation that law contains no less a moral and political agenda than any other definition of transgression may be correct, it provides no particular guidance regarding why we should choose one particular framework for defining the parameters of study over another. We suggest that the first step beyond this set of mutual accusations is to distinguish between the positivist concept of *lack of bias* and critical theory's concept of *reflexivity*. Within a positivist conception of social science *bias* is a preference for one set of social outcomes over another. This should be avoided in favor of a value-free science in which the researcher holds no brief with respect to the world in view.

The presumed attainability of a science without bias arises from the attempt in positivist epistemology to separate the powers of human reason from the inevitability of human commitment to the social world. This separation of reason from commitment, according to Habermas (1974:264), produces the goal of unbiased inquiry through which reason is applied to developing the technical means of control over environments and people, but from which the application of that same reason to inquiry regarding the purposes of that control is excluded. Within this framework, social scientists who reveal preferences for some social agendas over others are suspected of allowing ideology to distort science, that is, commitment is thought to compromise reason.

The positivist *commitment* to a world developed through technical application of scientific rationality, by contrast, in interpreted not as commitment but as reason:

Efficiency and economy, which are the definitions of this [positivist] rationality cannot, in turn, be themselves conceived as values, and yet, within the framework of positivism's understanding of itself, they can only be justified as though they were values (Habermas, 1974:269).

The search for a social science devoid of bias is a misdirected and futile endeavor. As Karl Heilbroner (1974:23) observes:

The position of the social researcher differs sharply from that of the observer of the natural world. The latter. . .is not morally imbedded in the field he scrutinizes. By contrast the social investigator is inextricably bound up with the objects of his scrutiny. . .bringing with him feelings of animus or defensiveness to the phenomenon he observes.

In contrast to positivist notions of unbiased science, critical reflexivity is a mode of analysis that recognizes the existence of moral preferences in ourselves and others, and demands of us that we analyze the nature and construction of those preferences so that they contribute to rather than detract from our ability to achieve the purposeful understanding we seek and the type of social world to which we are committed. Rather than following the path outlined by a positivist model of inquiry presumably shorn of moral commitments, the study of injurious actions by TNCs should be guided, we suggest, by principles of critical reflexivity. This perspective provides a theoretically-grounded way to expand the scope of study beyond the limits of the law, and to incorporate a positive commitment to the reduction of social injuries by corporate actors within the framework of research concerns.

Critical reflexivity according to Habermas (1973:15) develops when we examine what he terms taken-for-granted "validity claims" and "redeem or dismiss them on the basis of arguments." Because of their taken-for-granted nature, however, validity claims are only revealed through discourses where "participants, themes and contributions are not restricted except with reference to the goal of testing the validity claims in question," and where "no force except that of the better argument is exercised" (Habermas, 1973:108).

Law is a socially-and historically-legitimated authority system. The validity claims implicit in laws—including the assumption that law is the final arbiter of transgressive action—have been established not through the type of discourses described above, but through the historical interplay of a variety of economic and political forces. If law is used to define the scope of corporate crime studies, the possibilities for a critical understanding of transgressive actions is negated by the consequently unanalyzed history of power—relations imbedded in law. Moreover, alternative discourses which perceive the validity claims of established laws as problematic are omitted from our inquiry, further narrowing our ability to analyze the transgressive actions of TNCs from a critically-reflexive standpoint.

With respect to the study of corporate crime, critical reflexivity does not mean seeking out some set of definitions that are free of moral implications. We are never without preferences with respect to outcomes in the social world. However, we can begin to develop critical reflexivity by using and entering into less restricted discourses which question rather than accept those validity claims that either the law or other conceptions of human rights treat non-problematic. The evolving U.N. codes for the conduct of TNCs represent this type of expanded discourse, and offer a broader framework for the study of injurious actions by TNCs than does limiting our inquiry to the laws of nation states.

CONCLUSION: TOWARD A DEFINITION OF CORPORATE TRANSGRESSIONS

Where injurious actions by TNCs violate existing national laws there is little conceptual difficulty in placing them within the purview of corporate crime studies. However, only by moving beyond national laws can we begin to study transgressions that arise in the space between national legal systems. The study of injurious actions by corporations that operate at the level of the world-system requires a conception of transgression developed through discourse at the same level, and which is capable of adapting to changing forms of injurious corporate action. With this in mind we offer the following expanded framework for the study of corporate wrongdoing:

Corporate transgressions by TNCs encompass any action in pursuit of corporate goals which violates national laws, or international standards such as codes of conduct for TNCs developed within the U.N., or which results in social injury analogous in severity and source to that caused by corporate violations of law or international standards.

We have substituted the term corporate *transgressions* for the more common phrase corporate *crime* for two reasons. First, the term transgressions avoids the semantic and theoretical problems that arise when corporate actions that are not specifically adjudicable under law are defined as *crime*. Second, the concept of *transgression* retains a sense of fundamental wrongfulness similar to that associated with "crime." This references *our* commitment to the reduction of avoidable, injurious actions committed against people by organizations in the pursuit of capital accumulation. We prefer the concept of corporate transgression to that of "corporate deviance," which can encompass any action that offends any organized constituency, whether it be consumers or stockholders (Ermann and Lundman, 1982:16–19). The term corporate transgressions is less relativistic and better conveys, we feel, the severity of harm that can arise from the actions of TNCs.

The general principles outlined in the U.N. codes, as well as the specific provisions under each, provide a conceptual framework which allows us to expand the scope of inquiry without the epistemological hazards of definitions derived from personal conceptions of human rights. The U.N. codes represent the current stage of political struggle to refine the concept of human rights, and rights of national sovereignty, *vis-a-vis* large, transnational, corporate institutions. As such they are the appropriate reference point for understanding what constitutes transgressions by these institutions.

In addition, definitions of corporate transgressions evolved at a world level through a process in which all members of the world community participate represents a type of expanded discourse. This expanded discourse offers greater possibilities for the development of critical reflexivity where injuries by TNCs are concerned than do the laws of individual nations. The U.N. codes are not products of Habermas' ideal form of discourse conducted in the absence of all force except the better argument. However, they represent concepts of transgression negotiated in a context *freer* of the political pressures and limitation on viewpoints that surround the more hegemonic processes of national legislation. The discourse surrounding the U.N. codes incorporates a broader range of voices, some of which are silent within individual nation states. Representatives of the non-aligned developing nations, the developed free-market states, and the developed and developing planned-economy states have each had opportunities to articulate their conceptions of corporate transgression, and to negotiate for provisions consistent with their views (U.N. Chronicle, July, 1983:103). This interplay of perspectives provides a climate wherein the normally hidden validity claims of legal systems in different nations are revealed for critical assessment.

We recognize that truly equal input into the deviance-defining process is not easily or likely to be achieved in any political context, including the United Nations. However, the political process surrounding the development of the U.N. consumer and corporate codes brings together into a single communicative forum a wider range of participants and perspectives than national debates. Consequently, a broader range of validity claims regarding the control of corporate activities is revealed for examination than in national forums. For those whose interest is the definitional process underlying concepts of corporate deviance, the opportunity to examine the conflicting validity claims that arise within the context of international debate regarding the behavior of TNCs is invaluable.

The inclusion of injuries that are demonstrably analogous in severity and source to those which violate national laws or international standards—even if they do not violate these laws or standards—advances both the behavioral and the definitional research domains in the study of injurious corporate actions.[5] Corporate crime studies regarding the organization and causation of injurious corporate actions are primarily concerned with explaining and eventually controlling these injurious actions. As shown by cases such as Nestle's marketing of breast milk substitutes (Chetley, 1979), or the current spread of genetic engineering beyond the reach of existing national laws (Schneider, 1986a, 1986b), new forms of injurious corporate actions can emerge more swiftly than laws or standards aimed at controlling them. Excluding analogous forms of corporate injuries because they have not been politically defined as transgressive confounds the behavioral paradigm with inappropriate definitional criteria. It places the behavioral paradigm under the authority of political processes. Inclusion of analogous corporate injuries advances the behavioral paradigm within corporate crime studies in another way. It makes it possible to compare the organization and causation of injurious actions that are defined as transgressive with those that are not. Comparisons of this type will improve our understanding of the relationship between causation and control of corporate behavior.

Inclusion of analogous forms of corporate injury is essential for any real development within the definitional research domain. A necessary

---

[5]For elaborated discussions of analogous social injury see Kramer (1985) and Michalowski (1985:314–18).

component of any mature inquiry into the application of meaning to corporate behavior is comparative analyses of the processes whereby some corporate injuries are selected for control while others are defined as acceptable or necessary consequences of economic practices. Excluding injurious activities from definitional studies because they have not been politically defined as transgressive closes off this crucial area of inquiry. The study of injurious actions by TNCs can make substantial contributions to the definitional paradigm in corporate crime studies–but only if our conceptualizations do not prohibit us from examining the processes by which some forms of corporate injury are defined as transgressive at either the national or international level and others are not. In general, we suggest that researchers interested in the study of corporate crime by TNCs maintain a clear distinction between behavioral and definitional research domains, recognize the limitations of legal criteria for setting the scope of study, and expand existing frameworks to include both violations of international standards of corporate conduct and all other analogous forms of corporate transgression.

REFERENCES

Advertising Age
1984   "U.N. proposed regulations menacing to U.S. marketers." Advertising Age 55 (June): 58.

Amin, Samir
1974   Accumulation on a World Scale. New York: Monthly Review Press.

Barnet, Richard J. and Ronald E. Muller
1974   Global Reach: The Power of the Multinational Corporations. New York: Simon and Schuster.

Blake, David H. and Robert S. Walters
1976   The Politics of Global Economic Relations. Englewood Cliffs, NJ: Prentice Hall.

Blake, Michael
1980   A Case Study on Women in Industry. Bangkok: Asian and Pacific Centre for Women and Development.

Blum-West, Steve and Timothy J. Carter
1983   "Bringing white-collar crime back in: An examination of crimes and torts." Social Problems 30: 545–54.

Bonner, Raymond
1983   "U.S. ties to anti-Sandinistas are reported to be extensive." New York Times, April 3: A1.

Braithwaite, John
1984   Corporate Crime in the Pharmaceutical Industry. London: Routledge and Kegan Paul.
1985   "White collar crime." Annual Review of Sociology 11: 1–25.

Bull, David
1982   A Growing Problem: Pesticides and the Third World Poor. Oxford: Oxfam.

Burns, James J.
1984   "International siting priorities for a high technology firm." Industrial Development 153:11.

Caplan, Richard and Scott L. Malcomson
1986   "Giving the U.N. the business." The Nation 243 (August 16): 108–12.

Castleman, Barry
1975   "The flight of hazardous industries to unregulating countries." Report issued by the Maryland Public Interest Group.
1978   "How we export dangerous industries." Business and Society Review 27: 7–14.
1979   "The export of hazardous factories to developing nations." International Journal of Health Services 9: 569–606.

Cavanagh, John and Fredrick F. Clairmonte
1983   "From corporations to conglomerates." Multinational Monitor 4 (January):16–20.

Centre on Transnational Corporations
1985   Environmental Aspects of the Activities of Transnational Corporations: A Survey. New York: Centre on Transnational Corporations.

Chase-Dunn, Christopher K.
1978   "Core-periphery relations: The effects of core competition." Pp. 159–76 in Barbara H. Kaplan (ed.), Social Change in the Capitalist World Economy. Beverly Hills, CA: Sage.

Chemical Week
1981   "Codes of conduct: Worry over new restraints on multinationals." Chemical Week 129 (July 15): 15.

Chetley, A.
1979   The Baby Killer Scandal. London: War on Want.

Clinard, Marshall B.
1946   ''The black market.'' American Sociological Review 11: 250-70.

Clinard, Marshall B. and Peter Yeager
1980   Corporate Crime. New York: Free Press.

Coleman, James W.
1983   The Criminal Elite: The Sociology of White Collar Crime. New York: St. Martin's.

Conklin, John
1977   Illegal but Not Criminal: Business Crime in America. Englewood Cliffs, NJ: Prentice Hall.

CTC Reporter
1982   ''The United Nations Code of Conduct on Transnational Corporations.'' The CTC Reporter 12: 3-4, 23-26.

Cultural Survival
1982   ''Poisons in the Third World.'' Cultural Survival 6 (Winter): 3-10.

del Olmo, Rosa
1986   ''Aerobiologia y drogas.'' Paper presented at the Fourth Annual Latinamerican Conference of Critical Criminology, Havana.

Denzin, Norman K.
1977   ''Notes on the criminogenic hypothesis: A case study of the liquor industry.'' American Sociological Review 42: 905-20.

Dewar, Helen
1978   ''Study cites firms flight to Third World to avoid safeguards.'' Washington Post, June 30: A2.

Dollars and Sense
1984   ''High tech and health.'' Dollars and Sense 99 (September): 6-7.

Dowie, Mark and Tracy Johnston
1976   ''A case of corporate malpractice.'' Mother Jones 2 (November): 36-50.

Edelhertz, Herbert
1970   The Nature, Impact and Prosecution of White Collar Crime. Washington, DC: National Institute of Law Enforcement and Criminal Justice.

Ermann David M. and Richard J. Lundman
1982   Corporate Deviance. New York: CBS College Publishing.

Farberman, Harvey
1975   ''A criminogenic market structure: The automobile industry.'' Sociological Quarterly 16: 438-57.

Fernandez-Kelly, Maria
1983   For We Are Sold, I and My People. Albany: State University of New York Press.

Flamm, Kenneth
1985   ''The semiconductor industry.'' Pp. 38-138 in Joseph Grunwald and Kenneth Flamm (eds.), The Global Factory. Washington, DC: The Brookings Institution.

Fortune
1980   ''The corporation haters.'' Fortune 101 (June, 16): 126-36.

Frank, Andre Gunder
1975   On Capitalist Underdevelopment. London: Oxford University Press.

Fuentes, Annette and Barbara Ehrenreich
1983   ''The new factory girls.'' Multinational Monitor 4 (August): 5-10.

Geis Gilbert
1967   ''The heavy electrical equipment antitrust cases of 1961.'' In Marshall B. Clinard and Richard Quinney (eds.), Criminal Behavior Systems. New York: Holt, Rinehart and Winston.

Grunwald, Joseph and Kenneth Flamm
1985   The Global Factory. Washington, DC: The Brookings Institution.

Habermas, Jürgen
1973   Legitimation Crisis. Boston: Beacon Press.
1974   Theory and Practice. London: Heinemann.

Hamilton, Geoffrey
1983   ''International codes of conduct for multinationals.'' Multinational Business 12 (Summer): 1-10.

Hartung, Frank E.
1950   ''White collar offenses in the wholesale meat industry.'' American Journal of Sociology 56: 22-34.

Hazarka, Sanjoy
1984   ''Gas leak in India said to kill 410.'' New York Times, December 4: A1.

Heilbroner, Karl
1974   An Inquiry Into the Human Prospect. New York: Norton.

Heritage Foundation
1983 Multinationals: First Victim of the U.N. War on Free Enterprise. Washington, DC: Heritage Foundation.

International Labor Organization
1985 Women Workers in Multinational Enterprises in Developing Countries. Geneva: International Labor Office.

Jensen, Michael
1973 "Allende target of proposals." New York Times, June 22: A1.

Kenworthy, E. W.
1973 "Senate group finds ITT and U.S. at fault on Chile." New York Times, June 22: A1.

Kirkpatrick, Jeane
1983 "Kirkpatrick criticizes U.N. for 'class rule' ideology." Multinational Monitor 4 (January): 8.

Kramer, Ronald C.
1985 "Defining the concept of crime: A humanistic perspective." Journal of Sociology and Social Welfare 12: 469–87.

LaDou, James
1984 "The not-so-clean business of making chips." Technology Review 87: 23–36.

LaFeber, Walter
1984 Inevitable Revolutions: The United States in Central America. New York: Norton.

Langley, Lester P.
1985 Central America: The Real Stakes. New York: Crown.

Leonard, H. Jeffrey and Christopher J. Duerksen
1981 "Environmental regulation and the location of industry: An international perspective." Columbia Journal of World Business 15: 55–68.

Leonard, William N. and Marvin Weber
1970 "Automakers and dealers: A study of criminogenic market forces." Law and Society Review 4: 407–24.

Lim, Linda
1983 "Are multinationals the problem? No." Multinational Monitor 4 (August): 15.

Lindblom, Charles
1977 Politics and Markets. New York: Basic Books.

Mattelart, Armand
1983 Transnationals and the Third World. South Hadley, MA: Bergin and Garvey.

Medawar, Charles
1979 Insult or Injury. London: Social Audit.

Michaloswki, Raymond
1985 Order, Law, and Crime. New York: Random House.

Mintz, Morton
1985 At Any Cost: Corporate Greed, Women and the Dalkon Shield. New York: Pantheon.

Multinational Monitor
1984 "Profits climb; foreign investments fall." Multinational Monitor 5 (January): 11.

Nash, June
1979 "Men, women and the international division of labor." Paper presented at the annual meetings of the Latin American Studies Association, Philadelphia.

New York Times
1978 "Safety panel votes to ban export of Tris sleepwear." New York Times, May 7: A26.

O'Connor, David and Chia Siew Wong
1983 "Are multinationals the problem? Yes." Multinational Monitor 4 (August): 16.

Ong, A.
1983 "Global industries and Malay peasants in peninsular Malaysia." Pp. 426–39 in June Nash and M. P. Fernandez-Kelly (eds.), Women, Men and the International Division of Labor. Albany, NY: State University of New York Press.

Pearson, Charles and Anthony Pryer
1978 Environment: North and South. New York: Wiley Interscience.

Randall, Kenneth
1977 "Foreword." Pp. i–ix in James R. Basche Jr. (ed.), Production Costs, Trends and Outlook: A Study of International Business Experience. New York: Conference Board.

Robinson, John
1983 Multinationals and Political Control. New York: St. Martin's Press.

Schrager, Laura Shill and James F. Short, Jr.
1978 "Toward a sociology of organizational crime." Social Problems 25: 407–19.

Schneider, Keith
1986a "Argentina protests use of live vaccine by scientists of U.S. New York Times, November 11: A1.
1986b "Second gene-altered vaccine tested outside the U.S." New York Times, November 13: A28.

Schwendinger, Herman and Julia Schwendinger
  1970   "Defenders of order or guardians of human rights." Issues in Criminology 5: 123–57.

Sellin, Thorsten
  1938   Culture Conflict and Crime. New York: Social Science Research Council.

Shapiro, Susan
  1983   "The new moral entrepreneurs: Corporate crime crusaders." Contemporary Sociology 12: 304–307.
  1984   Wayward Capitalists. New Haven: Yale University Press.

Shover, Neal
  1980   "The criminalization of corporate behavior: Federal surface coal mining." Pp. 98–125 in Gilbert Geis and Ezra Stotland (eds.), White Collar Crime: Theory and Research. Beverly Hills, CA: Sage.

Simon, David R. and D. Stanley Eitzen
  1986   Elite Deviance. Second Edition. Boston: Allyn and Bacon.

Strauss, Robert
  1978.   Interview. Environment Reporter 9 (July): 451.

Sunkle, Oscar
  1973   "Transnational capital and national disintegration in Latin America." Social and Economic Studies 22: 132–71.

Sutherland, Edwin H.
  1940   "White collar criminality." American Sociological Review 5: 1–12.
  [1949] White Collar Crime. New York: Holt,
  1961   Rinehart and Winston.

Tappan, Paul
  1947   "Who is the criminal?" American Sociological Review 12: 96–102.

Tift, Larry and Donald Sullivan
  1980   The Struggle to Be Human: Crime, Criminology, and Anarchism. Sanday, Orkney, U.K.: Cinfuegos Press.

United Nations
  1978   Transnational Corporations in World Development. New York: U.N. Commission on Transnational Corporations.

U.N. Chronicle
  1983   "Despite further agreement on code work remains incomplete." U.N. Chronicle 20: 102–104.

U.S. Department of Commerce
  1981   U.S. Direct Investment Abroad. Washington, DC: U.S. Government Printing Office.
  1984   U.S. Direct Investment Abroad. Washington, DC: U.S. Government Printing Office.

Vaughan, Diane
  1983   Controlling Unlawful Organizational Behavior. Chicago: University of Chicago Press.

Vieira, Anna Da Soledade
  1985   Environmental Information in Developing Nations: Politics and Policies. Westport, CT: Greenwood Press.

Wallerstein, Immanuel
  1979   The Capitalist World-Economy. New York: Cambridge.

Weidenbaum, Murray
  1983   "The U.N.'s bid to play consumer cop." New York Times, June 26: E1.
  1984   "U.N.'s regulatory riptide poses threat to international trade." Christian Science Monitor, January 5: B5.

Weir, David and Mark Schapiro
  1981   Circle of Poison: Pesticides and People in a Hungry World. San Francisco: Institute for Food and Development Policy.

SECTION
4

PROBLEMS
IN CONTROLLING
INSTITUTIONALIZED CRIME

The articles in this section demonstrate the massive theft, and even destruction of human life, through such activity as environmental pollution, which go largely unpunished and uncontrolled due to the massive power of corporations and their complete control of government. The paper by McCormick shows how the long-term failure to prosecute antitrust violations has led to a failure to morally stigmatize these activities. According to the first paper by Szasz, the 1976 federal regulatory law did not control corporate pollution practices, and in his second essay, Szasz shows that there is a recurrent failure of scandals to halt government-corporate corruption. Dowie shows how executives at Ford Motor Company made a decision to maximize corporate profits at the expense of crash protection for the gas tank of the Ford Pinto, knowing it would result in predictable amounts of injury and death. Even so, no Ford executive has been convicted in criminal court for these activities. The ultimate demise of the Occupational Safety and Health Administration is traced by Calavita.

RULE ENFORCEMENT
AND MORAL INDIGNATION

Some Observations on the Effects
of Criminal Antitrust Convictions
upon Societal Reaction Processes

Albert E. McCormick, Jr.
Macon Junior College

THE PROBLEM

The roles of rule enforcement and formal labelling in the process of creating deviant careers has been relatively well-explored in recent years. A second aspect of rule enforcement, however, has rarely been studied—the effects of rule enforcement upon the maintenance of moral opprobrium toward not just the deviant, but also toward *deviant behavior categories*.

Concern with this aspect of deviance originated with Durkheim (1947:102), who suggested that punishment primarily serves to emphasize and reinforce prevalent values. An interesting phenomenon to investigate in light of this thought is the corporate offense, as this category of violation currently meets with weak, unorganized indignation. In the long-running controversy over the essential nature of corporate offenses, both proponents (notably Clinard, 1946; 1952; Hartung, 1950; and Sutherland, 1945) and opponents (notably Burgess, 1950; Kadish, 1963; and Tappan, 1947) of a criminal definition noted that violations in this area are not generally regarded as particularly reprehensible either by enforcement agencies or the public at large. A small number of impressionistic and empirical studies bear out this conclusion (Der-

showitz, 1961:288–289; Geis, 1968; Newman, 1957; Smith, 1961).

This pattern indicates that the moral opprobrium which initially led to the creation of this class of violations has not endured. A key factor in the neutralization of moral opprobrium toward corporate offenses is the pattern of formal response established in regard to such violations. The following analysis focuses upon the Sherman Antitrust Act, one of the first federal regulatory laws, in order to demostrate what social phenomena may occur when sanctions are rarely applied to a particular form of deviance.

HISTORICAL CONSIDERATIONS

Various practices of trade restraint have long been censured in English common law and American colonial statute law. Primarily civil in nature, enabling recovery of damages, this body of law was deemed sufficient to control irregular business behavior in an economy characterized by small entrepreneurship, where the effects of any single violation were limited and local (Jones, 1926; Thorelli, 1955:9–23). With the rapid transformation to centralized industrialism in the latter portion of the nineteenth century, the development of the corporation changed the economic and social order in ways that the existing economic laws could scarcely control. Those segments of society economically based upon the ownership of small independent property and oriented toward small town and rural life, found themselves increasingly displaced socially, politically, and economically by those whose wealth and power was based upon the salaries, investments, and profits of a corporate economy.

Specifically, grievances against corporations centered upon 1) oppressive and ruthless business practices, 2) fear of concentrated wealth and power, and 3) governmental policies granting special privileges to big business at the expense of other interest groups (Dudden, 1957:589). Corporations and monopolism were viewed as antithetical to the traditional American economic ideology of free competition, free enterprise, a relative diffusion of wealth and power, freedom of contract, laissez faire and the "natural laws" of economics (i.e., that free competition, coupled with unrestricted supply and demand, acted as the natural governors of prices and quality), and a concept of government whose sole purpose was impartially to protect those laws.

While the growth of the corporate system confronted traditional values, the reaction against big business coalesced during a long-running series of agricultural depressions marking the latter third of the nineteenth century (particularly affecting cotton and wheat growers in the South and Midwest). Expressing his discontent through various agrarian third party movements, the typical small farmer placed the blame for falling prices, rising costs, increased debts, and massive foreclosures upon the monopolistic control of corporations and trusts. Big business was accused, with some justification, of massive manipulations of the marketplace, aided by such governmental favors as protective tariffs, import quotas, lax incorporation laws, currency and taxation policies, and access to government-owned resources. Hence, seeing gigantism itself as an evil, radical agrarian groups—as Grangers, Populists— pressed for complete destruction of industrial combinations (McKee, 2906; Morgan, 1971: 11–20; Thorelli, 1955:143–151). A significant segment of society believed itself to be cruelly exploited, and reacted strongly, agitating for legislation to redress its grievances.

Such proposed legislation, however, was directed against another powerful interest group.

And unlike that of the agrarians, the economic and political strength of corporate interests was rapidly increasing. As the centralization of business and industry was obviously perceived as integral to the continued existence of this interest group, a counterreaction to antimonopolism quickly developed, taking the forms of what Rogers and Buffalo (1974:112–113) term "reinterpretation" and "redefinition." This counterreaction centered on 1) the social benefits to be derived from industrial combination, 2) a defense of concentrated wealth and power, and 3) a defense of governmental privilege extended to business.

With the rise of business combination, an ideological alternative to traditional economic and social concepts evolved, drawing heavily upon popularized versions of Social Darwinism. In this view, big business, corporations, and their derivative social effects represented a logical step in social evolution and the perfection of society. While certain "temporary" dislocations could occur during this transition, industrial combination would eventually benefit all segments of society through higher wages, quality products, increased production, lower costs, and (through the elimination of "cut-throat" competition) a stable economy. Further, corporate entrepreneurs, labelled "criminals of greed" by their opponents, saw themselves as rugged individualists, superior to the commoner in initiative, industry, and ability. Hence, the concentration of wealth and power in their hands represented the inevitable and deserved rewards of natural selection and survival of the fittest (see, for example, Carnegie, 1889:656). As the development of the corporate system was the next integral step in the evolution of society, not only must the system continue unrestricted, but also, when and where necessary, it must obtain government protection and assistance (Thorelli, 1955:116–117; Tipple, 1963:23–26).

This period of history was characterized by considerable tensions between rural agrarian and urban industrial society. Industrialism had created a unified economic system, but at the cost of cherished, traditional ideals. With innovation, efficiency, and productivity had come an impersonal monolith exhibiting conspicuous wealth, concentrated power, unfair competitive practices, and undue political influence. Political pressures to control big business, spurred by the rapid growth of Populism, led to the legislation of the Sherman Antitrust Act of 1890. This law made it a criminal offense to combine in restraint of trade or to monopolize, with original penalties for conviction maximized at one year's imprisonment and $5000 fine (since raised to $50,000). While certain remedial measures of a civil nature were available, principal responsibility for enforcement was invested in the Department of Justice.

For agrarian reformers, the purpose of the Sherman law was not only to eliminate specific practices that threatened competition. They perceived it as meant to restrict the influence of big business on economic and social life. For whatever end the Sherman Act was designed, however, its effectiveness as a control on behavior rested ultimately on its enforcement, not its legislation.[1]

THE NATURE OF ANTITRUST ENFORCEMENT

In order to establish the viability of recently enacted legislation (especially one initiating an entirely new field of criminal law) the Sherman law should have been widely and vigorously enforced from the outset. Without question, the most critical period for instituting a law as an effective behavior control is that immediately following its enactment. This, however, was not the case with the Sherman law. Even though a significant segment of the population had vehemently protested abusive corporate behavior, government administrations in the years immediately following the passage of the Sherman Act were reluctant to act. No extra funds for antitrust enforcement were voted by Congress, nor was a separate Anti-Trust Division created

within the Department of Justice until 1903 (Neale, 1968:28; Thorelli, 1955:534–537). During this time, the Justice Department initiated only twenty-two antitrust cases, of which six were criminal. Until 1903, only one criminal and three civil suits against *corporate* defendants were successfully prosecuted. Enforcement bias is even more clearly demonstrated by examining the success ratio of antitrust suits directed against labor during the same period. Of seven suits, criminal and civil, initiated against labor organizations, six were successfully concluded by the government (Faulkner, 1959:102).

Even had the government been more willing to prosecute antitrust violations, a key Supreme Court decision diminished effective antitrust enforcement. In the E. G. Knight case of 1895, the Court ruled that the Sherman Act extended only to monopolies in commerce, and did not include monopolies in manufacturing (Thorelli, 1955: 445–448).

The significance of this early enforcement pattern should be apparent. Since the government was either unwilling or unable to execute the antitrust law, it could not be taken as a serious effort to regulate corporate behavior. During the crucial period in which the Sherman law required massive, visible enforcement for it to become established as instrumental policy, only feeble token efforts were made. In consequence, corporate combination, consolidation, and monopolization not only continued, but increased, particularly near the turn of the century. This was accompanied by wider and stronger appeals for effective regulatory controls (Bills and Debates in Congress Relating to Trusts, 1903; Thorelli, 1955:289–368).

As indicated by Table 1, this public pressure eventually had its effect during the second term of Theodore Roosevelt, when government-instituted antitrust cases increased, as did the percentage of criminal cases. But this increased level of enforcement was modified by the courts, particularly with a series of decisions, culminating in 1911, involving the Standard Oil and American Tobacco Corporations. In this series of decisions, the courts ruled that the Sherman Act applied only to "unreasonable" combinations and did not prevent consolidation in and of itself.

---

[1]For a fuller understanding of the social, economic, and political conflict underlying the antitrust issue, see the Congressional debates and actions surrounding the legislation of the Sherman Act. See Bills and Debates in Congress Relating to Trusts (1903) and the Congressional Record (1890).

TABLE 1 Litigated Criminal Conviction and Sentencing Patterns in Antitrust Cases Brought by the Department of Justice, 1890–1969, by Five Year Periods*

Period Case Instituted	Total	Criminal Cases	All Convictions	Litigated Convictions[a]	Sentences Imposed and Length[b]	Characteristics of Case
1890–1894	9	4	0	0	0	
1895–1899	7	1	0	0	0	
1900–1904	6	1	1	1	0	
1905–1909	39	26	11	11	0	
1910–1914	91	37	21	12	1–4 hrs.	labor (union misconduct)
1915–1919	43	25	13	8	3–4 hrs.	labor
					1 yr.	labor-sabotage
					1 yr.	labor
1920–1924	66	25	15	14	5–NA	price fixing-labor
					10 days	labor
					10 mos.	labor
					8 mos.	labor
					1 yr.	labor
1925–1929	59	16	14	10	3–6 mos.	labor
					NA	price fixing-labor
					10 days	price fixing-violence
1930–1934	30	11	8	6	6–3 mos.	monopolization-violence
					6 mos.	monopolization-violence
					6 mos.– 2 yrs.	price fixing-violence
					2 yrs.	price fixing-violence
					2–5 yrs.	price fixing-labor-violence
					3–6 mos.	labor-violence
1935–1939	57	27	19	6	1–1 yr.	labor-violence
1940–1944	223	163	123	13	0	
1945–1949	157	58	50	9	0	
1950–1954	159	73	65	10	2–6 mos.	price fixing-labor
					9 mos.	price fixing-labor
1955–1959	195	97	86	21	2–90 days	price fixing-labor
					1 yr.	price fixing-labor
1960–1964	215	78	64	17	2–30 days	price fixing
					NA	price fixing
1965–1969	195	52	46	6	1–24 hrs.– 60 days	price fixing
Total	1551	694	536	144	26	

[a]All convictions minus accepted nolo contendere pleas*

[b]Excludes suspended sentences, remitted sentences, and probation.

*Adapted from Posner (1970:385, 390–391).

This nebulous "rule of reason" doctrine left the determination of what was lawful and reasonable to the courts. Many business combinations were permitted to grow and flourish, as long as they remained "reasonable" (Arnold, 1937:207–209). Where legislative attempts once had been made to prevent the concept of business consolidation from taking hold, it had gained the status of an institution and formal sanction in a few years.

It is instructive to observe the entire pattern of criminal enforcement of the antitrust laws. While containing civil remedies, the Sherman Antitrust Act and subsequent antitrust legislation essentially classifies violations as criminal. Notwithstanding, less than half (694, or 44.7%) of the 1551 antitrust cases instituted by the government from 1890 to 1969 have been criminal suits. Further, the proportion of criminal suits to all suits has fluctuated rather widely from administration to administration (converting the figures in Table 1 to percentages, from a low of 14.3% in the period 1895–1899 to a high of 73.1% in the period of 1940–1944), perhaps indicating strong political influence on enforcement policies. Surprisingly enough, once a criminal suit is initiated, there seems to be a strong tendency for it to result in conviction; about three-quarters of all criminal suits were determined in favor of the prosecution. But when compared to the total number of cases instituted, only 34.6% have resulted in criminal convictions. Upon breakdown into five-year periods, the rate of criminal conviction generally remained well below 30% until the advent of World War II and the rigorous enforcement of Attorney-General Thurmond Arnold.

Almost three-fourths (73.1%) of criminal antitrust convictions have been gained through the acceptance of pleas of nolo contendere (a figure presumably reflecting defendant judgments of relative costs in accepting or contesting charges, or tendencies to prosecute cases with overwhelming evidence). While this is not unusual court procedure, in a sense somewhat akin to plea bargaining, it nevertheless has tremendous importance in limiting notions of criminality. In pleading nolo contendere, defendants *do not admit* any criminal guilt. Rather, they merely refuse to contest the charges against them, accepting whatever punishment the court determines. Usually the courts, grateful for the elimination of expensive and time-consuming litigation, reduce the severity of punishment (as occurs with plea bargaining in the disposition of conventional offenses). Therefore, in the majority of cases ending in "conviction," the defendant was in actuality spared formal definition as a criminal. Court findings of antitrust criminality, as reflected by litigated convictions, included only 144 cases, or 20.8% of all criminal cases instituted.

The number of convicted criminals produced by antitrust enforcement is much smaller than that represented even by litigated convictions. Of the 536 cases resulting in some type of criminal conviction, only twenty-six (4.9%) have led to the actual imposition of a prison sentence (this figure, however, does not include cases resulting in probation or in suspended or remitted sentences). *No individual served a prison sentence for an antitrust violation during the first twenty years of enforcement.* Even more telling, the *first eleven* imprisonments for antitrust convictions involved *union and labor* defendants. Of these twenty-six cases in which sentences were imposed and served, twenty-three involved labor misconduct and/or violence. It was not until 1961 (with the Electrical Conspiracy case) that businessmen were actually imprisoned purely for price-fixing and monopolization. In view of the enforcement pattern outlined here, it is no wonder that the convicted defendants in the Electrical Conspiracy case expressed surprise and anger over their sentences, in spite of knowing the patent illegality of their behavior (see Geis, 1968, and Smith, 1961).

Not only are the application of criminal sanctions in antitrust cases rare, but imposed penalties seem to be exceedingly light. Criminal fines are so small as to be regarded, when levied, as "reasonable license fees" for engaging in illegal conduct (Dershowitz, 1961:285–287). As seen in the last column of Table 1, length of sentences tends to be much less than the maximum permitted by law. Even here, it may be readily observed that sentences given to businessmen tend to be shorter than those given in cases involving labor or violence. By 1961, only thirty-one individuals had been imprisoned under the provisions of the Sherman Act (Dershowitz, 1961:291), and even with the inclusion of antitrust penalties imposed subsequent to 1961, the total number of imprisoned businessmen is less than fifty. A similar infrequency of criminal proceedings and criminal punishment has been noted in litigations concerning other types of corporate offenses (Clinard, 1952; Hartung, 1950; Sutherland, 1949).

The data from Table 1 may be summarized as follows. Of 1551 antitrust prosecutions instituted in eighty years of enforcement, 45% have been criminal cases. While 35% of all cases instituted led to criminal conviction, only 9% of all cases were litigated convictions. Less than 2% of all cases resulted in served sentences, and virtually all of these involved defendants from the labor sphere. Therefore, taking all antitrust cases into consideration, only a handful of business-persons have suffered actual criminal stigmatization for illegal monopolistic activity and restraint of trade.

DISCUSSION

It is apparent, that in regard to the federal antitrust laws, there has been a noticeable lack of large-scale, sustained, and well-publicized enforcement. In direct consequence, no large, visible group of convicted, stigmatized individuals has been created. This, in turn, has had profound effects upon various aspects of the societal reaction process directed against illegal corporate activities.

Perhaps the first effect of antitrust legislation and early enforcement was to transform monopolization and restraint of trade from nonconforming to aberrant behavior (using these terms as defined by Merton, 1971). In the counterreaction to antimonopolism, briefly described earlier, a significant number of books and articles defending the centralization of business and industry appeared in popular literature prior to the legislation of the Sherman Act. This literature, much of it written by such industrial leaders as Carnegie and Rockefeller, essentially rejected many traditional socio-economic values and attempted to replace them with the "superior" socio-economic values consistent with corporate development. Various forms of restraint of trade, which at that time, of course, were not illegal, were openly admitted and defended by corporate interests (e.g., Rockefeller's well-known American Beauty Rose analogy).

The transformation from nonconformity to aberrance, however, was not abrupt or concomitant with the legislation of the Sherman Act. During the initial period of antitrust enforcement (1890–1903), various forms of restraint of trade occurred in a relatively open manner. This was attributable at least in part to a deflection of public interest to other political issues, the initial lack of vigorous government enforcement, and adverse court decisions (such as the E. C. Knight case). Popular literature still contained

articles and books staunchly defending trust activity. For example, as late as 1899, a book was published characterizing antitrust as a "crusade against prosperity" (Gunton, 1899). Overt resistance to antitrust efforts diminished only when public opposition to trusts reintensified toward the end of the 1890's. This renewed interest in the trust problem, with an even wider public base of support than that originally leading to antitrust legislation, eventually produced the "trust-busting" era of Roosevelt and Taft (Thorelli, 1955:309–351). At this point, restraint of trade activities was forced to become covert, although corporate interests continued—and still continue—to attack the feasibility and desirability of federal restrictions.

While the antitrust violator has been transformed from a nonconformist to an aberrant by legislation and token enforcement, the primacy of this deviant role has not otherwise been affected. The risk of getting caught is small, and penalties are negligible when compared to potential profit. There is thus little motivation for, or merit in, conforming to the law. It may be speculated that conformity would place many corporations at a disadvantage in the business world, if estimates of the extent of regulatory violations have any validity. Criminal sanctions against antitrust violations are almost nil. A violator, even if caught, risks little likelihood of social stigma. This stigma, if it were present, would serve in the well-defined labelling process, to create social distance between the offender and society, hinder and limit the legitimate behavior options available, and thus force an offender further away from the mainstream. But, the deterrent power created by the negative stigma of a formal criminal label is totally lacking with this class of offenses. As a result, while acknowledging the illegality of the behavior, violators remain convinced of their own virtuous conduct, enabling them to maintain a positive self-image. The phenomenon of self-esteem maintenance is well-noted throughout white collar crime literature. In effect, illegal corporate conduct in the business world, where pressures and rewards exist for its continuation, is covertly condoned (Baumhart, 1961). This, coupled with weak enforcement policies, allows violators to retain a self-image of noncriminality, the primacy of their deviant role, and permits simultaneously a relatively unrestricted field, both social and psychological, for further violation.

The nature of antitrust enforcement has had its effect not only upon the violator, but also upon the violation. The legislation of the Sherman Act both created a new classification of offenses, publicly affirmed activities in restraint of trade as deviant, *and*, perhaps more important, symbolically upheld the formal dominance of traditional socio-economic ideology. In this light, the antimonopoly movement may be viewed as what Gusfield (1963), in reference to the Temperance movement, termed a "symbolic crusade." Indeed, both the antimonopoly and Temperance movements emanated from efforts on the part of rural small-town American to maintain its social standing and to resist the economic, political, and ideological inroads of an urban industrialized society. This public affirmation of corporate activity as deviant was effective only on the level of establishing ideal cultural norms. In terms of attempting to institute real behavioral norms, the Sherman law was completely ineffective. Thus, the want of real, vigorous enforcement permitted the rise of a dual and contradictory economic value system. In this duality, dominant culture officially recognizes and pays lip service to the ideals of free competition, but practices private regulation and collectivism.

Therefore, in pragmatic terms, antitrust enforcement practices have failed to accomplish the essential function of rule enforcement: clearly to demonstrate what social rules and values are working and dominant. Inconsistent and haphazard implementation of the law has not only served to widen the disparity between real and ideal cultural norms, but has also created a large degree of rule ambiguity. With the exception of extreme cases, there are few clear guidelines to what business behavior is permitted or prohibited. This ambiguity is well-illustrated by the transformation of intent of the Sherman Act when it was initially implemented. It was the original purpose of antitrust proponents to make a law that would effectively combat predatory business practices, regardless of their form. In-

frequent government prosecution, implementation of the law as a method to control labor, and key, adverse court decisions quickly obscured the original intent. The ambiguity inherent in the antitrust law is symbolized by the "rule of reason" test. Nowhere is the term "reasonable" legislatively defined, therefore such definition is left to the courts and to judicial precedent. Such precedents are not lacking, but their effectiveness as unmistakable and realistic guidelines has been eroded by sporadic enforcement and extremely lenient adjudication.

The haziness regarding specific behavioral criteria in regulatory laws has created a certain degree of confusion and frustration in the implementation of business procedures (Lane, 1953:154–157). This in turn has functioned to exacerbate a general atmosphere of uncertainty and unpredictability, accompanied by, as Sutherland (1940:5) noted, resultant negative effects upon social organization (e.g., creation of distrust, lowering of social morale, increasing disrespect for law). On the other hand, the ambiguity inherent in this situation permits its exploitation. Behavior that would otherwise be prevented by closer scrutiny and regulation is permitted free rein. Hence, I suspect that regulatory enforcement policies, as practiced, are in reality designed to *maintain* a high potential for flexibility of action in nominally illegal areas.[2]

Perhaps central to the effects of enforcement patterns has been the disruption of the entire societal reaction process which first led to the legislation of antitrust laws. The enactment of prohibitory laws, designed to control particular segments of the population, requires the impetus of moral indignation on the part of interest groups possessing the power to designate the prohibitions. If laws are to be effectively maintained on both instrumental and symbolic levels, the intensity of disapproval must remain relatively stable. As part of the societal reaction process, rule enforcement serves not just to control be-

---

[2] It has been argued, for this very reason, that the Sherman Act itself was deliberately worded in an ambiguous manner. See Clark (1931), Fainsod and Gordon (1941), Seager and Gulick (1929), and Thorelli (1955), among others, for elaboration.

havior, but symbolically to reinforce and sustain opprobrium directed toward offender and offense. It is this critical function that the enforcement of antitrust laws has failed to fulfill.

This has occurred, in part, because enforcement has not established a continuous, readily identifiable group of violators against which society could symbolically (as through stigmatization, spoiling identities) react. Such a continuous group is required, as the maintenance of a high level of indignation rests upon the public repeatedly observing and participating in successful degradation processes. Simultaneously, there has been a failure to establish a continuous group of *victims,* which would not only supply a direct source of indignation, but also attract a certain amount of positive, sympathetic reaction from society at large. Nonenforcement, in addition to signifying the lack of an offense or an offender, implies also that no victim exists. Further, this subtle denial of victimization emanates from the most credible of sources: those who have been officially entrusted with the implementation and enforcement of the law. Essentially, enforcement has created nothing more against which society could react. No actions are taken which would serve to continue the process of *reaffirming* illegal corporate behavior as deviant.

Counterreaction has been a key element in neutralizing both intensity of enforcement and social indignation leading to enforcement demands. By influencing visibility and reporting of offenses (Dershowitz, 1961:288–289), manipulating community expectations through the propagandizing of themes focusing upon the necessity of a profit system, the role of business in combatting social problems, improvements in living standards (Seider, 1974:807–808), and affecting the organization and actions of enforcement agents (Hills, 1971:172–195), societal indignation and resistance directed toward illegal corporate activities has been steadily eroded. This evolution of public attitude has in no way been stemmed by enforcement, which, if vigorously committed to traditional socioeconomic values, may have counteracted this neutralization process. That is, concomitant with the movement toward a centralized economy was the rise of a new "big business" ideology, presenting society with alternatives to established traditional values. Initially, this alternative value set was considered deviant by important social segments which perceived themselves as its victims. Working from a position of power, through the dual action of managing public opinion and nullifying notions of victimization (essentially by propagating the message that the benefits of the new system far outweighed shortcomings) and directly negating the policies of effective enforcement, "big business" ideology gained legitimacy, if not ideally, at least pragmatically. Behavior originally perceived as aberrant to traditional custom eventually became part of the normative order and was regarded as integral to social organization. Thus, this behavior went through a process of *redefinition* (Rogers and Buffalo, 1974:113). The behavior has remained essentially the same, but society has changed in its reaction to the behavior, in this instance from an attitude of indignation to one of neutrality.

SUMMARY

Rule enforcement is a critical element in the ongoing societal reaction process. After a rule is created, both its instrumental and symbolic functioning are dependent upon the frequency, manner, and degree with which it is invoked against transgressors. Where enforcement is rare, the entire societal reaction process is disrupted and the rule itself becomes an anachronism.

The case history of antitrust regulation illustrates this general process: (1) moral indignation against illegal corporate activity was at one time high and (2) enforcement of the criminal laws designed to regulate and control such behavior, in practical terms, has been virtually nonexistent. Nonenforcement assisted the redefinition of corporate activities as legitimate (or semi-legitimate) and crucial to socioeconomic organization. Nonenforcement also shows that dominant society is not concerned with corporate deviance, nor perceives it as a significant threat to social order. In fact, the opposite argument may be offered, that vigorous enforcement of regulatory laws may potentially pose a very real threat to the present socio-economic system.

REFERENCES

Arnold, Thurmond W.
1937   The Folklore of Capitalism. New Haven: Yale University Press.

Baumhart, Raymond C.
1961   "How ethical are businessmen?" Harvard Business Review 39: 6-19, 156-176.

Bills and Debates in Congress Relating to Trusts
1903   Senate Document 147, Fifty-seventh Congress, Second Session, Washington, D.C.: U.S. Government Printing Office.

Burgess, Ernest W.
1950   "Comment." American Journal of Sociology 56: 32-34.

Carnegie, Andrew
1889   "Wealth." North American Review 148: 653-664.

Clark, John D.
1931   The Federal Trust Policy. Baltimore: Johns Hopkins Press.

Clinard, Marshall B.
1946   "Criminological theories of violation of wartime regulations." American Sociological Review 11: 258-270.
1952   The Black Market. New York: Rinehart.

Congressional Record
1890   Fifty-first Congress, First Session. Washington, D.C.: U.S. Government Printing Office.

Dershowitz, Alan M.
1961   "Increasing community control over corporate crime—A problem in the law of sanctions." Yale Law Journal 71: 280-306.

Dudden, Arthur P.
1957   "Men against monopoly: The prelude to trust-busting." Journal of the History of Ideas 18: 587-593.

Durkheim, Emile
1947   The Division of Labor in Society. Tr. George Simpson. Glencoe: Free Press.

Fainsod, Merle and Lincoln Gordon
1941   Government and the American Economy. New York: Norton.

Faulkner, Harold U.
1959   Politics, Reform, and Expansion 1890-1900. New York: Harper.

Gies, Gilbert
1968   "The heavy electrical equipment cases of 1961." Pp. 103-118 in Gilbert Geis (ed.), White-Collar Criminal. New York: Atherton.

Gunton, George
1899   Trusts and the Public. New York: Appleton.

Gusfield, Joseph
1963   Symbolic Crusade. Urbana: University of Illinois Press.

Hartung, Frank
1950   "White collar offenses in the wholesale meat industry." American Journal of Sociology 56: 25-32.

Hills, Stuart L.
1971   Crime, Power, and Morality: The Criminal Law Process in the United States. Scranton: Chandler.

Jones, Franklin D.
1926   "Historical development of the law of business competition." Yale Law Journal 35: 42-55, 207-234, 905-938.

Kadish, Sanford H.
1963   "Some observations on the use of criminal sanctions in enforcing economic regulations." University of Chicago Law Review 30: 423-449.

Lane, Robert E.
1953   "Why businessmen violate the law." Journal of Criminal Law, Criminology, and Police Science 44: 151-165.

McKee, Thomas H.
1906   The National Conventions and Platforms of All Political Parties. Baltimore: Friedenwald.

Merton, Robert K.
1971   "Social problems and sociological theory." Pp. 793-845 in Robert K. Merton and Robert A. Nisbet (eds.), Contemporary Social Problems. New York: Harcourt, Brace, and World.

Morgan, H. Wayne
1971   Unity and Culture. Baltimore: Penguin.

Neale, A. D.
1960   The Anti-trust Laws of the United States of America. New York: Cambridge University Press.

Newman, Donald J.
1957   "Public attitudes toward a form of white collar crime." Social Problems 4: 228-232.

Posner, Richard A.
1970   "A statistical study of antitrust enforcement." Journal of Law and Economics 13: 365-419.

Rogers, Joseph W. and M. D. Buffalo
 1974 "Fighting back: Nine modes of adaptation to a deviant label." Social Problems 22: 101–118.

Seager, Henry R. and Charles A. Gulick
 1929 Trust and Corporate Problems. New York: Harper.

Seider, Maynard S.
 1974 "American big business ideology: A content analysis of executive speeches." American Sociological Review 39: 802–815.

Smith, Richard Austin
 1961 "The incredible electrical conspiracy." Pp. 529–548 in Marvin E. Wolfgang, Leonard Savitz, and Norman Johnston (eds.), The Sociology of Crime and Delinquency. New York: Wiley.

Sutherland, Edwin H.
 1940 "White-collar criminality." American Sociological Review 5: 1–12.

 1945 "Is 'white collar crime' crime?" American Sociological Review 10: 132–139.

 1949 White Collar Crime. New York: Holt, Rinehart, and Winston.

Tappan, Paul W.
 1947 "Who is the criminal?" American Sociological Review 12: 96–102.

Thorelli, Hans B.
 1955 The Federal Antitrust Policy. Baltimore: Johns Hopkins Press.

Tipple, John
 1963 "The robber baron in the gilded age: Entrepreneur or iconoclast?" Pp. 14–37 in H. Wayne Morgan (ed.), The Gilded Age: A Reappraisal. Syracuse: Syracuse University Press.

CORPORATIONS, ORGANIZED CRIME, AND THE DISPOSAL OF HAZARDOUS WASTE

An Examination of the Making of a Criminogenic Regulatory Structure*

Andrew Szasz
University of California, Santa Cruz

The generation of hazardous waste is a necessary side effect of modern industrial production. Factories must cope daily with large accumulations of unrecyclable chemical byproducts generated by normal production techniques. The processing or disposal of these byproducts is a significant cost of production, a cost that, like all other costs of production, the prudent owner or manager minimizes.

Until recently, industrial hazardous waste was not legally distinguished from municipal garbage and other solid wastes. It was disposed of with ordinary garbage, at very low cost to the generator, mostly in coastal waters or in landfills unfit to adequately contain it. However, concern grew during the 1970s that improper disposal of hazardous waste was creating an environmental and public health burden of unknown but potentially massive scale. This concern finally moved some states and eventually the federal government to begin to legislate new

regulations. The centerpiece of this regulatory effort was the federal Resource Conservation and Recovery Act (RCRA) of 1976. On paper, RCRA mandated comprehensive mechanisms to guarantee the safe disposal of hazardous waste. It established standards and procedures for classifying substances as hazardous. It authorized the states to register corporate generators of hazardous waste and license hauling and disposal firms. It mandated the creation of a manifest system that would document the movement of hazardous waste "from cradle to grave," from the generator, through the hands of the transporter, to the shipment's final destination at a licensed disposal site.

By legally distinguishing hazardous waste from other wastes and by directing that such wastes be treated differently than municipal solid waste, the new regulations dramatically increased, almost overnight, the demand for hazardous waste hauling and disposal services. Unhappily, recent state and federal investigations have documented both that illegal waste disposal is widespread (U.S. General Accounting Office, 1985; U.S. House of Representatives, 1980) and that organized crime elements traditionally active in garbage hauling and landfilling have entered this burgeoning and potentially profitable new market (Block and Scarpitti, 1985; U.S. House of Representatives, 1980, 1981a). Although the exact extent of organized crime involvement in hazardous waste hauling

Andrew Szasz (1986) "Corporations, Organized Crime, and the Disposal of Hazardous Waste: An Examination of the Making of a Criminogenic Regulatory Structure." *Criminology* Vol. 24 (February): 1–27.

*I wish to gratefully acknowledge that this paper has benefited from comments by Frank Henry, Judith Gerson, Wendy Strimling, Vern Baxter, John Campbell, Carroll Estes, members of the Pew Writing Seminar, and several anonymous reviewers.

and disposal is uncertain,[1] the fact of that involvement is beyond question. A situation exists, then, in which corporations, some at the heart of the American economy, discharge their regulatory obligations under RCRA by entering into direct contractual relationships with firms dominated by organized crime. The goal in this paper is to analyze in detail the complex nature of this relationship between corporate generators of hazardous waste and elements of organized crime that are active in industrial waste disposal. This goal will be approached by analyzing the formation and implementation of RCRA legislation.

The subject of this paper speaks to two distinct criminological literatures: works that examine the relationship between legitimate and illicit enterprise and works that examine crimogenic market structures. Recent scholarship has chal-

lenged the commonsense distinction between legitimate business and organized crime. Schelling (1967), Smith and Alba (1979), Smith (1980), and Albanese (1982) all argue that the most fundamental aspect of organized crime is that it is a form of entrepreneurial activity and that its ethnic or conspiratorial nature is of secondary importance. Recent scholarship also challenges the equally widely held belief that the relationship between the underworld and legitimate business consists solely of the former exploiting the latter through extortion, racketeering, and so on (Drucker, 1981). At minimum, it is argued that the relationship is one of mutually beneficial interdependence (Martens and Miller-Longfellow, 1982). This is clearly supported by excellent case studies of labor racketeering (Block and Chambliss, 1981), organized crime on the waterfront (Block, 1982), and arson (Brady, 1983). Chambliss (1978:181–182) argues the even stronger view that organized crime can exist only because the structure of the legitimate economy and its accompanying political organization make its emergence possible and even inevitable. In a similar vein, Smith (1980) and Smith and Alba (1979) challenge the very distinction between business and organized crime and begin to dissolve that distinction in the common dynamic of a market economy. The study of organized crime participation in hazardous waste disposal presents an opportunity to once again examine this relationship between legitimate and illegitimate entrepreneurship.

The story of RCRA may also have links to the concept of criminogenic market processes. Farberman's (1975) and Leonard and Weber's (1977) studies of auto retailing and Denzin's (1977) study of the liquor industry showed that the normal operating logic of an industry may force some sectors of that industry into illegal activity in order to survive, much less thrive, in doing their part of the business. Needleman and Needleman (1979) subsequently expanded the concept by describing a second type of criminogenesis in which the criminal activity is not forced. It is, instead, an unwelcome drain on business, but it is unavoidable because the conditions that make it possible are necessary to the

[1]The extent of involvement is unclear for two reasons:

First, investigation has focused on the New York, Connecticut, and New Jersey region. This is a strategic site for investigation because so much hazardous waste is produced in the Tri-State area (for example, New Jersey ranks number one in the nation in annual hazardous waste generation) and because mob involvement in garbage in this region has been thoroughly documented. But, for the same reasons, this region may not be typical of the rest of the nation. Recent investigatory reporting concerning environmental pollution and political corruption in Louisiana (Getschow and Petzinger, 1984; Petzinger and Getschow, 1984a, 1984b; Snyder, 1985a, 1985b, 1985c, 1985d, 1985e, 1985f) shows that waste disposal is a corrupt business there as well, but that corruption grows out of the specific history of oil industry domination of that state's economy and its politics and appears to be quite different from patterns of corruption in the Northeast. This suggests that the post-RCRA relationship between corporate generators and waste disposers may be heavily influenced by variations in regional history predating RCRA.

Second, on a more theoretical level, the boundary between organized crime and legitimate business is, at points, somewhat ambiguous. Take, for example, SCA, the nation's third largest hazardous waste company. SCA undertook a vigorous acquisition program in New Jersey and quickly bought up about 20 garbage hauling and landfill companies. Some of these were formerly owned by organized crime figures. SCA is a corporation whose stock is traded on the New York Stock Exchange and its corporate board boasts outside directors associated with IBM, Houghton Mifflin Co., MIT, and the Boston Co. (U.S. House of Representatives, 1980, 1981a), but Congressional testimony indicates that when SCA bought mob-owned firms, it hired the former owners as managers and appears to have allowed them free hand to run their businesses as they had before acquisition.

overall functioning of that industry and could not be altered without fundamentally affecting how business is conducted in that industry. Needleman and Needleman discussed securities fraud as an example of what they call a "crime-facilitative," as opposed to a "crime-coercive" market sector. The fact that RCRA not only cannot prevent illegal hazardous waste dumping but has also attracted organized crime participation in illegal hazardous waste activity suggests that the concept of criminogenesis may be fruitfully extended to regulatory processes as well.

In the first sections of this paper, some background is presented on hazardous waste as a social issue and the nature and extent of organized crime involvement in hazardous waste hauling and disposal is summarized. At the core of the paper, the conditions that made this involvement possible are analyzed. It is shown that the most common explanations—lax implementation and enforcement by state and local officials—are incomplete. Analysis of the formation of RCRA legislation shows that corporate generators of hazardous waste were instrumental in securing a regulatory structure that would prove highly attractive to and well suited for organized crime participation. In other words, generators are deeply implicated in the creation of conditions that made their relationship to organized crime possible. This finding is used to critique two explanations of this relationship suggested during Congressional hearings, generator "ignorance" and generator "powerlessness." It is then argued that the relationship has two other important aspects: generators did not consciously desire or intend this outcome, but they nonetheless benefitted from it once it occurred. The paper concludes with a discussion of the relevance of the findings to the two areas of criminological research mentioned above.

THE ISSUE BACKGROUND: HAZARDOUS WASTE FACTS

The Environmental Protection Agency (EPA) defines waste products as "hazardous" if they are flammable, explosive, corrosive, or toxic. Major industries central to the modern national economy, such as the petroleum, chemical, electronic, and pharmaceutical industries, generate copious amounts of hazardous waste. Although there is still great uncertainty about the exact effect of industrial hazardous waste on public health (Greenberg and Anderson, 1984:84–105), improper management may result in explosions, fires, pollution of water resources, and other uncontrolled releases that put surrounding communities at risk and may result in physical harm ranging from skin irritation to increased incidence of cancer, lung disease, birth defects, and other serious illnesses.

How much hazardous waste has accumulated? How much is currently generated? Neither question can be answered confidently at this time. The generation and disposal of hazardous waste was completely unregulated until the late 1970s. In the absence of regulation, there was no systematic data-gathering effort. Consequently, there is great uncertainty about the magnitude and composition of hazardous waste accumulated up to the passage of the RCRA. Estimates have risen regularly as more sites are located and assessed. The EPA's most recent estimate is that there are 25,000 sites nationally that contain some hazardous waste. Of these, about 2,500 are priority sites judged by the EPA to be imminently hazardous to public health. More recent research by the General Accounting Office (GAO) and the Office of Technology Assessment (OTA) suggests that there may be 378,000 total sites nationally, perhaps 10,000 of them requiring priority attention (Shabecoff, 1985).

In theory, at least, the availability of data should have improved greatly following passage of the RCRA. Generators of hazardous waste were now required to create written documentation—the manifest—of the amount and content of every shipment of hazardous waste signed over to outside haulers and disposers. This documentation would be forwarded to state agencies following final disposition of each waste shipment. However, the actual quality of the data produced was compromised by several factors. First, there was little agreement over what substances should be defined as hazardous. Congressional and EPA testimony (U.S. Environmental Protection Agency, 1976, 1979; U.S. House of Representatives, 1975, 1976; U.S. Senate, 1974, 1979) shows that industrial spokesmen argued that too many substances had been unjustifiably included, while environmentalists argued that some materials had been improperly excluded. Second, firms generating less than one metric ton (2,200 lbs.) of hazardous waste per month are exempt from RCRA regulation (U.S. House of Representatives, 1983:56, 60). There are over four million privately owned industrial sites in the nation. The "small generator" exemption leaves all but a few tens of thousands of these sites out of RCRA's registration and manifest system. Third, some firms that generate significant amounts of hazardous waste have either failed to cooperate with EPA requests for data (Williams and Matheny, 1984:436–437) or have failed to identify themselves to the EPA as regulable generators (U.S. General Accounting Office, 1985:14–20). Fourth, even those firms that appear to comply with reporting requirements may not be reporting accurately the types and quantities of hazardous waste they generate (U.S. GAO, 1985:20–23). Consequently, knowledge of the amount and content of current hazardous waste generation is still imprecise. Estimates, like estimates of historical accumulation, have been rising. In 1974, the EPA was estimating hazardous waste generation at 10 million metric tons per year (U.S. Senate, 1974:70). In 1980, the EPA estimate had risen to 40 million metric tons. In 1983, new research led the EPA to nearly quadruple its estimate to 150 million metric tons (Block and Scarpitti, 1985:46), while the OTA was estimating 250 million metric tons per year (U.S. House of Representatives, 1983:1).[2]

Where does hazardous waste end up? In response to EPA inquiries in 1981, 16% of generating firms reported treating their wastes completely on site and another 22% reported treating part of their wastes on site. The remaining 62% contracted with other parties to handle all of their wastes (Block and Scarpitti, 1985:48–49). Where do transported wastes ac-

tually end up? The exemptions and noncooperation cited above leave an unknown fraction of total hazardous waste movement out of the paperwork of the manifest system (U.S. GAO, 1985:3–4, 14–24). The manifests that are filed are poorly monitored and vulnerable to undetected falsification (Greenberg and Anderson, 1984:242; U.S. GAO, 1985:25–31; U.S. House of Representatives, 1980:140, 1981b:124). Consequently, this question also cannot be answered with great certainty. On the basis of admittedly poor and incomplete data, the OTA estimates that no more than 10% to 20% of all hazardous waste is rendered harmless by incineration or by chemical or biological treatment. There are few facilities that can treat wastes in these ways and the price of treatment is much higher than the price of other means of disposal (U.S. House of Representatives, 1983:2, 5–6). The remaining 80% to 90% is either landfilled or disposed of illegally. Only a small proportion of hazardous waste goes into landfills that have the siting studies, proper containment practices, and continuous monitoring to be fully licensed by the EPA, since there are only 200 such landfills in the nation (Block and Scarpitti, 1985:49; U.S. House of Representatives, 1981b:187). Even these top landfills are only required by the EPA to keep wastes contained for 30 years (U.S. House of Representatives, 1983:2).[3] Most hazar-

---

[2]Methods of estimation are discussed in depth by Greenberg and Anderson (1984).

[3]It is generally admitted that even the best landfill is only temporary and inadequate: "No landfill can be made safe from all substances"—Albert Gore (U.S. House of Representatives, 1983:2). George J. Tyler, Assistant Commissioner of the New Jersey Department of Environmental Protection, speaking about the Lone Pine landfill in Freehold, New Jersey (U.S. House of Representatives, 1981b:188): "The landfill is leaking into the water, but so does every landfill in the country." The landfill at Wilsonville, Illinois, owned and operated by SCA (see Note 1), is, according to Dr. Raymond D. Harbison, a toxicologist, EPA consultant, and professor of pharmacology at Vanderbilt University, "the most scientific landfill in this country" (U.S. House of Representatives, 1981a:267). Geological and soil permeability feasibility tests were conducted before construction was begun. Trenches were carefully dug. Arriving waste is sampled and tested, then buried in either nonleaking 55 gallon drums or double-walled paper bags. Monitoring wells surround the site. Yet subsequent studies show that the soil is more porous than originally thought and water is seeping in at rates greater than predicted. Furthermore, the landfill is built over an aban-

dous waste goes to landfills that have only interim license to operate, landfills that are of much poorer quality and are likely to pollute the surrounding land and water within a few years.

Illegal hazardous waste dumping is even more likely to have adverse short-term environmental and public health consequences. The full extent of illegal hazardous waste disposal is not known. State officials interviewed by the GAO agreed that illegal disposal was occurring, but had no firm information on the scope of this activity (U.S. GAO, 1985:10). One study done for the EPA surveyed hazardous waste generators in 41 cities and estimated that one in seven generators had illegally disposed some of their wastes during the two years preceding the study (U.S. GAO, 1985:10). A wide array of illegal disposal practices have been documented. Waste shipments may end up commingled with ordinary garbage. A 20 cubic yard "dumpster" full of dry garbage can be made to absorb up to sixty 55 gallon drums of liquid hazardous waste (U.S. House of Representatives, 1980:63) and then be deposited in unlicensed municipal landfills never designed to contain hazardous waste. Liquid hazardous waste may be released along a roadway. An 8,000 gallon truck can be emptied in 8 minutes (U.S. House of Representatives, 1980:101). Shipments may simply be stockpiled at sites awaiting alleged transfer that never happens or at disposal facilities that have no real disposal capability (U.S. House of Representatives, 1980:10). Wastes may be drained into local city sewer systems, rivers, and oceans, or dumped in out-of-the-way rural spots (U.S. House of Representatives, 1980:93). Flammable hazardous waste may be commingled with fuel oil and sold as pure heating oil (U.S. House of Representatives, 1980:63–64) or sprayed on unsuspecting communities' roads for dust control (U.S. House of Representatives, 1980:151).

---

doned coal mine and feasibility tests underestimated the likelihood of "subsidence," land sinkage that may compromise the site's ability to keep substances safely contained. If this is the best site in the nation, the Office of Technology Assessment is right to worry that current efforts to clean up the worst abandoned sites under the Superfund program only transfer the problem to other places and future times (Shabecoff, 1985:31).

ORGANIZED CRIME PARTICIPATION IN THE HAZARDOUS WASTE DISPOSAL INDUSTRY

CONGRESSMAN ALBERT GORE: "At what point did companies picking up garbage begin to get into the toxic waste disposal business?"
HAROLD KAUFMAN: "To my knowledge, it's when the manifest system came out is when they found out the profit motive" (U.S. House of Representatives, 1980:8).

New Jersey Attorney General John J. Degnan pointed out to a Congressional audience that organized crime activity accounts for only a fraction of the illegal dumping taking place in the United States (U.S. House of Representatives, 1980:87). Nonetheless, organized crime was ideally suited to develop the methodology of illegal hazardous waste practices to the fullest. In those parts of the nation where garbage hauling and landfilling was historically controlled by organized crime, their movement into the newly created hazardous waste market was an obvious extension of current activity. In New Jersey, for example, organized crime had controlled the garbage industry through ownership of garbage hauling firms, through ownership of or control of landfills, and through labor racketeering (U.S. House of Representatives, 1981:1–45). The new regulations governing hazardous waste would have had to have been carefully written and tenaciously enforced were organized crime to be kept from applying this highly developed infrastructure to the new market. In fact, as will be shown below, the opposite happened and organized crime easily entered both the hauling and the disposal phases of the hazardous waste handling industry.

Hauling. Organized crime had dominated traditional garbage hauling in states like New York and New Jersey for decades. Once associates of organized crime owned a number of hauling firms in any geographical area, they established an organizational infrastructure that governed their relationships and ensured high profits. Threats and violence persuaded other firms to join that infrastructure and abide by its rules or to sell and get out. The keystone of this infrastructure was the concept of "property rights" or "respect." Municipal solid waste hauling contracts were illegally apportioned among haulers. Having a property right meant that a hauler held rights to continue picking up the contract at sites he currently serviced without competition from others. Other firms would submit artificially high bids or would not bid at all when a contract came up for renewal, thereby assuring that the contractor kept his traditional site. This system of *de facto* territorial monopolies permitted noncompetitive pricing and made the lowly business of garbage hauling a very lucrative activity. Property rights were recognized and enforced by organized crime authorities. Conflicts were adjudicated in meetings of the Municipal Contractors Association. Decisions of the MCA were enforced by threats and, if necessary, violence (U.S. House of Representatives, 1981a:1–42).[4] As is shown below, when the RCRA mandated the licensing of firms deemed fit to transport hazardous waste, mob-connected garbage haulers found it easy to acquire state permits and declare themselves to be hazardous waste haulers. Quite naturally, they brought their traditional forms of social organization with them. Individual haulers holding established property rights assumed that they would transfer those property rights to the new type of waste (U.S. House of Representatives, 1980:22). They also met as a group to set up a Trade Waste Association modeled after the Municipal Contractors Association to apportion and enforce property rights in the new market (U.S. House of Representatives, 1980:9–10, 1981a:1–12, 212).

Disposal. The manifest system requires that someone be willing to sign off on the manifest and declare that a waste shipment has been properly disposed of. This means, as Congressman Florio (Democrat, New Jersey) pointed out (U.S.

House of Representatives, 1980:30), that mob control over hauling is not enough: organized crime figures had to have ownership of, or at least influence over, final disposal sites. This requirement did not prove to be a serious stumbling block, however. Many landfills were already owned wholly or in part by organized crime figures, a legacy of past mob involvement in the garbage business. These sites readily accepted dubious shipments of hazardous waste thinly disguised as ordinary municipal waste (U.S. House of Representatives 1981a:228, 1981b). Landfill owners not directly associated with organized crime could be bribed to sign manifests for shipments never received or to accept hazardous waste that was manifested elsewhere (U.S. House of Representatives, 1980:70, 90). In addition, known organized crime figures started or seized control of a network of phony disposal and "treatment" facilities such as Chemical Control Corporation, Elizabeth, New Jersey; Modern Transportation, Kearny, New Jersey; and Duane Marine, Perth Amboy, New Jersey.[5] Licensed by the state, these outfits could legally receive hazardous waste and sign off on the manifest. They would then either stockpile it on site (where it would stay until it exploded, burned, or otherwise came to the attention of authorities) or dump it along roadways, down municipal sewers, into the ocean, or elsewhere (Block and Scarpitti, 1985:145, 158, 298; U.S. House of Representatives, 1980:25). In the extreme, actual ownership of or access to disposal sites was unnecessary for those willing to file totally fanciful manifests. Congressman Gore cited one case in which several major corporations signed over their

---

[4]Of parenthetical interest here is the methodological similarity between organized crime's property rights system in garbage and price-fixing by Westinghouse, General Electric, and other firms in the famous heavy electrical equipment price fixing scandal of 1961 (Geis, 1977).

[5]Modern Transportation, a firm that would ultimately receive half the manifested hazardous waste originating in northern New Jersey, was incorporated in 1972 by Richard Miele, co-owner with known organized crime figures of numerous garbage-related firms and landfills (Block and Scarpitti, 1985:297). Chemical Control Corporation was taken over by Johnny Albert, one of the organizers of the New Jersey Trade Waste Association (Block and Scarpitti, 1985:256–260; U.S. House of Representatives, 1980:10). Duane Marine was so enmeshed in organized crime networks and activities that its former employee, Harold Kaufman, became the central federal informant on these activities.

wastes to an out-of-state facility that subsequently was shown to simply not exist (U.S. House of Representatives, 1980:70, 135).[6]

ENABLING CAUSES: THE MAKING OF A VULNERABLE REGULATORY STRUCTURE

In retrospect, it is hardly surprising that, given the opportunity, organized crime would enter the newly created market for hazardous waste handling. It was an extension of their current business activity. They had the equipment and organization. They had both the know-how and the will to corrupt the manifest system. It was an attractive prospect. Both the potential size of the market and the potential profits were enormous. Even if they charged only a fraction of the true price of legitimate disposal, that price would be much higher than the price they charged to move the same stuff when it was legally just garbage, but their operating expenses would stay the same (if they commingled hazardous waste with ordinary garbage) or decrease (if they simply dumped). Why organized crime would want to enter into relationship with corporate generators when the opportunity presented itself needs no subtle unraveling. The more complex task is to determine what political and social-structural conditions made it possible for them to "colonize" the hazardous waste disposal industry.

Lax Implementation, Incompetent and/or Corrupt Enforcement

Explanations of organized crime presence in hazardous waste handling focused on lax implementation and improper enforcement. Congressional hearings produced dramatic evidence that, at least in New Jersey, the state where organized crime intrusion into hazardous waste is most thoroughly documented, the major provisions of the RCRA were poorly implemented and enforced. Interim hauling and disposal licenses were freely granted. The manifest system was not sufficiently monitored.

Interim Licensing. Congress had mandated an extended transition period during which both transporters and disposal firms would operate under temporary permits until an adequate national hazardous waste industry developed. Generators lobbied quite heavily on this point (U.S. EPA, 1976:238, 1979:153, 307; Gansberg, 1979) and Congress had to agree to this provision because the shortage of adequate hazardous waste facilities was so severe. American industry would have choked in its own accumulating wastes had it not been permitted to continue to use less-than-adequate means of disposal. A reasonable concession to economic realities, implementation of interim licensing was poorly managed. House of Representatives testimony shows that New Jersey issued hauling permits to any applicant who paid a nominal $50 fee (U.S. House of Representatives, 1980:14–15). Existing landfills and even totally bogus firms with no real disposal facilities found it equally easy to get interim disposal permits (U.S. House of Representatives, 1980:10).

HAROLD KAUFMAN (key FBI informant on mob involvement in hazardous waste disposal, testifying about his old firm, Duane Marine): "The State licensed us. We were the first ones licensed. . . ."

GORE: "And this was a chemical waste disposal facility, is that right?"

KAUFMAN: "Well, that is what it was called. It never disposed of anything, but you can call it that."

Manifest Oversight. Once a license was obtained, lax supervision of the manifest system made illegal and unsafe disposal of hazardous waste a relatively straightforward, low-risk ac-

---

[6]Albert Gore in the case of Capital Recovery: "The subcommittee's investigation has uncovered evidence that since August, 1976, major industrial companies, such as Koppers, Inc., in one case Exxon, Union Chemical Company in the state of New Jersey certified that over 270,000 gallons of chemical waste were delivered to an out-of-state facility in Wilmington, Delaware, named Capital Recovery. From all the available evidence, Capital Recovery is nothing more than a paper corporation. It has no offices or any site in Wilmington. There is no phone listing, no city or State real estate tax or business tax information no annual report has been filed. . ." (U.S. House of Representatives, 1980:135–136).

tivity (U.S. House of Representatives, 1980: 140).

GORE: "What enforcement efforts are you making to prevent the abuse of the manifest system?"

EDWIN STIER (New Jersey Division of Criminal Justice): "The only way the manifest system is going to be properly, effectively enforced is through the proper analysis of the information that comes from the manifest. . . . Anyone who assumes that a manifest system which looks good on paper can control the flow and disposition of toxic waste without the kind of support both technical and manpower support that is necessary to make it effective, I think, is deluding himself. [However] . . . we aren't looking specifically for manifest case violations. We aren't pulling every manifest in that is filed with the department of environmental protection and looking for falsification of manifests specifically because we don't have the time, the resources, or the specific lead information to do that."

Congressional testimony revealed that until 1980 New Jersey did not have a single person assigned to monitor the manifests being filed in Trenton (U.S. House of Representatives, 1981b:124). A recent study by the General Accounting Office (U.S. GAO, 1985:25–31) found that the manifest system does not detect illegal disposal, in part because of inadequate monitoring.

Congressional hearings also produced evidence suggesting that the relevant New Jersey agencies—the Interagency Hazardous Waste Strike Force, the Division of Criminal Justice, and the Division of Environmental Protection—were incapable of producing effective enforcement even when tipped off to specific instances of hazardous waste dumping (U.S. House of Representatives, 1980:144–146, 1981b:110–124). Block and Scarpitti (1985) present many other examples that appear to show corruption or, at best, ineptitude on the part of state officials responsible for investigation and prosecution of illegal hazardous waste practices.

Lax implementation and enforcement undoubtedly played a big role in facilitating or-

ganized crime entry into the hazardous waste disposal industry. There are, however, more fundamental conditioning factors that logically and temporally preceded these causes. RCRA is a regulatory structure ripe with potential for subversion. Why did Congress create a regulatory structure so vulnerable to lax enforcement? A review of RCRA's legislative history shows quite clearly that corporate generators moved decisively to shape the emerging federal intervention to their liking. They determinedly fought for and achieved a regulatory form that would demand of them the least real change and a form that would minimize their liability for potential violations of the new regulations.

Generators' Strategic Intervention in the Legislative Debate over the Form of Policy

Compared to the regulatory mechanism written into the final language of the RCRA, some potential alternative forms that were proposed and then rejected would have proved much less hospitable to noncompliance in general and to the entry of organized crime in particular. The federal government could have mandated specific treatment and disposal practices, or directed generators to treat all of their wastes themselves, or legislated that generators retain full responsibility for their wastes even if they assign them to other parties for shipping and disposal. Generators, led by representatives of major oil and chemical corporations, explicitly and vigorously opposed any such language. They hammered away with striking unanimity at two fundamental points: that the government should in no way interfere in firms' production decisions, and that generators should not be held responsible for the ultimate fate of their hazardous wastes.

Generators repeatedly warned Congress neither to appropriate to itself the power to intervene in production processes nor to require generators to follow specific waste treatment practices. They stressed, instead, that regulatory controls are more properly imposed at the stage of final disposition. Here are some representative statements:

We believe that the disposal of wastes ought to be regulated instead of regulating the nature and use of the product or the type of manufacturing process used (E.I. DuPont de Nemours and Co., U.S. Senate, 1974:454).

Authority to control production, composition, and distribution of products . . . would be devastating to free enterprise commerce (Dow Chemical, U.S. Senate, 1974:1478).

[Stauffer Chemical opposes generator permits which] would place controls on raw materials, manufacturing processes, products and distribution (Stauffer, U.S. Senate, 1974:1745).

. . . legislation should not impede the natural interaction of raw materials, market and other forces that ultimately control the nature, quality, price, and success of products developed in our free enterprise system (Union Carbide, U.S. Senate, 1974:1748).

No specific requirements or prohibitions should be set governing the recovery, reuse or disposal of industrial wastes. . . . Generators should be free to increase or decrease waste production rates, terminate waste production, treat their own wastes, and negotiate treatment or disposal service contracts in a free and competitive market (American Petroleum Institute, U.S. EPA, 1976:1406, 1410).

. . . the generator should be free to decide whether to treat or dispose of wastes (Manufacturing Chemists Association, U.S. EPA, 1976:565).

. . . economic incentive alone should determine the degree of waste recycle and recovery. . . . We are opposed to regulations specifying the kind and amount of processing and recycle of wastes [by the generator]. [The] greatest emphasis should be placed on establishing standards which assure that the ultimate disposal method is satisfactory (DuPont, U.S. EPA, 1976:72–73).[7]

Generator unanimity was equally impressive on the second issue of responsibility. They were willing to have limited responsibility, to label their wastes, and make sure they contracted only with firms approved by state authorities, but they vehemently opposed the idea that generators should bear legal responsibility for their wastes

from cradle to grave. They argued that responsibility should pass to the party in physical possession of the hazardous waste. Under such a system, they further pointed out, only the hauler and disposer need to be licensed and the government should not license generators. Here are some representative statements:

We agree that the generator has some responsibility in the area, . . . [i.e.] make some determination that the disposer is competent and has the proper permits for disposal. . . . However, the waste hauler and disposer have responsibility to assure, respectively, that the wastes are delivered for disposal at the proper location and are properly disposed. Irresponsible action is invited if the person holding the waste has no responsibility for it (DuPont, U.S. EPA, 1976:73–74).

[The generator should] confirm the competence and reliability of transporters, treaters and processors to whom the waste may be transferred. . . . Each transporter, treater and disposer should be responsible for his individual activities while the waste is in his possession (Monsanto, U.S. EPA, 1976:410–411).

MCA recommends that the responsibility for the waste should be associated with physical possession of the waste, so that the generator should not be held liable for negligence of the transporter and the disposer of the waste (Manufacturing Chemists Association, U.S. EPA, 1976: 565). We feel that permits should only be required of the disposal site operator (B.F. Goodrich, U.S. Senate, 1974:1441).

. . . permits for both generation and disposal of hazardous waste is doubly redundant. . . . A permit system for generators of wastes is unneeded and would tend to stagnate technology at the level prevailing at the time the permit was issued (Dow Chemical, U.S. Senate, 1974:1478–1479).

. . . we consider permits for the generation of hazardous wastes to be unneeded, and could result in unnecessary restriction of manufacturing operations (Union Carbide, U.S. Senate, 1974:464).[8]

The generators also lobbied for the other provisions to their liking—a narrow definition of

---

[7]Other companies and associations making the same argument during these hearings included Monsanto, Exxon, B. F. Goodrich, Alcoa, the Texas Chemical Council, and the Western Oil and Gas Association.

[8]The same point was also raised by Stauffer Chemicals, Marathon Oil, American Cyanamid, Berylco, Shell, Alcoa, the Texas Chemical Council, the Western Oil and Gas Association, the American Petroleum Institute, and the New Jersey Manufacturers Association.

what substances should be regulated as hazardous, flexible time frames for implementation, and less stringent rules for on-site disposal[9]—but the two points above were the heart of their legislative intervention. In the end, they didn't get everything they wanted. The government would make generators register with the EPA. On-site, generator self-disposal would be subject to the same rules that governed off-site disposal firms. However, the overall forms of RCRA passed by Congress embodied both of their major demands.

The Legacy of Generator Inattention and Inaction

The generators also contributed indirectly to the shaping of RCRA legislation through their historical lack of attention to proper hazardous waste disposal. The EPA estimated in 1974 that ocean dumping and improper landfilling cost about 5% of the price of environmentally adequate disposal and it reported that

Given this permissive legislative climate, generators of waste are under little or no pressure to expend resources for adequate management of their hazardous wastes (U.S. Senate, 1974:71).

Lack of generator demand for adequate disposal facilities discouraged the inflow of investment capital, and an adequate waste disposal industry had failed to develop by the time RCRA legislation was being debated. Had legislators ignored this situation and required an immediate shift to proper disposal, a production crisis could have been triggered as wastes accumulated and firms found few legal outlets for them. Industrial spokesmen predicted dire consequences. In a representative statement, a Union Carbide spokesman warned legislators:

Those wastes which are non-incinerable and have no commercial value must be disposed of. To deny opportunity for disposal would effectively eliminate much of the chemical process industry. Disposal in or on the land or disposal in the oceans are the only viable alternatives available. (U.S. Senate, 1974:461)

Neither individual officeholders nor whole governments stay in office long if they pass legislation which, even for the best and most popular of reasons, brings to a halt industrial sectors central to the national economy. Congressmen had to be realistic and mandate years of transition during which hazardous waste would be hauled and disposed by operators having only interim licenses. This reasonable concession to the reality of the situation, a legacy of generator inattention, created a loophole through which many less-than-qualified parties could legally participate as providers in the hazardous waste market.[10]

CORPORATE GENERATORS AND ORGANIZED CRIME: A COMPLEX RELATIONSHIP

The discussion of enabling causes leads from the surface explanation of lax implementation and enforcement back to the moment of creation of a regulatory structure ripe for subversion and subterfuge. Analysis of the formation of the RCRA shows that the actions of corporate

[9]The issue of flexible time frames was raised by the National Association of Manufacturers (U.S. House of Representatives, 1976:190) and Exxon (U.S. EPA, 1976:940). Arguing for a restricted definition of what is regulable hazardous waste were DuPont (U.S. EPA, 1976:69), the American Iron and Steel Institute (U.S. EPA, 1976:100), American Cyanamid (U.S. EPA, 1976:1550), B. F. Goodrich (U.S. Senate, 1974:1440), Stauffer (U.S. Senate; 1974:1746). Monsanto (U.S. EPA, 1976:406–407) and Dow (U.S. EPA, 1976:956) argued for fewer restrictions for on-site disposal.

[10]It should be noted that generators intervened not only in policy formation but also engaged in ongoing efforts to weaken regulatory impact during implementation. They appeared at EPA implementation hearings to emphasize that the criteria for declaring substances hazardous were still too broad, that proposed disposal requirements were too stringent, that interim standards were burdensome and inflexible, and that recordkeeping and reporting requirements were onerous. Especially active in this period were trade associations such as the Manufacturing Chemists Association, the Synthetic Organic Chemists Manufacturing Association, the American Petroleum Institute, and the National Paint and Coatings Association, as well as large individual corporations such as Dow and DuPont (U.S. EPA, 1979; U.S. Senate, 1979). EPA officials complained privately that "the millions of pages of testimony filed by representatives of industry on virtually each clause of every implementation proposal" created "a major obstacle" to timely implementation of RCRA (Shabecoff, 1979:1).

generators were principally responsible for the passage of such a vulnerable structure. This is the most basic aspect of the generator-organized crime relationship. Answers to two questions may flesh out the analysis: did corporate generators intend this outcome? And what effect did it subsequently have upon them? One may also ask how Congressional hearings did or did not deal with these issues. Discussion continues here with the latter line of exploration.

Congress Discusses the Role of Corporate Generators

Having thoroughly documented organized crime presence in the hazardous waste industry, Congressional scrutiny could have turned to the question of how generators, legitimate economic actors, relate to that presence. However, the issue of corporate behavior or corporate responsibility was, for whatever reason, never treated as a central topic of investigation during hearings.[11] There were only a few isolated attempts to broach the subject and probe it even a little. Two explanations were tentatively suggested during these brief interludes. These explanations are now critically examined in light of the facts already at hand.

Ignorance and "Good Faith." Congressman Gore suggested to Harold Kaufman, the former Duane Marine employee turned star witness, that perhaps companies used Kaufman's phony "disposal" firm knowingly as a front. In response, Kaufman articulated the theory of ignorance and good faith.

---

[11] A concrete measure of inattention: in four Congressional hearings on organized crime in hazardous waste, hearings totaling approximately 500 pages of transcript, a total of five corporations are identified by name: Exxon, Union Chemical Co., 3M, Koppers, Inc., and Monsanto. Discussion of corporate involvement was incidental to the main themes of the hearings, which was the fact of mob involvement and criticism of law enforcement efforts (U.S. House of Representatives, 1982). To their credit, Congressmen appeared somewhat more willing to raise the question of corporate responsibility than either federal regulatory officials or state legal authorities (see U.S. House of Representatives, 1980:20, 140, 1981a:12, 1981b:56, 103, 109–110, 153, 158, 1983:60).

MR. GORE: "You offered a front to companies that wanted to pretend they were disposing of toxic waste."

MR. KAUFMAN: "No, that wasn't true. That wasn't true."

GORE: "Well, explain it to me in your own words."

KAUFMAN: "You're blaming the companies; 99 percent of these companies in good faith thought that Duane Marine had the facility."

GORE: "I see."

KAUFMAN: "Because the State licensed us. We were the first ones licensed, Duane Marine. . . . these industrial people who in good faith wanted to follow the law, if they wanted to cheat, they wouldn't have brought the stuff to us, because we were charging a lot of money" (U.S. House, 1980:10).

KAUFMAN, later: "Forget about the generator. Let's not blame the people that are really trying to follow the manifest. . . . these companies operate in good faith—otherwise they wouldn't have called the people [i.e., Duane Marine], they would have thrown it in the nearest dump" (U.S. House, 1980:16).

According to this scenario, managers and owners see the license, the State's seal of approval, and believe in good faith that the shipment of hazardous waste that they sign over will be properly disposed of by responsible operators. They do not know that their wastes end up stockpiled on an Atlantic Coast pier, poured down a municipal sewer, or burned, commingled with fuel oil, in a school furnace. They do not know they are dealing with organized crime. They are in fact being cheated because they pay large amounts for treatment and disposal that are not performed.

The issue of subjective awareness cannot be decisively resolved without indepth interviewing of corporate managers in charge of waste disposal contracting, but the preponderance of circumstantial evidence makes claims of ignorance appear unconvincing. Organized crime control of garbage hauling and disposal had been considered a fact of life in New Jersey for decades. It had been the subject of numerous state hearings and investigations since 1958 (U.S. House of Representatives, 1981a:15–16, 36, 39). Organized crime's rapid entry into hazardous waste was so readily apparent that New Jersey established an Inter-Agency Hazardous Waste Strike Force to investigate and attack the problem in 1978, shortly after the new system of licensing and manifesting was begun. Management also knew—they themselves had stressed this fact when they had lobbied for extended transition periods in RCRA implementation—that there were few adequate hazardous waste facilities available, yet the feared shortage of disposal sites never materialized.

Rather than ignorance and good faith, these facts suggest that the rational industrial manager would have had ample reason to distrust the identity of their contractual partners. Had their suspicions been aroused, it would have been easy to hire investigators, as state and local officials had done, to follow some hazardous waste shipments and lay their doubts to rest:

CONGRESSMAN RINALDO: "Is there any way these plants or companies could have discovered on their own that Duane Marine was a front, a fraud. . .?"
KAUFMAN: "I guess they could have, sure. All they had to do was [go to Duane Marine and] see their stuff piled up and go to Chemical Control and see their stuff piled up" (U.S. House of Representatives, 1980:20).[12]

If managers and owners were indeed ignorant, that subjective state must either have been achieved through the hard work of vigilant inattention or have been the fruit of a profound lack of interest. Indeed, generators may have good material reasons to desire to stay ignorant.

---

[12]Albert Gore speaks on Capital Recovery, the phony Delaware disposal firm: "The companies I mentioned, Koppers, Exxon, Union Chemical Co., probably were unaware, *maybe that is overly generous*, but from what I can ascertain from those documents, it is quite likely that the hauler was the person aware of the ultimate disposal site. *The company should have been aware, but they may very well not have been aware* of the fact that the Capital Recovery facility was nonexistent" (U.S. House of Representatives, 1980:140, emphases added).

In its comments on the GAO's draft report on illegal waste disposal, the EPA states that the "key reason" why generators do not notify officials when they suspect that a waste shipment may have gone astray is "the unwillingness of the generator to "turn-in" its low-bid transporter. This is especially true for smaller volume generators who routinely have great difficulty finding transportation for their wastes" (U.S. GAO, 1985:62). But, more to the point, the subjective state of awareness of owners and managers is irrelevant because their right to be ignorant is structured into the regulatory scheme of the RCRA. As has been shown, the generator bears no obligation to know its contractual partner beyond assuring itself that the firm has been licensed, declared fit to handle hazardous waste by one of the states. Rather than attempt to argue what corporate actors know, do not know, could know, or should have known, one must remember that generators explicitly fought for RCRA language that entitled them to a state of ignorance.

Powerlessness. Kaufman and New Jersey Deputy Attorney General Madonna suggested a second theory that also tends to absolve the generator of responsibility. Even if the corporate generator knows that it is dealing with organized crime, the "property rights" system forces it into a passive, powerless position:

MADONNA: ". . . numerous customers of garbage or solid waste collectors who have attempted to secure alternative collectors, for whatever reason, have found that it is virtually impossible to obtain a different garbage man to pick up their garbage" (U.S. House of Representatives, 1981a:12).
CONGRESSMAN MARKS: "If a disposer of chemical waste sought a different company to haul those waste, could that person voluntarily change without there being a problem?"
KAUFMAN: "Not to my knowledge has it ever happened, because you see, most of the haulers of toxic wastes that are in the garbage business respect the same thing in toxics as solid, so he has no choice. He has a man there

and nobody will go in'' (U.S. House of Representatives, 1980:22).

This claim of generator powerlessness is also undermined by the previous discussion of the generators' role in the shaping of RCRA legislation. Individual generators, especially smaller firms, may indeed find themselves unable to shop around among hazardous waste haulers once the property rights system had assigned their site to a specific hauler, but the discussion above suggests that one must look beyond individual firms to see how corporate power was exercised collectively. Industries that produce the bulk of hazardous waste—oil, chemicals, pharmaceuticals, electronics—exert tremendous political power nationally and in states like New Jersey, where these four industries account for 36% of all industrial production (Governor's Commission, 1983:18). These lobbying powerhouses used their collective political power during legislative debate over the form of RCRA to create a structure that, subsequently, permitted the emergence of a "property rights" system that can impose its will on some individual generators. Claims of generator powerlessness cannot be accepted without profound qualification.

The details of corporate intervention during the formation of the RCRA undermine any explanation that absolves them of all responsibility, but generator actions do not, by themselves, convey the full complexity of the resultant relationship. Two issues remain: why did the corporate generators do it? And what were the consequences for them?

The Question of Intent

The cohesiveness and unanimity of generator intervention to shape RCRA legislation certainly shows that they intended *something*. Nonetheless, no evidence was found in the research discussed here to support an argument that generators consciously intended to create a context for organized crime entry into the industrial waste disposal business, or even that they understood that such an outcome was possible. Rather, it appears much more likely that they acted out of a general tendency to resist full social responsibility for the "externalities," the environmental and public health consequences, of industrial production, and that they do not much care what, if any, unintended consequences would follow.

Why were generators so vehement that Congress not force them either to change production techniques or to assume full legal responsibility for proper waste disposal? These actions find their meaning within the larger context of industrial response to the whole spectrum of environmental, so-called "social" regulations. Industrial groups active during the passage of RCRA have consistently opposed Congressional passage of every piece of recent social regulation, intervened to weaken their form when passage seemed inevitable, and mobilized to limit their impact once they were implemented. They have done so with regard to the EPA, the Occupational Safety and Health Administration (OSHA), the Toxic Substances Control Act (TOSCA), the Superfund law (CERCLA), surface mining regulation, and right-to-know laws.[13]

Policy committees composed of corporate leaders and elected officials often state that an intact environment and a healthy public are objectively in the long-run interest of the corporate sector. For example, the Governor's Commission on Science and Technology of the State of New Jersey (1983:18) recently stated that "The safe disposal of hazardous and toxic substances is of enormous concern; if the problem is not solved, it will severely limit industrial growth." But this understanding is not reflected in the individual or the collective behavior of industrial firms. Regardless of objective or long-term interest, their behavior indicates that they do not wish to "internalize" the true cost of the undesirable side effects of modern industrial production.[14] Both generator failure to pay for prop-

---

[13]For a discussion of similar industrial action to limit regulatory intervention in the area of worker safety and health, see Szasz (1982, 1984). Corporate vigilance concerning any government attempt to impose greater responsibility is both comprehensive and reveals exquisite attention to detail, especially by corporations and trade associations large enough to have the legal and lobbying staffing for ongoing analysis and intervention.

[14]There are always some owners and managers who advocate a more enlightened, long-range view of industrial interest

er waste disposal before RCRA and their talking points during RCRA legislative debate are manifestations of this posture. In some areas of regulation, such as worker safety and health, successful corporate intervention may delay passage of legislation, weaken its form, and lessen its impact through ongoing resistance to full implementation. But regulation of hazardous waste was a unique case because of the specific history of organized crime control of garbage. Because of this peculiar circumstance, corporate resistance to this regulation not only had the usual intended effect of avoiding the full internalization of responsibility and cost, it also had the effect—apparently unintended—of opening the door to mob colonization of the regulation-mandated market.

Even Unintended Outcomes Have Payoffs

Generators mobilized when it became apparent that the political moment for regulation of hazardous waste had decisively arrived. There was sufficient public awareness, fear, and organized demand that the government would legislate something. They perceived, though, that the onerousness of impending federal intervention would be minimized if they could (1) ensure that regulation would not interfere with production decisions, and (2) they would not be fully liable for all possible costs associated with the ultimate fate of their wastes. A manifest-and-disposal-licensing structure was the generators' best-case damage control strategy. Undoubtedly, the greatest benefit would accrue to the generators from their successful move to veto potentially more interventionist forms of regulation. The victory would hold the new regulation's impact to manageable proportions.

---

in environmental matters. Producers of pollution control equipment of course support stronger regulation because it increases demand for their product. Nonetheless, historical and content analysis of past regulatory initiatives supports the view that the majority of industrial spokesmen vigorously oppose increases in government regulation of their health externalities. Crenson (1971), in the case of municipal regulation of air pollution, and Williams and Matheny (1984), in the case of state regulation of hazardous waste, have both shown statistically that the local presence of industry inhibits the imposition of regulation.

However, the unintended effect of their legislative efforts then provided several important secondary benefits on top of the main payoff of defeating stronger forms of federal intervention.

Noninterruption of Vital Service. Industrial waste accumulates every day that a factory operates. It has to be dealt with. With passage of RCRA, firms faced new uncertainties in coping with their hazardous waste. They worried, quite realistically, that RCRA would uncover a fundamental shortage of legal off-site facilities at the same time that the new rules would require firms to upgrade their facilities if they wished to treat wastes themselves. Lax implementation of interim licensing allowed enough parties to enter the new market that potentially crisis-inducing bottlenecks of accumulating waste were avoided. This benefit accrued to industry as a whole and was of central importance in cushioning the potential adverse impact of the transition from an unregulated to regulated situation.

Cost. The transition to regulation also threatened an immense cost shock. As noted earlier, the EPA estimated in 1974 that firms were customarily paying no more than 5% of the price of adequate treatment (U.S. Senate, 1974:71). If generators discharged their RCRA obligations by dealing with shady haulers and phony disposal firms, they would typically pay a higher price for disposal than they had before RCRA, but these charges could still be significantly less than the full price of adequate treatment. The Congressional hearings uncovered several instances of such cost savings by generators (U.S. House of Representatives, 1980:189), but how often this benefit occurred was not fully explored.

Obfuscation of Origins. The final potential benefit follows from organized crime's facility at falsifying manifests. As hazardous waste travels through the maze of illegitimate haulers and disposers, it becomes equally impossible to trace its industrial origins or to locate its ultimate destination. Officials find that even if a waste shipment can be followed from the generator to a nondisposing "disposal" site like Duane Marine or Modern Transportation, its ultimate resting place still cannot be identified with any certainty.[15] Conversely, when improperly disposed wastes are found, it is nearly impossible to trace backward and identify their corporate origins (U.S. House of Representatives, 1981b:153, 158).[16] The Superfund law, passed shortly after RCRA, provides that the original generators of abandoned wastes be identified and forced to pay for remedial cleanup. According to the Office of Technology Assessment, remedial cleanup can cost 10 to 100 times the cost of initial proper disposal (U.S. House of Representatives, 1983:7). Therefore, a firm can expect to escape serious liabilities if manifest manipulation has successfully "orphaned" its wastes by obfuscating its origins.

DISCUSSION: CORPORATIONS, ORGANIZED CRIME, AND EXTERNALIZING CRIMINOGENESIS

As noted earlier, recent work has challenged the clear distinction between legitimate and illegitimate business, between corporate and organized crime. On the one hand, organized crime is described as entrepreneurial activity (Schelling, 1967; Smith, 1980; Smith and Alba, 1979; Albanese, 1982), and its most overtly deviant features—conspiracy, violence—are explained as organizational necessities for businesses that cannot turn to the legal structure to govern their internal relationships (Smith, 1980:375). Chambliss (1978:181) argues, furthermore, that it is "the logic of capitalism . . .[which makes] the emergence of crime networks inevitable." Others (Barnett, 1981) assert that the logic of capital constantly presses legitimate economic actors to violate socially defined limits of business conduct. Studies showing widespread illegal activity (including fraud, bribery, and pricefixing) by a majority of Fortune 500 corporations (Clinard, Yeager, Brissette, Petrashek, and Harries, 1979; Clinard and Yeager, 1980; Etzioni, 1985) support the view that the most powerful and legitimate enterprises routinely engage in highly rationalized criminal activity. The logical endpoint of this argument is the radical view that the process of capital accumulation is itself organized crime in some larger sense of that term.[17]

Challenging the commonsense distinction between business and organized crime has the merit of drawing attention to the definitional processes whereby society labels some economic acts as legitimate and others as deviant. But even if one agrees that this distinction is a product of social construction and is on some level ideological, one can say that the central dynamic disclosed in this paper depends on continued social and legal acceptance of the reality of that

---

[15]Modern Transportation, incorporated in 1972, quickly became the largest of New Jersey's 18 licensed disposal facilities. By 1980, it was receiving almost 50% of the hazardous waste manifested in northern New Jersey. The manifests allowed investigators to follow hazardous waste from generator to Modern Transportation, but they were unable to establish with any certainty where the waste actually went after arriving at this "disposal" firm that had no observable disposal facilities (Block and Scarpitti, 1985: 296–298; U.S. House of Representatives, 1981b: 115).

[16]The effectiveness of "orphaning" one's hazardous waste, letting it be hauled and dumped without adequate records, is shown by the difficulties EPA has had in identifying the generators of wastes found in Superfund sites. One such site, the Lone Pine landfill in Freehold, New Jersey, where large amounts of improperly stored hazardous waste are leaching into the Manasquan River, was examined in detail in the U.S. House of Representatives (1981b). Both state and EPA officials stated that they could not identify the original generators of the material at the landfill. One New Jersey official stated, "It is very difficult to enforce against chemical waste surreptitiously going to a landfill" (1981b:115). Richard Dewling, EPA Region II office, agreed that such information is often impossible to obtain because of insufficient data, stonewalling by guilty parties, and so on (1981b:158). As a result, Dewling reported that "To the best of our knowledge, there is no reliable information presently available on generators whose wastes have been illegally disposed of at Lone Pine" (1981b:153).

[17]This perspective, most commonly associated with Marxist sociology, rests on the view that one must go beyond current social definitions of what is crime and strive to develop a definition of crime based on a more abstract and theoretical vision of what constitutes moral human conduct and social need. The most succinct statement of this perspective is still Proudhon's dictum that "Private property is theft." In line with the topic of this paper, criticism of the environmental effects of capitalist industrial production often expresses the implicit view that such economic conduct is fundamentally "criminal." In this light, see Marx's remark (1967:269) that "Capital . . . is in practice moved as much and as little by the sight of the coming degradation and final depopulation of the human race, as by the probable fall of the earth into the sun."

definitional boundary. Widely accepted ideologies are more than pure illusion: they have important material consequences.

Exactly because there is a socially and legally recognized boundary between legitimate business and organized crime, ethically unacceptable activities that benefit legitimate businesses may happen without compromising their reputation because those acts are committed by and can be blamed on those whose social reputation is already sullied. Block and Chambliss's (1981) analysis of labor racketeering in trucking, restaurants, and the garment trades shows clearly that owners may gain great benefits, such as lower wages and labor peace, when labor unions are dominated by organized crime. Brady's (1983:11) excellent analysis of arson in Boston shows that arson is an outcome of

economic decisions undertaken by the banking, real estate, and insurance industries, as well as the racketeering organizations of organized crime syndicates. . . . [Although the actual arson is committed by organized crime,] banks often profit more than the racketeers . . . even without consciously joining in the conspiracy and without violating the law.

Societal acceptance of a definitional boundary between legitimate business and organized crime makes possible a type of criminogenic process different from the two types of criminogenesis defined by Needleman and Needleman (1979). Crimes that are functional for a particular industry are committed by actors that are not only not of that industry but are of a totally different economic world, the "underworld." One may think of this process as parallel to the process of externalizing the economic costs of production and call it "externalizing criminogenesis." What is externalized here is the legal liability and the social blame for those dirty little acts that quicken the wheels of commerce.

Analysis of the formation of hazardous waste disposal regulations captures such a criminogenic structure at the moment of its formation. In the mid-1970s, corporations faced the prospect of new legislation that would force them to bear the responsibility and cost of environmentally safe disposal of massive amounts of hazardous waste. They responded with a legislative campaign that

effectively limited their liability. The regulatory structure they advocated would prove to be highly vulnerable to the commission of disposal crime, but these crimes would be committed by others, not by the generators themselves. Even if generators did not intend this outcome, they were well served by it because illegal disposal activity effectively slowed the pace of change and cushioned the shock of transition from an unregulated to an increasingly regulated context.

REFERENCES

Albanese, Jay S.
    1982   What Lockheed and La Cosa Nostra have in common: The effect of ideology on criminal justice policy. Crime and Delinquency 28: 211–232.

Barnett, Harold C.
    1981   Corporate capitalism, corporate crime. Crime and Delinquency 27: 4–23.

Block, Alan A.
    1982   "On the Waterfront" revisited: The criminology of waterfront organized crime. Contemporary Crisis 6: 373–396.

Block, Alan A. and William J. Chambliss
    1981   Organizing Crime. New York: Elsevier.

Block, Alan A. and Frank R. Scarpitti
    1985   Poisoning for Profit: The Mafia and Toxic Waste in America. New York: William Morrow.

Brady, James
    1983   Arson, urban economy and organized crime: The case of Boston. Social Problems 31: 1–27.

Chambliss, William J.
    1978   On the Take: From Petty Crooks to Presidents. Bloomington: Indiana University Press.

Clinard, Marshall B., Peter C. Yeager, Jeanne M. Brissette, David Petrashek, and Elizabeth Harries
    1979   Illegal Corporate Behavior. Washington, D.C.: U.S. Government Printing Office.

Clinard, Marshall B. and Peter C. Yeager
    1980   Corporate Crime. New York: The Free Press.

Crenson, Matthew A.
    1971   The Un-Politics of Air Pollution: A Study of Non-Decisionmaking in the Cities. Baltimore: Johns Hopkins University Press.

Denzin, Norman K.
    1977   Notes on the criminogenic hypothesis: A case study of the American liquor industry. American Sociological Review 42: 905–920.

Drucker, Peter F.
    1981   What is business ethics? The Public Interest 63: 18–36.

Etzioni, Amitai
    1985   Shady corporate practices. New York Times. November 15.

Farberman, Harvey A.
    1975   A criminogenic market structure: The automobile industry. Sociological Quarterly 16: 438–457.

Gansberg, Martin
    1979   New Jersey Journal. New York Times. January 21.

Geis, Gilbert
    1977   The heavy electrical equipment antitrust cases of 1961. In Gilbert Geis and Robert F. Meier (eds.), White-Collar Crime: Offenses in Business, Politics, and the Professions (rev. ed.). New York: Free Press.

Getschow, George and Thomas Petzinger, Jr.
    1984   Oil's legacy: Louisiana marshlands, laced with oil canals, are rapidly vanishing. The Wall Street Journal. October 24.

Governor's Commission on Science and Technology for the State of New Jersey
    1983   Report of the Governor's Commission on Science and Technology.

Greenberg, Michael R. and Richard F. Anderson
    1984   Hazardous Waste Sites: The Credibility Gap. Piscataway, NJ: Center for Urban Policy Research.

Leonard, William N. and Marvin G. Weber
    1977   Automakers and dealers: A study of criminogenic market forces. In Gilbert Geis and Robert F. Meier (eds.), White-Collar Crime: Offenses in Business, Politics, and the Professions (rev. ed.). New York: Free Press.

Martens, Frederick T. and Colleen Miller-Longfellow
    1982   Shadows of substance: Organized crime reconsidered. Federal Probation 46: 3–9.

Marx, Karl
    1967   Capital: A Critique of Political Economy, Vol. 1. New York: International Publishers.

Needleman, Martin L. and Carolyn Needleman
    1979   Organizational crime: Two models of criminogenesis. Sociological Quarterly 20: 517–528.

Petzinger, Thomas, Jr. and George Getschow
    1984a   Oil's legacy: In Louisiana, big oil is cozy with officials and benefit is mutual. The Wall Street Journal. October 22.
    1984b   Oil's legacy: In Louisiana, pollution and cancer are rife in the petroleum area. The Wall Street Journal. October 23.

Shabecoff, Philip
    1979   House unit attacks lags on toxic waste. New York Times. October 14.
    1985   Toxic waste threat termed far greater than U.S. estimates. New York Times. March 10.

Schelling, Thomas C.
    1967   Economics and criminal enterprise. The Public Interest 7: 61–78.

Smith, Dwight C., Jr.
    1980   Paragons, pariahs, and pirates: A spectrum-based theory of enterprise. Crime and Delinquency 26: 358–386.

Smith, Dwight C., Jr., and Richard D. Alba
    1979   Organized crime and American life. Society 3: 32–38.

Snyder, David
    1985a   Toxic scars crisscross Louisiana. The New Orleans Times-Picayune. September 8.
    1985b   Early action was met with disbelief. The New Orleans Times-Picayune. September 8.
    1985c   Wastes choke scenic bayous of St. Charles. The New Orleans Times-Picayune. September 10.
    1985d   Chemical specter fills Cajun paradise with sense of fear. The New Orleans Times-Picayune. September 11.
    1985e   He won't be stopped, landfill operator warns. The New Orleans Times-Picayune. September 11.
    1985f   10-year struggle to shut down waste site stymied by state. The New Orleans Times-Picayune. September 12.

Szasz, Andrew
    1982   The dynamics of social regulation: A study of the formation and evolution of the Occupational Safety and Health Administration. Unpublished doctoral dissertation. Madison: University of Wisconsin.
    1984   Industrial resistance to occupational safety and health legislation: 1971–1981. Social Problems 32: 103–116.

U.S. Environmental Protection Agency
1976   Hazardous Waste Management: Public Meetings. December 2–11.
1979   Public Hearings on the Proposed Regulations Implementing Sections 3001 to 3004 of the Resource Conservation and Recovery Act. February 22–23.

U.S. General Accounting Office
1985   Illegal Disposal of Hazardous Waste: Difficult to Detect or Deter. Comptroller General's Report to the Subcommittee on Investigations and Oversight, Committee on Public Works and Transportation, House of Representatives.

U.S. House of Representatives
1975   Waste Control Act of 1975. Hearings held by the Subcommittee on Transportation and Commerce, Committee on Interstate and Foreign Commerce. April 8–11, 14–17.
1976   Resource Conservation and Recovery Act of 1976. Hearings held by the Subcommittee on Transportation and Commerce, Committee on Interstate and Foreign Commerce. June 29–30.
1980   Organized Crime and Hazardous Waste Disposal. Hearings held by Subcommittee on Oversight and Investigations, Committee on Interstate and Foreign Commerce. December 16.
1981a   Organized Crime Links to the Waste Disposal Industry. Hearings held by Subcommittee on Oversight and Investigations, Committee on Energy and Commerce. May 28.
1981b   Hazardous Waste Matters: A Case Study of Landfill Sites. Hearings held by Subcommittee on Oversight and Investigations, Committee on Energy and Commerce. June 9.
1982   Hazardous Waste Enforcement. Hearings held by Subcommittee on Oversight and Investigations, Committee on Energy and Commerce. December.
1983   Hazardous Waste Disposal. Hearings held by Subcommittee on Oversight and Investigations. Committee on Science and Technology. March 30 and May 4.

U.S. Senate
1974   The Need for a National Materials Policy. Hearings held by the Subcommittee on Environmental Pollution, Committee on Public Works. June 11–13, July 9–11, 15–18.
1979   Oversight of RCRA Implementation. Hearings held by the Subcommittee on Environmental Pollution and Resource Protection, Committee on Environmental and Public Works. March 28–29.

Williams, Bruce A. and Albert R. Matheny
1984   Testing theories of social regulation: Hazardous waste regulation in the American states. Journal of Politics 46: 428–458.

THE PROCESS AND SIGNIFICANCE
OF POLITICAL SCANDALS

A Comparison of Watergate and the "Sewergate"
Episode at the Environmental Protection Agency*

Andrew Szasz
University of California, Santa Cruz

In the spring of 1983, a major political crisis erupted at the U.S. Environmental Protection Agency (EPA). Weeks of front page coverage featured accusations of political favoritism, sweetheart deals, conflict of interest, misappropriation of funds and the destruction of evidence. Six congressional subcommittees announced investigations. The White House and Congress engaged in a struggle over control of information that ultimately threatened to set off a constitutional crisis. The crisis was highly embarrassing to the administration, and was ultimately resolved with mass firings and the installation of a new administrator, William Ruckelshaus, who promised to set the Agency back upon a proper course.

The removal of EPA head Anne Gorsuch (Burford) and 21 other political appointees provided an emotionally satisfying, cathartic closure

© 1986 by the Society for the Study of Social Problems. Reprinted from *Social Problems,* Vol. 33, No. 3, February 1986, pp. 202–217, by permission.

*I gratefully acknowledge funding for this research by a Summer Fellowship from the Rutgers University Research Council. Earlier versions of this paper were presented at meetings of the Eastern Sociological Society, 1984, and the American Sociological Association, 1985, and to the Rutgers Sociology junior faculty research brownbag. The final product benefited greatly from comments at these presentations and from the incisive comments of several *Social Problems* reviewers. Correspondence to: Sociology Board, University of California, Santa Cruz, CA 95064.

for the participants in the crisis. Agency staff who had been in open revolt against her cheered Ruckelshaus when he first met with them. Clenched fists, exultant signs of victory, were seen around the auditorium. Environmental lobbyists had new hope that the Agency would begin to function again. The Democrats who had spearheaded the congressional investigations and hearings basked in positive publicity. As the dramatic moment, the intense political spasm, passed, media coverage rapidly decayed and attention shifted toward new developments in domestic and foreign events. A lingering sense remained that, for the first time since the inauguration of the Reagan administration, the rush toward massive deregulation of environmental, health, and safety laws had been effectively blocked.

In the most immediate and evident sense, the crisis at the EPA was a manifestation of political conflict in a specific policy arena, the regulation of environmental pollution and other industrial health hazards. But, abstracted from its specific issue context, the crisis can also be examined as another instance of a more general phenomenon—political scandals that involve dramatization of corruption and the strategic orchestration of political embarrassment. The Watergate crisis of 1974 is the outstanding, even paradigmatic, example of this type of political phenomenon in the United States. Startling parallels between

Watergate and the 1983 crisis at the EPA strongly suggest that they belong to the same category of political events. In both cases, (1) the administration is accused of abuses of democratic procedures and other wrongdoings by political opponents, (2) the vulnerable administration attempts to quell the crisis through claims of executive privilege and other defenses, (3) the strategic orchestration of embarrassing accusations overwhelms these defenses, and (4) the situation is resolved by resignations.[1]

In this paper I explore the process and significance of such political events. I first describe my data and methods. Then I divide the discussion into two main parts—the course or trajectory of scandal, and the effects of scandal. I review the relevant literature on the cause and course of Watergate, present parallel Sewergate case material, and suggest a conceptual framework to describe the process of scandal. I then examine the extent to which the two episodes had any enduring political consequences and, based on my findings, discuss what function scandal may serve in contemporary political culture.

DATA AND METHODS

My analysis rests on a comparison of the Watergate and Sewergate episodes. Data on Sewergate came from media accounts and from in-depth interviews with participants in the EPA events. I reconstructed the overall course of events through a review of all articles appearing between December, 1982 and May, 1983 in *The Washington Post* and *The New York Times*. In the summer of 1983 I conducted interviews with the staffs of two congressional committees and with the staffs of several environmental organizations.

Interviewees were selected on the basis of their centrality to the action. I also interviewed a small snowball sample of five EPA professionals. An unstructured format was used in all interviews views to elicit information on the subjective aspects of Sewergate, interviewees' view of their role in the events, their professed motivations, and their perceptions of others' roles. Interviews lasted in length from one to six hours. No attempt was made to interview highly-placed EPA political appointees who were the target of scandal. I supplemented these interviews and media accounts with my research findings from previous studies of the history of the deregulatory movement (Szasz, 1984, 1986).

I then reviewed the literature on Watergate, an event that stimulated an outpouring of social science interest in political corruption and scandal (Williams, 1981). Investigators have sought to explain Watergate's cause (Bernstein, 1976; Brown, 1974; Candee, 1975; Chomsky, 1973; Lipset and Raab, 1973; Lyman, 1975; San Francisco/Bay Area Kapitalistate Group [Kapstate], 1975; Shrag, 1974; Vidich, 1975; Wrong, 1974), describe its course (Bennett, 1980; Lang and Lang, 1980; Kapstate, 1975; Shrag, 1974; Vidich, 1975), and evaluate its enduring effects (Bernstein, 1976; Chaffee, 1975; Committee on Research of the National Capital Area Chapter of APSA, 1976; Dennis and Webster, 1975; Fowlkes, 1977; Hawkins et al., 1975; McLeod et al., 1977; Wright, 1979; Zimmer, 1979). I then attempted to identify the most important parallels between my material on Sewergate and the findings in the Watergate literature.

Finally, I sought to describe these parallels theoretically. Analyses of Watergate loosely combined two very different theoretical traditions—structural theories of State and legitimacy (see especially Kapstate, 1975) and a theatrical framework implicitly derived from Goffman (1959, 1967; see especially Bennett, 1980; Lang and Lang, 1980; Shrag, 1974). I found that both theoretical traditions provide important insights and that a careful articulation of their intersection provides a powerful conceptual framework that captures the most salient features of political scandal.

---

[1]Watergate and Sewergate are not independent cases of some abstract, timeless category. The course of the latter event was shaped in part by the symbolic legacy left by the former: The legitimacy of the administration's claim of executive privilege in 1983 was undermined by the taint left on the doctrine from 1974. Reports of document shredding and the mysterious erasure of floppy diskettes at the EPA resonated with recollections of the Watergate coverup.

THE COURSE OF SCANDAL: TAKEOFF, GROWTH, CLIMAX, AND RESOLUTION

Major Themes in the Watergate Literature[2]

Students of Watergate differed widely over how best to approach the issue of enabling causes: What makes a scandal episode *possible*? How does scandal get under way? Since the commission of culpable acts appears to be necessary before opponents can attempt to launch a scandal, one debate raged over the question of why Nixon and his associates had acted as they had. Others insisted that explaining culpable acts is less important than exploring the circumstances that permit opponents to successfully orchestrate condemnation of those acts.

Why had Nixon and his men engaged in acts that could be made the raw material of accusation and scandal? Some authors agreed with popular discourse that culpable acts could be explained purely in terms of the participants' character structure (Wrong, 1974) or their inadequate moral development (Candee, 1975). Others went beyond individual character deficiency to more structural explanations. Lipset and Raab (1973) thought that the Nixon group's behaviors were not unique to them, but were just the most recent example of a recurring minor chord in the history of American political culture that they called the "paranoid style" of politics. Lyman (1975) argued that "dirty work" is part of the normal (if hidden) repertoire of all government bureaucracies and that past Presidents had often committed similar acts. Bernstein (1976), Brown (1974), and Shrag (1974) argued that such behavior had become the habitual and necessary tool of statecraft as the United States had become a world power and the Executive had grown to become the dominant branch of the federal government. Brown (1974), Chom-

sky (1973), and Kapstate (1975) argued that Nixon and his associates blundered and became vulnerable to scandal only because they used break-ins, wiretaps, and other so-called dirty tricks—often used with impunity against unpopular, disorganized, deviant, marginal and/or powerless segments of society—against mainstream opponents. The claim that officeholders engage in potentially scandalous behavior more or less regularly alters the terms of the debate over the cause of scandal. It suggests that attention must shift from attempts to explain culpable acts to examination of the opposition actors who make an issue of these acts and the conditions under which they do so successfully (Vidich, 1975:786).

Commentators were sharply divided about what made Watergate possible, or even how best to think about that question; but they were in much greater agreement in their description of the mature phase of the crisis, the period after takeoff had been achieved. Theatrical metaphors and concepts of legitimacy were freely combined to capture the main features of the scandal process. Nixon and his men faced the loss of personal legitimacy—loss of political face—as their involvement with the burglary became undeniable. They tried to shore up their collective presentation of self by offering a front of explanatory accounts (Bennett, 1980) and managed impressions (Lang and Lang, 1980). At the same time, they engaged in ever more complex backstage efforts to control and suppress destructive information to keep their front of professed innocence from breaking down. These backstage efforts—planning perjury, discussing illegal payoffs, "deep sixing" files, and erasing damaging audio tapes—were what came to be referred to as "the coverup."

Analysts describe the opposition as engaged in the opposite task of strategically defeating the Nixon group's attempts to bring the crisis to a halt, and as driving to complete the discrediting and defacing of the administration. Their task became progressively easier as the coverup began to unravel and new evidence of wrongdoing was gleefully displayed to the public. Some authors emphasized that the discrediting of political opponents had to be done with some tact and

---

[2] I treat the Watergate articles cited here as if they represent neutral academic discourse, although it is clear that many of them promote, more or less openly, the authors' political and ideological commitments. I have excluded articles that appear to be overwhelmingly ideological (see, for example, Ives, 1976), and articles promoting interpretations that were quickly refuted (Oglesby, 1974; Sale, 1973).

circumspection to ensure that it did not lead to a more profound loss of mass faith in the legitimacy of the political process as a whole (Kapstate, 1975; Vidich, 1975). The opposition accomplished this in the case of Watergate by intentionally limiting the scope of the public investigation and steering it away from topics that might open up a more profound critique of the State (Kapstate, 1975), by personalizing the wrongdoing and focusing attention exclusively on the unethical or illegal practices of individuals (Hentoff, 1977), and, of course, by claiming that the discrediting was being done exactly to protect the integrity of the political process.

As the crisis matured, analysts argued that both the Nixon group and its opponents pitched their every move with one eye to the opposition and the other to the national audience. The congressional hearing, which culminated in actual impeachment proceedings, became a "political soap opera" running daily on daytime television (Shrag, 1974). Congressional lawyers and investigators questioned witnesses in private and broke new ground. The congressmen, briefed by their staffs but pretending lack of knowledge, reenacted the discovery of new facts and registered shocked outrage in front of the live cameras.

The crisis reached its climax when this constant bombardment finally caused the Nixon group's facade of seamless collective innocence to break down. Administration members abandoned their attempts to continue as a team and turned on each other. This loss of expressive coherence, as well as the specific revelations of backstage activity and the "smoking pistol," signalled that the struggle to deface the regime had succeeded. All but a few of the most faithful recognized that the Nixon team could no longer be allowed to rule, that they must be thrust out of office and punished. Resignations, the vote to impeach, and jail terms followed. I now describe the parallel trajectory of events at the EPA in 1983.

The "Sewergate" Crisis at the EPA

Overall policy trends that had begun in the mid 1970s ensured that some kind of "deregulation" would be implemented following the 1980

elections regardless of the identity of the winners (Szasz, 1984, 1986). Nonetheless, the two major parties defined deregulation quite differently, and the GOP victory meant that the more extreme version favored by the small business sector and the ultraconservative fringe of the corporate sector would be implemented. The details would be determined by the identity of administrative appointees who were ultimately chosen on the basis of political considerations having little to do with the environment or regulation, *per se.* The ultraconservative wing of the party had to be given some appointments, but geopolitical and national considerations made it unrealistic and irresponsible to give them critical posts such as in the State, Treasury, or Defense Departments. Giving them the Department of Interior, the EPA, and similar agencies was an ideal political solution because of their visceral dislike for federal regulation. Anne M. Gorsuch, conservative Colorado state legislator and an associate of nationally-prominent, ultraconservative Joseph Coors, was appointed to head the EPA. The assistant administrator level was staffed with people who had worked for corporate and legal adversaries of regulation.[3] Thus, these specific individuals came to hold positions at the Agency as a result of a complex web of determinations. Once there, they brewed an explosive mixture by committing some ethically-questionable acts, pursuing extreme policy change in an unrelenting and uncompromising fashion, and willfully antagonizing other actors in the political process.

There is no doubt that the Reagan appointees at the EPA committed unethical and possibly illegal acts. Investigation eventually revealed that they were cozy with regulated firms, gave personal assurances of nonenforcement, agreed to "sweetheart deals" that allowed polluting industries to avoid full payment of cleanup costs, and manipulated waste site cleanup timetables to benefit Republican candidates in congres-

---

[3]Major figures in Sewergate came to the EPA from Johns-Manville, the asbestos manufacturer, from Exxon, and from the Aerojet General Corporation, a company involved in dumping at a California hazardous waste site that became the target of congressional investigation.

sional races. Several appointees failed to sequester themselves from Agency action involving former emloyers. However deplorable such behaviors were, they were probably not deviant enough, by themselves, to have been the raw material of scandal.[4] The appointees' real downfall was that their routine behavior created opponents who would gladly seize upon and exploit these few marginal behaviors.

Gorsuch and the other appointees acted as if they meant to bring every aspect of the Agency's work to a virtual standstill. They wholeheartedly supported deep cuts in the EPA budget made by the administration in both fiscal years 1982 and 1983, cuts which forced staff attrition and corroded the Agency's ability to do basic research, rulemaking, and enforcement. Gorsuch declared that regulatory rulemaking must wait for adequate scientific research, but EPA cut back on research. Enforcement was decentralized to the various states, but EPA decreased grants that support state enforcement activities. Enforcement procedures were repeatedly reorganized until confusion and inaction reigned. Many experienced professionals were laid off, others fled the Agency, and those who remained suffered from deep loss of morale.[5]

The environmental lobby had come out of the 1980 elections anticipating a major offensive against "their" agency. Well-funded, capable, and politically influential,[6] these organizations vigorously opposed administration policy from the earliest days; but, by themselves, they did not have the clout to block implementation of those policies. They stood ready to join any

opposition that might emerge to take on the administration. The Reagan appointees' behavior ensured that the environmental lobby would be joined by other forces with whom they could forge a formidable oppositional coalition. The appointees pursued their policies with abandon, audacity, and undisguised contempt for those who disagreed. Notably, they alienated two groups with whom they should have, instead, sought to develop working relationships: congressmen who oversee the Agency's work and the EPA's staff of career professionals and scientists. They perfunctorily rejected EPA accountability to congressional oversight committees. They isolated themselves from EPA professional staff and treated them like enemies. In interviews, the phrase I most often heard was that the Reagan appointees did not understand "how government works." They routinely and even defiantly violated the norms of behavior that grease interactions in a social world where people must continue to cooperate with present and future opponents. As a consequence, interviewees unanimously agreed, the Reagan team at EPA came to be despised by anyone who dealt with them. They were described as incompetent, mediocre, indiscrete, stupid, inexperienced, occasionally malicious, and corrupt. They were accused of being ideologues who were anti-information, anti-science and anti-analysis.[7]

Democratic congressmen had excellent reasons for participating in the anti-Gorsuch opposition. Genuine concern about environmental policies blended well with political calculation. Prominent environmental advocacy was good for the individual congressman's reputation. It was also good for the party since the administration's environmental actions were one of the few evident ways for Democrats to attack an otherwise popular President. Not surprisingly, then, the House committees with statutory oversight rights actively sought to generate damaging information through investigation and through soliciting leaks from disaffected EPA insiders. Hearings were then scheduled to publicize the findings,

---

[4]Even after the crisis boiled over, after months of uncontrolled leaking, congressional scrutiny by six subcommittees, and intensive investigatory reporting, *The New York Times* could still report (Taylor, 1983), "No evidence clearly establishing that any crime has been committed has yet been made public."

[5]Detailed documentation of these policies may be found in National Wildlife Federation (1982).

[6]Their influence is based on the perception that they speak for a highly organized constituency that transcends social class differences and whose desire for safe air, clean water, and unpolluted neighborhoods crosses traditional ideological divisions—a perception supported by opinion polls (see, for example, the Harris Survey, June 11, 1981; New York Times/CBS Poll, October 4, 1981).

---

[7]For a discussion of the potential for conflict within state apparatuses between political staff and scientific/technical personnel, see Campbell (1986).

and EPA officials were brought in for ritualized face-to-face confrontations.

The third source of resistance came from within the Agency itself. Some EPA staff would have opposed deregulatory actions under any circumstances; others were alienated by the way these policies were being pursued. Many staff had been fired and rumors of politically motivated "hit lists" circulated in the Agency. The staff's mood vacillated from demoralization to profound hatred. An oppositional staff culture developed. Solidarity was built through rumors, constant verbal opposition, and especially through humor.[8] Dissident staff acted strategically within the Agency to frustrate policy initiatives with which they disagreed. They took resistance outside the Agency, forming ongoing, semi-covert alliances with and efficiently leaking potentially damaging information to congressional investigators, environmental groups, and the media.

Although the opposition coalition achieved episodic media and public disapproval of EPA actions, a sustained uproar failed to develop. More was needed—more dirt or more drama—in order to keep the EPA on the front page long enough to really heat things up. Prospects for scandalmongering improved in late 1982. National attention had been drawn to the hazardous waste issue by news of the Dioxin contamination of Times Beach, Missouri. Toxic waste was an ideal focal issue. Polls showed that there was widespread concern about this issue and Congress had recently passed new toxic waste legislation—the Resource Conservation and Recovery Act, and the Superfund law.[9] The issue

was fresh and had not yet suffered the decay characteristic of the "issue attention cycle" (Downs, 1972).

In late 1982, congressional subcommittees, chaired by John D. Dingell (D-MI) and Elliott H. Levitas (D-GA), began to scrutinize EPA's implementation of the Superfund. Provided with a working fund of 1.6 billion dollars raised through a new tax on the chemical industry, the Superfund theoretically allowed the EPA to clean up abandoned hazardous waste sites expeditiously, and then to recover expenses from the original polluters through litigation. Armed with leaked information, the committees charged that EPA was not implementing the law and was striking sweetheart deals with polluting firms. They asked for all files concerning several Superfund sites in California and Indiana. The EPA declined, stating that the files contained "enforcement sensitive" material that might find its way into the hands of firms being targeted for enforcement. This claim provided the window of opportunity for the opposition because it was simply not believable. EPA officials were widely believed to be in friendly contact with the firms involved. It seemed implausible that congressional access to documents could give firms information that they did not have already. The committees seized the moment and issued subpoenas.

In response, the administration escalated and invoked the doctrine of executive privilege. The move had little to do with this specific conflict. Some members of the administration had been looking for a showdown with Congress over executive privilege, and refusing congressional scrutiny of EPA's Superfund activities was only the vehicle through which this confrontation was to be carried through.[10] It was a bad miscalculation. The opposition had a potentially viable

---

[8]Anti-Gorsuch and anti-Reagan cartoons were posted throughout the Agency. People wore buttons proclaiming that "Jane Wyman was Right." Intramural softball teams were given provocative names, such as the "Killer Trees," mocking Mr. Reagan's most remarkable statement on the causes of environmental pollution. Fake memos intended to foster ridicule of the bosses were anonymously reproduced and circulated.

[9]Support for cleanup of toxic wastes is not undermined by personal economic considerations. Unlike a factory worker who faces a potential conflict between the desire for health and the desire for income and job security (a conflict effectively exploited by employers), a homeowner living near a hazardous waste site does not bear the economic costs of

cleanup. Costs are borne by the Federal government or by responsible companies. The homeowner feels the cost indirectly, if at all, as a few pennies in additional inflation. The cleanup actually provides a direct economic benefit as property values are preserved.

[10]Anne Gorsuch Burford claimed this to be true in congressional testimony in October, 1983. Investigators for the House Judiciary Committee also blamed the Justice Department for the administration's actions vis-a-vis Congress (see footnote 16).

issue and the administration had failed to see that the executive privilege claim might push events over the threshold. The claim had the aroma of coverup and could be easily construed to mean that the administration was trying to hide serious wrongdoing. Even if it later proved not to be so,[11] perception can be more important than truth under certain circumstances. Furthermore, the executive privilege claim enlarged the symbolic terrain of the conflict from a struggle between a few subcommittees and the EPA into a struggle between Congress as a whole and the Executive Branch. On December 16, 1982, 55 Republican congressmen, motivated by the issue of congressional rights, joined the Democratic majority in voting a contempt citation for Gorsuch.

The same Justice Department that had instructed Anne Gorsuch to invoke the doctrine of executive privilege now had the incongruous constitutional duty to prosecute her for acting as its agent. It refused to do so and, instead, appealed to the federal courts to rule in its favor. The investigation of the Superfund had suddenly blown into a full-fledged constitutional crisis. The administration gambled that a favorable court order would both affirm executive privilege and bring congressional pressure on EPA to a halt. But on February 3, 1983, District of Columbia District Judge John Lewis Smith Jr. dismissed the Justice Department's suit and ordered the two sides to try to reach an accord. The decision left the situation open, without clear resolution.

Sensing the growing potential for political damage, administration officials moved to bring the situation under control. Rita Lavelle's "voluntary resignation" was announced the day after the court decision. Lavelle was a logical choice for scapegoating and ritual sacrifice. She headed the EPA program most directly under scrutiny and was already under investigation for perjury, conflict of interest, and harassment of a dissident at the Agency. The administration

also announced three separate internal investigations—by presidential counsel Fred Fielding, the FBI, and the Justice Department. The sacrificial firing of lower level personnel and promises of self-investigation are hallowed crisis-management tactics, but the firing of Lavelle went badly. Her purported resignation note was revealed to be a sham. She fought back, refused to accept responsibility and implicated others, including Edwin Meese. Rather than relieving pressure on the administration, the tactic backfired and made things even worse.

Sensing that they were gaining the upper hand, Democratic congressmen intensified the pressure. New allegations—political manipulation of cleanup timetables, financial mismanagement, use of government resources for personal business—were added to old allegations of nonimplementation, conflict of interest, and sweetheart deals. News of paper shredders at work at the Agency, perhaps shredding incriminating subpoenaed documents, led to charges of coverup. Four more subcommittees announced hearings and investigations. More subpoenas were issued. Every old and new charge, every denial and strategic move, was amplified through daily repetition in press conferences.[12] The goal of all this action was to keep the story constantly in the news and to keep the process going, not toward a preconceived endpoint, but for however much political gain could be wrung from it.

A major effort to abort the scandal was clearly necessary. The administration offered to turn over all subpoenaed documents to Congressman Levitas in a way that would save face by nominally preserving the claim of executive privilege. The administration was ready to surrender, but why should the congressional Democrats let it off the hook when, for the first time in two years, they had a situation which could be leveraged into something big? They rejected the offer and pressed their advantage. They made new allegations of political manipulation

---

[11]Inspection of subpoenaed materials after they were finally surrendered to Congress showed that the most damaging material—instances of political manipulation, *ex parte* contacts with regulated industries, favoritism toward appointees' former employers—had already been leaked.

[12]Between February 3, when Judge Smith handed down his decision, and February 21, when the administration's attempt to strike a deal with Congress fell through, media coverage expanded dramatically. *The New York Times* had the EPA on the front page 12 of the 19 days, ran 31 total stories, (an average of 1.63 per day), and ran four editorials.

of cleanup timetables, conflict of interest, and perjury. They charged that attorney general William French Smith had wrongly interfered with the contempt of Congress prosecution, and called for an investigation. The rhetoric escalated. Congressman Dingell claimed he had evidence of actual criminal misconduct.

Sewergate became even a bigger story than before.[13] Media coverage ceased striving for neutrality. *The New York Times* editorialized about the "cynicism, mismanagement, decay" at the Agency, called for Gorsuch's resignation, and quoted similar editorial demands from major newspapers around the nation.[14] The administration's room to maneuver had shrunk precipitously. More firings of lower level appointees were tried, but such moves could no longer bring things to a convincing or satisfying conclusion. The sheer duration of the uproar, the daily front page coverage, had created an atmosphere of crisis, an aura of untrustworthiness. Inside the EPA, work had ground to a halt. The Agency was in total uproar. Dissident staff gleefully discussed developments. Bets were placed on what day Gorsuch would resign.

The administration's facade of coherence began to come apart. Gorsuch (now Mrs. Burford) openly clashed with the Justice Department and White House staff. Even though she swore loyalty to Mr. Reagan the next day, the disorganization inside the administration could not be hidden. Republican congressmen voiced concern about public confidence and suggested that Burford would have to go. A new poll showed that 54 percent of the public thought that the President cared more about firms that violate anti-pollution laws than about enforcing those laws,[15] and White House aides "privately" (i.e. publicly, but anonymously!) worried that the

EPA was spoiling the "Good News" presidency. Sewergate had to be resolved before further damage was done. On March 9, 1983, Anne (Gorsuch) Burford resigned and the White House announced it would hand over all the documents requested by Congress. The congressmen tried to maintain momentum by redirecting their attack toward appointees still in office, but the administration was now moving decisively. More resignations were arranged. The White House admitted that some allegations had been correct. The appointment of William Ruckelshaus, the first head of EPA and someone with intact environmental credentials, to replace Gorsuch was both an admission that changes would have to be made and a tactic to get the EPA off the front page and, in the words of an anonymous advisor, "to kill the persistant notion that he [Mr. Reagan] sympathizes with big business on the environment" (Clines, 1983). These gestures left the opposition with nothing to do but savor the symbolic victory and voice cautious optimism that there would be real changes under Ruckelshaus. Media coverage faded as the story ran out of steam and the scandal episode drew to a close.[16]

DISCUSSION: THE PROCESS OF SCANDAL

In this section, I discuss the triggering and subsequent trajectory of scandal in more general terms. I review and expand upon some of the

---

[13]Between February 23, when congressmen rejected the compromise offer, and March 9, the day before Anne Gorsuch resigned, *The New York Times* had the EPA on the front page 13 of 15 days and ran a total of 46 stories, an average of more than three articles a day.

[14]See editorials in *The New York Times* February 16 and March 2. On March 6 the *Times* approvingly quoted similar editorials from the major dailies of Washington, Philadelphia, Kansas City, Miami, Arizona, Chicago, Detroit, and *The Wall Street Journal*.

[15]Washington Post/ABC Poll, March 5, 1983.

[16]In contrast to the period of most intense coverage (see footnote 13), *The New York Times* had the EPA on the front page only 10 days in the months of April and May, about one day in six. During those months, it ran 51 total stories, less than one a day. As of March, 1986, Democrats are engaged in another attempt to rekindle Sewergate. In December, 1985, the House Judiciary Committee released a 1,200 page document that charged Justice Department lawyers with misleading congressional committees and the federal court, and, invoking the Ethics in Government Act, called on the attorney general to appoint an independent counsel to investigate the charges (United Press International, 1985). In no great hurry to pursue itself, the Justice Department is, as of this writing, asserting that it has scrupulously complied with the law and is promising to complete its preliminary investigation of the Committee's report by late April (Shenon, 1986).

theoretical kernels in the Watergate literature that are either implicit or not fully articulated in order to suggest something akin to a Weberian ideal type of the scandal process.

Legitimation of States and Personal Legitimacy of Officeholders

Analyses of Watergate freely combined concepts derived from two very different traditions of sociological theorizing—structural theories of the State and concepts of interactional "face-work" associated with Erving Goffman (1959, 1967). It is clearly appropriate to apply both conceptual schemes to Watergate, an event that combined in real life a perceived threat to the legitimacy of the State and the unmasking, loss of face, and embarrassment of individuals. More generally, the intersection of the two theoretical traditions takes us to the heart of the scandal dynamic.

Sociologists and political scientists since Weber have emphasized that States must legitimate themselves, justify their domination, and cultivate consent. Legitimation is defined as the creation and maintenance of a certain emotional and/or cognitive condition among the pressing majority the population: "docility" (Edelman, 1980a:1); "diffuse mass loyalty, . . . an unspecific readiness to follow" (Habermas, 1973:36, 70); and the "consent to be governed" (Vidich, 1975:786). Recent writing on legitimation emphasizes, though, that in advanced capitalist societies States' efforts to sustain mass consent are fraught with difficulties and contradictions (Habermas, 1973; O'Connor, 1973; Offe, 1974; Offe and Ronge, 1975; Wolfe, 1977). At the very least, the modern democratic State must project a commitment to democratic values and to such expressive and evocative symbols as legality, honesty, fairness, and neutrality. To validate its claim to these values, the State has to provide its citizens with open debate and participation in formally democratic, fair, and neutral institutions administered by honest and competent personnel (Edelman 1980b:3; Habermas, 1973:37). The legitimacy of the State and the legitimacy of officeholders, then, are mutually interdependent. In Goffman's terms, state actors strive in-

dividually to present a proper political "face" expressing commitment to democratic values and procedures and collectively to carry out a "team performance" embodying these commitments. Adequately done, the performance simultaneously validates the actors—because they observe the rules and procedures expected of them—and reproduces the legitimacy of the State.

However, even though the legitimacy of the State and the legitimacy of officeholders are mutually dependent, they are not identical and totally coextensive. The strategic drawing of a distinction between the two is key to the scandal process. The State ceases to be a monolithic team putting on a unified performance characterized by tact, loyalty, discipline, and circumspection. It splits into antagonistic teams. Dramatically employing the distinction between the State and the persons who temporarily hold state office, one team accuses another team of violating the values and procedures upon which the enduring legitimacy of the State rests. The attacking team exposes "destructive information" that will "discredit, disrupt, or make useless" (Goffman, 1959:141) the performance and self-presentation of the targets. If successful, the attacking team delegitimates its opponent, ruining its performance and discrediting its line, and in the same gesture validates the values of the State. This is exactly the attractive and potent configuration sought by teams who attempt to trigger political dramas such as Watergate or Sewergate.

Political Phenomenology

Once political actors decide to foment scandal, how they and their intended victims engage each other is determined, in part, by their perception of the texture of mass political consciousness. The point of scandalmongering is to arouse the sensibilities of the political audience and turn them against one's enemies. Theoretically, the aggressors claim to act in the name of the purported popular will, projecting the image of an active, attentive, deeply-caring audience out there, in the darkness beyond the footlights of the Washington stage. But, in fact, everyone really acts as if the public is a distracted, inattentive audience most of the time. Politics is actually assumed to play a very peripheral role in the awareness of the public, to be phenomenologically in the background while the kaleidoscope of daily concerns occupies and preoccupies the center of awareness. This implicit assumption of a chronically distracted audience is the key to understanding the logic of both teams' tactical actions as one group tries to launch a scandal and the other moves to squelch it.

Triggering Scandal

The motivation to foment scandal lies in the highly favorable ratio of the low costs of failure to the potential benefits of success. Short of attempting and failing so often that one is labeled and loses credibility, failed attempts cost little because they are soon left behind and forgotten in the rapid flow of newsworthy events. In contrast, success promises increased exposure and political clout for both the whole organized opposition and for its individual members. We may expect, then, that an opposition team will readily coalesce and attempt to foment scandal whenever the opportunity presents itself.

What constitutes opportunity? The evident response is that there must be commission of procedural violations or violations of some central legitimating values. Without that, political struggle among state personnel must trudge through the ordinary channels of policymaking. However, consider a situation where there is widespread consensus about the policy goals that were furthered by those questionable acts. The social base for an emergent opposition is absent and attempts to foment scandal will fail.[17] In addition to a minimum of violations of procedures

or central values, latent disagreement over substantive policy must also be present to some degree. The case of Sewergate shows that if the substantive policy issue involved has great support and, therefore, there is strong potential for an opposition to coalesce, even relatively minor violations can be built into a very respectable scandal episode. Watergate shows that truly spectacular scandal can be produced when major political deviance occurs in the context of deepseated policy antagonisms.

However, it is premature to suggest some formula for necessary and/or sufficient conditions for successful scandalmongering and, in a sense, such an attempt would miss the point. Politics is a social practice lived by its active participants. Contemplating a campaign to ruin the reputation of an opponent, the political actor certainly evaluates the chances of success before committing valuable time, resources, and reputation to the effort. But, in the last analysis, scandalmongering is truly a *practice* in that one learns the chances of succeeding only in the act of trying. The proof of the pudding is in the eating.

Although there is no ironclad logic in deciding to attempt scandal, there is a clear logic that guides action once the effort is undertaken. As I suggested above, this logic is based on the assumption that mass political awareness is distracted and mass political memory is short. The task, then, is to cut through inattention, to capture attention, to organize and focus it, and then to keep it focused. Sustained presence in mass media is the key to success because it counteracts the effects of short collective memory and attention span, and because sustained coverage helps create the impression that something is indeed amiss. The attacking team is engaged, in essence, in a struggle to define the situation as extraordinary, to pile on the allegations and intensify the uproar until there is a qualitative shift in the definition of the political moment.

The task of the potential targets of scandal mirrors that of their opponents, and their behavior is guided by and counts on the same perception of chronic mass political inattention. To squelch the potential scandal, do anything, their actions seem to say, to get the story off the front page for a couple of days and the thing will die.

---

[17]This seems to have been the case in the recent Greenpeace case. French frogmen sank the Rainbow Warrior, a Greenpeace protest ship planning to lead a protest against French nuclear testing, and killed one crewman in the process. French media singlehandedly kept the heat on the French government. There were resignations, but the scandal fizzled quickly because both the French public and the political opponents of the current regime strongly support France's nuclear weapons program.

They respond to the threat with routine methods of perception management. They project a perception of the situation as ordinary, benign, and overblown. If this strategy works, the story drowns in the rapid flow of issues appearing and disappearing on the national political stage. But if these initial, routine methods fail, the target team is forced to move to more extraordinary measures of crisis management. This is a clear indicator that they have begun to lose the struggle over the definition of the political moment and that the scandal process has moved beyond its initial stages.

The Scandal Process in Full Bloom

The heart of the process involves continuing struggle over the definition of the situation as the political reputation of the targets is increasingly put at risk. For both sides, duration is everything. The scandal can be aborted at any moment if the target team's strategies of impression management succeed and the press drops the story. Everything the team at risk does is intended to accomplish this. The opposition must, on the other hand, foil every attempt by the target team, prevent closure of the event, intensify the pressure, and continue to capture media attention. Each failure forces the target team to try increasingly extraordinary, increasingly desperate measures to shore up its front and save the situation. It becomes more and more likely that the target team will blunder as the situation closes in on it. Its extraordinary measures can easily backfire and become the raw material of new attacks as they are labeled a coverup and declared to be evidence of probable guilt. Its public front becomes increasingly incredible, and its assurances that nothing is wrong increasingly unbelievable. The crisis reaches its point of no return when the target team begins to come apart. The line it has attempted to uphold is shredded. It is defaced, embarrassed, and can no longer govern plausibly without major repairs. The crisis is resolved only when wrongdoing is ritually admitted, major repairs are undertaken, and these measures are accepted as adequate by opposing forces and the media.

THE EFFECTS OF SCANDAL

Full-blown scandals are tremendously dramatic events. Watergate dominated headlines and national political discourse for over a year. For the first time in U.S. history, Congress voted articles of impeachment against a President. Sewergate was a top political story for five months. A popular President was discomfitted for the first time while the opposition savored victory. The analysis of political events, though, must go beyond their immediate theatricity to examine their enduring effects. Edelman (1980a) suggests that any state action may be evaluated either in terms of its effects on policy, the actual allocation of values or resources, or in terms of legitimation effects on the public's attitudes and beliefs. I now take the two instances of scandal and explore what enduring policy and legitimation effects they had, if any.

Policy Effects

Two articles (Bernstein, 1976; Committee on Research of the National Capital Area Chapter of APSA, 1976) empirically examined the substantive policy reforms that followed Watergate. They found that, with the exception of some reform of campaign financing laws, Watergate did not lead to fundamental reforms in government operations or activities. The committee of political scientists seemed genuinely surprised that there was so little real policy impact. Perhaps more should not have been expected. Although I argued above that deep-seated policy differences played a role in the magnitude and intensity of Watergate, the explicit focus of outrage was the "dirty tricks"—the grievous procedural violations—not the substantive policy differences (such as the conduct of the Vietnam War) that occasioned these violations. In contrast, the administration's opponents in Sewergate were motivated much more overtly by substantive policy differences and they seized opportunistically upon a few procedural deviations to try to force policy change. Given this, the failure to wring much substantive policy change from the scandal is all the more interesting.

EPA's performance following Sewergate did improve in limited terms. Ruckelshaus recruited assistants who were generally more competent and professional, and had more government experience than their predecessors. Staff no longer had to strategize against a hostile cadre of bosses in order to carry out even routine duties. Order and morale were restored, and the situation inside the Agency stabilized. There was some improvement in Superfund implementation, a bigger budget, more emergency cleanups, and more civil and criminal enforcement. But these were improvements only in comparison to the dismal state to which the Agency had sunk.

The scandal did not transform federal environmental policy in any fundamental sense. It could not do so because the crisis could not begin to break the grip of larger forces that shape and limit that policy. Deregulation is a long-term policy trend, part of an overall conservative political trend made possible by the national economic malaise of the 1970s. This larger contextual reality, rather than the identity of specific officeholders or even specific administrations, had been the major determinant of environmental and regulatory policy since the mid 1970s. It was not seriously challenged by the crisis. To break through this barrier, the opponents of the Reagan team at EPA would at least have had to question the increasingly-accepted linkage of social deregulation and national economic recovery. The environmental lobbies were most willing to go to this point, but neither the Democratic congressmen nor the national press were prepared to challenge the political consensus on the desirability of some sort of significant deregulation. That is why the most that could have been expected from the crisis was the adoption of the rationalized, balanced, corporate-style deregulation explicitly favored by Ruckelshaus.

Furthermore, the scandal did not even accomplish *that* modest improvement. Although the administration had moved to short-circuit the scandal through firings and grudging admissions of error, its basic line on the environment had not changed. It had at its disposal effective structural mechanisms to ensure that the new appointee at EPA could make no major changes.

Control over the agency's budget by the Office of Management and Budget (OMB) was one obvious mechanism. The Agency's capacity to function, curtailed by budget cuts and the loss of experienced professional staff, could only be restored by a hefty infusion of funds. Although there was a token increase in the Agency's budget, the funds necessary for rebuilding were not provided. The OMB was also authorized by Reagan's Executive Order 12291 to review, analyze and, if it so wished, reject agency rule-making. When Ruckelshaus took office it was generally agreed that he had to take action on the symbolic issue of acid rain if he was to re-establish the agency's credibility. But OMB sided with the interests of sulphur-emitting power plants and repeatedly forced Ruckelshaus to withdraw his acid rain proposals—a clear sign that OMB would enforce the administration's overall line on the environment regardless of who was running the Agency. The Agency went beyond the limits set by OMB only when forced to do so by federal court decisions favoring legal suits brought by environmental groups.

Sewergate also had no observable positive effect on efforts to renew either the Superfund or other basic environmental enabling legislation during the 1983–84 session of Congress. Administration officials, congressional Republicans, and corporate lobbyists successfully blocked action on these bills. The Clean Air and Clean Water Acts and other laws stayed in force through continuing resolutions; but, without formal renewal, the very legislative foundation of federal EPA policy remained uncertain as of the 1984 elections.[18]

Legitimation Effects

The participants in Watergate treated its legitimation aspects as if the crisis were the political analogue of a medieval passion play—the Passion of St. Democracy. Mass faith in the political

---

[18]In late 1985, the House and Senate passed widely differing versions of the Superfund bill. As of this writing, the two houses are far from resolving their differences and only emergency allocations are allowing the program to avoid total shutdown.

process is shaken only to be more deeply reaffirmed because the political process walks through the Valley of Death and is found not wanting. Sinners are damned and sacrificed for the sake of the salvation of the political system. The regime of discredited men is driven from office and belief in the fundamental justness of the political system is symbolically affirmed. Revelations of wrongdoing that might undermine the legitimacy of the State become, instead, the vehicle through which that legitimacy is restored and reaffirmed. The opposition presented itself to the nation in these terms—and even some of those vanquished and bound for jail verbally affirmed that the legitimacy of the political system had been restored.

Watergate did monopolize political discourse during its actual course, but empirical studies do not support the participants' view of its impact on mass attitudes. Studies indicate that there were short-term negative impacts and that these impacts did not endure long after the scandal was resolved. Chaffee (1975), Dennis and Webster (1975), Fowlkes (1977), Hawkins et al. (1975), and Zimmer (1979) appeared to find that Watergate deepened political disillusionment and distrust among children, young voters, college students, and the general public. Wright (1979) reported some tendency for voters in 1974 to turn against those congressmen who had been overtly loyal to Nixon. However, McLeod et al. (1977) showed that the purported attitudinal effects were in fact a continuation of secular trends that started in the 1940s and 1950s. Based on this analysis, they argued that Watergate's effect on political beliefs could not be demonstrated. They reexamined 1974 election results and revealed that the crisis had had no overall effect on them. They concluded (1977:195) that there is ''no overwhelming case for massive long-term effects . . . in terms of drastically altered political orientations and behaviors.''

Sewergate shows a similar pattern. Participants were sanguine about the episode's symbolic significance. However, even though the events temporarily dominated national political discourse, durable attitudinal effects did not follow. Congressmen and their aides asserted that the crisis had strengthened the legitimacy of the congressional oversight process. Environmental groups and agency dissidents enjoyed the increased stature that comes with victory. In contrast, the administration was depicted as having suffered serious embarrassment. Its front of honest, homespun conservativism had become a bit ragged by the end; its face was in rather bad repair.

But these consequences all proved to be short-lived. A lot of issues clamor for national media attention and the center stage in political discourse. The administration did enough to rehabilitate itself. Ruckelshaus, some said, was brought in to get the agency off the front page. He may not have done much more, but his ability to restore the semblance of normalcy and make modest improvements at the EPA insured that attention would turn elsewhere. Some political careers were ruined. Rita Lavelle went to jail for a few months and subsequent events demonstrated that Anne Gorsuch Burford could not be rehabilitated and appointed again to office. Other potential legitimation effects faded rapidly as the scandal dropped from the headlines and withdrew to the shadowy edge of collective political awareness. The immense landslide electoral victory enjoyed by Mr. Reagan a mere year and a half later certainly does not support any argument that the administration's loss of face during Sewergate caused it permanent damage.

CONCLUSION: WHY DO DRAMATIC POLITICAL EVENTS HAVE SUCH SMALL CONSEQUENCES?

The evaluation of the effects of Watergate and Sewergate suggests that even highly successful and complete instances of scandal may have little or no clear consequences. I conclude with a discussion of this paradox and explore what significance scandals may have in spite of their apparent tendency to evanesce and leave little obvious aftermath.

The absence of major policy effects is perhaps easier to understand than the absence of lasting legitimation effects. First of all, the essence of scandal is not primarily about policy, at least as it is publicly presented by the participants to the national audience. The opposition may well be motivated by disagreement over policy, and the presence of such disagreement may even be required before an effective opposition can emerge. But the stated focus of scandal is alleged violation of procedural norms and democratic values. The resolution does not require policy change, although it is not inconceivable that some policy change might follow as new officeholders replace those driven from office or if the scandal shifts the political balance long enough to push through some policy reform. Yet the content of State policy is rooted in factors deeper and more stable than the identity of specific officeholders or even whole administrations. For example, I showed above how, in spite of Sewergate, EPA policies were constrained by the overall perspective of the administration and, one step deeper, by a long-term conservative trend that promotes deregulation. It is possible to conceive of a scandal so immense that the government not only falls but the overall direction of current State policy is discredited. In practice, however, both opposing teams are likely to have strong motivations to resolve things long before it gets to that. Therefore, even if scandal occasions some policy change as a side effect, the magnitude of these changes is likely to be modest.

Scandal is centrally about the legitimacy of individuals and of the State, and there are observable legitimation effects during the actual course of events: At the height of Sewergate, polls showed that Mr. Reagan was disapprovingly seen as sympathizing with polluters (see footnote 15). In both events, personal reputations were ruined and political careers forcibly ended. However, the evidence suggests an absence of durable mass attitudinal effects.

Even highly dramatic events may leave little aftermath if the texture of mass political consciousness is, as I depicted it above, in a chronic state of distraction characterized by short collective memory and absence of historical continuity. Most political events tend to lose reality soon after they cease to capture media coverage; but scandal is special in that successful resolution of an episode actually facilitates forgetting. Resolution, as Wrong said (1974:501), is analogous to

a "ritual cleansing." The threatened pollution of the body politic has been fiercely, and successfully, confronted. The matter is resolved. The audience is reassured and encouraged to return to chronic inattentiveness as both sides recite reaffirming verbal formulas. It should not be surprising that Vidich found that Watergate left the citizenry in a state of "mechanical or routinized [consent] . . . based on habit and inertia" (1975:811). Both the stirring up of mass disapproval during a scandal episode and the rapid waning of such feelings after its resolution follow directly from the actions of the participants and are entirely consistent with their intentions. Properly resolved, scandal should leave no residue of hesitation about feeling nonspecific allegiance to the political process.

Finally, it is possible that this cycle of orchestrated outrage and return to obliviousness may serve to stabilize the political system in a way never consciously intended by any of the participants. Although commentators like to express dismay at political disinterest and nonparticipation, and condemn it as a failure of our political culture, no less a political theorist than Samuel Huntington worried recently in print that democracies may be ungovernable if citizens take their juridical right to participate too much to heart (Crozier et al., 1975). Distraction and nonparticipation may be the *sine qua non* of stable democracies. But nonparticipation is hard to reconcile with the pride citizens are encouraged to feel at being the epitome of a free and sovereign people. Scandal provides an antidote to the distress that may arise from this contradiction by providing compelling episodes of *spectator participation*.

Scandal may be more akin to professional wrestling than to a medieval morality play. In scandal, political bodies fly through the air, mete out incredible punishments, and crash noisily to the canvas. What purpose can such a spectacle serve?[19] Professional wrestling demands a suspension of disbelief in the phoniness of the match. If one can do this, one reaps the rewards of participating as a spectator in a "mythological

---

[19]For an excellent discussion of the spectacle of professional wrestling, see Barthes (1972).

fight between Good and Evil'' (Barthes, 1972: 23). Political scandal implicitly demands a suspension of disbelief, this time in the phoniness of what passes daily for democratic participation. One is rewarded with the feeling of witnessing and being swept up in important political events. Nonparticipation is replaced for the moment by exciting, spectator participation. Scandals may serve to stabilize the political system not primarily because they drive from office those who refuse to play by the rules, but because they periodically help repress the gnawing preconscious sense of impotence and restlessness that plagues nominally empowered but chronically passive, uninvolved citizens.

REFERENCES

Barthes, Roland
    1972   ''The world of wrestling.'' Pp. 15–25 in Mythologies. New York: Hill and Wang.

Bennett, W. Lance
    1980   ''Paradox of public discourse: A framework for the analysis of political accounts.'' Journal of Politics 42: 792–817.

Bernstein, Barton J.
    1976   ''Road to Watergate and beyond: The growth and abuse of executive authority since 1940.'' Law and Contemporary Problems 40: 58–86.

Brown, Bruce
    1974   ''Watergate: Business as usual.'' Liberation 18: 16–29.

Campbell, John
    1986   ''Legitimation meltdown: Weberian and neo-Marxist interpretations of legitimation crisis in advanced capitalist society.'' In Maurice Zeitlin (ed.), Political Power and Social Theory, Vol. 6. Greenwich, CT: JAI Press. In press.

Candee, Dan
    1975   ''Moral psychology of Watergate.'' Journal of Social Issues 32: 183–92.

Chaffee, Steven H.
    1975   ''Young voters' reactions to early Watergate issues.'' American Politics Quarterly 3: 360–85.

Chomsky, Noam
    1973   ''Watergate: A skeptical view.'' New York Review of Books September 20: 3–8.

Clines, Francis X.
    1983   ''White House seeks to peer beyond E.P.A. smoke.'' The New York Times. March 11.

Committee on Research of the National Capital Area Chapter of APSA
    1976   ''Watergate in retrospect: The forgotten agenda.'' Public Administration Review 36: 306–10.

Crozier, Michael J., Samuel P. Huntington and J. Watanuki
    1975   The Crisis of Democracy: Report on the Governability of Democracies to the Trilateral Commission. New York: New York University Press.

Dennis, Jack and Carol Webster
    1975   ''Children's images of the president and government.'' American Politics Quarterly 3: 386–405.

Downs, Anthony
    1972   ''Up and down with ecology—The issue attention cycle.'' Public Interest 28: 38–50.

Edelman, Murray
    1980a   ''Implementation as non-implementation.'' Paper presented at the Conference on Social Policy Evaluation, Tel Aviv, Israel.
    1980b   ''Mystifying political communications: The attribution of individual choice, blame and merit.'' Paper presented at the Conference on Language and Power, Bellagio, Italy.

Fowlkes, Diane L.
    1977   ''Realpolitik and play politics: The effects of Watergate and political gaming on undergraduate students' political interest and political trust.'' Simulation and Games 8: 419–38.

Goffman, Erving
    1959   The Presentation of Self in Everyday Life. Garden City: Doubleday.
    1967   Interaction Ritual: Essays in Face-to-Face Behavior. Chicago: Aldine.

Habermas, Jurgen
    1973   Legitimation Crisis. Boston: Beacon Press.

Hawkins, Robert P., Suzanne Purgee and Donald Roberts
    1975   ''Watergate and political socialization.'' American Politics Quarterly 3: 406–22.

Hentoff, Nat
    1977   ''Press as unindicted coconspirator.'' Social Policy 7: 62–64.

Ives, C. P.
1976   "Watergate: Two parables and a proposition." Modern Age 20: 141–52.

Lang, Gladys E. and Kurt Lang
1980   "Polling on Watergate: The battle for public opinion." Public Opinion Quarterly 44: 530–47.

Lipset, Seymour M. and Earl Rabb
1973   "An appointment with Watergate." Commentary 56: 35–43.

Lyman, Stanford M.
1975   "Legitimacy and consensus in Lipset's America: From Washington to Watergate." Social Research 42: 729–59.

McLeod, Jack M., Jane D. Brown and Lee B. Becker
1977   "Watergate and the 1974 congressional elections." Public Opinion Quarterly 41: 181–95.

National Wildlife Federation
1982   "Shredding the environmental safety net: The full story behind the EPA budget cuts." Washington, DC: National Wildlife Federation. February 4.

O'Connor, James
1973   The Fiscal Crisis of the State. New York: St. Martin's Press.

Offe, Claus
1974   "Structural problems of the capitalist state." German Political Studies 1: 31–57.

Offe, Claus and Volker Ronge
1975   "Theses on the theory of the state." New German Critique 6: 137–47.

Oglesby, Carl
1974   "In defense of paranoia." Ramparts 13: 15–50.

Sale, Kirkpatrick
1973   "The world behind Watergate." New York Review of Books. May 3: 9–16.

San Francisco/Bay Area Kapitalistate Group
1975   "Watergate, or the eighteenth Brumaire of Richard Nixon." Kapitalistate #3: 3–24.

Schrag, Peter
1974   "Watergate as entertainment." Social Policy 5: 23–26.

Shenon, Philip
1986   "Meese says inquiries focus on actions of U.S. officials." The New York Times. March 12.

Szasz, Andrew
1984   "Industrial resistance toward occupational safety and health legislation, 1971–1981." Social Problems 32: 103–16.
1986   "The reversal of federal policy toward worker safety and health: A critical examination of alternative explanations." Science and Society 50: 25–51.

Taylor, Stuart, Jr.
1983   "E.P.A. inquiries center on four issues." The New York Times. March 13.

United Press International
1985   "Panel urges special counsel in E.P.A. case." The New York Times. December 6.

Vidich, Arthur J.
1975   "Political legitimacy in bureaucratic society: An analysis of Watergate." Social Research 42: 778–811.

Williams, Robert J.
1981   "Political corruption in the United States: Review article." Political Studies 29: 126–29.

Wolfe, Alan
1977   The Limits of Legitimacy: Political Contradictions of Contemporary Capitalism. New York: Free Press.

Wright, Gerald C., Jr.
1977   "Constituency response to congressional behavior: The impact of the House judiciary committee impeachment votes." Western Political Quarterly 30: 401–10.

Wrong, Dennis
1974   "Watergate: Symptom of what sickness?" Dissent 21: 501–7.

Zimmer, Troy A.
1979   "Impact of Watergate on the public's trust in people and confidence in the mass media." Social Science Quarterly 59: 743–51.

PINTO MADNESS

Mark Dowie

One evening in the mid-1960s, Arjay Miller was driving home from his office in Dearborn, Michigan, in the four-door Lincoln Continental that went with his job as president of the Ford Motor Company. On a crowded highway, another car struck his from the rear. The Continental spun around and burst into flames. Because he was wearing a shoulder-strap seat belt, Miller was unharmed by the crash, and because his doors didn't jam he escaped the flaming wreck. But the accident made a vivid impression on him. Several months later, on July 15, 1965, he recounted it to a U.S. Senate subcommittee that was hearing testimony on auto safety legislation. ''I still have burning in my mind the image of that gas tank on fire,'' Miller said. He went on to express an almost passionate interest in controlling fuel-fed fires in cars that crash or roll over. He spoke with excitement about the fabric gas tank Ford was testing at that very moment. ''If it proves out,'' he promised the senators, ''it will be a feature you will see in our standard cars.''

Almost seven years after Miller's testimony, a woman, whom for legal reasons we will call Sandra Gillespie, pulled onto a Minneapolis highway in her new Ford Pinto. Riding with her was a young boy, whom we'll call Robbie Carlton. As she entered a merge lane, Sandra Gillespie's car stalled. Another car rear-ended hers at an impact speed of 28 miles per hour. The Pinto's gas tank ruptured. Vapors from it mixed quickly with the air in the passenger compartment. A spark ignited the mixture and the car exploded in a ball of fire. Sandra died in agony a few hours later in an emergency hospital. Her passenger, 13-year-old Robbie Carlton, is still alive; he has just come home from another futile operation aimed at grafting a new ear and nose from skin on the few unscarred portions of his badly burned body. (This accident is real; the details are from police reports.)

Why did Sandra Gillespie's Ford Pinto catch fire so easily, seven years after Ford's Arjay Miller made his apparently sincere pronouncements— the same seven years that brought more safety improvements to cars than any other period in automotive history? An extensive investigation by *Mother Jones* over the past six months has found these answers:

Fighting strong competition from Volkswagen for the lucrative small-car market, the Ford Motor Company rushed the Pinto into production in much less than the usual time.

Ford engineers discovered in pre-production crash tests that rear-end collisions would rupture the Pinto's fuel system extremely easily.

Because assembly-line machinery was already tooled when engineers found this defect, top Ford officials decided to manufacture the car anyway—exploding

Mark Dowie (1977) ''Pinto Madness.'' *Mother Jones* Vol. II, No. VIII (September/October): 18–24, 28–32. Reprinted by permission.

gas tank and all—*even though Ford owned the patent on a much safer gas tank.*

For more than eight years afterwards, Ford successfully lobbied, with extraordinary vigor and some blatant lies, against a key government safety standard that would have forced the company to change the Pinto's fire-prone gas tank.

By conservative estimates Pinto crashes have caused 500 burn deaths to people who would not have been seriously injured if the car had not burst into flames. Burning Pintos have become such an embarrassment to Ford that its advertising agency, J. Walter Thompson, dropped a line from the end of a radio spot that read, "Pinto leaves you with that warm feeling."

Ford knows the Pinto is a firetrap, yet it has paid out millions to settle damage suits out of court, and it is prepared to spend millions more lobbying against safety standards. With a half million cars rolling off the assembly lines each year, Pinto is the biggest-selling subcompact in America, and the company's operating profit on the car is fantastic. Finally, in 1977, new Pinto models have incorporated a few minor alterations necessary to meet that federal standard Ford managed to hold off for eight years. Why did the company delay so long in making these minimal, inexpensive improvements?

Ford waited eight years because its internal "cost-benefit analysis," *which places a dollar value on human life,* said it wasn't profitable to make the changes sooner.

Before we get to the question of how much Ford thinks your life is worth, let's trace the history of the death trap itself. Although this particular story is about the Pinto, the way in which Ford made its decision is typical of the U.S. auto industry generally. There are plenty of similar stories about other cars made by other companies. But this case is the worst of them all.

The next time you drive behind a Pinto (with over two million of them on the road, you shouldn't have much trouble finding one), take a look at the rear end. That long silver object hanging down under the bumper is the gas tank. The tank begins about six inches forward of the bumper. In late models the bumper is designed to withstand a collision of only about five miles per hour. Earlier bumpers may as well not have

been on the car for all the protection they offered the gas tank.

Mother Jones has studied hundreds of reports and documents on rear-end collisions involving Pintos. These reports conclusively reveal that if you ran into that Pinto you were following at over 30 miles per hour, the rear end of the car would buckle like an accordion, right up to the back seat. The tube leading to the gas-tank cap would be ripped away from the tank itself, and gas would immediately begin sloshing onto the road around the car. The buckled gas tank would be jammed up against the differential housing, which contains four sharp protruding bolts likely to gash holes in the tank and spill still more gas. The welded seam between the main body frame and the wheel well would split, allowing gas to enter the interior of the car.

Now all you need is a spark from a cigarette, ignition, or scraping metal, and both cars would be engulfed in flames. If you gave the Pinto a really good whack—say, at 40 mph—chances are excellent that its doors would jam and you would have to stand by and watch its trapped passengers burn to death.

This scenario is no news to Ford. Internal company documents in our possession show that Ford has crash-tested the Pinto at a top-secret site more than 40 times and that *every* test made at over 25 mph without special structural alteration of the car has resulted in an ruptured fuel tank. Despite this, Ford officials denied having crash-tested the Pinto.

Eleven of these tests, averaging a 31-mph impact speed, came before Pintos started rolling out of the factories. Only three cars passed the test with unbroken fuel tanks. In one of them an inexpensive light-weight metal baffle was placed so those bolts would not perforate the tank. (Don't forget about that baffle, which costs about a dollar and weighs about a pound. It plays an important role in our story later on.) In another successful test, a piece of steel was placed between the tank and the bumper. In the third test car the gas tank was lined with a rubber bladder. But none of these protective alterations was used in the mass-produced Pinto.

In preproduction planning, engineers seriously considered using in the Pinto the same kind of gas tank Ford uses in the Capri. The Capri tank rides over the rear axle and differential housing. It has been so successful in over 50 crash tests that Ford used it in its Experimental Safety Vehicle, which withstood rear-end impacts of 60 mph. So why wasn't the Capri tank used in the Pinto? Or, why wasn't that baffle placed between the tank and the axle—something that would have saved the life of Sandra Gillespie and hundreds like her. Why was a car known to be a serious fire hazard deliberately released to production in August of 1970?

Whether Ford should manufacture subcompacts at all was the subject of a bitter two-year debate at the company's Deaborn headquarters. The principals in the corporate struggle were the then-president Semon "Bunky" Knudsen, whom Henry Ford II had hired away from General Motors, and Lee Iacocca, a spunky young turk who had risen fast within the company on the enormous success of the Mustang. Iacocca argued forcefully that Volkswagen and the Japanese were going to capture the entire American subcompact market unless Ford put out its own alternative to the VW Beetle. Bunky Knudsen said, in effect: let them have the small-car market; Ford makes good money on medium and large models. But he lost the battle and later resigned. Iacocca became president and almost immediately began a rush program to produce the Pinto.

Like the Mustang, the Pinto became known in the company as "Lee's car." Lee Iacocca wanted that little car in the showrooms of America with the 1971 models. So he ordered his engineering vice president, Bob Alexander, to oversee what was probably the shortest production planning period in modern automotive history. The normal time span from conception to production of a new car model is about 43 months. The Pinto schedule was set at just under 25.

Design, styling, product planning, advance engineering and quality assurance all have flexible time frames, and engineers can pretty much carry these on simultaneously. Tooling, on the other hand, has a fixed time frame of about 18 months. Normally, an auto company doesn't begin tooling until the other processes are almost

over. *But Iacocca's speed-up meant Pinto tooling went on at the same time as product development.* So when crash tests revealed a serious defect in the gas tank, it was too late. The tooling was well under way.

When it was discovered the gas tank was unsafe, did anyone go to Iacocca and tell him? "Hell no," replied an engineer who worked on the Pinto, a high company official for many years, who, unlike several others at Ford, maintains a necessarily clandestine concern for safety. "That person would have been fired. Safety wasn't a popular subject around Ford in those days. With Lee it was taboo. Whenever a problem was raised that meant a delay on the Pinto, Lee would chomp on his cigar, look out the window and say 'Read the product objectives and get back to work.' "

The product objectives are clearly stated in the Pinto "green book." This is a thick, top-secret manual in green covers containing a step-by-step production plan for the model, detailing the metallurgy, weight, strength and quality of every part in the car. The product objectives for the Pinto are repeated in an article by Ford executive F. G. Olsen published by the Society of Automotive Engineers. He lists these product objectives as follows:

1. True subcompact
   Size
   Weight
2. Low cost of ownership
   Initial price
   Fuel consumption
   Reliability
   Serviceability
3. Clear product superiority
   Appearance
   Comfort
   Features
   Ride and handling
   Performance

Safety, you will notice, is not there. It is not mentioned in the entire article. As Lee Iacocca was fond of saying, "Safety doesn't sell."

Heightening the anti-safety pressure on Pinto engineers was an important goal set by Iacocca known as "the limits of 2,000." The Pinto was not to weigh an ounce over 2,000 pounds and not to cost a cent over $2,000. "Iacocca enforced these limits with an iron hand," recalls the engineer quoted earlier. So, even when a crash test showed that that one-pound, one-dollar piece of metal stopped the puncture of the gas tank, it was thrown out as extra cost and extra weight.

People shopping for subcompacts are watching every dollar. "You have to keep in mind," the engineer explained, "that the price elasticity of these subcompacts is extremely tight. You can price yourself right out of the market by adding $25 to the production cost of the model. And nobody understands that better than Iacocca."

Dr. Leslie Ball, the retired safety chief for the NASA manned space program and a founder of the International Society of Reliability Engineers, recently made a careful study of the Pinto. "The release to production of the Pinto was the most reprehensible decision in the history of American engineering," he said. Ball can name more than 40 European and Japanese models in the Pinto price and weight range with safer gas-tank positioning. Ironically, many of them, like the Ford Capri, contain a "saddle-type" gas tank riding over the back axle. *The patent on the saddle-type tank is owned by the Ford Motor Co.*

Los Angeles auto safety expert Byron Bloch has made an in-depth study of the Pinto fuel system. "It's a catastrophic blunder," he says. "Ford made an extremely irresponsible decision when they placed such a weak tank in such a ridiculous location in such a soft rear end. It's almost designed to blow up—premeditated."

A Ford engineer, who doesn't want his name used, comments: "This company is run by salesmen, not engineers: so the priority is styling, not safety." He goes on to tell a story about gas-tank safety at Ford:

Lou Tubben is one of the most popular engineers at Ford. He's a friendly, outgoing guy with a genuine concern for safety. By 1971 he had grown so concerned about gas-tank integrity that he asked his boss if he could prepare a presentation on safer tank design. Tubben and his boss had both worked on the Pinto and shared a concern for its safety. His boss gave him the go-ahead, scheduled a date for the presenta-

tion and invited all company engineers and key production planning personnel. When time came for the meeting, a total of two people showed up—Lou Tubben and his boss.

"So you see," continued the anonymous Ford engineer, "there *are* a few of us here at Ford who are concerned about fire safety." He adds: "They are mostly engineers who have to study a lot of accident reports and look at pictures of burned people. But we don't talk about it much. It isn't a popular subject. I've never seen safety on the agenda of a product meeting and, except for a brief period in 1956, can't remember seeing the word safety in an advertisement. I really don't think the company wants American consumers to start thinking too much about safety—for fear they might demand it, I suppose."

Asked about the Pinto gas tank, another Ford engineer admitted: "That's all true. But you miss the point entirely. You see, safety isn't the issue, trunk space is. You have no idea how stiff the competition is over trunk space. Do you realize that if we put a Capri-type tank in the Pinto you could only get one set of golf clubs in the trunk?"

Blame for Sandra Gillespie's death, Robbie Carlton's unrecognizable face and all the other injuries and deaths in Pintos since 1970 does not rest on the shoulders of Lee Iacocca alone. For, while he and his associates fought their battle against a safer Pinto in Dearborn, a larger war against safer cars raged in Washington. One skirmish in that war involved Ford's successful eight-year lobbying effort against Federal Motor Vehicle Safety Standard 301, the rear-end provisions of which would have forced Ford to redesign the Pinto.

But first some background:

During the early '60s, auto safety legislation became the *bête-noire* of American big business. The auto industry was the last great unregulated business, and if *it* couldn't reverse the tide of government regulation, the reasoning went, no one could.

People who know him cannot remember Henry Ford taking a stronger stand than the one he took against the regulation of safety design. He spent weeks in Washington calling on members of Congress, holding press conferences and recruiting business cronies like W. B. Murphy of Campbell's Soup to join the anti-regulation battle. Displaying the sophistication for which today's American corporate leaders will be remembered, Murphy publicly called auto safety "a hula hoop, a fad that will pass." He was speaking to a special luncheon of the Business Council, an organization of 100 chief executives who gather periodically in Washington to provide "advice" and "counsel" to government. The target of their wrath in this instance was the Motor Vehicle Safety Bills introduced in both houses of Congress, largely in response to Ralph Nader's *Unsafe at Any Speed.*

By 1965, most pundits and lobbyists saw the handwriting on the wall and prepared to accept government "meddling" in the last bastion of free enterprise. Not Henry. With bulldog tenacity, he held out for defeat of the legislation to the very end, loyal to his grandfather's invention and to the company that makes it. But the Safety Act passed the House and Senate unanimously, and was signed into law by Lyndon Johnson in 1966.

While lobbying for and against legislation is pretty much a process of high-level back-slapping, press-conferencing and speech-making, fighting a regulatory agency is a much subtler matter. Henry headed home to lick his wounds in Grosse Pointe, Michigan, and a planeload of the Ford Motor Company's best brains flew to Washington to start the "education" of the new federal auto safety bureaucrats.

Their job was to implant the official industry ideology in the minds of the new officials regulating auto safety. Briefly summarized, that ideology states that auto accidents are caused not by *cars*, but by people and highway conditions.

It is an experience to hear automotive "safety engineers" talk for hours without ever mentioning cars. They will advocate spending billions educating youngsters, punishing drunks and redesigning street signs. Listening to them, you begin to think that it is easier to control 100 million drivers than a handful of manufacturers. They show movies about guard-rail design and advocate the clear-cutting of trees 100 feet back from every highway in the nation. If a car is un-safe, they argue, it is because its owner doesn't maintain it properly.

In light of an annual death rate approaching 50,000, they are forced to admit that driving is hazardous. But the car is, in the words of Arjay Miller, "the safest link in the safety chain."

Before the Ford experts left Washington to return to drafting tables in Dearborn they did one other thing. They managed to informally reach an agreement with the major public servants who would be making auto safety decisions. This agreement was that "cost-benefit" would be an acceptable mode of analysis by Detroit and its new regulators. And, as we shall see, cost-benefit analysis quickly became the basis of Ford's argument against safer car design.

Cost-benefit analysis was used only occasionally in government until President Kennedy appointed Ford Motor Company President Robert McNamara to be Secretary of Defense. McNamara, orginally an accountant, preached cost-benefit with all the force of a Biblical zealot. Stated in its simplest terms, cost-benefit analysis says that if the cost is greater than the benefit, the project is not worth it—no matter what the benefit. Examine the cost of every action, decision, contract, part, or change, the doctrine says, then carefully evaluate the benefits (in dollars) to be certain that they exceed the cost before you begin a program or pass a regulation.

As a management tool in a business in which profits count over all else, cost-benefit analysis makes a certain amount of sense. Serious problems arise, however, when public officials who ought to have more than corporate profits at heart apply cost-benefit analysis to every conceivable decision. The inevitable result is that they must place a dollar value on human life.

Ever wonder what your life is worth in dollars? Perhaps $10 million? Ford has a better idea: $200,000.

Remember, Ford had gotten the federal regulators to agree to talk auto safety in terms of cost-benefit. But in order to be able to argue that various safety costs were greater than their benefits, Ford needed to have a dollar value figure for the "benefit." Rather than coming up with a price tag itself, the auto industry pressured the National Highway Traffic Safety Administration to do so. And in a 1972 report the agency determined that a human life lost on the highway was worth $200,725 [Table 1]. Inflationary forces have recently pushed the figure up to $278,000.

Furnished with this useful tool, Ford immediately went to work using it to prove why various safety improvements were too expensive to make.

Nowhere did the company argue harder that it should make no changes than in the area of rupture-prone fuel tanks. Not long after the government arrived at the $200,725-per-life figure, it surfaced, rounded off to a cleaner $200,000, in an internal Ford memorandum. This cost-benefit analysis argued that Ford should not make an $11-per-car improvement that would prevent 180 fiery deaths a year.

This cold calculus [Table 2] is buried in a seven-page company memorandum entitled "Fatalities Associated with Crash-Induced Fuel Leakage and Fires."

TABLE 1. What's Your Life Worth? Societal Cost Components for Fatalities, 1972 NHTSA Study

Component	1971 Costs
Future productivity losses	
Direct	$132,000
Indirect	41,300
Medical costs	
Hospital	700
Other	425
Property damage	1,500
Insurance administration	4,700
Legal and court	3,000
Employer losses	1,000
Victim's pain and suffering	10,000
Funeral	900
Assets (lost consumption)	5,000
Miscellaneous accident cost	200
Total per fatality: $200,725	

Here is a chart from a federal study showing how the National Highway Traffic Safety Administration has calculated the value of a human life. The estimate was arrived at under pressure from the auto industry. The Ford Motor Company has used it in cost-benefit analyses arguing why certain safety measures are not "worth" the savings in human lives. The calculation above is a breakdown of the estimated cost to society every time someone is killed in a car accident. We were not able to find anyone, either in the government or at Ford, who could explain how the $10,000 figure for "pain and suffering" had been arrived at.

TABLE 2 Benefits and Costs Relating to Fuel Leakage Associated with the Static Rollover Test Portion of FMVSS 208

Benefits
Savings: 80 burn deaths, 180 serious burn injuries, 2,100 burned vehicles.
Unit cost: $200,000 per death, $67,000 per injury, $700 per vehicle.
Total benefit: 180 × ($200,000) + 180 × ($67,000) + 2,100 × ($700) = $49.5 million.

Costs
Sales: 11 million cars, 1.5 million light trucks.
Unit cost: $11 per car, $11 per truck.
Total cost: 11,000,000 × ($11) + 1,500,000 × ($11) = $137 million.

The memo goes on to argue that there is no financial benefit in complying with proposed safety standards that would admittedly result in fewer auto fires, fewer burn deaths and fewer burn injuries. Naturally, memoranda that speak so casually of "burn deaths" and "burn injuries" are not released to the public. They are very effective, however, with Department of Transportation officials indoctrinated in McNamarian cost-benefit analysis.

All Ford had to do was convince men like John Volpe, Claude Brinegar and William Coleman (successive Secretaries of Transportation during the Nixon-Ford years) that certain safety standards would add so much to the price of cars that fewer people would buy them. This could damage the auto industry, which was still believed to be the bulwark of the American economy. "Compliance to these standards," Henry Ford II prophesied at more than one press conference, "will shut down the industry."

The Nixon Transportation Secretaries were the kind of regulatory officials big business dreams of. They understood and loved capitalism and thought like businessmen. Yet, best of all, they came into office uninformed on technical automotive matters. And you could talk "burn injuries" and "burn deaths" with these guys, and they didn't seem to envision children crying at funerals and people hiding in their homes with melted faces. Their minds appeared to have leapt right to the bottom line—more safety meant higher prices, higher prices meant lower sales and lower sales meant lower profits.

So when J. C. Echold, Director of Automotive Safety (chief anti-safety lobbyist) for Ford, wrote to the Department of Transportation—which he still does frequently, at great length—he felt secure attaching a memorandum that in effect says it is acceptable to kill 180 people and burn another 180 every year, *even though we have the technology that could save their lives for $11 a car.*

Furthermore, Echold attached this memo, confident, evidently, that the Secretary would question neither his low death/injury statistics nor his high cost estimates. But it turns out, on closer examination, that both these findings were misleading.

First, note that Ford's table shows an equal number of burn deaths and burn injuries. This is false. All independent experts estimate that for each person who dies by an auto fire, many more are left with charred hands, faces and limbs. Andrew McGuire of the Northern California Burn Center estimates the ratio of burn injuries to deaths at ten to one instead of the one to one Ford shows here. Even though Ford values a burn at only a piddling $67,000 instead of the $200,000 price of life, the true ratio obviously throws the company's calculations way off.

The other side of the equation, the alleged $11 cost of a fire-prevention device, is also a misleading estimation. One document that was *not* sent to Washington by Ford was a "Confidential" cost analysis *Mother Jones* has managed to obtain, showing that crash fires could be largely prevented for considerably *less* than $11 a car. The cheapest method involves placing a heavy rubber bladder inside the gas tank to keep the fuel from spilling if the tank ruptures. Goodyear had developed the bladder and had demonstrated it to the automotive industry. We have in our possession crash-test reports showing that the Goodyear bladder worked well. On December 2, 1970 (*two years before* Echold sent his cost-benefit memo to Washington), Ford Motor Company ran a rear-end crash test on a car with the rubber bladder in the gas tank. The tank ruptured, but no fuel leaked. On January 15, 1971, Ford again tested the bladder and

again it worked. The total purchase and installation cost of the bladder would have been $5.08 per car. That $5.08 could have saved the lives of Sandra Gillespie and several hundred others.

When a federal regulatory agency like the National Highway Traffic Safety Administration (NHTSA) decides to issue a new standard, the law usually requires it to invite all interested parties to respond before the standard is enforced—a reasonable-enough custom on the surface. However, the auto industry has taken advantage of this process and has used it to delay lifesaving emission and safety standards for years. In the case of the standard that would have corrected that fragile Pinto fuel tank, the delay was for an incredible eight years.

The particular regulation involved here was Federal Motor Vehicle Safety Standard 301. Ford picked portions of Standard 301 for strong opposition back in 1968 when the Pinto was still in the blueprint stage. The intent of 301, and the 300 series that followed it, was to protect drivers and passengers *after* a crash occurs. Without question the worst postcrash hazard is fire. So Standard 301 originally proposed that all cars should be able to withstand a fixed-barrier impact of 20 mph (that is, running into a wall at that speed) without losing fuel.

When the standard was proposed, Ford engineers pulled their crash-test results out of their files. The front ends of most cars were no problem—with minor alterations they could stand the impact without losing fuel. "We were already working on the front end," Ford engineer Dick Kimble admitted. "We knew we could meet the test on the front end." But with the Pinto particularly, a 20-mph rear-end standard meant redesigning the entire rear end of the car. With the Pinto scheduled for production in August of 1970, and with $200 million worth of tools in place, adoption of this standard would have created a minor financial disaster. So Standard 301 was targeted for delay, and, with some assistance from its industry associates, Ford succeeded beyond its wildest expectations: the standard was not adopted until the 1977 model year. Here is how it happened:

There are several main techniques in the art of combating a government safety standard: a) make your arguments in succession, so the feds can be working on disproving only one at a time; b) claim that the real problem is not X but Y (we already saw one instance of this in "the problem is not cars but people"); c) no matter how ridiculous each argument is, accompany it with thousands of pages of highly technical assertions it will take the government months or, preferably, years to test. Ford's large and active Washington office brought these techniques to new heights and became the envy of the lobbyists' trade.

The Ford people started arguing against Standard 301 way back in 1968 with a strong attack of technique b). Fire, they said, was not the real problem. Sure, cars catch fire and people burn occasionally. But statistically auto fires are such a minor problem that NHTSA should really concern itself with other matters.

Strange as it may seem, the Department of Transportation (NHTSA's parent agency) didn't know whether or not this was true. So it contracted with several independent research groups to study auto fires. The studies took months, often years, which was just what Ford wanted. The completed studies, however, showed auto fires to be more of a problem than Transportation officials ever dreamed of. A Washington research firm found that 400,000 cars were burning up every year, burning more than 3,000 people to death. Furthermore, auto fires were increasing five times as fast as building fires. Another study showed that 35 per cent of all fire deaths in the U.S. occurred in automobiles. Forty per cent of all fire department calls in the 1960s were to vehicle fires—a public cost of $350 million a year, a figure that, incidentally, never shows up in cost-benefit analyses.

Another study was done by the Highway Traffic Research Institute in Ann Arbor, Michigan, a safety think-tank funded primarily by the auto industry (the giveaway there is the words "highway traffic" rather than "automobile" in the group's name). It concluded that 40 per cent of the lives lost in fuel-fed fires could be saved if the manufacturers complied with proposed Standard 301. Finally, a third report was prepared for NHTSA. This report indicated that the Ford Motor Company makes 24 per cent of

the cars on the American road, yet these cars account for 42 per cent of the collision-ruptured fuel tanks.

Ford lobbyists then used technique a)—bringing up a new argument. Their line then became: yes, perhaps burn accidents do happen, but rear-end collisions are relatively rare (note the echo of technique b) here as well). Thus Standard 301 was not needed. This set the NHTSA off on a new round of analyzing accident reports. The government's findings finally were that rear-end collisions were seven and a half times more likely to result in fuel spills than were front-end collisions. So much for that argument.

By now it was 1972; NHTSA had been researching and analyzing for four years to answer Ford's objections. During that time, nearly 9,000 people burned to death in flaming wrecks. Tens of thousands more were badly burned and scarred for life. And the four-year delay meant that well over 10 million new unsafe vehicles went on the road, vehicles that will be crashing, leaking fuel and incinerating people well into the 1980s.

Ford now had to enter its third round of battling the new regulations. On the "the problem is not X but Y" principle, the company had to look around for something new to get itself off the hook. One might have thought that, faced with all the latest statistics on the horrifying number of deaths in flaming accidents, Ford would find the task difficult. But the company's rhetoric was brilliant. The problem was not burns, but . . . impact! Most of the people killed in these fiery accidents, claimed Ford, would have died whether the car burned or not. They were killed by the kinetic force of the impact, not the fire.

And so once again, the ball bounced into the government's court and the absurdly pro-industry NHTSA began another slow-motion response. Once again it began a time-consuming round of test crashes and embarked on a study of accidents. The latter, however, revealed that a large and growing number of corpses taken from burned cars involved in rear-end crashes contained no cuts, bruises or broken bones. They clearly would have survived the accident unharmed if the cars had not caught fire. This pattern was confirmed in careful rear-end crash tests performed by the Insurance Institute for Highway Safety. A University of Miami study found an inordinate number of Pintos burning on rear-end impact and concluded that this demonstrated "a clear and present hazard to all Pinto owners."

Pressure on NHTSA from Ralph Nader and consumer groups began mounting. The industry-agency collusion was so obvious that Senator Joseph Montoya (D–N.M.) introduced legislation about Standard 301. NHTSA waffled some more and again announced its intentions to promulgate a rear-end collision standard.

Waiting, as it normally does, until the last day allowed for response, Ford filed with NHTSA a gargantuan batch of letters, studies and charts now arguing that the federal testing criteria were unfair. Ford also argued that design changes required to meet the standard would take 43 months, which seemed like a rather long time in light of the fact that the entire Pinto was designed in about two years. Specifically new complaints about the standard involved the weight of the test vehicle, whether or not the brakes should be engaged at the moment of impact and the claim that the standard should only apply to cars, not trucks or buses. Perhaps the most amusing argument was that the engine should not be idling during crash tests, the rationale being that an idling engine meant that the gas tank had to contain gasoline and that the hot lights needed to film the crash might ignite the gasoline and cause a fire.

Some of these complaints were accepted, others rejected. But they all required examination and testing by a weak-kneed NHTSA, meaning more of those 18-month studies the industry loves so much. So the complaints served their real purpose—delay; all told, an eight-year delay, while Ford manufactured more than three million profitable, dangerously incendiary Pintos. To justify this delay, Henry Ford II called more press conferences to predict the demise of American civilization. "If we can't meet the standards when they are published," he warned, "we will have to close down. And if we have to close down some production because we don't meet standards we're in for real trouble in this country."

While government bureaucrats dragged their feet on lifesaving Standard 301, a different kind of expert was taking a close look at the Pinto— the "recon man." "Recon" stands for reconstruction; recon men reconstruct accidents for police departments, insurance companies and lawyers who want to know exactly who or what caused an accident. It didn't take many rear-end Pinto accidents to demonstrate the weakness of the car. Recon men began encouraging lawyers to look beyond one driver or another to the manufacturer in their search for fault, particularly in the growing number of accidents where passengers were uninjured by collision but were badly burned by fire.

Pinto lawsuits began mounting fast against Ford. Says John Versace, executive safety engineer at Ford's Safety Research Center, "Ulcers are running pretty high among the engineers who worked on the Pinto. Every lawyer in the country seems to want to take their depositions." (The Safety Research Center is an impressive glass and concrete building standing by itself about a mile from Ford World Headquarters in Dearborn. Looking at it, one imagines its large staff protects consumers from burned and broken limbs. Not so. The Center is the technical support arm of Jack Echold's 14-person anti-regulatory lobbying team in World Headquarters.)

When the Pinto liability suits began, Ford strategy was to go to a jury. Confident it could hide the Pinto crash tests, Ford thought that juries of solid American registered voters would buy the industry doctrine that drivers, not cars, cause accidents. It didn't work. It seems that citizens are much quicker to see the truth than bureaucracies. Juries began ruling against the company, granting million-dollar awards to plaintiffs.

"We'll never go to a jury again," says Al Slechter in Ford's Washington office. "Not in a fire case. Juries are just too sentimental. They see those charred remains and forget the evidence. No sir, we'll settle."

Settlement involves less cash, smaller legal fees and less publicity, but it is an indication of the weakness of their case. Nevertheless, Ford has been offering to settle when it is clear that the company can't pin the blame on the driver of the other car. But, since the company carries $2 million deductible product-liability insurance, these settlements have a direct impact on the bottom line. They must therefore be considered a factor in determining the net operating profit on the Pinto. It's impossible to get a straight answer from Ford on the profitability of the Pinto and the impact of lawsuit settlements on it—even when you have a curious and mildly irate shareholder call to inquire, as we did. However, financial officer Charles Matthews did admit that the company establishes a reserve for large dollar settlements. He would not divulge the amount of the reserve and had no explanation for its absence from the annual report.

Until recently, it was clear that, whatever the cost of these settlements, it was not enough to seriously cut into the Pinto's enormous profits. The cost of retooling Pinto assembly lines and of equipping each car with a safety gadget like that $5.08 Goodyear bladder was, company accountants calculated, greater than that of paying out millions to survivors like Robbie Carlton or to widows and widowers of victims like Sandra Gillespie. The bottom line ruled, and inflammable Pintos kept rolling out of the factories.

In 1977, however, an incredibly sluggish government has at last instituted Standard 301. Now Pintos will have to have rupture-proof gas tanks. Or will they?

To everyone's surprise, the 1977 Pinto recently passed a rear-end crash test in Phoenix, Arizona, for NHTSA. The agency was so convinced the Pinto would fail that it was the first car tested. Amazingly, it did not burst into flame.

"We have had so many Ford failures in the past," explained agency engineer Tom Grubbs, "I felt sure the Pinto would fail."

How did it pass?

Remember that one-dollar, one-pound metal baffle that was on one of the three modified Pintos that passed the pre-production crash tests nearly ten years ago? Well, it is a standard feature on the 1977 Pinto. In the Phoenix test it protected the gas tank from being perforated by those four bolts on the differential housing.

We asked Grubbs if he noticed any other substantial alterations in the rear-end structure of the car. "No," he replied, "the [baffle] seems to be the only noticeable change over the 1976 model."

But was it? What Tom Grubbs and the Department of Transportation didn't know when they tested the car was that it was manufactured in St. Thomas, Ontario. Ontario? The significance of that becomes clear when you learn that Canada has for years had extremely strict rear-end collision standards.

Tom Irwin is the business manager of Charlie Rossi Ford, the Scottsdale, Arizona dealership that sold the Pinto to Tom Grubbs. He refused to explain why he was selling Fords made in Canada when there is a huge Pinto assembly plant much closer by in California. "I know why you're asking that question, and I'm not going to answer it," he blurted out. "You'll have to ask the company."

But Ford's regional office in Phoenix has "no explanation" for the presence of Canadian cars in their local dealerships. Farther up the line in Dearborn, Ford people claim there is absolutely no difference between American and Canadian Pintos. They say cars are shipped back and forth across the border as a matter of course. But they were hard pressed to explain why some Canadian Pintos were shipped all the way to Scottsdale, Arizona. Significantly, one engineer at the St. Thomas plant did admit that the existence of strict rear-end collision standards in Canada "might encourage us to pay a little more attention to quality control on that part of the car."

The Department of Transportation is considering buying an American Pinto and running the test again. For now, it will only say that the situation is under investigation.

Whether the new American Pinto fails or passes the test, Standard 301 will never force the company to test or recall the more than two million pre-1977 Pintos still on the highway. Seventy or more people will burn to death in those cars every year for many years to come. If the past is any indication, Ford will continue to accept the deaths.

According to safety expert Byron Bloch, the older cars could quite easily be retrofitted with gas tanks containing fuel cells. "These improved tanks would add at least 10 mph improved safety performance to the rear end," he estimated, "but it would cost Ford $20 to $30 a car so they won't do it unless they are forced to." Dr. Kenneth Saczalski, safety engineer with the Office of Naval Research in Washington, agrees. "The Defense Department has developed virtually fail-safe fuel systems and retrofitted them into existing vehicles. We have shown them to the auto industry and they have ignored them."

Unfortunately, the Pinto is not an isolated case of corporate malpractice in the auto industry. Neither is Ford a lone sinner. There probably isn't a car on the road without a safety hazard known to its manufacturer. And though Ford may have the best auto lobbyists in Washington, it is not alone. The anti-emission control lobby and the anti-safety lobby usually work in chorus form, presenting a well-harmonized message from the country's richest industry, spoken through the voices of individual companies—the Motor Vehicle Manufacturers Association, the Business Council and the U.S. Chamber of Commerce.

Furthermore, cost-valuing human life is not used by Ford alone. Ford was just the only company careless enough to let such an embarrassing calculation slip into public records. The process of willfully trading lives for profits goes back at least as far as Commodore Vanderbilt, who publicly scorned George Westinghouse and

his "foolish" air brakes while people died by the hundreds in accidents on Vanderbilt's railroads.

The original draft of the Motor Vehicle Safety Act provided for criminal sanction against a manufacturer who willfully placed an unsafe car on the market. Early in the proceedings the auto industry lobbied the provision out of the bill. Since then, there have been those damage settlements, of course, but the only government punishment meted out to auto companies for non-compliance to standards has been a minuscule fine, usually $5,000 to $10,000. One wonders how long the Ford Motor Company would continue to market lethal cars were Henry Ford II and Lee Iacocca serving 20-year terms in Leavenworth for consumer homicide.

This article was published in September of 1977, and in February 1978 a jury awarded a sixteen-year-old boy, badly burned in a rear-end Pinto accident, $128 million in damages (the accident occurred in 1973 in Santa Ana, Calif.). That was the largest single personal injury judgment in history.

On May 8, 1978, the Department of Transportation announced that tests conducted in response to this article showed conclusively that the Pinto was defective in all respects described in the article and called for a recall of all 1971 to 1976 Pintos—the most expensive recall in automotive history.

THE DEMISE OF THE OCCUPATIONAL SAFETY AND HEALTH ADMINISTRATION

A Case Study in Symbolic Action*

Kitty Calavita
Middlebury College

Since its birth on April 28, 1971, the Occupational Safety and Health Administration (OSHA) has been criticized by both U.S. labor and management for its inefficiency and lack of meaningful impact.[1] Many scholars argue that, at its inception, OSHA served at best a symbolic function; it was intended to placate labor and not alter significantly workplace conditions (Berman, 1978; Deutsch, 1981a; Donnelly, 1982; Page and Munsing, 1974; Sheskin, 1982). Nonetheless, when the administration of President Ronald Reagan came to power in January, 1981, it immediately began debilitating OSHA and a number of other regulatory agencies, in many cases even rescinding existing standards.

The question then arises: Why the "overkill," if OSHA played a largely symbolic role in the first place? This paper is an attempt to answer that question. It is, in effect, a case study in the dismantling of symbolic action.

The OSHAct (29 U.S.C., Sections 651-78 [1970]) was signed into law by President Richard Nixon on December 29, 1970, creating for the first time a comprehensive federal agency designed to ensure U.S. workers of a safe and healthy work environment. Located within the Department of Labor, OSHA has primary responsibility for establishing and enforcing standards related to worker safety and health. The act explicitly encourages individual states to establish programs which may be subsidized by the federal government and may pre-empt the federal program; to qualify, each state must provide OSHA with evidence that their program is at least as effective as the federal agency.

The passage of the OSHAct in 1970 was in large part a response to protests by rank-and-file workers against the working conditions that annually kill at least 100,000 U.S. workers and disable 390,000 others (U.S. Department of Health, Education, and Welfare, 1972).[2] The act was thus perceived to be a major victory for labor. As this paper will show, however, the

©1983 by the Society for the Study of Social Problems. Reprinted from *Social Problems*, Vol. 30, No. 4, April 1983, pp. 437-448, by permission.

*An earlier version of this paper was presented at the annual meeting of the Law and Society Association, Toronto, 1982. The author thanks Patrick Donnelly and the editors of *Social Problems* for their helpful comments. Correspondence to: Department of Sociology/Anthropology, Middlebury College, Middlebury, Vermont 05753.

[1]Robert Crandall (1982:5), a senior fellow with the Brookings Institution who became a member of Reagan's regulatory reform team, generalizes such criticisms of OSHA to include the Environmental Protection Agency (EPA), the Food and Drug Administration (FDA), and the National Highway Traffic Safety Administration (NHTSA), declaring that in general the regulatory policies of these agencies consist of "purposefully inefficient statutes."

[2]These estimates are conservative since only those illnesses that have been ascertained to be directly related to work are included, thereby excluding (1) many health conditions whose onset occurs only after many years; and (2) the related illnesses of family members and those residing in communities surrounding the offending worksite.

establishment of OSHA represents less a final victory for labor than the beginning of a 10-year struggle on the safety and health front. Its dismantling can only be understood within this context.

This paper is divided into four parts. First I review the concept of symbolic action and the evidence that OSHA was an example of such action. Second I look at the deregulation fever that swept Washington, beginning during the Carter administration in 1979 and escalating during the first years of the Reagan administration. Third I document the gutting of seven OSHA standards under Reagan, as well as cuts in the agency's budget that thwart efforts to organize and educate workers. Finally I trace workers' gains under OSHA and link the cutbacks at OSHA to these gains, both material and ideological.

OSHA AS SYMBOLIC ACTION

Scholars from a variety of traditions have used the concept of "symbolic action." Burke stressed the symbolic component of political language as a device with which to disguise politically distasteful, but economically useful, action: "It is the normally prayerful use of language to sharpen up the pointless and blunt the too sharply pointed" (1954:393). According to Burke, politicians use symbolic action, in the form of political rhetoric, to appease the public, while engaging in action that is incompatible with that rhetoric.

Arnold (1937) noted the purely symbolic effect of much regulatory legislation:

The effect of this statement of the ideal [the federal anti-trust law of 1890] and its lack of enforcement was to convince reformers either that large combinations did not exist, or else that . . . they were about to be done away with (1937:208). . . . Historians now point out that Theodore Roosevelt never accomplished anything with his trustbusting. Of course he didn't. The crusade was not a 'practical' one. . . . Since the organizations were demanded, attempts to stop their growth became purely ceremonial. The anti-trust laws, being a preaching device, naturally performed only the functions of preaching (1937:211).

While Edelman (1964; 1977) fleshes out aspects of symbolic action only alluded to by Arnold and Burke, his definition of the concept varies from one context to another. He occasionally suggests that all significant political action is symbolic:

Practically every political act that is controversial . . . is bound to serve in part as a condensation symbol. It evokes a quiescent or an aroused mass response because it symbolizes a threat or reassurance (1964:7).

More frequently, however, Edelman calls "symbolic" all political action which has little or no impact on objective conditions, but which serves the purpose of placating certain groups:

If the regulatory process is examined in terms of a divergence between political and legal promises on one hand and resource allocations on the other, the largely symbolic character of the entire process becomes apparent (1964:22).

Several sociologists of law have integrated the concept of symbolic legal action into a dialectical-structural model of law; in so doing, they have avoided some of the theoretical ambiguities that flaw Edelman's work. Chambliss (1979), Stearns (1979), Whitt (1979), and others have suggested that fundamental and inherent contradictions in the political economy are frequently the moving force behind significant legal developments. Law, from this perspective, represents the state's attempt to resolve the conflicts deriving from these contradictions. One such contradiction in western capitalist democracies is that between capital accumulation on the one hand and political stability and state legitimation on the other. The state must provide for and protect the conditions for capital accumulation, yet it must simultaneously appear to be class-neutral. In other words, while it must often be class-biased in providing optimum conditions for profit maximization, the capitalist state must maintain a semblance of impartiality if it is to retain its legitimacy and minimize social protest. The conflicts which arise from this contradiction create a dilemma for the state: Must it promote the immediate interests of capital and, by thus demonstrating its class-bias, jeopardize the stability of the political system? Must it shore up the political status quo by interfering with the short-term interests of capital in the interest of long-term survival? Or does it have a third, less painful option?

Stearns (1979), in her examination of occupational safety and health laws in Sweden, concludes that a third option is often the best temporary solution to such dilemmas. Protests and political demands can often be placated with symbolic activity which does not significantly threaten even the short-term interests of the industries involved. In Sweden, a Social Democratic government was able to demonstrate its concern for the working class while allowing uninterrupted capital accumulation, by launching a highly visible—but effectively symbolic— occupational safety and health drive in 1970. Largely in response to wildcat strikes among miners in 1969, the government dramatically increased the size of the occupational safety and health bureaucracy, while simultaneously reducing the number of actual inspections made by its officials.

Donnelly (1982:18), focusing on the role of party politics in the creation of symbolic laws, argues that the OSHAct of 1970 was a symbolic gesture by the Nixon administration aimed at gaining the support of rank-and-file workers for the 1972 presidential election. Page and Munsing (1974:668) underscore the purely symbolic effect of this law and conclude that "the lofty goals of the 1970 Act . . . offer . . . little more than rhetoric to the American worker." Deutsch (1981a:3) argues that "the OSHAct came into being as a political act" and that the agency was deftly used by Nixon in an attempt to elicit political support from industry and labor simultaneously.

Declared by Nixon "perhaps one of the most important pieces of legislation to pass in this Congress" (Public Papers of the Presidents, 1970:1160), the bureaucracy to which the OSHAct gave birth was in many ways stillborn. In fact, the Nixon administration, intent on securing the endorsement of organized labor through the establishment of an occupational safety and health agency, was less intent on its

actual effectiveness. As a memo published by the Senate Watergate Committee reveals, a high-ranking Nixon official guaranteed the business community in 1972 that "no controversial standards [would] be proposed by the Occupational Safety and Health Agency during the coming four years of the Nixon administration" (quoted in Navarro, 1977:17).

Congressional under-funding of the National Institute of Occupational Safety and Health (NIOSH), whose task it was to supply OSHA with recommendations for standards, compounded OSHA's early impotence. In an interview with the *New York Times*, Dr. Marcus M. Key, NIOSH's director through mid-1974, was blunt: "Our present laboratory space isn't even adequate for any kind of research. It's substandard. . . . I don't think NIOSH is a viable organization at this time." Leaders from labor, government, industry, and academia agreed: "The realities of current administration funding have deprived it [NIOSH] of much-needed muscle" (quoted in Brody, 1974:20).

Between 1970 and 1974, NIOSH made only 18 recommendations for standards, of which OSHA adopted only one, which established a maximum legal level of exposure to asbestos in 1972. Meanwhile, a General Accounting Office report to the Senate Committee on Labor and Public Welfare in 1973 estimated that U.S. industries use or produce up to six hundred new toxic substances every year, and that by 1973 approximately 25,000 such toxic substances were being used or generated. Citing budget inadequacies and hiring freezes as partially responsible for NIOSH's "slow progress," the report drew attention to deficiencies in the implementation of the OSHAct (General Accounting Office, 1973). While pressure from organized labor has resulted in the development of several important new regulations, by 1980 OSHA was generating only about three standards per year.

Enforcement was another problem. At the rate that inspectors were visiting workplaces during OSHA's first year, Brody (1974:20) calculated that it would take them two hundred years to inspect every U.S. workplace. Furthermore, fines for violations of OSHA standards have rarely been severe enough to act as deterrents. The OSHAct set the maximum legal penalty for a serious violation at $1,000. The average fine for a serious violation in 1976 was $620.02; for all violations the average penalty was $37.44. As Boden and Wegman (1978:45) point out:

Given that manufacturing and construction sites have only a ten percent chance of being inspected, the average employer would expect to pay that amount over a ten-year period. Those whose violations would cost more than $3.74 per year to correct would be better off waiting until after they were inspected.

In the early 1970s, U.S. labor leaders began protesting OSHA's unwillingness to adopt expensive or controversial standards, its ineffective enforcement policies, and Congressional under-funding. Kenneth Peterson, the legislative representative of the American Federation of Labor–Congress of Industrial Organizations (AFL–CIO), told the 1973 Senate Committee on Appropriations: "After two years of operations under the Occupational Safety and Health Act, the entire program has never gotten off the ground" (U.S. Congress Senate 1973:6427). John J. Sheehan, representing the United Steelworkers of America, was somewhat more cynical: "We are greatly disturbed that the Administration is deliberately choking off the federal OSHA program. . . . It is our contention that . . . the Administration is *deliberately underfunding* and misguiding OSHA" (1973: 6433, italics in original). Anthony Mazzocchi, legislative director of the Oil, Chemical, and Atomic Workers International Union, said in an interview with the *New York Times*, "The act has done a great deal to improve workers' perception about the situation, but it hasn't yet done much to improve the situation" (quoted in Brody, 1974:20).

Recognition of OSHA's lack of impact even surfaced in business circles. The Research Institute of America, a New York–based business consulting firm, conducted a survey in 1973 on the consequences of the OSHAct for business. It told the Senate Committee on Appropriations for fiscal year 1974, "Despite all the drawbacks, weaknesses, and bureaucratic blunders, the history of the law in the past two years has shown

it to be *simply not that bad for business*. 'Comply or close' has not proven to be the small company's bête noire, as anticipated" (U.S. Congress: Senate 1973:6419, italics in original). An article in *Fortune Magazine* in 1979 concluded, "The huge outlays to meet OSHA's safety requirements have yet to result in any measurable improvement in safety"[3] (Alexander, 1979:127).

EARLY SIGNS OF DEREGULATION

In 1979, there were clear indications of the emerging deregulatory mood of policy-makers, as Congress adopted a more restrictive mentality vis à vis many of the regulatory agencies it had created, some of which, like the Federal Trade Commission (FTC), had been in place since early in this century. At least 150 regulatory reform bills were introduced in Congressional committees in one session alone in 1979. Although only a handful of these bills were ultimately passed into law, the sheer volume of such proposals was indicative of the emerging mentality.

Among the first agencies to be affected by deregulation were the FTC and the Environmental Protection Agency (EPA). In Senate Commerce Committee Hearings in 1979, Committee Chair Howard Cannon warned FTC director Michael Pertschuk: "I want to go on record today advising the members of the FTC as well as other regulatory agencies [that] this Commerce Committee has jurisdiction over, that we will be conducting the most vigorous oversight your agency has probably ever experienced" (quoted in Alexander, 1979:126). In May, 1980, the FTC became the first regulatory

---

[3]Alexander was referring here specifically to *safety* regulations designed to reduce the accident rate, rather than to health standards which focus on the minimization of work-related illnesses. OSHA has frequently been criticized for an overemphasis on relatively trivial details of the work environment which are only peripherally connected to safety, while overlooking more substantial health hazards (Mendeloff, 1979). This focus on the more easily modified features of the workplace has resulted in (1) the expenditure of funds by industry to comply with some of these regulations, while not significantly affecting either the production process or profit margins; and (2) little or no change in illness or accident rates.

agency to have its proposals subject to Congressional veto—an apparent legislative reaction to the enthusiastic regulatory activities of Pertschuk. In early 1981, Reagan replaced Pertschuk with James Miller III, an adamant deregulation enthusiast, thereby further neutralizing the FTC.

In 1981, Congress cut the EPA's budget by 20 percent in what House Speaker Thomas P. (Tip) O'Neill called a "radical demolition program" (quoted in Hornblower, 1982:16). O'Neill's fears were echoed by Russell E. Train, former EPA director under two previous Republican administrations:

The EPA is rapidly being destroyed as an effective institution. . . . Environmental statutes may remain in full force on the books, but the agency charged with their implementation will be a paper tiger (quoted in Hornblower, 1982:16).

Statistics on EPA enforcement activities underline the urgency of these warnings. In 1980, 43 suits were filed by the EPA against companies for violation of hazardous waste standards; in 1981, the number dropped to seven; in the first quarter of 1982, no suits had been filed (Hornblower, 1982:17).

One month after President Ronald Reagan came to power in January, 1981, he signed Executive Order 12291. This required all regulatory agencies to send any proposed new rules and standards costing $100 million or more to the Office of Management and Budget (OMB) for cost-benefit analysis. As a result, the OMB does not have outright veto power over these agencies, but as Crandall (1982:3) put it, "It is administration policy that rules not be proposed without OMB's blessing—and the agency administrators serve at the pleasure of the President." In its first year as watchdog, the OMB reviewed 2,715 existing regulations, required minor changes in 134, and returned 91 to the appropriate agencies for major overhauls (Crandall, 1982:3).

OSHA AS A TARGET OF DEREGULATION

The debilitation of OSHA was a top priority of the new Reagan administration. In January,

1981, Reagan's newly-appointed Secretary of Labor, Raymond Donovan, withdrew for "re-evaluation" seven safety and health standards promulgated in the last months of President Jimmy Carter's administration. He did this without consulting OSHA's outgoing director, Eula Bingham, or any other existing staff, and before Thorne Auchter had even been named as incoming OSHA director. These seven "midnight rules"—so-called because they were established very late in the Carter administration—tackled key areas of concern to U.S. workers. In each case, the "re-evaluation" of these standards was followed by recisions or substantial modifications.

1. *Labeling of hazardous chemicals:* On February 12, 1981, before Auchter had been installed as new OSHA director, Secretary of Labor Donovan unilaterally revoked a rule, passed one month earlier, which would have required all toxic chemicals used in the workplace to be labeled. The Reagan administration is considering a new labeling standard, emphasizing the employer's right to withhold trade secrets and to use discretion in deciding how and when to conduct the hazard evaluation research on which labeling would be based (Piller, 1982:9). Furthermore, Reagan's proposal explicitly states that any new federal labeling standard will pre-empt the more stringent state laws recently passed in California, New York, Connecticut, and a number of other states, thereby contradicting his "new federalism" rhetoric. Even the Reagan proposal may not be approved by the OMB. According to one OMB spokesperson, ". . . it's a major rule which would affect a large number of companies, both large and small. We do have our doubts about it" (quoted in Engel, 1982:59).

2. *Indiana's health and safety plan:* In April, 1980, OSHA under Carter's director Eula Bingham, began plans to decertify Indiana's state safety and health plan due to its lack of trained personnel, the systematic failure of its inspectors to identify hazards, and the persistent miscalculation of penalties (Engel, 1981a:42). In March, 1981, Reagan's OSHA team rescinded the decertification proposal, ensuring the sur-

vival of Indiana's plan and leaving Indiana's workers with little protection.

3. *Cancer policy:* OSHA had taken nearly three years to construct a new cancer policy under President Carter's administration. Finally passed in January, 1981, the new policy stipulated simply that once a potentially carcinogenic substance had been found to pose a "significant risk," regulation would ensue. It further required the publication of an "annual candidates list" of suspected carcinogens. Reagan's OSHA revoked the policy on March 27, 1981. The new administration has been considering a substitute for almost two years, but agency administrators have suggested that it will probably not be available until the end of 1983 (*Occupational Hazards*, 1982b:63).

4. *Walk-around pay:* This ruling, passed in January, 1981, entitled employees who accompanied OSHA staff on inspections of their worksites to their normal wages, without which workers would be financially penalized for exercising their legal rights to accompany OSHA inspectors. On May 29, 1981, Auchter rescinded the walk-around pay rule.

5. *Cotton dust standard:* The cotton dust standard, passed in mid-1980, would have prevented an estimated 21,000 cases of brown lung disease a year (Verespe, 1980:54), and was hailed by labor as a major breakthrough. The standard was immediately contested by industry and, at the time of Auchter's appointment to OSHA, was being considered by the U.S. Supreme Court. In March, 1981, Auchter requested that the Supreme Court drop the case and send the standard back to OSHA for re-evaluation. The Supreme Court refused and on June 17, 1981, upheld the cotton dust rule (*American Textile Manufacturers Institute, Inc., et al. v. Donovan*, 1981), opening the way for OSHA enforcement. Instead, one month after the court decision, OSHA withdrew the standard indefinitely for an "economic feasibility analysis" (Palisano, 1981: 68).

6. *Lead standard:* On November 14, 1978, OSHA had established a maximum legal exposure level for airborne concentrations of lead. Like the cotton dust rule, it was immediately contested in court. On August 15, 1980, the Washington, D.C. Court of Appeals upheld the standard (*The United Steelworkers of America v. Marshall*, 1980). Four months after the Reagan administration came to power, however, Auchter asked the U.S. Supreme Court to vacate the lower court's finding. The Supreme Court refused to hear the case; however, in December, 1981, OSHA amended the lead standard to allow 39 industries where workers are exposed to high levels of lead to institute only what controls they deemed "feasible." In addition, the compliance deadline has been extended to two-and-a-half years. In the meantime, the entire lead standard is being re-evaluated (*Occupational Hazards*, 1982a:39).

7. *Hearing conservation rule:* Passed on January 13, 1981, this rule required employers to provide hearing protectors for workers exposed to noise levels above a certain eight-hour, time-weighted average. Auchter delayed the effective date of the hearing conservation rule three times. While most of the provisions finally took effect on August 22, 1981, OSHA ordered a stay on certain aspects of the rule related to monitoring and testing (Palisano, 1981:73).

The attack on OSHA didn't stop with the death and/or postponement of these "midnight rules." Three weeks after Auchter took over in February, 1981, OSHA publicized its new cost-benefit approach, which made time-consuming "economic feasibility analyses" within the agency compulsory before proposing any new standard to the OMB.

A few weeks later, Auchter withdrew from distribution three OSHA films, three pamphlets, and two slide shows which he felt "established a biased point of view" (Auchter, 1981:100). He announced that he planned to burn 100,000 copies of one pamphlet, which documented the hazards of cotton dust, because it was not "neutral in tone, content, and approach" (quoted in Pinsky, 1981:8). Particularly offensive to Auchter was the cover photograph of a victim of brown lung disease.

Perhaps even more critical than this cancellation of standards, delays, and censorship, is OSHA's increased emphasis on "voluntary compliance." In October, 1981, OSHA unveiled its new "targeting" strategy, which exempts high-risk industries from the automatic inspection to which they had previously been liable. The new plan, called PRIME, for Positive Results Through Intensive Management Efforts, bases inspection on company records of rates of work-days lost due to injuries; in effect, 73 percent of U.S. manufacturing firms have rates low enough to avoid inspection under this new policy (Engel, 1981b). Besides depending on honest record-keeping, this criterion ignores both fatalities and illnesses which are likely to occur many years after workers are exposed to hazardous substances.

Other "voluntary safety programs" exempt still more workplaces from OSHA's orbit. One program, called STAR, for Sharing the Accountability for Regulation, allows employers to set up labor-management health and safety committees (with no legal or enforcement capabilities) in exchange for a guarantee of inspection waivers.[4] PRAISE, for Positive Results Achieved in Safe Employment, exempts certain low-hazard industries whether they have such committees or not (Engel, 1981b).

Finally, on February 1, 1982, OSHA announced it would no longer respond automatically to complaints from workers, as the OSHAct called for. Action would be taken only where a "violation threatens immediate physical harm or imminent danger," and OSHA officials would assess such danger by calling the employer (quoted in Crawford, 1982:5).

Organized labor has not been involved in any of these policy changes at OSHA. In fact, for the first time since OSHA's inception, there were *no* top-level discussions between AFL–CIO officials and either Secretary of Labor Donovan or OSHA Director Auchter from February to December, 1981 (Gerstenzang and Rothberg, 1981:A8).

The effects of deregulation on OSHA were apparent one year into the Reagan administration. The number of workplace inspections dropped 18 percent in 1981, compared with the 1980 rate; follow-up inspections (crucial, since without a determination of employer compliance, there is no enforcement) were down 73 percent. Serious citations declined 37 percent; willful citations (signifying non-compliance, detected by a follow-up visit) declined 80 percent. Fines were reduced by 65 percent. Prior to 1981, approximately 23 percent of all citations were contested by the employer; in 1981, only 8 percent were so contested. At the same time, the backlog of unanswered complaints from workers rose by 121 percent (Crawford, 1982:5).

Severe budget reductions have struck the final blow to OSHA. Congress cut the agency's 1982 budget by 25 percent, to $191 million, forcing a 30 percent reduction in the number of OSHA inspectors, from 1,700 in 1981 to 1,200 in 1982 (Bernstein, 1982:19). NIOSH's budget was cut almost 40 percent, from $81.5 million in 1981 to $50 million in 1982. NIOSH training and education centers were closed entirely in 1982 for lack of funds. Congress cut in half the budget for New Directions, an OSHA grant program which provides colleges, universities, unions, and trade associations with courses on occupational safety and health (Palisano, 1982). Even Secretary of Labor Donovan—a staunch supporter of Reagan's budget cutbacks—admitted of the 1982 occupational safety and health budget: "We're no longer cutting into fat; we're cutting into muscle" (quoted in Palisano, 1982:58).

WORKER GAINS UNDER OSHA

While symbolic political action may have little initial impact, it does provide a vehicle for incremental change over time, as demonstrated by workers' gains under OSHA. Ten years after the formation of this agency, labor had secured a number of isolated victories in the area of occupational safety and health. Among the most

---

[4]In early 1980, Senator Richard Schweiker (Republican, Pennsylvania) and Senator Harrison Williams (Democrat, New Jersey) introduced a controversial bill, ironically entitled the OSHA Improvement Act (S.2153), which was based on this same principle of the substitution of internal safety and health committees for OSHA inspections. Protest from organized labor ultimately defeated the Schweiker–Williams Bill, only to have it replaced in 1981 by this OSHA-inspired "voluntary compliance" strategy.

dramatic of these gains were: (1) a limit on exposure to asbestos, passed in 1972, which prevents between 630 and 2,500 deaths a year (Verespe, 1980:54); (2) a limit on worker exposure to vinyl chloride, passed in 1974, which prevents an estimated 2,000 deaths a year and which had been condemned by the plastics industry as totally unfeasible and ''an economic disaster'' (Mendeloff, 1979:54);[5] (3) the 1978 lead standard (recalled for re-evaluation); (4) the February, 1980, U.S. Supreme Court decision upholding the right of workers to refuse to perform tasks they believe pose an ''imminent danger of death or serious injury'' (*Whirlpool Corporation v. Marshall,* 1980); (5) the 1980 cotton dust standard (recalled); (6) the 1981 walk-around pay rule (revoked); and (7) the 1981 chemical labeling standard (revoked).

Not the least of labor's victories have been in the area of education and information. As Lloyd McBride, President of the United Steelworkers of America in 1980, put it: ''OSHA has uncorked a bottle of knowledge on workplace hazards and unleashed an educational process which has awakened workers to the dangers they confront on the job'' (quoted in Verespe, 1980:54).

In 1972, the first local Committee on Occupational Safety and Health (COSH) was formed in Chicago (CACOSH) as a coalition of workers, trade unions, and health and legal specialists concerned with safety and health on the job. Since its formation, two dozen other such COSH groups have been organized; the most active are in Philadelphia, Boston, New Jersey, San Jose, Los Angeles, and New York (Berman, 1981:104). These groups have been influential in training rank-and-file workers in safety and health issues; providing the services of volunteer doctors, hygienists, lawyers, and other specialists to workers on the shop floor; and increasing public awareness by focusing media attention on occupational safety and health issues.

In addition to these educational functions, COSH groups have successfully spearheaded a number of lobbying campaigns, including that

which ultimately defeated the Schweiker–Williams ''OSHA Improvement Act'' of 1980. The Chicago group led a successful drive to obtain workers' compensation in Illinois for partial hearing loss. The Philadelphia group organized the 1980 campaign to pressure OSHA to establish the chemical labeling standard (Berman, 1981:107).

Other such grass-roots, union-oriented coalitions include the Brown Lung Associations, located in North and South Carolina; the Asbestos Victims of America; the White Lung Association; the Women's Occupational Health Resource Center; and the Coalition for Reproductive Rights of Workers (CRROW). This latter group was formed in 1980 to fight the policies of American Cyanamid, General Motors, DuPont, and B. F. Goodrich, which had ''resolved'' their hazardous substances problems by excluding fertile women from certain jobs. Fearful of lawsuits related to birth defects, these companies in some cases coerced their female employees to submit to sterilization in order to keep their jobs. Responding to the complaints of CRROW and other such coalitions, OSHA in 1980 fined American Cyanamid $10,000 for its sterilization policies (Howard, 1980:2).

Since its formation in 1978, New Directions has provided a substantial share of the funding for these and other organizations. Moreover, it has provided unions with professionally trained experts by offering training and educational programs. Before 1978, U.S. unions employed a total of 15 staff persons devoted to safety and health, and only half of them had any professional training. By 1981, there were 100 professionally trained union staff engaged full time in safety and health issues (Deutsch, 1981a:4).

According to Deutsch (1981a:4), the OSHA grant program has had ''a very substantial impact, like dropping a small pebble in a pond and watching the outward ripple effect.'' This has been evident in an increased awareness of and organizational activity for the labor movement in general. In organizing effectively around safety and health, workers have increasingly found that democracy in the workplace is the fundamental issue. Deutsch (1981b:124) quotes

---

[5]For a case study of the evolution of this standard, see Northrup et al. (1978:291–418).

Robert Sass, director of Occupational Safety and Health for the province of Saskatchewan, Canada, who argues that workers must have three rights in order to ensure that employers comply with safety and health regulations: "the right to know about dangers in the work environment," "the right to participate in the day-to-day detection, evaluation, and reduction of workplace hazards," and "the right to refuse to work in conditions known or believed to be unusually dangerous without fear of repercussion." Moreover, the mental health of workers is inextricably tied both to the degree of self-determination in the workplace and to the decision-making processes that determine *unemployment* casualties. The path of occupational safety and health activism, then, ultimately leads directly and powerfully to the more fundamental and explosive social issue of industrial democracy.

MATERIAL AND IDEOLOGICAL ASPECTS OF SYMBOLIC ACTION

If OSHA was created largely as a symbolic act, why has it been the target of such vitriolic deregulation? The answer, I believe, is that the Reagan administration is trying to offset—and in some cases even roll back—the incremental material and ideological changes that have occurred since OSHA was established. On one hand, specific regulations, such as the cotton dust and lead standards, have been attacked; on the other, the agency's education and information function has been undermined, which will critically alter the balance of knowledge between labor and management. Remember that several of the revoked "midnight rules," such as the walk-around pay rule and the chemical labeling standard, concerned the workers' "right-to-know," as did the pamphlets and films censored by Auchter. And the most severe budget cuts fell at NIOSH and the grant programs, from which COSH groups and other grass-roots coalitions had benefitted.

In other words, while the OSHAct may have begun as a token gesture to workers and had little immediate impact, it ultimately provided both

a vehicle within which organized labor could hammer out sporadic concessions *and* a rallying point around which the awareness and knowledge of workers was heightened. The recent rollbacks must be seen within this context, as an effort to undo these gains. As Steve Wodka, international representative and OSHA liaison for the Oil, Chemical and Atomic Workers (OCAW), argues:

If OSHA had gone on the last three years like its first six, the agency would be so meaningless no one would have given a hoot. OSHA finally began to be effective and cost industry some money, so business is trying to clip its wings (quoted in Verespe, 1980:51).

More perplexing is the fact that even OSHA's symbolic component—its concessionary ideology—is being steadily eroded. The agency, which in 1970 was created to convince workers that the White House heard and responded to their grievances, today seems intent on erasing that message. Not only are incremental advances being revoked, they are being revoked with all the fanfare normally reserved for the *creation* of symbolic law. Consider, for example, the announcement that pamphlets describing brown lung disease were to be burned en masse; or the closed-door meetings at which standards were frozen and then rescinded.

To understand these events, it might be helpful to consider the advantage and disadvantage of symbolic action from the state's point of view. The advantage is that symbolic action tells workers that the state is responsive to their demands; the disadvantages is that it gives workers a sense of power, a sense that they can successfully precipitate change. In other words, while symbolic action may not substantially affect material conditions, at least not initially, it may significantly modify *ideological* conditions, by telling workers: "Your collective action has pressured us into a response." As an industrial hygienist with the United Steelworkers of America put it: "The most important lesson is that you can win" (quoted in Howard, 1980:2).

Not surprisingly, then, the retrenchments at OSHA have both a material and an ideological dimension, and are designed above all to put labor on the defensive after a decade of progress. The factors which make such retrenchments possible are both economic and political. With the United States experiencing a deep recession and the highest unemployment rates since the 1930s, organized labor is suffering from profound economic vulnerability. As Berman (1978:36) warned with almost uncanny foresight in 1978:

> . . . it is doubtful that the advances of the past decade can be preserved, let alone extended, in the context of a capitalist system where real wages have been stationary or declining, the proportion of unemployed and marginalized workers continually creeps upward, multinational firms increase their power over U.S. and foreign production. . . . There is no reason to believe that working conditions can improve if the overall standard of living of the working class is being pushed back.

The fragmentation of political issues and disintegration of traditional political blocks has compounded labor's vulnerability. With the proliferation of single-issue interest groups, such as those concerned with nuclear disarmament, budget deficits, and tax reform, it may no longer be strategically necessary for political aspirants to woo organized labor as an electoral bloc.

The Reagan administration has taken advantage of this vulnerability by retracting the concessionary image of previous years. As labor's advances on the occupational safety and health front are rolled back with a showy disregard for labor input, the ideological message is clear. Just as the creation of OSHA was a symbolic concession to workers and served to confirm the responsiveness of the state to labor needs, the blatant debilitation of OSHA, at a time of labor vulnerability, serves symbolically to reverse that message, and to place labor firmly on the defensive.

CONCLUSION

I have attempted to explain the irony that OSHA—originally a symbolic gesture—is now a major target of the deregulators in the White House, in Congress, and in the agency itself. I argue that although OSHA began as a token

gesture to labor, it ultimately provided a vehicle for real material and ideological gains on the safety and health front, and that it is in order to curb these advances that the agency has been cut back. This understanding of the evolution of symbolic law, from essentially meaningless political action to a tool with which labor can carve out incremental advances, helps explain the motivation behind the deregulation fervor; however, it is the current recession and the erosion of the economic and political power of labor that permits these deregulators to carry out their mission.

If this analysis is correct, two conclusions follow.

1. The dramatic recisions and cutbacks within OSHA and other federal regulatory agencies can not be fully explained in terms of President Reagan's, or any other individual's, politics. While Reagan's attitudes and politics undoubtedly have facilitated and accelerated the rollbacks, his influence is neither a necessary nor a sufficient condition for deregulation. This conclusion is further substantiated by the fact that it was in the pro-business administration of Nixon that OSHA was *established*, and that Congressional warnings of its forthcoming deregulation predated Reagan.

2. In the absence of economic recovery and an accompanying resuscitation of the power of U.S. labor, the deregulation of OSHA, the FTC, the EPA, and other federal agencies, will continue and may even be accelerated. As long as workers in the United States must struggle to retain their jobs, and unions are coerced into endorsing contracts containing "give-back" concessions to industry, a continuing erosion can be expected, both in the material advances made by labor under the auspices of OSHA and in the symbolic message that the OSHAct originally carried.

REFERENCES

Alexander, Tom
1979 "It's round-up time for the runaway regulations." Fortune Magazine 180(11): 126–132.

Arnold, Thurman W.
1937   The Folklore of Capitalism. New Haven: Yale University Press.

Auchter, Thorne
1981   "Interview." Occupational Hazards 43(10): 100.

Berman, Daniel M.
1978   Death on the Job. New York: Monthly Review Press.
1981   "Grassroots coalitions in health and safety: The COSH groups." Labor Studies Journal 6(1): 104–113.

Boden, Les, and David Wegman
1978   "Increasing OSHA's clout: Sixty million new inspectors." Working Papers (May/June): 43–49.

Brody, Jane
1974   "Many workers still face health peril despite law." New York Times, March 4: 20.

Burke, Kenneth
1954   A Grammer of Motives. New York: Prentice-Hall.

Chambliss, William J.
1979   "Contradictions and conflicts in law creation." Pp. 3–27 in Steven Spitzer (ed.), Annual Review of the Sociology of Law. Greenwich, Connecticut: Jai. In press.

Crandall, Robert W.
1982   "Twilight of deregulation." The Brookings Bulletin 18(3–4): 1–5.

Crawford, James
1982   "Briefing: An OSHA without teeth." In These Times, April 7–13: 5.

Deutsch, Steven
1981a   "Introduction: Theme issue on occupational safety and health." Labor Studies Journal 6(1): 3–6.
1981b   "Extending workplace democracy: Struggles to come in job safety and health." Labor Studies Journal 6(1): 124–132.

Donnelly, Patrick
1982   "The origins of the Occupational Safety and Health Act of 1970.." Social Problems 30(1): 13–25.

Edelman, Murray
1964   The Symbolic Uses of Politics. Chicago: University of Illinois Press.
1977   Political Language: Words That Succeed and Policies That Fail. New York: Academic Press.

Engel, Paul
1981a   "Midnight rules: Now you see 'em . . . now you don't." Occupational Hazards 43(7): 42–44.
1981b   "1982: Targeting tops OSHA priority list." Occupational Hazards 43(12): 59–62.
1982   "Close-up on OSHA's proposed new chemical labeling standard." Occupational Hazards 44(4): 55–59.

General Accounting Office
1973   Report to the Senate Committee on Labor and Public Welfare: Slow Progress Likely in Development of Standards for Toxic Substances and Harmful Physical Substances Found in Workplaces, 7. Washington, D.C.: U.S. Government Printing Office.

Gerstenzang, James, and Donald Rothberg
1981   "Reagan unfetters U.S. business." San Diego Union, December 28: sec.A, p. 8.

Hornblower, Margaret
1982   "The EPA: A case of depression?" National Wildlife 20(5): 16–19.

Howard, Robert
1980   "Reproductive rights in the workplace." In These Times, September 3–9: 2.

Mendeloff, John
1979   Regulating Safety: An Economic and Political Analysis of the Occupational Safety and Health Policy. Cambridge: MIT Press.

Navarro, Vincente
1977   "Occupational safety and health vs. the right of capital accumulation." In These Times, December 6–12: 17.

Northrup, Herbert R., Richard L. Rowan, and Charles R. Perry
1978   The Impact of OSHA. Labor Relations and Public Policy Series #17, Industrial Research Unit, The Wharton School, Philadelphia: University of Pennsylvania.

Occupational Hazards
1982a   "OSHA communique" 44(2): 39–40.
1982b   "Showdown looms over OSHA's cancer policy, 44(4): 60–63.

Page, Joseph A., and Peter N. Munsing
1974   "Occupational health and the federal government: The wages are still bitter." Law and Contemporary Problems 38(4): 651–668.

Palisano, Peg
1981 ''Reagan's OSHA team—They hit the ground running.'' Occupational Hazards 43(10): 67–74.
1982 ''Reaganomics: Belt-tightening begins at federal safety and health agency.'' Occupational Hazards 44(3): 56–61.

Piller, Charles
1982 ''Business applauds proposal.'' In These Times, August 11–24: 9.

Pinsky, Mark I.
1981 ''Textile firms want to spread the blame.'' In These Times, May 6–12: 8.

Public Papers of the Presidents
1966 Milwood, New York: Kraus–Thompson
–71 Organization Press.

Sheskin, Arlene
1982 ''Leviathan undone? Deregulation and regulation in the corporate state.'' Paper presented at the annual meeting of the Law and Society Association, June 2, Toronto.

Stearns, Lisa
1979 ''Fact and fiction of a model enforcement bureaucracy: The labor inspectorate of Sweden.'' British Journal of Law and Society 6: 1–23.

U.S. Congress: Senate
1973 ''Cuts in OSHA programs.'' Senate Hearing Before the Committee on Appropriations. Department of Health, Education, and Welfare. House Report 8877, 93rd Congress, 1st Session, Part 7: 6409–6490.

U.S. Department of Health, Education, and Welfare
1972 President's Report on Occupational Safety and Health. Washington, D.C.: U.S. Government Printing Office.

Verespe, Michael A.
1980 ''Has OSHA improved?'' Industry Week, August 4: 48–56.

Whitt, Allen
1979 ''Toward a class-dialectical model of power.'' American Sociological Review 44(1): 81–99.

Cases Cited

American Textile Manufacturers Institute, Inc., et al. v. Donovan, 49 U.S.L.W. 4720, 1981.

The United Steelworkers of America v. Marshall, 49 U.S.L.W. 2155, 1980.

Whirlpool Corporation v. Marshall, 48 U.S.L.W. 4189, 1980.

Codes Cited

Occupational Safety and Health Act, 29 U.S.C., Sections 651–78, 1970.

SOCIAL SCIENCE ETHICS IN STUDYING INSTITUTIONALIZED CRIME

The first article in this section argues that, because leaders of business and government are in positions of public trust, they have no rights of privacy as enjoyed by others. The second article states that when social scientists study the powerful, it is typically the case that respondents can take care of themselves. Both selections argue for a more aggressive role for social science research to uncover the abuses of the powerful.

THE PROTECTION OF HUMAN SUBJECTS
A Reexamination of the Professional Code of Ethics*

John F. Galliher
University of Missouri at Columbia

LIMITATIONS IMPOSED BY THE CODE

The ASA Code of Ethics (*American Sociologist*, 1968:318), as adopted several years ago, contains three rules dealing directly or indirectly with the subjects' right of privacy. Rule number 3 of the Code reads: "Every person is entitled to the right of privacy and dignity of treatment. The sociologist must respect these rights." Rule number 4 also has a bearing on the question of the subjects' right of privacy: "All research should avoid causing personal harm to subjects used in research." Rule number 5 begins as follows: "Confidential information provided by a research subject must be treated as such by the sociologist."

Rule 3 implies that one must never conduct research without voluntary subject cooperation, while rule 5 indicates that the sociologist's use of data must not exceed the limits set by the subject. Rule 4, a more general mandate, proscribes causing personal harm and discomfort to research subjects, presumably including dis-

closure of any information about them against their wishes. These rules are not a dramatic departure for our discipline and probably reflect the longstanding values of most sociologists, and it has only recently become clear the extent to which such rules impose limitations on our profession.

These limitations have become increasingly evident, not because of developments within sociology, but due to events outside the discipline. Recently, several dramatic disclosures involving the operation of government and big business have been made by Jack Anderson, well-known investigative reporter and syndicated columnist, who relied on key informants in government and business to smuggle out highly-revealing information. No less noteworthy was Daniel Ellsberg's decision to reveal the classified documents depicting the United States' entry into the war in Viet Nam. Many feel the efforts of Anderson and Ellsberg have made significant contributions to our understanding of the operation of government and big business, even though their techniques involve some duplicity. Certainly those people and groups who were the objects of these disclosures were not aware of Anderson's and Ellsberg's activities nor would they have allowed the information to be disclosed had they been consulted.

There has been some precedent for similar duplicity in social science research since Bettelheim's (1943) well-known study of Jews in

John F. Galliher (1973) "The Protection of Human Subjects: A Reexamination of the Professional Code of Ethics." *The American Sociologist* Vol. 8 (August): 93–100.

*I am grateful to my colleagues in the Department of Sociology who have helped me with this paper, and I am especially indebted to James L. McCartney who initially suggested that I put these ideas in writing and who made many helpful comments on earlier drafts of the paper.

German concentration camps. In reading Bettelheim's study, one gets the impression that he obtained neither the permission of his fellow prisoners nor of the prison staff, and that the latter was most certainly not aware of his research. Obviously, such secrecy was required. More recently, in a study of police behavior, Black and Reiss (1970:65) admit to "systematic deception" of officers whose behavior they observed. They indicated to the officers that they were only interested in *citizen reaction toward the police* when, in fact, they were studying *police treatment of citizens*. Black and Reiss apparently felt that this subterfuge was required since it is well-documented that there is a widespread concern among police to maintain secrecy from outsiders (Westley, 1956; Stoddard, 1968; Savitz, 1970; Reiss, 1968).

Recently, Rainwater and Pittman (1967:365–366) issued a challenge to sociologists to increase the accountability of elites in business and government. They concluded that:

Sociologists have the right (and perhaps also the obligation) to study publicly accountable behavior. By publicly accountable behavior we do not simply mean the behavior of public officials (though there the case is clearest) but also the behavior of any individual as he goes about performing public or secondary roles for which he is socially accountable—this would include businessmen, college teachers, physicians, etc.; in short, all people as they carry out jobs for which they are in some sense publicly accountable. One of the functions of our discipline, along with those of political science, history, economics, journalism, and intellectual pursuits generally, is to further public accountability in a society whose complexity makes it easier for people to avoid their responsibilities.

Presumably, Rainwater and Pittman would applaud the efforts of Anderson and Ellsberg, as well as those of Bettelheim and Black and Reiss, even though all engaged in forms of subterfuge required for their investigations and would applaud other similar research on conduct in accountable roles. Unfortunately, the ASA Code of Ethics, while somewhat vague, doesn't seem to specify any circumstances under which subterfuge or duplicity in dealing with persons in the course of our investigations might be permitted.

COMMENTARY ON THE CODE

Lofland (1961:366) has defended disguised participant observation as a legitimate research technique. He dismissed the idea of professional rules which would prohibit such techniques.

A professional rule to this effect would not only make for great past, present and future loss of the discipline, but would be an active violation of many people's moral standards who think that there are some groups, such as professional crime and fascist groups, that should be studied whether they are asked and give permission or not. In other words, in accepting this rule, we could not study "bad" groups, which, as it happens, are also especially likely to be "groups that do not want to be studied."

Roth (1962:283) also expressed opposition to a body of rules prohibiting secret research because: "All research is secret in some ways and to some degree—we never tell the subjects 'everything'." Moreover, he (284) argued that:

If the possibility of disrespect for an organization or group is at issue, we are faced with the question of just when a collection of people becomes a self-identifiable group that may have considered itself being researched on. Would this mean that groups which are consciously organized deserve more consideration than those which are not?

During the initial consideration of the Code of Ethics, Becker (1964) expressed doubt about the usefulness of such a body of regulations. He astutely observed that on many issues such a code must be vague and equivocal because there is no consensus within the discipline on many critical problems unique to social science. It is especially interesting that the one example that Becker cited of such issues was the use of undercover research roles.

A different opinion of subterranean research is found in Erikson's (1967:373) conclusions:

It is unethical for a sociologist to *deliberately misrepresent* his identity for the purpose of entering a private domain *to which he is not otherwise eligible*; and second, that it is unethical for a sociologist to *deliberately misrepresent* the character of the research in which he is engaged.

The only conceivable argument in favor of such experimentation is that the knowledge derived from it is worth the discomfort it may cause. And the difficulties here are that we do not know how to measure the value of the work we do or the methods we employ in this way. . . . Sociologists cannot protect their freedom of inquiry if they owe the rest of the community (not to mention themselves) an accounting for the distress they may have inadvertently imposed on people who have not volunteered to take that risk (368).

Research of this sort is liable to damage the reputation of sociology in the larger society and close off promising areas of research for future investigators. . . . Any research tactic which attracts unfavorable notice may help diminish the general climate of trust toward sociology in the community as a whole (368–369).

The NIH's social science grant review committee sponsored a conference on ethical issues involving the protection of subjects and, in contrast to Erikson's belief that the value of certain research can never be assessed, the participants generally agreed that the risks and potential harm of research must be balanced against the possible contributions to science and human welfare (Sykes, 1967:10). Even so, problems created by deceptive experiments were a central theme of the discussions and ethical problems of participant observation and of gaining access to groups by the use of false credentials were also criticized (9). A number of participants felt that the involvement of the federal government in funding social science research introduced new responsibilities and constraint, in part because the use of public funds for research implied new responsibilities to the public (10).

All participants, however, were not eager to generate new controls on social science research. Festinger (Sykes, 1967:9) reminded his colleagues that besides protecting subjects, they might want to remember "the hard-won freedom of scientific inquiry and the social benefits of research in the social sciences." Also, at least one participant suggested that some important scientific discoveries have required flouting the norms of the time and place (10); the issue of illegal dissection of human corpses was used as an illustration.

Later, the report of the ASA Committee on Professional Ethics, which included the Code (*American Sociologist*, 1968:316), was published. It recognized some areas of "unfinished business" which were "impossible to resolve," including the following questions:

To what extent can public figures claim the same rights of privacy as ordinary citizens? To what extent does the injunction about the confidentiality of research sites prevent legitimate criticism of organizations that have cooperated in the research? . . . Clearly, much more thought and analysis must be devoted to such questions, and others as well.

However, since the Committee's report, such thought and analysis apparently have not developed; and, having heard of no opposition from other sociologists to the attempt to protect human subjects, through the Code, one may wonder if their silence indicates that they see these rules as reasonable, necessary, and perhaps moral and humane as well.[1]

THE EMPIRICAL CONSEQUENCES OF PROFESSIONAL MORALITY

Perhaps the image that many sociologists conjure up when considering such categorical imperatives governing research is that of the ignorant and vulnerable ADC mother, the prison inmate, or the undergraduate student, all defenseless against the scheming sociologist armed with his one-way mirrors and trick questions. Kelman (1967) and Bonacich (1967) comment on the need to protect student subjects, while Rainwater and Pittman (1970) and Erikson (1967:371) discuss the problems of protecting the poor and relatively powerless segments of society. This image is unquestionably well-founded, for only these types of people do, in fact, need protecting from sociologists and other social scientists as well. However, in studies dealing with the activities of the more powerful and affluent, the same quality and measure of protec-

---

[1]Roth (1969) and Friedrichs (1970) have, however, raised more general questions about the utility of the Code of Ethics.

tion is not required since, unlike ADC mothers and undergraduates, these people are often members of groups or organizations that have elaborate screening devices to insure that those sociologists who have contact with them operate in the research setting only as agreed to by prior arrangement. If one does not honor these arrangements, it is recognized that the host organization, group, or individual will cease to cooperate. These groups also seek to filter out researchers and projects that are potentially embarrassing. (For examples of such self-protective reactions, see Record, 1967; Goldner, 1967; and Daniels, 1967). Moreover, Roth (1962:284) raises the possibility that, because these formal organizations are more easily identifiable than other groups, their interests may be more easily protected by the Code.

Lowry (1972:437) observes that America is increasingly a closed society in which secrecy is a dominant concern of all types of organizations. Even so, he suggests that the myth of an open society where information is freely exchanged still prevails and that the hiatus between the myth and reality is not recognized by many social scientists. Indeed, belief in an open society is reflected in the Code of Ethics which implies that much significant data are available for the asking.

The organizational affiliations of elites are often the avenues for the wielding of power. The Code, and the professional morality it reflects, ostensibly protect *individuals* but, in fact, serve to protect powerful *groups* as well. The individualistic orientation of the Code ignores the organization as a unit of analysis and, as a consequence, makes no special provision for the study of social groups. Since it is impossible to betray the group without also betraying individuals, sociologists have failed to hold actors accountable in their organizational and occupational roles. Missing from the Code is some discussion of whether only people in their roles as private citizens are to be protected, or if this protection also extends to actors filling roles in government and business. Using this distinction, it appears that some social scientists have ignored the occupational and organizational roles of the more affluent in government and business and transgressed the private roles of the poor.

Since the relatively new formal Code of Ethics, as well as longstanding professional morality of most sociologists, seem to require the cooperation of our subjects, the only secret information obtainable is from individuals and groups who are too ignorant and/or powerless to demand the necessary limitations upon the researchers. Much more is known about the indiscretions and alleged pathologies of the ignorant, poor, and powerless than any other groups higher in the stratification system. Apparently the poor and powerless are least able to keep their private lives private from the social scientist. As a consequence of our professional ethics, therefore, the image we portray of American society is highly distorted. What the social scientist then describes is a great deal about the personal lives of the poor and powerless and little about the secrets of the more affluent. Even if only the aggregate characteristics of the poor are described, such information may still have adverse effects on the group. For example, a description of the work and sex habits or modes of family organization of poor Blacks may influence government social welfare policy, adversely affecting the subject group. The detailed view of the poor, together with the veneered image of the more affluent, can be used to legitimize a highly economically stratified and racist society. The imagery suggests that the poor are poor because they are the most pathological.

Our relatively detailed knowledge of the poor and powerless seems to indicate that the notion of consent may be inadequately developed to offer them adequate protection. It is likely that they do not as readily understand the aims of social science research as others and may not be as sensitive to the possible political consequences of their participation in such research. Moreover, in our increasingly organization-centered society, heads of organization can frequently control the participation of subordinates in research on their organizations. In such settings, consent is usually not secured from each actor but rather is assumed if secured from the organization's leader(s). This not only strips subordinates of the modicum of privacy provided by anonymity but also protects organizational elites.

In sum, the postulates reflected in our professional Code of Ethics that (1) all subjects require protection and (2) that our professional guidelines, in fact, offer adequate protection where needed, are open to serious question.

While all people may be worthy of the same respect as human beings, it does not necessarily follow that their activities merit the same degree of protection and respect. As indicated earlier, Lofland (1961:366) questioned possible prohibitions on the undercover study of fascist groups. It is questionable whether the files of the American Nazi Party are deserving of the same respect as any other data source; must one secure the active cooperation of the Ku Klux Klan, or for that matter of the Pentagon, before conducting research in their organizations or with their personnel? While doing research in South Africa, van den Berghe (1967:185) concluded: ''From the outset, I decided that I should have no scruples in deceiving the government. . . .'' The question is, how much honor is proper for the sociologist in studying the membership and organization of what he considers an essentially dishonorable, morally outrageous, and destructive enterprise? Is not the failure of sociology to uncover corrupt, illegitimate, covert practices of government or industry because of the supposed prohibitions of professional ethics tantamount to supporting such practices?

PROFESSIONAL MORALITY AND METHODOLOGY

The sociologist's professional ethics, which require the active cooperation of the subject, are reflected in the types of research problems developed in which power differentials are not, in effect, made problematic. These research problems have, in turn, influenced the types of methodologies employed. Young (1971:279) contends that:

The dynamics of the greater part of contemporary methodology, based as that methodology is on tact, consensus, cooperation, persuasion, and establishment sponsorship, are compatible with a managed society—managed on behalf of the large-scale organizations of business, government, military, industry, finance, and education.

These dominant sociological methods include widespread use of interviews and questionnaires and increasing reliance on statistical analysis (Brown and Gilmartin, 1969). Accordingly, in an unusually candid and enlightening statement, Fichter and Kolb (1953:547) suggest that statistical analysis is preferable for sociological research because it protects subjects, especially leading members of the group, by reporting only aggregate characteristics. In any event, during the past thirty years, there has been a great elaboration of statistical techniques which are the creation of a social science which both emphasizes the cooperation of subjects and the use of interview and questionnaire data. Since sociologists assume the cooperation of subjects, they have concentrated upon data that are easily observable, and have ultimately collected data that are easily enumerated. The use of data which can be readily counted encourages the search for large numbers and a burgeoning of statistical techniques.

On the other hand, techniques which don't require subject cooperation have not been developed and elaborated at least in part because they have not been considered professional. Many sociologists would probably argue that such techniques are not only unethical but can also involve the social scientist in ''politics'' and, therefore, are the province of the political activist and the newspaperman but not the professional social scientist. Ironically, it is the sociologists themselves who have helped politicize their craft by treating methodological and empirical problems of data collection as political or ethical questions.

CONCLUDING DISCUSSION

The irony of the attempt to protect human subjects through a Code of Ethics is that this very Code encourages an approach to data that can be used to legitimize a highly stratified society. Far from protecting those who are vulnerable, the Code serves to aid those least in need of our concern. Becker and Horowitz (1972:48) observe that sociological research has generally serviced elites at the expense of the less powerful:

Prison research has for the most part been oriented to problems of jailers rather than those of prisoners; industrial research, to the problems of managers rather than those of workers; military research, to the problem of generals rather than those of privates. . . . Wherever someone is oppressed, an "establishment" sociologist seems to lurk in the background, providing the facts which make oppression more efficient and the theory which makes it legitimate to a larger constituency.

Becker and Horowitz (1972:55) then conclude:

A sociology that is true to the world inevitably clarifies what has been confused, reveals the character of organizational secrets, upsets the interests of powerful people and groups.

ALTERNATIVE RULES

What is required to give a more balanced and accurate description of the workings of society are supplementary data from methodology not based on cooperation of subjects. To help facilitate such research, the following changes in rules 3, 4, and 5 of the Code are offered for consideration:

Rule 3.

From: Every person is entitled to the right of privacy and dignity of treatment. The sociologist must respect these rights.

To: Every person is entitled to equal privacy and dignity of treatment as a private citizen. However, equal protection may require unequal treatment of different types of subjects. More elaborate warnings and explanations may be required in dealing with economic and racial minorities and others who are poorly educated and likely to be ignorant of the research process than with other citizens. The sociologist must make the judgment regarding the amount of explanation required for adequate subject protection. When actors become involved in government and business or other organizations where they are accountable to the public, no right of privacy applies to conduct in such roles.

Rule 4.

From: All research should avoid causing personal harm to subjects used in research.

To: All research should avoid causing personal harm to subjects used in research unless it is evident that the gain by society and/or science is such that it offsets the probable magnitude of the individual discomfort. The revelation of wrongdoing in positions of public trust shall not be deemed to cause "personal harm" within the meaning of this rule.

Rule 5.

From: Confidential information provided by a research subject must be treated as such by the sociologist.[2]

To: Confidential information provided by a research subject must be treated as such by the sociologist unless it is evident that the gain by society and/or science is such that it offsets the probable magnitude of the individual discomfort. The revelation of wrongdoing in positions of public trust shall not be deemed to be "confidential information" within the meaning of this rule.[3]

The latter two proposals reflect the balance of interests perspective regarding research risks

---

[2]The remaining sections of rule 5 can be deleted. They are:

Even though research information is not a privileged communication under the law, the sociologist must, as far as possible, protect subjects and informants. Any promises made to such persons must be honored. However, provided that he respects the assurances he has given his subjects, the sociologist has no obligation to withhold information of misconduct of individuals or organizations.

If an informant or other subject should wish, however, he can formally release the researcher of a promise of confidentiality. The provisions of this section apply to all members of research organizations (i.e., interviewers, coders, clerical staff, etc.), and it is the responsibility of the chief investigators to see that they are instructed in the necessity and importance of maintaining the confidentiality of the data. The obligation of the sociologist includes the use and storage of original data to which a subject's name is attached. When requested, the identity of an organization or subject must be adequately disguised in publication.

[3]Other sections of the code, such as the rules concerning disclosure of the sources of financial support and acknowledgment of research collaboration and assistance, are not problematic. Moreover, the existence of a Code of Ethics for sociology is useful, if for no other reason than furtherance of public relations, since it keeps sociology professionally abreast of other social sciences including psychology and anthropology, which have such bodies of rules.

agreed to at the NIH conference mentioned above. In these two cases, the professionals' judgment of "the gain by society and/or science" will be directly related to the amount and significance of new information available. The significance of this information will in turn often be a function of how harmful the subject activity is viewed by the researcher.

Unlike the original rules, the suggested revisions are not vague categorical imperatives but rather explicitly require the use of professional judgments. That professional sociologists, in fact, do make such judgments is reflected in numerous and diverse types of research (Glazer, 1972).

Techniques which might be used under such a revised Code could include, but would not be limited to, the use of key informants, and confidential records, both of which are, of course, the stock in trade of the investigative reporter. Participant observation is a well-known sociological method which, when conducted in a clandestine manner, is also useful as a subterranean technique. Elsewhere, it has been suggested that sociologists set about analyzing "accidents" and even causing "scandals," both of which can reveal the nature of societal elites (Molotch and Lester, 1972). The lawsuit involving cross-examination of subpoenaed witnesses is another research tool not requiring voluntary cooperation of subjects (Young, 1971:279–280).

However, it must be recognized that the use of these methodologies will very likely create problems for sociologists in a number of their environments. We can expect that some judges will place sociologists in jail who fail to reveal their informants as is increasingly true of newspaper reporters. One need only refer to the recent jailing of Samuel Popkin (Kovach, 1972:1, 40), the Harvard political scientist, who refused to tell a federal grand jury how he knew about details of the Pentagon papers before their public disclosure. Social scientists are even more vulnerable than journalists because the former do not enjoy the constitutional guarantees of freedom of the press. Moreover, many universities are likely to become embarrassed and intolerant of such research activities under pressure from outraged leaders in business and government. In con-

demning the use of such techniques, Erikson (1967:368–369) has correctly observed that employing such methods will also probably change sociology's relations with the general public, including potential subjects, thereby altering the conditions and increasing the difficulty for traditional research.

Research employing clandestine methodologies must not require vast expenditures of money since funding support will not likely develop for this type of research. Such techniques not only can challenge existing power arrangements but also violate the guidelines of most funding agencies. The Institutional Guide to Department of Health, Education, and Welfare Policy on Protection of Human Subjects (National Institutes of Health 1971:7–8), for example, requires "informed consent" from all human subjects and clearly prohibits subterranean techniques. If we are convinced by our methodologies that useful research, of necessity, requires vast sums of money, then our purview will be further narrowed by the partialities of financial sponsors. In any event, perhaps the use of such techniques will allow some sociological research to remain independent of the influence of government and private foundations over the development of ideas within our discipline. While it is not questioned that funding agencies have made possible much important research in sociolgy, it has nevertheless been established that only selected types of research are supported (McCartney, 1970; Galliher and McCartney, 1973; Tibbitts, 1962:900; Coser, 1955:5–6).

Even after giving due weight to all the likely costs and risks to the profession, the unavoidable question sociologists must answer is whether a sociology that only poses approved questions in an approved fashion is either empirically or morally sound. Moreover, Erikson's (1967:368–369) warnings about risking our freedom of inquiry by using clandestine research methods may also be taken to suggest that freedom of inquiry exists only so long as no attempt is made to employ this "freedom" by conducting research outside of approved and safe boundaries. Erikson's foreboding may well represent a correct assessment of the situation, yet it seems wiser to recognize these problems as constraints on our research which require thoughtful consideration than to continue to believe in an academic freedom that does not exist.

REFERENCES

American Sociologist
1968 "Toward a code of ethics for sociologists." 3 (November): 316–318.

Becker, H. S.
1964 "Against the code of ethics." American Sociological Review 29 (June): 409–410.

Becker, H. S. and I. L. Horowitz
1972 "Radical politics and sociological research: Observations on methodology and ideology." American Journal of Sociology 78 (July): 48–66.

Bettelheim, B.
1943 "Individual and mass behavior in extreme situations." The Journal of Abnormal and Social Psychology 38 (October): 417–452.

Black, D. J. and A. J. Reiss Jr.
1970 "Police control of juveniles." American Sociological Review 35 (February): 63–77.

Bonacich, P.
1970 "Deceiving subjects: The pollution of our environment." American Sociologist 5 (February): 45.

Brown, J. S. and B. G. Gilmartin
1969 "Sociology today: Lacunae, emphases, and surfeits." American Sociologist 4 (November): 283–291.

Coser L. A.
1955 "The functions of small-group research." Social Problems 3 (July): 1–6.

Daniels, A. K.
1967 "The low-caste stranger in social research." Pp. 267–296 in Gideon Sjoberg (ed.), Ethics, Politics, and Social Research. Cambridge, Mass.: Schenkman.

Erikson, K. T.
1967 "A comment on disguised observation in sociology." Social Problems 14 (Spring): 366–373.

Fichter, J. H. and W. L. Kolb
1953 "Ethical limitations on sociological reporting." American Sociological Review 18 (October): 544–550.

Friedrichs, R. W.
1970 "Epistemological foundations for a sociological ethic." The American Sociologist 5 (May): 138–140.

Galliher, J. F. and J. L. McCartney
1973 "The effects of funding on juvenile delinquency research." Social Problems 21 (forthcoming).

Glazer, M.
1972 The Research Adventure. New York: Random House.

Goldner, F. H.
1967 "Role emergence and the ethics of ambiguity." Pp. 245–266 in Gideon Sjöberg (ed.), Ethics, Politics, and Social Research. Cambridge, Mass.: Schenkman.

Kelman, H. C.
1967 "Human use of human subjects: The problem of deception in social psychological experiments." Psychological Bulletin 67 (January): 1–11.

Kovach, B.
1972 "Harvard professor jailed in Pentagon papers case." New York Times (November 22): 1, 40.

Lofland, J.
1961 "Comment on 'initial interaction of newcomers in alcoholics anonymous'." Social Problems 8 (Spring): 365–367.

Lowry, R. P.
1972 "Towards a sociology of secrecy and security systems." Social Problems 19 (Spring): 437–450.

McCartney, J. L.
1970 "On being scientific: Changing styles of presentation of sociological research." American Sociologist 5 (February): 30–35.

Molotch, H. and M. Lester
1972 "Accidents, scandals and routines: Resources for conflict methodology." Paper presented at the 67th Annual Meeting of the American Sociological Association, New Orleans.

National Institutes of Health
1971 Institutional Guide to DHEW Policy on Protection of Human Subjects. Washington, D.C.: DHEW Publication No. (NIH) 72–102.

Rainwater, L. and D. J. Pittman
1967 "Ethical problems in studying a politically sensitive and deviant community." Social Problems 14 (Spring): 357–366.

Record, J. C.
  1967 "The research institute and the pressure group." Pp. 25-49 in Gideon Sjoberg (ed.), Ethics, Politics, and Social Research. Cambridge, Mass.: Schenkman.

Reiss, A. J., Jr.
  1968 "Police brutality—Answers to key questions." Trans-action 5 (July–August): 10-19.

Roth, J. A.
  1962 "Comments on 'secret observations.'" Social Problems 9 (Winter): 283-284.

  1969 "A codification of current prejudices." The American Sociologist 4 (May): 159.

Savitz, L.
  1970 "The dimensions of police loyalty." American Behavioral Scientist 13 (May–June, July–August): 693-704.

Stoddard, E. R.
  1968 "The informal 'code' of police deviancy: A group approach to 'blue-coat crime.'" The Journal of Criminal Law, Criminology and Police Science 59 (June): 201-213.

Sykes, G. M.
  1967 "Feeling our way: A report on a conference on ethical issues in the social sciences." American Behavioral Scientist 10 (June): 8-11.

Tibbitts, H. G.
  1962 "Research in the development of sociology: A pilot study in methodology." American Sociological Review 27 (December): 892-901.

van den Berghe, P. L.
  1967 "Research in South Africa: The story of my experiences with tyranny." Pp. 183-197 in Gideon Sjoberg (ed.), Ethics, Politics, and Social Research. Cambridge, Mass.: Schenkman.

Westley, W. A.
  1956 "Secrecy and the police." Social Forces 34 (March): 254-257.

Young, T. R.
  1971 "The politics of sociology: Gouldner, Goffman, and Garfinkel." American Sociologist 6 (November): 276-281.

SOCIAL SCIENTISTS'
ETHICAL RESPONSIBILITIES
TO SUPERORDINATES
Looking Upward Meekly*

John F. Galliher
University of Missouri—Columbia

Social scientists have recently been exhorted to study superordinate people and groups. The anthropologist Laura Nader (1969:289–301) observes that "scientific adequacy," or complete description, requires that social scientists "study up" as well as down. She argues that social scientists already know a good deal about the poor, so that the time has come to "study up" in the stratification system. Nader continues by arguing that "democratic relevance" also requires studying up since "citizens need to know something about the major institutions, government or otherwise, that affect their lives."

Sociologists Rainwater and Pittman (1967:365–366) have challenged others in their own and related disciplines to increase the accountability of elites in business and government. They have concluded that:

Sociologists have the right (and perhaps also the obligation) to study publicly accountable behavior. By publicly accountable behavior we do not simply mean the behavior of public officials (though there the case is clearest) but also the behavior of any individual as he goes about performing public or secondary roles for which he is socially accountable—this would include businessmen, college teachers, physicians, etc.; in short, all people as they carry out jobs for which

they are in some sense publicly accountable. One of the functions of our discipline, along with those of political science, history, economics, journalism, and intellectual pursuits generally, is to further public accountability in a society whose complexity makes it easier for people to avoid their responsibilities (1967:365–366).

Considering anthropologists, Nader resolves the question as follow:

For the most part anthropologists working in the United States can be said to have worked on the private sphere: we study families, small groups, those aspects of communities which are more private than public. We should not necessarily apply the same ethics developed for studying the private, and even ethics developed for studying in foreign cultures (where we are guests), to the study of institutions, organizations, bureaucracies that have a broad public impact (1969:304–305).

And more specifically, she concludes:

Furthermore, it could be argued that access to bureaucratic organizations (such as governmental agencies) frequented by the wealthy and powerful should be open to social scientists by virtue of laws which protect public access to information affecting the public interest (1969:302–303).

Considering psychological research, Ruebhausen and Brim argue:

. . . privacy is in conflict with other valued social interests, such as informed and effective government,

*Thanks are due Richard Hessler and James McCartney for help in exploring the obligations we all have to each other.

law enforcement and free dissemination of the news . . . public figures, particularly those who appeal to the public for elective office, have impliedly consented to the yielding up of some areas of private personality (1966:424–431).

And several years ago I (Galliher, 1973) suggested that the American Sociological Association so alter its Code of Ethics as to support the right of sociologists to conduct research on the behavior of those in public positions where they are accountable to all citizens. Such calls for accountability do not necessarily assume that public officials are inherently evil but merely that their high position gives them power which can be abused. Publicly, social scientists have not objected to the general idea of such research, but simply ignored it. The American Sociological Association has disregarded my suggestion for altering the Code of Ethics. Although devoted to ethical problems in social science research, a recent issue of *The American Sociologist* (August, 1978) did not touch on the subject (researching the publicly accountable) although the sixteen contributors included some of the most prominent scholars associated with the social science study of ethics. Given their traditional concerns with more individualistic issues (Kelman, 1972), one can understand why psychologists might overlook power and public accountability, even in discussions of the relationship between power and research ethics, but clearly it is within the purview of anthropology, political science and sociology.

A hint as to why this avoidance takes place is in the controversy found in the report of the American Sociological Association Committee on Professional Ethics. In drafting the Association's Code of Ethics the committee recognized some areas of ''unfinished business'' which were ''impossible to resolve'':

To what extent can public figures claim the same rights of privacy as ordinary citizens? To what extent does the injunction about the confidentiality of research sites prevent legitimate criticism of organizations that have cooperated in the research? . . . Clearly, much more thought and analysis must be devoted to such questions, and others as well (American Sociologist, 1968:316).

The Committee could not resolve these issues so it dropped them. Agreement on a general level about the role of social science research in the accountability of public officials did not lead to agreement on specifics. For example, the American Anthropological Association was recently faced with a dramatic case of questionable professional morality which was uncovered when a student pilfered a professor's files (Wolf and Jorgensen, 1970; 1971). Apparently the chair and one member of the Anthropological Association's Ethics Committee raised questions of propriety with those anthropologists named in these files as participants in United States government counterinsurgency research. Shortly thereafter the Executive Board of the American Anthropological Association reprimanded both for this action (Orlans, 1973:68–69). The action of the Board undoubtedly makes it appear to some that it will not tolerate attempts to hold Association members publicly accountable, if discrediting information comes from pilfered files, even when documents show involvement in attempts to aid in genocidal foreign policy. However, sociologists should be the last to condemn the conflict in other professions since the American Sociological Association has resolved the problem of professional ethics by appointing an Ethics Committee, while providing no funds for investigation, and so there is no record of it having decided on a single case (Barber, 1977). Sociologists haven't made any mistakes because they haven't done anything.

Sociology, anthropology, psychology and political science developed new codes of ethics in the 1960's and 1970's (American Sociologist, 1968; American Anthropological Association, 1971; American Psychologist, 1963; P.S., 1968), and at least in the case of sociology this was a clear consequence of the threat of federal controls (Galliher, 1975). None of these codes nor the AAUP Statement on Academic Freedom make any provisions for public accountability, although the latter does state: ''The teacher is entitled to full freedom in research and in the publication of the results, . . .'' (Academic Freedom, 1940:49). It goes on to say: ''A university or college may not place any restraint upon the teacher's freedom in investigation''

(1940:52). Yet over the past decade there has been a steady increase in federal controls on university researchers' activities through efforts to *protect human subjects*. These new controls on research "limit both research and consequent criticism of local officials" (Galliher, 1978:251), for there is no allowance in these federal controls for public accountability (Code of Federal Regulations, 1977). The attitude implied by both the federal guidelines and professional codes of ethics is that public accountability can best be left to the mass media, but surely the First Amendment guarantee of freedom of the press does not necessarily exclude social scientists and their journals, such as the *American Anthropologist,* the *American Sociological Review* or the *American Political Science Review.*

DEFINITIONAL PROBLEMS

If research subjects' rights of privacy must be protected, it must first be determined who qualifies as a research subject. Are groups as well as individuals defined as subjects? If groups have rights that must be protected, as Shils (1973) claims was true according to the Department of Health, Education and Welfare–approved guidelines at Berkeley, then research on the powerful seems impossible, for people often become powerful through their groups, as in the case of Pentagon generals and General Motors presidents. Yet Shils reports that DHEW-approved guidelines prohibited the study of any group, explicitly including churches, universities and prisons, without their informed consent, when the research risks placing "the reputation or status of a social group or an institution in jeopardy" (1973:292). Such restrictions will necessarily constrain social science research, focused as it is on the understanding of groups and organizations. There is also the knotty problem of who can speak for the group? If one relies on the traditional practice of allowing organization leaders to give or withhold research entry, then public accountability of such leaders is impossible. Moreover, if others are asked about these superordinate persons, who are the research subjects: the elites or the respondents

themselves? For example, an opinion survey question might have asked respondents if they felt former President Nixon knew about the Watergate burglary before it occurred. The subject of the research in this example is clearly Richard Nixon, but the research subjects are the citizens chosen in a sample.

There are other definitional problems. If it is not always clear how we shall define research subjects, it is equally unclear who qualifies as a superordinate or an elite who should be held accountable for a public performance. Rainwater and Pittman explicitly include business executives, college professors and physicians. But Black and Reiss (1970:65), by snooping on the behavior of police officers, seem to extend the definition. Clearly, Henry Ford II is an elite and is superordinate to almost all Americans. It is equally clear that the chronically unemployed, lower-class ghetto dwellers are not elites and are superordinate to few other citizens, if any. Between those two extremes the definition of superordinate becomes problematic. For example, the beat patrolman is superordinate to some citizens but is only a marginally middle-class wage earner who does not set governmental policy (Galliher, 1971). The question is, should police officers lose their rights of privacy when performing their public role? If we agree with Rainwater and Pittman that physicians are superordinates who should be publicly accountable, is the same true of registered nurses? And if nurses are to be held publicly accountable, how about ambulance drivers and hospital orderlies? If professors can be held publicly accountable (and I feel they should be), how about graduate teaching assistants? If business or government executives can be held publicly accountable, is this true of all people in business and government? In fact, does this mandate of Rainwater and Pittman extend to a large proportion of all citizens and include anyone who serves the public, not just obvious targets such as physicians and corporation heads, but also waitresses and cooks, cab and bus drivers, and garbage collectors? We have then a ready-made justification for holding almost anyone accountable to the social scientist. This seems somewhat absurd on the face of it, but if we choose not to hold nurses, cops, and assembly line foremen accountable, we may be closing off avenues for learning about the abuses of power of physicians, police chiefs, and industry heads, for it is often only through these lower-level superordinates that we can learn about the abuses of power of high-level policy makers.

TEMPEST IN A TEAPOT: DEBATE ABOUT METHODS

Whether it is useful and necessary to conduct research on elites, however defined, has not been the main bone of contention. Rather, attention has focused on the appropriateness of the methods for collecting the data, usually without a similar concern with the political, theoretical and philosophical significance of such methodologies. By alleging that certain methodologies are simply not scientific, one can ostensibly disallow the researchers on professional and intellectual grounds, rather than admitting to political reasons.

It has become popular for social scientists to condemn Humphreys (1970) for disguised observation of gay men in homosexual encounters and Douglas (1977) for his research on a nude beach. Unfortunately, both Humphreys and Douglas have not studied the powerful but have trivialized clandestine observation and thereby made it easy prey for opponents. In a *Psychology Today* article, Warwick (1975:105) asserts, "It is highly doubtful that any study involving deception ultimately promotes human welfare." And, he continues, "The dangers in bracketing the civil liberties of some citizens seem too obvious to deserve comment"—but he does. He continues in this and another statement (Warwick, 1974) that approval of clandestine research (such as I have advocated, 1973) uses the same ends-justifying-the-means reasoning used by former President Richard Nixon and his White House friends. However, the means-ends distinction seems to obscure rather than clarify this issue because those who claim that methods involving deception are never justified have elevated the means of the research to an end.

Warwick (1974) challenges my claim (1973: 97) that techniques which do not require subject cooperation are not considered fully professional by sociologists, then demonstrates the claim is accurate by his considerable ire. In the same essay that rankles him, I concluded: "Ironically, it is the sociologists themselves who have helped politicize their craft by treating methodological and empirical problems of data collection as political or ethical questions." Warwick fits this very mold. In response to my essay he (Warwick, 1974:106) concludes: "Government must step in to prevent the most flagrant abuses. . . ." In reply (Galliher, 1974), I matched his scorn by belittling his concern for the privacy of public officials. Yet I now recognize that if I were to write the essay so as to shed more light (and less heat) on the issues, I would not put so much emphasis on clandestine techniques of data collection.

Warwick (1974:158) was quite right in observing that I ignored the body of information available on important people "mainly because there are more people watching them," as shown in the work of Arthur Schlesinger, Jr. He also correctly observes that one can use existing records of congressional hearings as did I. F. Stone. There are, however, limits to the value of these latter public documents, for their use often presumes that the truth is spoken on the House and Senate floor and in hearing rooms. Moreover, it is noteworthy that in his rebuttal Warwick relies on the examples of Schlesinger, a historian, and Stone, a journalist, and he admits: "The fact of the matter is that sociologists, with few exceptions, have not made use of often very revealing public material" (1974:159). The practices of historians and journalists are really beside the point when considering sociologists. Most sociologists do not consider the study of existing records, as practiced by Schlesinger or Stone, to be fully professional, and their judgment is based on technical rather than ethical considerations. Sociology, more than history and perhaps some other social sciences, has been drowning in a sea of arcane statistical techniques (McCartney, 1970; Brown and Gilmartin, 1969). These statistics usually require a search for large numbers which must be easily gathered or observed. Sociologists seldom get around to discussing the ethical consequences of research as conducted by Stone or Schlesinger because it does not meet their technical requirements.

However, I was a little melodramatic in discussing clandestine methods; and, without overemphasizing my influence, some of the heat of the debate which ensued (also see Lundman and McFarlane, 1976; Christie, 1976) is probably my responsibility and a product of my distrust of government after the late 1960's and 1970's. It is not just that government should be monitored, but I implied that it is the people's enemy:

While all people may be worthy of the same respect as human beings, it does not necessarily follow that their activities merit the same degree of protection and respect. As indicated earlier, Lofland questioned possible prohibitions on the undercover study of fascist groups. It is questionable whether the files of the American Nazi Party are deserving of the same respect as any other data source; must one secure the active cooperation of the Ku Klux Klan, or for that matter of the Pentagon, before conducting research in their organizations or with their personnel? While doing research in South Africa, van den Berghe concluded: 'From the outset, I decided that I should have no scruples in deceiving the government. . . .' The question is, how much honor is proper for the sociologist in studying the membership and organization of what he considers an essentially dishonorable, morally outrageous, and destructive enterprise? Is not the failure of sociology to uncover corrupt, illegitimate, covert practices of government or industry because of the supposed prohibitions of professional ethics tantamount to supporting such practices (Galliher, 1973:96; internal citations omitted)?

I suggested the use of key informants and confidential records, scandals, and court subpoenas, and clandestine participant observation—all except the last used in the Watergate investigation. Countering what some may see as my verbal swashbuckling is the work of Frederick Wiseman (see Friedenberg, 1971), who has made muckraking films about a high school, a mental hospital, a police department, and a military boot camp. He has found that people in official positions will sometimes volunteer damning in-

formation because they are so sure that theirs is the only reasonable position.

Obviously, the high-ranking do not always volunteer damning information, and it is especially unlikely when their behavior involves criminal activity. There are, moreover, "obstacles and objections" (Nader, 1969:301–302) to research on elites. "The powerful are out of reach on a number of different planes: they don't want to be studied; it is dangerous to study the powerful; they are busy people. . . ." Similarly, Gans (Woodward, 1974:78) comments about economic as opposed to political leaders: "Since the rich don't let themselves be studied, and it's pretty hard to get into a fancy club on your own, sociologists go where they have easier access." For example, Domhoff (1975) relied heavily on key informants in his research on private ruling-class retreats. High-ranking people do not want social scientists around, in part merely because the latter are lower-ranking. Even with limited resources, a researcher can spend a summer in Harlem; but few, if any, social scientists have the money or prestige to be welcome as participant observers in prestigious eastern clubs or in a General Motors board meeting. Nader recognizes that scholars cannot use participant observation when studying up, but recommends the use of personal documents, memoirs and interviews. The composite picture then from looking at the work of Nader, Wiseman and Warwick is that even eschewing more aggressive and clandestine techniques, social scientists could do a lot more with established methods to learn about the powerful.

ACTUAL RESEARCH ON SUPERORDINATES

Because social scientists have been bogged down in disputes about methodology, they do not usually get past the talking stage and into actual research. According to Nader (1969:303), anthropologists have not had an intense interest in social reforms in their research because of their usual cultural relativism and commitment to being value free, and perhaps also due to their thinking that sociologists are doing this type of research. But we typically are not. The point of ignorance of the powerful is forcefully emphasized by Green (1971) in citing the lack of any independent academic study of an organization such as Standard Oil of New Jersey, a mammoth corporation with vast national and international influence.

Oddly, until called on to prepare this essay, I had not reflected on my own field research experiences among powerful Americans during the past decade, to test my ideas about research ethics and methods. In interviewing state government officials, civil servants and business leaders in Nebraska (Galliher et al., 1974), Utah (Galliher and Basilick, 1979) and most recently in Nevada, I have found few refusals and little hostility in studies of the origins of criminal laws, even when the details of such interviews are discrediting to respondents. In beginning each study, I was quite willing—and even eager—to use duplicity, but it never was necessary. There was never any information that was not freely available. In Nebraska, for example, I found a blatant case of special interests being served by a criminal law. A Nebraska prosecuting attorney active in Republican party politics freely told me that, to protect his son, a reduced penalty for marijuana possession was passed into law and made retroactive to the date of his son's arrest. My research experiences with governors, state senators and other state officials, as well as with corporation heads leads me to believe that Wiseman is correct. Powerful people seem so convinced of their own righteousness and so sure of their power that they usually talk freely.

In my research, however, I have been careful to try to present myself as someone as much like my respondents as possible. I have gotten a haircut and shaved my beard and worn a business suit and necktie. While I was in Utah, I wore only white shirts, in keeping with the usual Mormon garb. My success as a researcher was manifest in a zero rate of refusal from Mormons and several invitations to dinner, as well as invitations to join their church. Stone (1962) observes that in our manner of dress we create a presentation of self, and by wearing suits and white shirts, I feel I was less than completely honest. My tactics in this regard go beyond the usual practice of dressing so as not to distract or annoy respondents. Another possible dilemma is that even without naming the individual involved, it is sometimes impossible to describe events and attitudes without indicating the source as, for example, in discussing a governor's timing and rationale for a veto or a Senate finance committee chairman's techniques and reasons for pushing a bill through his committee. Clearly the information itself can only come from one source. Surely governors, senators and presidents must realize this and recognize that this lack of privacy necessarily comes from a public role.

Yet in some studies of elites or superordinates, greater stealth (than merely shaving) may be necessary in collecting information. The Watergate story would probably have been impossible to write if all information had to pass White House censors or federal guidelines for the protection of human subjects. Duster et al. report on clandestine research sponsored by the Department of Housing and Urban Development (HUD) to determine the extent of racial discrimination by realtors. Black and white couples answered newspaper advertisements and blacks experienced "documentable discrimination by rental agents three out of four times" (Duster et al., 1979:136). Obviously informed consent is not possible in such research. Further, the study of organized crime by most social scientists is laughable because such research usually relies on government reports (Galliher and Cain, 1974). In his actual field research into organized crime, Chambliss (1978) relied heavily on key informants to learn about the behavior of powerful people (this tactic was also true in the Watergate story). Yet in spite of journalists' success in the Watergate story, the field of public accountability should not be left to the press, in part because the free press in the United States is not really *free*. A handful of giant corporations own a larger and larger percentage of newspapers and television stations, and fewer and fewer American cities have competing daily newspapers. These patterns suggest a growing monopoly ownership of the American mass media. Moreover, at its best, social science offers a unique type of interpretation of events not usually found in the more individualistically oriented American journalism.

CONCLUSION

In conclusion, both technical problems and moral considerations are associated with the practice of fieldwork with superordinates. Technical problems involve the search for complete description, and without more adequate description social science theories will be hopelessly miscast. The moral consideration is whether public officials are deemed to have the same rights of privacy as other citizens; if the answer is affirmative, then it seems unclear what part social scientists or any other group can play in the task of holding public officials accountable, or in examining and fully understanding their social world.

The Code of Ethics of the American Sociological Association is, for example, a moral mandate that contains a claim of what sociology as a discipline is, can be, and should be. The Code also reflects an implicit theory of the workings of society, or description of social order, which is bereft of any hint of stratification, whether racial, sexual or economic. Since the Code makes no mention of social stratification, one can assume that sociologists feel social stratification is irrelevant to the ethical concerns of social scientists. Looking only at the rights of individual research subjects implies an overly technical, individualistic and nonsociological definition of rights, ignoring as it does the structural environment in which the research takes place.

Wax (1977), however, recognizes how initial access to human subjects necessarily involves consideration of stratification and power differences, such access often being controlled by elites. Then he observes that federal regulations like professional codes ignore such issues:

In contrast to the foregoing complexities, the federal system for the protection of human subjects is framed about a contractarian model in which the actors are conceived as free and unattached individuals who meet for a specific and temporary purpose. The model assumes that the researcher has influence, power, and

knowledge such as to intimidate the subject, and a major purpose of the regulations is to compensate for the imbalance of power by requiring that the subject be provided with more information both as to the activity that is planned and as to the alternative courses of action which are open to him (1977:325).

Cassell (1979) contends that the relationship between the researcher and subject has been oversimplified and incorrectly generalized from medical research to the social and behavioral sciences. She claims that this error may be due to the biomedical language in which persons are identified as *subjects* of research despite the power differentials between researchers and those researched among the scientific disciplines.

Having established that ethical issues in the protection of human subjects are seldom related to social stratification, what is the consequence of making such a linkage? Attempting to associate what social scientists know about the nature of the effects of social stratification with protection of human subjects would lead one to conclude that not all actors are equally free to make informed choices about research participation and therefore not all actors require the same protection. Presumably, those who are least free require the most protection. Does anyone really believe that corporation presidents or United States presidents need the same warnings and protection from social scientists as do undergraduates or ghetto dwellers? Must Jimmy Carter or Henry Ford II really be told that their participation in a study is voluntary? Indeed to give such equal warnings may help maintain unequal protection of human subjects.

For social scientists, moral considerations or dilemmas include not only obligations to the individual studied and to one's government, but also to all the citizens in one's society and those of other societies. If we are to deal fairly with peoples of other cultures and with American economic and racial minorities, unequal treatment of some others may be required. As reasoned in Affirmative Action Programs, powerless and deprived groups must be given special consideration to help rectify the effects of past discrimination which have put them at a great disadvantage. Specifically in social science research, if all research subjects are told the same thing about the research, some poor people may still feel coerced in ways that the more affluent are not. Anthropologists and sociologists undoubtedly look a great deal like social workers or police detectives who routinely disrupt the lives of the poor (Coser, 1978). Therefore, special efforts may be necessary to give the poor the same freedom of choice the more affluent have always had. According to this reasoning, superordinates are not necessarily due the same degree and type of consideration by researchers as are other more deprived and powerless individuals.

Even more basic to such issues, if one makes ethical judgments about social stratification, one may conclude that not all actors merit the same degree of respect. In racist societies such as South Africa or the United States, do social scientists have any ethical obligation to attempt to redress these wrongs through their research? If the answer is yes, then in such societies perhaps social science cannot operate ethically by always avoiding harm to *all* subjects. Perhaps those executives of corporations owning slum dwellings should be embarrassed, harassed and ultimately discredited by social science research. The same is true of others who profit from, and contribute directly to, racism and economic exploitation (e.g., the Duster et al. case involving realtors who refuse to rent to minorities). If we agree that social stratification and its consequences are relevant ethical concerns of social science, then to remain silent implicitly endorses this stratification. Few social scientists would be likely to claim that stratification is irrelevant to their science. Many sociologists probably have not reacted against the restrictive federal guidelines because they are more interested in intricate statistical manipulation of existing data than in actual data collection (Duster et al., 1979:138).

Perhaps a reason for the lack of clarity regarding the specifics of professional ethics is that we have not usually addressed the underlying issue of the general ethical goals of social science. Usually such general considerations are eschewed in favor of analyses of specific ethical problems encountered in research. Such general questions might include: What is the use of social science? Are the products of social science to be equally available to the very rich and to the very poor and to all nations equally, including South Africa? Do social scientists have a vision of a just or ethical social ordering toward which they strive in their research? Is it possible, even if we assume that all individuals have rights as research subjects, that some rights are in conflict with and prior to others? The report on the confrontation of demonstrators and police in Chicago during the National Democratic Convention of 1968 is, in fact, entitled *Rights in Conflict* and refers to the conflict between the "right to dissent and a community's right to protect its citizens and property" (Walker, 1968:vi). During epidemics, for example, conflict exists between the right of the general public to safety and the rights of individuals who on religious grounds refuse immunization. In the case of social science research, it may be that many people's rights to physical survival could depend in part on a social scientist overriding another person's rights as a research subject. The social scientist might agree to do so, unless the choice of the research method is elevated to an end in itself. Such a case might involve the analysis and publication of the illegal practices of a slum landlord or a realtor who refuses to rent to minorities. Duster et al. conclude:

. . . the blanket application of these [federal] rules obscures conflicts of interest . . . are the subjects to be protected the thousands of Americans who consume or the business people who work the system? . . . In some situations "informed consent" may in fact impede the protection of some human subjects, for example, when the question before the researchers—and the public—involves possible unethical behavior, like fraud and discrimination. . . . To mechanically apply to powerful institutions a bureaucratic rule originally meant to protect the powerless forgets the reason behind the reform (1979:140–141).

In regard to such a case, Bennett observes that many of those who invoke the right of privacy are "the people who do have something to hide, from outright crime to malevolence. . . . Their secrets impinge on the welfare of others and the moral imperative may demand their exposure" (1967:375). Attempting to achieve the greatest good or well-being for the greatest number of people is one rule of thumb for placing priorities on rights which are in conflict. Certainly one's right to free speech is overriden by the personal safety of others and prohibits one from falsely yelling "fire" in a crowded theatre. However, such considerations fall short of a complete answer because as Vaughan and Sjoberg (1978) observe, such an orientation may not adequately draw attention to the concerns of numerical minorities. This discussion merely suggests that ethics are based on a sense of social justice and cannot be created bereft of such considerations.

Cassell (1978) repeats a question often raised in judging the ethical merits of research. These judgments are often made by weighing the risks to human subjects against the potential benefit of the research. Cassell focuses the question more precisely:

In cases involving deception, there is a conflict between the potential harm of the invasion of privacy, and the emerging value of the public's 'right to know.' There is no clear solution to this conflict through abstract analysis, nor is there a clear formula for the risk-benefit calculus (1978:137).

And Cassell asks doubtfully, "When one person or group benefits from the risks of another, can risk and benefit be weighed against each other" (1978:139)? Only by considering the public's right to know about the activities of those in positions of public trust is the analysis of otherwise private details generally considered acceptable and even necessary in democratic states.

There may seem to be an irony about asking for greater freedom for social scientists while at the same time asking that professors be held publicly accountable. Social scientists are at present held publicly accountable by the federal government for their research with human subjects, but exercise very little professional freedom. Public accountability is only appropriate in those roles where occupants are free to exercise some professional discretion. Public accountability without the exercise of professional discretion lends itself to political coercion and harassment.

Finally, is there *ever* a justification for a social scientist deceiving *any* research subject? The easiest and of course the conventional answer to this question is to assert that deception is never tolerable because, if deception is sometimes held to be tolerable, one must then specify under what conditions this holds true. But if one contends that deception by social scientists is never tolerable, is it (a) because deception of research subjects at all times is wrong when done by anyone including journalists, or (b) because of the unique nature of social science? If one chooses (b) as the grounds for opposition to clandestine techniques, one must then specify in what ways social science is unique.

If clandestine research is never tolerable in the United States, is it justifiable in South Africa or in Nazi Germany? Most social scientists possibly would agree that in these latter two examples some deception is justified, for in these settings social research is likely to be possible only with deception. More importantly, the variation in judgments regarding the appropriateness of deception in investigations shows how research ethics imply a specific political climate. If only the extreme circumstances of South Africa and Nazi Germany are believed to justify covert research, then the myriad of American professional codes of ethics and government regulations which prohibit deception indicate that—in spite of United States' traditions of genocide of Native Americans, racism, sexism and grinding poverty—the largely middle-class, Caucasian members of professional associations and government regulatory agencies do not feel that circumstances in America are extreme enough to warrant deceptive research practices.

REFERENCES

Academic Freedom and Tenure Committee
1940   "Statement of principles." Bulletin of the American Association of University Professors 26 (February): 49-54.

American Anthropological Association
1971   "Principles of professional responsibility" (adopted May).

American Psychologist
1963   "Ethical standards of psychologists." 18 (January): 56-60.

American Sociologist
1968   "Toward a code of ethics for sociologists."
       3 (November): 316–318.

1978   (August) Volume 13.

Barber, Bernard
1977   "Report of the Committee on Ethics."
       Footnotes 5 (February): 8.

Bennett, Chester C.
1967   "What price privacy?" American
       Psychologist 22 (May): 371–376.

Black, Donald J. and Albert J. Reiss, Jr.
1970   "Police control of juveniles." American
       Sociological Review 35 (February): 63–77.

Brown, Julia S. and Brian G. Gilmartin
1969   "Sociology today: Lacunae, emphases,
       and surfeits." American Sociologist 4
       (November): 283–291.

Cassell, Joan
1978   "Risk and benefit to subjects of
       fieldwork." American Sociologist 13
       (August): 134–143.

1979   "Ethical principles for conducting
       fieldwork." Paper presented at the con-
       ference on "Ethical Problems of
       Fieldwork," Asilomar Conference Center,
       Pacific Grove, California, April 22–25.

Chambliss, William J.
1978   On the Take: From Petty Crooks to
       Presidents. Bloomington: Indiana Univer-
       sity Press.

Christie, Robert M.
1976   "Comment on conflict methodology: A
       protagonist position." Sociological
       Quarterly 17 (Autumn): 513–519.

Code of Federal Regulations
1977   Protection of Human Subjects. 45 Public
       Welfare CFR Part 46, Revised October 1.

Coser, Ruth Laub
1978   "Comment." American Sociologist 13
       (August): 156–157.

Domhoff, G. William
1975   The Bohemian Grove and Other Retreats.
       New York: Harper and Row.

Douglas, Jack D., Paul K. Rasmussen and Carol Ann
Flanagan
1977   The Nude Beach. Beverly Hills: Sage.

Duster, Troy, David Matza and David Wellman
1979   "Field work and the protection of human
       subjects." American Sociologist 14
       (August): 136–142.

Friedenberg, Edgar Z.
1971   "The films of Frederick Wiseman." The
       New York Review of Books 17 (October
       21): 19–22.

Galliher, John F.
1971   "Explanations of police behavior: A critical
       review and analysis." Sociological
       Quarterly 12 (Summer): 308–318.

1973   "The protection of human subjects: A
       reexamination of the professional code of
       ethics." American Sociologist 8 (August):
       93–100.

1974   "Professor Galliher replies." American
       Sociologist 9 (August): 159–160.

1975   "The ASA code of ethics on the protec-
       tion of human beings: Are students human
       too?" American Sociologist 10 (May):
       113–117.

1978   "The life and death of liberal
       criminology." Contemporary Crises 2
       (July): 245–263.

Galliher, John F. and Linda Basilick
1979   "Utah's liberal drug laws: Structural foun-
       dations and triggering events." Social
       Problems 26 (February): 284–297.

Galliher, John F. and James A. Cain
1974   "Citation support for the Mafia myth in
       criminology textbooks." American
       Sociologist 9 (May): 68–74.

Galliher, John F., James L. McCartney and Barbara Baum
1974   "Nebraska's marijuana law: A case of
       unexpected legislative innovation." Law
       and Society Review 8 (Spring): 441–455.

Green, Philip
1971   "The obligations of American social scien-
       tists." The Annals of the American
       Academy of Political and Social Science
       394 (March): 13–27.

Humphreys, Laud
1970   Tearoom Trade: Impersonal Sex in Public
       Places. Chicago: Aldine.

Kelman, Herbert C.
1972   "The rights of the subject in social
       research: An analysis in terms of relative
       power and legitimacy." American
       Psychologist 27 (November): 989–1016.

Lundman, Richard J. and Paul T. McFarlane
1976   "Conflict methodology: An introduction
       and preliminary assessment." Sociological
       Quarterly 17 (Autumn): 503–512.

McCartney, James L.
1970 "On being scientific: Changing styles of presentation of sociological research." American Sociologist 5 (February): 30–35.

Nader, Laura
1969 "Up the anthropologist—Perspectives gained from studying up." Pp. 284–311 in Dell Hymes (ed.), Reinventing Anthropology. New York: Random House.

Orlans, Harold
1973 Contracting for Knowledge. San Francisco: Jossey-Bass.

P.S., Newsletter of the American Political Science Association
1968 "Ethical problems of academic political scientists." 1 (Summer): 3–28.

Rainwater, Lee and David J. Pittman
1967 "Ethical problems in studying a politically sensitive and deviant community." "Social Problems 14 (Spring): 357–366.

Ruebhausen, Oscar M. and Orville G. Brim, Jr.
1966 "Privacy and behavioral research." American Psychologist 21 (May): 423–437.

Shils, Edward
1973 "Muting the social sciences at Berkeley." Minerva 11 (July): 290–295.

Stone, Gregory P.
1962 "Appearance and the self." Pp. 86–118 in Arnold M. Rose (ed.), Human Behavior and Social Processes: An Interactionist Approach. Boston: Houghton Mifflin.

Vaughan, Ted R. and Gideon Sjoberg
1978 "Comment." American Sociologist 13 (August): 171–172.

Walker, Daniel
1968 Rights in Conflict. (The Walker Report to the National Commission on the Causes and Prevention of Violence.) New York: Bantam Books.

Warwick, Donald P.
1974 "Who deserves protection?" American Sociologist 9 (August): 158–159.

1975 "Social scientists ought to stop lying." Psychology Today 8 (February): 38, 40, 105–106.

Wax, Murray L.
1977 "On fieldworkers and those exposed to fieldwork: Federal regulations and moral issues." Human Organization 36 (Fall): 321–329.

Wolf, Eric R. and Joseph G. Jorgensen
1970 "Anthropology on the warpath in Thailand." The New York Review of Books 15 (November 19): 26–35.

1971 "Anthropology on the warpath: An exchange." The New York Review of Books 16 (April 8): 43–46.

Woodward, Kenneth L.
1974 "Secrets of the very rich." Newsweek (October 7): 78.